A Companion to European Romanticism

Blackwell Companions to Literature and Culture

This series offers comprehensive, newly written surveys of key periods and movements and certain major authors, in English literary culture and history. Extensive volumes provide new perspectives and positions on contexts and on canonical and post-canonical texts, orientating the beginning student in new fields of study and providing the experienced undergraduate and new graduate with current and new directions, as pioneered and developed by leading scholars in the field.

A COMPANION TO

European Romanticism

Edited by Michael Ferber

This companion describes the way in which the Romantic Movement swept across Europe in the early nineteenth century, transforming literature, music, painting, religion, philosophy, politics, and personal relationships. It is the first book of its kind to focus on the whole of European Romanticism, moving between the national literatures of Britain, France, Germany, Italy, Poland, Russia, and Spain on the one hand, and common themes, subjects, forms, and sources on the other. Subjects addressed range from Orientalism, capitalism, and nature, to the revival of the lyric and the influence of the French Revolution. The volume also includes cross-disciplinary contributions on literature and music, literature and painting, and the general system of Romantic arts. There are over 30 essays in all, written by leading Romanticism scholars from America, Australia, Britain, France, Germany, Italy, and Switzerland.

The Editor

~∰⊙

Michael Ferber is Professor of English and
Humanities at the University of New
Hampshire. His previous publications include
The Social Vision of William Blake (1985),
The Poetry of William Blake (1991), *The Poetry
of Shelley* (1993), *A Dictionary of Literary
Symbols* (1999), and an anthology, *European
Romantic Poetry* (2005).

b

A COMPANION TO

EUROPEAN
ROMANTICISM

EDITED BY MICHAEL FERBER

Blackwell
Publishing

BLACKWELL PUBLISHING
350 Main Street, Malden, MA 02148-5020, USA
9600 Garsington Road, Oxford OX4 2DQ, UK
550 Swanston Street, Carlton, Victoria 3053, Australia

First published 2005 by Blackwell Publishing Ltd

1 2005

Library of Congress Cataloging-in-Publication Data

A companion to European romanticism / edited by Michael Ferber.
p. cm.—(Blackwell companions to literature and culture; 38)
Includes bibliographical references and index.
ISBN-13: 978-1-4051-1039-6 (hardcover : alk. paper)
ISBN-10: 1-4051-1039-2 (hardcover : alk. paper) 1. Romanticism.
I. Ferber, Michael. II. Series.

PN603.C65 2005
809'.9145—dc22

2005022100

A catalogue record for this title is available from the British Library.

Set in 11/13pt Garamond 3
by SPI Publisher Services, Pondicherry, India

For further information on
Blackwell Publishing, visit our website:
www.blackwellpublishing.com

Contents

Contents

Notes on Contributors

Simon Bainbridge is Professor of Romantic Studies at Lancaster University, UK, and author of the monographs *Napoleon and English Romanticism* (Cambridge University Press, 1995) and *British Poetry and the Revolutionary and Napoleonic Wars: Visions of Conflict* (Oxford University Press, 2003). He has also published his work in journals such as *Romanticism*, *Romanticism on the Net*, and *The Byron Journal*. He is a past president of the British Association for Romantic Studies.

Michael Basker is Reader in Russian and Head of Russian Studies at the University of Bristol. He has written widely on Russian poetry, particularly of the early twentieth century, and is currently a coeditor of the Russian Academy of Sciences' 10-volume *Complete Works* of Nikolai Gumilev. Among his publications on Pushkin are an annotated edition of *The Bronze Horseman* (Bristol Classical Press, 2000), an Introduction and extensive notes to the revised Penguin Classics translation of *Eugene Onegin* (2003), and translations of some of Pushkin's critical and historical writing in *The Complete Works of Alexander Pushkin* (Milner, 2000-3).

Susan Bernofsky, the author of *Foreign Words: Translator-Authors in the Age of Goethe* (2005), works on German Romanticism, Modernism, and translation history and theory. She has published articles on Friedrich Hölderlin, Walter Benjamin, Friedrich Schleiermacher, August Wilhelm Schlegel, and Robert Walser, and is currently at work on a book on Walser.

E. H. and A. M. Blackmore have edited and translated 13 volumes of nineteenth-century French literature. Their *Selected Poems of Victor Hugo* (University of Chicago Press) received the American Literary Translators' Prize and the Modern Language Association Scaglione Prize for Literary Translation. Their other publications include literary criticism, psycholinguistics, and studies of grammatical awareness.

Inger S. B. Brodey is an Assistant Professor in Comparative Literature and Adjunct Professor in Asian Studies at the University of North Carolina at Chapel Hill. She has published widely on Jane Austen, Laurence Sterne, Johann W. von Goethe, and Natsume Soseki, including *Rediscovering Natsume Soseki* (2000). A forthcoming work entitled *Ruined by Design* focuses on the history of the novel and the philosophy and aesthetics surrounding the culture of sensibility.

Margaret Brose is currently Professor of Italian and Comparative Literature at the University of California at Santa Cruz, where she is also Director of the Italian Studies Program, and will be Director, University of California Education Abroad Programs in Italy, 2005-7. She previously taught at the University of Colorado and Yale University, and has been a Visiting Professor at Stanford University. She has written widely on all periods of Italian literature. In 2000 she was awarded the Modern Language Association Marraro-Scaglione Prize for the outstanding publication in Italian Literary Studies for her book, *Leopardi sublime: la poetica della temporalità* (1998). She is presently working on a book entitled *The Body of Italy: Allegories of the Female Figure.*

Frederick Burwick has taught at UCLA since 1965, and during that time has also enjoyed eight years in visiting positions in Germany at the universities of Würzburg, Siegen, Göttingen, and Bamberg. He has lectured at the universities of Heidelberg, Cologne, Giessen, Leipzig, and Jena in Germany as well as Oxford and Cambridge in England. He is author and editor of 20 books and over a hundred articles and reviews, and his research is dedicated to problems of perception, illusion, and delusion in literary representation and theatrical performance. As a director, he has brought to the stage Friedrich Dürrenmatt's *The Physicists* (in 2000), Christian Dietrich Grabbe's *Jest, Satire, Irony, and Deeper Meaning* (in 2002), and many other plays of the Romantic era.

Peter Cochran is the editor of the *Newstead Abbey Byron Society Review.* He has lectured on Byron in London, Oxford, Cambridge, Newstead, Glasgow, Liverpool, Versailles, Salzburg, Yerevan, and New York, and published numerous articles on the poet. He is author of the Byron entry in the *New Cambridge Bibliography of English Literature* (1999), and of the entries on J. C. Hobhouse and E. J. Trelawny for the new *Oxford Dictionary of National Biography* (2004).

Barbara T. Cooper is Professor of French at the University of New Hampshire. She is a specialist in French drama of the first half of the nineteenth century and the works of Alexandre Dumas père. She has edited Dumas's *The Three Musketeers* (2004) and a volume of the *Dictionary of Literary Biography* on *French Dramatists, 1789-1914* (1998) and published numerous articles in professional journals and books.

Michael Ferber is Professor of English and Humanities at the University of New Hampshire. He has written two books on William Blake, one on Percy Shelley, and *A Dictionary of Literary Symbols* (1999); most recently he has edited and partly translated an anthology of *European Romantic Poetry* (2005).

Derek Flitter is Head of Hispanic Studies at the University of Birmingham, UK. He has published extensively on Spanish Romanticism and its relationship with other periods of literature and ideas, including *Spanish Romantic Literary Theory and Criticism* (Cambridge 1992), *Teoría y crítica del romanticismo español* (Cambridge 1995) and the jointly authored *Don Álvaro et le drama romantique espagnol* (Dijon 2003). His latest book, *Spanish Romanticism and the Uses of History: Ideology and the Historical Imagination*, is to appear in 2005. He contributed to the new *Cambridge History of Spanish Literature* and is completing the Romanticism volume for Palgrave's European Culture and Society series.

Lilian R. Furst, Marcel Bataillon Professor of Comparative Literature at the University of North Carolina at Chapel Hill, is the author of *Romanticism in Perspective* (1969), *Romanticism* (1969), *Counterparts* (1977), *The Contours of European Romanticism* (1979), *European Romanticism: Self-Definition* (1980), and *Fictions of Romantic Irony* (1984). More recently she has worked on realism and on literature and medicine.

Piero Garofalo is Assistant Professor of Italian at the University of New Hampshire. He has published extensively on Italian Romanticism including articles on Berchet, Leopardi, Manzoni, Niccolini, and Pellico. He is the coauthor of *Ciak ... si parla italiano: Cinema for Italian Conversation* (2005) and coeditor of *Re-Viewing Fascism: Italian Cinema, 1922-1943* (2002).

Heike Grundmann is a Lecturer in English and Comparative Literature at the University of Munich and has also taught at the University of Heidelberg. She has published a book on the hermeneutics of remembering and articles on Shakespeare, Coleridge, Kleist, and others. Her current research project deals with "Fools, Clowns, and Madmen in Shakespeare's Plays."

John Hamilton is Assistant Professor of German and Comparative Literature at Harvard University. He is the author of *Soliciting Darkness: Pindar, Obscurity, and the Classical Tradition* (2004).

Elizabeth Wanning Harries teaches English and Comparative Literature at Smith College in Northampton, Massachusetts, where she is Helen and Laura Shedd Professor of Modern Languages. Her book *The Unfinished Manner: Essays on the Fragment in the Later Eighteenth Century* was published in 1994; a related article is " 'Excited Ideas': Fragments, Description, and the Sublime," in *Del Frammento*, ed. Rosa Maria Losito (2000). Recently she has been writing about European fairy tales; her book *Twice upon a Time: Women Writers and the History of the Fairy Tale* came out in paperback in 2003.

Jocelyne Kolb is a Professor of German Studies at Smith College. She has published on European Romanticism and literary revolution in the works of Goethe, Byron, Heine, and Hugo; on the relationship of music and literature in the works of Hoffmann, Heine, and Thomas Mann; and on literal and figurative constructions of Jewishness in Lessing, Heine, and Fontane.

Roman Koropeckyj is an Associate Professor of Slavic Languages and Literatures at UCLA. He is the author of *The Poetics of Revitalization: Adam Mickiewicz Between*

Forefathers' Eve, part 3 and Pan Tadeusz (2001) as well as articles on Polish and Ukrainian literatures.

Kari Lokke is Professor of Comparative Literature at the University of California, Davis. She is the author of *Gérard de Nerval: The Poet as Social Visionary* (1987), *Tracing Women's Romanticism: Gender, History and Transcendence* (2004) and coeditor, with Adriana Craciun, of *Rebellious Hearts: British Women Writers and the French Revolution* (2001). Research and teaching interests include women poets of the Romantic era, Romantic aesthetics and historiography, and theories of myth.

Michael Löwy has been Research Director in Sociology at the National Center for Scientific Research (CNRS), Paris, since 1978 and Lecturer at the Ecole des Hautes Etudes en Sciences Sociales, Paris, since 1981. His publications include *Georg Lukàcs: From Romanticism to Bolshevism* (1981), *Redemption and Utopia: Libertarian Judaism in Central Europe* (1992), *On Changing the World: Essays in Political Philosophy, from Karl Marx to Walter Benjamin* (1993), *The War of Gods: Religion and Politics in Latin America* (1996), *Fatherland or Mother Earth? Essays on the National Question* (1998), and *Romanticism Against the Tide of Modernity* with Robert Sayre (2001).

James C. McKusick is Professor of English and Dean of the Davidson Honors College at the University of Maryland, Baltimore County. His books include *Green Writing: Romanticism and Ecology* (Palgrave, 2000), *Literature and Nature: Four Centuries of Nature Writing*, coedited with Bridget Keegan (Prentice-Hall, 2001), and *Coleridge's Philosophy of Language* (Yale University Press, 1986). He has also published more than 20 articles and over two dozen reviews in such journals as *Eighteenth-Century Studies*, *English Literary History*, *European Romantic Review*, *Keats-Shelley Journal*, *Modern Philology*, *Nineteenth-Century Contexts*, *Romantic Circles*, *Studies in Romanticism*, *University of Toronto Quarterly*, and *The Wordsworth Circle*.

Fabienne Moore is Assistant Professor of French in the department of Romance Languages at the University of Oregon in Eugene. She received her PhD in Comparative Literature at New York University in 2001. She is completing her first book on *The Dynamics of Prose and Poetry in Eighteenth-Century France. A History of "Poèmes en Prose."* Her next project, *Chateaubriand's Lost Paradises*, connects Chateaubriand's haunting theme of the Fall with his travels to the New World and the Orient to show how his descriptions and meditations anticipate today's postcolonial discourse.

Virgil Nemoianu is William J. Byron Distinguished Professor of Literature and Ordinary Professor of Philosophy at the Catholic University of America in Washington, DC. He has also taught at the Universities of California (Berkeley and San Diego), Bucharest (Romania), Cincinnati, and Amsterdam. His *The Triumph of Imperfection*, to be published by the end of 2005 by the University of South Carolina University Press, is a study of early nineteenth-century European literary and cultural discourses.

James Parsons is Professor of Music History at Missouri State University. He edited and contributed two essays to *The Cambridge Companion to the Lied* (2004). He has lectured in the United States, Great Britain, and Germany, and has published on the music of Mozart, Johann Friedrich Reichardt, Beethoven, Schubert, and Hanns Eisler for such publications as *Beethoven Forum* and the *Journal of the American Musicological Society*. He is currently working on a book-length study of twentieth-century German song for which he was awarded fellowships from the National Endowment for the Humanities and the Fulbright Commission.

Roger Paulin has been Schröder Professor of German at Cambridge since 1989. He is the author of *Ludwig Tieck* (1985), *The Brief Compass: The Nineteenth-century German Novelle* (1985), and *The Critical Reception of Shakespeare in Germany* (2003)

Thomas Pfau is Eads Family Professor of English and Professor of German at Duke University. His publications include *Idealism and the Endgame of Theory* (1994), *Wordsworth's Profession* (1997), *Lessons of Romanticism* (1998), and *Romantic Moods: Paranoia, Trauma, Melancholy, 1780-1840* (2005). His essays have appeared in numerous collections and journals, including *MLN*, *Journal of the History of Ideas*, *Studies in Romanticism*, *Romanticism*, and *New Literary History*. At present he is embarking on a new project that explores the Romantic conception of *Bildung* as a matrix for the production of aesthetic forms and social knowledge across numerous nineteenth-century disciplines (biology, instrumental music and musical aesthetics, the novel, speculative philosophy, and dialectical materialism) between 1780 and 1914.

Robert Reid is Reader in Russian Studies at Keele University. His research centers on nineteenth-century Russian literature, particularly the Romantic period. His publications in this area include *Problems of Russian Romanticism* (Gower, 1986); *Pushkin's "Mozart and Salieri"* (Rodopi, 1995); *Lermontov's "A Hero of Our Time"* (Bristol Classical Press, 1997); and *Two Hundred Years of Pushkin* (Rodopi, 2003).

Diego Saglia is Associate Professor of English Literature at the Università di Parma, Italy. His main research interest is British literature of the Romantic period, also in its connections with Continental Romanticisms, and especially such areas as exoticism, the culture of consumption and luxury, the Gothic, gender and women's verse, legitimate drama and historical tragedy, representations of war, and national ideologies. He is the author of *Poetic Castles in Spain: British Romanticism and Figurations of Iberia* (2000), and his articles on Romantic literature have appeared in *ELH*, *Studies in Romanticism*, *Nineteenth-Century Literature*, *Notes and Queries*, *Comparative Literature Studies*, *Studies in the Novel*, and the *Keats-Shelley Journal*. His latest publication is a book-length study of British Orientalism, *I discorsi dell'esotico: l'oriente nel romanticismo britannico* (2002).

Robert Sayre is an American who lives and teaches in France at the University of Marne-la-Vallée. He has written on various topics in modern French, English, and American literatures, notably involving Romanticism. He is coauthor, with Michael

Löwy, of *Révolte et mélancolie: le romantisme à contre-courant de la modernité* (1992), which has more recently appeared in a revised, augmented English translation: *Romanticism Against the Tide of Modernity* (2001).

Fiona Stafford is a Reader in English at Somerville College, Oxford, who works on eighteenth- and nineteenth-century literature, and on the relationships between English, Scottish, and Irish writing. Her books include *Starting Lines in Scottish, Irish and English Poetry, from Burns to Heaney* (2000), *The Last of the Race: The Growth of a Myth from Milton to Darwin* (1994), and *The Sublime Savage: James MacPherson and the Poems of Ossian* (1988).

Jonathan Strauss is Associate Professor and Chair of French and Italian at Miami University. He is the author of *Subjects of Terror: Nerval, Hegel, and the Modern Self* (1998) and numerous articles on subjects in French literature from the eighteenth through twentieth centuries. The editor of a special edition of *Diacritics* (Fall 2000) on attitudes toward death in nineteenth-century France, he is currently completing a book entitled *Human Remains: An Essay on the Materiality of the Past*.

Patrick Vincent is Professor of English and American Literature at the University of Neuchâtel, Switzerland. He is the author of *The Romantic Poetess: European Culture, Politics and Gender, 1820-1840* (2004).

Benjamin Walton is Lecturer in Music at the University of Bristol. Recent publications include articles in *19th-Century Music*, the *Cambridge Opera Journal*, and a chapter for the *Cambridge Companion to Rossini* (2004). He is currently completing a book on music, politics, and society in Restoration France.

Introduction

Michael Ferber

The Word "Romantic"

In 1798, among the Schlegel circle in Jena, the word "romantic" (German *romantisch*) was definitively attached to a kind of literature and distinguished from another kind, "classic" (*klassisch*); it was soon attached to the Schlegel circle itself as a "school" of literature, and the rest is history. But the word already had behind it a good deal of history, which made it the almost inevitable choice.

Nonetheless the word came down to the Schlegels and their friends through some interesting accidents. It is one of the oddities of etymology that "romantic" ultimately derives from Latin *Roma*, the city of Rome, for surely the ancient Romans, as we usually think of them, were the least romantic of peoples. It is then a pleasant irony of cultural history that one of the distinctive themes of writers (and painters) whom we now call Romantic was the ruins of Rome – as in Chateaubriand's *René* (1802), Wilhelm Schlegel's "Rom: Elegie" (1805), Staël's *Corinne* (1807), Byron's *Childe Harold's Pilgrimage*, Canto 4 (1812), Lamartine's "La Liberté ou une nuit à Rome" (1822), and so on – while a large share of the Italian tourism industry today depends on the image of Rome as The Romantic City. Indeed the romantic ruins of ancient Rome could be taken as an emblem of the meaning and history of the word "romantic" itself.

The odd turn in its etymology took place in the Middle Ages. From the adjective *Romanus* had come a secondary adjective *Romanicus*, and from that the adverb *Romanice*, "in the Roman manner," though that form is not attested in the literature. Latin speakers in Roman Gaul would have pronounced *romanice* something like "romansh" and then "romants" or "romaunts." By then the Franks had conquered Gaul and made it "France," but the Franks spoke a Germanic language akin to Dutch, so "romants" (spelled *romauns*, *romaunz*, *romance*, and several other ways) was enlisted to distinguish the Roman or Latin language of the Gallo-Romans from "French" or Frankish of their conquerors. Eventually, of course, the Franks gave up their language and adopted the *romauns* language, and the word "French" switched its reference to what we now call Old French, the descendant of vulgar Latin spoken in France. Yet *romauns* remained in use to distinguish that spoken or vernacular form of Latin (that is, "French") from the older, more or less frozen, form of Latin used by the church and court. ("Romance" is still the adjective for all the daughter languages of Latin: French, Italian, Spanish, Portuguese, Romanian, and the rest.)

Romauns had also been applied to anything written in Gallo-Roman Old French and, even after "French" had replaced it as the name for the language, it remained in use for the typical kind of literature written in it, that is, what we still call "romances," the tales of chivalry, magic, and love, especially the Arthurian stories. These romances are the ancestors of the novel, and the word for "novel" in French became *romant* and then *roman*. German, Russian, and other languages have borrowed the French term for "novel," but English took its term from Italian *novella*, that is, *storia novella*, "new (story)," and limited "romance" first to the original medieval works and then to a particular kind of novel: for example, Scott's *Ivanhoe: A Romance*, Hawthorne's *Blithedale Romance*, or the "Harlequin Romances" of today.

Romant or *roman* formed several adjectives, such as *romantesque* and *romanesque*, the latter now used in art history to refer to the style preceding Gothic, and German *romanisch*. By the seventeenth century *romantique* appeared in French and "romantick" in English, but they did not catch on until the mid-eighteenth century, largely under the influence of James Thomson's *The Seasons* (1726-46), translated almost immediately into the main European languages, where we find "romantic Mountain," "romantic View," and clouds "roll'd into romantic Shapes." By the 1760s Wieland and Herder are using *romantisch* in Germany, and Letourneur and Girardin are using *romantique* in France, sometimes, as Thomas Warton did in his *Romantic Fiction* (1774), to refer to kinds of literature.

When Friedrich Schlegel and his circle began writing of *romantische Poesie* and the like, they were hearkening back to the old use of *romauns* as a term distinct from "Latin," for one of the emergent meanings is its contrast with "classic," that is, Greek and Latin literature. Friedrich Schlegel did not quite use "Romantic" as a period term. He denied that he identified "Romantic" with "modern," for he recognized some contemporary writers as classical; rather, "I seek and find the Romantic among the older Moderns," he wrote, "in Shakespeare, in Cervantes, in Italian poetry, in that age of chivalry, love and fable, from which the phenomenon and the word itself are derived" (*Dialogue on Poetry*, 1800, trans. Lilian Furst, in Furst 1980: 8-9). In his circle, however, *romantisch* became nearly identified with "modern," or "Christian," while sometimes it was narrowed to a sense connected to *Roman* as "novel" and meant "novelish" or "novelic," the novel being a characteristically modern genre.

Thus launched as a term for a trend in literature, and for those who launched the term itself, "romantic" within a decade or two was received and debated throughout Europe. It is worth remembering, in view of the indelible label later generations have given them, that in Britain neither the exactly contemporaneous "Lake School" (Wordsworth, Coleridge, Southey, Lamb), nor the next generation (Byron, Shelley,

Keats, Hunt), nor anyone else called themselves Romantics at the time. Thanks especially to Madame de Staël's *De l'Allemagne* (*On Germany*) (1813), which reported on her encounters with the "Romantic" school as well as with Goethe and Schiller, the romantic–classic distinction entered European discussion permanently. By 1810 *romanticeskij* was in use in Russia, by 1814 *romantico* in Italy, by 1818 *romantico* in Spain. In his 1815 Preface to the *Poems* Wordsworth distinguished between the "classic lyre" and the "romantic harp"; these instruments became common synec-doches for contrasting artistic commitments, as in Victor Hugo's "La Lyre et la harpe" (1822), though he does not use "classic" or "romantic" to define them. As period terms, "classic" (or "neoclassic") and "romantic" remain standard today in literary history, art history, and, to a lesser degree, in music history.

Defining Romanticism

Since almost the moment they appeared as the name of a school of literature, the words "Romantic" and "Romanticism" in various languages have been explained, queried, re-explained, criticized, defended, mocked, withdrawn, reasserted, finally laid to rest, and revived from the dead, too many times to count. In the twentieth century, scholarly essays for or against this label – I shall consider the terms one label, and capitalize them – so often began by quoting long lists of completely disparate definitions, alike only in the confidence with which they were put forth, that it became a generic requirement of such essays, which for that very reason I can forgo here. (I will give a different sort of list in a moment.) It was not the term itself that was at stake, though some have argued for a different one; it was not even the fact that specialists completely disagreed on their definitions, though that was embarrassing enough; it was the suspicion, made explicit by A. O. Lovejoy in his famous article "On the Discrimination of Romanticisms" (1924, reprinted 1948), that the term referred to nothing at all. In Lovejoy's formulation, "The word 'romantic' has come to mean so many things that, by itself, it means nothing. It has ceased to perform the function of a verbal sign" (1948: 232).

Lovejoy's essay carried many scholars with him, but very few, I think, gave up using the term. It was, and remains, too deeply entrenched, too familiar, in the end too attractive, to be discarded. Here, as evidence, is a list of titles of books that have appeared in the last 30 years or so:

Romanticism: An Anthology (1994, 1998)
Romantic Women Poets 1770-1838 (1995)
Romantic Women Poets: An Anthology (1997)
Women Romantic Poets 1785-1832: An Anthology (1992)
Poesía Romántica (1999)
La Poésie romantique française (1973)
Romantic Art (1978) (reprinted in 1994 as *Romanticism and Art*, a slight retreat)

German Romantic Painting (1980, 1994)
British Romantic Painting (1989)
Romanticism (on art) (1979)
Romanticism (again; on art) (2001)
The Romantic Movement (1994)
Nineteenth-Century Romanticism in Music (1969, 1988)
Romantic Music (1984)
The Romantic Generation (on music) (1995).

Perhaps with Lovejoy's anathema echoing in their minds, several editors have avoided
the misleading implication that their anthologies contain only Romantics (the one
called *Romanticism: An Anthology* includes Godwin and Paine, for instance) and
shunted the word into a period category:

The New Oxford Book of Romantic Period Verse (1993)
Romantic Period Writings 1798-1832: An Anthology (1998)
British Women Poets of the Romantic Era: An Anthology (1997)
Great German Poems of the Romantic Era (1995) (the German title is *Berühmte Gedichte
der deutschen Romantik*, which is more ambiguous)
Gedichte der Romantik (1988) (also ambiguous)
Painting of the Romantic Era (1999).

One sees their point, but it doesn't really get around Lovejoy's strictures, and it raises
a new question, to which I shall return, concerning the aptness of certain historical
labeling. I have noticed only one major anthology in English that goes all the way
with Lovejoy: *British Literature 1780-1832*. A prominent French anthology, *Anthologie
de la poésie française du XIX siècle*, is filled with poets usually called Romantics from
Chateaubriand to Baudelaire.

   With very few exceptions, then, scholars have continued to embrace the term that
Lovejoy said meant nothing. It probably does little harm that we use the word in titles
of books and university courses, as long as we remind readers and students from time to
time that the word is rather vague, somewhat arbitrary, and under dispute. And our
periodic efforts to ventilate the arguments over the word and its application probably
does some good as well, by demonstrating the complexities of cultural history or
"genealogy," as a term somewhat arbitrary in origin got pressed into service in various
polemics, institutionalized in universities and professional associations, and so on.

   I am not alone, however, in feeling a little uncomfortable with this situation,
familiar though it is. People do ask us, after all, what Romanticism was, who the
Romantics were, when it started and ended (if it ended), and the like. Was Blake
a Romantic? Was Byron? Leopardi? Hölderlin? Pushkin? Baudelaire? Not that
we need feel obliged to offer a sound-bite-sized answer to these questions, but we
ought to have a shorter and more obliging one at hand than a history of the
vicissitudes of the term. The task does not seem hopeless, and I have a modest

proposal or two for altering the framework in which we usually think about the subject. They might at least tidy up the situation so we can take stock of the problem more clearly.

I think we first need to ponder what a definition is, the definition of definition, if that's not begging the question, and to do so we must return to Lovejoy. In his article Lovejoy presents three groups that have been called "romantic": the school of Joseph Warton, the Jena circle around the Schlegels, and a group of one, Chateaubriand. He can find no common denominator, no single significant trait the three groups share. "Romanticism A," he writes, "may have one characteristic presupposition or impulse, X, which it shares with Romanticism B, another characteristic, Y, which it shares with Romanticism C, to which X is wholly foreign" (Lovejoy 1948: 236). We can illustrate his claim with a Venn diagram, and round out his claim by showing that B and C might share a trait Z wholly foreign to A.

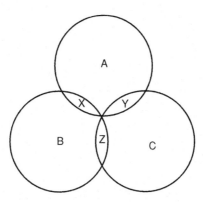

Now an easy answer to Lovejoy would be to say that the Warton school is a case of "pre-Romanticism" or "sensibility," as is Chateaubriand for the most part, but I will set that aside. Another would be to adduce several other groups, such as the Lake School (Wordsworth, Coleridge, Southey), the Cockney and Satanic Schools (Byron, Shelley, Keats, Hunt), the later Romantics in Germany (e.g., Brentano, Eichendorff, Chamisso), the Hugo *cénacle* in France, and perhaps Mickiewicz and Pushkin, to see how many other significant traits emerge. Something like this second course, I find, is a fruitful way to proceed: Lovejoy's evidence, for all his erudition, is too slender. But there is a more interesting point. Lovejoy assumes that a term lacks a definition if there is no one characteristic trait that the term always refers to, and that assumption is too narrow.

In his famous reply to Lovejoy, René Wellek (1949) proposes three traits or "norms" shared by those authors whom we still call Romantic: imagination for the view of poetry, nature for the view of the world, and symbol and myth for poetic style. Some whom we want to call Romantic, he concedes, elude one criterion or another: Byron did not see the imagination as the fundamental creative power, and "Blake stands somewhat apart" with regard to nature (surely an understatement). But the three norms are found quite widely across European literature, and those who display one of them usually display the others.

Wellek's argument has also carried many scholars with him, though Geoffrey Hartman may have been right to say that the debate is a standoff (Hartman 1975: 277). If it is a standoff, however, it may be the fault of a common trait between the two sides, for Wellek shares with Lovejoy the same notion of definition, except that in Wellek's view it is not one trait we are looking for but three. (Or rather, since the three are interlinked, they are really one, though a fairly complicated one, which may not be fully expressed in each Romantic.) Wellek's case is embarrassed by the exceptions he cites, however: if Byron is not a Romantic, or only two-thirds of a Romantic, then we had better go back to the dictionary.

The Lovejoy–Wellek debate has been replayed many times (for surveys see, for example, Remak 1961, McGann 1983, Parker 1991), almost invariably under the same rules: the search, or the abandonment of the search, for a common denominator. It seems to me a better way forward is to adopt Wittgenstein's notion of "family resemblances." In a family of 10 people, for instance, there may be five or six distinctive facial or bodily features that recur among them, but it might turn out that two or even three members share none of them. They might each have two of the traits, but the other members of the family each have four or five of them, so there are many overlaps, and when you have had a good look at, say, five members of the family, you can pick out the other five from a crowd. A definition based on this idea would amount to a list of distinctive traits, with some ranking as to importance and generality, but no one trait, maybe not even two or three, would be decisive.

Such a list might well begin with Wellek's three norms, and then several others of comparable sweep that have been put forward recently, followed by eight or ten more concrete ones:

imagination for the view of poetry
nature for the view of the world
symbol and myth for poetic style
"natural supernaturalism" (Carlyle, via M. H. Abrams 1971) or perhaps "spilt
    religion" (T. E. Hulme 1936)
"a profound change, not primarily in belief, but in the spatial projection of reality"
    (Northrop Frye 1963: 5)
"internalization of quest romance" (Harold Bloom 1971)
lyricization of literature
the fragment as privileged form
disdain for Newtonian science and utilitarianism
history or development as framework for biology, sociology, law, etc.
themes: the uniqueness of childhood; the dignity of primitives, solitaries, noble
    savages, outcast poets; night as the setting for deepest imaginative truth; incest as
    ideal; ruins, especially by moonlight; etc.

metaphors: lamp or fountain, as opposed to mirror; Aeolian harp and "correspondent breeze"; organism as opposed to machine; volcanoes; etc.

And I will toss in one more metaphor that I've noticed recently: poets as eagles. It seems to be a distinctive habit of Romantic writers in at least Britain, Germany, France, and Russia to compare themselves and each other to eagles. Since ancient times poets have been nightingales, swans, or larks, but with the main exception of Pindar poets did not presume to liken themselves to eagles until the later eighteenth century, when large flocks of them gather in the skies of poetry and circle there until about 1850, after which they rapidly thin out. It may seem trivial, but there they are in Blake, Words-worth, Mary Robinson, Byron, Shelley, Hemans, Goethe, Schiller, Hölderlin, Lamar-tine, Hugo, Sainte-Beuve, Tastu, Vigny, Alfieri, Coronado, and Pushkin, not to mention those I have missed, all standing for the poet or genius or creative enthusiasm. Eagles come oddly close to the single X that Lovejoy could not find!

Such a roster will look somewhat like the table of "elements" of West European Romanticism offered by Henry H. H. Remak, where he lists such items as folklore, medievalism, individualism, nature, and *Weltschmerz* and notes whether they were strong features in five national literatures. His proposal deserves better than the weak response it has received: reconsidered in the light of Wittgenstein's idea, and with some new features to consider, it seems promising. He concludes from it that "the evidence pointing to the existence in Western Europe of a widespread, distinct and fairly simultaneous pattern of thoughts, attitudes and beliefs associated with the connotation 'Romanticism' is overwhelming" (Remak 1961: 236).

Of course definitions should be fairly brief, and the family-resemblance approach could tend toward prolix "thick descriptions," but it seems to me our discussions would be more fruitful under this aegis than under the compulsion to search for the single decisive feature or set of features. Moreover, though it may not seem so at first, the more writers one considers the easier it is to discern recurring traits. Lovejoy offered three groups; one should look at eight or ten. For that reason, and for the way they would highlight forms and styles as opposed to themes or symbols, I suggest we bring painting and music under consideration as well. The painters and composers are as various and distinctive, no doubt, as the writers, but when they are brought onto the stage I think certain family traits stand out, such as the "musicalization" of the other arts, the rise of short forms, and the prominence of deliberate fragments. (I make a case for a Romantic "system" of the arts in the final chapter in this volume.) And of course certain Romantic literary themes persist, such as the consecration of the artist in self-portraiture, virtuoso performances (Paganini, Liszt, Chopin), and "confes-sional" music (Berlioz's *Symphonie fantastique* and *Lélio*); landscape painting and music that evokes an outdoor setting (notably in Berlioz and Liszt), not to mention settings of songs about nature and wandering; and Orientalism.

It is usually harmless enough to refer to the years 1789 to 1832, or 1820 to 1850, depending on the country, as the "Age of Romanticism" or "The Romantic Period": it will be clear that one is conferring a certain distinction on a major trend in literature or all the arts but is not necessarily claiming that it or they had a monopoly. Yet one can easily slide without thinking into a notion of cultural homogeneity or at least the assumption that everything was touched by "the spirit of the age," in Hazlitt's phrase, or the *Zeitgeist*. Strained efforts to show that Austen or Landor or Godwin was a Romantic often show this unexamined assumption at work. A recent claim, now withdrawn, that there was a distinct "women's Romanticism" in England, whose main features were flatly opposed to those of "men's Romanticism," seemed in the grip of the same idea. In any period there will be various norms, trends, tastes, or schools, and at times none of them will be dominant. Just when Romanticism became dominant, as most scholars think it did, is not easy to decide. In England we often open the period at 1789, the date of Blake's *Songs of Innocence* that also nicely coincides with the beginning of the French Revolution, but Blake went unnoticed until well after his death and is not altogether a Romantic anyway. 1798 looks like another good starting date, the year of Wordsworth and Coleridge's *Lyrical Ballads* that happily coincides with the formation of the Jena group. But it took some years for their book to make its mark; it was not a bestseller. It might not be until 1812, then, when Byron awoke to find himself famous for *Childe Harold*, that we can rightly claim that Romanticism became the dominant complex or norm, though Byron would have been astonished to hear it. The closing date of English Romanticism is often taken to be 1832, with the Reform Bill as the marker but with a sense that the recent deaths of the three younger Romantics (and Blake) put an end to something. But is Tennyson not a Romantic? And the Brontës? Surely Romantic norms were spreading everywhere even as new norms were taking shape. What we call (meaninglessly) the Victorian era might rightly be called Romantic. Yeats called himself one of the last Romantics, but may well have been mistaken. An era when millions of people flock to see *The Lord of the Rings* might forgivably be called Romantic still. Looking to other countries, and to the other arts, the same complexities recur and compound each other.

The lesson in all this is simply to keep distinct the uses of "Romantic" as a complex or system of norms and "Romantic" as a period. We can still usefully debate the meaning of the former along the lines I have suggested, and trace its anticipation in earlier periods and its persistence into later periods, that is, periods other than that of its first full flowering. This volume, by and large, confines itself to this "classic" period of Romanticism, but I have not tried to impose any definition of Romanticism as a system or even suggest that contributors should have one of their own. Some contributors may tend toward Lovejoyan skepticism, others toward Wellekian optimism, but I think I can trace through most of these excellent essays some striking family resemblances in the midst of a rich and colorful variety.

REFERENCES

Abrams, M. H. (1971). *Natural Supernaturalism.* New York: Norton.

Bloom, Harold (1971). "The Internalization of Quest Romance." In *The Ringers in the Tower.* Chicago: University of Chicago Press, pp. 13-35.

Frye, Northrop (1963). "The Drunken Boat: The Revolutionary Element in Romanticism." In N. Frye (ed.), *Romanticism Reconsidered.* New York: Columbia University Press, pp. 1-25.

Furst, Lilian R. (1980). *European Romanticism.* London: Methuen.

Hartman, Geoffrey (1975). "On the Theory of Romanticism." In *The Fate of Reading and Other Essays.* Chicago: University of Chicago Press.

Hulme, T. E. (1936). *Speculations.* New York: Harcourt, Brace & World.

Lovejoy, A. O. ([1924] 1948). "On the Discrimination of Romanticisms." In *Essays in the History of Ideas.* Baltimore: Johns Hopkins University Press, pp. 228-53.

McGann, Jerome J. (1983). *The Romantic Ideology.* Chicago: University of Chicago Press.

Parker, Mark (1991). "Measure and Countermeasure: The Lovejoy-Wellek Debate and Romantic Periodization." In David Perkins (ed.), *Theoretical Issues in Literary History.* Cambridge, MA: Harvard University Press, pp. 227-47.

Remak, Henry H. H. (1961). "West European Romanticism: Definition and Scope." In Newton P. Stallknecht and Horst Frenz (eds.), *Comparative Literature: Method and Perspective.* Carbondale, IL: Southern Illinois University Press, pp. 223-59.

Wellek, René (1949). "The Concept of 'Romanticism' in Literary History." *Comparative Literature,* 1: 1-23, 147-72.

1

On Pre-Romanticism or Sensibility: Defining Ambivalences

Inger S. B. Brodey

The Gap Between Enlightenment and Romantic Literature

On September 3, 1967, at 2 a.m., Swedish government and transportation officials executed a nationwide edict to switch traffic from driving on the left side of the street to the right. With military precision (and, in fact, the assistance of the army), the Swedish government distributed a 30-page document to each individual household, stopped all traffic for five hours, rearranged signage, and allowed traffic to resume on the opposite side of the street from the previous day.

Although there have been times in history where matters of culture or taste have seemed to reverse themselves suddenly, seldom do historical periods begin or end with such militaristic precision. The transition in Europe from Enlightenment Classicism to Romanticism has frequently been described in dichotomous terms – opposing, for example, Enlightenment or classical preference for rational order and symmetry with Romantic preference for spontaneity, fragmentation, and organicism. Indeed, the traits of Romantic and Enlightenment thought seem so dichotomous that it is hard to imagine the mechanisms of a transition between them. What suits the convenience of historians and their students, however, also tends to suit the historical self-understanding of individual epochs that define themselves in contrast to that which preceded them. Accordingly, in order to benefit from periodicization or even to identify the dominant traits of what Erwin Panofsky called the "mental habit" of an age, or what Michel Foucault called *"episteme,"* one must often ignore family characteristics: large undercurrents of shared assumptions.

The second half of the eighteenth century in England, and also largely in Germany and France, has long been victim of a tug-of-war between the classical and the Romantic, between the Enlightenment and Romanticism. English letters has had no "Storm and Stress" period, no established name to give to a long transition between periods that appear so different in nature. As a result there has been a tendency for Romanticism – already so voluminous and variable that the term can hardly bear its own weight – to swallow half of the eighteenth century as well, through the term "Pre-Romantic," a term that stems from observations made in the 1930s of conspicuous parallels between European music and literature of the 1740s to the 1790s.

There has also been much dispute about the exact dates to attach to Sensibility. On the one hand, there are scholars who are engaged in extending the earlier boundary: such scholars have tried to claim that Sensibility is a subset of Enlightenment, including Jessica Riskin's (2002) recent work on medical discourse in Sensibility, where she claims that French and American Enlightenment thought was imbued with the language and philosophy of Sensibility. Other scholars are engaged in extending the later boundary, not only those who call it Pre-Romanticism, but also scholars such as Julie Ellison (1990), who has claimed that Romanticism itself is an episode within Sensibility.

In Germany, Pre-Romantic movements in music have been separated into *Sturm und Drang* (represented by artists such as Joseph Haydn) and the *empfindsamer Stil* (represented by artists such as C. P. E. Bach). There is a complex relationship between these musical modes and the *Frühromantik*, *Empfindsamkeit*, and the Jena school of Romanticism in literature and philosophy. While it will not be a goal of this essay to untangle this web of movements, most scholars would name the *Sturm und Drang* or "Storm and Stress" movement as the most conspicuous manifestation of pre-Romanticism in German literature, featuring the extremely influential *Die Leiden des jungen Werthers* by Goethe (1774).[1] In France, Pre-Romanticism also has numerous manifestations, including *sensibilité*, and the *comédie larmoyante*, exerting influence over French literary styles in both the novel and theater. In English literature, Pre-Romantic manifestations include both Sensibility and the Gothic (or Gothick) – largely overlapping, yet seemingly distinguishable movements. The relationship between the Gothic and Sensibility, in particular, is one that has not yet been fully explored. Another confounding element in discussions of Sensibility in England and beyond is its relation to sentimentalism. Sensibility became a dominant aspect of Pre-Romanticism, distinguishing itself from sentimentalism (a much broader term) in its combination of assumptions about human psychology and anatomy. Again, it is not possible here to distinguish between these many Pre-Romantic cousins, but instead this essay will focus on Sensibility, primarily in the English novel of 1740-90, but also as Sensibility is manifested in French *sensibilité* and German Storm and Stress.

However one refers to or defines the dominant European literary taste of 1740-90, the literature of this period has not fared equally well at the hand of critics. Marilyn Butler, for example, calls Sensibility a "weak trial run for Romanticism" (Butler 1982: 29). While definition through hindsight has a long tradition, including the term "Middle Ages," yet even if it is true that Pre-Romanticism "preceded and anticipated Romanticism," as Gary Kelly (2004: 904) writes, can one not say that any period which precedes generally also anticipates subsequent periods? We can certainly find anticipation of Romantic literary notions and style as early as Plato, Montaigne, or Cervantes, if we choose to call them anticipation. Charles Rosen (1995), for example, cites many seventeenth-century analogues to Pre-Romantic traits in music. In French literature, Lafayette, Racine, and Scudéry all bear resemblances to the sentimental impulses of pre-Romantic literature, or to the literature of *sensibilité*.

Generally the term pre-Romanticism is vaguely derogatory and associated with pseudo-Romanticism, suggesting inferior content, or a period not worthy of the name of what succeeded and surpassed it: "a trough between two creative waves" (D. J. Enright 1957: 391-2) or the "the swamps between the Augustan and Romantic heights" (Todd 1986: 142). I would argue, however, that if the period is "swamplike," this is due to a lack of definite boundaries rather than a lack of brilliance or historical significance. Geographically disparate and lacking a manifesto or concrete set of goals, the culture of Sensibility may indeed seem overly amorphous: Northrop Frye's term "the Age of Sensibility" seems to oversimplify the issues of periodicization. Many scholars have used terms like the Culture of Sensibility, the Cult of Sensibility, or simply spoken of Sensibility as a movement. More recently, several cultural historians have come to see Sensibility as "the specifically cultural aspect or expression of a broad, late-eighteenth-century movement for social, economic, or political reform, linked to both the Enlightenment and Romanticism but distinct from them" (Kelly 2004: 904-5).

This is however not a new opinion: scholars as varied as Arthur Lovejoy, Erwin Panofsky, Christopher Hussey, M. H. Abrams, Martin Battestin, Michel Foucault, and Charles Taylor have all located a highly significant, aesthetic and philosophical watershed at the midpoint of the eighteenth century across Britain and continental Europe. Although the interpretations of this shift vary, they all describe the movement away from Augustan and neoclassical symmetry and order towards a new interest in asymmetry and irregularity. In the aesthetic terms of Edmund Burke, or of landscape gardening, Sensibility is involved more with the serpentine curves and studied irregularity of the picturesque than with the awe-inspiring and precipitous sublime: it is not yet opening up the realm of the monstrous, characteristic of Romanticism *per se*.[2] For the purposes of this essay, I will use the term Sensibility rather than pre-Romanticism because it treats the literary, aesthetic, and philosophical developments as important in their own right rather than as premonition of future developments. Without trying to claim that Sensibility is a distinct period (since periodicization is fraught with danger and absurdity), I will instead attempt to show that Sensibility, as a geographically disparate but temporally fairly coherent movement, provides a convenient way of understanding the cluster of transitions that occurred in the second half of the eighteenth century in Britain as well as most of Central and Northern Europe.

These five decades are a crucial turning point in such diverse fields as political philosophy, natural science, epistemology, theology, aesthetics, and moral philosophy; it witnessed great changes in general attitudes towards privacy, nature, subjectivity, language, and the self. While it will not be part of the goal here to establish causality, or to establish which discipline first influenced others, we will turn to certain of these developments to help explain the fundamental assumptions shared by most of the authors involved in the literature of Sensibility. We will pay particular attention to the ways in which the authors of Sensibility were consciously distinguishing themselves from their literary and philosophical predecessors, regardless of underlying, persistent family resemblances.

On Sensibility and its Traits

Within the literature of Sensibility, the dominant genres tended to be poetry, drama, and especially the novel. Novels also began to change in form, as the tendencies grew in Germany, France, and England towards first-person narratives, fictional letters or memoirs, self-conscious narrators, and content with a deeper psychological edge. The increased use of the self-conscious narrator is particularly significant for understanding the growing self-reflexivity and concerns about the difficulties of self-representation that helped shape narrative techniques of the literature of Sensibility. Representative novelists include Laurence Sterne, Henry Mackenzie, Charlotte and Henry Brooke, Charlotte Smith, Frances Sheridan, and Mary Wollstonecraft in England and Scotland; Johann W. Goethe, Jean Paul (Johann Paul Friedrich Richter), E. T. A. Hoffmann, Wilhelm Heinse, and Karl Philipp Moritz in Germany; and Jean-Jacques Rousseau, l'abbé Prévost, Jean-François Marmontel, and Bernardin de St Pierre in France. If it is true that from the 1740s to the 1770s, the Culture of Sensibility was predominantly shaped by the novel of the time, then it is also the case that it was largely shaped by *foreign* novels in translation. In the recent *Encyclopedia of the Romantic Era*, for example, Gary Kelly (2004) argues that it was the translation into English of Rousseau, Prévost, and St Pierre (among others) that spurred Sensibility in England, while Robert J. Frail (2004) argues that it was the translation of Defoe and Richardson (along with the poets Thomson and Young) into French that spurred Pre-Romanticism in France. In fact, as French "Anglomania" intensified after 1750, English novels appeared by the hundreds and such frenchified English novels were often called *"le genre triste"* (Frail 2004: 907).[3] As novels of Sensibility swept Europe in the 1760s and 1770s at the height of the movement, Werther became a household name in England, and Clarissa and Yorick became familiar presences in both Germany and England.

The developments in the novel relate to concurrent trends in moral philosophy, philosophy of language, and aesthetics; together, these trends describe an interesting and pervasive mode of thought that flourished during this critical period. The rise of empiricism, the growing distrust of unaided reason, the elevation of the passions – especially as guides to moral behavior – a new faith in the natural goodness of humankind, and increasing emphasis on the faculties of sympathy and imagination, combined to shape the drastically new moral self which accompanied Sensibility. At the same time, one can detect a peculiar skepticism concerning language – a growing distrust of the referential and communicative powers of language, so that words no longer are the trustworthy allies of either reason or emotion.

To summarize, there are six clusters of ideas that seem to be most characteristic of the culture of Sensibility, influencing its literary styles and content: (1) ethical thought that stressed the significance of feeling over reason for moral behavior, resulting in a new psychology that stressed the ethical, didactic, and emotional effect of the faculty of sight; (2) scientific theories that stressed the biological basis of emotion and sympathy; (3) an emphasis on the importance of independence from authority, whether construed in political, cultural, religious, or aesthetic terms; (4) a consistent preference for rural simplicity over urbanity; (5) intense concern over the possibility of human intimacy and effective (affective) communication, especially as an antidote to solipsism; and, finally, (6) a deep ambivalence about the desirability of order and system. The second of these traits could be seen as a continuation of Enlightenment or neoclassical rationalism and love of system, and the last two ideas tend to lessen in subsequent decades with the transition to Romanticism, whereas items 1, 3, and 4 do not in isolation distinguish Sensibility from Romanticism.

Moral Sentiments and Virtue-breeding Visions

One of the most infamous hallmarks of the literature of Sensibility is the prevalence of lachrymose outbursts, such as those that fill the pages of Henry Mackenzie's *The Man of Feeling* or Goethe's *Die Leiden des jungen Werthers*. Generally the protagonist is a "sensitive soul" or "man of feeling" who is placed in conflict with either "men of the world," who think of worldly gain, or the prototypical Enlightenment "man of letters" who argues with great faith in reason, but little heart. Unlike protagonists of many other periods, the man of feeling is judged by the degree to which his soul is moved by sights and tales of virtue and suffering. To some extent his virtue is proved by his weakness in other traditional roles: he possesses neither public authority, nor martial skill, nor conventional heroic strength of will. Regardless of whether male or female, the protagonists of Sensibility reject reason as a guide to moral behavior; instead their authors show that sympathy and their pure hearts are less fallible guides to moral behavior. The sympathy which these characters readily feel and display is often stimulated by a tableau of virtue in distress. Novels of Sensibility are sprinkled generously with such visual tales and tableaux of suffering to serve as stimuli for the virtuous feelings of protagonist and reader alike.

In direct opposition to classical and Augustan thought, feeling takes the place of reason as the supreme human faculty; feeling rather than reason now provided the only hope of community within the tenets of Sensibility. Whereas Enlightenment or neoclassical thought required vision for the perception of a rational, eternal order, Sensibility's use of sight tends towards *affect* – especially the possibility of sympathy evoked by visions of suffering. This also differs from its use in Romantic thought, where, just as the emphasis in poetic imagery is often on night rather than day, the "inner eye," or what the imagination "sees" often seems more significant than what the eye could witness in daylight.

Already in late seventeenth-century England, Locke had begun to pave the way for these developing ideas about reason. When Locke asks the crucial question in his *An Essay Concerning Human Understanding*: "Whence has [the mind] all the materials of Reason and Knowledge?" his response is especially illuminating:

> To this I answer, in one word, From EXPERIENCE: In that, all our Knowledge is founded; and from that it ultimately derives it self. Our Observation employ'd either about *external, sensible Objects; or about the internal Operations of our Minds, perceived and reflected on by our selves, is that, which supplies our Understandings with all the materials of thinking.* (Locke 1975: 104, my emphasis)

Locke's division of "EXPERIENCE" into "Observation" of both "external, sensible Objects" and "internal Operations of our Minds" draws a strong connection between "SENSATION" and "REFLECTION" (Locke 1975: 105). In doing so, he establishes to an unprecedented degree the importance of the senses and the passions to the process of "thinking." The sensations and passions do not themselves rule thought or reason, but they come *first* in the process and provide thought with its fodder. Without them we are incapable of thought.[4]

The third Earl of Shaftesbury, often taken as the official philosopher of Sensibility, carried the displacement of reason by feeling several steps further, as he began to substitute an "ethics of feeling" for the dominant "ethics of rationalism." Shaftesbury aestheticized morality to an unusual degree:

> To philosophise, . . . is but to carry good-breeding a step higher, for the accomplishment of good breeding is, to learn whatever is decent in company or beautiful in arts; and the sum of philosophy is, to learn what is just in society and beautiful in Nature and the order of the world. (Shaftesbury 1900, II: 255)

He was confident that human beings could achieve both virtue and happiness by harmonizing their passions and by cultivating the delicacy and aristocratic nobility of "taste."[5] Compared to taste, other faculties like judgment, unaided reason, and conscience based on discipline were powerless: "After all," he wrote, "'tis not merely what we call principle, but . . . taste that governs men. . . . Even conscience, I fear, such as is owing to religious discipline, will make but a slight figure where this taste is set amiss" (Shaftesbury 1900, II: 265).[6]

Hume, Adam Smith, and Rousseau, following Shaftesbury, all carefully excluded unaided reason from their discussion of virtue; they achieved this by displaying the inherent weakness of unaided reason and by taking additional steps to raise the passions to an exalted status previously held exclusively by reason. Hume, for example, wrote that "I shall endeavour to prove *first*, that reason alone can never be a motive to any action of the will; and *secondly*, that it can never oppose passion in the direction of the will" (Hume 1978: 413). By this Hume does not mean that reason is insignificant in our actions, but instead that it does not have the psychological *power* of passion. Only passion can oppose passion, just as "morality... is more properly felt than judg'd of" (1978: 470). Law, reason, and discipline cannot move us to virtue; only such *virtuous passions* as sympathy and benevolence can do so: "Our sense of duty always follows the common and natural course of our passions" (p. 484). The most shocking aspect of Hume's philosophy in this regard was not so much his claim that reason generally does not control the passions, but his refusal to accept the idea that reason *should* (Lovejoy 1961: 181).

The word "sentiment" became a vehicle for the *synthesis* of reason and emotion which proved key to moral philosophers such as Hume and Smith and separated them from Shaftesbury: for these mid-century philosophers, "sentiment" denoted intellec-tualized emotion or emotionalized thought. Thus, in his *Theory of Moral Sentiments*, Smith could speak of, for example, the "heart" rather than the mind of the impartial spectator judging our actions, and also of "our *hearts* [having to] adopt the *principles* of the agent" (Smith 1982: 39, my emphasis). Over and over again Smith attributes traditionally rational functions, such as judging and adopting principles, to the tender heart of the spectator. Thus the rise in moral authority that the passions had gained by this time showed itself in the changing meaning of the word "sentiment."

When reason loses its moral authority and becomes less normative, "sentiment," that curious combination of emotion, reason, and sensation, rises to take its place as the representative of our natural and normative inner self. Along with this changing notion of the self follows a new perception of our position within nature and nature within us. Taylor calls this change the "Deist shift":

> For the ancients, nature offers us an order which moves us to love and instantiate it, unless we are depraved. But the modern view, on the other hand, endorses nature as the source of right impulse or sentiment. So we encounter nature..., not in a vision of order, but in experiencing the right inner impulse. (Taylor 1989: 284)

Whereas for Aristotle, for example, the goal is for *phronèsis* to guide the passions according to an understanding of the good, this modern view differs radically in that there is no hierarchical order to apprehend or apply (Taylor 1989: 283-4). Instead, the moral agent needs to look inside to gauge his or her own "inner impulses"; no disengaged reason, no other voice is necessary – simply the promptings of one's own *sensible* heart.

As the literature of Sensibility flourished, the ethics of feeling continued to dominate, as evidenced by the emphasis on intense friendship or ardent romantic love as indicators of the ability to feel, and continued emphasis on expressivism and using narrative techniques to affect emotion in the audience. While the Augustan tendency towards didacticism did not fade fully in England until the nineteenth century, the nature of didactic lessons changed, and authors manipulated readers' emotional responses in order to achieve a sentimental education of the audience, presumed immune to the effects of direct argumentation.

Sensible Bodies, Sensitive Nerves

If vision loomed large as a sense that enabled the sensitive soul to sympathize with others, then the nerves figured even more prominently as the conveyors of emotion within the sensitive soul's anatomy. Potential for virtue, in other words, seems to have been proportionate to the functioning of one's nervous system. Preoccupation with bodily mechanisms of emotion and experience stem from the Enlightenment materialist epistemology described above, and much discourse in philosophy and natural science was devoted to finding the biological basis of emotion, particularly as located in the nerves and senses. Thus the new psychology that stressed the ethical, didactic, and emotional effect of the faculty of sight rests upon the foundation of the sensory origin of ideas, first made popular by John Locke, and propagated in literature through the works of Laurence Sterne, Samuel Richardson, and Jean-Jacques Rousseau.

The definition of *"Sensibilité (morale)"* from Diderot's *Encyclopédie* illustrates well what was comprised in this new ideal:

> Tender and delicate disposition of the soul which renders it easy to be moved and touched. Sensibility of soul, which is rightly described as the source of morality, gives one a kind of wisdom concerning matters of virtue and is far more penetrating than the intellect alone. People of sensibility because of their liveliness can fall into errors which Men of the world would not commit; but these are greatly outweighed by the amount of good that they do. Men of sensibility live more fully than others.... Reflection can produce a man of probity: but sensibility is the mother of humanity, of generosity; it is at the service of merit, lends its support to the intellect, and is the moving spirit which animates belief. (my translation)

However, it is remarkable to students today that Diderot felt the need to include separate "medical" and "philosophical" entries for Sensibility in his *Encyclopédie* (1751-65). Here is a brief excerpt from the medical entry written by a natural scientist: "the faculty of sensing, the cause of feeling, or feeling itself in the organs of the body, the basis of life and what assures its continuance, animality *par excellence*, the finest, the most singular phenomenon of nature."

Poetry eulogizing Sensibility also often emphasized its physical origins in the tingling nerves and fibers of the human body:

> Hail, sacred source of sympathies divine,
> Each social pulse, each social fiber thine;
> Hail, symbols of the God to whom we owe
> The nerves that vibrate, and the hearts that glow.

The above excerpt from Samuel Jackson Pratt's poem *Sympathy* (1781), shows a common conception that the physical impulses of sensibility are imbedded in human nature by God, and are the key to sociability and fellow-feeling. Frances Brooke, in her sentimental novel *Emily Montague* (1769), also displays the intimate connection between Sensibility's psychology and its ethics: women do not achieve religion and virtue through "principles found on reason and argument" but instead through "elegance of mind, delicacy of moral taste, and a certain quick perception of the beautiful and becoming in everything" (Brooke 1985: 107).

"Sensibility," a word that was quite rare until the middle of the century, took on multiple meanings including "perceptibility by the senses, the readiness of an organ to respond to sensory stimuli, mental perception, the power of the emotions, heightened emotional consciousness, and quickness of feeling" (Hagstrum 1980: 9).[7] This keen response could be stimulated by either *beauty* or *suffering*: in other words, "sensibility" took over not only aesthetic terrain but also the moral terrain of "what would once have been called charity" (Lewis 1967: 159). As "sympathy" and "sensibility" replace "charity," the emotions in the "sensible" spectator become more important than any actions that this virtuous observer may take to alleviate suffering. Personality and spontaneous, overflowing feeling replaced character, plans, discipline, and, eventually, action; nerves and glands came to bear greater ethical significance than muscles. This crucial shift in ethics and aesthetics affected the protagonists of Sensibility.

"[F]ar more penetrating than the intellect alone," Sensibility's ideal portrays the dramatic fall of unaided or "disengaged" reason that we have described above. Reflection no longer has direct contact with the will, and the passions and nerves carry more potent (eventually even more accurate) information than reasoning. Mary Wollstonecraft describes Sensibility as "the result of acute senses, finely-fashioned nerves, which vibrate at the slightest touch, and convey such clear intelligence to the brain, that it does not require to be arranged by the judgment."[8] As the passions grow reasonable and even moral, the need arises to *cultivate* rather than suppress them. We have seen the effects of this trend in the pedagogy of seeing and feeling emphasized both in landscape gardening and the sentimental novel. Sensibility's moral psychology brought with it an emphasis on receptivity or sensitivity to external behavior and sights, whether the landscape garden, the Alps, or the sight of human suffering at home. In short, "sensibility," a word which has largely disappeared from our vocabulary today, and when used means little more than "emotional viewpoint," had a glorious past. During this half century, it meant little less than the essential spark of life, virtue, and humanity.

Natural Goodness, Originality, and the Rustic Soul

The words "sentiment" and "sensibility" provide a bridge between the epistemological, linguistic, and ethical issues of the period. The multiple meanings of the word "sensible," in fact, helped contribute to the mid-century rise in an optimistic conception of natural human goodness. Both the terms "sentimental" and "sensibility" show a significant and unprecedented ability to bundle reason, passion, and virtue into one tidy package. The peculiar confluence of two of the main meanings of the word "sensible" – that is, the minimalist (1) "conscious . . . aware" and the rarified (2) "having sensibility; capable of delicate or tender feeling" – enables the creation of a naturally virtuous hero or heroine and expresses the potential for great optimism by suggesting that virtue is as natural to us as sensing or waking.[9] Inherent in such easy access to virtue is, however, also the possibility for great disappointment. For if virtue is so natural, how does one explain its (very frequent) absence? Eighteenth-century writers therefore sought for new guides to moral behavior, since they observed that reason and virtue, as traditionally understood in classical or Christian terms, did not seem to be doing the job. This combination of euphoric optimism and great fear or pessimism is a pervasive feature of Sensibility.

Somewhat oddly, it was a mid-seventeenth-century philosopher, long since dead, who figured most prominently as the philosophical opposition for Sensibility. Explicitly or implicitly, the ideas of Thomas Hobbes and his *Leviathan* (1660) fueled the culture of Sensibility; philosophers and other authors united in the desire to prove him wrong about the inescapably selfish nature of human beings. While philosophers in the common sense school struggled to lower the threshold for natural virtue, for example, novelists of Sensibility sought to illustrate examples of the untaught nature of virtue, and attention was drawn to the anthropological discoveries of the "noble savage" in the voyages of Captains Cook and Bougainville, among others. Two of the ways in which this attention to natural goodness figures prominently in the hallmarks of the literature of Sensibility are the consistent preference for rural simplicity over urbanity and the importance placed on independence from institutional authorities.

Sensibility coincides with a dramatic rise in folklore movements across Europe and Britain. Across the genres of literature, one can see a growing emphasis on nature, natural simplicity, the ordinary, everyday rustic life, and also kindness to animals. The new moral aesthetic left no room for more urban forms of virtue: urbane sophistication was untrustworthy; erudition was formed for abuse; civility was another form of dishonesty; and those with education were seen as most skilled in deception. Three works – in the French-speaking world, Rousseau's *Discours sur l'origine et les fondements de l'inégalité parmi les hommes* (1755); in England, Thomas Percy's *Reliques of Ancient English Poetry* (1765); and in Germany, Herder's *Von Deutscher Art und Kunst* (1773) – were especially significant in building a vogue for folk culture and folk literature. Some authors, most notably James Macpherson in his *Poems of Ossian* (1760-63), were so eager to include examples of ancient, untrained, natural simplicity and virtue that the authors resorted to forgery in order to claim the historical authenticity of the texts and the protagonists, while others took to the fields to find poems written by talented milkmaids. The pursuit of natural goodness, and the desire to prove Hobbes wrong, also spurred an emphasis on the importance of originality or independence from authority and traditional institutions. Depending on the individual authors, this was construed in either political, aesthetic, cultural, or religious terms. Authors stressed the inadequacies of old hierarchies, praised a reliance on self-taught knowledge, promoted skeptical irreverence towards theories and institutions. In French literature, this often took the form of freedom from Classicism and its rigid aesthetic rules, as well as from traditional religious and social constraints. In Germany, it could be seen, for example, in the growing popularity of Pietism, a brand of Protestantism that emphasizes spiritual intensity and direct communication with a personal deity in preference to mediation by institutions and clergy. These reformist or oppositional aspects of Sensibility have led many authors to place Sensibility in the camp of French revolutionaries.[10]

Each in a different context, Edward Young, Jean-Jacques Rousseau, and Johann W. Goethe, all wrote about the importance of originality and the corrupting and diminishing effects of society, draining individuals of their authenticity. In his *Discours sur les sciences et les arts* (1750), Rousseau complains of the homogenizing effect of society upon our passions:

> Before art had shaped our manners and taught our passions to speak an artificial language, our customs were *rustic* but natural; ... Today, more subtle study and a more refined taste have reduced the art of pleasing to a system; a vile and misleading uniformity prevails in our manners, so that one would think all minds had been cast in the same mold. Unremittingly, politeness requires this; decorum legislates that; unceasingly we follow these forms rather than our own genius. (Rousseau 1971a: 54, my translation)

Nine years later, in his *Conjectures on Original Composition* (1759), Edward Young similarly complains of the contemporary lack of originality in a society that seems to require uniformity: "Born Originals how does it come to pass that we die Copies!" (1759: 42). With a memorable line that could almost be a paraphrasing of Young's credo, Rousseau opens his *Social Contract* ([1762] 1971b): "Man was born free, but is everywhere in chains." And in his *Die Leiden des jungen Werthers*, Goethe's eponymous protagonist shows fictionally the fate of those who try to remain authentic originals despite the pressure of society to conform to regulations and homogenizing expectations, whether in terms of social conventions or ethical standards: his struggles bring him to the brink of madness and, ultimately, to suicide. Reason, established etiquette, logic, self-conscious moderation, and mathematical proportion eventually came to be seen by devotees of Sensibility as enemies of the "right inner impulse" which would only be quenched or diffused by such censorship.

One of the primary features of the "mental habit" of Sensibility seems to have been an assumption (or fear) of the impossibility of the coexistence of authority, authentic feeling, and virtue in any given individual, as well as doubt as to whether virtuous people can conform their expressions to the political and social conventions of society without sacrificing their own authenticity and, therefore, virtue. In other words, despite the moral sense school's attempts to portray virtue as increasingly natural and accessible, virtue actually became rarer, in a sense, as the culture of Sensibility progressed. The rarity or scarcity of virtue and authentic feeling was denoted in a number of ways, including the drive to look further and further afield for its exemplars. Finally we end up with an ironic return to a universe that seems strikingly Hobbesian, as the "sensitive soul" or "man of feeling" becomes increasingly rare and embattled.[11] Authors of novels of Sensibility thus felt pressure to portray heroes who were also victims of society – Shaftesburian souls, forlorn in a Hobbesian universe.

The Language of Feeling

As inheritors of John Locke's disturbing epistemological findings, and lacking a concomitant moral confidence in the duty to organize and categorize and speak, authors of the culture of Sensibility grew painfully aware of the limitations of both the representative and communicative powers of language. Given its own ambivalent attitude towards words and definition and its consciousness of the difficulties of self-representation, perhaps it would only be appropriate that this disputed period remain nameless. As Laurence Sterne warns, through the voice of Tristram Shandy, "to define is to distrust"; however, to speak is, inevitably, to generalize.

Just as reason was under heavy fire in the second half of the eighteenth century, language was as well: language's referential and communicative powers, the possibility of objectivity for the human mind, and the possibility of translation were all topics that spurred heated intellectual debate among such major figures as Locke, Shaftesbury, Diderot, Hume, and Smith. Diderot, Rousseau, and Herder showed that by allowing feelings to be passed through the ordering, but stultifying, funnel of discourse, we lose the authenticity of the instantaneous "flash" of feeling. Thus the culture of Sensibility sought to represent through gestures, visual art, and fragmentation what could no longer be articulated through syntactic completion and with a reliance on logic or discursive reason.

Out of these movements in philosophy, linguistics, and aesthetics emerges a new character. Shaftesbury's gentleman of taste; Hume and Smith's man of sympathy or moral sentiments; Rousseau, Voltaire, and Diderot's noble savage; Mackenzie's man of feeling; Sterne's sentimental traveler, and Goethe's Werther, all share the essential attributes of the hero of Sensibility: unspoiled natural virtue, an unusually keen perception, and a deep capacity to feel.[12] In addition, all of the fictional heroes and heroines from Diderot to Goethe share great difficulty expressing their deep, naturally virtuous feelings in the conventional language of society. In fact, their difficulty speaking becomes a measure of their sensibility: in being men of feeling, they are explicitly not men of words.

The intense concern over the (im)possibility of human intimacy and communication, was exacerbated by concern over human tendencies towards solipsism, so effectively illustrated by Laurence Sterne in his *Tristram Shandy*. Solipsism, in fact, became such a hallmark of Sensibility that Keats and Hazlitt both denigrated Sensibility's purposeless and solipsistic self-consciousness. In a philosophical dispute that, in effect, resembled a linguistic corollary to the dispute over Hobbes and natural goodness, authors were torn between the demand for intense self-consciousness and awareness of the dangers of solipsism, between self and society. For novelists of Sensibility this formed not only an intriguing philosophical problem, but also an opportunity to exercise new narrative techniques, particularly following the eccentricities of Sterne. First-person, self-conscious narrators became much more common, largely through the work of Sterne, Tieck, and Diderot, and authors generally experimented with the self-conscious mediation of sentiment via language. A "rhetoric of silence" resulted from this desire to represent what could no longer be articulated directly – that is, to preserve natural expression uncensored by the authority of words, logic, grammar, and closure.

The Architecture of the Novel of Sensibility

As we have seen from these excerpts of philosophy and psychology from the second half of the eighteenth century, aspects of human nature that had previously been considered unruly and disorderly rose to distinction, as the passions grew to displace reason as the more trusted guides to moral behavior. The irregular, the fragmented, the unintended, the unruly, the nervous, the hysterical – tokens of human depravity to neoclassical eyes – became not only aesthetically desirable, but morally superior to regularity, completion, and order. Artists of Sensibility were thus in a paradoxical position of having to pursue and "compose" decay, ruination, and irregularity in order to capture authentic feeling. In the case of novels of Sensibility, authenticity and artifice, disorder and order are intricately interwoven. When, as in the case of Sensibility's aesthetic code, authenticity is equated with disorder, and artifice with order, authors must respond by combining structure with the pointed avoidance of structure in order to articulate their story and evoke the proper emotions in the reader. Authors in mid-to-late eighteenth-century England, France, and Germany, writing novels of Sensibility, in other words, responded to the same aesthetic and cultural demands as the architects of the follies, the artificial architectural ruins that became popular across Europe alongside Sensibility.

Just as scenes of pathos, depictions of unqualified virtue, promotion of subjective responses in the reader, and tableaux of emotionally laden situations became commonplace hallmarks of the novel of Sensibility, the six ideas developed above led to the need for new narrative strategies. For example, the aesthetic associated with Sensibility demanded of its literature that those who speak well cannot possibly feel, and those who feel most deeply invariably stammer and fragment their speech; in other words, according to Sensibility's moral and aesthetic code, eloquence had become a moral indicator of hypocrisy or heartlessness. Responding to these challenges, authors such as Laurence Sterne, Johann W. Goethe, and Henry Mackenzie developed a new strategy: they constructed purposely fragmented novels with elaborate narrative frames that could divide the responsibility for authorship among the characters and thereby allow the protagonists to tell their own stories without seeming to organize them, protecting them from accusations of coldness or insensibility. They succeeded in hiding their role as "men of words" in order to protect their status as "men of feeling." As a result, the five decades of Sensibility witnessed strong innovations in the form of the novel, particularly its narrative techniques.

The novel was a natural locus for issues central to Sensibility, because of the conflicts over narration and the difficulties of self-representation. In other words, the growing distrust of reason discussed above also corresponded to a distrust of omniscient narration, which gradually grew incompatible with sensibility. A narrator who was *not* self-conscious, and therefore not a participant in the action and feelings of the novel, could be seen as anonymous, heartless, and bringing a random imposition of the author's authority. Only spontaneous speech, "uncensored" by strict grammatical rules and "untainted" by practical purpose or preconceived plans, could count as authentic or sincere. Traditional narrative was equated with cold-hearted rationality and worldliness, especially if the narrative is explicitly written as a final product, with the intent of publication.

Both Sterne and Goethe use an intruding narrator to create an additional frame of authorship in their texts and to protect themselves and their protagonists from the taint of coherent narrative and from accusations of such base practicality. In *A Sentimental Journey*, Yorick is the narrator as well as the central character in his travels; in *Werther*, Werther also narrates his own story – this time, in the form of letters. Goethe provides a self-conscious narrator, the *Herausgeber*, who acts as editor and compiler of Werther's letters. The *Herausgeber* forms a second narrative frame, especially noticeable since his is the first and last voice of the text. All three of these narrators contribute to the fragmentary nature of the narrative because they are self-conscious about their writing and the difficulties associated with producing an organized, unified text. These complicated linguistic and narratorial requirements were not limited to these two novels, but instead exhibit responses to Sensibility's central concerns as enumerated above. Henry Mackenzie's *The Man of Feeling*, the third in the triumvirate of most popular novels of Sensibility, appeared in 1771, three years after *A Sentimental Journey*, and three years before *Werther*. Mackenzie borrows many techniques from Sterne and his innovations foreshadow Goethe's *Werther* as well. Mackenzie's combination of themes and narrative techniques used by Sterne and Goethe will further illustrate the ideas associated with these techniques. By transferring authorship and authority to their self-conscious narrators, Sterne, Mackenzie, and Goethe attempt to bridge the gap between men of feeling and men of words. The fragmentation and chaotic elements of the novels can therefore be attributed to the narrator agents, while the authors themselves can still maintain an invisible control over, and mastery of, the text.

In *The Man of Feeling* Mackenzie's decision to leave the narrating of Harley's story to others is precisely not a return to an authoritative narrator, such as the one in Fielding's *Tom Jones*; instead, Mackenzie goes to great lengths to undermine any appearance of order, control, or objective detachment on the part of his narrators. Mackenzie's novel uses no fewer than three narratorial frames to mask the authorship of those whom it seeks to portray as "men of feeling." Just like Goethe's *Werther*, it has multiple narrators, only Mackenzie uses *three* layers of editors who account for its fragmentation as well as its order.

Upon examination, we can see that each of the three central voices in this novel – the three central "I"s – represents a separate "feeling heart" through its fragmentation. Although Harley does not narrate his own story, the narrators transcribe his spoken words and (somewhat unaccountably) his private thoughts at great length. Mackenzie shows his response to the demands of the culture of Sensibility by sacrificing authenticity in plot, at such times, for the sake of authenticity of emotion: it is more important that Harley *not* be a man of words, than that the reader understands *how* the narrator could possibly have known his feelings. On a rare occasion, Harley does write of his (unproclaimed) love: in Chapter XL, we find a pastoral poem that Harley has laboriously written; however, he promptly uses it to lift a hot tea kettle, and forgetfully leaves it on the handle. The narrator, Charles, finds it there, and later records: "I happened to put it in my pocket by a similar act of forgetfulness" (Mackenzie 1987: 113). It is clear that Mackenzie will go to great, and almost comic, lengths to stress the unpremeditated nature of these men's actions; therefore, their status as men of feeling cannot be sullied with imputations of "rational" or "artificial" motives. The narrator-participant Charles must not think of himself as narrator during the time frame that his narration depicts, lest the reader find him cold, hypocritical, or untrustworthy. Thus, somewhat ironically, he must display a lack of foresight in order to gain the "sensible" reader's trust. Charles (we learn his name on the last page), repeatedly evinces traditional narratorial omniscience, but this omniscience is masked by his personal subjectivity: Charles loves Harley, and his great affection for him prevents him (according to his own account) from presenting the narrative in an orderly fashion.

Many of the major gaps and silences in the narrative, however, stem from neither Charles's delicate sensibility nor Harley's distrust of words: instead their source is on another plane of narrative altogether. They are the result of the actions of "the unfeeling curate" who, as we learn in the introduction, finding Charles's story worthless ("the hand is intolerably bad, I could never find the author in one strain for two chapters together: and I don't believe there's a single syllogism from beginning to end"), has used Charles's story as wadding for his rifle when he hunts (Mackenzie 1987: 5). Of course, the curate's objections to the narrative style reveal precisely the story's worth in terms of sensibility: a strong hand would betoken a cold heart, and more adherence to story or plot would signify insincerity. The curate's mangling of the document, forming the third narrative frame for the story, is the palpable reason the novel begins with "Chapter XI" and has chapter headings such as "The Fragment," yet the narrative gaps of the manuscript actually function as gaping wounds inflicted by a Hobbesian society upon the sensitive Shaftesburian soul.

In one sense, the multiple narrative frames of the novel of Sensibility have one simple goal: repeated deferral of responsibility for authorship (or passing the buck, if you will) from author to fictional editors as well as from protagonist to fictional editors. The greater the number of individuals (fictitious or not) whose sensibility and authenticity needed to be protected as well as portrayed, the greater the number of editorial frames the works required. This may give us another way of understanding the appeal of translated novels to the culture of Sensibility. When works were translated into a new language, the original author occasionally became a new natural hero or heroine of Sensibility; a new editorial frame was added in the course of the new translation or edition of the work, claiming how the translator discovered this exquisite gem that would otherwise have been overlooked by the unfeeling populace at large. In other words, the effect of translation was not only thematically appropriate, but it also added another archaeological layer to the complex narrative strategies preferred by readers during the five decades when Sensibility flourished.

Defining Ambivalence

Throughout this essay, I have suggested central ambivalences or tensions within the ideas that helped shape the novel of Sensibility. It may be that such fundamental ambivalence, or simultaneous optimism and pessimism, is one of the most important hallmarks of Sensibility – at the same time, it is also a token of the movement's instability and lack of coherence. In the preceding pages, we have looked at the desire for order and system coexisting with the relish of spontaneity; the distrust of reason argued most persuasively and rationally by philosophers; the desire for narration that seeks to hide all traces of narrative authorship; and the insistence upon natural goodness accessible to all, yet which is poignantly rare and fragile. In most of these cases, Sensibility started as a reaction against Enlightenment confidence in the powers of reason and education, but ultimately resulted in an ironic reversal, showing the continuity of family traits by pursuing similar goals under different terms. An example would be the continuance of didacticism, but its transformation into a pedagogy of seeing and feeling, rather than a pedagogy of abstract reasoning.

Sensibility's "double vision" consists of a persistent tension between extreme optimism and fearful pessimism, between revolutionary fervor and nostalgic conservatism, between democratic and hierarchical impulses, between egalitarianism and elitism, between virtue as natural and virtue as highly cultivated, between ruins and carefully constructed buildings, between narratives and fragments. Although the distinction is far from glamorous, Sensibility may also be distinguished from Romanticism by its heartfelt ambivalence, stemming at least from the events of the French Revolution and subsequent Terrors, simultaneously intrepid and fearful. This brings us back again to Hobbes, against whom the culture of Sensibility largely defined itself. A Hobbesian understanding of human nature became necessary as a foil or a backdrop to the unfolding of this Shaftesburian soul – the man of feeling – as virtue *in* distress gradually contorted itself into the virtue *of* distress.

Perhaps this lends new meaning to the negative treatment Sensibility has received at the hands of critics, particularly in relation to Romanticism. Critics frequently use such terms as "half-hearted" or "weak" to describe Sensibility: just as Marilyn Butler described sensibility as a "weak trial run for Romanticism" (Butler 1982: 29). D. J. Enright once wrote that "between the self-assured work of the Augustans and the energetic and diverse movements of the Romantic revival came a period of half-hearted, characterless writing" (Enright 1957: 391-2). Marshall Brown, too, describes Pre-Romanticism as "a problem, rather than an ambition" (Brown 1991: 99). But is that lack of Romantic univocalism necessarily a weakness? I would argue that Sensibility's double vision, hypocritical as it may seem at times, expresses a basic human ambivalence that is at least partly an enlightened response to the events of the French Revolution. Sensibility was an interesting experiment in attempting to express both optimistic revolutionary fervor and conservative nostalgic concerns for order and stability without falling into either disastrous extreme – in political terms, avoiding both anarchy and totalitarianism. Ambivalence is not a glamorous distinction, but perhaps it is one with a wisdom of its own.

NOTES

1 Interestingly, this work is also sometimes categorized under the movement "*Empfindsamkeit*."

2 This is true especially in French and English versions of Pre-Romanticism; the German example is more complicated. The *Sturm und Drang* movement was more involved in the sublime, storms, and darker, emotional concepts than the French and English versions of Sensibility. Although contemporaries like Hoffman called all three composers "*romantisch*," Mozart and Haydn can be considered Pre-Romantic, whereas Beethoven can be seen to represent Romanticism because he opens up the realms of the monstrous and immeasurable.

3 In music, representatives of Sensibility would include Haydn and Mozart; in painting, Constable, Turner, Claude, Poussin, Greuze, and Piranesi; and in landscape gardening, the Englishmen Repton and Whately.

4 At this point, however, we must distinguish between the seventeenth-century Locke and the eighteenth-century Locke: that is, we must try to separate his own position from the conclusions that were drawn from him later in the eighteenth century. For Locke, "disengaged reason" still rules supreme and provides the only way we gain our rightful

place in the providential order (Taylor 1989: 265): "To Locke all men are by nature rational and God, 'commands what reason does'" (Aarsleff 1982: 175). Later in the eighteenth century, Locke was, of course, considered to have knocked the pedestal out from under Reason (a conclusion which was not unmerited by some of Locke's claims), but he himself did not consider that to be the case. (Cf. Nuttall 1974: 13-19, for a discussion of the eighteenth-century interpretations of the implicit solipsism in Locke's teaching, as well as Locke's foreshadowing of nineteenth- and twentieth-century existentialism.) Although elements of his thinking did indeed have the effect of shaking the confidence in "disengaged reason," his purpose in illustrating the potential distortions of human understanding was to protect Reason and Knowledge from abuse.

5 "Taste" (as well as another of his favorite terms, "relish") is another term that, despite a primary designation of aesthesis, and a physical origin, describes a process that includes elements of both passion and thought. And just like "sentiment" and "sensibility," it is endowed in the eighteenth century with moral qualities as well. For Shaftesbury, it did not carry the subjective meaning it does today.

6 Bishop Butler protested that conscience could not survive without judgment, discipline, authority, or a standard which stood outside and opposed itself to the individual, and suggested that such thinking as Shaftesbury's offered no protection against human weakness and vice (Bredvold 1962: 19). However, voices such as Bishop Butler's and Samuel Johnson's were outnumbered by those who had greater faith in the "internalization" of virtue.

7 Lewis remarks that its most pervasively popular meaning, was "a more than ordinary degree of responsiveness or reaction; whether this is regarded with approval (as a sort of fineness) or with disapproval (as excess)" (Lewis 1967: 159).

8 Quoted in Warren (1990: 31).

9 Definitions of "sensible" from *Oxford English Dictionary*, 2nd edn.

10 For further discussion of Whig and Tory interpretations of Sensibility, see Markman Ellis (1996).

11 Brissenden also views this paradoxical situation as central to Sensibility (e.g. Brissenden 1974: 21); in fact, it is the inspiration for the title of his book *Virtue in Distress*.

12 See Bredvold (1962: 24-5) and Brodey (1999 passim).

REFERENCES AND FURTHER READING

Aarsleff, Hans (1982). *From Locke to Saussure: Essays on the Study of Language and Intellectual History*. Minneapolis: University of Minnesota Press.

Bredvold, Louis I. (1962). *The Natural History of Sensibility*. Detroit: Wayne State University Press.

Brissenden, R. F. (1974). *Virtue in Distress: Studies in the Novel of Sentiment from Richardson to Sade*. New York: Barnes and Noble.

Brodey, Inger Sigrun (1999). "The Adventures of a Female Werther: Austen's Revision of Sensibility." *Philosophy and Literature* 23 (1): 110-26.

Brooke, Frances (1985). The *History of Emily Montague*. Ottawa and Don Mills, ON: Carleton University Press.

Brown, Marshall (1991). *Preromanticism*. Stanford, CA: Stanford University Press.

Burke, Edmund (1968). *A Philosophical Enquiry into the Origin of our Ideas of the Sublime and Beautiful*, ed. James Boulton. Notre Dame, IN and London: University of Notre Dame Press.

Butler, Marilyn (1982). *Romantics, Rebels, and Reactionaries: English Literature and Its Background, 1760-1830*. Oxford and New York: Oxford University Press.

Diderot, Denis and Robinet, Jean-Bapiste René (1751-65). *Encyclopédie ou Dictionnaire raisonné des sciences, des arts et des métiers*. Paris: Briasson.

Ellis, Markman (1996). *The Politics of Sensibility: Race, Gender, and Commerce in the Sentimental Novel*. Cambridge, UK: Cambridge University Press.

Ellison, Julie (1990). *Delicate Subjects: Romanticism, Gender, and the Ethics of Understanding*. Ithaca, NY and London: Cornell University Press.

Enright, D. J. (1957). "William Cowper." In Boris Ford (ed.), *Pelican Guide to English Literature*. Harmondsworth, UK: Penguin.

Frail, Robert J. (2004). "Pre-Romanticism, France." In Christopher John Murray (ed.), *Encyclopedia of the Romantic Era: 1760-1850*. New York and London: Fitzroy Dearborn, p. 907.

Frye, Northrop (1963). "Towards Defining an Age of Sensibility." In Northrop Frye, *Fables of Identity*. New York: Harcourt Brace, pp. 130-7.

Goethe, Johann Wolfgang von (1989). *Die Leiden des jungen Werthers*. In E. Trunz (ed.), *Goethes Werke: Hamburger Ausgabe*. München: C. H. Beck.

Hagstrum, Jean H. (1980). *Sex and Sensibility: Ideal and Erotic Love from Milton to Mozart*. Chicago: University of Chicago Press.

Hume, David (1978). *A Treatise on Human Nature*. Oxford and New York: Clarendon Press and Oxford University Press.

Hussey, Christopher (1967). *The Picturesque: Studies in a Point of View*. London: Frank Cass.

Kelly, Gary (2004). "Pre-Romanticism: Britain." In Christopher John Murray (ed.), *Encyclopedia of the Romantic Era: 1760-1850*. New York and London: Fitzroy Dearborn, pp. 904-5.

Lewis, C. S. (1967). *Studies in Words*. Cambridge, UK: Cambridge University Press.

Locke, John (1975). *An Essay Concerning Human Understanding*. Oxford: Clarendon Press.

Lovejoy, Arthur O. (1961). *Reflections on Human Nature*. Baltimore, MD: Johns Hopkins Press.

Mackenzie, Henry (1987). *The Man of Feeling*. Oxford and New York: Oxford University Press.

Nuttall, A. D. (1974). *A Common Sky: Philosophy and the Literary Imagination*. Berkeley: University of California Press.

Pratt, Samuel Jackson (1781). *Sympathy, a Poem*. London: T. Cadell.

Riskin, Jessica (2002). *Science in the Age of Sensibility: The Sentimental Empiricists of the French Enlightenment*. Chicago and London: University of Chicago Press.

Rosen, Charles (1995). *The Romantic Generation*. Cambridge, MA: Harvard University Press.

Rousseau, Jean-Jacques (1971a). "Discours sur les sciences et les arts (First Discourse)." In Jean-Jacques Rousseau, *Oeuvres complètes*. Paris: Du Seuil, pp. 52-68.

Rousseau, Jean-Jacques (1971b). "Le Contrat social: Livre I." In Jean-Jacques Rousseau, *Oeuvres complètes*. Paris: Du Seuil, pp. 515-80.

Shaftesbury, Anthony, Earl of (1900). *Characteristicks of Men, Manners, Opinions, Times*. London: Grant Richards.

Smith, Adam (1982). *The Theory of Moral Sentiments*. Indianapolis: Liberty Classics.

Taylor, Charles (1989). *Sources of the Self: The Making of the Modern Identity*. Cambridge, MA: Harvard University Press.

Todd, Janet (1986). *Sensibility: An Introduction*. London and New York: Methuen.

Warren, Leland E. (1990). "The Conscious Speakers: Sensibility and the Art of Conversation Considered." In Syndy McMillen Conger (ed.), *Sensibility in Transformation: Creative Resistance to Sentiment from the Augustans to the Romantics, Essays in Honor of Jean H. Hagstrum*. Rutherford, NJ: Fairleigh Dickinson University Press, pp. 25-42.

Young, Edward (1759). *Conjectures on Original Composition. In a Letter to the Author of Sir Charles Grandison*. London: A. Millar and R and J. Dodsley.

2

Shakespeare and European Romanticism

Heike Grundmann

From Classic Unities to Natural Genius

We owe some of the best Shakespearean criticism ever written to the Romantics. Between 1808 and 1818, August Wilhelm von Schlegel, Samuel Taylor Coleridge, and William Hazlitt among others wrote lectures and essays that were revolutionary and detailed at the same time, and still have not lost their freshness of insight for the modern reader. It was on the basis of Shakespeare's work that the Romantics inaugurated close psychological analysis ("character criticism"), and developed the study both of the history of the stage and of the national and political setting in which a work of art is situated. Their turning to "practical criticism," a close reading of texts, originated in the attempt to understand textual structures as "organic wholes," centered and unified in a "germ" that had only to be laid open to give meaning to the entire work of art. The history of modern criticism and the emergence of a new hermeneutics became almost identical with the history of Shakespeare interpretation throughout Romanticism.[1]

The need to defend Shakespeare against the disparagement he had suffered from neo-Classicist critics such as Voltaire led to a rejection of the rules that had hitherto been regarded as prerogatives for dramatic art: the "Aristotelian" unities of time, place, and action; decorum and verisimilitude; the differentiation of (high) tragedy and (low) comedy according to the social status of their characters. Obviously, Shakespeare's work ran directly contrary to these definitions of "good taste," and the generation that was in its youth at the end of the eighteenth century used him as their battle-cry in fending off French hegemony and turning the old system of values upside down.

Despite differences in approach, the Romantics were united in their animosity to the totalitarianism of Napoleonic rule as well as the prescriptionism of the French Academy. Their all-encompassing defense of Shakespeare against the strictures of neo-Classicism meant that barbaric genius was reinterpreted as conscious artistry, the supernatural in his plays was given a psychological and philosophical justification, the seemingly wild masses of mixed characters and actions in his plays were interpreted as well-wrought structures, or else defended as a perfect mirror of a chaotic and confused reality. His mixture of the grotesque and sublime, high and low, comic and tragic was seen as a realistic and truthful depiction of the panorama of the world. As German idealism permeated the spirit of the English Romantic age, reality came to be located in the interplay of the intellectual and imaginative faculties of the mind, no longer in a fixed external reality. The introspective and idealistic tendencies of Romanticism found their perfect mirror image in the character of Hamlet, who was interpreted as a paralyzed Romantic and subjected to psychoanalysis: it is the abstracting and reflecting self of the philosopher that inhibits his practical activity in the world. In the microcosm of the continental reception of Shakespeare we can observe the struggle between the Classic and the Romantic: the English poet became the vanguard of a revolution of sensibility and taste that involved the discovery of the vitality of national literature and a Rousseauistic appeal to subjective analysis and introspection. Shakespeare gave the Romantics all they were craving for: a world that confronted great kings with fools and destitute beggars, characters that were as inconsistent as real human beings are, combining melancholia and obsession, madness and high intellectuality, sublime goodness and grotesque evil – the whole gamut of experience set against the artificial puppeteering of an anaemic Classicism.

"Strong Imagination" – British Romanticism

Creative imagination, genius, and nature are closely associated with one another in the beliefs of the British Romantics, and yet these tenets can be traced back well into the eighteenth century, when writers such as Edward Young and Alexander Gerard laid the groundwork for the Romantics by exploring the creative power of imagination with recourse to Shakespeare.[2] Even as early as in Milton's "L'Allegro" Shakespeare is "fancy's child," warbling "his native wood-notes wild"; he is the natural genius, despite having (or because he had) only "small Latin and less Greek." As neoclassical criticism in Britain did not represent so monolithic an obstacle to the younger generation as Voltaire represented for French Romanticism, the British Romantics rather synthesize and refine what has gone before.[3] John Dryden (1631-1700), for example, distinguishes between art and nature, genius and learning when he refers to Shakespeare:

> All the images of nature were still present to him, and he drew them not laboriously, but luckily; when he describes any thing, you more than see it, you feel it too. Those who accuse him to have wanted learning give him the greater commendation: he was naturally learned; he needed not the spectacles of books to read nature; he looked inwards and found it there. I cannot say he is every where alike; were he so, I should do him injury to compare him with the greatest of mankind. He is many times flat,

insipid; his comic wit degenerating into clenches, his serious swelling into bombast. But he is always great when some great occasion is presented to him.... (Dryden [1668] 1962, 1: 67)

Though praise is mingled here with condemnation of his faults (bombast, triteness), Shakespeare increasingly becomes the unquestioned hero of British cultural consciousness. In Dr Johnson's preface to his edition of the plays, published in 1765, Shakespeare is "above all writers, at least above all modern writers, the poet of nature; the poet that holds up to his readers a faithful mirrour of manners and of life" (Johnson 1968: 62). Even before the advent of Romanticism proper English neo-Classicists use Shakespeare's disregard of rules as an exemplum of their rejection of French insistence on abstract codification. The demand for editions and the omnipresence of quotations from his plays in everyday speech, as well as the success of Garrick's productions at Drury Lane after 1747, testify to Shakespeare's continued supreme status as poet of the English people. The summation of the neoclassical adherence to Shakespeare was Garrick's Jubilee at Stratford in 1769, which also marked the beginning of a new age of bardolatry.[4]

In the aftermath of the French Revolution and its terrors, the English middle class needed a national figure of identification. This led to the "gentrification" of Shakespeare, an ideological maneuver that turned a deer poacher into the prosperous middle-class businessman in Stratford-upon-Avon, who even applied for a coat-of-arms.[5] The "Tory history of England," a conservative ideology of history opposed to revolutionary change, found material proof in Shakespeare – both in the histories and in *Macbeth* and *King Lear*. In his *Reflections on the Revolution in France* (1790), Edmund Burke (1729-97) depicts the imprisonment of the French royal couple as analogous to the night of murder in *Macbeth*; and in his 1805 *Prelude* William Wordsworth (1770-1850) also alludes to *Macbeth* when associating revolutionary atrocities with his memories of lying awake in Paris shortly after the September massacres:

> And in such way I wrought upon myself,
> Until I seemed to hear a voice that cried,
> To the whole city, "Sleep no more." (*The Prelude*, Book X, lines 75-7)

This conservative backlash, which regards the liberating eradication of royal tyrants as comparable to the regicide in *Macbeth*, where bad conscience cries in the murderer's head: "Sleep no more" (*Macbeth* II, ii, 35), is typical of the appropriation of Shakespeare by many British Romantics, who tended to forget the revolutionary fervor of their own youth. In allusion to Henry Fuseli's (1741-1822) famous painting, caricaturists represented the Jacobins and their sympathizers as the three witches in *Macbeth*, or the rebels in the *Tempest*. During the war against France, *Henry V* was used for nationalistic purposes, and J. P. Kemble's historicizing and antiquarian performances established Shakespeare as part of the national heritage. Sir Walter Scott's (1771-1832) novels strengthened this equation of Shakespeare with British history by using extensive intertextual references to connect his own representation of history with Shakespeare's. When he has the young Charles II disparage Shakespeare's histories (he is not willing to read *Richard II* in *Woodstock*, he is hinting at the dangers of ignoring the wisdom of these plays.

Liberal intellectuals like Tom Paine and William Cobbett reacted with disparagement of Shakespeare. Cobbett sees in his plays "wild and improbable fiction, bad principles of morality and politicks, obscurity in meanings, bombastical language" (quoted in Schabert 2000: 621). But John Thelwall and other "Jacobin" critics still searched for a possibility of identification with Shakespeare. William Hazlitt's (1778-1830) *Characters of Shakespear's Plays* (1817) shows the struggle of an admirer of Shakespeare's artistic achievement with his own misgivings about his assumed royalism. In his discussion of Shakespeare's histories Hazlitt points out their advocacy of a hierarchical state governed by the established authorities and the discrepancy between the power relations depicted and the idea of a just order. Interpreting *Coriolanus*, Hazlitt claims that Shakespeare could understand the plight of the people because of his sympathetic nature; and yet "the language of poetry naturally falls in with the language of power." Apart from giving an analytical insight into the course of history, great art is necessarily elitist, concludes Hazlitt.[6]

A much more conservative kind of criticism can be encountered in the work of Samuel Taylor Coleridge (1772-1834), who argues for a formal, apolitical, philosophical approach. In the age of Johnson, Shakespeare was admired for his mimetic truth to created nature (*natura naturata*); in that of Coleridge himself, as he writes in "On Poesy or Art," he was admired rather for his grasp of the living principle at the heart of nature (*natura naturans*):

> If the artist copies mere nature, the *natura naturata*, what idle rivalry! If he proceeds only from a given form, which is supposed to answer to the notion of beauty, what an emptiness, what an unreality there always is in his productions, as in Cipriani's pictures! Believe me, you must master the essence, the *natura naturans*, which presupposes a bond between nature in the higher sense and the soul of man. (Coleridge 1907, 2: 257)

Coleridge adopts the ideas of A. W. Schlegel, who regarded Shakespeare's work as the outcome of a central synthesizing creative power in the person of the poet, and in his *Biographia Literaria* (1817) calls this creative principle "imagination."[7] Shakespeare's histories are explained with regard to the "germ" that gives unity to the matter of history, and the discovery of this center should be the goal of Shakespeare criticism, evading thereby ideological issues as well as Classicist demands for obedience to rules that lie outside the work of art. Coleridge, like Schlegel, differentiates between mechanical and organic form, and defines Shakespeare's art as unconscious inspiration directed by intellectual consciousness: "And even such is the appropriate excellence of her [Nature's] chosen poet, of our own Shakespeare, himself a nature humanised, a genial understanding directing self-consciously a power and an implicit wisdom deeper than consciousness" (Coleridge 1960, 1: 198). Whereas Johnson defined

Shakespeare as a genius unconscious of his powers, the bard is now regarded as a conscious artist who works according to an organic principle that is yet deeper than consciousness.

Following his own theory in his "practical criticism," Coleridge gives detailed analyses of many opening scenes, which he regards as the "germ" out of which the unity of the whole can be developed. He also points out individual words in order to prove that each part is essential to the whole: key words such as "again" in the first scene of *Hamlet*, "honest" in *Othello*, "crying" in Prospero's account of his flight from Milan with the infant Miranda, encompass the meaning of the whole (Coleridge 1960, 1:18, 46-7, 2: 135. See also Bate 1986: 14). In his combination of practical criticism with a belief in the "organic unity" of the work of art, as developed in chapter 15 of the *Biographia Literaria* (1817), Coleridge became an early proponent of what would later be called New Criticism. Coleridge, who coined the word "psychoanalytical," also instigated and participated in the Hamlet fever that held many intellectuals in its grip throughout the nineteenth century and relates character interpretation to idealistic philosophy: "Hamlet's character is the prevalence of the abstracting and generalizing habit over the practical. . . . I have a smack of Hamlet myself, if I may say so" (Coleridge June 15, 1827, [1835] 1990, 2: 61).

According to Coleridge, Shakespeare's supreme artistry is due to his "Protean" nature, the ability to transcend slavish copy by creative imitation, to sympathize with his characters while still remaining detached:

> While the former [Shakespeare] darts himself forth, and passes into all the forms of human character and passion, the one Proteus of the fire and the flood; the other attracts all forms and things to himself, into the unity of his own IDEAL. All things and modes of action shape themselves anew in the being of MILTON; while SHAKSPEARE becomes all things, yet for ever remaining himself. (Coleridge 1907: 27-8)

The essentials of Coleridge's aesthetics are represented by an impersonal author who is yet sympathetic, organic unity of the work of art, and a close relationship between poetry and philosophy. The image of Shakespeare as Proteus was one of the most fruitful concepts among the Romantic Shakespearean critics (Bate 1986: 15ff.). Hazlitt based his criticism on the principle of sympathy (in opposition to the criticism of A. W. Schlegel, whom he admired but found overtheoretical) and claims accordingly that Shakespeare had "a perfect sympathy with all things," yet was "alike indifferent to all," that he was characterized by "the faculty of transforming himself at will into whatever he chose: his originality was the power of seeing every object from the exact point of view in which others would see it. He was the Proteus of the human intellect" (Hazlitt 1930-4, 8: 42). These remarks are the forerunners of Keats's belief that men of genius "have not any individuality, any determined Character," but are like chameleons (Keats 1965, 1: 184).

Despite the success of great actors and actresses such as Sarah Siddons, John Kemble, and Edmund Kean, antitheatrical prejudice was rampant and the fitness of

Shakespeare's plays for the stage was a contested issue. Charles Lamb attempts to reduce Shakespeare to an ideal substratum and argues that the embodiment of his characters on stage amounts to a debasement: "instead of realising an idea, we have only brought down a fine vision to the standard of flesh and blood";[8] the reader's imagination on the contrary purifies the drama from human and moral implications. On the stage, characters such as Macbeth, Richard III, and Iago are criminals, but in the reading process their spiritual qualities – ambition, the poetic language, and the sublimity of their vision – are revealed. Hazlitt, on the contrary, realized that appreciation of Shakespeare on the stage depended simply on the quality of the actors and their representation of the text.[9]

Whereas Romantic criticism attains an integral understanding of Shakespeare, creative imitation of his work is concentrated on single visions, images, and stylistic specialties – the very greatness of Shakespeare seems to have exerted an inhibiting influence on British dramatic productivity in the nineteenth century. Attempts to create a neo-Elizabethan drama end up in closet dramas such as Robert Southey's *Wat Tyler*, Coleridge's *Remorse* and *Zapolya*, Wordsworth's *Borderers*, Shelley's *Charles I* and Keats's *Otho the Great*. Only Shelley's play *The Cenci* (1819) transcends mere imitation and fulfills the demand expressed in the preface to bind the imagery to the passion. Shelley also rewrites Shakespeare's *Richard II* into *Charles I* by putting Gaunt's patriotic death speech into the mouth of the freedom fighter John Hampden, thereby turning it from a defense of national freedom into a defense of individual freedom. Lord Byron (1788-1824) changes Macbeth in his drama *Manfred* (1817) into the hero of an autonomous imagination, Ann Radcliffe widens Macbeth's visions into passages of gothic terror in *The Italian* (1797), Keats (1795-1821) deploys Shakespearean imagery in his poems "The Eve of St. Agnes" (1819) or "On Sitting Down to Read *King Lear* Once Again," and William Blake (1757-1827) chooses single images as topics for his illustrations. Most Romantic poets take lines, imagery, and stylistic features of Shakespeare, making their own work into a web of references in admiration of the bard, but also to cope with their own feeling of inferiority and belatedness.[10]

German *"Shakespearomanie"*

The feeling of belatedness and lack of a great national literature of their own induced in German writers an enthusiastic Shakespeare cult, which exceeded the bardolatry of the other countries on the continent and from the start combined admiration with identification and appropriation (*Aneignung*). In contrast to the British reception of their national poet in the nineteenth century, the Germans regarded Shakespeare as exemplary of the democratic and progressive liberal cultural life of England and tried to incorporate him as a third "German classic" into their own culture.

This wholehearted embrace of Shakespeare was inhibited at first by French rationalist criticism (Voltaire, Boileau), which gave Germany a Classicist image of Shakespeare. Johann Christoph Gottsched (1700-66), approaching Shakespeare from a didactic point of view, criticized him for his irregularity, mixture of kings and beggars, violation of the unities, and lack of clarity. Tragedy was meant for moral improvement of the audience and therefore should not depict free-reigning passions but stoic endurance (Pascal 1937: 3ff.). Gotthold Ephraim Lessing's (1729-81) 17th *Litteraturbrief* of 1759 reverses these dramatic values. Whereas Gottsched set out from moral intention, Lessing made the first principle of tragedy the excitement of passion ("*Erregung der Leidenschaft*") and sympathetic identification of the spectator with the hero ("*Mitleiden*"). As tragedy must have in his view a subjective, emotive value, he condemns the Procrustean influence of the French classical drama (Corneille) and holds Shakespeare up as a model.[11] J. J. Eschenburg's translations were replaced by Christoph Martin Wieland's (1733-1813) translation of 22 plays which appeared between 1762 and 1766, and from this time Shakespeare became the common property of all educated Germans.

A new generation, later designated as *Sturm und Drang* (Storm and Stress),[12] comprising Gerstenberg, Klinger, Lenz, Herder, Goethe, and Schiller, worshiped Shakespeare for his evocative power to involve the audience in the action. In their rebellion against the bureaucracy and despotism of German provincialism and political quietism Shakespeare meant for them an intellectual revolution, a liberation of senses, feeling, and imagination. With Johann Gottfried Herder's (1744-1803) essay on Shakespeare of 1773, historical criticism was inaugurated: Greek drama is the product of the climatic and geographical position of Greece and its national culture and tradition, while Shakespeare is the product of the north and of entirely different cultural conditions: "Thus Sophocles's drama and Shakespeare's drama are two things which in a certain respect have scarcely the name in common."[13] This was not only a new view of the *querelle des anciens et des modernes*, liberating modern authors from the oppressive comparison with the Greeks, but also an attempt at description and interpretation instead of accusation or defense of Shakespeare; Herder "would rather explain him, feel him as he is, use him, and – if possible – make him alive for us in Germany" (Bate 1992: 39).

The admiration of the *Sturm und Drang* authors did not remain merely theoretical, in that Shakespeare's language of passion, daring imagery, and twisted syntax had a deep impact upon their own dramatic practice. These angry young men adopted less Shakespeare's plots than his characters, especially those of his great villains (Richard III, Iago, Macbeth), and used scenes and motifs (the balcony scene in *Romeo and Juliet*, the graveyard scene from *Hamlet*, the madness of Ophelia) in their own work for their pictorial as well as their dramatic effect. A prominent example, the speech of the disadvantaged evil brother Franz Moor in Friedrich Schiller's (1759-1805) first play *The Robbers* (1781), merges the nihilism of the bastard Edmund with the diabolical hypocrisy of Richard III's rebellion against his natural destiny of ugliness:

I have no small cause for being angry with Nature, and, by my honour! I will have amends. – Why did I not crawl first from my mother's womb? why not the only one? why has she heaped on me this burden of deformity? on me especially? just as if she had spawned me from her refuse. Why to me in particular this snub of the Laplander? these negro lips? these Hottentot eyes? [...] No! no! I do her injustice – she bestowed inventive faculty, and sets us naked and helpless on the shore of this great ocean, the world – let those swim who can – the heavy may sink. To me she gave naught else, and how to make the best use of my endowment is my present business. Men's natural rights are equal; claim is met by claim effort by effort, and force by force – right is with the strongest – the limits of our power constitute our laws. (Schiller 1953: 18ff., my translation)

Promethean rage against the injustice of nature and against patriarchal authority, expressed in a staccato of questions and exclamations, makes the ancestry of Schiller's language evident. Shelley will learn this play by heart, Wordsworth and Coleridge use it as a dramatic springboard, and Verdi in 1846 uses it as a source for his opera *I Masnadieri* – in homage to Schiller as well as to Shakespeare. Schiller's work abounds with characters similar to Shakespearean characters: obvious parallels are the elder Moor and Gloucester/ Lear; Don Carlos and Hamlet; Fiesko and elements of Caesar and Coriolanus; in the *Wallenstein* trilogy Gräfin Terzky and Lady Macbeth, Illo at the Banquet and Lepidus (in *Anthony and Cleopatra*); MacDonald and Deverous and the murderers in Richard III.[14] *Sturm und Drang* drama is the drama of idealistic young heroes (such as Karl Moor, Goethe's Götz von Berlichingen, Schiller's Ferdinand von Walter, Klinger's Simsone Grisaldo and Guelfo) thwarted by a society dominated by corruption and evil. Usually their fight for freedom and love is frustrated, and a yearning for withdrawal into the idyllic can be discerned in many of the plays. The restrictive conditions of the political situation in Germany forced these authors to create men whose desire to act is frustrated, idealists and sentimentalists who remain ineffectual in their endeavors. This attitude also had its effect on the staging of Shakespeare in Germany: he was produced in prose translations, in which coarse characters and bawdy puns were excised, often by using Garrick's versions with imposed happy endings.

   Johann Wolfgang von Goethe (1749-1832) had begun his career as a *Sturm und Drang* author, hailing Shakespeare enthusiastically in his early speech *"Zum Schäke-spears Tag"* ("On Shakespeare's Birthday," 1771), in which he claims that the new subjectivity, unencumbered by rules, can create characters that pulsate with the life of Nature: "Nature, Nature! nothing is so much Nature as Shakespeare's characters!" (Goethe 1986-, 1.2: 413, my translation). He disdains the unity of place as "incarcerating" (*"kerkermäßig ängstlich"*), the unities of action and time as "cumbersome shackles of our imagination" (*"lästige Fesseln unsrer Einbildungskraft"*) (ibid., p. 412). But when he goes to Weimar in 1775 to serve at the court of Herzog Karl August, a shift in his attitude to society and social conventions gradually turns him into a "Classicist" (*Klassiker*) who develops a new regard for order (albeit the order of nature). And yet the famous analysis of *Hamlet* in *Wilhelm Meister's Apprenticeship* (1796) has always been regarded as the starting point for the Romantic reception of Shakespeare, which grew out of the famous characterization of Hamlet as being in his sensitivity and introspectiveness too weak to carry out the demand for action that is imposed on him: "Shakespeare tried to describe a great deed laid on a soul not adequate to the task."[15] The Hamlet passages are groundbreaking as the first example of the so-called "character criticism" that will dominate the Romantic approach to Shakespeare. In his position as director of the reorganized Weimar theater, however, Goethe retreated more and more from psychological realism, propagating a stylized formal acting mode defined in his "Rules for Actors" (1803) and an unrealistic style of declamation without much movement. Admittedly, in a 1795 production he allowed Hamlet to die and restored the gravedigger scene (both of which elements had been traditionally omitted), but the dominant "classical" tendency of the Weimar theater shows itself in the production of Schiller's free translation of *Macbeth* in 1800, when the incantations of the witches are linked with the chorus of antique tragedy and Goethe had the witches played by beautiful young maidens.[16] Goethe's own translation, or rather trimming, of *Romeo and Juliet* of 1811 was a mutilation of the original. In his essay "Shakespeare and no End!" (1813-16) Goethe defends his way of producing Shakespeare on the Weimar stage. In strong opposition now to the views put forward by A.W. Schlegel, Goethe maintains that Shakespeare is above all a poet to be read and no poet of the theater, because only "what is immediately symbolical to the eye" is theatrical and these moments of union are rare in his work: "Shakespeare's whole method finds in the stage itself something unwieldy and hostile" (Bate 1992: 7). For the reader, the frequent changes of scene are no drawback, but for the spectator they are confusing. Shakespeare is lacking in "action evident to the senses" ("*sinnliche Tat*"), the events and scenes of the plays are "better imagined than seen" (Bate 1992: 6). Yet this criticism is tempered by extravagant praise, as this essay also contains what is in effect the "classical" restatement of the earlier *Sturm und Drang* encomium in its affirmation of Shakespeare's universal significance – he is unique in that he combines the despotic idea of fate and necessity that dominates the drama of antiquity with the modern concept of individual volition, thereby reconciling liberty with necessity ("*Wollen*" and "*Sollen*").

The next generation, called in Germany the "Early Romantics" (*Frühromantiker*), no longer attempted to "better" the poet, but rather to understand him, to emphasize the theatrical abilities of Shakespeare. These writers constituted a close-knit coterie of poets and critics, writing half-esoterically only for a very small public so that their periodical *Athenäum* tended to be aphoristic and obscure. A. W. Schlegel fought for productions of Shakespeare in their original form despite misgivings about their public reception. Their greatest achievement, however, was the still unsurpassed Schlegel–Tieck translation of Shakespeare's plays. Schlegel's translations of 17 of the plays between 1797 and 1810 broke new ground in attempting to reproduce Shakespeare's blank verse and idiom in a German as close to the English original as possible, and although they met with some opposition at the time, they have attained canonical status and given Germany the Shakespeare most people still read, know, and perform today.[17] Their popularity has been to a large extent responsible for Shakespeare's having been claimed by Germans as "their" leading dramatist, and his plays are performed on the German stage more than those of any other writer.

The "Early Romantic" criticism of Shakespeare follows similar lines. Ludwig Tieck's (1773-1853) famous introduction to his translation of *The Tempest*, "Shakespeare's Treatment of the Marvellous" (1793), praises Shakespeare's comedies for their complete and consistent unreality, their dreamlike quality which until then had been subjected to severe condemnation. The rehabilitation of the fantastic not only saved plays such as *A Midsummer Night's Dream* and *The Tempest* from the accusation of lacking probability and realism, but influenced the German Romantic comedy, which deploys fantastic characters and events in abundance. Tieck's own works, such as *Puss in Boots* (1797), *Prince Zerbino* (1798), and *The World Upside Down* (1799), are set in a fairy-tale world; Clemens Brentano's (1778-1842) *Ponce de Leon* (1804) is an imitation of *As You Like It*; and Joseph von Eichendorff's *The Wooers* (1833) imitates *Twelfth Night*.[18] Tieck, who had visited England in 1817 and subsequently became a theater critic in Dresden, also wrote a defense of Shakespeare as a poet of the theater, "Remarks on some Characters in *Hamlet* and about the Way they can be Presented on the Stage" (1823), disputing the persistent notion that Shakespeare had not been a dramatic poet.[19]

In 1796, August Wilhelm Schlegel (1767-1845) began his series of essays on Shakespeare with the object of proving the formal consistency of his work, the unity of every detail with the whole, and also (for the first time) exploring Shakespeare's sources. In his famous essay "On Shakespeare's Romeo and Juliet," published in Schiller's journal *Die Horen* (1797), Schlegel shows the artistry of the composition of this play, which is based on binary oppositions: the enmity of the Capulets and Montagues is mirrored in the antagonism of servants and minor characters and in the relationship of Romeo and Juliet. Comic characters, such as Mercutio and the Nurse, whose parts had been excised and mutilated for ages, are now elevated from the status of superfluous comic elements and *"possenhafte Intermezzisten"* (farcical intermezzists; Goethe 1986-, 11: 184) to that of structurally necessary devices, namely as contrastive foils.

Both August Wilhelm and his brother Friedrich Schlegel (1772-1829) regarded Shakespeare as an example of technical excellence instead of mere natural genius, as the *Sturm und Drang* authors had claimed. In an aphorism in the *Athenäum* of 1798, Friedrich Schlegel characterizes Shakespeare as the most "systematic" and "correct" author, correctness meaning here the conscious construction of all parts in the spirit of the whole, and claims that the deliberateness of construction (*Absichtlichkeit*) makes him a supremely conscious artist (quoted in Pascal 1937: 141). A. W. Schlegel's famous and highly influential *Lectures on Dramatic Art and Literature* (1808-11), held in Vienna when the city was under Napoleonic siege, give an outline of the society and culture of Shakespeare's period and derive the nature of his drama from the political climate of the Elizabethan period – the age of exploration and heroism, which was far superior to his listeners' own time. This brilliant example of historicostructural criticism was further developed in the series of lectures on Shakespeare held in 1806 in Dresden by the economist and literary historian Adam Müller (1770-1829). In his theory Müller (writing almost like a precursor of Mikhail Bakhtin) differentiates "monological" from "dialogical" drama. Sentimental dramas, based on audience identification and a simple scheme of reward and punishment, are distinguished from Shakespeare's infinitely more complex histories, which he calls "dialogical," because they prevent simple identification and confront the audience with an abundance of possible meanings and positions.[20]

Strangely enough, while Shakespeare became more and more ingrained into Germany's national culture and performances that were true to the original were more frequent in Germany than in England, Romantics such as Friedrich Schlegel and the idealist philosopher F. W. J. von Schelling (1775-1854) began to criticize Shakespeare's pessimism and lack of metaphysical consolation, preferring the Spanish poet of the *siglo d'oro* Calderón de la Barca (1600-81). This paradigmatic change was due to a yearning for ultimate meaning and harmony that could not be satisfied by Shakespeare's openness and multivocality and that had indeed induced many Romantics to convert to Catholicism. From about 1815 onwards Shakespeare ceases to be the slogan of an aesthetic that is regarded as progressive and becomes more and more the subject of literary scholarship without a close connection to contemporary developments in literature.[21]

French École Romantique – *Shakespeare c'est le drame*!

To a greater degree than Johnson in England and Gottsched in Germany, Voltaire (François Marie Arouet, 1694-1778) was the enemy in opposition to whom the French Romantics had to define themselves. Ambivalent utterances by the early Voltaire, who appreciated Shakespeare's greatness despite his barbarism and breaking of the rules, had given way to an increasing inclination to disparage Shakespeare in order to assert the supremacy of Corneille and Racine. While still calling Shakespeare a genius, he is unequivocal about his faults in the 18th of his *Lettres philosophiques* (1734): "He had a genius full of force and fecundity, of the natural and the sublime, without the least glimmer of good taste and without the least knowledge of the rules."[22] Just as Voltaire's knowledge of Shakespeare evidently comprised only a small canon (*Hamlet*, *Julius Caesar*, and *Othello*), Shakespeare seems to have been virtually unknown to his contemporaries. Voltaire even opposed La Place's translation of Shakespeare into French out of fear that widespread accessibility of the English "*Gille de la foire*" (crier in the marketplace) would undermine good taste. In contrast to the effect J. J. Eschenburg's translations (1775-82) had in Germany, not even Pierre Félicien Le Tourneur's pioneering Shakespeare translations (1776-82) succeeded in enlarging the canon; for more than 50 years Shakespeare remained a sleeping beauty in a country paralyzed by neo-Classicism. An exception to the mood of his time, Le Tourneur appreciates in the *Preface* to his translation (like the *Sturm und Drang* authors) the historical embeddedness of a work of art, and thereby paves the way for a later Romantic re-evaluation of Shakespeare: "*Pour mieux apprécier les travaux de tout Artiste, il faut les reporter au siècle où il a vécu, et comparer ses succès avec ses moyens*"

(In order to best appreciate a writer's work one must go back to the period in which he lived and compare his success with his means), he writes, and states with regret "*Shakespeare est vraiment inconnu en France*" (Shakespeare is really unknown in France; Le Tourneur 1990: 55).

Early proponents of the French "school" of Romanticism, such as François René de Chateaubriand (1768-1848), could not shake free from the manacles of Voltaire's criticism, but in his *Mélanges littéraires* (1801), despite criticism of Shakespeare's faults, he betrays his enthusiasm when he describes the "Striking Beauties of Shakespeare" and expresses his doubts of the value of neo-Classic rule (Chateaubriand 1837: 267-78; see also excerpts in LeWinter 1963: 73-81). A turn of the tide sets in with Louis Sébastien Mercier (1740-1814), whose treatise "*Du Théâtre, ou Nouvel Essai sur l'art dramatique*" (1773) attacks Voltaire and stresses the superiority of natural genius over artificial rules (unity of interest), and with Mme de Staël's (1766-1817) classic work *De la littérature considérée dans ses rapports avec les institutions sociales* (1800). Mme de Staël rehabilitates Shakespeare by reaccentuating the relation between art and nature, as well as by defining literature as dependent on national, historical, and geographical parameters: "Shakespeare opened a new literature; it was borrowed, without doubt, from the general spirit and colour of the north: but it was he who gave to the English literature its impulsation, and to their dramatic art its character" (in Bate 1992: 73).

Art no longer is supposed to impose an atemporal ideal order on the chaos of reality, but to give an "authentic" representation; Classicist *bienséance* is replaced by naturalness, one-dimensional heroes by complex characters. These paradigmatic shifts appear familiar to readers of German criticism, and indeed Mme de Staël became one of the most influential promoters of the lectures A. W. Schlegel had held at Vienna. These lectures may have appealed to her because of their anti-Napoleonic thrust, as she herself had been exiled by Napoleon in 1803 and again in 1806. Her final banishment from France was the result of her seminal work *De l'Allemagne* (1810), in which she openly espoused German culture and gave a survey of German Romanticism.[23] She follows Goethe in claiming that Shakespeare's "pieces deserve more to be read than to be seen" in order to appreciate their underlying ideas, and points out Shakespeare's popular, "democratic" appeal: "In England, all classes are equally attracted by the pieces of Shakspeare. Our finest tragedies, in France, do not interest the people" (Mme de Staël, *On Germany*, in Bate 1992: 82).

The difficulty of making Shakespeare palatable to the taste of an audience attuned to Classicism became vividly clear in July 1822 when a performance of *Othello* by English actors in Paris was drowned out by the cries of an enraged audience: "Down with Shakespeare! A lieutenant of Wellington!" The angry crowds had to be dispersed by the cavalry, yet this memorable event induced Stendhal (Marie Henri Beyle, 1783-1842) to publish an article in the *Paris Monthly Review* in October of the same year that later became the first chapter of his notorious pamphlet *Racine et Shakespeare* (1823).[24] Stendhal presents a witty dispute between "The Academician" and "The Romantic" on the question whether Shakespeare rather than Racine should become the model for drama. "The Romantic" clearly states that the observation of the unities of place and time " . . . is a French habit, a deeply rooted habit, a habit of which we can rid ourselves with difficulty, because Paris is the salon of Europe and gives it its tone; but I say that these unities are in no way necessary to produce a profound emotion and true dramatic effect" (Stendhal, *Racine et Shakespeare*, in Bate 1992: 218). The unities are superfluous in a drama that achieves "moments of perfect illusion," as the spectator's imagination is "concerned solely with the events and the development of passions that are put before his eyes," without thinking about the probability of an action that encompasses months of real time in a two-hour performance; in this respect Shakespeare is superior (ibid., pp. 221-3). Modern drama must liberate itself from the Procrustean bed of neo-Classicism and follow the model of Shakespeare in his disregard for the unities, his combination of verse and prose, the heroic and the quotidian.

Stendhal prepared the way for the great, albeit brief, influence of Shakespeare on French literature that set in with Victor Hugo's (1802-85) preface to his drama *Cromwell* (1827). This famous attack on Classicism places Shakespeare in a line of succession with Homer and the Bible; whereas Homer lived in the age of epic and the Bible was written in the age of the lyric, we are now living in the age of the drama – and *"Shakespeare, c'est le drame"*: "We have now attained the culminating point of modern poetry. Shakespeare is the Drama; and the drama, which combines in one breath the grotesque and the sublime, the terrible and the absurd, tragedy and comedy, is the salient characteristic of the third epoch of poetry, of the literature of to-day" (Hugo 1896, in Bate 1992: 225).

Hugo proclaims the liberty of art as opposed to the despotism of systems, laws, and rules, and even slaps Voltaire in the face by praising the mixture of the sublime and the grotesque in the gravedigger scene in *Hamlet*, a scene that the great arbiter of taste had condemned most ferociously. Hugo's conviction that "the grotesque is one of the supreme beauties of the drama" is put into practice in his panoramic historical novel *Les Misérables* (1845-62) and his gothic masterpiece *Notre-Dame de Paris* (1831), which is still unsurpassed in its depiction of carnivalesque medievalism and as a psychological study of religious and sexual obsession. These narrative works brought him the title of the "Shakespeare of the novel" (Lamartine). His first attempt to put his insights into dramatic practice in his verse play *Cromwell* (published 1827, but first performance not until1956) failed because of the play's "epic" proportions: the sheer number of characters (the Protector Cromwell alone is provided with *four* fools!), the many comic and grotesque scenes that were intended to give a first-hand feeling of life at the time of the English Civil War, and the use of the alexandrine verse made the play unsuited for stage performance.

Although *Cromwell* remained a closet drama, contemporary French audiences gained increasing access to performances of Shakespeare's plays. Charles Kemble and Harriet Smithson, acting in *Hamlet* and *Romeo and Juliet* at the Odéon in Paris, were not only celebrated by intellectuals such as Eugène Delacroix (who was to paint scenes from *Hamlet*, *Macbeth*, and *Othello*), Alexandre Dumas (who would later adapt *Hamlet*),

Théophile Gautier, Charles-Augustin Sainte-Beuve, Alfred de Vigny, and Hugo himself, but they were "the trigger for the explosion of French Romanticism" (Bate 1992: 27). Hector Berlioz, whose work (most notably his *Roméo et Juliette* symphony) gives testimony to Shakespeare's influence, vividly captured the impact of this performance of *Hamlet* (where he watched his future wife in the role of Ophelia) in his *Mémoires*:

> Shakespeare, coming upon me unawares, struck me like a thunderbolt. The lightning flash of that discovery revealed to me at a stroke the whole heaven of art, illuminating it to its remotest corner. I recognized the meaning of grandeur, beauty, dramatic truth, and I could measure the utter absurdity of the French view of Shakespeare which derives from Voltaire [. . .] I saw, I understood, I felt . . . that I was alive and that I must arise and walk. (Berlioz 1969: 95)

The aesthetic battle was just about to start, and the first performance of Hugo's perhaps most influential verse drama *Hernani ou L'Honneur castillan* (1830), written not in alexandrines but in the irregular *vers coupé*, was marked by a violent clash between Classicists and Romantics in the audience, which would enter theater history as the *Bataille d'Hernani*.[25] Under the leadership of Théophile Gautier the Romantics decided this battle in their favor, and the aesthetic revolution instigated by the success of *Hernani* became an important precedent for the political revolution later in 1830, when riots in a theater spread to the streets and after three days of violence Charles X abdicated and fled the country. Aesthetics merged with politics, and yet the hailing of a revolutionary taste in art did not necessarily tie in with a progressive political attitude. As early as in 1821, François Guizot (1787-1874) can argue from an almost conservative position in his introduction to a newly revised edition of Shakespeare translations: "At the present day, all controversy regarding Shakspeare's genius and glory has come to an end. No one ventures any longer to dispute them; but a greater question has arisen, namely whether Shakspeare's dramatic system is not far superior to that of Voltaire." [26]

Guizot gives a detailed sociohistorical analysis of the emergence of Shakespeare's drama out of traditional English forms of popular culture and holidays. He claims that "a theatrical performance is a popular festival" and explains the origin of drama by recourse to the games, May festivals, banquets, Morris dances, and Robin Hood performances of medieval and early modern British country life. Theater is "among the people and for the people" and once it loses its connection to its roots – when it is appropriated by the "superior classes" – it will decline. As in Hugo, this argument is deployed to explain the juxtaposition of the comic and the tragic in Shakespeare: "The comic portion of human realities had a right to take its place wherever its presence was demanded or permitted by truth; and such was the character of civilisation, that tragedy, by admitting the comic element, did not derogate from truth in the slightest degree" (Guizot in Bate 1992: 210). Hamlet and the gravediggers, Falstaff and Henry V, Macbeth and the porter, high and low belong together, and "without this intervention of the inferior classes, how many dramatic effects, which contribute power-fully to the general effect, would become impossible!" (ibid., p. 215). Guizot traces the heterogeneity of Shakespeare's characters back to the "democratic" liberal spirit of English society under Elizabeth I, which he claimed should become the model for a French national egalitarian theater, yet this promotion of the people in drama did not lead the same author to support the people in political matters. Although after 1830 he became Minister for Education, then Foreign Minister, and eventually Prime Minister, he resisted extensions of the franchise and in February 1848 he fell from power and became the victim of another revolution.[27] Although the French Romantic movement included some of the greatest intellectuals of the period, it remained largely a shift of aesthetic paradigm, which established Shakespeare securely as supreme dramatist, but was ineffectual in the long run. Critics such as Guizot and Mézières could remain conservatives while still admiring Shakespeare, as he had ceased to be the center of controversy. When in 1864 Victor Hugo expressed his Romantic enthusiasm for Shakespeare in his introduction to translations of Shake-speare by his son, the countermovement against Romanticism had already set in with Hippolyte Taine's rational and scientific approach to literature and history.

Further Developments

The French Classicist influence determined both dramatic practice and Shakespeare's reception in Italy, Russia, Eastern Europe, and to a certain degree Spain as well. Not until Ugo Foscolo's (1778-1827) ranking of Shakespeare with Alfieri, Sophocles, and Voltaire as a great tragedian was he regarded as worthy of study in Italy. In his epistolary novel *Ultime lettere di Jacopo Ortis* (1802), the suicidal hero, who suffers from the torn condition of the state of Italy, asserts that Shakespeare "possessed" his imagination and "fired" his heart. But his voice alone was not strong enough to supersede the ambivalent Voltairean attitude toward Shakespeare. In 1814, Madame de Staël's *De l'Allemagne* was published in translation and made disciples of younger writers such as Michele Leoni and Giacomo Leopardi. Translations and critical prefaces followed in abundance, and Shakespeare was again used to overthrow the classical critical doctrine, particularly the three unities.[28] Alessandro Manzoni (1785-1873), who ranked Shakespeare with Virgil, became the major Shakespeare critic in Italy as well as one of his advocates in his own works. *I Promessi sposi* (1827), one of the most important novels of Romantic literature, shows this influence clearly. In his "Letter to M. Chauvet on the Unity of Time and Place in Tragedy" Manzoni contrasts *Othello* with Voltaire's *Zaïre*, claiming that Shakespeare's breach of the unity of time makes his play much more convincing, because it allows Othello's jealousy to develop, while Voltaire, operating within the narrow confines of his 24 hours, must depend on chance. He dispenses with the unity of place as well by claiming that the imagination will help the audience to follow the fictional characters on the stage from one place to another: "it is the mind of the spectator which follows them – he has no travelling to do except to imagine to himself that he is traveling [sic]. Do you think that he has come to the theatre to see real events?"(*Lettere*, Manzoni 1843: 257-60, in LeWinter 1963: 133). Creative imitation can be seen at work in the libretti of the time, which took Shakespeare's subjects and abbreviated and simplified them in order to further the democratic art of the Risorgimento, which would become fully realized in Giuseppe Verdi's operas (*Macbetto*, 1847, *Otello* 1887, *Falstaff* 1893).

Russia, which imitated French cultural centralism, painting, architecture, and lifestyle, followed the Classicist French example in literature as well, and most translations of Shakespeare were based on French or German precursors (La Place, Ducis, Eschenburg) (see Levin 1993, Stríbrný 2000). A Russian nationalist and "Romantic" consciousness arose in 1812 in the war against Napoleon, which created a hitherto unknown solidarity between the leaders and the governed and developed into a veritable Russian Hamletism after the crushing of the Decembrist revolt in 1825. The failed revolutionary hopes clearly had an impact on Mikhail Lermontov (1814-41), the greatest Russian Romantic poet, who imitates Hamlet's poetic language of weakness, indecisiveness, and irresoluteness, for instance in his poem "Duma" ("Meditation").

For Aleksandr Sergeevich Pushkin (1799-1837) it was not the revolutionary author of *Macbeth* and *Julius Caesar*, nor of *Hamlet,* but Shakespeare as the poet of the people – the creator of Falstaff – that attracted him. Reading Shakespeare in Le Tourneur's translation (he knew English only from 1828 onwards, after four months of studying it), he used his knowledge of Shakespeare to help him put the catastrophe of December 14, 1825 in perspective: the role of chance in the course of world history, the illegitimacy of power, and the right of the people to revolt were the pre-eminent elements of his reception of Shakespeare. After having read "The Rape of Lucrece" he parodies it in his own poem "Count Nulin." Because mere chance governs history, the rape of Lucrece could have been avoided if she had just given Tarquinius a box on the ears. Then the kings would not have been expelled by Brutus and world history would have taken another direction. *Boris Godunov* (1825) is intended as a drama of the people and employs single lines taken from Shakespeare's plays as well as clearly Shakespearean scenes depicting the masses of the people on stage. Boris Godunov himself is a highly mixed character, combining elements of a tragic loving father, an evil murderer, a hypocrite and a Christ figure, a cowardly usurper and a legitimate monarch all in one: "Shakespeare's characters, unlike Molière's types, are not governed by one single passion, one single vice, but are living beings, governed by many passions and many vices; the varying and manifold characters are developed in front of the spectators according to circumstances" (Pushkin, quoted by Etkind 1988: 253, my translation).

In his essay *La Vie de Shakespeare* (1821) Pushkin summarized his ideas on Shakespeare (which are based on the work of François Guizot), holding Shakespeare to be the absolute opposite of Classicist and aristocratic systems: he is the representative of democracy; the restoration in France after 1815 is comparable to the Elizabethan age; history is not the biography of kings, but the creation of the people; history has a moral, and Shakespeare represents artistic, political, and moral freedom (Etkind 1988, Parfenov and Price 1988). This antifeudal, subversive Falstaffian Shakespeare found his way into the new genre that asserted its supremacy by the middle of the century, the novel, and especially in the work of Ivan Turgenev and Fyodor Dostoevsky.

NOTES

1 Jonathan Bate (1986: 6) states: "The rise of Romanticism and the growth of Shakespeare idolatry are parallel phenomena." He also quotes Friedrich Schlegel: "Shakespeares Universalität ist wie der Mittelpunkt der romantischen Kunst" (Schlegel 1967: aphorism 247).

2 Works such as Edward Young's *Conjectures on Original Composition* and Alexander Gerard's *Essay on Genius* especially influenced the German discussion on imagination and genius, beginning with the *Sturm und Drang* movement.

3 Jonathan Bate stresses this close connection in his introduction both to *Shakespeare and the English Romantic Imagination* (1986) and to his anthology *The Romantics on Shakespeare* (1992).

4 On the history of the Shakespeare cult see Dávidházi (1998) and Felperin (1991).

5 de Grazia (1991) shows how Edmond Malone played down the image of Shakespeare as poet from the people.

6 Hazlitt, "A Letter to William Gifford, Esq." (Hazlitt 1930-4, vol. 9: 13). Hazlitt's subversive reading of *Measure for Measure* as a criticism not of sexual lust, but instead of "want of passion" aroused the wrath of the critical establishment. See Bate (1992: 24).

7 On the issue of influence or plagiarism see McFarland (1969).

8 Lamb, "On the Tragedies of Shakspeare, considered with reference to their fitness for stage representation" (essay in the *Reflector*, 1811). See the extract in Bate (1992: 111-27).

9 On Hazlitt's ambivalent attitude see Bate (1992: 32).

10 For a comprehensive account of Shakespeare's influence on the language and imagery of the British Romantics in their poetic practice, see Bate (1986).

11 See Number 17 of his *Briefe die neueste Litteratur betreffend* (February 16, 1759) and his *Hamburgische Dramaturgie*, part 2, piece 63 (January 12, 1768). The relevant passages can be found in Pascal (1937: 50-2).

12 This movement of the 1770s is different from what is regarded as Romanticism in Germany, yet the "Storm and Stress" movement has been related to early Romanticism abroad and shows many similarities with it. Schlegel contests this view when he differentiates between the unconscious naïveté of these authors and the consciousness of the real Romantics.

13 Herder, "Shakespeare," first published in an anonymous collection of five essays edited by Herder, *Von deutscher Art und Kunst* (*On German Character and Art*). See Herder (1985). Reprinted in Bate (1992: 39-48, 40).

14 Coleridge, who translated *The Piccolomini* and *The Death of Wallenstein*, regarded these plays as the closest modern equivalents of Shakespeare.

15 This line runs in German: "eine große Tat auf eine Seele gelegt, die der Tat nicht gewachsen ist," *Wilhelm Meisters Lehrjahre. Ein Roman* (Goethe 1986-, 5.4: 245, my translation). At a later period of German history, Georg Herwegh will see in Hamlet's inability to act the epitome of the German "malaise" and Ferdinand Freiligrath will claim "Deutschland ist Hamlet" (Germany is Hamlet).

16 See Williams (1990: 88-107). *Macbeth* was produced with great success, and repeated in 1804, 1806, 1808, and 1810.

17 For a concise summary of the debate and Tieck's role in it, see Habicht (1993) and Zybura (1994).

18 Heinrich von Kleist in his drama *The Schrof-fenstein Family* (*Die Familie Schroffenstein*) of 1803, combines Shakespeare with Rousseau and gives a gothic rendering of the tragic tale of Romeo and Juliet's love and death.

19 Tieck also was the first in Germany to investigate the nature of the Shakespearean stage and to study the playwrights contemporary with Shakespeare in his *Letters on Shakespeare* (*Briefe über Shakspeare*) in 1800. See Pascal (1937: 29, 133).

20 See his "*Fragmente über William Shakespeare*" ("Fragments concerning William Shakespeare") in his "*Vorlesungen über die dramatische Kunst*" ("Lectures on Dramatic Art"). A translation from his *Vermischte Schriften über Staat, Philosophie und Kunst* (*Diverse Writings on Philosophy, Art and State*) is available in Bate (1992: 83-7).

21 A witty element within the burgeoning Shakespeare scholarship of the nineteenth century is to be found in Heinrich Heine's (1797-1856) prose piece "Shakespeare's Maidens and Women" (1839) which is enlightening and full of the sharp irony of a master satirist.

22 "Il avait un génie plein de force et de fécondité, de naturel et de sublime, sans la moindre étincelle de bon goût et sans la moindre connaissance des règles" (Voltaire 1964: 104).

23 Bate (1992: 10). On the historical and biographical circumstances of her writing see Isbell (1994) and Posgate (1969).

24 See Bate (1992: 26). On the topic of Shakespeare on the French stage see Lambert (1993).

25 The play shows the influence both of Corneille's *Cid* and of Schiller's *Robbers* and the characters depicted are a mixture of heroism and evil weaknesses. For a description of this battle see Gautier ([1874] 2000).

26 From *On the Life and Works of Shakspeare* (1821), repr. in Guizot (1852), in Bate (1992: 203).

27 For an account of his conservative attitude see Bate (1992: 30).

28 A good summary of Shakespeare's reception in Italy, France, Russia, Poland, Germany and other countries as well as an excellent bibliography can be found in Schabert (2000: 609-90).

REFERENCES AND FURTHER READING

Bate, Jonathan (1986). *Shakespeare and the English Romantic Imagination*. Oxford: Clarendon Press.

Bate, Jonathan (1992). *The Romantics on Shakespeare*. London: Penguin.

Berlioz, Hector ([1870] 1969). *The Memoirs of Hector Berlioz*, trans. David Cairns. New York: Knopf.

Chateaubriand, François René de (1837). *Sketches of English Literature*. London: Henry Colburn.

Coleridge, Samuel Taylor ([1835] 1990). *Table Talk Recorded by Henry Nelson Coleridge*, ed. Carl Woodring, 2 vols. London and Princeton, NJ: Routledge and Princeton University Press.

Coleridge, Samuel Taylor (1907). *Biographia Literaria*, 2 vols., ed. J. Shawcross. Oxford: Clarendon.

Coleridge, Samuel Taylor (1960). *Coleridge's Shakespearean Criticism*, 2 vols., ed. Thomas M. Raysor. London: Constable.

Dávidházi, Péter (1998). *The Romantic Cult of Shakespeare. Literary Reception in Anthropological Perspective*. Basingstoke, UK: Macmillan.

de Grazia, Margreta (1991). *Shakespeare Verbatim: The Reproduction of Authenticity and the 1790 Apparatus*. Oxford: Clarendon Press.

Dryden, John ([1668] 1962). "Of Dramatic Poesy." In George Watson (ed.), *Of Dramatic Poesy and other Critical Essays*, 2 vols. London: Dent, pp. 70-130.

Etkind, Efim (1988). "Shakespeare in der russischen Dichtung des Goldnen Zeitalters." In Roger Bauer (ed.), *Das Shakespeare-Bild in Europa zwischen Aufklärung und Romantik*, Jahrbuch für internationale Germanistik, vol. 22. Bern: Peter Lang, pp. 241-61.

Felperin, Howard (1991). "Bardolatry Then and Now." In Jean I. Marsden (ed.), *The Appropriation of Shakespeare. Post-Renaissance Reconstructions of the Works and the Myth*. Hemel

Hempstead, UK: Harvester Wheatsheaf, pp. 129-44.

Gauthier, Théophile (2000). *Histoire du romantisme.* In *Victor Hugo par Théophile Gautier, choix de textes,* ed. Françoise Court-Pérez. Paris: H. Champion.

Goethe, Johann Wolfgang von (1986). *Essays on Art and Literature,* ed. John Gearey, trans. Ellen von Nardroff and Ernest H. von Nardroff. Frankfurt: Suhrkamp.

Goethe, Johann Wolfgang von (1986-). *Sämtliche Werke nach Epochen seines Schaffens,* 21 vols., Münchner Ausgabe, ed. Karl Richter et al. München: Carl Hanser Verlag.

Guizot, François (1852). *Shakspeare et son temps,* trans. as *Shakspeare and his Times.* London: R Bentley.

Habicht, Werner (1993). "The Romanticism of the Schlegel-Tieck Shakespeare and the History of Nineteenth Century German Shakespeare Translation." In Dirk Delabastita and Lieven D'Hulst (eds.), *European Shakespeares. Translating Shakespeare in the Romantic Age.* Amsterdam: Benjamins, pp. 45-54.

Hazlitt, William (1930-4). *The Complete Works of William Hazlitt,* ed P. P. Howe, 21 vols. London: Dent.

Herder, Johann Gottfried (1985). "On German Character and Art." In H. B. Nisbet (ed.), *German Aesthetic and Literary Criticism: Winckelmann, Lessing, Hamann, Herder, Schiller and Goethe,* trans. Joyce P. Crick. Cambridge, UK: Cambridge University Press.

Hugo, Victor ([1827] 1896). *Preface to "Oliver Cromwell,"* trans. I. G. Burnham. London.

Isbell, John C. (1994). *The Birth of European Romanticism. Truth and Propaganda in Staël's "De l'Allemagne" 1810-1813.* Cambridge, UK: Cambridge University Press.

Johnson, Samuel (1968). *Johnson on Shakespeare,* ed. Arthur Sherbo, Yale edn. of the *Works of Samuel Johnson,* vols. 7-8. New Haven, CT: Yale University Press.

Keats, John (1965). *The Letters of John Keats 1814-1821,* 2 vols., ed. H. E. Rollins. Cambridge, MA: Harvard University Press.

Lamb, Charles (1903-14). *The Works,* ed. Edward V. Lucas, 11 vols. London: Methuen.

Lambert, José (1993). "Shakespeare en France au tournant du XVIII siècle. Un dossier européen." In Dirk Delabastita and Lieven D'Hulst (eds.), *European Shakespeares. Translating Shakespeare in the Romantic Age.* Amsterdam: Benjamins, pp. 25-44.

Levin, Yuri D. (1993). "Russian Shakespeare Translations in the Romantic Era." In Dirk Delabastita and Lieven D'Hulst (eds.), *European Shakespeares. Translating Shakespeare in the Romantic Age.* Amsterdam: Benjamins, pp.75-90.

LeWinter, Oswald (ed.) (1963). *Shakespeare in Europe.* New York: World Publishing Co.

Le Tourneur, Pierre Félicien (1990). *Préface du Shakespeare traduit de l'anglois,* ed. Jacques Gury. Geneva: Droz.

Manzoni, Alessandro (1843). *Opere complete,* ed. Niccolò Tommaséo Paris: Baudry.

McFarland, Thomas (1969). *Coleridge and the Pantheist Tradition.* Oxford: Clarendon Press.

Müller, Adam (1817). *Vermischte Schriften über Staat, Philosophie und Kunst,* 2nd edn. Vienna: Heubner & Volke.

Parfenov, A. and Price, H. G. (eds.) (1988). *Russian Essays on Shakespeare and his Contemporaries.* Newark: University of Delaware Press.

Pascal, Roy (1937). *Shakespeare in Germany (1740-1815).* Cambridge, UK: Cambridge University Press.

Posgate, Helen B. (1969). *Madame de Staël.* New York: Twayne.

Schabert, Ina (ed.) (2000). *Shakespeare Handbuch.* Stuttgart: Alfred Kröner.

Schiller, Friedrich (1953). *Die Räuber.* In Herbert Stubenrauch (ed.), *Schillers Werke,* Nationalausgabe, vol. 3. Weimar: Hermann Böhlaus Nachfolger.

Schlegel, August Wilhelm von ([1815] 1846). *A Course of Lectures on Dramatic Art and Literature,* trans. John Black, revised A. J. W. Morrison. London: G. Bohn.

Schlegel, August Wilhelm von (1962-8). *Kritische Schriften und Briefe,* ed. Edgar Lohner, 6 vols. Stuttgart: Kohlhammer.

Schlegel, Friedrich (1967). *Charakteristiken und Kritiken I (1796-1801),* ed. and introd. Hans Eichner. In *Kritische Friedrich-Schlegel-Ausgabe,* ed. Ernst Behler et al., vol. 2. München: Paderborn.

Staël, Germaine de (1991). *De la littérature,* ed. Gérard Gengembre. Paris: Flammarion.

Staël, Germaine de (1998-9). *De l'Allemagne,* chron. and introd. Simone Balayé, 2 vols. Paris: Flammarion.

Stendhal ([1823] 1968). *Racine et Shakespeare*. Nendeln, Liechtenstein: Kraus.

Stríbrný, Zdenek (2000). *Shakespeare and Eastern Europe*. Oxford: Oxford University Press.

Voltaire (1964). *Lettres philosophiques ou Lettres anglaises*, ed. and introd. Raymond Naves. Paris: Garnier Frères.

Williams, Simon (1990). *Shakespeare on the German Stage, vol. I: 1586-1914*. Cambridge, UK: Cambridge University Press.

Zybura, Marek (1994). *Ludwig Tieck als Übersetzer und Herausgeber*. Heidelberg: Universitätsverlag Winter.

3

Scottish Romanticism and Scotland in Romanticism

Fiona Stafford

The imagination of Northern men soars beyond this earth, on which they live; it soars through the clouds on the horizons that are like the mysterious gateway from life to eternity. (Germaine de Staël 1820)

Scotland seems to have been hitherto the country of the Useful rather than the Fine Arts. We are more prone to study realities than appearances...(William Hazlitt 1822)

Madame de Staël, surveying European literature at the turn of the nineteenth century, saw a continent divided by geography, climate, and politics. In the warm South, writers, basking in the lovely Mediterranean sunlight, had been filling their poems with color and voluptuous imagery since the days of Homer. By contrast, the frozen wastes of the North, fostering a fierce independence and seriousness, had given rise to the most original and sublime poetry. Whatever the legacy of classical Greece or Renaissance Italy, Northern Europe was the true homeland of the modern Romantic imagination, its ultimate ancestor, the ancient Scottish bard, Ossian.

With such unreserved contemporary affirmation of Scotland's importance to Romanticism, it is somewhat startling, then, to find William Hazlitt spitting with indignation over the practical, utilitarian attitudes he perceived north of the Border. "Scotland," he observed, "is of all other countries in the world perhaps the one in which the question, 'What is the use of that?' is asked oftenest. But where this is the case, the Fine Arts cannot flourish" (Hazlitt ([1822] 1930-4, 18: 168). While de Staël celebrated the "Northern imagination that delights in the seashore, in the sound of the wind, the wild heaths," Hazlitt lamented "the cold, dry, barren soil," where native talent was "pinched and nipped into nothing" by public opinion and Kirk Assemblies.[1] Far from being the natural cradle of the creative imagination, Scotland was, for Hazlitt, its early grave.

Such polarized views demonstrate at once the complexity of Scotland's relationship to Romanticism. Seen by some as a symbol for free, imaginative expression, it struck others as narrowly provincial, intolerant, and altogether barren. Hazlitt's view of the arts being oppressed by Presbyterianism is similar to John Keats's reaction: "These Kirkmen have done Scotland harm – they have banished puns and laughing and kissing."[2] For Keats, part of Robert Burns's tragedy was that "his disposition was southern" and his naturally "luxurious imagination" was forced into self-defense against inclement surroundings. Hazlitt's chilly image of "cold, dry, barren soil" is also reminiscent of Byron's *English Bards and Scotch Reviewers*, where the hopes of aspiring poets are "nipped in the bud by Caledonian gales."[3] Scotland might be widely regarded as the land of the sublime, but it was also seen as an inhospitable environment where sensitive plants were likely to perish under the severe influences of the Kirk and the critics. And yet Byron's satire is itself complicated by his own Scottish ancestry and by his frequent reference to poetry inspired by Scotland. As Byron, heir to an English barony but born and educated in Scotland, was well aware, there was no neat North/South, critical/creative divide: the relationship between Scotland and imaginative writing was more complicated altogether. In many instances, the assertion of creative freedom was a direct response to the more utilitarian or condemnatory aspects of Scottish culture while, conversely, Romantic admiration for Scotland might encompass a deep respect for plain speaking and solemnity.

Even those most exasperated by the narrowness they perceived in Scottish culture were also aware of the irresistible magnetism of the North. Keats's remarks on the Kirkmen were made during his personal exploration of the country of Scott, Burns, and Ossian. In Scotland he found beautiful heaths, magnificent glens, and above all, mountains, which combined "to strengthen more my reach in Poetry, than would stopping at home among Books even though I should reach Homer" (letter to Benjamin Bailey, July 22, 1818, in Keats 1958, I: 342). Like Keats and Byron, William Wordsworth was also deeply wounded by reviews in the Edinburgh periodicals, but this did nothing to diminish his enthusiasm for Scotland. Many of his most beautiful lyrics, including "The Solitary Reaper," "Yarrow Unvisited," or "Stepping Westward," were inspired by successive tours and a profound interest in Scotland. Wordsworth celebrated the plain truths and deep wisdom of rural Scotland in figures such as the Leech Gatherer and the Pedlar, while in the opening book of *The Prelude*, he lingered on the idea of William Wallace as a subject for epic poetry. Despite his deep attachment to England, Wordsworth eventually admitted that "I have been indebted to the North for more than I shall ever be able to acknowledge" (letter to Allan Cunningham, November 23, 1825, in Selincourt 1978: 402). And even Hazlitt, despite his outburst at the exhibition of Scottish art, was both an eloquent champion of Burns and a regular contributor to the *Edinburgh Review*. Romantic Scotland might be a center of skeptical criticism, religious intolerance, and utilitarian attitudes, but it was also a land of poetry, truth, and visionary possibility.

Ossian, Enlightenment, and Romanticism

Although Madame de Staël's image of Ossian as the spiritual ancestor of modern poetry suggests a strain of Scottish Romanticism that is at odds with the skeptical, down-to-earth attitudes prevailing in Edinburgh, James Macpherson's ancient bard derived as much from modern urban culture as from the Highlands. Throughout the Romantic period, readers across Europe and America thrilled to the freedom of a lost Celtic world but, as they did so, they were also enjoying a literary text whose form and content was shaped by the politics and aesthetics of mid-eighteenth-century Scotland. The apparently oppositional strains of imaginative release and practical improvement were fused in Macpherson's poetry to produce a powerful, and yet elusive, image that contributed greatly to later Romantic perceptions of Scotland. *The Poems of Ossian* are crucial to an understanding of Scotland and Romanticism not merely because of their extraordinary influence on European writers, artists, and musicians, but also because they represent an early incarnation of some of the aesthetic ideas that came to characterize the Romantic movement (Gaskill 1994). *Ossian* carried across Europe not only an idea of Scotland, but also Scottish ideas, and is therefore an obvious starting point for this chapter.

The Poems of Ossian took their raw materials from the Gaelic heritage of Highland Scotland, but the form and tone of the published texts were shaped by the Scottish Enlightenment. Macpherson grew up in the Highlands, experiencing the devastation surrounding the 1745 Jacobite Rising, but his literary aspirations developed at Aberdeen, where he sat at the feet of distinguished philosophers, imbibing an admiration for classical literature and a sense of "the various purposes it serves in Life" (Gerard 1755: 28).[4] If *The Poems of Ossian* can in some ways be seen as a reaction against the heavily utilitarian emphasis of his university education, they are also, in part, a natural consequence. For it is unlikely that Macpherson would have attempted to publish translations of the poetry circulating in his local community, had it not been for the primitivist ideals and fascination with early literatures that he acquired as a student, and shared with the influential figures he subsequently encountered in Edinburgh.

At Aberdeen, under the influence of Thomas Blackwell, the study of classical literature encouraged admiration for the physical strength and spontaneous energy of the earliest societies, whose vigor poured out in powerful poetry. A similar preoccupation with antiquity stimulated intellectual debate in Edinburgh and Glasgow, where a proper understanding of the beginnings of human society was deemed essential to modern progress. The brilliant thinkers who gathered in the intellectual societies, including David Hume, Adam Smith, Lord Kames, and Adam Ferguson, were all fascinated by the origins of civil society, of political and economic systems, racial difference and human behavior in general.[5] The transformation of language, especially, from its simplest articulations to the complexity of modern prose, seemed central to human development; and linguistic theories drew variously on classical texts and evidence from contemporary travelers. James Burnet, Lord Monboddo, examined accounts of peoples as diverse as the Polynesians and the Hurons in his ambitious, six-volume analysis *Of the Origins and Progress of Language* (1773-92). Spatial and temporal differences were often similarly conflated, as remote, contemporary societies came to be regarded as living representations of the savage or barbarous stages of humankind.

Such enthusiastic research into the origins of civilization, into ancient languages and alternative societies, inevitably stimulated interest in the history of Britain and Ireland, and the indigenous Celtic languages. For the Highland student, James Macpherson, exposure to the research interests of modern Scottish scholars meant, paradoxically, a return to the traditional culture of his Gaelic-speaking home. In the Highlands and islands of Scotland, one of the oldest known languages was still in daily use, while the heroic legends of the ancient Celts might yet be heard by the fire during long winter nights. The collection and translation of traditional Gaelic material was an obvious objective for Scottish intellectuals, eager at once to develop their knowledge of social progress and to establish the superiority of Scotland to England whenever the opportunity arose. Macpherson's work on *The Poems of Ossian* resulted from the complicated interweaving of his own Highland background with contemporary academic interest in recovering some vestiges of ancient Scottish society, a pursuit that seemed especially urgent as Highland culture receded rapidly in the wake of Culloden, and the English language spread further and further north.

When Macpherson came to present his first renditions of Gaelic verse to the English-speaking public, as *Fragments of Ancient Poetry* in June 1760, he naturally emphasized their importance as records of early society. The epic poem that he hoped to rescue as a result of further research was similarly presented as a precious relic which "might serve to throw considerable light upon the Scottish and Irish antiquities" (Macpherson 1996: 6). Some 18 months later, *Fingal, An Ancient Epic Poem in Six Books* came suitably prefaced by a substantial "Dissertation concerning the Antiquity of the Poems of Ossian," and buttressed with extensive footnotes, drawing parallels with classical epic and emphasizing the historical significance of the various poems. "The Songs of Selma," for example, had a note describing the annual feast of the Bards and the original social function of the verse. Whatever the public might think of the poetry, it was clear that the translator expected his work to be judged by philosophical and historical measures. Here was poetry that had possessed a central role in early society, and which offered modern readers unique insight into the manners of their ancestors.

Macpherson's presentation of his translations was strongly influenced by his Edinburgh patrons, and especially Hugh Blair. As the first Professor of Rhetoric and Belles Lettres in Edinburgh, Blair can be seen as Scotland's first true literary critic, while his work on *Ossian* is a foundational text for the distinguished reviewing culture of Edinburgh in the Romantic period.[6] For although Blair's tone was very much more sympathetic than that of later reviewers, such as Francis Jeffrey, his attitude to literature was informed by a strong sense of its usefulness to society and importance to the nation. The *Critical Dissertation on the Poems of Ossian*, originally published in 1763 to accompany *Fingal*, begins with a sociological justification for reading ancient poems as a record of the early stages of modern nations. Almost immediately, however, Blair introduced ideas of passion, feeling, and imagination, emphasizing the "vehemence and fire" of the earliest poetry, and the "picturesque and figurative" quality of its language (Blair 1996: 345). Rather than presenting an opposition between artistic creation and social function, Blair argued that the usefulness of ancient poetry lay in its expression of imaginative freedom and undisguised passion. Blair, though a minister of the High Church and a university professor, employed his critical skills not for nipping early poetry in the bud, as later readers might expect, but rather for nurturing a sympathetic understanding of its true value. Although he adopted a broadly historical approach to *Ossian*, reverting frequently to speculation on the "infancy of society," Blair's *Critical Dissertation* was also promoting a new kind of poetry, based on aesthetic ideals that diverged significantly from the neo-Classicism of the previous century.

Blair's elevation of conciseness, simplicity, and figurative language over diffuseness, artful transitions, and abstract personification mark an important turn in the tide of literary taste. His emphasis on language that is at once limited in range, and yet profoundly moving, looks forward to ideas later developed by Wordsworth in the Preface to *Lyrical Ballads*. His celebration of natural man living closely in touch with his landscape ("the desart," says Fingal, "is enough for me, with all its woods and deer," Blair 1996: 354) also corresponded closely to the new Rousseauistic admiration for humankind uncorrupted by modern urban lifestyles and commercial values. Above all, Blair saw in Ossian the ideal of sublimity, which had so recently been analyzed by Edmund Burke, and which would become central to German Romantic aesthetic thought, after Kant.[7] Sublimity was the keynote of the ancient bard of Scotland, and although Blair emphasized the moral character of the Ossianic sublime, his prose warms to the idea of a natural genius in native surroundings:

> Amidst the rude scenes of nature, amidst rocks and torrents and whirlwinds and battles, dwells the sublime. It is the thunder and lightning of genius. It is the offspring of nature, not of art. It is negligent of all the lesser graces, and perfectly consistent with a certain noble disorder. It associates naturally with that grave and solemn spirit, which distinguishes our author. (Blair 1996: 395)[8]

The ancient Bard was not only passionate and spontaneous, but also grave and solemn: a prophetic figure, whose words resonated with the sublime authority of natural power. Since the sublime dwelt in the ruder scenes of nature, the mountains of Scotland were the perfect setting.

As sublimity became celebrated more widely, and the taste for rocks and torrents and whirlwinds grew, so did the popularity of *Ossian*. Throughout Europe, readers were enraptured by the strange rhythmic prose and the distinctive melancholy tone. Macpherson may have presented "The Songs of Selma" as an example of an interesting old custom, but for many of his readers it was the poetry that mattered: "Star of the descending night! Fair is thy light in the west! Thou liftest thy unshorn head from thy cloud: thy steps are stately on thy hill. What dost thou behold in the plain? The stormy winds are laid. The murmur of the torrent comes from afar. Roaring waves climb the distant rocks" (Macpherson 1996: 166). This was the very poem that Goethe translated and presented to Friederike Brion, and which, in his 1774 *Die Leiden des jungen Werthers*, he made the sorrowful Werther read with Lotte shortly before his suicide (see Lamport 1998). And while Werther is perhaps not exactly an ideal reader, the way in which Goethe incorporates *Ossian* into his hugely popular sentimental novel is symptomatic of its appeal in the late eighteenth century. Not only were people reading the texts, but many were also sufficiently enthused to compose imitations, fresh translations, and dramatic adaptations. Nor was the creative impulse confined to writers: artists from Cotman and Kauffman to Ingres and Turner painted Ossianic subjects, while Schubert, Mendelssohn, Brahms, and Schumann were among the many musicians inspired by *Ossian* (Okun 1967, Fiske 1983, Daverio 1998). With every fresh creative response came a renewed idea of Romantic Scotland.

At the same time, Macpherson's texts provoked enormous and long-running critical controversy. For every reader enchanted by *Ossian*, there must have been another who regarded the translations as fraudulent, their antiquity incredible. The controversy over the authenticity took so long to resolve that the issue was still being debated in the pages of the *Edinburgh Review* some 40 years after the original publications.[9] If Blair's *Critical Dissertation* did much to foster the development of literary appreciation in Scotland, the disagreement over the authenticity and ultimate value of *Ossian* gave rise to a much more hard-hitting style of critical judgment. Macpherson's work represents a curious fusion of the imaginative and utilitarian strains in Scottish culture, but its reception also reveals deep divisions between a sentimental enthusiasm on one hand, and a very unsentimental skepticism on the other.

Scottish Romanticism

For late eighteenth-century readers, Ossian's poems revealed man in his natural condition – rooted in his native landscape and expressing powerful, but often tender emotions in the simple language that flowed from his heart. At the same time, the dominant voice was that of an old man lamenting the times of old, while the Highland landscape is blasted with images of ruin and desolation. This pervading sense of loss and imminent oblivion was an important part of Ossian's appeal to an age of sensibility. It was also quietly reassuring to readers who might still harbor fears of the wild Highlands for physical or political reasons. The elegiac nature of Ossian's poems nevertheless gave Scotland's claim to literary greatness a somewhat insubstantial and backward-looking air. The Celtic Bard was trapped in antiquity, his broken poems – or "Fragments" – accessible only through Macpherson's notoriously unreliable English translations. Many of the qualities admired by readers of *Ossian*, however, found new vitality and contemporary significance in the work of Scotland's greatest Romantic poet: Robert Burns.

Burns responded to the new aesthetic appetite by creating poems that brimmed with feeling and celebrated a close and fruitful relationship with nature. Everything in Burns's work was fresh, fertile, and concrete. Unlike the venerable, but somewhat decrepit, Ossian, Burns was a self-styled "simple Bard" reveling in the here and now, and making poems from everyday Scottish life.[10] If Blair's critical ideas anticipated later Romantic poetic manifestos, Burns's *Poems, Chiefly in the Scottish Dialect*, published in the Ayrshire town of Kilmarnock in 1786, demonstrated the new ideals in action. Here was "low and rustic life" in all its glory, captured in poetry that expressed the essential passions and aimed explicitly to "touch the heart" (Wordsworth 1992: 60, "Epistle to John Lapraik, An Old Scotch Bard," in Burns 1968, I: 87). Burns was a man, speaking to others in the real language of rural Scotland, as his series of verse epistles to other local poets makes clear:

> But Mauchline Race Or Mauchline Fair,
> I should be proud to meet you there;
> We'se gie ae' night's discharge to care,
>   If we forgather,
> An' hae a swap o'rhymin-ware,
>   Wi' ane anither. ("Epistle to John Lapraik" Burns 1968, I: 88)

Burns creates a poetry of democratic sociability, which reflects the colloquial language of his home and remains grounded insistently in his local area. He admired Ossian, but his own work drew on the very different traditions of Lowland Scotland: "The Epistle to J. L***k," for example, draws on Allan Ramsay's sequence of verse epistles, which had similarly debated the nature of Scottish poetry in the distinctive stanzas known as "Standard Habbie" (Ramsay 1974).[11]

At a time when many Scottish writers were laboring to demonstrate their skills in elegant standard English, Burns's feisty celebration of Scottish forms and words is a striking statement of independence. Part of *Ossian's* appeal to the Edinburgh literati was that as an English translation from Gaelic, the published poems conformed to acceptable linguistic standards, while remaining essentially Scottish. Burns, on the other hand, advertised his country's spoken language in his very choice of title. The opening poem in his groundbreaking collection did include an Ossianic speaker, but rather than adopt the lofty, melancholic tones of Macpherson, Burns set up a comic canine dialogue between the local landowner's dog, Caesar, and the ploughman's collie, Luath, named "After some dog in *Highlan Sang,/* Was made lang syne, lord knows how lang" ("The Twa Dogs," Burns 1968, I: 138). Although a suitable footnote directs readers to "Ossian's Fingal," the satiric tone of the verse makes it clear that for this poet, contemporary rural Scotland is far more interesting than third-century Caledonia.

In "The Vision," too, the Ossianic divisions of poems into "Duans"[12] and the motif of the visiting Muse are both undermined by her very physical entrance: "When click! The *string* the *snick* did draw;/ And jee! The door gaed to the wa'" (Burns 1968, I: 104). Burns's supernatural is carefully naturalized, as the speaker's "musing-deep, astonish'd stare" is answered by a Muse, Coila, who adopts "an elder Sister's air." Fraternal feelings soon give way to a different kind of admiration, once the Muse's tartan robe slips open to reveal "half a leg": the inspiration offered by Coila, though political, literary, and serious, has a vital sexual dimension, rather similar to the feeling inspired by "darling Jean" in the "Epistle to Davie, a brother poet." Unlike the sustained otherworldliness of Macpherson's Celts, Burns treats supernatural figures with an earthy enthusiasm or a brusque irreverence, as when the devil is addressed as an "auld, snick-drawing dog," who "came to Paradise incog" ("Address to the Deil," ibid.:171). In Burns's comic masterpiece, "Tam o'Shanter," Satan and sexuality are conjured up with unforgettable energy in the mock-moral tale of drunken Tam.

Keats may have lamented the repressive influence of the "Kirkmen" on Burns, but it is also possible to see these essential aspects of provincial Scottish society providing a vital catalyst for his work. Burns's most vigorous satires, such as "Holy Willie's Prayer" or "The Holy Fair" were responses to a certain brand of harsh Presbyterianism, while his repeated celebration of whiskey, wit, and women derived much of their force from a self-conscious outrageousness before po-faced morality. Nevertheless, as Liam McIlvanney points out, it was Burns's own Presbyterianism that had instilled in him "the principles of independence which animate his satires on the Kirk": his reaction against the repression and hypocrisy of certain elders was part and parcel of his own democratic faith (McIlvanney 2003: 162). The no-nonsense, argumentative strains in Scottish culture emerge in Burns's comic treatment of literary, religious, and social convention, contributing a vital new tone to traditional material. Far from being thwarted by his environment, Burns drew on and resisted the world around him; and contemporary readers were compelled by the energy and varied tones of what they assumed to be "simple" verse.

The comedy in Burns's work was also a crucial enabler of sentiment, allowing him to produce poems that were moving rather than mawkish. To write sympathetically on the destruction of a mouse's nest would be a challenge for any writer, but Burns succeeds through addressing the dispossessed mouse as vigorously as he speaks to the devil: "Wee, sleekit, cowrin, tim'rous *beastie*, / O, what a panic's in thy breastie!" ("To a Mouse," Burns 1968, I: 127). The colloquial diction, the chiming rhyme, and the bouncy rhythm of the lines keeps the sentiment in check, while allowing the poem to develop into a startling meditation on the human condition. Burns's poetry has moments of profound melancholy: as Wordsworth observed, "His 'Ode to Despondency' I can never read without the deepest agitation" (letter to Coleridge, February 27, 1799, in Selincourt 1967, I: 255-6). But the feelings of despondency are all the deeper for the sharply contrasting comic and satiric poems that lie around. Francis Jeffrey, scourge of so many Romantic poets, praised Burns for both his comedy and his "simple and unpretending tenderness" (Jeffrey 1809). In an age which had spawned a host of sentimental novels and poetic effusions, Burns possessed a rare ability to convey tenderness in ways that rang true. For Hazlitt, Burns "was not a sickly sentimentalist, a namby-pamby poet," but shared with Shakespeare "something of the same magnanimity, directness and unaffected character" (Hazlitt ([1822] 1930-4, 5: 128). "Unpretending" and "unaffected" were key terms in the contemporary reception of Burns, who increasingly stood for natural genius and native truth.

Given the critical elevation of naturalness, spontaneous expression, and distinctive native character, it is perhaps unsurprising that in the eyes of both Hazlitt and Jeffrey, Burns's greatest legacy lay in his songs. The notion that music was part of human-kind's expressive nature, and that the earliest poetry had been accompanied by music, was commonplace in Scottish Enlightenment thought and can also be seen in the background of the Romantic critical response to Burns. In Hazlitt's lecture "On Poetry in General," for example, he dwelt on the "connection between music and deep-rooted passion," and the capacity for lyrical poetry to utter emotions of the soul (Hazlitt [1822] 1930-4, 5: 12). Later in the series, theory gave way to the living examples of Burns's love songs, which took "the deepest and most lasting hold of the mind" (ibid.: 140). Celebration of Burns's songs arose partly from the new post-Enlightenment aesthetics, which were in turn affirmed and given concrete artistic expression. Burns's own fame in the Romantic period owed much to the widespread interest in his hard life and premature death, but he lived on most persistently in songs such as "My Luve is Like a Red, Red Rose," "Mary Morison," or "John Anderson." Scottish song had been popular throughout Britain for at least a century before Burns's publications, but his contribution was unparalleled and took on new life in nineteenth-century Europe when brilliant composers adapted his work. The very qualities admired by Hazlitt and Jeffrey made his lyrics perfect for lieder, as Roger Fiske has commented: "His genius was for crystallising a simple situation into a moment of delight or sorrow" (Fiske 1983: 157). Burns's work was also instrumental in the elevation of the Romantic lyric, as the pre-eminent genre for expressing the deepest emotions, undisguised by artificial conventions.

Contemporary admiration for Burns's songs stemmed partly from their connection with local tradition. Throughout the eighteenth century, collections of Scottish song had been gathered for publication by editors keen to demonstrate the value of native art forms within the newly united kingdom of Great Britain. Songs and ballads were part of the old oral tradition, which relied on living poets and singers to perform the lyrics and pass them on to new generations. Often the authorship of a song had been lost on its way through the centuries, and so it seemed to embody not only the prized qualities of early poetry, but also the shared emotions and values of the community in which it survived. For Hazlitt, Burns's songs drew inspiration from the old ballads of Scotland, which represented a vital link to the national past:

We seem to feel that those who wrote and sang them (the early minstrels) lived in the open air, wandering on from place to place with restless feet and thoughts, and lending an ever-open ear to the fearful accidents of war or love, floating on the breath of old

tradition or common fame, and moving the strings of their harp with sounds that sank
into a nation's heart. (Hazlitt [1822] 1930-4, 5: 140)

The qualities that Blackwell had imagined in Homer, and Blair had glimpsed
through the translations of Ossian, were now widely associated with the "early
minstrels" of the British Isles. Hazlitt's enthusiasm reflects the late eighteenth-
century elevation of the minstrel figure, which followed Percy's important collection
of traditional ballads, *Reliques of Ancient English Poetry* (1765). A much more immediate and specifically Scottish influence, however, was Sir Walter Scott, whose literary
fame was founded on his own collection, *Minstrelsy of the Scottish Border*.

Scott, like Burns and Macpherson, had, from his earliest days, absorbed the legends
and songs of his local area. His decision to publish an edition of Border poetry was
similarly prompted by current literary interests, however, and especially by the vogue
for Gothic ballads in the 1790s. As Scott translated some of Bürger's popular ballads
and assisted Matthew Lewis in the compilation of *Tales of Wonder*, he recognized the
possibility of a wider audience for the songs and stories of his own country. While
Lewis was interested in ballads for their sensational stories and market value, Scott's
activities as a collector and creator were part of his deep attachment to the land where
his family had lived for generations. The growing interest in the Scottish Highlands
also strengthened Scott's determination to record and publicize the distinctive ballads
of the Lowlands. Macpherson had seen the effect on Gaelic poetry of the rapid changes
in eighteenth-century Highland life; Scott was similarly aware of the fragility of the
popular poetry of the Borders. The survival of oral literature required performers
capable of memorizing, adapting, and carrying the old songs into the minds and
hearts of new audiences. In his introduction to the *Minstrelsy*, Scott described the
"town-pipers" of the Border towns, who used to spend the spring and harvest
traveling through the local district, entertaining the community with songs (Scott
1931: 65-6). The footnotes signal the end of a long tradition, however, as they record
the recent deaths of Robin Hastie, the last town-piper of Jedburgh, and John Graeme,
"the last of our professed ballad reciters." What Scott was attempting to preserve in
his edition was a long-lived, but suddenly doomed tradition. He was, in a sense,
taking on the role of the vanished minstrel or town-piper, and transmitting the
ancient ballads to new homes.

Like the intellectuals who had sent Macpherson into the Highlands to recover what
was left of ancient Gaelic poetry, Scott's aim was partially preservation. Like Macpherson, too, he encouraged a rational, historical approach to the ballads, by prefacing
his collection with a substantial essay on the history and manners of the Borders, and
introducing individual pieces with contextual detail. And like Macpherson, again, his
editing involved some creative embellishment. *Minstrelsy of the Scottish Border* included
not only traditional ballads, such as "The Twa' Corbies," "The Battle of Otterbourne,"
or "Johnny Armstrong," but also more recent imitations and songs such as Jean
Elliot's "Flowers of the Forest." Although he has been criticized for some of these
editorial decisions, the immediate popularity of the volume and the demand for an

expanded edition show that Scott's desire to widen the admiration for Border songs was rapidly fulfilled.

Scott's *Minstrelsy* was among a number of important collections that combined to make Scottish song one of the nation's most important contributions to European Romanticism. It also demonstrates once more the importance of the local oral traditions to the most successful Scottish writers of the period. For Scott's own narrative poem, *The Lay of the Last Minstrel*, grew directly from his work as a ballad collector, and, like the *Minstrelsy*, carried Border legend into thousands of contemporary homes. Its astonishing success prompted Scott to turn to the emotive topic of Flodden Field for *Marmion*, before moving further north to the Trossachs for the story of *The Lady of the Lake*. The huge success of Scott's novels eventually eclipsed the fame of his poetry, but in the early nineteenth century, Scott's long, narrative poems were phenomenal best sellers. Nor should his later development as a novelist be seen as a move away from poetry. For Scott, collection and creation, verse and prose, were all complementary, and his best work combined the various facets of his talent. Scott's biographer, John Gibson Lockhart, particularly admired the introductory essays in the *Minstrelsy*, and records John Wilson's comment on the public excitement over the anonymity of *Waverley*: "I wonder what all these people are perplexing themselves with: Have they forgotten the *prose* of the *Minstrelsy?*" (Lockhart 1882, II: 132).

Scott's *Minstrelsy of the Scottish Border* was full of prose passages; his first novel, *Waverley*, is packed with references to poetry. The young hero, Edward Waverley, is "wild and romantic...with a strong disposition towards poetry," and is therefore primed to enjoy the old ballads he hears from David Gellatly and relish the stirring Highland songs of Flora MacIvor (Scott 1981: 56). Scattered throughout the narrative are snatches of "Chevy Chase," "Charlie is my Darling," "Hardiknut," and a host of other songs and ballads, which root the fiction firmly in the familiar tradition of Scottish song. At the same time, the novel includes alternative perspectives, such as that of Baron Bradwardine, who "piqued himself upon stalking through life with the same upright, starched, stoical gravity" and whose literary tastes are diametrically opposed to Waverley's (ibid.). Scott is also at pains to check popular Romantic stereotyping of the Highlanders, making Fergus MacIvor observe, "A simple and unsublimed taste now, like my own, would prefer the jet d'eau at Versailles to this cascade with all its accompaniments of rock and roar" (ibid.: 109). Far from conforming to Ossianic ideals, Fergus is witty, sophisticated and "unsublimed."

The flexible form of the novel allowed Scott to combine both the powerful imaginative attractions of the Highlands and the more skeptical, comic tone that was equally characteristic of Scottish culture, in one internally varied work. The different elements fuse to generate a dynamic narrative that is comic and yet moving, entertaining but still serious. As in the poetry of Burns, where comedy enables sentiment, Scott's gently ironic and self-consciously literary tone allows for the inclusion of moments of high Romantic fantasy and also of deep melancholy. The almost Shandyan touch of "Postscript, which should have been a Preface" lightens the final revelation of the novel's underlying purpose, which is strongly reminiscent of his earlier efforts as a collector of poems. In the closing pages, readers discover that *Waverley*, like the *Minstrelsy of the Scottish Border*, arose from Scott's attachment to his native country, and his acute sense of massive and irreversible transformation: "There is no European nation which, within the course of half a century, or little more, has undergone so complete a change as this kingdom of Scotland" (Scott 1981: 340).

Scott's desire to record the details of his changing nation drove him to write novel after novel, each drawing energy from the great variety of Scottish life, history, and landscapes. The fluidity of prose fiction allowed him to introduce a huge cast of characters from every area, class, and period, and to incorporate the multiple voices and forms of contemporary Scotland. Scott's prolific publication and enormous popularity did much to establish the novel as the major literary genre of the nineteenth century. He also made Scotland a subject for fiction, just as Maria Edgeworth had presented Ireland in her influential novels of Irish life. Scott's example was followed by John Galt, who helped to popularize the subgenre of the "regional novel" in his appealing depictions of rural Ayrshire, *Annals of the Parish* (1821). Far more innovative, however, was the work of James Hogg, who mirrored Scott by rising to fame as a poet before becoming increasingly known for his prose fiction.

Hogg was a collector of traditional Scottish stories and supplied Scott with many Border ballads for the *Minstrelsy*. His own writing plays persistently on the borders between collecting and creating, mixing traditional tales with his own compositions and frequently assuming different roles for his poetic and prose narratives. His *Winter Evening Tales* (Hogg 2002) for example, a volume of regional short stories and novellas published in 1820, is advertised as a series "Collected among the Cottagers in the South of Scotland," as if to cast Hogg as an editor rather than an author. In his most famous work, *The Private Memoirs and Confessions of a Justified Sinner* (1824), the "editor's narrative" is almost as long as the sinner's memoir, so that the two accounts comment on each other, refusing any single perspective or conclusive judgment. Authorship in Hogg's work is repeatedly questioned, with the responsibility for the narrative being deferred to untraceable origins. Although the contemporary image of Hogg as the "Ettrick Shepherd" smacks of late eighteenth-century aesthetic ideas of natural individuals in rural surroundings, Hogg's originality lies in his highly sophisticated challenges to the very idea of an author as the single-handed creator of a text. Hogg's fiction, like Scott's, celebrates the variousness of Scottish life, but where Scott generally developed a consistent omniscient narrator, Hogg frequently disguises any separate narrative voice and makes the teller an integral part of the tale. If Scott included characters who represented different strands in Scottish society, Hogg chose to adopt their very voices, setting the words of the manic "sinner" against the apparently objective account of the mysterious "editor." Hogg was as alert to the contradictory impulses of his environment as any writer of the period and in a torrent of unpredictable poems, short stories, and novels, he reflected the full complexity of Romantic Scotland.

Scotland in Romanticism

The compelling idea of Scotland in the Romantic period derived not only from Scottish pens and presses, but also from the descriptions published by visitors. From the late eighteenth century onwards, as mountain scenery became more fashionable and Highland travel safer, people were drawn to see for themselves the magnificent scenery of north-western Scotland. Although there were earlier accounts, such as Martin Martin's *Description of the Western Islands*, it was not until the 1770s that travel in Highland Scotland began to seem a realistic possibility for those unfamiliar with the region. Smollett's fictional travelogue, *The Expedition of Humphry Clinker*, and Samuel Johnson's own account of his *Journey to the Western Islands of Scotland* did much to arouse interest in Scotland, while the descriptions published by the naturalist, Thomas Pennant, and the picturesque tourist, William Gilpin, guided armchair travelers to the most remarkable scenes. Pennant's *Tour*, for example, included Joseph Banks's description of the phenomenal caves in the Hebridean island of Staffa, which came as a revelation to him and to subsequent readers: "Compared to this what are the cathedrals or palaces built by men!" Banks exclaimed, "Mere models or playthings, imitations as diminutive as his works will always be when compared to those of nature" (Pennant 1774: 262). The secrets of the western islands were being unveiled to the reading public for the first time, and seemed to surpass any of the known wonders of Britain. It is not surprising, then, that by the time Keats visited Fingal's Cave in 1818, he was almost as astonished by the number of tourists as by the natural wonder that had attracted them to Staffa:

> 'Tis now free to stupid face
> To cutters and to fashion boats,
> To cravats and to petticoats. ("Not Aladin Magian," Keats 1970: 375)

In spite of his dismay, however, Keats was profoundly struck by his journey; the images he garnered rapidly bore fruit in his great epic fragment "Hyperion," where the fallen Titans lie on "Couches of rugged stone," surrounded by the "solid roar/ Of thunderous waterfalls and torrents hoarse" (ibid.: 416).

The interest in Fingal's Cave demonstrates the multiple attractions of Romantic Scotland; for while many were following Banks's scientific lead and visiting a remarkable geological phenomenon, the popularity and controversy surrounding *Ossian* gave special interest to any site associated with the ancient Celtic heroes. Staffa is one of the highlights of Sarah Murray's *A Companion and Useful Guide to the Beauties of Scotland*, published in 1799 to assist intrepid travelers. In a breathless description of her visit, excitement over Ossian mingles with amazement at the physical spectacle, "I was almost overcome with astonishment and delight, on viewing the parts around the outside of the boat cave, and I remained in silent amazement at every succeeding object that met the eye" (Murray 1982: 133). The thrill of visiting the cave of the ancient Celtic hero is only one element of an excitement, mounting at the sight of the physical formations: "a round projection of most beautiful compact prisms descending from the magnificent crown or dome of small pillars in every direction...to a solid rough base of basaltes." Science and poetry united in Staffa, and visitors were staggered by the force of the feelings aroused. Ossianic sublimity found its natural counterpart in Fingal's Cave, but the emotion induced in countless Romantic visitors, like Sarah Murray, was religious wonder: "Never shall I forget the sublime, heaven-like sensations with which Fingal's Cave inspired me...Staffa produced the highest pitch of solemn, pious, enthusiastic sensation I ever felt or ever can feel in this my house of clay."

The solemnity of the Scottish landscape frequently elicited religious language from its visitors. Dorothy Wordsworth's *Recollections of a Tour Made in Scotland in 1803* includes a number of almost visionary moments, when the restlessness of the journey is stilled, and the scene sinks into the memory. Unlike Sarah Murray's excitement over the physical landscape, however, the scenes that moved Dorothy Wordsworth most deeply were often those in which a solitary human figure is silhouetted against an austere hillside. As she crossed a bleak, treeless tract in the Borders, she saw her first Highlander, dressed in his bonnet and grey plaid and recalls the "scriptural solemnity in this man's figure, a sober simplicity which was most impressive" (Selincourt 1941, I: 214). A few miles later on, she was even more struck by a shepherd boy: "on a bare moor, alone with his sheep, standing, as he did, in utter quietness and silence, there was something uncommonly impressive in his appearance, a solemnity which recalled to our minds the old man in the corn-field" (ibid.: 216). The Wordsworths' tour of Scotland, like Keats's later trip, was largely a literary pilgrimage to the places associated with Burns, Ossian, Wallace, and the Border songs and ballads. What they found in Scotland, however, was not just confirmation of the reality of places and people that had lived in their imaginations for many years. Dorothy's *Journal*, and the poems written by Wordsworth, reveal a journey that was literary in its inspiration – and in its results. In addition to verses written after visiting the grave of Burns, or on not visiting the famous river Yarrow, there are poems which, like the journal, record memorable encounters and local stories. Wordsworth's celebration of Scotland in his *Poems in Two Volumes* added greatly to the attraction of Scotland in the Romantic period, and for later travelers such as Keats, the visit to Burns's country was deepened by the knowledge that the Wordsworths and Coleridge had also made the journey and added their own contribution to the idea of Romantic Scotland.

Although the Scotland that emerges from Dorothy Wordsworth's *Recollections* more than fulfills the contemporary expectation of solemn scenery, mysterious figures, mist and mountains, such Romantic motifs do not make up the whole picture. In addition to the visual delights, imaginative fascination, and physical hardship, she also records numerous references to friendly encounters and generous hospitality. Though hampered by their inability to speak Gaelic, the Wordsworths came away with memories not just of striking figures on hillsides, but also of warm welcomes and human anecdotes. Nor was their literary pilgrimage confined to graves, as is clear from the account of the happy meeting with Scott, who recited part of his unpublished *Lay of the Last Minstrel.*

As Scott's fame grew, enabling him to purchase and improve a large house on the banks of the Tweed, Abbotsford became something of a magnet for literary tourists. Not only Wordsworth, but also Joanna Baillie, Felicia Hemans, Maria Edgeworth, Thomas Moore, and Washington Irving were entertained at Abbotsford, while Hogg, Lockhart, Constable, and Ballantyne were regular visitors. Scott turned himself into a Scottish laird and his house into a baronial castle, packed with heraldic decorations and suits of armor. As Mark Girouard has observed, "the romanticism which produced Scott's novels and the romanticism which turned him into a Scottish laird were essential to each other" (Girouard 1981: 40). It may be a Romanticism that seems far removed from the radical, democratic thrust of so much Romantic writing, but it is just as much part of the period and evolves from a similar late eighteenth-century enthusiasm for a heroic past where people lived close to nature. For the pursuit of nature in the Romantic period meant not only admiration of spectacular scenery or of simple people in rural surroundings, but also hunting, shooting, and fishing. Those who visited Scott were as likely to be drawn by the salmon fishing or the famous Abbotsford Hunt as by his poetry.

While Romantic tourists set off for Scotland in search of waterfalls, rocks, and poetic flights, many journeyed north attracted by reports of rich fare and abundant game. Gilpin may have guided readers towards the romantic banks of the Tay, but tour-writers such as Colonel Thornton were sharing first-hand knowledge of the ptarmigan, grouse, and deer. If Wordsworth was moved by the poverty and simplicity of life in rural Scotland, Thornton was struck by its luxury "what few possess, viz. roebucks, cairvauns, hare, black game, dottrel, white game, partridges, ducks and snipes; salmon, pike, trout, char, par, lampreys and eels" (Thornton [1804] 1974: 227).

Determined tourists traveled to Scotland in the late eighteenth and early nineteenth century, attracted by Scottish poetry and novels and by the descriptions written by earlier visitors. Undeterred by demanding terrain and challenging weather, they followed routes familiar from their reading, and yet responded very variously to what they saw. While many were deeply moved by the mountain landscapes and sublime solemnity of Scotland, others were satisfied by the physical rewards of walking, riding, and blood sports. Some were excited by seeing the habitat and behavior of unfamiliar birds and animals, others were more interested in how they tasted. The Scots themselves, who live on in their own writings and in writings about them, regarded their country in equally diverse ways: while some drew endless inspiration from their land and its traditions, others moved away, returning only through books.

Romantic Scotland was at once a wild place where the imagination could roam freely, and a barren landscape inhabited largely by the wildlife. It was both an intellectual powerhouse, where educated people tackled the obstacles to modern progress energetically, and a country characterized by religious austerity and opposition to change. It was a place where people gathered to exchange views and friendship, and an underpopulated land renowned for the solitariness of its people. United with England since 1707, it was a nation increasingly proud of its distinctive achievements, and yet burdened by a sense of linguistic inferiority and physical remoteness. Though apparently consisting of oppositions and contrasts, the Scotland of Romanticism is really multifaceted: shifting, dazzling, and as various as its weather. Since Romanticism is itself notoriously elusive and open to debate, Scotland offers numerous possibilities for further exploration of the Romantic movement – and the Romantic period.

Notes

1 "l'imagination du Nord, celle qui plaît sur le bord de la mer, au bruit des vents, dans les bruyères sauvages" (de Staël 1820: 258; Hazlitt, ibid.).

2 Letter to Tom Keats, July 7, 1818, in Keats (1958, I: 319).

3 Byron (1980-93, I: 242). On the contemporary Scottish reviewers, see Demata and Wu (2002).

4 For fuller discussion, see Stafford (1988: 24-39).

5 For a useful introduction, see Broadie (1997), Sher (1985).

6 On the importance of Scottish literary criticism in this period, and Blair in particular, see Crawford (1992, 1998).

7 Burke's *A Philosophical Inquiry into the Origin of our Ideas of the Sublime and the Beautiful* was published in 1757; Immanuel Kant's *Observations on the Feeling of the Sublime and the Beautiful* was published in 1764, though his mature analysis, published in 1790 in *The Critique of Judgement* is more familiar to Romanticists. For useful discussion and other important texts, see Ashfield and de Bolla (1996).

8 On the importance of the Celtic Bard for ideas of national identity, see Katie Trumpener's excellent study, *Bardic Nationalism* (1997).

9 In 1805, two major publications relating to the controversy appeared: Henry Mackenzie (ed.), *Report of the Highland Society of Scotland. Appointed to Enquire into the Nature and Authenticity of the Poems of Ossian*; and Malcolm Laing (ed.), *The Poems of Ossian &c, containing the Poetical Works of James Macpherson*. Walter Scott reviewed the *Report* in the *Edinburgh Review*, VI (1805): 429-62.

10 The epigraph on the title page of Burns's *Poems Chiefly in the Scottish Dialect* (Kilmarnock, 1786) read: "The Simple Bard, unbroken by rules of Art, / He pours the wild effusions of the heart: / And if inspir'd, 'tis Nature's powers inspire; / Her's all the melting thrill and her's the kindling fire."

11 On the "Standard Habbie," later known as the "Burns stanza," see Dunn (1997).

12 As Burns (1968) notes, "Duan, a term of Ossian's for the different divisions of a digressive Poem." See his *Cath Loda*, vol. 2 of MacPherson's translation.

References and Further Reading

Ashfield, Andrew and de Bolla, Peter (eds.) (1996). *The Sublime: A Reader in British Eighteenth-Century Aesthetic Theory.* Cambridge, UK: Cambridge University Press.

Blair, Hugh (1996). "A Critical Dissertation on the Poems of Ossian." In James Macpherson, *The Poems of Ossian*, ed. Howard Gaskill. Edinburgh: Edinburgh University Press, pp. 343-400.

Broadie, Alexander (ed.) (1997). *The Scottish Enlightenment*. Edinburgh: Canongate.

Burns, Robert (1968). *The Poems and Songs of Robert Burns*, ed. James Kinsley, 3 vols. Oxford: Clarendon Press.

Byron, Lord (1980-93). *English Bards and Scotch Reviewers*. In Jerome J. McGann (ed.), *The Complete Poetical Works*, 7 vols. Oxford: Clarendon Press.

Crawford, Robert (1992). *Devolving English Literature*. Oxford: Clarendon Press.

Crawford, Robert (ed.) (1998). *The Scottish Invention of English Literature*. Cambridge, UK: Cambridge University Press.

Daverio, John (1998). "Schumann's Ossianic Manner." *Nineteenth-Century Music*, 21 (3): 247-73.

Demata, Massimiliano and Wu, Duncan (eds.) (2002). *British Romanticism and the Edinburgh Review*. London: Palgrave.

Dunn, Douglas (1997). " 'A Very Scottish Kind of Dash': Burns's Native Metric." In Robert Crawford (ed.), *Robert Burns and Cultural Authority*. Edinburgh: Edinburgh University Press, pp. 58-85.

Fiske, Roger (1983). *Scotland in Music: An European Enthusiasm*. Cambridge, UK: Cambridge University Press.

Gaskill, Howard (1994). "Ossian in Europe." *Canadian Review of Comparative Literature*, 21: 644-54.

Gerard, Alexander (1755). *A Plan of Education in the Marischal College and University of Aberdeen*. Aberdeen: James Chalmers.

Girouard, Mark (1981). *The Return to Camelot: Chivalry and the English Gentleman*. New Haven, CT and London: Yale University Press.

Hazlitt, William ([1822] 1930-4). *The Complete Works of William Hazlitt*, ed. P. P. Howe, 21 vols. London and Toronto: Dent.

Hogg, James (2002). *Winter Evening Tales*, ed. Ian Duncan. Edinburgh: Edinburgh University Press.

Jeffrey, Francis (1809). "Review of R. H. Cromek, *Reliques of Robert Burns*." *Edinburgh Review*, 13: 249-76.

Keats, John (1958). *The Letters of John Keats*, ed. Hyder Rollins, 2 vols. Cambridge, MA: Harvard University Press.

Keats, John (1970). *The Poems of John Keats*, ed. Miriam Allott. London: Longman.

Lamport, Francis (1998). "Goethe, Ossian and Werther." In Fiona Stafford and Howard Gaskill (eds.), *From Gaelic to Romantic: Ossianic Translations*. Amsterdam and Atlanta, GA: Rodopi, pp. 97-106.

Lockhart, John Gibson (1882). *Memoirs of Sir Walter Scott*, 10 vols. Edinburgh: A. and C. Black.

McIlvanney, Liam (2003). *Burns the Radical: Poetry and Politics in Late Eighteenth-Century Scotland*. East Linton, UK: Tuckwell.

Macpherson, James (1996). *The Poems of Ossian*, ed. Howard Gaskill. Edinburgh: Edinburgh University Press.

Murray, Sarah (1982). *A Companion and Useful Guide to the Beauties of Scotland*, ed. W. F. Laughlan. Hawick, UK: Byway Books.

Okun, H. (1967). "Ossian in Painting." *Journal of the Warburg and Courtauld Institute*, 30: 327-56.

Pennant, Thomas (1774). "Account of Staffa." In *A Tour in Scotland and Voyage to the Hebrides*. Chester: John Monk.

Ramsay, Allan (1974). "Familiar Epistles between Lieutenant William Hamilton and Allan Ramsay." In A. M. Kinghorn and A. Law (eds.), *Poems by Allan Ramsay and Robert Fergusson*. Edinburgh and London: Scottish Academic Press, pp. 17-27.

Scott, Walter ([1802-3] 1931). *Minstrelsy of the Scottish Border*, ed. Thomas Henderson. London: Harrap.

Scott, Walter (1981). *Waverley; or 'Tis Sixty Years Since*, ed. Claire Lamont. Oxford: Clarendon Press.

Selincourt, Ernest de (ed.) (1941). *The Journals of Dorothy Wordsworth*, 2 vols. London: Macmillan.

Selincourt, Ernest de (ed.) (1978). *The Letters of William and Dorothy Wordsworth: The Later Years, Part 1, 1821-1828*, rev. edn. Alan G. Hill. Oxford: Clarendon.

Sher, Richard B. (1985). *Church and University in the Scottish Enlightenment*. Edinburgh: Edinburgh University Press.

Staël, Germaine de (1820). *De la Littérature, considérée dans ses rapports avec les institutions sociales*. In *Œuvres complètes de Mme la baronne de Staël*, 8 vols., vol. IV. Paris: Treuttel et Würtz.

Stafford, Fiona (1988). *The Sublime Savage: James Macpherson and the Poems of Ossian*. Edinburgh: Edinburgh University Press.

Thornton, Thomas ([1804] 1974). "A Sporting Tour Through the Northern Parts of England and the Highlands of Scotland." In A. J. Younson (ed.), *Beyond the Highland Line: 3 Journals of Travel in Eighteenth Century Scotland*. London: Collins, pp. 207-47.

Trumpener, Katie (1997). *Bardic Nationalism: The Romantic Novel and the British Empire* (Princeton, NJ: Princeton University Press.

Wordsworth, William ([1800] 1992). Preface to *Lyrical Ballads*, ed. Michael Mason. London: Longman.

4

Byron's Influence on European Romanticism

Peter Cochran

In 1837 Adam Mickiewicz wrote:

> The epoch between 1815 and 1830 was a happy one for poets. After the great war, Europe, tired of battles and congresses, bulletins and protocols, seemed to become disgusted with the real, sad world, and lifted its eyes towards what it thought of as the ideal world. At that point Byron appeared. Rapidly, in the regions of the imagination, he took over the place which the Emperor had recently occupied in the regions of reality. Destiny, which had never ceased to furnish Napoleon with pretexts for continual warfare, favoured Byron with a long peace. During his poetic reign, no great event occurred to distract the attention of Europe, wholly taken up with its English reading. (Swidzinski 1991: 9)

The Byron around whom the second most powerful myth in nineteenth-century Europe formed was not the author of those poems which we most value today. This is not just because *Don Juan, Beppo*, and *The Vision of Judgement* are harder to translate than *Childe Harold, The Giaour*, or *Manfred* (though they do seem to be) but because the myth which they partially contradict was already too well developed across Europe when Byron wrote them. His letters, too, which we regard so highly, were unknown to all but their recipients before 1830 – and even then they were published in incomplete texts.

Amédée Pichot's prose translations of Byron[1] constituted the most important vehicle for the dissemination of the poet's reputation through Europe, a process which they initiated, in part, during his lifetime. Their relationship with Byron's real corpus is good in outline, useless in terms of style and tone; but great writers, being great readers, could, if they had no English, see past their monotony and intuit what the original must be like. This seems especially the case with Pushkin, whom I take to be the greatest writer of the period.

Lamartine, Musset, and Pushkin all got to know Byron through Pichot. Goethe, Heine, de Vigny, Espronceda, Lermontov, and Stendhal, however, having English, would have disdained doing so – and when Mickiewicz gave Pushkin a single-volume Byron it was an English-language edition, published by Brœnner of Frankfurt. Mickiewicz translated Byron from the original. But Pichot's, while not the best translation of Byron, remains historically the most important. It seems likely to me – though I can't prove it – that several "translations" into other languages were created from it.

Byron – or rather, European Byronism – seems to have answered two needs: the need for what was perceived as a revolutionary voice, both literary and political, with which to identify, and the need for what was perceived as a similar revolutionary voice from which to recoil in horror. His heroes – Harold, Selim, Conrad, and so on – who in truth pose no great threat to any political establishment, were read and recreated eagerly as if they did. *Manfred*, whose protagonist, in not relying on the Devil to destroy himself, and in rejecting Christian solace to save himself, really did pose an ideological threat to the establishment, was read even more eagerly. As George Sand writes, Manfred is "...Faust délivré de l'odieuse compagnie de Méphistophélès" (Faust delivered from the odious company of Mephistopheles; Sand 1839: 612). Byron's life, as it was understood via international rumor, added the thrill of mysterious personal transgressions – even Goethe thought Byron was a murderer (Goethe 1970, II ii: 186-9). *Don Juan*, in changing the world's perception of Byron's solemnity, did nothing to change its perception of his radicalism; and his sensational death in Greece capped all of the foregoing with an unanswerable martyrdom in one of the very causes he had been seen to propagate.

The myth of Byron was multifold – like Don Juan, he was all things to all people. He was, to some, a posturing dandy of magnificent panache; to others, a poet of passion and guilt such as had not been read, in any language, since Shakespeare; to others, reading *Manfred*, a soul defying all powers, both celestial and infernal, to the point of death and beyond – it is difficult for us today to appreciate the impact the play had. To others, he was one who had rejected the certainties of the Enlightenment, substituting for them, not so much an alternative certainty, as a variety of new ways in which to express the profoundest uncertainty. As Richard Cardwell puts it, "[Byron's work] opposed the central presumption which underlies the history of Western civilisation, that to the central questions about the nature and purpose of men's lives, about morals, about death, and the hereafter, true, objective, universal and eternal answers could be found" (Cardwell 1997: 9).

To other observers, Byron was the greatest living critic of political chicanery and hypocrisy, and the greatest prophet of the doom of imperialism, at a time, after 1815, when chicanery, hypocrisy, and imperialism seemed to rule all Europe; lastly, he was an active champion of freedom against oppression, who passed the final test: he put his life where his words were, and died for his beliefs. Paul Trueblood writes: "...Byron's death at Missolonghi in 1824 had a catalytic effect on the struggle for political liberty and nationalism throughout Europe... More than the writings of any other major Romantic poet Byron's political poetry... reflects the revolutionary upheavals of the peoples all over the Continent seeking political freedom and national identity" (Trueblood 1981: 200-1). Whether that effect seems, from our perspective, to have been benign or otherwise, is a question for debate (Tessier 1997: 6). We cannot hold Byron responsible for the frightening subsequent history of Continental chauvinism.

There were even some readers – very important readers, as I hope I shall show – who regarded Byron above all as a master of satire and of comic inventiveness: the biggest anti-Romantic of them all. Different nations and different writers combined these factors in whatever proportions suited them best, or in whatever proportions the regimes under which they lived were prepared to countenance. But no matter how repressive the regimes, the myth was all-powerful – Byron as both writer and thinker, doer and actor, was (except to his own class, in his own country) a universal revolutionary idol and role-model, whose status no one (except, again, his own compatriots) could diminish.

He was preoccupied with the figures of Faust and of Don Juan – he wrote the most radical rewritings of the myths in their entire history. In this he was set apart from all his English "Romantic" contemporaries, but followed and answered by many Continental writers (though few of them appreciated his originality). Just as his Don Juan renders impossible an idealization of womanhood – for Byron, women are the predators – so Manfred, his Faust, renders impossible any thought that nonhuman powers are to blame for the hero's, and mankind's, fate.

There was justice in what happened. Of all English writers in the Napoleonic and post-Napoleonic period, Byron owed most both to his immediate and to his more distant European predecessors. He is the most European of the English so-called "Romantic" writers. It was thus natural that he should be assimilated as an influence in return. The depth and breadth of his influence is, however, startling. In 1909 Arthur Symons wrote, "[Byron] filled Europe, as no other poet in the history of Literature has filled Europe" (Symons 1909: 249). What I shall try to examine in this chapter is not only direct influence, but the way in which Byron created a literary and political climate in which like-minded writers could be more confidently true to themselves.

Russia: Pushkin and Lermontov

A sadder way of putting it is this: early nineteenth-century European literature is strewn with the corpses of men who thought that they'd been influenced by Byron. In many cases, they really had been influenced by him. For example: in the eighth chapter of Pushkin's *Eugene Onegin* (published 1833), Tatyana, the heroine, who has earlier in the poem flung herself at the protagonist, only to be rebuffed, sees him once more across the room at a St Petersburg reception:

Ей нравится порядок стройный
Олигархических бесед,
И холод гордости спокойиой,
И зта смесь чинов и лет.
Но зто кто в толпе избранной
Стоит безмолвный и туманный?
Для всех он кажется чужим.
Мелькают лица перед ним,
Как ряд докучных привидений.
Что, сплин иль страждущая спесь
В его лице? Зачем он здесь?
Кто он таков? Ужель Евгеннй?
Ужели он? .. Так, точно он.
--- Давно ли к нам он занесён?

Всё тот же ль он иль усмирился?
Иль корчит так же чудака?
Скажите, чем он возвратился?
Что нам предстравит он пока?
Чем ныне явится? Мельмотом,
Космополитом, патриотом,
Гарольдом, квакером, ханжой,
Иль маской щегольнёт иной,
Иль просто будет добрый малый,
Как вы да я, как целый свет?
Но крайней мере, мой совет:
Отстать от моды обветшалой.
Довольно он морочил свет... (*Onegin* VIII vii-viii)

(She likes the stately disposition
Of oligarchic colloquies,
Their chilly pride in high position,
The mix of years and ranks she sees.
But who is that among the chosen,
That figure standing mute and frozen,
That stranger no one seems to know?
Before him faces come and go
Like spectres in a bleak procession.
What is it—martyred pride or spleen
That marks his face? ... Is that Eugene?
That figure with the strange expression?
Can that be he? It is, I say.
"But when did fate cast him our way?

"Is he the same, or is he learning?
Or does he play the outcast still?
In what new guise is he returning?

> What role does he intend to fill?
> Childe Harold? Melmoth for a while?
> Cosmopolite? A Slavophile?
> A Quaker? Bigot?—might one ask?
> Or will he sport some other mask?
> Or maybe he's just dedicated,
> Like you or me, to being nice?
> In any case, here's my advice:
> Give up a role when it's outdated.
> He's gulled the world . . . now let it go."
> "You knew him them?" "Well, yes and no." (Pushkin 1995: 188)

The matter of *Childe Harold* and the Turkish Tales is here being held at a satirical distance, but aided by a style derived from *Don Juan*. Onegin really has modeled himself on the futile Byronic hero, just as Pushkin's earlier works *A Prisoner in the Caucasus* and *The Fountain of Bakhchisari* (*Кавказкий Пленник* and *Бахчисарайский Фонтан*, 1822 and 1824) had modeled themselves on the poems in which he first appeared. However, just as Tatyana steels herself against the attraction she still feels for him by adopting a pose of amused dispassion, so Pushkin could only contextualize one heavy Byronic style by adopting another, light one. Pushkin's most overt act of homage to Byron is the neglected *Little House at Kolomna* (*Домик в Коломне*), a comic hymn to the female sexual impulse in ottava rima, modeled on *Beppo*.

After years struggling against Tsarist oppressiveness in all its forms, Pushkin died in a wretched duel which he provoked himself.

Byron was regarded with deep suspicion by the Tsarist authorities. All translations of his work were censored; John Murray's guidebooks warned against trying to smuggle your copy of *Don Juan* through the Russian customs (Custine 1991: 252 n.16).

Pushkin's successor was also killed in a duel, and was less critically in Byron's shadow than Pushkin had been. Mikhail Lermontov became emotional when he thought of Byron:

> Я молод; но кипят на сердце звуки,
> И Байрона достигнуть я б хотел;
> У нас одна душа, одни и те же муки;
> О если б одинаков был удел!
> Как он, ишу забвенья и свободы,
> Как он, ребячестве пылал уж я душой,
> Любил закат в горах, пенящиеся воды,
> И бврь земных и бурь небесных вой. (Lermontov 1961: 136)

(Though young, sounds boil within me, / And it is Byron I wish to emulate: For we inherit one soul and like torments, / Oh could but our fate also be the same. // Like him,

I seek oblivion and freedom, / Like his, my soul in childhood was aflame, / I loved a mountain sunset, foaming waters, / And heaven and earth aloud with tempest's roar. (trans. Tatyana Wolff.)

Pechorin, the protagonist of Lermontov's *A Hero of Our Time* (1840), has small, delicate hands, curly hair, and a pale, noble brow; at 25 he is bored with society, learning, warfare, and women; he enjoys dressing as a stylish Asiatic tribesman, adores the novels of Scott, and prefers to doubt everything. He also has a destructive influence on the lives of nearly everyone he meets. It comes as no surprise when he describes himself as one of those who start life expecting to end up as Alexander the Great, or Lord Byron (Lermontov 1966: 53-4, 67-8, 113, 135, 158, 184).

Germany: Heine and Goethe

Heinrich Heine celebrated Byron's death in an aptly sombre manner:

> Eine starke, schwarze Barke
> Segelt trauervoll dahin.
> Die vermummten und verstummten
> Leichenhüter sitzen drin.
>
> Toter Dichter, stille liegt er,
> Mit entblöatem Angesicht;
> Seine blauen Augen schauen
> Immer noch zum Himmelslicht.
>
> Aus der Tiefe klingts, als riefe
> Eine kranke Nixenbraut,
> Und die Wellen, sie zerschellen
> An dem Kahn, wie Klagelaut.

(A stout, black bark sails sadly along. In it sit the masked and silent pall-watchers. / The dead poet lies still, his face unshrouded; his blue eyes still gaze up at the light of heaven. / Sounds rise from the deep, as if a water-sprite's ailing bride were calling, and the waves break against the bark, like lamentations.) (Heine 1968: 118)

When he heard of Byron's death, Heine referred to him as having been "mein Vetter" (my cousin; Heine 1970: 163). But it was not the Haroldian Byron that Heine – who, unlike Pushkin, knew English – admired most. A few stanzas from *Deutschland. Ein Wintermärchen* (1844) will show the affinity with the later, facetious Byron. In the poem, Heine, returning from France, sees German soil for the first time in years, and is entranced by the singing of a little German girl:

Ein Hochzeitkarmen ist mein Lied,
Das bessere, das neue!
In meiner Seele gehen auf
Die Sterne der höchsten Weihe –

Begeisterte Sterne, sie lodern wild,
Zerfließen in Flammenbächen –
Ich fühle mich wunderbar erstarkt,
Ich könnte Eichen zerbrechen!

Seit ich auf deutsche Erde trat,
Durchströmen mich Zaubersäfte –
Der Riese hat wieder die Mutter berührt,
Und es wuchsen ihm neu die Kräfte.

II
Während die Kleine von Himmelslust
Getrillert und musizieret,
Ward von den preußichen Douaniers
Mein Koffer visitieret.

Beschnüffelten alles, kramten herum
In Hemden, Hosen, Schnupftüchern;
Sie suchten nach Spitzen, nach Bijouterien,
Auch nach verbotenen Büchern.

Ihr Toren, die ihr im Koffer sucht!
Hier werdet ihr nichts entdecken!
Die Contrebande, die mit mir reist,
Die hab ich im Kopfe stecken. (Heine 1991, I: 65-76, II: 1-12)

(My song is an epithalamion, my new song, my better song! I feel stars of the highest grace rising in my soul. / They burn with a savage fire, and their rays turn into torrents of flame! I feel my powers growing in a marvelous way; I feel wonderfully strengthened, as though I could burst oak trees asunder! / Since I set foot in Germany, magic powers are streaming through me; the Giant has touched the Mother, and has gained new skills. / II. / While the little girl trilled and made her heavenly music, the Prussian customs officers looked through my luggage. / They nosed through the lot, shirts, coats, snot-rags; looking for lace, for jewels – also for forbidden books. / You morons, searching my trunk! You won't find anything there – the *contrebande* I bring with me is hidden in my head.)[2]

The stanzas show a movement from a mock early-Byronic exaltation, via a later-Byronic dip into bathos with the description of the minutiae inspected by the customs officer, to another later-Byronic defiance, a pride in the poet's ability to see further than the provincial boors who would muzzle him. Heine's imitation of the Englishman's satire is more flattering than the condescension of Goethe, who, in *Faust*

Part II, portrays Byron as Euphorion, talented offspring of his protagonist and Helen of Troy, a child who takes off, flies too near the sun, and disappears in "ein Lichtschweif" (*Faust* II, iii) – a streak of light. Goethe, acknowledged as a genius well before Byron, died in a comfortable old age: Heine died slowly of spinal tuberculosis, exiled from home (though, like Byron, he never had one) in his Parisian "mattress-grave."

Italy

An Italian poem which shows how a writer from that country could transform the verifiable Byron into a more accommodating one is Francesco dall'Òngaro's 1837 *Il Venerdì Santo* (Good Friday). Dall'Òngaro started adult life as a priest, but quit the cloth to follow the Risorgimento. In his poem Byron ("Giorgio") sits one evening in the Euganaean Hills with Allegra ("sua figlia d'amore"). In his inscrutability, he resembles one of his own earlier heroes:

> . . . sotto le brune
> Ciglia sinistro scintillò lo sguardo,
> Nel suo mantello si ravvolse e indarno
> Il suo vicino sel cercò da presso. (Dall'Òngaro 1837: 19)

(. . . under the dark brow his sinister gaze flashed, he gathered himself in his mantel and vainly did [even] his nearest neighbor look for him.)

Allegra sings an *Ave Maria*, in strange echo of his own in *Don Juan* IV:

> Ave, Maria: questa è l'ora tranquilla
> Che il tuo nome gentil mi parla al cor;
> Or ti saluta colla sacra squilla
> L'aura del vespro accarezzando i fior. . . (Dall'Òngaro 1837:24)

(Hail, Mary: this is the calm hour when your sweet name speaks to my heart; now the evening breeze greets you with its sacred tune . . .)

But for dall'Òngaro, as for most Italian poets, there is no light relief, no critical comment. Father and daughter hear the sound of Good Friday worship in the distance, as if from *Cavalleria Rusticana*, or, with greater relevance, from *Faust* Part I scene vi, except that dall'Òngaro invests his Easter scene with far greater Christian meaning than does Goethe. Witnessing the annual procession, "Giorgio" is transported. After explaining what Good Friday means, he tells Allegra that he will take her back to England, where

Ada ed Allegra entrambe
Innocenti del pari ed infelici
Di me vi sovverete ed io di voi
Sia che in terra io travagli, o in ciel riposi . . . (Dall'Òngaro 1837: 51).

(Ada and Allegra, neither knowing any unhappiness, you will remember me, and I you,
whether I work on earth or sleep in heaven . . .)

. . . if she will only be patient; for he has first to go to Greece:

Non lungi
Dall'Italia è una terra, inclita un tempo
Per armi e per virtù, per quanto al mondo
Può far altero e venerato un suolo.
Testè per lunga servitù prostrata
Dell'antiche sue glorie e de' suoi fati
Immemore la vidi, e maledissi.
Or, dal sonno riscossa, i suoi tiranni,
Disfida a sanguinosa ultima guerra.
Stringe coll'una man la croce bianca,
Coll'altra il ferro onde il divin vessillo
Sugli aerei pinacoli riponga
Dove d'Ali la curva luna splende.
Tu resterai pregando, io là del sacro
Adorabile segno i dritti augusti
Vendicherò . . . (Dall'Òngaro 1837: 52-3).

(Not far from Italy there is a land, once glorious for arms and virtue, respected
throughout the world. I witnessed her long-worn-out servitude, and, unmindful of
her ancient glories and of its destiny, I saw her and cursed her. Now, having recovered
from sleep, and from her tyrants, she is waging one last bloody war. With one hand she
holds the white cross, with the other the divine standard, placed on the lofty battle-
ments from which flies the crescent moon of Ali. You will remain here praying, I shall
be victorious in the sacred sign of the mighty laws.)

Dall'Òngaro's scenario is not so very ludicrous. He has read not only his Moore, but
his Medwin and his Blessington, and has amassed from them sufficient evidence of
Byron's admiration for Catholicism to give his vision credibility ("Quel loro purga-
torio è una cara dottrina" – compare Medwin 1966: 80.) Our view of "Giorgio"'s
aspirations is colored by the knowledge of what happened to father and daughter in
reality.

Italy's most important poet of the period – Giacomo Leopardi – does not seem to
have held Byron in any esteem, or even to have read him much; but Byron (much of
whose work was banned in early nineteenth-century Italy) was a potent literary and

moral force during the Risorgimento. Here is an extract from the diary of Cesare Abba (published 1882), one of Garibaldi's Thousand: "Trovammo un cavallo disteso morto sul margine del sentiero, e si disse che era di Bixio: il quale irato, perchè ci nitriti poteva scoprirci al nemico, gli aveva scaricata nel canio la sua pistola. Byron, sempre Byron! Lara l'avrebbe fatto anche lui" (Abba 1918: 79). (We found a horse lying dead by the side of the path and they said it was Bixio's, who had been enraged because its neighing could have revealed our presence to the enemy and had blown its brains out with his own pistol. Byron, always Byron! Lara would have done the same; Abba 1962: 53.)

Spain: Espronceda

The "Spanish Byron" was José de Espronceda, who died of diphtheria and syphilis in 1842. His most Byronic poems are the unfinished *El Diablo mundo*, which, like *Don Juan*, denies life any universal meaning or harmony; and *El estudiante de Salamanca*, his version of the Don Juan legend, published in 1840. In its second part the heroine, Elvira, pens a letter (in ottava rima) to the depraved protagonist Don Felix de Montemar, who has seduced and betrayed her:

> A Dios por siempre, a Dios: un breve instante
> siento de vida, y en mi pecho el fuego
> aún arde de me amor; mi vista errante
> vaga desvanecida..., calma luego
> ¡oh muerte! Mi inquietud...¡Sola...expirante...!
> Ámame; no, perdona: ¡inútil ruego!
> A Dios, a Dios, ¡tu corazón perdí!
> ¡Todo acabó en el mund para mí!
>
> (For ever fare thee well; I have I know
> One moment brief of life, and still love's fire
> Glows in my heart; mine eyes they wander slow,
> My sight grows dim...So soothe now, vision dire,
> My fretful soul!...Alone...To death I go!
> Oh love me!...No, forgive!...Oh vain desire!
> Goodbye, I could not hold thy heart in fee!
> ...So all is ended in the world for me!) (Espronceda 1991: 64-5)

It is like, and yet unlike, Donna Julia's letter to Juan at the end of the first canto of Byron's epic, which Espronceda knew in the original; he had, with many liberals, been exiled in England by the government of Ferdinand VII "of grateful memory" (Byron 1980-93, V: 83). Unlike Julia, Elvira dies, and the poem's terrifying second half shows Don Felix descending like Manfred into the shades, led by her ghost – where Manfred has only the shortest of meetings with Astarte, however, Don Felix is punished by being forced to make love to Elivira's sentient corpse for the rest of eternity. It is a debt to Byron, being paid with creative inversions and variations. Byron's problem was whether to punish Don Juan by damning him or marrying him off – Espronceda does both at the same time.

Once Espronceda passed away, Spanish Byronism ceased.

France: Stendhal and Musset

Of the numerous French writers who borrowed from Byron, Stendhal and Musset stand out. Consider this, from Stendhal's *Le Rouge et le noir* (1830):

Julien la serra dans ses bras avec la plus vive passion; jamais elle ne lui avait semblé si belle. Même à Paris, se disait-il confusément, je ne pourrai rencontrer un plus grand caractère. Elle avait toute la gaucherie d'une femme peu accoutumé à ces sortes de soins, et en même temps le vrai courage d'un être qui ne craint que des dangers d'un autre ordre et bien autrement terribles.

Pendant que Julien soupait de grand appétit, et que son amie le plaisantait sur la simplicité de ce repas, car elle avait horreur de parler sérieusement, la porte de la chambre fut tout à coup secouée avec force. C'était M. de Rênal.

—Pourquoi t'es-tu enfermée? lui criait-il.

Julien n'eut que le temps de se glisser sous le canapé.

— Quoi! Vous êtes tout habillée, dit M. de Rênal en entrant; vous soupez, et vous avez fermé votre porte à clef.

Les jours ordinaires, cette question, faite avec toute la sécheresse conjugale, eût troublé Mme de Rênal, mais elle sentait que son mari n'avait qu'à se baisser un peu pour apercevoir Julien; car M. de Rênal s'était jeté sur la chaise que Julien occupait un moment auparavant vis-à-vis le canapé.

La migraine servit d'excuse à tout. Pendant qu'à son tour son mari lui contait longuement les incidents de la poule qu'il avait gagnée au billard du Casino, une poule de dix-neuf francs ma foi! ajoutait-il, elle aperçut sur une chaise, à trois pas devant eux, le chapeau de Julien. Son sang-froid redoubla, elle se mit à se déshabiller, et, dans un certain moment, passant rapidement derrière son mari, jeta une robe sur la chaise au chapeau. (Stendhal 1964: 257-8)

(Julien clasped her eagerly, passionately in his arms; never before had she seemed so beautiful as now. Even in Paris, his bemused mind was thinking, I can't possibly meet anyone with a nobler nature. She showed all the awkward embarrassment of a woman little used to attentions of this kind, but she showed at the same time the true courage belonging to one who is only frightened by dangers of another, and very much more terrible order.

While Julien was eating his supper with a keen appetite and his mistress was joking with him about the frugality of his meal, the door of the room was all at once violently shaken. It was M. de Rênal.

"Why have you locked yourself in?" he called out to her loudly. Julien had only time just to slip under the sofa.

"What? you're completely dressed," said M. de Rênal as he entered, "you're having supper and you've locked the door!"

On any ordinary day, such a question, addressed to her with all his usual conjugal curtness, would have made Mme de Rênal feel upset, but now she was conscious that her husband had only to stoop down a little to catch sight of Julien. M. de Rênal had flung himself into the chair on which Julien had been sitting a moment before and which was directly facing the sofa.

Her headache served as an excuse for everything. While M. de Rênal was giving her in his turn a long and detailed account of how he had won the pool at billiards in the Casino – "A pool of nineteen francs, by Jove," he added, – she noticed Julien's hat on a chair three feet away. With formidable presence of mind, she began to undress and at a given moment, passing rapidly behind her husband, she flung a dress over the chair with the hat on it.) (Stendhal 1965: 237-8)

From the proximity of cuckold and cuckold-maker, to the tell-tale item of clothing, and the wickedness of the observation that, the nearer discovery comes, the more cool and mendacious the adulteress gets, the comedy is pure Byron – from *Don Juan* canto I, again. Madame de Rênal is not as loquacious in her lying as Julia is; she doesn't have to lie, for Monsieur de Rênal accuses her of nothing; but we're confident that, if put on the spot, she could. Stendhal is playing witty games with *Don Juan*, as his epigraphs hint. The difference between Julien and Juan is that where Juan reads Boscan and Garcilasso, Julien fortifies himself with the *Mémoire de Ste Hélène* and the bulletins of the Grande Armée, and at first loves Napoleon far more than he does Madame de Rênal.

Stendhal, alone amongst writers mentioned in this essay, met Byron – at Milan in 1816. He was witness to the scene of Dr Polidori's arrest at La Scala, when the doctor unwisely asked an Austrian soldier to remove his hat. Stendhal's English was excellent.

French Byronism began with Alfonse de Lamartine's "L'Homme," in *Méditations poétiques* (1820):

> Toi, dont le monde encore ignore le vrai nom,
> Esprit mystérieux, mortel, ange ou démon,
> Qui que tu sois, Byron, bon ou fatal génie,
> J'aime de tes concerts la sauvage harmonie
> Comme j'aime le bruit de la foudre et des vents
> Se mêlant dans l'orage à la voix des torrents! (Lamartine 1956: 5)

(You, whom the world is still unable to name, mysterious spirit, mortal, angel or demon, whoever you are, Byron, good or bad spirit, I love the savage harmony of your music, as I love the way the thunderbolt and winds mix during the storm, together with the noise of the torrents! . . .)

The paradox in France was that Romanticism was reactionary: Classicism was the style of the radicals. Lamartine was a radical (of sorts); but he did not admire the later satirical work of Byron, which he characterized as "l'école du rire."

The hero of Prosper Mérimée's *Carmen*, Don José, is much more Byronic – more grim, brooding, and guilt-ridden – than his operatic version. Mérimée and Stendhal introduced Alfred de Musset to *Don Juan*, and the effect was deeper and longer-lasting than that of any others I have to chronicle. In *Namouna* (1829) Musset wrote:

> Eh! Depuis quand un livre est-il donc autre chose
> Que le rêve d'un jour qu'on raconte un instant;
> Un oiseau qui gazouille et s'envole; – une rose
> Qu'on respire et qu'on jette, et qui meurt en tombant; –
> Un ami qu'on aborde, avec lequel on cause,
> Moitié lui répondant, et moitié l'écoutant?
>
> Aujourd'hui, par exemple, il plaît à ma cervelle
> De rimer en sixains le conte que voici.
> Va-t-on le maltraiter et lui chercher querelle?
> Est-ce sa faute, à lui, si je l'écris ainsi?
> Byron, me direz-vous, m'a servi de modèle.
> Vous ne savez donc pas qu'il imitait Pulci?
>
> Lisez les Italiens, vous verrez s'ils les vole.
> Rien n'appartient à rien, tout appartient à tous.
> Il faut être ignorant comme un maître d'école
> Pour se flatter de dire une seule parole
> Que personne ici-bas n'ait pu dire avant vous.
> C'est imiter quelqu'un que de planter des choux. (Musset 1998: 330-1)

(Eh! Since when has a book been anything other than a day-dream which one relates in an instant? A bird which warbles, and then flies off? A rose which one smells and then throws away, and which is dead before it hits the ground? A friend one bumps into, to whom one chats, half listening to him, half replying to him? / Today, for example, I took it into my head to write the tale before you in sestets. Are you really going to abuse it by searching for its sources? Is it really its fault, that I write it in the way I do? You will tell me that Byron has served me for a model. Don't you know that he imitated Pulci? / Read the Italians – you'll see they stole. Nothing belongs to nothing, everything belongs to everything. You'd have to be as ignorant as a schoolteacher to flatter yourself that you'd said a single word that hadn't been said before. Even to plant cabbages is to imitate someone.)

The arrogance, the conversational tone – quite unlike the chaste, rhetorical alexandrines of Lamartine, who idolized Byron without in the least imitating him – the reader-insulting insouciance: the implication that poetry isn't a serious business: all belie the seeming disclaimer of Byronic influence – specifically, the influence of *Beppo* and of *Don Juan* – which Musset, after all, doesn't actually deny, even though *Namouna* is not in ottava rima.

Poland: Mickiewicz

In Poland, the more nationhood was threatened, the more important Byron became; and by the mid-1830s, Polish nationhood was officially no more, obliterated by Russia. The fact drove a wedge between Pushkin and his friend, Adam Mickiewicz.

Mickiewicz once committed himself to writing, "It is only Byron that I read, and I throw away any book written in another spirit, because I detest lies" (Robinson 1938: 131 n.143). Despite such confidence, there were serious differences of belief between the two poets; the Catholic Mickiewicz could not come to terms with the nihilistic Byron. Mickiewicz made a version of *The Giaour*, which turns all that poem's anti-Christian sneers into statements of immaculate faith. But on less controversial Oriental ground he could create pictures of emptiness, gloom, and decay equal to anything of his idol's. Here is one of his Crimean Sonnets, *Bakczysaraj (Bakhchisarai*, 1826). It refers to the ruined harem of Khan Girey, which Pushkin had himself mourned at the end of his early poem, *The Fountain of Bakhchisarai* (compare also Byron, *The Giaour*, 287-351):

> Jeszcze wielka, już pusta Girajów dziedzina!
> Zmiatane czołem baszów ganki i przedsienia,
> Sofy, trony potęgi, miłości schronienia
> Przeskakuje szrańcza, obwija gadzina.
> Skróś okien różnofarbnych powoju roślina,
> Wdzierając się na głuche ściany i sklepienia,
> Zajmuje dzieło ludzi w imię przyrodzenia
> I pisze Balsazara głoskami "RUINA".
>
> W środku sali wycięte z marmuru naczynie;
> To fontanna haremu, dotąd stoi cało
> I perłowe łzy sącząc woła przez pustynie:
> "Gdzież jesteś, o miłości, potęgo i chwało?
> Wy macie trwać na wieki, zródło szybko płynie,
> O hańbo! wyście przeszły, a zródło zostało" (Mickiewicz [1826] 2005)

(Those halls of the Gireys – still vast and great! –
Are galleries where desolation falls;
Those varicolored domes, those crumbling halls
Where proud pashas upon rich divans sate:

Retreats of love and palaces of state –
Here now the locust leaps, the serpent crawls,
And bindweed Ruin writes, as on the walls
The hand of doom once traced Belshazzar's fate.

Within, the marble fountain made to hold
The harem waters still unbroken stands,
Which shedding pearly fears, 'neath shattered panes,
Cries: "Where are ye, O Glory, Love, and Gold?
You should endure, while streams waste into sands.
O shame, ye pass – the gazelle's spring remains!") (translation from <http://daisy.
htmlplanet.com/amick.htm>)

Mickiewicz's most-read poem, *Pan Tadeusz* (it is Poland's national epic) was published
in Paris in 1834 – the same year as his *Giaour* translation. It shows the influence, not
of the Turkish Tales, as in *Bakczysaraj,* but of *Don Juan* and of *Eugene Onegin*, in its
detailed depiction of rural Lithuanian society (Poland and Lithuania were one country
between 1386 and 1772) and the social, hunting, wooing, dressing, wedding, and
gastronomic rituals practiced there a generation previously. Its authorial voice sometimes intrudes, but, unlike Byron's, bestows an Olympian calm on the narrative. Like
Onegin, it is a novel in verse; like *Don Juan*, it takes recent history as its subject, and
has as hero a Walter Scott-type innocent caught up in political and amatory escapades,
the significance of which he cannot judge – which may be a good thing, as the action
predates and anticipates Russia's attempted destruction of Polish nationalism in the
1830s.

Like Byron in the English cantos of *Don Juan*, Mickiewicz's nostalgia for a society
which is no more is tempered by his satirical awareness of that society's failings. His
landowners are as litigious and quarrelsome as they are patriotic: they argue over the
merits of hunting dogs, pillage one another's estates, condescend to the poor, and
challenge one another to duels, almost as happily as they massacre Muscovites, or join
with Napoleon against the Tsar. The venerable old man who shows most knowledge
of ancient Lithuanian social customs in Book XII has already been established as the
tale's most deadly knife-thrower in Book V.

Although *Pan Tadeusz* is far less enthralling erotically than *Don Juan*, the scene
in Book V in which the hero sees the older of the two heroines, Telimena, writhing
about in what seems romantic despair, only to find on advancing that she is
being attacked by ants, has nothing to fear from a comparison with anything in
Don Juan:

> Widać z jej ruchów, w jakiej strasznej jest męczarni;
> Chwyta się za pierś, szyję, za stopy, kolana;
> Skoczył Tadeusz myśląc, że jest pomieszana
> Lub ma wielką chorobę. Lecz z innej przyczyny
> Pochodziły te ruchy.
>   U bliskiej brzeziny
> Było wielkie mrowisko, owad gospodarny
> Snuł się wkoło po trawie, ruchawy i czarny;
> Nie wiedzieć, czy z potrzeby, czy z upodobania
> Lubił szczególnie zwiedzać Świątynię dumania;

Od stołecznego wzgórka aż po zródła brzegi
Wydeptał drogę, którą wiodł swoje szeregi.
Nieszczęściem, Telimena siedziała śród dróżki;
Mrówki, znęcone blaskiem bieluchnej poñczoszki,
Wbiegły, gęsto zaczęły łaskotać i kąsać,
Telimena musiała uciekać, otrząsać,
Na koniec na murawie siąść i owad łowić.

Nie mógł jej swej pomocy Tadeusz odmówić;
Oczyszczając sukienkę, aż do nóg się zniżył,
Usta trafem ku skroniom Telimeny zbliżył -
W tak przyjaznej postawie, choć nic nie mówili
O rannych kłótniach swoich, przecież się zgodzili;
I nie wiedzieć jak długo trwałaby rozmowa,
Gdyby ich nie przebudził dzwonek z Soplicowa –

(Her motions showed her fearful agonies;
She clasped her neck, her feet, her hair, her breast.
Tadeusz leapt forth thinking her possessed
Or in some sickness. But that was not why
She rushed about.
Beneath a birch nearby,
There lay a mighty ant-hill whence a mass
Of nimble creatures swarmed across the grass.
Impelled by need perhaps or delectation,
They specially loved the Shrine of Meditation,
And from their hill-town to the fountain's banks
Had trodden a path by which they led their ranks.
Unhappily Telimena sat across
This path. The ants attracted by the gloss
Began to invade her stockings shining white
And swarm up them to tickle and to bite.
Telimena tried by running to detach them,
But had to sit down on the grass and catch them.
Tadeusz seeing her in this distress
Could not refuse to aid her helplessness.
He brushed her gown, bent to her feet, and now
By chance his lips came nearer to her brow
In such a tender posture that though not
A word was said, their quarrel was forgot.
Their converse might have gone on – who can tell? –
Had they not heard the Soplicowo bell –) (Mickiewicz 1998: 222-5)

However, Telimena's aim is to seduce Tadeusz away, as Calypso seduces Odysseus, or
Alcina seduces Ruggiero, from his virtuous homeland to the depravities of St Petersburg, so the poem cannot allow their relationship to flourish: in any case, Tadeusz's

father wants his son married to the poem's younger heroine, Zosia, so that their families may be reconciled. At one point in Book VIII Telimena appears to Tadeusz ghost-like, just as the Duchess of Fitz-Fulke does to Juan in Canto XVI. She bears the same emotional relationship to Zosia as Fitz-Fulke or Adeline Amundeville might have borne to Aurora Raby, had *Don Juan* been continued.

Mickiewicz died of cholera in Constantinople, trying to raise a brigade to fight the Russians.

Conclusion

Perhaps it would be good to end by reminding ourselves what the early nineteenth-century English establishment thought of Byron. My last quotation is by the Rev. John Todd, first Professor of English at University College London, from his 1830 book *The Students' Guide*:

> Byron . . . is doomed to be exiled from the libraries of all virtuous men. It is a blessing to the world that what is putrid must soon pass away. The carcase hung up in chains will be gazed at for a short time in horror; but men will soon turn their eyes away, and remove even the gallows on which it is hung.[3]

NOTES

1 *Œuvres de Lord Byron*, 10 vols. Paris 1819-21, trans. "A.-E. de Chastopalli" (Amédée Pichot and Eusèbe de Salle); 10 vols. Paris 1821-2; 5 vols. Paris 1820-2; 15 vols. Paris 1821-4; 8 vols. Paris 1822-5, including a *notice prélimi-naire* by Charles Nodier; *Œuvres nouvelles*, 10 vols. Paris 1824; 13 vols. Paris 1823-4; 20 vols. Paris 1827-31 (6th edition: includes translation of Medwin's *Conversations*); 6 vols. Paris 1830, 1830-5, 1836; 1 vol. Paris 1837; Paris 1842 (11th edition); 1872 ("15th edition").

2 All translations are by Peter Cochran unless otherwise stated.

3 Quoted in Chambers (1925: 19). Todd, writing as "Oxoniensis", had in 1822 published a pamphlet against Byron's *Cain*: "A Remonstrance Addressed to Mr. John Murray, Respecting a Recent Publication."

REFERENCES AND FURTHER READING

Abba, Giuseppe Cesare (1918). *Da Quarto al Volturn/ Noterelle d'uno dei Mille*, ed. Nicola Zanichelli, 12th edn. Bologna.

Abba, Giuseppe Cesare (1962). *Abba, The Diary of One of Garibaldi's Thousand*, trans. E. R. Vincent. Oxford: Oxford University Press.

Butler, E. M. (1956). *Byron and Goethe: Analysis of a Passion*. London: Bowes and Bowes.

Byron, Lord (1980-93). *The Complete Poetical Works*, ed. Jerome J. McGann and Barry Weller. Oxford: Oxford University Press.

Cardwell, Richard A. (ed.) (1988). *Byron and Europe*. Special issue, *Renaissance and Modern Studies*, 32.

Cardwell, Richard A. (ed.) (1997). *Lord Byron the European: Essays from the International Byron Society*. Lewiston, NY: Edwin Mellen Press.

Cardwell, Richard A. (ed.) (2005). *The Reception of Byron in Europe*, 2 vols. London: Thoemmes Continuum.

Chambers, R. W. (1925). *Ruskin (and Others) on Byron*. Oxford: Oxford University Press.

Custine, Marquis de (1991). *Letters from Russia*, trans. and ed. Robin Buss. London: Penguin.

Dall'Òngaro, Francesco (1837). "Il Venerdì Santo, Scena della vita di L. Byron." *Canto di Francesco dall'Ongaro*. Padova: Cartalier.

Espronceda, José de (1991). *The Student of Salamanca*, trans. C. K. Davies, intro. Richard Cardwell. Warminster, UK: Aris and Phillips.

Estève, Edmond (1907). *Byron et le Romantisme français. Essai sur la fortune et l'influence de l'œuvre de Byron en France de 1812 à 1850*. Paris: Hachette.

Gassenmeier, Michael, Kamolz, Katrin, Gurr, Jens, and Pointner, Frank-Erik (eds.) (1996). *The Literary Reception of British Romanticism on the European Continent*. Essen: Die Blaue Eule.

Goethe, Johann Wolfgang von (1965). *Goethes Briefe*, ed. Bodo Morawe. Hamburg. Christian Wegner Verlag.

Goethe, Johann Wolfgang von (1970). *Ueber Kunst und Alterthum*, 6 vols. Bern: Herbert Lang.

Greenleaf, Monika (1994). "Pushkin's Byronic Apprenticeship: A Problem in Cultural Syncretism." *Russian Review*, 53 (3): 382-39.

Guerrazzi, Francesco Domenico (1969). *Pagine autobiografiche*, ed. Gaetano Ragonese.

Heine, Heinrich (1968). *Heinrich Heine, Selected Verse*, ed. and trans. Peter Branscombe. Harmondsworth, UK: Penguin.

Heine, Heinrich (1970). *Werke/Briefe*, vol. 20, ed. F. H. Eisner.

Heine, Heinrich (1991). *Deutschland ein Wintermärchen*, ed. Werner Bellman. Leipzig: Reclam.

Hoffmeister, Gerhard (1983). *Byron und der europäische Byronismus*. Darmstadt: Wissenschaftliche Buchgesellschaft.

Lamartine, Alphone de ([1820] 1956). "L'Homme – à Lord Byron." In *Méditations poétiques*. Paris: Garnier.

Lermontov, Mikhail (1961). "к***." In *М.Ю.Лермонтов Стихотворения* I. Leningrad: Nauk.

Lermontov, Mikhail (1966). *A Hero of Our Time*, trans. Paul Foote. London: Penguin.

Medwin, Thomas (1966). *Conversations of Lord Byron*, ed. Ernest J. Lovell. Princeton, NJ: Princeton University Press.

Mickiewicz, Adam ([1826] 2005). *Bakczysaraj*. Text from <http://monika.univ.gda.pl/~literat/amwiersz/0037.htm>.

Mickiewicz, Adam (1956). *Adam Mickiewicz 1798-1855. Selected Poems*, ed. Clark Mills. New York: Voyages Press.

Mickiewicz, Adam (1998). *Pan Tadeusz*, trans. Kenneth R. Mackenzie. New York: Hippocrene Books.

Musset, Alfred de (1998). *Namouna*. In *Premières poésies*, ed. Jacques Bony. Paris: Garnier-Flammarion.

Peers, E. Allison (1920). "Sidelights on Byronism in Spain." *Revue Hispanique*, L: 359-66.

Pushkin, Alexander (1963). *The Letters of Alexander Pushkin*, ed. and trans. J. Thomas Shaw, 3 vols. Philadelphia: University of Pennsylvania Press; Bloomington: Indiana University Press.

Pushkin, Alexander (1975). *Eugene Onegin*, trans. Vladimir Nabokov. Princeton, NJ: Princeton University Press.

Pushkin, Alexander (1995). *Eugene Onegin*, trans. James E. Falen. Oxford and New York: Oxford University Press.

Pushkin, Alexander (1986). *Pushkin on Literature*, ed. and trans. Tatiana Wolff. Stanford, CA: Stanford University Press.

Robertson, J. G. (ed.) (1925). *Goethe and Byron*. London: Publications of the English Goethe Society.

Robinson, Charles E. (ed.) (1982). *Lord Byron and Some of His Contemporaries: Essays from the Sixth International Byron Seminar*. Newark: University of Delaware Press

Robinson, H. C. (1938). *Henry Crabb Robinson on Books and Their Writers*, ed. Edith J. Morley, 3 vols. London: Dent.

Sand, George (1839). "Essai sur le drame fantastique: Gœthe, Byron, Mickiewicz." *Revue des Deux Mondes*, December 1: 593-645.

Stendhal (1964). *Le Rouge et le noir*, ed. Michel Crouzet. Paris: Garnier-Flammarion.

Stendhal (1965). *Scarlet and Black*, trans. Margaret R. B. Shaw. London: Penguin.

Swidzinski, Jerzy (1991). *Puszkin i Ruch Literacki w Rosji*.

Symons, Arthur (1909). *The Romantic Movement in English Poetry.* New York: Dutton.

Tessier, Thérèse (1997). "Byron and France: A Survey of the Impact of the Poet's Personality and Works." In Richard A. Cardwell, (ed.) *Lord Byron the European: Essays from the International Byron Society.* Lewiston, NY: Edwin Mellen Press, pp. 1-20.

Trueblood, Paul Graham (ed.) (1981). *Byron's Political and Cultural Influence in Nineteenth-Century Europe, A Symposium.* London: Macmillan.

5

The Infinite Imagination: Early Romanticism in Germany

Susan Bernofsky

German Romanticism was anything but a unified movement. What we think of today as "Romanticism" is a more or less arbitrary assemblage of chronologically overlapping groups of writers distributed across several German cities, as well as a handful whose association with these others may have consisted of little more than a partially shared sensibility. Of the various Romanticisms that flourished in Germany around the turn of the nineteenth century and in the few decades thereafter, none has been more influential than what is generally referred to as "early Romanticism," a group of writers and thinkers who can be defined as a movement without much difficulty since, for the most part, they knew one another, collaborated on projects, and shared a set of ideals and aesthetic principles. Often referred to as the "Jena Romantics," this group, whose main activities took place between 1795 and 1800, clustered around the brothers Friedrich and August Wilhelm Schlegel and included their wives Dorothea and Caroline, the young nobleman Friedrich von Hardenberg who wrote under the name Novalis, and the philosopher Friedrich Schelling. The writer Ludwig Tieck and the philosopher and theologian Friedrich Schleiermacher, both of whom lived in Berlin, also associated with the Jena Romantics and formed part of their circle.

Precursors and Intellectual Context

The intellectual background of early Romanticism can be traced back, most immediately, to Johann Georg Hamann with his religious enthusiasm and acquired distrust of rationality, and above all to Johann Gottfried Herder. Herder, who himself had been much influenced by Rousseau, privileged sentiment over reason in his writings and cultivated a profound interest in the specific characteristics of different cultures, which led him to study national traditions and "primitive" poetry. Every national literature, he believed, was a reflection not only of its age but of the particular *Volk* that had engendered it, and thus he judged it senseless to imitate the works of another people; rather, he believed, the writers of a nation should study how, for instance, the works of the ancient Greeks reflected both their nation and the age, and from this comparison learn how to produce works relevant to their own time and context.

Herder was associated, along with Goethe and Schiller, with the *Sturm und Drang* (Storm and Stress) movement, which can be said to have given birth to Romanticism, but while the two movements shared certain tastes (valuing sentiment over reason, intensity over order, individual freedom over social stability, longing over fulfillment), there were also key points in which they diverged. Storm and Stress literature emphasized the suffering of the individual under the established social order, but it tended to accept as given both the oppressive social framework and the aesthetic categories associated with it. Goethe's 1774 *Die Leiden des jungen Werthers* (The Sorrows of Young Werther), an epistolary novel which is arguably the greatest work of the Storm and Stress, is radical in its subject matter (a young man's love for a woman who happens to be betrothed and then married to another; an act of suicide with which the reader is invited to concur) but naturalistic in its presentation and formally straightforward. By contrast, Friedrich Schlegel's great Romantic novel *Lucinde* (1799), written a quarter of a century later, is radical in both its subject *and* its form: Schlegel presents his paean to free love as an often chaotic medley of narrative collage with scarcely a page of realistic storytelling to be found in it anywhere. The writers of both the Storm and Stress and Romanticism revered Shakespeare as a genius, but the former saw him as a figure of unbridled passion, the latter as a brilliant craftsman and artist.

Most of the early Romantics (Novalis was eventually an exception) professed a profound admiration for Goethe's writings, and initially they were indebted to Schiller as well. Schiller, who had been a professor of history at the University of Jena since 1788, was instrumental in making Jena – a small town near Weimar – the center of early Romanticism by encouraging August Wilhelm Schlegel to move there in 1796 to collaborate more closely on Schiller's journal *Die Horen* (The Horae) which published, among other things, Schlegel's influential "Brief über Poesie, Silbenmaß und Sprache" (Letter on Poetry, Meter, and Language). Novalis studied briefly under Schiller as a young man and greatly revered him.

Certain of Schiller's writings contain decidedly proto-Romantic elements. His early play *Die Räuber* (The Robbers, 1781) features a conflict between two brothers, one of whom, Franz Moor, exemplifies the dangers of a rationality not tempered by feeling; the play was rightly understood as critical of Enlightenment ideals. His important *Briefe über die ästhetische Erziehung des Menschen* (Letters on the Aesthetic Education of Man, 1795) describe two categories of degeneration: savagery and barbarism, the former produced by a surfeit of feeling in the absence of thought, and the latter by an unfeeling rationality. Clearly these ideas, like those of Hamann and Herder, influenced the young writers Schiller mentored.

By the time early Romanticism came on the scene, Goethe had turned from Storm and Stress to Classicism. The literature of Classicism was initially perceived by the young writers in Jena as no more antithetical to their project than Storm and Stress had been. The Classicism of Goethe and Schiller, after all, emphasized the value of art and personal freedom as antidotes to the alienation of modern life, and at first this shared set of concerns largely outweighed those tendencies of Classicism that were less congenial to the Romantics, such as the insistence on disciplined, even rigid, literary forms and the use of order and pattern to express what for the younger writers would become formally unfettered subjectivity. Romanticism was first conceived as an extension of the views of the Classicists taken to their logical extremes. August Wilhelm Schlegel, for example, did not present Romanticism as opposed to Classicism until his series of Berlin lectures on literature and art in 1801-4, when he began to argue for the existence of two separate literary traditions with different goals and aesthetic principles. Those authors such as Corneille, Racine, and Molière who had modeled themselves on the Roman classics, he argued, differed not just in degree but in kind from those whom the Romantics claimed as their literary forebears: Pindar, Sophocles, Dante, Boccaccio, Cervantes, Calderón, and, of course, Shakespeare.

The antithesis between Weimar Classicism and Jena Romanticism developed only gradually, by way of the Romantics' explicit and implicit attacks on the idea of Aristotelian mimesis (Behler 1993: 3). Where the Classicists revered the Romans, the Romantics turned for inspiration to the ancient Greeks. They also came to see the often monolithic works of the Classicists, with their emphasis on aesthetic harmony and symmetry, as characterized by an inappropriate imposition of order. Every achievement, every work that was "finished" and codified, would eventually run afoul of the emerging Romantic ethos of the progressive and the infinite, the sense that all art – like all philosophy and criticism – was a work eternally in progress, something infinitely *becoming*. Romanticism, then, was oriented less toward the past than toward the future. Rather than seeing language as referentially linked to the world, the young Romantics extolled its figurative potential, its treasures of metaphor and allegory. At the same time, paradoxically, all the spheres rejected by Romanticism were also incorporated into it, for the sake of the ironic tensions to which this bringing together of contradictory complementaries gave rise. In the end, the Romantic notion of absolute literature became so pure as to transcend any actual work that had been written (Behler 1993: 7).

Two thematic areas in which early Romanticism differed from both Storm and Stress and Classicism were knowledge and religion. While the Romantics, like the Storm and Stress writers, distrusted the ability of reason alone to describe the world, they were certainly not opposed to rationality and logical thought – indeed, they were passionate readers of philosophy, including the difficult philosophical works being written by their contemporaries (see Thomas Pfau's chapter in this volume). Whereas Enlightenment thought had construed the Fall of Man as an ultimately positive event, one that forced individuals to become intellectually and morally self-reliant (since to be truly good, one must will oneself to be good), for the Romantics it was an absolute fall from grace, the destruction of all the unity and harmony that had ever existed in the world. While Storm and Stress characters tended to suffer from an absence of divine succor, a sense of having been abandoned by God, the early Romantics saw God everywhere (in part subsumed into Nature), and thus the general tenor of their works was not mournful but rather joyous, a delight at the infinite possibilities offered by the world. God in Classicism was omnipresent as well, but more as an abstract, benign force than as part of Nature.

The Romantics maintained their reverence for Goethe even as their work developed in a direction very different from his. Goethe himself never officially embraced Romanticism, but neither did he dismiss it outright. His oft-quoted remark equating the Romantic with "the sick" was made in reference to a specific mediocre work and was certainly never intended as a barb against his neighbors in Jena. With Schiller, matters stood differently. In 1797 he and Friedrich Schlegel traded devastating critiques of one another's work and eventually broke off all contact.

Another important influence on the young Romantics was the philosopher Johann Gottlieb Fichte, a protégé of Kant's who began teaching in Jena in 1794 and made a strong impression on Friedrich Schlegel, particularly with his 1794 lectures on the vocation of the scholar: Fichte declared it to lie in the very nature of man (as opposed to God) never to achieve that for which he strives – the goal he aims for can only be endlessly approximated. Fichte's *Wissenschaftslehre* (translated sometimes as "The Science of Knowledge," sometimes as "The Theory of Science") posits a self that is not merely a transcendental condition for knowledge (as in Kant) but a creative activity and the root of all reality – a notion that would come to influence Friedrich Schlegel's concept of irony. Unlike Schiller, Fichte maintained his enthusiasm for revolution in general and the French Revolution in particular even after it had devolved into the Reign of Terror. Eventually (in 1799) he was forced to resign his teaching post after a scandal arose over charges that his philosophy was atheistic.

The other Jena philosopher important to the Romantics was Schelling, who was only 23 years old in 1798 when he was given a university post at Fichte's recommendation. As a 15 year old, he had entered the Theological Seminary of the University of Tübingen, where he befriended fellow students Georg Wilhelm Friedrich Hegel and Friedrich Hölderlin. Schelling's philosophy was based on Fichte's idea of the pure ego as the unique metaphysical principle, but he differed from Fichte in his concept of Nature. Schelling proposed a philosophical model based on the dual, complementary but opposed standpoints of subject and object, or spirit and Nature, which coexist, supplementing and supporting one another, without either being able to encompass the other.

Jena Romanticism did not fully develop until after a cross-pollination with Berlin, where, on a sojourn in 1797, Friedrich Schlegel made the acquaintance of Ludwig Tieck, Wilhelm Heinrich Wackenroder, and Friedrich Schleiermacher. Berlin at the time was a burgeoning center of intellectual activity, with important literary salons hosted invariably by women, many of them Jewish, which brought together writers, artists, and philosophers for long evenings of discussion. Henriette Herz, who was a friend of Schleiermacher's and translated at least one book that appeared under his name, and Rahel Levin (Rahel Varnhagen after her later marriage), were two of the most prominent hostesses. In 1798, August Wilhelm followed Friedrich to Berlin, where the two of them founded the journal *Athenäum*, which continued to appear until 1800 and by many accounts was itself one of the major achievements of early Romanticism. The *Athenäum* published some of the most important works of the new "school" including Novalis's series of fragments *Blütenstaub* (Pollen). When Friedrich Schlegel returned to Jena in 1799, Wackenroder and Tieck followed him. Schleiermacher remained behind in Berlin, where he held a position as a pastor (as well as an appointment at the Charité, a public hospital), and took over the editorship of the *Athenäum*. When the University of Berlin was founded in 1810 by the brothers Wilhelm and Alexander von Humboldt, he joined its faculty in theology.

The Schlegels and Novalis: Universal Poetry

Of all the early Romantics, the one who has cast the longest shadow as viewed from the twenty-first century is clearly Friedrich Schlegel, whose great contribution was to propose and adumbrate an inextricable linkage between poetry and criticism. "A distinctive characteristic of modern poetry," he wrote in 1808, "is its precise relationship to criticism and theory and the crucial influence they exert on it" (Ein unterscheidendes Merkmal der modernen Dichtkunst ist ihr genaues Verhältnis zur Kritik und Theorie, und der bestimmende Einfluß der letzteren; Schlegel 1972: 361).[1] Though he published a book of poems in 1800, he is best known for his critical essays, his novel *Lucinde* (1799), and the two sequences of fragments he published in the *Lyceum der Schönen Künste* (1797) and the *Athenäum* (1798). *Lucinde* quickly gave rise to both a scandal and a debate. Schleiermacher published (anonymously) a defense of the novel, but the book was widely decried as immoral and lacking in literary value (a judgment that persisted well into the twentieth century). *Lucinde's* notoriety stemmed largely from the fact that it appeared to be a *roman à clef*, with figures readily associable with Schlegel himself, Dorothea (who was not yet his wife), his brother August Wilhelm, Caroline, and Novalis, suggesting that the philosophically tinged lasciviousness put forth in the novel was autobiographical. "We embraced one another," the narrator reports, "with equal measures of exuberance and religion" (Wir umarmten uns mit eben so viel Ausgelassenheit als Religion; Schlegel 1963: 8). Meanwhile the book was seen as thumbing its nose at the whole institution of the novel; while it certainly has structural principles of its own, it eschews linear narration for a mix of genres, full of detours and digressions from the ostensible narrative, self-proclaimed allegorical passages, and sections of philosophical reflection that touch on subject matters which many of the book's readers at the time must have considered undignified. *Lucinde* remained a fragment; Schlegel's plans for a second volume were never carried out.

But Schlegel is known primarily as a critic, one whose legacy reaches into the present, in large part because his work was taken up by Walter Benjamin, above all in his 1919 dissertation *Der Begriff der Kunstkritik in der deutschen Romantik* (The Concept of Aesthetic Criticism in German Romanticism; Benjamin 1973). Schlegel is the author of a seminal essay on Goethe's *Wilhelm Meister* ("*Über Goethes Meister*," which was quickly dubbed "the *Übermeister*") as well as studies of Greek poetry, Lessing, "incomprehensibility" (*Unverständlichkeit*), the nature of criticism, and poetry. For Schlegel, the true work of the critic is not the evaluation of individual works.[2] Criticism, like poetry itself, is a constantly evolving activity, one that takes place within the subject, which is thereby elevated above the constrictions of society and its value-assigning mechanisms. Criticism, as he saw it, also had the task of uniting many different spheres: reason with the imagination, intellect with feeling, the outer world with the inner life of the individual, not to mention all the different arts and other sorts of human endeavors. Thus the three great events he considered to have transformed the world are drawn from three quite different realms: the French Revolution, the publication of Fichte's *Wissenschaftslehre*, and Goethe's *Wilhelm Meister*.

Friedrich Schlegel received public recognition as a scholar-critic early on, in 1795 when he was only 23, and quickly became a sought-after contributor to various contemporary journals including *Deutschland* as well as the *Lyceum der Schönen Künste* and Schiller's *Die Horen*. In fact, much of our notion of early Romanticism comes from Schlegel's famous fragments, particularly Fragment 116 (of the *Athenäum* fragments), which is perhaps the single most important statement of Romantic poetics:

Die romantische Poesie ist eine progressive Universalpoesie. Ihre Bestimmung ist nicht bloß, alle getrennten Gattungen der Poesie wieder zu vereinigen und die Poesie mit der Philosophie und Rhetorik in Berührung zu setzen. Sie will und soll auch Poesie und Prosa, Genialität und Kritik, Kunstpoesie und Naturpoesie bald mischen, bald verschmelzen, die Poesie lebendig und gesellig und das Leben und die Gesellschaft poetisch machen, den Witz poetisieren und die Formen der Kunst mit gediegnem Bildungsstoff jeder Art anfüllen und sättigen und durch die Schwingungen des Humors beseelen. Sie umfaßt alles, was nur poetisch ist, vom größten wieder mehrere Systeme in sich enthaltenden Systeme der Kunst bis zu dem Seufzer, dem Kuß, den das dichtende Kind aushaucht in kunstlosen Gesang. [...] Nur sie kann gleich dem Epos ein Spiegel der ganzen umgebenden Welt, ein Bild des Zeitalters werden. Und doch kann auch sie am meisten zwischen dem Dargestellten und dem Darstellenden, frei von allem realen und idealen Interesse, auf den Flügeln der poetischen Reflexion in der Mitte schweben, diese Reflexion immer wieder potenzieren und wie in einer endlosen Reihe von Spiegeln vervielfachen. [...] Andere Dichtarten sind fertig und können nun vollständig zergliedert werden. Die romantische Dichtart ist noch im Werden; ja das ist ihr eigentliches Wesen, daß sie ewig nur werden, nie vollendet sein kann. Sie kann durch keine Theorie erschöpft werden, und nur eine divinatorische Kritik dürfte es wagen, ihr Ideal charakterisieren zu wollen. Sie allein ist unendlich, wie sie allein frei ist und das als ihr erstes Gesetz anerkennt, daß die Willkür des Dichters kein Gesetz über sich leide. Die romantische Dichtart ist die einzige, die mehr als Art und gleichsam die Dichtkunst selbst ist: denn in einem gewissen Sinn ist oder soll alle Poesie romantisch sein. (Schlegel 1972: 37-8)

Romantic poetry is a progressive, universal poetry. Its aim isn't merely to reunite all the separate species of poetry and put poetry in touch with philosophy and rhetoric. It tries to and should mix and fuse poetry and prose, inspiration and criticism, the poetry of art and the poetry of nature; and make poetry lively and sociable, and life and society poetical; poeticize wit and fill and saturate the forms of art with every kind of good, solid matter for instruction, and animate them with the pulsations of humor. It embraces everything that is purely poetic, from the greatest systems of art, containing within themselves still further systems, to the sigh, the kiss that the poetizing child breathes forth in artless song. [. . .] It alone can become, like the epic, a mirror of the whole circumambient world, an image of the age. And it can also – more than any other form – hover at the midpoint between the portrayed and the portrayer, free of all real and ideal self-interest, on the wings of poetic reflection, and can raise that reflection again and again to a higher power, can multiply it in an endless succession of mirrors. [. . .] Other kinds of poetry are finished and are now capable of being fully analyzed. The romantic kind of poetry is still in the state of becoming; that, in fact, is its real essence: that it should forever be becoming and never be perfected. It can be exhausted by no theory and only a divinatory criticism would dare try to characterize its idea. It alone is infinite, just as it alone is free; and it recognizes as its first commandment that the will of the poet can tolerate no law above itself. The romantic kind of poetry is the only one that is more than a kind, that is, as it were, poetry itself: for in a certain sense all poetry is or should be romantic. (Schlegel 1991: 31-2)

Romantic poetry, in Schlegel's description, is all-encompassing: it embraces all forms, all genres, even nature and society, and by definition is a work in progress, not a completed edifice. Thus the series of fragments (not yet complete, and always rearrangeable) is the ideal Romantic form (in the words of Rudolf Gasché, "a manifesto of Romantic exigency"; Gasché 1991: ix). Indeed, as Schlegel's *Athenäum* fragments attest, the form even defied the notion of individual authorship: Schlegel's own fragments were interspersed with some by other hands (including August Wilhelm, Schleiermacher, and Novalis). In the copy of the *Athenäum* owned by Rahel Levin Varnhagen (and now in the collection of the Staatsbibliothek preußischer Kulturbesitz in Berlin), handwritten notes in the margins identify a number of the fragments written by authors other than Schlegel. The work of art, then, transcends even the individual artist: it is universal, eternal, infinite, communal and eternally in flux.

Two crucial concepts in Schlegel's criticism are reflection and irony. Irony, he proposes in *Lyceum* Fragment 42, may be defined as "logical beauty." This is not the mere rhetorical gesture to which the term "irony" can also be applied; Schlegel's "divine breath of irony" suffuses ancient and modern poems alike: "Es lebt in ihnen eine wirklich transzendentale Buffonerie. Im Innern die Stimmung, welche alles übersieht, und sich über alles Bedingte unendlich erhebt, auch über eigne Kunst, Tugend oder Genialität: im Äußern, in der Ausführung die mimische Manier eines gewöhnlichen guten italienischen Buffo" (Schlegel 1972: 12) ([They are] informed by a truly transcendental buffoonery. Internally: the mood that surveys everything and rises infinitely above all limitations, even above its own art, virtue, or genius; externally, in its execution: the mimic style of an averagely gifted Italian *buffo*; Schlegel 1991: 6-7).

Romantic irony as here defined is structural, a mood, position, or subjective potential, a liberation (perhaps only briefly) from the received tradition and social contract that would presume to determine value. Irony as a stance for the artist is not an escape from reality – it requires the tension between reflection and social reality, including the distance from one's own artistic production. As Friedrich Schlegel "defines" it, "Ironie ist die Form des Paradoxon. Paradox ist alles, was zugleich gut und groß ist" (Irony is the form of paradox. Paradox is everything simultaneously good and great; *Lyceum* Fragment 48, Schlegel 172: 8). Schlegel's formulation, itself apparently paradoxical, reflects the form of what it is describing. That which is "good" partakes of the (social) framework of value, that which is "great" rises above it. To be both "good" and "great" at once is to stand simultaneously within and beyond this sphere. Irony, then, is the form of this double standing and is closely linked with Schlegel's concept of "reflection," which also looks in two directions at once: the thought is at once the thought of the thing and of the thought's thinking of the thing, producing a structure of infinite regression (or, more accurately, since Romanticism is about growth and increase rather than falling away) of *progression*.

August Wilhelm Schlegel, Friedrich's older brother who also assisted in his education, is not now known for his own literary writings (though he did write poetry and published a play, *Ion*, in 1803). One of his two major contributions to early Romanticism was his series of public lectures on literature, by means of which he drew attention to the new Romantic writers, presenting their work as the logical culmination of a tradition of writing that stood distinctly apart from French and French-influenced Classicism. The other was his brilliant translation of 17 of Shakespeare's plays, which are still canonical today and serve as the source of sayings and quotations just as the originals do in English. The first 16 of these plays – including *Hamlet*, *A Midsummer Night's Dream*, *The Tempest*, and *Romeo and Juliet* – appeared between 1797 and 1800, with a final translation (*Richard III*) following in 1810. (For more on the role of Shakespeare reception in Romanticism, see Heike Grundmann's chapter in this volume.)

Novalis began his law studies in 1790, at the age of 18, studying first in Jena and then in Leipzig, where he and Friedrich Schlegel became friends. In 1794 he received his degree and shortly afterward took up a post in the family trade, working as a salt-mine administrator, but through a series of visits and letters maintained contact with the rest of the circle, particularly Friedrich Schlegel. Novalis's life was tragically short. In 1797 he was deeply shaken by the death, after long illness, of his beloved fiancée Sophia von Kühn, and in 1801 himself succumbed to lung disease.

Where both the Schlegel brothers were, in different ways, scholarly, historical, and systematic in their work, Novalis was mystical and metaphysical. For him, this meant pursuing a mode of philosophy not indebted to a historical consciousness of philosophical tradition. He carefully studied the works of Fichte (sometimes in the company of Friedrich Schlegel), and then those of Kant and Schelling, seeking in them a framework he could use to develop his own brand of philosophy. As he announced to Schlegel, he had every intention of outphilosophizing Schelling, by developing a "religion of the visible universe" (quoted in Behler 1993: 181), which would unite the world we see and the world beyond our grasp, subjectivity and objectivity into a universal, symbolic whole. Feeling no obligation to be systematic in his reflections, Novalis combined philosophy and poetry freely, making frequent use of the terms "Romantic," "mystical" and "infinite":

> Der Sinn für Poësie hat viel mit dem Sinn für Mystizism gemein. Er ist der Sinn für das Eigenthümliche, Personelle, Unbekannte, Geheimnißvolle, zu *Offenbarende*, das Nothwendigzufällige. Er stellt das Undarstellbare dar. Er sieht das Unsichtbare, fühlt das Unfühlbare etc. Kritik der Poësie ist Unding. Schwer schon ist es zu entscheiden, doch einzig mögliche Entscheidung, ob etwas Poësie sey, oder nicht. Der Dichter ist wahrhaft sinnberaubt – dafür kommt alles in ihm vor. Er stellt im eigentlichsten Sinn *Subj{ect} Obj{ect}* vor – *Gemüth und Welt*. Daher die Unendlichkeit eines guten Gedichts, die Ewigkeit. Der Sinn für P[oësie] hat nahe Verwandtschaft mit dem Sinn der Weissagung und dem religiösen, dem Sehersinn überhaupt. Der Dichter ordnet, vereinigt, wählt, erfindet – und es ist ihm selbst unbegreiflich, warum gerade so und nicht anders. (Novalis 1960: 685-6)

> (The sense for poetry has much in common with that for mysticism. It is the sense for the peculiar, personal, unknown, mysterious, for what is to be *revealed*, the necessary-accidental. It represents the unrepresentable. It sees the invisible, feels the unfeelable, etc. Criticism of poetry is an absurdity. Although difficult to decide, the only possible distinction is whether something is poetry or not. The poet is truly deprived in this sense – instead, everything happens within him. He represents in the most genuine manner *subject-object – mind and world*. Hence the infinity is a good poem, the eternity. The sense for poetry has a close relationship with the sense for augury and the religious sense, with the sense for prophecy in general. The poet organizes, unites, chooses, invents – why precisely so and not otherwise, is incomprehensible even to himself.) (quoted in Behler 1993: 183)

Novalis is now known primarily for his collection of 114 fragments entitled *Blüten-staub* (Pollen) which was published in the *Athenäum* in 1798, for the novel *Heinrich von Ofterdingen*, and for his long poem *Hymnen an die Nacht* (Hymns to the Night) – the last two of these works were published only posthumously. The fragments that comprise *Blütenstaub* closely resemble those of Friedrich Schlegel (indeed, several of them are now believed to have been written by Schlegel), yet while Schlegel understood his collections of fragments as themselves finished works in a genre to be understood as quintessentially Romantic, fragments for Novalis were stepping-stones, brief glimpses into an ongoing work-in-progress and part of the larger development of his thought. *Blütenstaub* is preceded by an epigraph: "Friends, the soil is poor, we must sow seeds in abundance if we are to enjoy even meager harvests" (Freunde, der Boden ist arm, wir müßen reichlichen Samen Ausstreun, daß uns doch nur mäßige Erndten gedeihn; Novalis 1989: 296). (Ernst Behler, one of the most important scholars of Romanticism, notes that "Novalis" is a Latin rendering of the poet's family name, "Hardenberg" or "fallow land"; Behler 1993: 43). These "seeds" or reflections are records of Novalis's attempt to establish a model for a human thinking presence in the world, one that is in equal measure poetic and philosophical and that

declares itself most often metaphorically, by analogy. "Our entire capacity for perception," he writes, "resembles the eye"; "We will never fully grasp ourselves, but what
we will and can do with regard to ourselves goes far beyond grasping" (Unser
sämtliches Wahrnehmungsvermögen gleicht dem Auge; Ganz begreifen werden wir
uns nie, aber wir werden und können uns weit mehr, als begreifen; Novalis 1989:
296-7).

The principal topics around which Novalis's work is structured are religion, love,
poetry, and death. *Hymnen an die Nacht*, a six-part poem written mainly in prose and
published in the *Athenäum* in 1800, tells of a longing for a "holy, ineffable, mysterious
night" (der heiligen, unaussprechlichen, geheimnisvollen Nacht) and for death,
intertwined realms of beauty, love (including erotic love), innocence, and oneness
with Nature and with God. The poem melds earthly love with religious feeling; its
final stanza proclaims a journey "to my sweet bride, / To Jesus, my beloved"
(Hinunter zu der süßen Braut, / Zu Jesus, dem Geliebten; Novalis 1989: 196,
207). In Novalis's essay "Die Christenheit oder Europa" (Christianity or Europe), a
crucial document of the early Romantics' move towards Catholicism, he attacks
Protestantism and the post-Reformation civilization of Europe as coldly rationalistic
and contrasts them with a vision of Catholicism drawn from the Middle Ages: an age
of political and spiritual unity and peace. Friedrich Schlegel would embrace Catholicism several years later (converting, along with his entire family), and a number of the
younger generation of Romantics followed his example.

Novalis's novel *Heinrich von Ofterdingen* was to have been a massive work, but what
we have of it is only its first volume and a fragment of the second. The tale of a young
man's quest to become a poet, it has often been compared to Goethe's *Wilhelm Meister's
Apprenticeship*, a novel Novalis initially admired and later rejected as bourgeois,
prosaic, and hostile to everything mystical and poetic. *Heinrich von Ofterdingen* contains a good deal of historical realistic writing (it is set during the Middle Ages in the
time of the Crusades and includes, for instance, an encounter with miners who speak
of their work), but it also features fantastic encounters with the supernatural, dreams
that impinge on reality, and interspersed poems. The goal of Heinrich's philosophical
and poetic aspirations is emblematized by a blue flower with a girl's face he sees in a
dream – this is the famous blue flower of Romanticism – which he later recognizes as
bearing the face of Mathilde, daughter of the bard Klingsohr who becomes his
mentor. The fairy-tale elements of the novel were, in Novalis's plan for its completion,
gradually to have taken over the novel, forming a synthesis of the prosaic and the
mythical, the mundane and the supernatural. (For a more detailed analysis, see the
chapter in this volume by Roger Paulin.)

Other Major Figures in Early Romanticism

Among the Berlin Romantics, Ludwig Tieck was one of the best-known writers of his
day, but the only works of his still widely read are his supernatural fairy tales *Der

blonde Eckbert (Blond Eckbert, 1797) and *Der Runenberg* (The Rune Mountain, 1804), and to a lesser extent his satirical, humorous plays, especially *Der gestiefelte Kater* (Puss in Boots, 1797). He is widely (though erroneously) assumed to have collaborated with August Wilhelm Schlegel on the latter's canonical Shakespeare translations, still known in Germany as "The Schlegel–Tieck Shakespeare"; in fact, his principal contribution to the project was to recruit his daughter Dorothea Tieck and a young acquaintance, Wolf Graf Baudissin, to translate the plays Schlegel hadn't got around to so that Schlegel's publisher in Berlin, Reimer, would be able to issue a complete edition of Shakespeare's works in German. Tieck introduced revisions into the text of Schlegel's translations to which the latter objected so bitterly in a letter to his publisher that they were subsequently removed. Tieck's own 1801 translation of *Don Quixote*, however, was well received. His early novel *Franz Sternbalds Wanderungen* (Franz Sternbald's Wanderings, 1798), set like *Heinrich von Ofterdingen* in the Middle Ages, was dismissed as an unsuccessful imitation of *Wilhelm Meister*.

Tieck also edited (adding material of his own) his friend Wilhelm Heinrich Wackenroder's important work of aesthetic theory, *Herzensergießungen eines kunstlieben-den Klosterbruders* (Outpourings of an Art-loving Friar, 1797), which appeared only months before its author's untimely death. (Tieck's editorial additions are generally held not to sit well with the rest of the book.) Wackenroder writes of art (and poetry and music) in a manner tinged with longing for a bygone age in which artistic enthusiasm was not yet enervated by reason, and art and religion were closely allied. Thus the artists he writes of – including the Renaissance painters Michelangelo, Leonardo da Vinci, and Raphael, as well as Dürer, who is given pride of place at the book's center – can be understood as parallel to the Romantic canon of literary forebears established by August Wilhelm Schlegel. The *Herzensergießungen* influenced the other Romantics as well in their turn toward the Medieval period and Catholicism.

Friedrich Daniel Ernst Schleiermacher was trained in philosophy and classical philology as well as theology and is now known for his translations of Plato and his pioneering work on hermeneutics (the theory of interpretation) as well as his writings on religion. His project of translating Plato's dialogues was originally planned as a collaboration with Friedrich Schlegel, with whom Schleiermacher shared living quarters during Schlegel's sojourn in Berlin from 1797 to 1799. Schleiermacher's most influential work on the philosophy of religion, "Über die Religion: Reden an die Gebildeten unter ihren Verächtern" (On Religion: Speeches Addressed to its Cultured Detractors, 1799), was written at the behest of his fellow Romantics and argued for the validity of multiple forms of religion, including those that eschew the notion of human immortality and even the existence of God. His ideas about hermeneutics brought together linguistic, psychological, and philosophical interpretation with biblical exegesis, and were deeply indebted to Herder. Schleiermacher's 1813 essay "Über die verschiedenen Methoden des Übersetzens" (On the Different Methods of Translating) is the most important work of translation theory from this period (others were written by Wilhelm von Humboldt and Goethe).

The women of early Romanticism authored relatively little – which is hardly surprising for women at this time – and thus are known to us primarily through their letters and what biographical information has come down to us. The wives of both Schlegel brothers, however, were influential members of the circle, and one of them, Dorothea, wrote a novel that appeared under her husband's name. Dorothea, née Brendel Mendelssohn, was the daughter of the Enlightenment philosopher Moses Mendelssohn. She left her first husband, the banker Simon Veit, for Friedrich Schlegel, who was eight years her junior, and she is generally assumed to have been the model for the title figure in Schlegel's scandalous novel *Lucinde*. Dorothea Schlegel's own novel, *Florentin*, the tale of a passionate young man, is not considered a major work of Romantic literature, though it does employ various self-conscious narrative devices (albeit grafted onto an otherwise conventional storyline).

Caroline Schlegel, née Michaelis, the daughter of a Göttingen professor, was widowed young after the death of the physician Johann Franz Wilhelm Böhmer. She inspired the love of both Schlegel brothers, but eventually married August Wilhelm in 1796 after having taken part in the Mainz Republic – a group of German intellectuals petitioned the French National Assembly in 1793 to have Mainz integrated into the French Republic – an adventure that left her both pregnant and (briefly) incarcerated. As August Wilhelm's wife, she is known to have collaborated closely with him on many of his lectures and on his great Shakespeare translations (the manuscripts show both their handwritings), work for which she was never officially credited (Bernays 1981). Eventually their marriage soured and in 1801 she married the much younger Friedrich Schelling.

Three great authors of the period who intersected only marginally if at all with the early Romantics but are sometimes classed among them are Friedrich Hölderlin, Heinrich von Kleist, and Jean Paul Richter (known simply as Jean Paul). Hölderlin, the greatest poet of the age, studied theology at the seminary in Tübingen as a young man along with Hegel and Schelling, and spent time in Jena in 1794 and 1795, where he had contact with Schiller, met Goethe, and attended Fichte's lectures. He is known to have met Novalis in May 1795 at the home of the philosopher Friedrich Immanuel Niethammer when he came to Jena to visit Schiller, but their contact does not seem to have gone beyond this one encounter (Behler 1993: 14, 17). Like the Jena Romantics, Hölderlin was fascinated by the literature and culture of the ancient Greeks. He sought to emulate them not directly, but through a complex understanding of cultural individuality. He wrote frequently in classical forms and spoke of the impoverishment of the "Hesperian age," in which all traces of the Hellenic unity of life and art, forged in a world in which humans had direct access to the gods and divine understanding and guidance, had been lost. Hölderlin's poetry is characterized by a profound (and untranslatable) syntactical complexity, one that owes its character to the Greek language. Indeed, Hölderlin also translated from the Greek – Sophocles and Pindar above all – and his translations display a syntax even more intricate in part than the Greek originals. Hölderlin's *Hyperion oder der Eremit in Griechenland* (Hyperion or the Hermit in Greece, 1797-9) is a novel comprised of letters written to a

German named Bellarmin ("the good German") by his Greek friend Hyperion, who has returned to his homeland in a time of war, during the Greek struggle in 1770 to escape Turkish rule. The novel thematizes the contrasts between both the Golden Age of Ancient Greece and the impoverished present, on the one hand, and the inherent unity of Nature and the fractured state of humankind and human society, on the other. The book's famous penultimate section contains a scathing condemnation of the German national character: "Barbarians of long standing who have become more barbaric still through their diligence and science and even their religion, profoundly incapable of any sort of divine feeling . . . " (Barbaren von Alters her, durch Fleiß und Wissenschaft und selbst durch Religion barbarischer geworden, tiefunfähig jedes göttlichen Gefühls; Hölderlin 1992, I: 754). This discomfort with the German bourgeois status quo and the longing for a state of absolute transcendence – oneness with Nature, unity with the gods, and the return of a lost age – are concerns Hölderlin shared with his contemporaries in Jena.

The works of Heinrich von Kleist and Jean Paul also contain elements reminiscent of early Romanticism. Kleist's stories and plays in particular valorize feeling over rationality and speak of human inability to attain certain knowledge of the world; like the Romantics, he was reading Kant and Fichte. Kleist and Jean Paul both turned against the aesthetic program of Weimar Classicism; Jean Paul even parodied Goethe's *Wilhelm Meister* in his Bildungsroman *Titan* (1800–3). But neither figure interacted with the members of the Romantic circle – they arrived on the scene a few years later than the others, for one thing – and the Romantics' central literary-utopian project of universal progressive poetry finds no reflection in their work.

One important area in which the work of the Jena Romantics diverges from that of Kleist and Hölderlin is their sense of God's presence in Nature as a benign, meaning-bringing force. In Kleist's work, by contrast, God appears as a force beyond human comprehension whose effects often appear arbitrary, possibly even malevolent. And Hölderlin's poetry is one long lament over the destitution of a humankind that has been abandoned by the gods – the Greek deities and Jesus Christ often appear in his work as part of a single continuum. In Hölderlin's work, flashes of divinity may still appear in Nature, but these glimpses are fleeting, and all that is left for us to do is hope for a return to an age of divine grace, something that can perhaps be facilitated by the work of poets.

Conclusion

What all the various figures of early Romanticism had in common was the belief that the prevailing literary and philosophical edifices of eighteenth-century Enlightenment, Idealism, and Classicism were inadequate to represent the complexities not only of the human spirit but of a society still wracked by revolution and upheaval. In their place, they set about producing what Behler (1993: ix) describes as "a rupture within the system of mimesis and representation that had dominated European aesthetic thought." The Romantics' underlying distrust of logic, coherence, and completion inspired both philosophical systems based on eternal becoming and works of literature that resisted the traditional strictures of form. As Walter Benjamin wrote in his dissertation, "The Romantics did not, like the Enlightenment, conceive of form as a rule for producing beauty in art that must necessarily be followed if the work was to have a pleasing or edifying effect. Rather, they saw form neither as a rule nor as independent of rules" (Benjamin 1973: 71). The quintessentially early Romantic forms of the fragment, the journal, and the novel combining bits and pieces drawn from a wide range of different genres, provided the basis for a group of works which crossed the boundaries established by both Storm and Stress and Classicism to produce a new sort of art that, rather than rejecting these earlier "stages of development," made them the fertile soil for blue flowers of many sorts.

The Jena circle of Romantics effectively disbanded in 1800. Novalis was on his deathbed. Friedrich Schlegel submitted his dissertation at the University of Jena and began to lecture there, but with little success, and soon thereafter he left with Dorothea for Dresden and then Paris. Caroline Schlegel divorced August Wilhelm Schlegel to marry Schelling, and only a few years afterward August Wilhelm accepted an invitation from Madame de Staël, author of the stunningly successful *De l'Allemagne*, to join her household in Coppet on Lake Geneva, as an advisor to her and tutor to her children. For all intents and purposes, then, early Romanticism was over – but though it lasted barely five years, it left behind an intellectual and artistic legacy that continues to influence the way we think about literature and art to this day.

NOTES

1 All translations are mine unless otherwise noted.

2 An early note by Schlegel, often quoted out of context, does state that the task of the critic is to determine the value of works of art, but this is a position from which he soon departs and to which he never returns.

REFERENCES AND FURTHER READING

Behler, Ernst (1993). *German Romantic Literary Theory*. Cambridge, UK: Cambridge University Press.

Benjamin, Walter (1973). *Der Begriff der Kunstkritik in der deutschen Romantik*, ed. Hermann Schweppenhäuser. Frankfurt/M: Suhrkamp.

Bernays, Michael (1981). "Vorrede und Nachwort zum neuen Abdruck des Schlegel-Tieckschen Shakespeare." *Preussische Jahrbücher* 68 (3): 524-69.

Gasché, Rudolf (1991). "Foreword: Ideality in Fragmentation." In Friedrich Schlegel, *Philosophical Fragments*, trans. Peter Firchow. Minneapolis and Oxford: University of Minnesota Press.

Hölderlin, Friedrich (1992). *Sämtliche Werke und Briefe*, ed. Michael Knaupp. Munich: Hanser.

Novalis (1960). *Schriften: Die Werke Friedrich von Hardenbergs*, 3, ed. Richard Samuel with

Hans-Joachim Mähl and Gerhard Schulz. Stuttgart: Kohlhammer.

Novalis (1989). *Dichtungen und Fragmente*, ed. Claus Träger. Leipzig: Reclam.

Schlegel, Friedrich (1963). *Lucinde*, ed. Karl Konrad Polheim. Stuttgart: Reclam.

Schlegel, Friedrich (1972). *Schriften zur Literatur*, ed. Wolfdietrich Rasch. Munich: Deutscher Taschenbuch Verlag.

Schlegel, Friedrich (1991). *Philosophical Fragments*, trans. Peter Firchow. Minneapolis and Oxford: University of Minnesota Press.

6

From Autonomous Subjects to Self-regulating Structures: Rationality and Development in German Idealism

Thomas Pfau

The Sociality of Reason: Rationality, Autonomy, and Community in Kant

Responding to a number of seventeenth- and eighteenth-century philosophical projects (Cartesianism, Leibnizian theories of preformation, Lockean empiricism, and Humean skepticism), the writings of German Idealism develop fundamentally new, emphatically *systematic* conceptions of subjectivity. In their own diverse and progressive pursuit of this project, the main representatives of German Idealism (Kant, Fichte, Schelling, and Hegel) thereby also bring about a transformation of the very meaning of "system" and, ultimately, of philosophy itself as it evolves from Kant's "critical" to Hegel's "speculative-historical" modeling of reason. Notwithstanding its highly specialized, ostensibly hermetic discursive profile, German Idealism remains embedded within much broader shifts that drastically alter the late eighteenth- and early nineteenth-century understanding of agency (*Subjektivität*), sociality (*Öffentlichkeit*), and (self-)cultivation (*Bildung*). A sociological sketch of these wider currents will indicate how and for what reasons the emphatically dynamic, mobile, and developmental conceptions of agency unfolded by Kant, Fichte, Schelling, and Hegel took on such rigorously technical characteristics and why in particular these writers chose to place emphasis on the formal criteria – that is, on the "conditions" of evidence, explicitness, and justification always in play when we speak of a subject. Seen within a broader sociological analysis of modernity, German Idealism constitutes but one of numerous "expert systems" (such as the emergent disciplines of legal theory, hermeneutics, aesthetics, linguistics, or probability theory), all of them rapidly consolidating themselves as quasi-autonomous, "professional" languages at the end of the eighteenth century (see Giddens 1990: 55-63, Ziolkowski 1990: 3-17, 218-308, Sheehan 1989: 145-73). While the philosophical arguments of German Idealism have long been understood to represent a major break with Cartesian rationalism or Humean skepticism, their Weberian (Protestant) work ethic of a self-generating subject axiomatically tied to a developmental model of rationality and, by that very token, to its own progressive socialization, also situates the technical expertise of a Kant or a Hegel in the broader plot of modernity.

The canonical texts of German Idealism – from Kant's three *Critiques* (1781-90) via Fichte's various drafts of the *Science of Knowledge* or his *Reden an die Deutsche Nation* (1808), Schelling's versions of a *Philosophy of Nature* (1797-9) and his *System of Transcendental Idealism* (1800) to Hegel's *Phenomenology* (1807), *Logic* (1815), *Encyclopedia* (1817), and his *Philosophy of History* (1822-3) – can be read as *reflexes* of a particular phase (late Enlightenment and Romanticism) within the evolving story of modernity. For a long time, that story itself was told as one of progressive secularization, as "a vision of an ultimate end, as both *finis* and *telos*, . . . provid[ing] a scheme of progressive order and meaning, a scheme which has been capable of overcoming the ancient fear of fate and fortune" (Löwith 1949: 18). Against Max Weber's and Karl Löwith's influential portrayal of modernity as such a process of secularization – a thesis often thought to have received its first and most consummate articulation in the philosophy of Hegel – Hans Blumenberg has urged a reading of post-Reformation modernity as a series of "reoccupations" of original Judaeo-Christian problems. On this reading, the Cartesian *cogito* does not so much amount to a secular break with Ockham's nominalism. Rather, Descartes is read as offering a more fulsome rearticulation of the problem of a dualism that Ockham himself had already inherited from the Gnostics (Blumenberg 1983: 37-76; see also Taylor 1989: 143-58, Pippin 1999: 22-8). For Blumenberg, Judaeo-Christian thought and secular modernity remain connected by a set of fundamental questions; what differs are primarily their strategies of how to shape answers to these questions – less in an effort to settle them once and for all than, pragmatically, to legitimate their own, obviously changed historical situation.

In this barest outline, Blumenberg's thesis would ask sensibly that we read the conceptual innovations of Kantian and post-Kantian Idealism as a distinctive phase in a larger and ongoing struggle with defining a legitimate and internally cohesive model of agency, a narrative whose beginnings may at least date back to St Augustine. Not coincidentally, beginning with Kant's *Critique of Pure Reason*, the framework within which Idealist philosophy seeks to locate the reception of its specific narratives is always that of a full-scale *conversion* of the reader's sense of his or her self and its relation to the world. To read the philosophical narratives of Kant, Fichte, Schelling, or Hegel within post-schismatic modernity's overall quest for self-legitimation is not, however, to approach the principal texts of German Idealism as mere *reflexes* of a particular set of social, economic, and cultural forces. Rather, the objective will be to articulate Idealism's specific contribution of new and especially plausible languages of self-description and self-legitimation. We should give due weight to the fact that, beginning with Kant, the philosophical legitimation of a new type of agency is no longer the exclusive province of a narrow scholarly elite, nor indeed does it unfold as a recondite, scholastic inquiry deemed safe by hereditary political elites. Instead, the group seeking and attaining legitimacy through the discursive and conceptual projects of Kant, Fichte, and Hegel are the liberal-democratic, professional, middle-class communities and nation states of Western Europe as they consolidate themselves between 1780 and 1830. Kantian "autonomy," Fichtean "vocation" (*Bestimmung*), and the Hegelian "state" all aim to secure the intrinsic rationality and vicarious sociality of the modern, disaggregated individual. In one way or another, the philosophical systems in question all aim to provide a materially altered subject with both the impetus and a logical trajectory for transforming itself into a legitimate and progressively more self-conscious *social* agent. Hence, far from being hemmed in by extrinsic (socioeconomic and political) forces, German Idealism itself constitutes such a force in its own right, a particularly sophisticated idiom within a broad network of innovative discourses and, thus, as part of a variegated conceptual armature marshaled by the emergent middle-class, liberal-democratic, and bureaucratic nation state so as to understand its historical epoch and legitimate its own standing within it. Not coincidentally, the following brief glimpse into Kant's critical method at work shows several of its key concepts – such as transcendental reflection, transcendental aesthetics (space/time), and a strictly formal concept of moral agency – intimately entwined with much broader socioeconomic transformations of the late Enlightenment.

Kant's 1781 *Critique of Pure Reason* opens not so much with an outright rejection of the concept of experience but with the curious hypothetical statement that "experiential knowledge might quite possibly be already something composite [*ein Zusammengesetztes*] of what we receive by way of intuition and what is spontaneously furnished by our cognitive faculties [*Erkenntnisvermögen*]." The involvement of the latter, meanwhile, is said to constitute "an additive [*Zusatz*] that we cannot distinguish from the basic matter of experiential data until extended practice has drawn our attention to this circumstance and has schooled us to make discriminations in this manner" (Kant 1969: 41-2). Kant's opening remarks already advance *two* claims that reciprocally confirm one another: first, that the possibility of knowledge rests on something logically prior to the deceptive primacy of experiential data and also prior to our intuitive mechanisms for the reception of such data; and, second, that in order to grasp such a counterintuitive theory of knowledge, we must effectively abandon all hope for speedy proof and submit to the "extended discipline" (*lange Übung*) of transcendental reflection. Ultimately, Kant's *Critique* proposes itself as the only available manual for this new type of cognitive proficiency. For Kant's *Critique* "*constructs* theoretical entities that serve his purpose. There is no empirical confirmation of Kant's hypothesis, however, since what counts as experience, and also as confirmation, is created by our acceptance of that hypothesis" (Rosen 1987: 25). In this manner, the Kantian project of a "critique" of reason, of setting limits to the kinds of claims that can responsibly and autonomously be made by and for the modern individual, comes at the expense of a pervasive disorientation that, in the domain of empirical, socioeconomic phenomena a sociologist like Anthony Giddens has called "disembedding," a " 'lifting out' of social relations from local contexts of interaction and their restructuring across indefinite spans of time-space" (Giddens 1990: 21).

In his "transcendental doctrine of elements" for the *Critique of Pure Reason*, Kant famously asserts that time and space do "not represent any property of things in themselves" but, in fact, constitute solely "the form of all appearances of outer sense . . . [or] the subjective condition of sensibility, under which alone outer [or, in the case of time, inner] intuition is possible for us" (Kant 1969: 71). Such a position both reflects and reinforces a transformation – fueled by increasingly abstract and complex forms of economic production and legal-bureaucratic administration – already well advanced in England yet also, if more slowly, underway in Germany. Just as the clock came to express "a uniform dimension of 'empty' time," we can observe the concurrent "separation of *space* from *place*," with the latter becoming "increasingly *phantasmagoric* . . . [as] locales are thoroughly penetrated by and shaped in terms of social influences quite distant from them" (Giddens 1990: 17-19; on time, see also Sheehan 1989: 799). With time and space conceived as abstract or, in Kant's language, "transcendental" conditions of possibility for intuition, the definition of rationality shifts from Cartesian self-awareness to a logic of strictly equivalent measures. Time is no longer rhythmic in ways so eloquently captured at the opening of Johann Huizinga's *Waning of the Middle Ages*. Rather, once divided into strictly abstract and equivalent chronological measurements, this new, abstract time exemplifies a rationality that everywhere "excises the incommensurable; not only are qualities dissolved in thought, but men are brought into actual conformity" (Adorno and Horkheimer 1972: 12).[1]

For another example, we turn to the conception of the "public sphere" that Kant sets forth in his political essays of the mid-1780s, and that he was to develop in greater detail and at the level of "transcendental" argument in his 1790 work *Critique of Judgment*). His advocacy of "*sapere aude!*" ("Have courage to use your own understanding!") pivots above all on "the freedom to use reason *publicly* in all matters." Kant's division of the modern individual into a private *subject* and a public *citizen* institutes a potentially schizophrenic split between the subject's nonnegotiable private obedience to institutional demands and its equally nonnegotiable "freedom" and "civic duty" as a public "scholar [to] make use of reason before the entire *literate* world" (Kant 1983: 42, 43). Kant's affirmation of subjectivity as inherently autonomous and self-determined in its "public" sense presages the transcendental concept of moral agency that he was to set forth a year later in his *Grounding for the Metaphysics of Morals* (1785). Here the use of reason is not predicated on a dogmatic or metaphysical assertion of independence. Rather, inasmuch as it is an object of "critique," reason in Kant at all times is to be understood as a complex developmental project. A first step of philosophy's agenda thus will be "to realize what has been involved all along in thinking, judging and acting. [It is only] by realizing how much of the shape of our experience and action is 'up to us,' not 'determined' by what we find in the world or by the passions or human nature, that the modern insistence on autonomy can be best defended" (Pippin 1999: 49).

At the same time, Kant's apparent conjunction of "public," "scholar," and "literate" also reveals the domain of rationality to be fundamentally comprised of disembodied published writing as it operates within and steadily reinforces the modern definition of the "public sphere" as that of an anonymous print culture. Yet the seemingly recondite, because highly specialized, language associated with "expert systems" (Giddens) such as Kantian moral and political theory can be easily misconstrued. For even as Kantian "scholars" remain obedient to the quotidian demands of political and institutional authorities, their manner of conveying to the public rational reflections as printed matter reveals "abstraction" to point less to the recondite technicality of Kantian discourse than to its covert claim for universal authority. Implicitly, Jürgen Habermas remarks, "the issues discussed became 'general' not merely in their significance, but also in their accessibility: everyone had to *be able* to participate" (Habermas 1994: 37).[2] The subterranean universalism of Kant's critical philosophy is thus matched, in his political writings, by a hypothesis concerning the gradual dissemination of rational patterns throughout political and social life. Such patterns – which, like the transcendental claims of Kant's critical philosophy, remain equally beyond verification or falsification – are no longer driven by a conscious intentionality but manifest themselves as a self-regulating, structural movement or development. As Kant puts it, "what strikes us as complicated and unpredictable in the single individual may in the history of the entire species be discovered to be the steady progress and slow development of its original capacities" ("Idea for a Universal History," in Kant 1983: 29). This "structural transformation of the public sphere" (to borrow Habermas's titular phrase) as a dialectical progression and development (with coemergent disciplines of demography and probability theory as just two of its conceptual entailments) is particularly in evidence in the rise of literacy, itself a sociological premise for Kant's hint at "a strange, unexpected pattern in human affairs" whereby the world of conceptual innovation and free, rational exploration "gradually reacts on a people's mentality (whereby they become increasingly able to *act freely*) and . . . finally even influences the principles of government" ("What is Enlightenment?" in Kant 1983: 46).[3]

Pivotal for any understanding of German Idealism is the notion of "autonomy," which Kant defines as "the ground of the dignity of human nature and of every rational nature" (Kant 1981: 41). Arguably, evidence for a truly self-determining, autonomous agency can only be achieved *ex negativo*, that is, by excluding any empirical objects or intentional objectives (outcomes, motives, desires, etc.) from the moral evaluation of an action. "In every case where an object of the will must be laid down as the foundation for prescribing a rule to determine the will, there the rule is nothing but heteronomy. The imperative is then conditioned . . . [and] hence can never command morally, i.e., categorically" (1981: 47). Having posited the modern subject's spontaneous (free), quasi-legislative authority over all empirical phenomena in the *Critique of Pure Reason*, Kant had also, at least implicitly, asserted the intrinsic *universality* of his subject's representations of phenomenal experience and the moral good. Behind the formal austerity of the categorical imperative – that is, the demand that the maxims informing a specific action must be imagined as valid principles for universal legislation – lurks a radical, as it were "leveling," theory of community. Homologous with "reason" (*Vernunft*) itself, community serves both as the distant *telos* to whose realization all individual practice (if it is to count as "moral") must be committed *and* as the (seemingly present) source of legitimation for moral agency. Kant's reconceptualization of moral agency succinctly dramatizes how philosophy itself establishes a new understanding of "modernity" around 1780 yet, in so doing, also compels its new, "disembedded" subject to experience all the more acutely its precarious situation. "Human life has become, in a collective sense, completely self-determining, but . . . in a way that is thereby completely contingent" (Pippin 1999: 35). In his *Grounding for the Metaphysics of Morals*, Kant acknowledges as much when, in an aside often ignored by readers today, he expressly rejects the consideration of happiness from his theory of moral agency: "The principle of one's own happiness is most objectionable," not only because "experience contradicts the supposition that well-being is always proportional to well-doing" but, more importantly, because "this principle contributes nothing to the establishment of morality, inasmuch as making a man happy is quite different from making him good" (Kant 1981: 46). To the contingent and hence specious good of happiness, Kant opposes the "ontological concept of perfection" as the rational principle of morality. It is a notion subsequently amplified as the "postulates" (God, freedom, and immortality) in the *Critique of Practical Reason*.

> The production of the highest good in the world is the necessary object of a will determinable by the moral law. But in such a will the *complete conformity* of dispositions with the moral law is the supreme condition of the highest good. The conformity must therefore be just as possible as its object is, since it is contained in the same command to promote the object. Complete conformity of the will with the moral law is, however, *holiness*, a perfection of which no rational being of the sensible world is capable at any moment of his existence. Since it is nevertheless required as practically necessary, it can only be found in an *endless progress* toward that complete conformity, and in accordance with principles of pure practical reason it is necessary to assume such a practical progress as the real object of our will. This endless progress is, however, possible only on the presupposition of the existence and personality of the same rational being continuing *endlessly* (which is called the immortality of the soul). (Kant 1997: 102; see Pinkard 2002: 60-1).

Far from a metaphysical creed or dogma, Kant's shrewd introduction of such a postulate ("a theoretical proposition . . . not demonstrable as such") reveals how finite subjects must at all times *construct* those theoretical notions that will motivate and direct them (in their capacity as moral agents) to advance and implement the objective of reason. Postulates of "pure practical reason" thus seek to confer a certain measure of intuitive specificity on the underlying ontological idea of "perfection," even as Kant readily concedes that the idea of "perfection" necessarily "presuppose[s] the morality that it has to explain." Still, man-made postulates such as perfection remain preferable to a "divine concept" of the moral good, simply because "we cannot intuit divine perfection" (Kant 1981: 64-7).[4] By conceiving of "perfection" as the highest, "ontological" objective of life, and through its autonomous "construction" in the modality of "postulates," individuals afford themselves a categorical (noncontingent) motive for positively aspiring (rather than incidentally conforming) to the status of a disinterested moral agent. Kant's transgenerational conception of reason *qua* "immortality" thus exemplifies his overall position that moral agents must construct such theoretical notions as will induce them, as empirical and necessarily imperfect beings, to merge their contingent inclinations with the project of reason.

Probing the Grounds of Rationality: Self-consciousness as Process in Fichte and Schelling

It is this position – mirrored by Kant's insistence on the "communicability" of aesthetic judgments in the *Critique of Judgment* – which throws into relief the intrinsically developmental logic of Kantian thought and which, more than anything else, shaped virtually every philosophical and literary project of the Romantic period.[5] Johann Gottlieb Fichte (1762-1814) radicalizes above all Kant's notion of reason as autonomous and self-generating. Decisive for Fichte proved a dispute regarding the legacy of Kant's critical philosophy that unfolded in 1792. It featured, on one side, Karl Leonard Reinhold, whose *Elementarphilosophie* sought to distil from Kant's *Critiques* a widely applicable philosophical method predicated on what Reinhold called "the fact of consciousness." On the other side, much to the surprise of Fichte (then a committed Kantian), G. E. Schulze, a professor of philosophy at Helmstedt (and writing under the pseudonym "Aenesidemus") developed an incisive critique not only of Reinhold's premises but, to a certain extent, also of Kant's own system. Of the entire Reinhold–Aenesidemus debate, which has received ample critical attention, only one aspect can be taken up, and in so doing I follow Terry Pinkard's succinct account.[6] G. E. Schulze exposed "a massive inconsistency in Reinhold's account of self-consciousness, since Reinhold required all consciousness to involve representations, and a self-conscious subject therefore had to have a representation of itself, which, in turn, required a subject to relate the representation of the subject to itself, which, in turn, implied an infinite regress" (Pinkard 2003: 106). So as to recover from the apparent refutation not only of Reinhold's "fact" of self-consciousness but, by implication, the suddenly unsustainable distinction between conscious representations and things in themselves (*noumena*) at the very heart of Kant's first *Critique*, Fichte concedes that self-consciousness cannot be explained as a self-relation or Kantian synthesis at all. Self-awareness cannot originate in reflection, and the self can never be anchored in any reflexive comparison of the knowing subject with an objectified representation (*Vorstellung*) or image (*Bild*) that it has produced of "itself." For to seek self-awareness and self-confirmation through "reflexive determinations" (*Reflexionsbestimmungen*) presupposes that the reflecting self can recognize the *unity* of the knower (subject) and the known (self) and, moreover, that it is capable of repossessing that very recognition as affirming its very own (and not someone else's) *identity*. In response to this impasse, as Dieter Henrich and Manfred Frank have shown, Fichte shifts the conception of self-knowledge from one of relation to one of *production*, with "the act of production . . . taken to be a real activity, while the product is taken to be the knowledge of this act."[7]

Fichte's strictures on the scope and reach of reflection, which can never lay foundations but only clarify appearances *a posteriori*, was to be significantly extended and intensified by Novalis (Novalis 2003).[8] Already Fichte's performative model of self-consciousness as the supposed center and circumference of all philosophical knowledge encounters difficulties. Both the conversion of a subjective act of positing (*Tathandlung*) into an actual knowledge of the product (consciousness) and the further recognition of that product as identical with the producer's "self" succumb to a circular logic; for each step effectively presupposes that the original act of positing be transparent unto itself. As Fichte puts it, "the self is to posit itself, not merely for some intelligence outside it, but simply *for itself;* it is to posit itself *as* posited by itself. Hence, as surely as it is a self, it must have the principle of life and consciousness solely within itself" (Fichte [1794] 1970: 241).[9] As Helmut Müller-Sievers puts it in his fine account of the ascendancy of "epigenetic" over "preformationist" models of theory: "To the Kantian fallacy of a preformed I that can never get at its own origin Fichte thus opposes the reciprocal structure of an intellectual intuition in which the totality of the I is given while its constituent parts are still distinguishable" (Müller-Sievers 1997: 68).[10] And yet, even within the closed circuitry of Fichte's *Science of Knowledge* as one of autoproduction, the progressive determination of the "I" as self still entails an element of difference. "Since in . . . reflection the self is not conscious of itself, the reflection in question is a mere feeling" (Fichte 1970: 261).[11] Even an epigenetic "I" conceived as capable of generating from within itself the distinct qualities of intuition and reflection, as well as its own knowledge of them, presupposes a certain awareness of its own unity by the positing "I" or, in Fichte's words, premises all "determination" (*Bestimmung*) on a certain "feeling of determinability" (*Gefühl von Bestimmbarkeit*). For the formal unity of the self's performative self-generation must itself be mediated, that is, *re*cognized and *re*claimed by the resulting subject *as its own* identity.

The *identity* of the Fichtean "I" – that is, the predication of the individual on an absolute foundation, of contingent self-awareness on humanity as a shared condition and destiny – requires that that "I" recognize the formal *unity* of its constitutive materials (namely, intuition and concept) as the very foundation of its own being and so recognize itself as part of the greater plot of rationality in its unfolding. It is this experience of its own "determinability," according to Fichte, which manifests itself at first in affective form. That is, what philosophy calls an "intellectual intuition" attains phenomenal distinctness only in the subject's "feeling" of its own potential determinability (*Bestimmbarkeit*). Novalis puts it most succinctly: "Philosophy is originally a feeling." Aside from having anchored the subject in an "immediate" and seemingly indisputable ground – of transcendental function in Fichte's system, though strikingly reminiscent of empiricist models of "sensation" – not much has been accomplished. For the "feeling" of determinability must itself once again be recognized by the "I" *as its own* foundation or identity, and yet as Novalis so laconically remarks: "Feeling cannot feel itself" (1978, II: 18). It is a crucial, albeit to Fichte most unwelcome, qualification, whereby "feeling" succumbs to the vagaries of representation, figurative expression, and interpretive contingency. Involuntarily, Fichte here finds himself retracing Kant's deduction from the first *Critique* (particularly the pivotal chapter on the "transcendental schematism") and Kant's later, more explicit conception of "feeling" as a subjective universal in the realm of aesthetic production and judgment.[12] Thus Fichte admits that in order to "raise feeling to consciousness" the imagination must produce an "image" (*Bild*) of that feeling, one whereby consciousness would be enabled to recognize its immediate "feeling of determinability" in objective form and thus take hold of a knowledge that had previously slumbered in the encrypted form of an "intellectual intuition" (Fichte 1964-, II, 3: 297). In anticipation of Schelling's and Goethe's conception of an *Urbild*, Fichte stipulates that such an image must be produced by the subject's imagination, a claim that ensures the ascendancy of aesthetics over logic in the business of transcendental philosophy.

And yet once again the problem of reflective recognition intrudes. For what, other than mere desire (which may afford consciousness transient pleasures, though surely no coherent self), could possibly underwrite the objective authenticity of the image that the imagination had produced? How could the self recognize the image as a genuine representation of *its own* "feeling" of determinability? And how can an image paradoxically charged with mediating this supposedly "immediate feeling of determinability" for the "I" (and thus promoting that "I" to outright self-awareness) be recognized as having *delivered* proof rather than having contrived it? [13] Fichte's own reflections – carefully edited out from the 1794 *Wissenschaftslehre* – falter on just that point as he worries: "the (productive) imagination itself is a faculty of the Self. Couldn't it be the only grounding faculty [*Grundvermögen*] of the Self?" (Fichte 1963-, II, 3: 298).[14] Is the imagination a "faculty" of a rational, logically deducible subjectivity, or does it merely figuratively conjure or *project* a self whose most abiding characteristic it is to think of itself as firmly, rationally grounded? Mocking the reasoning whereby "*Ich* and *Geist* are but the Christian and Sirname [sic] of his weak Iness [sic], J. G. Fichte," Coleridge was to remark sometime after 1815 that Fichte's had not shown his notion of immediacy (or feeling) "to be more comprehensible than the *Anschauung*, & the precious mechanis[m] of *Selbstbewusstsein* substituted for it." As he sums up his case, "how could Fichte have *made* these abstractions of Reason, Feeling, intuitive space, but from some absolute Entity? And what entitled him to abstract?" Admittedly, though, Coleridge's qualms about Fichte's theory pertain not so much to "the *doctrine,* as to the Chasms in the Proof of it," and the latter would appear endemic to all talk of self-consciousness (Coleridge 1980, II: 610-11, 607).

Ever the "notorious and inveterate foundationalist," as Daniel Breazeale puts it, Fichte would continue to argue that the ultimate ground capable of comprising and uniting intuition and concept, content and form, substance and accident in one subjective *identity* is to be located in what he calls "intellectual intuition" (Breazeale 2000: 186). This problematic aspect of Fichte's Idealism has recently received much attention. Terry Pinkard convincingly shows how Fichte's notion of "intellectual intuition" effectively concedes the unavailability of objective "ground" for the self. Yet, in following Robert Brandom's influential arguments, Terry Pinkard also suggests that the seemingly indemonstrable, even mythical, nature of an "intellectual intuiti" need not necessarily be read as Fichte conceding defeat. Rather, with this term the *Science of Knowledge* advances not so much epistemological, let alone ontological claims for the self's "truth" as it merely asserts the self's "normative status" and effectively collapses rationality into normativity. As Pinkard puts it, "one cannot give a causal, or, for that matter, any other non-normative explanation of the subject's basic normative act of attributing entitlement to itself and to other propositions." And yet, any normative act derives its authority from the possibility of its contestation. Hence, the initial positing of the "I" by itself must simultaneously provide for the possibility of "incorrectness" vis-à-vis the normative "self" so posited. That is, implicit in a reading of Fichtean "positing" as the establishment of a "norm" is the possibility of that norm's negation by something else. Acknowledging as much, Fichte calls that something else the "non-I" (*nicht-Ich*), though he also hastens to restrict this "non-I" to the purely formal-logical status of an external "check" (*Anstoß*). Even such a minimalist conception of the "non-I," however, entangles Fichte in the logical contradiction of an "I" claiming rational authority and normative status for itself while simultaneously positing "some things as not having their normative status posited by the "I" (Pinkard 2002: 114-15; see also Brandom 1994: 3-55).

Fichte's logically inconsistent (dis)qualification of Nature as mere "non-I" – an unorganized and irrational externality – prompted F. W. J. Schelling (1775-1854) to embark on a different course. The objective was not so much to reject Fichte's entire system, to which Schelling had responded quite positively in his early publications between 1794 and 97, as it was to expand the dynamic conception of the Fichtean subject into the seemingly inert and "other" sphere of nature (see Frank 1985: 23-71).[15] In his *Naturphilosophie,* Schelling fundamentally seeks to disarm the logical tension between an "I" making normative claims for itself and, at the same time, attributing nonnormative and, by implication, irrational status to its Other, Nature. For Schelling, the objective became to discover within the realm of nature the same developmental model that had enabled the subject of the *Science of Knowledge* to attain progressively greater explicitness *as a Self* by means of what Fichte had called "reflexive determinations" (*Reflexionsbestimmungen*). As the principal means of philosophical practice, reflection could not content itself with thinking nature in merely formal terms, that is, as the *in*essential Other *against* and *by means of* which the self posits itself. To be sure, Schelling remarks in *Ideas for a Philosophy of Nature* (1797), "as soon as man sets himself in opposition to the external world . . . reflection first begins; he separates from now on what Nature had always united. . . . But this separation is only *means*, not *end*." Any philosophy that unsettles the "equilibrium of forces and of consciousness" by a free act of conscious reflection will also have to re-establish this equilibrium in the end; for "*mere* reflection . . . is a spiritual sickness in mankind" (Schelling 1988: 10-11). The only way to remedy the very split between self and other whereby philosophy itself became possible is to locate the same spontaneous and free developmental trajectory that characterizes human intelligence within the seemingly separate domain of nature. As Schelling was to summarize it in his *System of Transcendental Idealism* (1800), "intelligence will be able to intuit itself only in an object that has an internal principle of motion [*Bewegung*] within itself. . . . Hence the intelligence must intuit itself . . . as a living organization. But now it appears from this very deduction of life, that the latter must be common to all organic nature, and hence that there can be no distinction between living and nonliving organizations in nature itself" (Schelling 1978: 124).

Arguably, Schelling's initial attempts at constructing nature as the three-dimensional expression of an inherently dynamic intelligence in his 1797 *Ideas for a Philosophy of Nature* ran afoul of the empirical approaches favored by the scientific community of his time. Only two years later, however, Schelling returned with a more rigorous systematic formulation of what Dieter Sturma has called "the idea of a genetic isomorphism of nature and spirit," an idea that also proves strikingly prescient of Darwinian and neo-Darwinian thought (Sturma 2000: 225). Beyond its prescience of the kind of evolutionary thinking that was to dominate much of nineteenth- and twentieth-century theory, Schelling's *First Draft Toward a Systematic Philosophy of Nature* (*Erster Entwurf eines Systems der Naturphilosophie*) of 1799 also merits our attention because its conceptions of "movement" and "development" (*Bewegung* and *Entwicklung*) stand in particularly instructive contrast to Hegel's model in Part 2 of his 1817 *Encyclopedia*. For Schelling, it would be impossible to think of nature as an unconditional "being" (*Seyn*) "unless we could discover within the very concept of being the hidden trace of freedom. . . . Looked upon from a higher viewpoint, this being itself is nothing but nature's continual activity as it has congealed in its product." Schelling adamantly opposes any "primitive" reifying view of nature: "everything in nature must be understood as something that has become [*ein Gewordenes*]." The key question, then, becomes why an infinitely active nature should ever assume a particular material *Gestalt*. Given that, as Schelling puts it, "nature abhors all individuality and strives continually toward the absolute," the explanation for why we are nonetheless presented with definite and necessarily inadequate material entities has to be sought in the same logic of "development" (*Entwicklung*) that allows us to think of nature as "evolution" (*Evolution*) (*Erster Entwurf eines Systems der Naturphilosophie*, in Schelling 1982: 13, 33).

Schelling's argument here strikingly prefigures Richard Dawkins's reinterpretation of Darwin's theory of survival, according to which the individual being's preoccupation with its own survival is not driven by a desire to preserve its body but, rather, by a need for transmitting the genetic information contained in the body – a plot of which the individual organism, even a human one, need not be conscious at all (Dawkins 1989: 12-45). Thus Schelling remarks that the "metamorphoses through which various kinds of insects pass are *almost exclusively determined* by the development of their gendered individuality [*Geschlecht*]." Once a definite gender and sexual maturity has been attained, "the metamorphoses cease," and it appears that the butterfly, having evolved beyond its larval stages, "seems to have assumed this ultimate developmental stage solely for the purpose of propagating its species." Schelling's speculative concept of development thus accords individual entities and their morphological *Gestalt* only an instrumental, quasi-transitional role in a much larger evolutionary plot whose rationality we must ultimately locate in its continuous prolongation, an objective that can only be realized if there is something to transmit. Like the *Bildungsroman* – one may think of Goethe's *Wilhelm Meister's Apprenticeship* or his ironic subversion of didactic poetry in the "Metamorphosis of the Plants" – nature individualizes itself solely because it is only "at the peak of individuation that sexual maturity will be attained," which in turn ensures the prolongation of the process of rational organization that defines the totality of nature (*Entwurf*, in Schelling 1882: 45, 48n, 49n). As it "advances the development of individual forms, nature is by no means concerned with the individual – on the contrary, it aims at the annihilation [*Vernichtung*] of the individual." For as soon as "the common objective [*das Gemeinschaftliche*] has been secured, nature will abandon the individual, . . . indeed will proceed to treat it as an impediment [*Schranke*] of its activity, one that it works to destroy. For the individual must appear as the means, and the species as the end of nature" (ibid.: 50n, 51). Schelling proceeds to analyze how every developmental stage, as it manifests itself in the definitive *Gestalt* of a given organism, is but a "phenomenon" of a logical process consumed with its own continuity and coherence. Long before Darwin, Schelling also remarks on how the "developmental drive" (*Bildungstrieb*) is in principle absolutely free but, in fact, is constrained and given direction by "external conditions." Only through the latter does a given organism's internal "embryonic disposition" (*Keim oder Anlage*) acquire a sense of developmental direction and purpose. With this explanation for "why each organism can only ever reproduce itself ad infinitum" – that is, due to some "primordial restriction imposed [by external contingency] on its developmental drive" – there is no further justification for metaphysical or theological conceptions of nature as "preformation. . . . For the entire diversity of organisms and [their] component parts reveals nothing but the manifold directions in which the developmental drive is constrained to express itself at any given stage of development." For Schelling as for Goethe, with whom he was in close contact between 1799 and 1803, all formation [*Bildung*] thus occurs through *epigenesis* (that is, through metamorphosis or dynamic evolution)" (ibid.: 54n, 56, 60-1).[16] The concept of "development" has now evolved from a characteristic of the Enlightenment individual's rational and spontaneous self-determination to the simultaneously historical and systematic organization of all being.[17]

Negotiating Difference: Reason, Modernity, and Pragmatism in Hegel

As early as his long 1797 review essay of Fichte's *Science of Knowledge*, Schelling had begun to develop a protodialectical conception of philosophy that instituted a reflexive divide between "consciousness" and "spirit." As he puts it:

> every act of the soul is also a determinate stage of the soul. . . . Thus, through its own products – imperceptible to the common eye, [yet] clear and distinct to that of the philosopher – the soul marks the path on which it gradually reaches self-consciousness. The external world lies unfolded before us, so that we may rediscover within it the history of our spirit. ("Treatise Explicatory of the Idealism in the *Science of Knowledge*," in Schelling 1994: 90)

Yet to read Schelling's *Naturphilosophie* as introducing "a 'pre-history' of reason" (Sturma 2000: 218; see also Frank 1985: 97-107) into German philosophy also demands clarification of some fundamental philosophical issues on which Schelling's later philosophy was to differ emphatically from that of Hegel. It was left to Hegel to develop a comprehensive systematic account of the transforming relation between mere "opining" (*Meinen*) – that is, the discriminations ventured by our "natural consciousness" or "understanding" (*Verstand*) – and a fully socialized rationality (*Vernunft*) defining of philosophical "spirit" (*Geist*) proper. Already in his seminal 1801 *Difference between Fichte's and Schelling's System of Philosophy*, Hegel offers the following, programmatic qualification of a philosophy that remains entirely confined within the domain of the understanding and, on that basis, argues for the necessary and irremediable discontinuity between our forever partial, rational engagement of the phenomenal world and the forever ineluctable domain of the noumenal:

> The intellect, as the capacity to set limits, erects a building and places it between man and the Absolute, linking everything that man thinks worthy and holy to this building, fortifying it through all the powers of nature and talent and expanding it *ad infinitum*. The entire totality of limitations is to be found in it, but not the Absolute itself. [The latter] is lost in the parts, where it drives the intellect in its ceaseless development of manifoldness. But in its striving to enlarge itself into the Absolute, the intellect only reproduces itself *ad infinitum* and so mocks itself. Reason reaches the Absolute only in stepping out of this manifold of parts. The more stable and splendid the edifice of the intellect is, the more restless becomes the striving of life that is caught up in it as a part to get out of it, and raise itself to freedom. (Hegel 1977a: 89-90)

Presaging the critique of Enlightenment thought later undertaken by Nietzsche, Freud, and Adorno, Hegel pointedly comments on the "restlessness" of a "life" confined within the understanding's fragmented representation of being held and associated primarily with Kant's critical philosophy and its subjectivist extension in

Fichte's *Science of Knowledge*. By the time of the *Phenomenology* – itself the crucial transitional work in Hegel's oeuvre – the question as to how to grasp the meaning of the "absolute" is posed in markedly different ways than in his earlier writings. No longer does the "absolute" denote a merely negative void (as was the case in Kant's *Critique of Pure Reason*) inaccessible to the understanding's forever reactive, partial, and merely accumulative representations of being as the *other* of the thinking subject. Rather, the "absolute" comes to encompass the entire logic of successive paradigms of knowledge of which the individual subject can never be fully cognizant. As the "Preface" to the *Phenomenology* famously puts it:

> The Truth is the whole. But the whole is nothing other than the essence consummating itself through its development. Of the Absolute it must be said that it is essentially the *result*, that only in the *end* is it what it truly is; and that precisely in this consists its nature, viz. to be actual, subject, the spontaneous becoming of itself. (Hegel 1977b: 11)

In developing this gnomic pronouncement, Hegel's *Phenomenology* rearticulates what Schelling had first claimed vis-à-vis Fichte and Kant, namely, that the principal tool of the understanding, the "concept" (*Begriff*) stands not in radical separation from being (*Sein*) but is fundamentally on a continuum with being inasmuch as the latter has to be thought as forever developing. Hegel thus redefines philosophy's overall self-conception by insisting on the necessary "incompleteness" of the kind of conception of the world held by the understanding at a given point in historical time. Doing so allows Hegel to move beyond Kant's dualist (in its origins Gnostic) assertion of a categorical "incompatibility" between the noumenal (nonintuitable) totality of Reason and the understanding's contingent perspective (*Vorstellung*) on the phenomenal world (Pippin 1991b: 533).[18] Inasmuch as the concept can only ever furnish partial knowledge of "actuality" (*Wirklichkeit*) and remains susceptible to error, it must not be mistaken as a static implement, to be indifferently applied to a putatively separate realm of phenomena ("nature"). The challenge or, in Hegel's Protestant work ethic, the "labor" (*Arbeit*) of philosophy thus "consists not so much in purging the individual of an immediate, sensuous mode of apprehension . . . but rather in just its opposite, in freeing determinate thoughts (*Gedanken*) from their fixity. . . . [For] fixed thoughts have the 'I', the power of the negative, or pure actuality, for the substance and element of their existence." To tease the developmental logic, the intrinsic "dynamism" (*Bewegung*) out of thought is the great task of speculative dialectics:

> Thoughts become fluid when pure thinking . . . recognizes itself as a moment, or when the pure certainty of self abstracts from itself – not by leaving itself out, or setting itself aside, but by giving up the *fixity* of its self-positing. . . . Through this movement the pure thoughts become *Notions* (*Begriffe*), and are only now what they are in truth, self-movements (*Selbstbewegungen*), circles, spiritual essences, which is what their substance is. (Hegel 1977b: 19-20; see also Hegel 1952: 30-1)

What is here being said of an individual's cognitive relationship toward being also holds true of more complex *systems* of thought, including those put forward by Kant, Fichte, and also Schelling. The autonomous and spontaneous selves developed by these two thinkers, "critical" articulations of Enlightenment subjectivity, Hegel insists, must themselves be reflexively understood and absorbed as mere "moments" into a dynamic process of intellectual development (*Bildung*). Hegel thus aims not to refute but, rather, to sublate (*aufheben*) Kant's and Fichte's philosophies from their initial status as *doxa* or "opinion" (*Meinung*) to their truthful position within the developmental economy of philosophy as a "system." For however theoretically circumspect, Enlightenment rationality had always unfolded as a form of an "opinion" and thus necessarily had "fixated on the antithesis of truth and falsity." Hence, for Hegel, it could never actually "comprehend the diversity [*Verschiedenheit*] of philosophical systems as the progressive unfolding of truth, but rather sees in them simple contradictions [*Widerspruch*]" (Hegel 1977b: 2, translation modified; see also Hegel 1952: 10). In what amounts to a categorical break with Kant's and Fichte's premise of a radical discontinuity between subjective rationality and the realm of the noumenal or Being (*Sein*), Hegel premises his own correction of the Enlightenment project on a fundamentally new understanding of "difference." For Hegel, the logical category of "difference" no longer operates disjunctively – by positing an ontological incompatibility between two kinds of being. For to deploy it in that manner necessarily (and dogmatically) posits a realm of being supposedly independent of any specific subjective viewpoint and the discursive networks through which discrete viewpoints must continually be negotiated. With "substance" no longer operating as a foundational philosophical category in Hegel's system, "difference" – like time itself – now serves to organize different conceptual models or viewpoints *into a succession*. As Hegel puts it in the *Logic*, in observing that two things differ *in some specific respect* we institute "difference" (*Unterschied*) as a matter "of reflection, not [as] the otherness of determinate being." Whatever otherness an intelligence notices is "the otherness of an essence" (*das Andere des Wesens*) and not "the other as other of an other, existing outside it" (Hegel 1969: 417, translation modified; Hegel 1986, II: 46). In this manner, "difference" is repositioned as a key term within a narrative that progressively unmasks each instance of object-perception (*Wahrnehmung*) as but a transitional "normative" position taken up by one agent and entered, with varying degrees of success, into social, intersubjective circulation. Rather than *dissociating* discrete entities, "difference" in Hegel *organizes relations* over time by articulating the "diversity" (*Verschiedenheit*) of intellectual states and conceptual models (including the earlier, disjunctive paradigm of Enlightenment rationality) as a logical and historical sequence.

Hence Hegelian reflection repositions Kant's distinction between the noumenal and phenomenal as a particular "moment" in the trajectory of rationality to full awareness of its freedom, which will ultimately lead it to recognize that distinction as one that was not found (any more than objects are "found") but made. Hegel bluntly applies this position to his discussion of nature in the *Encyclopedia*: "Nature's essential and distinctive characteristic is to be the Idea in the form of otherness [*die Idee in ihrem Anderssein*]" (Hegel 1970: 15). As Terry Pinkard puts it, "in showing that the normative demands made by 'consciousness' (that is, the norms governing judgments about objects of which we are aware), we are driven to comprehend that our mode of *taking* them to be such-and-such plays just as important a role in the cognitive enterprise as do the objects themselves or our so-called direct awareness of them" (Pinkard 2002: 225). Hegel thus unmasks various epistemological stances, including the category of "perception," as covertly creating its "object" in the very act of venturing specific normative assertions about it. The act of "perception" (*Wahr/nehmung*; literally, "a taking-for-truth") thus surreptitiously constructs an object by venturing certain predicates "about" it, predicates that reflection will eventually come to reinterpret as norms for an intersubjective understanding. For in the end, "there is no 'outside' or extra-conceptual *explicans* [but] . . . only what we have come to regard as an indispensable *explicans*, and the narrative (i.e., Hegel's *Phenomenology*) we need to give concerns that 'coming to regard' " (Pippin 1999: 72).[19] It is in "self-consciousness" that the subject has progressed from a critical employment of the concept to a putatively other perceptual object to a reflexive "dismantling" (*Auseinanderlegung*) of the concept itself. To do so, however, is to shift one's intellectual concern from the intended "correspondence" between the concept and the object to an explication of the concept *for another* self-conscious being. As Hegel dramatizes in a series of stages, any theory of self-consciousness is implicitly a theory of intersubjectivity. Whereas in perception "consciousness is to itself the truth," self-consciousness now recognizes the "*singleness* . . . [and] *empty inner being* of the Understanding . . . [to be] no longer essences but moments of self-consciousness." The critical, reflexive distancing vis-à-vis the concept as a mere tool of the understanding produces a self-conscious subject *and* simultaneously casts its emergence as "essentially the return from *otherness* [*Anderssein*]."

In its very mode of being, then, Hegelian self-consciousness "is movement" (*Bewegung*) and "life," a paradigmatic shift from the inertia of merely perceiving consciousness that also explains why a number of readers have interpreted the *Phenomenology* as a developmental narrative or *Bildungsroman*. The formerly heteronomous "object" of perception, which is the negation of self-consciousness, "through this reflection into itself . . . has become life." Through a series of further reflexive steps, self-conscious subjectivity ultimately recognizes that a truly corresponding point of reference for its cognitive striving can ultimately only be found in another, equally self-aware being: "Self-consciousness achieves its satisfaction only in another self-consciousness. . . . Only so is it in fact self-consciousness; for only in this way does the unity of itself in its otherness become explicit for it" (Hegel 1977b: 104-5, 106, 110).[20] As Terry Pinkard summarizes this crucial transition: "Hegel's resolution of the Kantian paradox was to see it in social terms. Since the agent cannot secure any bindingness for the principle simply on his own, he requires the *recognition* of another agent of it as binding on both of them" (Pinkard 2002: 227).[21] As Jean Hyppolite had noted long before, "the condition of self-consciousness is the existence of other self-consciousnesses." Only "this mutual recognition, in which individuals recognize each other as reciprocally recognizing each other, creates the element of spiritual life" (Hyppolite 1974: 163, 166). The quasi-contractual logic that begins to permeate Hegel's argument with the section on "self-consciousness" also hints why Hegel was the only German Idealist to develop a comprehensive theory of language, and some closing reflections on the relation between dialectic movement and linguistic form are in order.

What the *Phenomenology* calls "spirit" is in the end precisely this ongoing, inter-subjective negotiating of those norms or "notions" (*Begriffe*) that are to be taken as the binding, communal "reality." Much has been said about the organizational peculiarities of Hegel's *Phenomenology* and its uneasy fusion of systematic and historical claims. Part BB, entitled "Spirit" thus effectively makes up the entire second half of the book as Hegel dialectically configures the three phases of the spirit – spirit in its imme-diacy, in alienation from itself, and as self-certainty – with the three historical stages of classical antiquity, feudal modernity up to the French Revolution, and the modern secular state since Napoleon. Each of the many transitions that comprise this histor-ical part of Hegel's *Phenomenology* occurs when a community of subjects, having posited a coherent view of their world, reflexively understand this view to have been a discursive construct and hence open to dynamic change. In arriving at a reflexive understanding of their own opinions as intrinsically linguistic, formal constructs – that is, as expressions of their own, intellectual "freedom" rather than as facsimiles of being – the subjects of a discursive community also begin to perceive a deep-structural connection between the "expression" (*Äußerung*) and the eventual "jettisoning" (*Entäusserung*) of their specific worldview. This recognition, in turn, produces their "alienation" (*Entfremdung*) from previous opinion, which is now reposi-tioned as but a moment in the simultaneously logical and historical development of a metasubjective "spirit."

For an example, one may turn to the struggle between the "noble consciousness" and an emergent theory of the modern state, as it is charted in the section on "Self-Alienated Spirit: Culture [*Bildung*]" of the *Phenomenology*. Hegel there shows how for the noble representative of a civic-humanist order the function of language exclusively inheres in "*law* and *command*, and in the actual world, in *counsel* only [and thus] has the essence for its content." Yet precipitated by other emergent social and intellectual formations (i.e., the rising professional, middle classes and their commitment to a more abstract and egalitarian idea of *civitas*), the "noble consciousness" of the feudal subject is constrained to adopt new forms of self-legitimation, which in turn impels it to reflect upon and thus distance itself from the paradigm of the noble individual. Characteristic of the latter was above all the aristocratic *habitus* of authoritative "speech [whereby] the pure self . . . *qua independent, separate individuality* comes into existence, so that it exists for others." Yet precisely this form is also its limitations, since it lacks the permanence and, seen as a medium, lacks universality inasmuch as all speech is local, occasional, and ephemeral; for "that it is *perceived* or *heard* means that its *real existence dies away* [*verhallt*]" (Hegel 1977b: 308-9, 1952: 362-3).[22] With its claim that "alienation takes solely place in language," Hegel's phenomenological analysis of spirit as its own history thus posits language as the very catalyst for the reflexive movement that is history. In its three dimensions – a) as the form of a specific content; b) as the reflexive content of that very form; and c) as a semiotic medium connecting and reconciling these two positions – language constitutes the very infrastructure of Hegelian reflection. As the very "medium of reflection" (*Reflexionsmedium*), to borrow Walter Benjamin's expression, language serves as the very circuitry of a systemic (i.e., no longer subjective) model of "intelligence." Indeed, as close readings of the second half of the *Phenomenology*, part III of the *Encyclopedia*, or all of Hegel's *Aesthetics* richly confirm, language is homologous with rationality itself, something that in the late work of Hegel presents itself as a dynamic and self-regulating structure of progressive and increasing complexity. Hegel's philosophy thus closely mirrors or presages a number of discursive and intellectual formations arising either simultaneously with it or following later in the twentieth century, such as the rise of the developmental novel (*Bildungsroman*), the rise of structuralist (rather than agency-driven) models of social description, and above all the "linguistic turn" of philosophy typically said to have begun with Wittgenstein and Heidegger and widely credited with having profoundly reconfigured the relationship between aesthetics, literary studies, historical inquiry, and philosophy.

NOTES

1 Especially poignant instances of the abstract category of space superseding the local and contingent meaning of place would be the capitalization of land as "real estate" via parliamentary acts of enclosure in England or the sweeping geographic and legal reorganization of Germany under the *Reichsdeputationshauptschluss* of 1803 and the subsequent introduction of uniform law (the *Code Napoléon*). See Sheehan (1989: 14-40, 235-73); see also Nipperdey (1996: 11-68).

2 Giddens notes that "notions coined in the meta-languages of the social sciences routinely re-enter the universe of actions they were initially formulated to describe or account for." As he puts it, "Modernity is itself deeply and intrinsically sociological" (Giddens 1990: 15, 43).

3 Evidence of the accelerating rate of literacy can be found in the number of new titles on display at the Leipzig book fair: 960 in 1700, 2,600 in 1780, and over 5,000 in 1800. See Sheehan (1989: 153) and Pinkard (2002: 7).

Likewise, German as a vernacular rapidly displaces Latin as the official language of scholarship during the eighteenth century, with the ratio of Latin to German publications dropping from 1:2 in 1700 to 1:10 in 1780; still, advanced literacy lags significantly behind England and France; see Engelsing (in Sheehan 1989: 157), who estimates that no more than 5 percent of Germans around 1780 possessed a high level of literacy.

4 On the relation of Kantian "morality" to institutional, organized religion, see Pinkard's (2002) splendid survey of *German Philosophy: 1760-1860*, pp. 58-65.

5 For a close and sustained reading of Kant's *Critique of Judgment*, see Rodolphe Gasché (2003) *The Idea of Form*, especially pp. 42-59.

6 On this debate, see Beiser (1987: 226-84), Pinkard (2002: 105-8), and the essays by A. von Schönborn and Michael Baur in Baur and Dahlstrom (1999); see also Breazeale (1996) and Cassirer (1974). Fichte's review of "Aenesidemus" can be found in Fichte (1988).

7   Notwithstanding Fichte's eagerness to escape the aporias of reflection in his quest for autonomous self-constitution free of all presuppositions, "elements of the reflection theory are... insinuating themselves into Fichte's counter-proposal. [Thus...] we do not yet see how we can use the productive act's encounter with itself to make this knowledge intelligible" (Henrich 1982: 26).

8   On Novalis's remarkably perceptive critique of Fichte in the six groups of manuscripts that make up the *Fichte Studies*, see Von Molnar (1987: 39-43) and Bowie (1997: 65-80). William O'Brien reads the *Fichte Studies* as the "decisive point... at which Romanticism turns away from Idealistic philosophy, or more precisely, turns back upon it in order to analyze it as language, and ultimately, as a fiction" (O'Brien 1995: 78).

9   Characteristically, Novalis will rewrite that Fichtean sentence as "The self must posit itself as actively presenting" (*Das Ich muß sich, als darstellend setzen*; Novalis 1978, II: 194), with the emphasis now placed on the temporalized, progressive, and intrinsically aesthetic nature of "positing."

10 Notwithstanding his fundamental departure from Fichte's system, Novalis and all early Romantics share the epigenetic premise: "How can a person have a sense of something if he does not have the germ of it within himself. What I am to understand must develop organically within me – and what I seem to learn is only nourishment – stimulation of the organism" (Novalis 1999: 25). Even more clearly, the *Fichte Studies* comment on the logic of origination: "Origination asserts a self-engendering, a causality that is its own cause" (*Entstehen drückt eine Selbsthervorbringung, eine Causalität, die sich selbst Causalität ist... aus*; Novalis 1978, II, 208).

11 On this problem in Fichte's early *Science of Knowledge*, see Müller-Sievers (1997: 65-89).

12 William O'Brien's study offers the most extensive account of Novalis's linguistic theory (O'Brien 1995: 77-118), though he appears unaware of the structural affinity between Novalis's semiotic speculations and his critique of Idealist models of reflection as *ordo inversus*. The latter concept figures more prominently in Winfried Menninghaus's reading of Romantic theories of reflection and representation (Menninghaus 1987: 74-98); see also Gasché (1986: 23-54).

13 Ulrich Pothast remarks that Fichte's theory "constructs the 'I' as one that knows itself, to be sure, though only at the expense of its internal consistency. The theory succeeds inasmuch as it shows that without the premise of certain paradoxes, i.e., incompatible situations, no 'I' deserving of that name could ever be constructed. Fichte's theory may be characterized as a self-consciously paradoxical one" (Pothast 1971: 44, my translation).

14 Though he makes no mention of Fichte's "Über Geist und Buchstaben in der Philosophie," a crucial intertext for any discussion of semiotics and linguistic theory relative to the *Wissenschaftslehre*, William O'Brien rightly notes how Fichte, "who took the step [towards semiotics] first, had also recoiled from it" (O'Brien 1995: 101).

15 Frank also acknowledges Hölderlin's significant contribution to Schelling's critique of Fichte. Of particular significance here are Hölderlin's letters to Schelling and his early essays, especially "Judgment and Being." See Hölderlin (1987: 37-8 and 124-6 [letter to Hegel]). On Schelling's early writings, see Bowie (1994: 12-29) and Cassirer (1974, III: 217-84).

16 In his autobiographical miscellany, *Tag- und Jahreshefte*, Goethe recalls reading Schelling's *Entwurf* around 1800 (Goethe 1981, X: 450). Goethe's famous didactic poems, *Metamorphosis of the Plants* and *Metamorphosis of the Animals* fall in the same period, roughly June 1798, though the latter poem remained fragmentary and did not attain its eventual form until 1806. See Goethe (1981, I: 199-203); see also Goethe's occasional poem, "Weltseele," eponymous with Schelling's 1799 treatise (Goethe 1981, I: 248).

17 Hegel's "Philosophy of Nature," which forms Part II of the 1817 *Encyclopedia of the Philosophical Sciences*, most cogently challenges Schelling's construction of nature as a separate developmental structure, ostensibly running parallel to the development of human intelligence, and recognizable for the latter

qua "intuition." As Hegel puts it, "in the Philosophy of Nature, people have fallen back on intuition (*Anschauung*) and set it above reflective thought; but this is a mistake, for one cannot philosophize out of intuition. What is intuited must also be thought" (Hegel 1970: 12). Schelling in turn responded with an incisive critique of Hegel's conception of Being (*Sein*) in his 1827 *Lectures on Modern Philosophy*, charging that for Hegel "being" as the "starting point" of all philosophical reflection is held to something "strictly negative, deficient, an emptiness" (*ein bloßes Minus, als ein Mangel, eine Leere*) which, paradoxically, is nonetheless "to be overcome and filled with content" by the autotelic process of thought (Schelling 1976: 419). On Schelling's critique of Hegel, see Manfred Frank's excellent *Der unendliche Mangel an Seyn* (1975: 32-119).

18 Pippin quickly inflects this ultimately crude view of Kantian dualism, particularly as regards Kant's conception of moral agency; see Pippin (1991b: 537-41).

19 See also Martin Heidegger (*Hegel's Phänomenologie des Geistes*). Heidegger had already emphasized Hegel's unmasking of "perception" (*Wahr/nehmen;* literally, "a taking-for-truth") as part of the overall project of a "Science of the Experience of Consciousness" – that being the original title for the *Phenomenology.*

20 On different, often radically incompatible readings of the *Phenomenology*, see the opening of Pippin (1993).

21 Pinkard here summarizes his earlier, expansive and thorough reinterpretation offered in *Hegel's Phenomenology: the Sociality of Reason* (Pinkard 1994).

22 See also §§ 440-64 of the *Encyclopedia*, where Hegel further develops his linguistic theory; see Hegel (1978: 78-217). The most expansive meditation on the dynamic relationship between "spirit and letter" (*Geist* and *Buchstabe*) is arguably offered in Hegel's *Aesthetics.* On Hegel's linguistic theory, see Derrida (1980) and Smith (1988).

REFERENCES AND FURTHER READING

Adorno, Theodor and Horkheimer, Max (1972). *Dialectic of Enlightenment*, trans. John Cumming. New York: Continuum.

Baur, Michael (1999). "The role of skepticism in the emergence of German idealism." In Michael Baur and Daniel O. Dahlstrom (eds.), *The Emergence of German Idealism.* Washington: Catholic University of America Press, pp. 63-91.

Beiser, Frederick C. (1987). *The Fate of Reason: German Philosophy from Kant to Fichte.* Cambridge, MA: Harvard University Press.

Blumenberg, Hans (1983). *The Legitimacy of the Modern Age*, trans. Robert M. Wallace. Cambridge, MA: MIT Press.

Bowie, Andrew (1994). *Schelling and Modern European Philosophy.* Cambridge, UK: Cambridge University Press.

Bowie, Andrew (1997). *From Romanticism to Critical Theory: The Philosophy of German Literary Theory.* London and New York: Routledge.

Brandom, Robert (1994). *Making It Explicit: Reasoning, Representing, and Discursive Commitment.* Cambridge, MA: Harvard University Press.

Breazeale, Daniel (1996). "The Theory of Practice and the Practice of Theory: Fichte and the 'Primacy of Practical Reason.'" *International Philosophical Quarterly* 36 (1): 47-64.

Breazeale, Daniel (2000). "The Spirit of the *Wissenschaftslehre.*" In Sally Sedgwick (ed.), *The Reception of Kant's Critical Philosophy.* Cambridge, UK: Cambridge University Press, pp. 171-98.

Cassirer, Ernst ([1920] 1974). *Das Erkenntnisproblem in der Philosophie und Wissenschaft der Neueren Zeit.* Darmstadt: Wissenschaftliche Buchgesellschaft.

Cassirer, Ernst (1981). *Kant's Life and Thought*, trans. James Hayden. New Haven, CT: Yale University Press.

Coleridge, Samuel Taylor (1980). *Marginalia*, ed. George Whalley and H. J. Jackson, 5 vols. Princeton, NJ: Princeton University Press.

Dawkins, Richard (1989). *The Selfish Gene*. Oxford: Oxford University Press.

Derrida, Jacques (1980). "The Pit and the Pyramid: Introduction to Hegel's Semiology." In *Margins of Philosophy*, trans. Alan Bass. Chicago, University of Chicago Press, pp. 69-108.

Fichte, Johann Gottlieb (1964-). *Werke*, ed. Reinhard Lauth and Hans Jacob. Stuttgart-Bad Cannstatt: Frommann.

Fichte, Johann Gottlieb ([1794] 1970). *Science of Knowledge*, trans. Peter Heath and John Lachs. New York: Appleton-Century-Crofts.

Fichte, Johann Gottlieb (1987). *The Vocation of Man*, trans. Peter Preuss. Indianapolis: Hackett.

Fichte, Johann Gottlieb (1988). *Fichte: Early Philosophical Writings*, ed. and trans. Daniel Breazeale. Ithaca, NY: Cornell University Press.

Frank, Manfred (1975). *Der unendliche Mangel an Seyn: Schellings Hegelkritik und die Anfänge der Marxschen Dialektik*. Frankfurt: Suhrkamp.

Frank, Manfred (1985). *Eine Einführung in Schellings Philosophie*. Frankfurt: Suhrkamp.

Frank, Manfred (1989). *Einführung in die frühromantische Ästhetik*. Frankfurt: Suhrkamp.

Gasché, Rodolphe (1986). *The Tain of the Mirror: Derrida and the Philosophy of Reflection*. Cambridge, MA: Harvard University Press.

Gasché, Rodolphe (2003). *The Idea of Form: Rethinking Kant's Aesthetics*. Stanford, CA: Stanford University Press.

Giddens, Anthony (1990). *The Consequences of Modernity*. Stanford, CA: Stanford University Press.

Goethe, Johann Wolfgang von (1981). *Werke*, ed. Erich Trunz. Munich: Beck.

Habermas, Jürgen (1994). *The Structural Transformation of the Public Sphere: An Inquiry into a Category of Bourgeois Society*, trans. Thomas Burger and Frederick Lawrence. Cambridge, MA: MIT Press.

Hegel, G. W. F. (1952). *Phänomenologie des Geistes*, ed. J. Hoffmeister. Hamburg: Meiner.

Hegel, G. W. F. (1969). *Hegel's Science of Logic*, trans. A. V. Miller. Oxford: Oxford University Press.

Hegel, G. W. F. (1970). *Hegel's Philosophy of Nature*, trans. A. V. Miller. Oxford: Oxford University Press.

Hegel, G. W. F. (1977a). *The Difference between Fichte's and Schelling's System of Philosophy*, trans.

H. S. Harris and Walter Cerf. Albany, NY: SUNY Press.

Hegel, G. W. F. (1977b). *Phenomenology of Spirit*, trans. A. V. Miller. Oxford: Oxford University Press.

Hegel, G. W. F. (1978). *Hegel's Philosophy of Subjective Spirit*, trans. and ed. M. J. Petry. Dodrecht, Netherlands and Boston: Reidel.

Hegel, G. W. F. (1986). *Wissenschaft der Logik*, ed. Eva Moldenhauer and Karl Markus Michel, 2 vols. Frankfurt am Main: Suhrkamp.

Heidegger, Martin (1980). *Hegel's Phänomenologie des Geistes*. Frankfurt: Klostermann.

Henrich, Dieter (1982). "Fichte's Original Insight." *Contemporary German Philosophy* 1: 15-53.

Hölderlin, Friedrich. *Essays and Letters on Theory*, trans. and ed. Thomas Pfau. Albany, NY: SUNY Press.

Hyppolite, Jean (1974). *Genesis and Structure of Hegel's Phenomenology of Spirit*, trans. S. Cherniak and J. Heckman. Evanston, IL: Northwestern University Press.

Kant, Immanuel (1969). *Critique of Pure Reason*, trans. Norman Kemp-Smith. New York: Macmillan.

Kant, Immanuel (1981). *Grounding for the Metaphysics of Morals*, trans. James W. Ellington. Indianapolis: Hackett.

Kant, Immanuel (1983). *Perpetual Peace and Other Essays*, trans. and ed. Ted Humphrey. Indianapolis: Hackett.

Kant, Immanuel (1997). *Critique of Practical Reason*, trans. and ed. Mary Gregor. Cambridge, UK: Cambridge University Press.

Löwith, Karl (1949). *Meaning in History: The Theological Implications of the Philosophy of History*. Chicago: University of Chicago Press.

Menninghaus, Winfried (1987). *Unendliche Verdopplung: die frühromantische Grundlegung der Kunsttheorie im Begriff absoluter Selbstreflexion*. Frankfurt am Main: Suhrkamp.

Müller-Sievers, Helmut. *Self-Generation: Biology, Philosophy, and Literature Around 1800*. Stanford, CA: Stanford University Press.

Nipperdey, Thomas (1996). *German History from Napoleon to Bismarck, 1800-1866*. Princeton, NJ: Princeton University Press.

Novalis (Friedrich von Hardenberg) (1978). *Werke, Tagebücher und Briefe*, ed. Hans-Joachim Mähl

122   *Thomas Pfau*

and Richard Samuel, 3 vols. Munich and Vienna: Hanser.

Novalis (1999). *Philosophical Writings*, trans. and ed. Margaret M. Stoljar. Albany, NY: SUNY Press.

Novalis (2003). *Fichte Studies*, trans. and ed. Jane Kneller. Cambridge, UK: Cambridge University Press.

O'Brien, William A. (1995). *Novalis: Signs of Revolution*. Durham, NC: Duke University Press.

Pinkard, Terry (1994). *Hegel's Phenomenology: The Sociality of Reason*. Cambridge, UK: Cambridge University Press.

Pinkard, Terry (2001). *Hegel*. Cambridge, UK: Cambridge University Press.

Pinkard, Terry (2002). *German Philosophy, 1760-1860: The Legacy of Idealism*. Cambridge, UK: Cambridge University Press.

Pippin, Robert B. (1991a). "Hegel, Modernity, and Habermas." *Monist* 74 (3): 329-57.

Pippin, Robert B. (1991b). "Idealism and Agency in Kant and Hegel." *The Journal of Philosophy* 88: 532-41.

Pippin, Robert B. (1993). "You Can't Get There From Here: Transition Problems in Hegel's *Phenomenology of Spirit*." In Frederick Beiser (ed.), *The Cambridge Companion to Hegel*. Cambridge, UK: Cambridge University Press, pp. 52-85.

Pippin, Robert B. (1999). *Modernism as a Philosophical Problem: On the Dissatisfactions of High European Culture*, 2nd edn. Oxford: Blackwell.

Pothast, Ulrich (1971). *Über einige Fragen der Selbstbeziehung*. Frankfurt am Main: Klostermann.

Rosen, Stanley (1987). *Hermeneutics as Politics*. New York: Oxford University Press.

Schelling, Friedrich Wilhelm Joseph (1976). *Schriften von 1813-1830*. Darmstadt: Wissenschaftliche Buchgesellschaft.

Schelling, Friedrich Wilhelm Joseph (1978). *System of Transcendental Idealism*, trans. Peter Heath.

Charlottesville, VA: University Press of Virginia.

Schelling, Friedrich Wilhelm Joseph (1982). *Schriften von 1799-1801*. Darmstadt: Wissenschaftliche Buchgesellschaft.

Schelling, Friedrich Wilhelm Joseph (1988). *Ideas for a Philosophy of Nature*, trans. Errol E. Harris and Peter Heath. Cambridge, UK: Cambridge University Press.

Schelling, Friedrich Wilhelm Joseph (1994). *Idealism and the Endgame of Theory: Three Essays by F. W. J. Schelling*, ed. and trans. Thomas Pfau. Albany, NY: SUNY Press.

Schönborn, Alexander von (1999). "Karl Leonhard Reinhold : '... endeavoring to keep up the pace *mit unserem Zeitalter*.' " In Michael Baur and Daniel O. Dahlstrom (eds.), *The Emergence of German Idealism*. Washington: Catholic University of America Press, pp. 33-62.

Sheehan, James J. (1989). *German History, 1770-1866*. Oxford: Clarendon Press.

Smith, John (1988). *The Spirit and its Letter*. Ithaca, NY: Cornell University Press.

Sturma, Dieter (2000). "The Nature of Subjectivity: The Critical and Systematic Function of Schelling's Philosophy of Nature." In Sally Sedgwick (ed.), *The Reception of Kant's Critical Philosophy: Fichte, Schelling, and Hegel*. Cambridge, UK: Cambridge University Press, pp. 216-31.

Taylor, Charles (1989). *Sources of the Modern Self: The Making of the Modern Identity*. Cambridge, MA: Harvard University Press.

Von Molnar, Géza (1987). *Novalis: Romantic Vision, Ethical Context*. Minneapolis: University of Minnesota Press.

Ziolkowski, Theodore (1990). *German Romanticism and its Institutions*. Princeton, NJ: Princeton University Press.

7

German Romantic Fiction

Roger Paulin

The Romantic Novel

Is it open-ended?

The German Romantic novel seems to have no sense of an ending. Too often (exceptions are rare) it breaks off, it fragments, it dissolves into discursiveness, it abandons linearity for the tangential. So many are actually unfinished or deliberately left in a state of disarticulation: Tieck never gave us part three of *Sternbald*; Novalis died before he could complete *Heinrich von Ofterdingen*; Brentano left *Godwi* in a state of fragmentary suspension; Arnim never finished *Die Kronenwächter* (The Guardians of the Crown); Hoffmann withheld the "real" ending of *Kater Murr* (Tomcat Murr); Dorothea Schlegel even rejected the very notion of a "satisfactory conclusion" for *Florentin*. Others, close to the Romantic movement but not of it, like Hölderlin in *Hyperion*, promise "more to come" and fail to deliver. Some of Eichendorff's characters find satisfaction and repose, whereas others are destined to continue their anabases beyond the last pages of the novel.

The popular novel of the period 1795-1815, by contrast, knew where it was going, especially the Gothic variety. No amount of "venerable eleutherarchs and ghastly confederates holding midnight conventions in subterranean caves" (Thomas Love Peacock's witty dismissal of the genre in *Nightmare Abbey*) could prevent the hero or heroine from emerging triumphant, virtue intact and marriage secured. But would we really prefer *Wippo von Königstein*, *The Double Ursuline Nun*, or *Elise von Eisenthurm* (actual titles from 1800)?

Alternatively, we could turn to Jean Paul's huge novel of 1800-3, *Titan* (large novels are a feature of this period). For it is both completed and of considerable literary quality. Jean Paul is the Romantics' older contemporary and his novels are the most read and the most influential of the time. True, in the closing apotheosis, as in seventeenth- or eighteenth-century novels of political intrigue and education, the hero Albano discovers that he is a prince, he finds a kindred spirit with whom he can share his throne, and he looks forward to wise and beneficent rule. But at what a cost! To achieve this, he has to learn his real identity, see human coldness destroy his first love, and (this is an age of sentimental male bondings) experience ecstatic friendship and its dissipation. Albano is the *ingénu*, the unwritten page, destined for rank and greatness, but only at the end of processes involving pain, renunciation, and rejection. The antihero is Roquairol, the "child and product of his age," ridden by *ennui* and *mal du siècle*. who represents the anarchy of passion. Three female characters induct Albano into the more subtle terrain of the sentiments; he learns ethereality and exaltation, infatuation and temptation, until head and heart are reconciled. Lest we should think that Jean Paul makes it easy for us, we have a plot, intricate by most standards, which opens in mid-story and needs to turn back on itself (a central symbol is a labyrinthine garden with *trompe l'oeil* and spirals): identities are withheld, intrigues are plotted, mysterious and numinous figures beckon and deceive, mechanical devices suggest manipulations by unfeeling and impersonal forces. Add to this the set-piece descriptions of the Italian landscape, with its classical and heroic connotations, and the denseness of the novel's structure becomes apparent. Does it even end where it purports to? No, Jean Paul adds a "comic appendix" that satirizes Fichte's epistemology (a character with a split identity occurs in the main plot), and a balloonist whose levitations are symbolic of his disdain for the follies and inanities of the world on which he looks down. These ascents remind us, in their episodic structure and their hard look at humanity, of Klingemann's *Die Nachtwachen des Bonaventura* (The Night Watches of Bonaventura; see below).

Goethe as influence

Jean Paul, our suggested alternative to the unfinished Romantic novel, thus involves hard going (800 pages), convolutions of plot, and complex interplay of characters. The reader must sustain a heavy application of platonic Idealism and sentiment, with its rhetorical accompaniment. Jean Paul is a writer whom the Romantics cannot overlook, with whom they critically engage, to whom they allude (and whom they satirize). Even more than to Jean Paul, they defer to the greatest living German writer, Goethe. Does he, as a novelist, provide a model for a novel with an ending? *Werther*, the world-famous novel of 1774, certainly ends, but with *éclat* and scandal, in the suicide of the hero. Werther as a character casts a long shadow, and it falls on many a Romantic hero. Where there are mood swings, stopping the ears to reason, melancholic broodings, nature enthusiasms, and cosmic despairs, Werther is somewhere in the background. But as many authors of European Romanticism were to discover – Chateaubriand, Constant, and Foscolo among them – *Werther* is inimitable. Much of its engagement with sentimental religious culture cannot be transferred to a younger generation. Furthermore, it subverts one of the eighteenth century's favored narrative forms: the epistolary novel. For we have Werther's letters only, not their answers. We have insight into his and others' states of mind only through his vision.

Then, towards the end, the narrator, where letter-writing no longer can be sustained, breaks open the device and steps directly into the account.

The young Ludwig Tieck may have wished to write his own *Werther* with his novel *William Lovell* (1795-6), the first important novel by a member of the Romantic generation. It lacked the original's dense brevity (there are three volumes). It could not sustain the self-projection that Goethe extends to his hero (there are, as said, no replies to Werther's letters). The conventional epistolary form has to be restored so that perspectives on the hero can be opened up and ironies introduced. Lovell, the young Englishman adrift on the continent, believes he is acting through the "will" that gives him his name. He is not: the secret agency of others is manipulating his every move. There is another major difference. Werther, to give him his due, causes harm to others only as his mind is fully deranged; he does not seize the object of his desires when he could, and retreats instead into deluded notions of reunion in the afterlife. Lovell lives for the here and now; he embraces a career of libertinage precisely to lose his innocence and to be initiated into the refinements of debauchery. There is something here of the French novel of pursuit and seduction, Laclos's *Les Liaisons dangereuses* or Restif's *Le Paysan perverti*. But it is also fair to say that all the introspections known to the century pass here as in review, all the absolute claims of the heart and self. While this may produce momentary exaltation, it also involves emptiness and despair, the sense of living out a cliché. The self becomes the arbiter of all behavior: but it is a self directed by a malevolent secret society bent on his destruction. Wickedness has its due punishment, but one feels that there is no moral order upholding this retribution. There is no Albano figure as in Jean Paul's *Titan*, only Roquairol. Tieck sensed, at the age of 22, that he had pushed the limits of both epistolary and Gothic novels to their extremes; no German writer of talent would wish to fall back on the conventional novel in letters. He had created an antihero who, even more than Werther, was in a sense living out the plots of others' narratives, the fictional world of the late Enlightenment as against Werther's Homer and Ossian.

Goethe's *Wilhelm Meisters Lehrjahre* (Wilhelm Meister's Apprenticeship; 1795-6), the novel of his maturity, appears at just the right moment for the young Romantic generation. It provides them with some patterns for their own writing of fiction, notably the young hero in search of development (*Bildung*) and personal fulfillment. It furnishes them with a legitimation for their endeavors, once the great Goethe has pointed the way. But Goethe is only marginally interested in the so-called proprieties of conventional novel writing, and he is not noted for his ability to sustain a plot from inception to end. Indeed, in *Wilhelm Meister* a great deal is left open or even unsaid. The Romantic novel takes much of what it likes from Goethe, without necessarily touching the substance. A hero who moves out of conventional society into the Hogarthian world of actors and their itinerant existence might appeal; but his later development, laid down by a secret society with firmly Enlightenment aims, and his integration into the prerevolutionary landed classes, might not.

Goethe cannot, of course, resist the standard cliché of the Gothic novel, the secret society, best known to German readers through Karl Grosse's *Der Genius*, the novel mentioned in *Northanger Abbey* in its translation as *Horrid Mysteries*. Gothic fiction, English in origin, migrates to Germany and returns in new guise as the novel or tale of terror. In Germany, Schiller had dignified the genre with his *Der Geisterseher* (The Ghost-Seer; 1789) a gripping tale that found attentive readers among the Romantics (including Hoffmann); but it, too, remained unfinished. While the Romantics, in their turn, did not necessarily accept that their heroes should have a destination and fulfillment similar to Wilhelm Meister's – indeed some of their early novels are written against the grain of such readings – nevertheless mysterious, alluring, preferably androgynous young heroines (based on Goethe's Mignon) or equally unfathomable, fate-ridden hermits, playing the harp for preference (Goethe's Harfner), crop up at many turnings, their origins obscure and darkly terrible. Where Goethe interspersed his text with just one or two of his finest lyrics (e.g., "Kennst du das Land?"), they, especially their great poets Brentano and Eichendorff, were prodigal in sustained lyrical interludes in their fiction, much of highest quality. Where Goethe had no compunction in breaking the flow of his narrative with discussions (about Hamlet) or interleaved subplots, the Romantics made a principle of multifariousness of form and style within the novel framework.

Theoretical considerations

This formal prodigality is not merely a homage to *Wilhelm Meister*: it is grounded in theoretical discussions of what a novel is and may be. *Wilhelm Meister* is for many of Goethe's contemporaries the proof that the German novel has come of age and that the wide-ranging theoretical discussions about the nature of the genre have come to fruition. It is a paradox that, as novel production in Germany increases (120 titles in 1790, 375 in 1800), there is an accompanying debate, of growing intensity, about its legitimacy and indeed its very nature. The Romantic novel has to be seen against this background. More perhaps than in other national literary cultures the theoretical discussion concentrated on the novel's affinities with other literary genres. Was it the successor to the epic, assuming the universality of that dignified genre, but relating to the needs of modern men and women? Or was it not also related to the drama, in its structure and its urging forward to an outcome? Was it not related to both genres in its examination of human nature and human development? Could its very nature not be summed up in that German word "*Werden*" which means "becoming," not "being." This discussion indicates that the debate was being partly driven by conventional poetics. *Wilhelm Meister*, on the other hand, could be hailed as a successful experiment surmounting such restricting considerations. Goethe's novel contained a short theoretical discussion which defined itself and its hero in terms of "expressed notions" (*Gesinnungen*) and "events" (*Begebenheiten*); unlike the drama, it had less to do with characters and deeds. The hero would find himself involved in processes where his role was more passive than active, his undertakings more of a hindrance to the progress of the plot than a catalyst; there would be more scope for chance than for personal assertion. Schiller, whose *Der Geisterseher* had collapsed on this very question of outside manipulation of events, particularly praised the delicacy and lightness of touch with which Goethe had brought his hero to where he wanted him to be. Friedrich Schlegel, in the most important Romantic critique of *Wilhelm Meister*, went even further and declared the inner organization of the novel to be consonant with the very principles underlying the work of art: wholeness, universality, the seamless growing of the individual parts into one organism (*Gewächs*). This, he went on to say, joined by Novalis, was because conventional notions of order and narrative propriety are kept in a permanent state of suspense (*schweben*), none obtruding to upset the delicate balance between unconsciousness and reflection, stated purpose and irony.

These statements on *Wilhelm Meister* elide easily into general definitions of "Romantic art" and the "Romantic work of art." When Friedrich Schlegel, looking for a term to accommodate these, lighted upon the word *Roman*, he was prompt to point out that this term did not indicate a literary genre as such, but an "element of poetry." Such Romantic poetry always referred beyond itself to a higher, indivisible unity; it embodied both chaos and order, purpose and ironic self-reflection. In formal terms, it was mixed, a synthesis (but not a mere accumulation) of all genres, *Universalpoesie* – as had been the *Don Quixote* of the great Romantic "archpoet," Cervantes. Schelling's view of the novel as a "tableau," a "mirror of the world," where episodes cohere to a higher unity, is related to this, or Karl Solger's notion of the coherence in a "totality" of the most disparate elements in human nature, and their formal expression.

Theory and experiment

But could one express all this in a real novel? Almost as he was formulating his theory of the novel, Friedrich Schlegel wrote one, as if to demonstrate the congruity of idea and reality: *Lucinde* (1799). It did not immediately achieve the desired effect: readers were affronted by the sexual candor of some situations or they expected some kind of sustained narrative and were disappointed in finding none. Schlegel's friend, the theologian Friedrich Schleiermacher, defended it in terms which were consonant with Romantic aesthetics but for which the nineteenth century, by and large, was not ready. It was only "narrative" in the sense that it had a beginning and an end; for the rest, it was a series of reflections – which could be extended into infinity – about itself; it engaged the reader in a dialogue about its own composition. The reader was not to find here the relatively gradual progress of *Wilhelm Meister*; instead, there would be interpolations, leaps, fugues – in short, a seeming chaos. Chaos was indeed what Schlegel wanted, only, paradoxically, a "systematic chaos" of higher artistry. He was seeking to give expression to "poetry without end," not of course infiniteness itself, but intimations, touches, *échappées de vue*, sparks of imagination that gave insight into such fullness: what he called "arabesques."

If *Lucinde* sought to question cherished notions of character and narratorial sequence, it similarly strove to challenge accepted views of the relationship between man and woman. Where conventional morality relegated to separate compartments the physical and sensual and the spiritual and the intellectual, Schlegel posited their unity. The dominance of the male as lover or as artist is overturned: Lucinde is Julius's equal and each partakes of the other's nature. Love which finds such fulfillment is poetic, is moral, is religious; indeed for Schlegel the very principle of Romantic poetry is love, its expression a "hieroglyph of the One eternal love."

Friedrich Schlegel's wife, Dorothea Mendelssohn (the Lucinde of his novel) also had notions of a Romantic novel. This was *Florentin* (1801). She had, however, more realistic expectations of her readers' capacity to tolerate experimentation. There are here the requisites borrowed from elsewhere and familiar in Tieck or Hoffmann or Eichendorff: castles in forests, livid skies rent by lightning, hunting horns (or guitars) ready to hand and words to accompany them. They become the symbolic accompaniment of wanderings, forays into the unknown, quests for identity, searches for an underlying meaning of existence as yet imperfectly revealed. Thus Florentin, a young aristocrat on his way to join the American wars of independence, is detained instead by a noble family, learns the draw of male friendship and female compan-ionship, shares in philanthropic schemes. We learn in a long interpolation that his *"Wanderjahre"* have taken in Italy, France, and England, and an artistic vocation. Interspersed letters and verses add to the variety of perspectives. But Dorothea resolutely refuses to round the narrative off with a "satisfying ending"; it stops instead in mid-story. The rest is left open-ended, to be completed in the reader's thoughts or dreams. This, she says, is infinitely preferable to the usual conclusions in marriage or death.

Clemens Brentano's novel *Godwi oder das steinerne Bild der Mutter* (Godwi, or The Stone Image of the Mother), published in the same year (1801) is altogether more radical and more "Romantic." The subtitle, *ein verwilderter Roman* (a novel run wild) promises loss of form in the conventional sense that narrative threads are lost, characters and their unresolved secrets and fates are introduced, letters are exchanged which have little immediate communicative function. The notion of the individual seems to have lost its congruity as it retreats into a variety of perspectives. Prose gives way to poetry (some of Brentano's best) or dramatic verse as narrative gives way to evocation. Is this therefore the "Romantic novel par excellence," as some critics aver? Or does it represent what actually happens when Romantic aesthetic ideas, as confidently formulated by Friedrich Schlegel, are fleshed out in the writing of fiction? Is Romantic irony – where the moment of creative awareness carries in it the sense of its own mutability, where perfection of form is referred to chaotic counterprocesses – here simply destructive of form? Is Schlegel's "higher unity" or "bond of ideas" lost amid the shifting perspectives and changing identities? Has the writing of fiction itself become both a theoretical and a practical impossibility?

These questions – part of the ongoing critical discussion of *Godwi* – raise serious issues of form and comprehensibility. And yet a pragmatic reading of this novel is possible: in Part One, Godwi (and others) are searching for the key to the mystery of the statue, the opening up of childhood visions of the dead mother; in Part Two they find their resolution, where characters, once shrouded in obscurity, are revealed and identified. It might be said that all this has been achieved at a considerable cost, but that one or two of Brentano's finest poems atone for the fractures in the main narrative.

Yet the reader of this nearly impenetrable novel will find in it discussions of the nature of art as mediator, as the suffusion of color into reality, as thought and form in harmonious balance, as transference or translation. These principles can be applied to the search for identity, self-knowledge, and fulfillment of the characters and relate thus to the central symbol of the statue and the unveiling of its secret.

Art and history

Although there are artist figures in Brentano's novel (and those of many others), they are not here of central concern. What happens when an artist becomes the object and hero of the novel? The depiction of the artist, historical or fictitious, in drama or narrative (*Künstlerdrama*, *Künstlerroman*) is a feature peculiar to German literature in the generation preceding the Romantics. Goethe's *Torquato Tasso* (1789) or Heinse's *Ardinghello* (1787) are the archetypes, where modern artistic sensitivity or awareness is transferred into a historical setting.

Ludwig Tieck's *William Lovell* had been a kind of anti-*Bildungsroman*, a novel of seduction and sensual gratification leading to chaos and void. With *Franz Sternbalds Wanderungen* (Franz Sternbald's Wanderings; 1798), Tieck was to follow much closer the patterns of *Wilhelm Meister*: a hero, an artist, was to get somewhere, achieve something, and find himself; his wanderings and adventures would end in fulfillment and maturity. That, at least, was the underlying idea. But Tieck broke off the novel two thirds through and could never bring himself to complete it. Yet the differences between Goethe's and Tieck's novels are equally apparent. They might be summed up as follows: German present versus German past; development versus circularity; irony and sophistication versus deliberate naïveté; increasing doubts about art versus the conscious cultivation of art. The view of art expressed in Tieck's novel was at odds with the uncompromising Classicism which he at that time saw Goethe as professing. Against this domination by classical antiquity and the pre-eminence of the plastic arts, Tieck posits the German and Italian Renaissance, the world of sixteenth-century Nuremberg, Venice, or Renaissance Rome. Art is not a system or a doctrine; it is an article of faith, the object of worship, accepted with childlike devotion. An artist so inspired – Franz Sternbald is one – will in one crucial way never "grow up." The many wanderings and adventures and encounters (some erotic) which he undergoes would (had the novel been finished) have landed him back in Nuremberg, his original views merely confirmed. His anabases and searchings, through a world of changing sensations and disguises, might have answered the question: who am I? He might have been reunited with the girl whose image haunts him as the object of memory and longing.

The history – we meet the pious and sober Albrecht Dürer in his Nuremberg studio, and Lukas van Leyden – is vague and stereotyped: Northern worth versus the enticements of the South. The sensitivities of the characters – Sternbald's melancholy and longing – are essentially modern. The discussions on art center on religious painting (a Romantic preoccupation) but also on landscape depiction, and as such they point forward to Philipp Otto Runge and Caspar David Friedrich. But to many of the novel's readers – who included Brentano, Arnim, Eichendorff, and Runge – the "message" was more important than any historical accuracy. The *present*, our world tainted with Enlightenment utilitarianism, must be referred to the *past*, and such a referral will reinstill in modern artists the simple-heartedness and devotion of earlier ages. Certainly the young German painters in Rome, known as the Nazarenes, read the novel as the bible of a religious cult of art.

Tieck's close friend Novalis (Friedrich von Hardenberg) also sought to produce a novel that would go beyond the scope of *Wilhelm Meister* and celebrate the artist while taking in the sweep of history. It was to be his *Heinrich von Ofterdingen* (1802), in two parts, the second unfinished. Not all Romantic readers of *Wilhelm Meister* shared Friedrich Schlegel's enthusiasm, and Novalis was no exception. Goethe's novel seemed to end in prose; Novalis's would end in poetry, indeed in an apotheosis that would usher in a golden age. The setting would not be Tieck's age of Dürer and Raphael, but the high Middle Ages, with its legends, its chivalry, its crusades, and its estates. Its adherence to history would be marginally closer than Tieck's, but each event and each encounter was to function at the same time as a prefiguration of a higher, spiritual process, the key to the opening up of *"das Wunderbare"* and the reign of poetry.

Heinrich differs from Wilhelm Meister in that he has in his mind a vision of poetry. He must meet persons – merchants, an oriental slave girl, a miner, a hermit, a poet, and finally his love Mathilde – who confront him with the individual processes (nature, war , history, love) of which poetry is the whole manifestation. The interpolated stories and poems mirror his progress from "Expectation" (Part One) to "Fulfillment" (Part Two). (Novalis's novel has none of the lyrical effusiveness of *Sternbald*.) A dream is to be fulfilled; the real processes of life are to be subsumed under poetry. Indeed, the unfinished second part is intended to lead the hero through the experienced reality of the things adumbrated in song and story, until all things are brought together, biblical-style (*apocatastasis panton*), in a new Jerusalem. In this way, the hero's "development" involves the Romantic interiorizing and spiritualizing of all pragmatic experience ("*Weg nach Innen*"), imparting to events a higher mythological sense and destination. In this, history and poetry are seen as an indivisible process.

For Novalis, but much less for Tieck, the past is subsumed under mythology, and the novel has the function of plotting the process whereby reality and imagination, historical past and timeless myth, coalesce. For Tieck, the historical background may remind us of past models of artistic piety (Dürer, Raphael), but his notion of the artist is essentially modern. Yet in works of nonfiction, editions of medieval poetry and epic, Tieck was to make the crucial link between an integrated past, where poetry, chivalry, church, and state cohered as one organism, and a present where these were either lost or fragmented. In Arnim, Hoffmann, and Eichendorff, who usher in a second phase of the Romantic novel, we see these ideas worked out in fiction. Either it seeks to forge the link between historical past and present (Arnim) or it places modern men and women and their society and their anxieties in the foreground (Eichendorff, Hoffmann, and Arnim).

Not surprisingly, both Tieck and Novalis kept their distance from the popular medievalizing fiction of the day, the *Ritterromane*. Yet this flourishing subgenre was also to find its way into Romantic circles with Friedrich de La Motte-Fouqué and his much-read *Der Zauberring* (The Magic Ring) or *Sintram*, loosely based on medieval or Nordic romance. Fouqué is a naïve and prolific writer who knows how to dress up the Middle Ages in a guise that will appeal to a vogue for all things past. It is a step from this medievalizing dressing up to Achim von Arnim's "historical novel" *Die Kronen-wächter* (The Guardians of the Crown; first part 1817, second published posthumously 1854). Coming relatively late in the movement, it relates only loosely to Tieck and Novalis, and almost not at all to *Wilhelm Meister*. Novalis had seen historical processes urging towards fulfillment, to the now restored paradise, ending in the unsayable and the inexpressible. Tieck had placed Franz Sternbald in a past society, but that setting was at most vague and at all times subordinate to questions of artistic development. Arnim is in the strict sense no more "historical" than Fouqué; he borrows un-ashamedly from Gothic fiction (the secret society again); he elides folk motifs and those of higher poetry. His aim is not to evoke the past as it was, like Scott, but as he believes it could have been. To this end, Arnim takes elements from all manner of sources to present a sixteenth century of his own making, the time of Faust and Maximilian, Dürer and Luther, with little regard for chronology and with at most a tortuous narrative thread. His two heroes are scions of the Hohenstaufens; but that once mighty dynasty is now a secret brotherhood devoted to worldly gain and with little sense of its historical mission. The adventures and encounters of the heroes are there to demonstrate how they, too, seek and only partially find, a sense and purpose in shifting times, with peasants' wars and changing allegiances. In all this, it is the poet-seer who is able to show the underlying processes of history. Like Novalis's novel, it is poeticized *Heilsgeschichte*, the story of human salvation; but Arnim concentrates less on fulfillment than on lost origins and on strivings towards a redemption yet to be achieved.

The social message

Unlike Novalis's novel, *Die Kronenwächter* is sharply focused on historical turmoils and upheavals; these point forward symbolically to the collapse of values in Arnim's own time in the wake of Napoleon, and he highlights those features that will lead eventually to the restoration of moral and spiritual values in the nation. This is an essentially conservative message, and Arnim's earlier novel, *Gräfin Dolores* (Countess Dolores; 1810), applied it to contemporary society. If *Die Kronenwächter* presents us with colorful tableaux and action piled upon action, *Gräfin Dolores* seems to enact *Universalpoesie* (it contains, in addition to the main plot, a short novel, several stories, various dramatic interludes, ballads, and lyrical "impromptus"). It reflects – perhaps as an extreme example – the insouciance towards outer form that characterizes the

German Romantic novel, requiring the reader to find an inner symbolic order. Goethe's last novel, *Wilhelm Meisters Wanderjahre* (Wilhelm Meister's Journeyman Years; 1829), while different thematically in almost every respect from Arnim's, displays a similar multiperspectivity and openness to form. Arnim's plot moves between Germany and Sicily, and takes in, apart from the main characters, a host of ancillary figures and what befalls them. This is clearly not the world of the earlier *Wilhelm Meisters Lehrjahre*; but it might be closer in one crucial respect to Goethe's middle novel, *Die Wahlverwandtschaften* (Elective Affinities; 1808). For that novel had dealt (among other things) with problems of love and marriage in modern aristocratic society. Arnim found its message ambiguous and wished to reinforce it with his own novel of marriage, adultery, and penance. Where Goethe left open any question of the wider social implications of his story of fatal attractions, Arnim was intent on making his novel a mirror of the *Zeitgeist* and its several manifestations, raffish and impious, spiritual and ascetic. The loss of spiritual values that is typical of postrevolutionary society contrasts with the awareness of family, religion, and nation, as the basis of a renewal. It is the same underlying belief in a historical process that informs *Die Kronenwächter*, but here with the focus on the contemporary stage of its unfolding.

Joseph von Eichendorff was a great admirer of *Die Gräfin Dolores*. He elevated it as a model of "*Gesinnung*," that inward moral and religious attitude that gives all true poetry its *raison d'être*, its life and its vitality; he saw its poet set in a great tree of life, raised above the affairs of humankind, as an intermediary between humankind and God. Eichendorff's novels *Ahnung und Gegenwart* (Intimation and Present; 1815) and its later companion piece, *Dichter und ihre Gesellen* (Poets and Their Companions; 1835), are "Romantic" on a surface level: they revel in mystery, disguise, mistaken identity, labyrinthine landscapes, enchanted gardens, distant echoes of hunting horns. Yet the seeming chaos of relationships and the fluctuations in settings are subject to a hidden order. Characters are led, as if by chance, but in reality by design, to encounters where they learn to understand their own selves, and where they have come from. The views out into nature are in reality "prospects" of a higher level of existence. symbolized by the Christian emblems of the sun or the cross. The "*Ahnung*" and "*Gegenwart*" of the title thus point as narrative principles to the present – a society, like Arnim's, that has lost its way and no longer recognizes spiritual values – and to a transfiguration of that present through intimations of a higher order of things. The hero, Count Friedrich, must confront the dark side of human nature, resist the allurements of passion, plunge himself into the turmoil of the times, before retreating into the safe haven of a monastery. But other characters find their fulfillment either in poetry or even in active practical life. *Dichter und ihre Gesellen* is differently focused: it takes four poets or would-be poets and confronts them with the dichotomies of art and life. One opts for the Romantic enticements of Italy; one prefers a shifting identity within a wandering troupe of actors; one finds solace in the church; one finds no anchorage in life and seeks death. There is no doubt where Eichendorff's own conservative sympathies lie, yet each of these conflicts and their various resolutions, is presented as real and credible in the terms of the novel.

Psychic terror, and parody

Jean Paul's *Titan* and Arnim's *Gräfin Dolores* each contain a character who takes his own life while acting out a role on the stage. It is *Wilhelm Meister* taken to extreme, the stage becoming a symbol of a world theater of absurdity and nothingness, real death preferable to its mere stage enactment. These images, and many others, that became the vocabulary of European *mal du siècle* and *Weltschmerz*, occur as a ground bass in August Klingemann's *Die Nachtwachen des Bonaventura* (Night Watches of Bonaventura; 1804). These 16 night watches rehearse, in seemingly capricious order, the inanities of human existence. They are "night pieces" (*Nachtstücke*) à la Breughel, to remind us of the dark side of humanity, its crimes and inhumanities covered by darkness. Bonaventura the night watchman – a foundling, the devil presiding over his birth – is less a real character than a wearer of masks. If these scenes have any coherence as a novel, it is as a series of reflections that could continue ad infinitum, as "arabesques," witnessing to the structure of the universe in its fullness. But a fullness of what? Of appearance that has no substance, of an ego constantly consuming itself (a parody of Fichte), as fiction, not as reality, a cosmic bad novel, a tragedy, a tragicomedy, a puppet play directed by Harlequin or an incompetent stage director (God) to whose whims we are subjected. Or playing out a role, never living in real substance, mechanically, consumed with *ennui*. From role playing and theater, it is but a step to the radical denial of any sense of existence. The last "watch" ends with the word "*Nichts*!"

Die Nachtwachen des Bonaventura coheres at most as a narrative in cycles of despair with recurrent motifs, E. Th. A. Hoffmann's novel *Die Elixiere des Teufels* (The Devil's Elixirs; 1815-17), by contrast, follows much more the patterns of popular fiction that have us on the edge of our chairs. But the novel bears only a superficial relationship to *Der Genius*, or M. G. Lewis's *The Monk* (which Hoffmann certainly knew). Nevertheless the novel is hard to put down, packed as it is with incidents in breathless sequence (intrigue, murder, rape), involving the church (the pope, no less), the state (a princely court) and their intertwining relations. The monk Medardus, who believes he has drunk the devil's elixirs and then embarks on a career of wickedness and deceit, is led into a tangle of relationships whose solution we as readers are agog to find out. But the "terror" is not provided by the stock-in-trade of Gothic motifs, those "ghastly confederates": it is the terror in the hero's own mind, his sense of the loss of self, indeed of seeing his own self, his own *Doppelgänger*. So great is Medardus's consternation at these confrontations that we, too, share in his mental anguish: we have no reason to believe that he is not the one who is carrying out the deeds. We suspend disbelief because the narrator is using the first person and we allow ourselves to accept his explanation or motivation. His self, he says, has fallen into the hands of mysterious forces (the words "fate," "machine," or "tool" are used without much distinction) who merge him into alien figures and alienate him from his own personality. Medardus is weighed down with the burden of guilt for misdeeds which, he senses, are the workings of those inscrutable "forces." Yet, in the end, a *Doppelgänger*, Medardus's darker self, Viktorin, proves to be the real perpetrator, his own brother, whose origins are similarly veiled in mystery. But it is essential to the narrative that Medardus feels the guilt for this catalogue of crimes and that it becomes the substance of his own confession. They are not related for our perverse delectation, but to establish, as best can be done, the congruities of cause and effect, of guilt and penance. The narrator keeps us in suspense, so that we feel at the end all the more the effect of redemption and the resolution of the tangled skein of his life's story. The agency of Medardus's deeds, readily attributed to those "forces" or even to "the sins of the fathers," is countered by the appeal to conscience and consciousness. Medardus learns that people must live with the consequences of their actions, even in ascetic renunciation. Thus this Gothic "Confessional of the Black Penitent" also ends with a very Catholic call to penance, and a kind of transfiguration.

Yet not all of the novel is borne along by such edifying considerations. Humor is a countervailing factor. There is the character called Belcampo, a barber, responsible for changing appearances, who stands back from his own bizarre character by subjecting it to laughter. This is his remedy for the personality split that so terrifies Medardus. Hoffmann's other novel, *Kater Murr* (Tomcat Murr; 1820-1) makes these two levels of self-awareness into the structural principle of its composition. And yet this most bizarre of Romantic novels does not fall into the convenient categories of either humor or terror. Its title is that of the eponymous hero, a learned tomcat with literary pretensions; indeed it is the diary of a literary nobody, a *Bildungsroman* of education in banality, social climbing (on roofs), and philistinism. The parody – and very funny it is – shows us a life, uncomplicated in itself, in which every element can be accounted for. But interleaved by accident into the cat's life is the fragmentary and tortured account of the musician Kreisler, at a court (more satire), with its attendant intrigues and love relationships. If Murr's life is "complete," Kreisler's falls apart, fugitive, torn between art and love, sardonic, melancholic. The humorous parody gives way to bitter satire, emotional confusion, but also to glimpses of a higher artistic existence as yet unfulfilled. Humor, both bright and black, is perhaps the only unifying principle in this novel. However, the figure of Meister Abraham, the manipulator of machines and apparatuses (and the owner of the cat), stands in both camps. Hoffmann devotes two-thirds of his novel to Kreisler; he rounds off Murr's life with an obituary, whereas Kreisler's ends in mystery and confusion, with no resolution of the claims of art and reality. It is the one side of the Romantic message, from *Sternbald* and *Godwi*, to *Kater Murr* and thence to *Dichter und ihre Gesellen*, that points out beyond itself in open form, unfinished messages, and unresolved prospects. Poetry, as all of these novels tell us, will not allow itself to be inhibited by narratorial constraints.

Short Fiction (*Novelle*)

The complexity and many-sidedness of Romantic notions of personality, artistry, history, and society are best evidenced in the Romantic novel (and to some extent the Romantic drama). As we saw, this can occasionally subject the novel form to strains which it cannot easily sustain, or the novel is seen in such commodious and universal terms that conventional compositional features (such as an ending) may be suspended. As a movement, German Romanticism is caught up in political and social events between 1795 and 1815. The élan for some longer poetic projects (*Sternbald*, *Kronenwächter*) cannot be sustained in these upheavals and they remain fragmentary. Paradoxically, however, German Romantic theory saw the fragment always in relation to the whole, never in isolation; it saw excrescences on the whole (arabesques) as pointing to the universal richness and fullness of poetic creation. In those terms, therefore, we are able to supply in our minds the continuations or fulfillments and "divine" the endings. Thus *Heinrich von Ofterdingen* traces selectively the processes of nature, history, art, and love that are intended to come together in one poetic synthesis at the end. Franz Sternbald's commitment to art will remain constant and integrated even when those wanderings reach their (as yet unreached) goal. The glimpses of the legendary Hohenstaufen castle in *Die Kronenwächter* intimate that higher historical processes will some day unite the contingent and the imagined. Kreisler's existence at the end of *Kater Murr*, by contrast, suggests an endless and unsatisfied quest for a resolution of life and art. But Hoffmann is too interested in Kreisler to leave it at that: the *Kreisleriana* in his collection of short fiction, *Fantasiestücke*, are part of that further existence, although not related to the plot of *Kater Murr*.

It has been traditional in criticism to see the less accessible Romantic novel as at most an adjunct to the much more readable and readily amenable short prose fiction of the Romantics, pearls in a chain, unlike the inchoate mass of the larger fiction. Romantic theory (Friedrich and August Wilhelm Schlegel both had views on the subject) did seize on the *Novelle* as part of its notion of *Universalpoesie*, stressing the needs of the moment, the urgency for action, as against the more gradual processes of the novel. But it also saw the *Novelle* as having affinities with the drama, and with the fairy tale: there was no wish to contain its scope within one category. The *Novelle*, essentially, draws on the same wellsprings of poetry as any other genre.

The injunction to record brief and extraordinary incidents in concentrated form had been part of the history of the European short story (*novela/novella/nouvelle/Novelle*) since the Renaissance. Similarly, it had been expected to relate to its own society, but to that which was out of the ordinary inside that framework. Goethe, with his collection of 1795, *Unterhaltungen deutscher Ausgewanderten* (Conversations of German Emigrés) in the same year as the first part of *Wilhelm Meister*, had illustrated very neatly the contrast between these two different, but related, modes of focus. Goethe's later *Die Wahlverwandtschaften* and *Wilhelm Meisters Wanderjahre*, by contrast, were to be novels structured around interspersed *Novellen*. *Novellen*, seen in this structural context, form part of the pattern of episode and subsection that we have seen in Arnim's *Die Gräfin Dolores* and in Eichendorff's two novels. In Arnim's case, one interspersed story is a continuation of the series of tales told in his earlier *Novelle* collection, *Der Wintergarten* (The Winter Garden; 1808), taken from earlier chronicled sources. Similarly, his *Novelle* collections of 1812 and later take up combinations of characters and situations, often bizarre and grotesque, in combinations reminiscent of the first part of *Die Gräfin Dolores*. The reference to times of historical crisis, revolution, *Zeitgeist*, that informs these stories, also makes a link with the novel. Similarly, the theme of wandering, seeking one's fortune, moving between the German homeland and the exotic delights of Italy, that inform both of Eichendorff's novels, are brought together in consummate form in his well-known story, *Aus dem Leben eines Taugenichts* (From the Life of a Good-for-nothing), while the sinuous landscape that symbolizes the enticements of the flesh is the focus of the story *Das Marmorbild* (The Marble Statue). One can extend this pattern to other authors. Novalis's story, *Die Lehrlinge zu Sais* (The Initiates at Sais; 1798), a symbolized dialogue on the philosophy of nature, relates forward to the theme and structure of *Heinrich von Ofterdingen*. Brentano's "run wild" narrative in *Godwi*, with its deliberately torn lines of communication, corresponds in simpler fashion to the levels of communication and the tragic misunderstanding underlying the later story *Vom braven Kasperl und dem schönen Annerl* (Of Honest Kasperl and Fair Annerl). The many stories for which Hoffmann is famous are often individual points of focus of the great themes of the novels: visions of terror, disturbed personality, plays on identity and consciousness, flights of imagination, satire (*Der Sandmann* [The Sandman], *Ignaz Denner*, *Ritter Gluck* [Chevalier Gluck], *Das Fräulein von Scuderi*, *Meister Floh* [Master Flea]). It is also fair to say that his best-known stories of fantasy and its fulfillment (*Der goldne Topf* [The Golden Pot], *Prinzessin Brambilla* [Princess Brambilla]) move far beyond the confines set by the two novels.

Similarly, the stories for which Ludwig Tieck is best known (*Der blonde Eckbert* [Fair-Haired Eckbert], *Der Runenberg*, *Liebeszauber* [Love's Enchantment]), like *Franz Sternbalds Wanderungen*, take up the question: who am I? Where Sternbald's encounters, in their multiformity of experience, contribute to self-revelation, the stories focus on one particular meeting, a confrontation with the unknown in oneself. The revelations of self in these *Novellen* are fatal; they open up abysses of memory, of the past, blurred lines between imagination and reality, where the mind cracks and madness and death beckon.

These themes, also present on a different level in the Gothic elements of the Romantic novel, are part of the Romantic extension of the *Novelle* repertoire beyond its habitual arsenal of extraordinary (but true) happenings, into areas where the traditional patterns of explanation no longer hold. At their most uncompromising, Heinrich von Kleist's stories explore the tragic potential of the *Novelle*, tragic because the certitudes or reconciliations of the European tradition are no longer valid and human frailty and misunderstanding replace an underlying world order. It is, however, to this day a matter of debate whether Kleist can rightly be called a Romantic.

Some Romantic authors, notably Tieck, Arnim, and Hoffmann, wished their stories to be read as a collective identity, with the framework pattern familiar from Boccaccio and others. Through this, we meet the society of narrators and auditors and their expectations; we see the relationship between them and the stories they are given to relate. The "tale of terror," such as Tieck's *Der blonde Eckbert*, can thus coexist with gentler and more appealing narratives, even with fairy tale. The disturbing effects of the one are relativized by the appeal to a different level of imagination. With these collections, Tieck's *Phantasus*, Arnim's *Der Wintergarten*, Hoffmann's *Die Serapionsbrü-der* (The Serapion Fraternity), the way is open for the fairy tale collection as an exclusive genre: the Grimm brothers' fairy tales (*Kinder- und Hausmärchen*; 1812-22). But that is another story altogether.

References and Further Reading

Behler, E. (1993). *Romantic Literary Theory*. Cambridge, UK: Cambridge University Press.

Blackall, E. A. (1983). *The Novels of the German Romantics*. Ithaca, NY and London: Cornell University Press.

Heiderich, M. W. (1982). *The German Novel of 1800. A Study of Popular Prose Fiction*. Berne: Peter Lang.

Paulin, R. (1985). *The Brief Compass. The Nineteenth-Century German Novelle*. Oxford: Clarendon.

Purver, J. (1989). *Hindeutung aus das Höhere. A Structural Study of the Novels of Joseph von Eichendorff*. Frankfurt am Main: Peter Lang.

Saul, N. (1984). *History and Poetry in Novalis and in the Tradition of the German Enlightenment*. London: Bithell Series of Dissertations/MHRA.

Saul, N. (ed.) (2002). *Philosophy and German Literature 1700-1990*. Cambridge, UK: Cambridge University Press.

Steinecke, H. and Wahrenburg, F. (eds.) (1999). *Romantheorie. Texte vom Barock bis zur Gegenwart*. Stuttgart: Reclam.

Swales, M. (1977). *The German Novelle*. Princeton, NJ: Princeton University Press.

8

The Romantic Fairy Tale

Kari Lokke

The only thing Luo was really good at was telling stories. A pleasing talent, to be sure, but a marginal one, with little future in it. Modern man has moved beyond the age of the *Thousand-and-One Nights*, and modern societies everywhere, whether socialist or capitalist, have done away with the old storytellers – more's the pity. (Dai Sijie 2001)

"The poet . . . either *is* nature or he will *seek* her. The former is the naïve, the latter the sentimental poet" writes Friedrich Schiller in his 1795 *Naïve and Sentimental Poetry* (Schiller 1966: 110). In this brief formula, Schiller offers a succinct definition of European Romanticism, emphasizing its acute consciousness of the disappearance of the natural world into urbanization, industrialization, and the artificiality of "civilization." For Schiller, the sentimental poet gives expression to a longing for nature that resembles the nostalgia of the adult for the child, the sick for the healthy, the "civilized" for the "simple." Though Schiller himself defined the naïve and sentimental as universal, ahistorical types while at the same time also identifying the sentimental with the modern and the naïve with the ancient, future critics and poets historicized Schiller's categories such that the sentimental poet became virtually synonymous with the Romantic era artist. Influenced by the sociopolitical perspectives of Germaine de Staël's *De la littérature* (1800) and the historicism of Friedrich Schlegel's conception of the Romantic in his *Athenäums-Fragmente* (1798) and *Gespräch über die Poesie* (1799), August Wilhelm Schlegel's *Vorlesungen über die dramatische Kunst und Literatur* (1808) canonized and simplified Schiller's sentimental/naïve opposition into the categories of Romantic/classic, culture/nature, North/South, spirit/body, melancholy/joy, Christian/pagan. This understanding of the Romantic, disseminated through Staël's *De l'Allemagne* (1811) and through Coleridge's lectures and writings, then gave impetus to the crucial theoretical works and definitions of European Romanticism written by its poetic practitioners: Hugo's *Préface de Cromwell* (1827), Stendhal's *Racine et Shakespeare* (1832), Heine's early and appreciative essay "Die

Romantik" as well as his later hostile polemic *Die romantische Schule* (1832-3) and Baudelaire's *Le Salon de 1846*. Conceptions of Romanticism based in Schiller's categories of the naïve and sentimental are still prevalent today in works as varied as Hans Robert Jauss's *Literaturgeschichte als Provocation*, M. H. Abram's *Natural Supernaturalism*, and Juliet Sychrava's *Schiller to Derrida: Idealism in Aesthetics*.

Nostalgia for Nature and Romantic Reflexivity

Acknowledging the enormous impact of Schiller's typology, this chapter surveys a literary phenomenon characteristic of and in some senses unique to the Romantic era – the effort of the individual, self-conscious poet to imitate and recreate the effect of folk art that is the product of a collective, popular, and anonymous voice. Or, as Schiller would put it, it examines the striving of the sentimental poet to become nature, to emulate the naïve in his or her own work through a kind of spiral-like movement that allows a return to origins, a conscious innocence. This effort takes many forms, from William Blake's *Songs of Innocence* (1789) whose naïveté Blake himself highlighted in the later *Songs of Experience* (1794), to the well-known attempt in William Wordsworth and Samuel Taylor Coleridge's *Lyrical Ballads* (1798) to narrate incidents from common or "low and rustic life" in simple "language really used by men." My focus here is the incorporation of folklore motifs, characters, and plotlines into the *Kunstmärchen* (art fairy tale), *conte de fée*, or *conte merveilleux* (wonder tale) that flowered in the Romantic era. This quintessentially Romantic genre takes many forms, both lyrical and narrative, poetic and fictional, and is distinguished by the poetic license taken by the writer with the original folkloric materials and by the highly self-conscious irony of the narrative voice (see Jocelyne Kolb's chapter on Romantic Irony).

Romantic nostalgia for nature and "the primitive" has its eighteenth-century roots in Jean-Jacques Rousseau, whose entire oeuvre can be read as a challenge to Enlightenment faith in historical and social progress. Rousseau's *Discours sur l'origine de l'inégalité* (1755) famously posits a hypothetical state of nature characterized by a peace and harmony that is destroyed by the historical development of human society. Similarly, his earlier *Discours sur les sciences et les arts* (1750) accuses poets and philosophers, in their attempts to civilize humanity, of corrupting virtue and contributing to the moral decline of the human race. And his *Essai sur l'origine des langues* (1781) glorifies Homer's "divine songs" and early oral poetry in general as vigorous, passionate language of the heart in contrast to the "more exact and clear, but more sluggish, subdued, and cold" (Rousseau 1990: 249) written word of modern Europe. Indeed, Schiller's essay on the naïve and sentimental is perhaps, above all else, an attempt to vindicate human capacity for self-improvement and perfectibility in the face of Rousseau's charge in the *Discourse on Inequality* that it may be "the source of all man's miseries," drawing man "out of that original condition, in which he would spend calm and innocent days" and making him "his own and Nature's tyrant"

(Rousseau 1990: 149). The writers of *Kunstmärchen* and *contes merveilleux/contes de fée* can be said to join Schiller in their creation of artifacts that seek to unite the sentimental and the naïve, to honor and recapture this lost innocence self-consciously.

In between Rousseau's essays and that of Schiller, Johann Gottfried Herder enters this cosmopolitan conversation in his *Über Ossian und die Lieder alter Völker* (1772). Styling himself as a German Rousseau in his "enthusiasm for the savage," Herder celebrates what he terms the "spirit of nature" in ancient poetry – its energy, immediacy of feeling, and liveliness in contrast to the "falseness, weakness, and artificiality" of the poetry of his day (Herder 1993: 456, 474; my translations). Modern poets seem crippled and lame, according to Herder, when held up to the vigor and power of Homer and Ossian (whom he took to be an authentic third-century bard of the Scottish Highlands, rather than the construct created from Gaelic ballads collected and reworked by Herder's contemporary James Macpherson that he turned out to be). Herder's admiration for Ossian and for the folk poetry collected in Thomas Percy's antiquarian *Reliques of Ancient English Poetry* (1765) combined with nationalistic antipathy to the cultural hegemony of French Classicism compels him to issue an impassioned call to his compatriots to begin the vital task of collecting this cultural treasure before it vanishes altogether. German folklore, Herder asserts, can hold its own against even the best of the Scottish ballads or romances he so admires:

> Folk songs from more than one province are familiar to me, songs that in the liveliness of their rhythms, the naïveté and strength of their speech yield nothing to those of other countries; but who collects them? Who concerns himself with them? Concerns himself with songs of the people? In our streets and alleys and fish markets? In the unschooled roundelay of the country folk? . . . who would want to collect them – who would have them published for our critics who can measure out and scan syllables so well? We'd rather, as a diversion, read our new beautifully printed poets. (Herder 1993: 480; my translation)

Beyond its echoes in Schiller, Herder's rhetoric powerfully influenced the next generation of German intellectuals, the German Romantics, who took up Herder's challenge to commit the German oral tradition to the written page. The second generation, or Heidelberg Romantics, Clemens Brentano and Achim von Arnim, collected folk songs in the early years of the nineteenth century that were published in 1805 under the title of *Des Knaben Wunderhorn* (The Boy's Magic Horn) and were accompanied by a programmatic essay on folksongs written by Arnim. Volumes Two and Three followed in 1808. Arnim's nationalistic essay bemoans the disappearance of folksongs in England, Italy, and above all in France, which he deems poorest in its fund of surviving folk culture. With powerful ecological symbolism, Arnim warns against the loss of its oral tradition, a loss he equates with both the destruction of nature and a flattening movement toward uniformity of culture. "When the summits of high mountains are once deforested, rain washes the soil down and no timber will grow again. That Germany will not be squandered away in this fashion is the aim of our endeavor" (Arnim 1992: 169; my translation).

Joining Arnim and Brentano in this effort to preserve German folk culture were their friends and colleagues Jacob and Wilhelm Grimm whose two volumes, *Kinder-und Hausmärchen, gesammelt durch die Brüder Grimm* (1812, 1815), have remained the most widely read and best loved collections of European folk tales to this day. Following Herder, Wilhelm Grimm in his Preface to the 1819 edition emphasizes the need to preserve a vanishing oral culture. "It is probably just the right time to collect these tales, since those who have been preserving them are becoming ever harder to find" (Tatar 2003: 264). And, like Arnim, Grimm sees their task as a metaphorical preservation of (cultivated) nature – preserving seeds from a crop devastated by storms as "seed for the future" (Tatar 2003: 264). In the late eighteenth century, Johann Karl August Musäus had published *Volksmärchen der Deutschen* (1782-7), but, as John Ellis has observed, a crucial difference between the two is immediately evident from their titles. Musäus's tales are announced as having been written by him, whereas "the Grimms apparently collected theirs" (Ellis 1983: 6). Indeed the 1819 Preface includes a tendentious attack on previous anthologizers who used folktales as the raw material for their own embellished and reworked creations as violators of what he sees as the simplicity, innocence, and purity of authentic folk art. For most of the last two centuries, then, the Grimm brothers have been viewed as having heeded Herder's call to seek out folk tales in the streets, alleys, fish markets, and farms and record them, as anthropological pioneers in the science of collecting folklore. Furthermore, Ellis notes, the Grimm brothers "presented the *Kinder und Hausmärchen* to their public essentially as a monument of national folklore" (Ellis 1983: 6).

In fact, it's now clear the Grimm brothers significantly rewrote the original tales and that the sources for many of their fairy tales turned out to be young, literate, and middle-class friends and relations of the Grimm brothers or descendants of French Huguenots who offered them versions of Charles Perrault's tales, rather than the German peasants touted by Jacob and Wilhelm Grimm. This fact says less about their desire to perpetrate a fraud on the public – Ellis's argument – than it does about the overwhelming cultural pressure they felt, in the midst of the Napoleonic Wars, to recreate and preserve the authentic, pure, naïve spirit of Germanic folklore.[1] Nevertheless, given the enormous worldwide popularity of the Grimm brothers' fairy tales and the rich, global tradition of rewritings they have stimulated, one is compelled to conclude that they were overwhelmingly successful in preserving this folk-tale tradition as "seed for the future," though not in the protoanthropological and nationalistic sense they had perhaps originally intended.

Realms of the *Kunstmärchen*: Aesthetics, Metaphysics, Psychology, Sociology

Similarly, the self-conscious *Kunstmärchen* may also be said to be a creation unique to the Romantic era that it has bequeathed to the future. It is difficult to overestimate either the significance of the fairy tale for the development of German Romantic aesthetics or the wealth and richness of the form as it took shape in the hands of its many practitioners. In their own writings, the earlier Jena Romantics (the Schlegels, Schelling, Novalis, and Tieck) and the Heidelberg Romantics were free from the concerns for strict authenticity and faithfulness to folk tradition reflected in the Grimm brothers' presentations of the *Kinder- und Hausmärchen* to their public. As I have suggested, they in fact reveled in the self-reflexivity that characterized their artful fairy tales. Novalis (Georg Friedrich Philipp von Hardenberg), central Romantic theorist of the *Kunstmärchen*, defined it as the quintessence of literature, the highest art: "The fairy tale is as it were the canon of poetry – everything poetic must be fairy tale like" (Novalis 1960, III: 449; my translation). For Novalis, the ideal fairy tale, like the dream, purifies reality and takes it to a higher power, thus revealing a spiritual nature beyond mundane or empirical reality: "A fairy tale is actually like a dream – without coherence. An ensemble of wondrous things and occurrences – for example, a musical fantasy – the harmonious result of an Aeolian harp – nature itself" (Novalis 1960, III: 454; my translation).

According to Novalis, even the novel should transform itself into fairy tale as it develops. Thus his *Heinrich von Ofterdingen*, though unfinished and posthumously published in 1802, includes in its last pages a celebration of a return to the prelapsarian innocence of a world of flowers and childhood, a rejuvenation manifested in a "green mysterious carpet of love" (Novalis 1964: 163) that covers the earth: "Deep down, childhood is close to earth, while clouds are perhaps the manifestation of a second, higher childhood, of paradise regained, and hence let their showers fall so beneficently on this other childhood" (Novalis 1964: 164). A *Bildungsroman* written in reaction or protest against Goethe's cynical and worldly *Wilhelm Meisters Lehrjahre* (1795) which Novalis termed "odious, a *Candide* against poetry" (Novalis 1964: 7), *Heinrich von Ofterdingen* tells the tale of its hero's search for a mystical blue flower associated with an ideal love, Mathilde. Mathilde's father, the wise poet Klingsohr, relates the fairy tale (begun separately in 1799 and later inserted into the novel) that concludes Part I of the novel and constitutes the climax of the novel as it stands.

Structured by the interactions among a host of allegorical, archetypal characters, the Klingsohr *Märchen* depicts the transformation of the universe by the spirit of poetry embodied in a little girl named Fable, the child of Mind and Ginnistan (Imagination). Replete with the hermetic, neoplatonic, and alchemical symbolism so prominent in the genre of the Romantic fairy tale as a whole, it also reveals the influence of Schiller's philosophy of history and Jacob Boehme's mysticism. The Klingsohr cosmos is composed of three realms. The upper kingdom, ruled by

Arcturus, is an icy northern world of eternal light inhabited by the princess Freya, Arcturus's beautiful daughter who suffers from the cold in this frozen realm. The middle world is home to Mind and Heart and their child Eros as well as Mind's child by Ginnistan, Fable. The two other inhabitants are Sophia or Wisdom and her opposite, a sour and sullen chronicler, the Scribe, identified by Novalis as "petrifying and petrified Reason." In the dark, cavernous lower world guarded by a mysterious Sphinx, live the three Fates, allies of the evil Scribe, who true to their names, are ancient hags spinning and cutting the threads of life.

The rejuvenation and transfiguration of the Klingsohr cosmos is sparked by Arcturus's command to his soldier Iron to cast his sword into the world so that, paradoxically, "they may know where peace (Freya) lies" (Novalis 1964: 123). The sword, transformed by Ginnistan into an ouroboros, changes the child Eros into a young man who, accompanied by Ginnistan, embarks upon his search for Freya. In their absence, the wicked Scribe and his cronies take over the middle realm and Fable takes action against them through a complex series of journeys. She claims her lyre in the kingdom of Arcturus, solves the riddle of the Sphinx, and defeats the Fates in the underworld. In the middle realm, the Scribe has set fire to her foster mother Heart; the funeral pyre reaches to the sun and consumes it in an apocalyptic conflagration that ultimately signals the end of time. Fable then gathers the ashes of Heart in a vessel and Sophia distributes them in a communion ritual to all present. The fairy tale concludes as the boundaries between the realm of Arcturus and the middle kingdom vanish, Eros is united with his beloved Freya, and the entire cast of characters celebrates "an eternal festival of spring" (Novalis 1964: 147). War is banished to an alabaster and black marble chessboard; the Fates and their Sphinx are captured in porphyry and basalt statues as their kingdom rises from below. Fable's earlier prophecies are fulfilled as she proclaims in conclusion: "The kingdom of eternity is founded, / By love and peace all strife has been impounded, / The dreams of pain are gone, to plague us never, / Sophia is priestess of all hearts forever" (Novalis 1964: 148).

If Novalis, after a period of inordinate admiration of Goethe's *Wilhelm Meister*, ultimately rejected it as "repulsive" and "foolish," "a satire on poetry [and] religion" (Novalis 1964: 6), he was, on the other hand, strongly influenced by Goethe's own *The Fairy Tale* published in 1795, an enigmatic text that can be said to introduce the genre of the *Kunstmärchen* in the German Romantic period. Like the Klingsohr *Märchen*, Goethe's tale portrays a world divided into separate realms that must be united and brought into harmony in order to usher in a new golden age of peace, beauty, and eternal youth. A motley cast of characters inhabits this whimsical world, among them two will-o'-the-wisps, a pug dog, a canary, a hawk, a bumbling giant, and a beautiful green serpent that moves freely and beneficently in all realms. A river divides the universe of the tale in two; on the one bank of the river the mundane lives of an old man and old woman proceed; the other side is home to a beautiful Lily, lonely and ideal, whose touch is fatal. This river must be bridged, just as a subterranean temple inhabited by four kings must be brought to light if the world is to be rejuvenated and redeemed.

A melancholy Knight who concludes his pilgrimage to the Lily by throwing himself at her and seeking death in her touch initiates the tale's narrative crisis. Forming a magic circle around the Knight's corpse, taking her tail in her mouth and creating an ouroboros, hermetic symbol of eternal life, the green serpent, in overt contrast to Judeo-Christian symbolism, is the agent of redemption in this tale. Her reconciling role is akin to that of Fable in the Klingsohr cosmos. Instructed by the old man, the Lily touches the snake with one hand and the Knight with the other, bringing him back to life. The snake subsequently dissolves into a sea of precious gemstones that are thrown into the river, precipitating the surfacing of the subterranean temple, with its four kings of gold, silver, iron, and alloy, representing wisdom, light, power, and love respectively. A magnificent bridge rises out of the river from foundations formed by the precious stones of the snake, resolving all tensions and transcending divisions. Thousands of foot travelers traverse the river as complete social harmony reigns:

> The great roadway in the middle was alive with livestock and mules, riders and carts, all of which seemed to stream past each other in both directions without any trouble at all. Everyone marvelled at such ease and splendour and the new king and his bride [the Knight and the Lily] were as delighted with the animation and activity before them as they were with their mutual love. (Goethe 2000: 29)

True to what might be termed Goethe's "Classicism" and to his "pagan" rejection of Christian dualism, even the agent of destruction, the bumbling giant whose shadow creates havoc among this stream of people on the bridge, is transformed and fixed to the ground as a sundial, darkness thus coming to serve order and light. The fairy tales of both Goethe and Novalis, in their abstract, universalizing combinations of the social and the cosmic, offer, among other things, metaphysical responses to the cataclysmic upheaval and violence represented by the French Revolution. In Novalis, we find a celebration of the revolutionary, even apocalyptic, potential of poetry as against reason, whereas in Goethe's more conservative world, interdependence and cooperation reign, there is a place for everything, and everything eventually finds or is put in its place.

In contrast to the metaphysical and alchemical allegories/symbols of Goethe and Novalis, Ludwig Tieck's masterpiece in the *Kunstmärchen* genre, *Blond Eckbert* or *Eckbert the Fair* (1797), offers a remarkable contribution to proto-Freudian depth psychology as a study in narcissism, repetition compulsion, and the return of the repressed. It is the story of a reclusive childless couple, the knight Eckbert and his wife Bertha. Eckbert's decision to ask his wife to share her strange life story with a friend, Philipp Walther, represents his effort to escape self-absorption and isolation. As Tieck writes,

> There are times when it troubles a man to keep a secret from a friend, a secret which, until then, had been guarded with the utmost care; his soul is overcome by an

irresistible desire to confide completely, to bare its innermost emotions to that friend, so that their friendship can become even closer. It might be the case, in such moments, that those more tender souls will come to appreciate one another more, yet, sometimes, it might also drive one party to shy away from acquaintance with the other. (Tieck 2000: 35-6)

Bertha's narrative plays upon the prototypical fairy tale plot, at the same time that, in an ironic gesture typical of the German *Kunstmärchen*, she explicitly warns her listeners "not to take my story for a fairy tale, however strange it may sound" (Tieck 2000: 36). The child of quarrelsome, impoverished parents, Bertha is a clumsy otherworldly child who is beaten by her father even as she dreams of instant riches that she can then shower on her abusive parents. After running away from home, she takes refuge in the woodland cottage of an uncanny old woman who teaches her how to spin and to take care of her household animals, a dog and a magical bird that lays eggs containing pearls and precious gems. When Bertha reaches 14, her witchlike guardian praises her diligence and obedience, but also sets the innocent girl up for her fall by warning her never "to stray from the true path: punishment will follow, no matter how late" (Tieck 2000: 43). In her world of *Waldeinsamkeit* (forest solitude), the imaginative girl also learns to read, dreams of handsome knights, and realizes that her dreams are within her reach if she dares to steal the magic bird and run away. Thus Tieck's self-conscious tale is an allegory of the Romantic movement itself, highlighting its awareness of the loss of innocence that inevitably results from the knowledge gained through books. Without moralizing, *Blond Eckbert* further dramatizes, in its whirlpool-like plot, the dangers of absorption in the solitary imagination.

In telling her tale to Philipp Walther, Bertha also confesses to murder, for she admits chaining and abandoning the dog to a certain death and then strangling the magic bird when its obsessively repeated song becomes the voice of her guilty conscience. Eckbert fulfills her fairy tale dreams of a handsome knight, but their marriage turns out anything but happily ever after once Bertha has revealed her secret past to their friend. Mysteriously, in bidding her good night, Walther refers to the name of the dog she had abandoned, Strohmian, and she is filled with "unspeakable terror" (Tieck 2000: 48) at the realization of his uncanny connection to her fate. Now Eckbert's only friend becomes a source of torment and threat. Eckbert kills him with a crossbow when out hunting one day, as Coleridge's Ancient Mariner shoots the albatross, having taken aim at Walther unconsciously, "without knowing what he was doing" (Tieck 2000: 48). Bertha simultaneously dies, and Eckbert is left alone, prey, as was Bertha, to continual self-reproach. Eckbert is befriended by a young knight named Hugo, only to have the same drama repeated. Compelled to confess his crime to Hugo, Eckbert afterwards imagines that Hugo is none other than Walther and he abandons forever "the notion of friendship, the desire for human contact" (Tieck 2000: 50).

Retreating into the woods, he rides aimlessly only to discover that he has retraced exactly Bertha's youthful journey. Face to face with the uncanny old woman, he learns that Walther and Hugo were merely products of her shape-shifting powers and that Bertha his wife was actually his sister who had been removed from his family at birth by a stepmother. The reader is compelled to question, along with Eckbert, the reality of all that happens to him: "[A]t times, his life seemed more akin to a strange fairy tale than reality, . . . and [h]e often felt that he must be insane and that everything was simply a wild figment of his imagination" (Tieck 2000: 49, 50). Eckbert expires, crazed by the realization of the "awful solitude" (Tieck 2000: 51) in which he has lived his life and admitting that he had indeed always suspected some horrible secret at the root of his melancholy marriage. In *Blond Eckbert*, Tieck creates an exemplary embodiment of the uncanny described by Freud as a feeling both strange and familiar produced by the surfacing of that which should have remained hidden. He also creates a remarkable study of existential solitude as the ultimate reality, the profound secret behind efforts at friendship and human communion. We recognize here the profoundly modern insights accorded the *Kunstmärchen* by virtue of its self-reflective presentation of folkloric themes.

If *Blond Eckbert* is Tieck's best-known tale, it is certainly not alone among his works in its reliance on folkloric structures and motifs. In fact, folkloric motifs and narrative structures are central to much of his work, from his early stories, *Almansur* (1790) and *Abdallah* (1792) to his epistolary novel *William Lovell* (ca. 1795-6) up to the fairy tales *Der Runenberg* (1801) and *Die Elfen* (1811). As if to acknowledge the centrality of the fairy tale not just to his own oeuvre but to Romantic aesthetics as a whole, during the years 1812-16, Tieck gathered together his earlier works in a frame novel, *Phantasus* which was modeled after Boccaccio's *Decameron* and Straparola's *The Pleasant Nights* (1550-3), the first known collection of European fairy tales united by a frame narrative. *The Pleasant Nights* features a group of exiled Milanese aristocrats seeking to entertain themselves by recounting fairy tales to one another. *Phantasus* brings together a group of landed gentry for the enjoyment of polite conversation and Romantic *Geselligkeit* (sociability) in an elegant and relaxed country house setting. The openness of this context allows room for the character Ernst's proto-Freudian forebodings of the troubling psychic sources of the *Märchenhaft* that might also be said to constitute a compendium of Romantic literary modes – sublime, grotesque, gothic, and fantastic:

> It is not just on the deserted heights of Gotthard that our spirit is filled with horror. . . even the most beautiful place has ghosts that stride through our heart, chasing such strange forebodings, such confused shadows through our imaginations, that we flee them and seek to lose ourselves in the hustle and bustle of the world. In this way, poems and fairy tales come into being in our inner selves as we seek to populate the vast emptiness, the terrible chaos with figures and to decorate the unpleasant room artistically; these pictures cannot then, however, deny the character of their creator. In these natural fairy tales the lovable is mixed with the horrific, the strange with the childish, such that our fantasy is perplexed to the point of poetic madness until this madness itself is let loose and freed in our inner self. (Tieck 1985: 112-13; my translation)

Phantasus contains not just Tieck's haunting fictional reworkings of folkloric themes, but also his plays based upon fairy tale motifs such as *Bluebeard, Little Red Riding Hood,* and *Puss in Boots,* the latter an exuberant, comic celebration of the nonrational in art and a farcical satire of contemporary theatrical tastes.

Just as Tieck had found Boccaccio and Straparola useful models, so Clemens Brentano wrote to Achim von Arnim, his coeditor of *Des Knaben Wunderhorn,* in December 1805 that he wanted to rework Basile's Neapolitan fairy tales, the *Pentameron* (1634) into a collection for German children. In the years 1805-17, Brentano completed 15 fairy tales and began four others. Eight of these completed tales were based upon motifs from the *Pentameron* and were woven together with a (fragmentary) frame tale entitled "The Fairy Tale of Fairy Tales." The rest of the tales feature motifs from the Rhine region and were gathered together in a collection that was also to remain incomplete. Indeed, Brentano showed no real concern for the publication of his tales and later denounced them as frivolous and sinful after his conversion to Catholicism. With his permission, they were finally published posthumously in 1846-7. In contrast to Novalis's metaphysical daring and Tieck's psychological depth, Brentano's tales resist analysis in their insistently performative quality and, as Marianne Thalmann has suggested, are reminiscent of *commedia dell'arte* and Punch and Judy shows.[2] His tales are further distinguished by their musicality, richness of wordplay, and the quirkiness of their humor which features comminglings of animal and human, nature and culture, chaos and order that border on what we would now term the absurd.

If Straparola and Basile were important models for Tieck and Brentano respectively in creating the frame tales for their *Märchen,* perhaps the most influential frame tale of all was *The Thousand and One Nights,* translated into French by Antoine Galland, published in 10 volumes between 1704 and 1717, and immediately disseminated throughout Europe. This literary historical fact helps explain the Orientalizing undercurrent that runs through so many Romantic fairy tales from Novalis's Klingsohr tale that identifies the imagination with Ginnistan (Hindostan) to the presence of the Bhagavad-Gita and hieroglyphics in Hoffmann's *The Golden Pot.* Thus Wilhelm Heinrich Wackenroder's *A Wondrous Oriental Fairy Tale of a Naked Saint* (1797), the most obvious example of the Romantic *Kunstmärchen*'s Orientalism opens: "The Orient is the home of all that is marvelous. In the ancient childlike views prevailing there, one finds strange signs and riddles still unsolved by Reason which considers itself so much more clever. Thus, for example, one often finds strange creatures living in the desert whom we would call mad, but who are there revered as supernatural beings" (Wackenroder 1983: 47). This "naked saint," a figure of Romantic madness and alienation, feels himself chained to a turning wheel in order to ensure the passage of time; in the end he is freed and transcends time itself by giving himself up to the spirit of music and love.

Despite their significant differences, the fairy tales of Goethe, Novalis, Tieck, Wackenroder, and Brentano have one notable trait in common — the universality and ahistoricity of their settings that align them with the "once upon a time" of the traditional folk fairy tale. With the works of E. T. A. Hoffmann, on the other hand, the Romantic fairy tale takes a step into the very specific social world of bourgeois nineteenth-century Germany. Indeed it is the tension between the magical and the mundane, the poetic and prosaic, the artistic and the worldly, the supernatural and the rational that forms the heart of Hoffmann's oeuvre. The richness of Hoffmann's imagination – his psychological perspicacity combined with a devastating sense of social satire, his compelling plots offset by vibrant symbolism – has rendered him the best-known and most influential of the practitioners of the Romantic *Kunstmärchen*. In France, Nodier, Nerval, Gautier, Baudelaire, Balzac, Dumas, and Sand all admired him enormously and owe him a great debt. In Russia the same can be said of Dostoevsky and Gogol. Carlyle's English translations of Hoffmann likely influenced Dickens. And the work of Poe and Hawthorne, from *Murders in the Rue Morgue* to *Rappaccini's Daughter*, is inconceivable without him, though the often unrecognized importance of Tieck's influence on these two American writers should also be acknowledged.

Folkloric and fairy-tale motifs abound in all of Hoffmann's works. In his most famous tale, *The Sandman*, the central literary example in Freud's essay on *The Uncanny*, for example, we read of the main character's sadistic nursemaid's version of the well-known bedtime story for children in which the Sandman throws sand into the eyes of naughty children so that their eyes will spring out of their heads and can be fed to his owl-like children. Hoffmann explicitly termed seven of his stories *Märchen*, presumably because of the preponderance of marvelous or supernatural elements in them and because of their tendency toward the happy endings that predominate in fairy tales: *The Golden Pot* (1814), *The Nutcracker and the Mouse King* (1816), *The Strange Child* (1817), *Little Zachary Named Cinnabar* (1818), *Princess Brambilla* (1820), *The King's Bride* (1820), and *Master Flea* (1822).

The Golden Pot, subtitled *A Modern Fairy Tale* and often considered to be Hoffmann's masterpiece in the *Kunstmärchen* genre, tells the tale of Anselmus, an unworldly and bungling student from Dresden, torn between his ambitions for a court councilor position and his longing for a realm of poetry and ideal beauty, between his attraction for a lively, flesh and blood woman named Veronica and the seductions of a gold-green snake named Serpentina. The text is divided into 12 sections entitled "vigils," as if to suggest that both the intrusive, tormented narrator and the reader are engaged in night watches of a dreamlike spirit world. In fact, as in many Hoffmann tales, the epistemological status of the perceptions of the main character is perhaps *the* central theme of the text, as the narrator makes clear:

> Gentle reader, make an effort while you are in the fairy region full of glorious marvels, where both the highest rapture and deepest horror may be evoked, where the earnest goddess herself lifts her veil so that we think we see her face, but a smile often glimmers beneath her glance, a playful teasing smile that enchants us just as that of a mother playing with her dearest children. While you are in this region that is revealed to us in dreams at least, try, gentle reader, to recognize the familiar shapes which hover around

you in the ordinary world. Then you will discover that this glorious kingdom is much closer to you than you ever imagined. It is this kingdom which I now strive with all my heart to reveal to you through the extraordinary story of Anselmus. (Hoffmann 1969: 32-3)

This fairy region, governed by the principles of alchemy and theosophy, is inhabited by a spirit named Phosphorous and his fire lily bride; their union produces the spark of thought and a fall from innocence that is ultimately repeated in the next generation when Serpentina's father, the archivist Lindhorst, an elemental fire spirit or salamander, is exiled to earth for marrying a snake against the will of Phosphorous, now the spirit realm's ruler. Lindhorst allows Anselmus access to this kingdom of dreams through his greenhouse/library/archive. Here in this room of azure and emerald reverberating with the sounds of birdsongs and crystal bells, it is Anselmus's task to copy perfectly a hieroglyphic, Orientalist manuscript, a book of nature found rolled up in the leaves of exotic palm trees.

If Lindhorst can marry off his three serpent daughters by finding for them youths of "childlike poetic nature" (Hoffmann 1969: 67) who understand their songs and believe in "the marvels of nature," or rather, in their own "existence amid these marvels" (Hoffmann 1969: 66), then he will be allowed to return home to Atlantis, the realm of the marvelous, accompanied by his son-in-law Anselmus. This tension between the everyday and the marvelous, the poetic and the prosaic, brings Anselmus to the brink of madness and nervous breakdown as he imagines himself imprisoned in a glass bottle that distorts his vision as punishment for spilling a blot of ink on the sacred document. In an effort to wrest Anselmus from the power of the salamander and the seductions of Serpentina, Veronica enlists the help of the witch Frau Rauerin, an earth spirit and the female counterpart of the archivist Lindhorst. Meanwhile Veronica's rationalist father fears that Anselmus is perpetually drunk or crazy and ends up himself succumbing to the effects of a steaming bowl of hot punch. In the end, Anselmus remains true to his ideals and is rewarded with the love of Serpentina and entrance into Atlantis, the Kingdom of Marvels. Veronica marries Registrar Heerbrand, who all along has clearly functioned as Anselmus's double, and lives happily ever after as Frau Court Councilor Heerbrand. The tale's conclusion, then, is read alternatively as recording Anselmus's suicide by drowning when, succumbing to madness, he throws himself into the glassy mirror of the waters of the Elbe, or as the resolution of the conflicts between the mundane and the ideal through poetry. The final sentence of *The Golden Pot* strongly supports the latter interpretation: "Is the bliss of Anselmus anything else but life in poetry, poetry where the sacred harmony of all things is revealed as the most profound secret of Nature?" (Hoffmann 1969: 92). Hoffmann's work, then, represents a culmination of the *Kunstmärchen* as an art form; *The Golden Pot* encompasses Brentano's whimsy and musicality, the psychological depth of Tieck and the metaphysical and cosmological daring of Novalis.

The most significant French practitioner of the Romantic-era *conte de fée*, Charles Nodier, was inspired by the work of Hoffmann as well as that of Goethe, Tieck, and

Arnim. In the preface to his best known and best loved tale, *La Fée aux miettes* (1832), Nodier evokes the charms of the tale-telling gifts of a Jura village patriarch, only to assert ultimately that in the current age of skepticism, authors must place their fantastic tales in the mouth of a lunatic if they are to gain the requisite credence. Accordingly, Michel, the hero of *La Fée aux miettes*, is a naïve carpenter whom the narrator finds in a Glasgow lunatic asylum. Michel is in search of a magical mandrake root that sings. In the epilogue we learn of Michel's grotesque fairy friend's connection to the singing mandrake; she eventually frees him from the asylum to marry her double, his ideal love, Belkiss, the Queen of Sheba, widow of King Solomon. (We see here once again the significance of Galland's *Thousand and One Nights*, for which Nodier wrote a preface in 1822 as well as the presence of Freemasonic lore, so prominent in both French and German Romanticism.) Finally, as in *The Golden Pot*, the aim of Nodier's tale is to reveal poetry's ability to reveal the inseparability of earthly and heavenly, mundane and magical worlds and the loves that inhabit them.

Half-forgotten Dreams and Elemental Spirits: Legacies of the Romantic Fairy Tale

After Hoffmann, fairy tale motifs and structures migrate increasingly into other genres beyond the *Kunstmärchen* per se – lyric and narrative poetry, drama, essay, novella, and short story. The sense of melancholy longing for an irretrievable past is also heightened, as we witness in Heinrich Heine's famous Lorelei lyric from "Die Heimkehr" (1823–4), about a beautiful siren whose singing lures sailors to their death:

> Ich weiß nicht, was soll es bedeuten,
> Daß ich so traurig bin;
> Ein Märchen aus alten Zeiten,
> Das kommt mir nicht aus dem Sinn.
>
> Die Luft ist kühl und es dunkelt,
> Und ruhig fließt der Rhein;
> Der Gipfel des Berges funkelt
> Im Abendsonnenschein.
>
> Die schönste Jungfrau sitzet
> Dort oben wunderbar,
> Ihr goldnes Geschmeide blitzet,
> Sie kammt ihr goldenes Haar.
>
> Sie kämmt es mit goldenem Kamme,
> Und singt ein Lied dabei;
> Das hat eine wundersame,
> Gewaltige Melodei.
>
> Den Schiffer im kleinen Schiffe
> Ergreift es mit wildem Weh;

Er schaut nicht die Felsenriffe,
Er schaut nur hinauf in die Höh.

Ich glaube, die Wellen verschlingen
Am Ende Schiffer und Kahn;
Und das hat mit ihrem Singen
Die Lorelei getan. (Heine 1969, I: 129-30)

Whereas the practitioners of the *Kunstmärchen* are fascinated with self-conscious development of experimental techniques and mechanisms to capture and illuminate the naïve, Heine above all else mourns its loss here. Identifying himself as a wild or crazed child seeking to conquer his fear of the dark through the recitation of folk songs, the poet's persona also reveals the desire for the naïve to be inseparable from a longing for a culturally repressed feminine that inevitably takes its revenge.

In a lighter and more humorous vein, Heine's essays *Elementargeister* (1835-6) and *Die Götter im Exil* (1853) manifest his appreciation for folklore as a vehicle for keeping alive the Germanic myth and Greco-Roman paganism that were demonized by the advent of Christianity. These essays have an ironic charm unique to Heine in the manner that their tongue-in-cheek representations and descriptions of mythical beings and elemental spirits matter of factly assert their unequivocal reality. *Elementargeister* begins by evoking the oral transmission from generation to generation of Germanic folklore as the lifeblood of German literature: "In Westphalia, the former Saxony, not everything that is buried is dead. When one walks through the ancient oak groves there, one hears the voices of olden times; one hears the echo of profound magic spells, in which more abundance of life flows than in all of Mark Brandenburg" (Heine 1969, III: 523; my translation). The spirit of Germanic folklore takes the form, for Heine, of an old woman buried alive by Saxon forces in their flight from Charlemagne's troops: "People say that the old woman still lives. Not everything that is buried in Westphalia is dead" (Heine 1969, III: 523; my translation). Once again for Heine, as with his Lorelei, the folkloric world is strongly associated with a female realm excluded from and perceived as threatening by official Christian dogma. Accordingly, many of the elemental spirits evoked by Heine are feminine: undines, melusines, and nixes (water), elves and willis (earth), and swan maidens (air). Heine's haunting remarks about these swan maidens who remove their feathered gowns to bathe, revealing and making themselves vulnerable as women, typify his stance in these essays. "Here we find traces of the oldest life of magic. Here are the sounds of Nordic paganism, that, like half forgotten dreams, find wonderful resonance in our memories" (Heine 1969, III: 538; my translation). For Heine, the female flight of these maidens was originally something remarkable and worthy; Christianity sullied and corrupted it into the flight of repugnant witches on broomsticks.

These female elemental spirits – water spirits or undines in particular – based in the lore of Paracelsus's *Liber de nymphis, sylphis, pygmaeis et salamandris et de caeteris spiritibus* (1591), are a rich source of inspiration for a wide variety of Romantic literary genres. Huguenot Friedrich de la Motte Fouqué's *Undine* (1811) transforms the Melusine of chapbook legend and of Jean d'Arras's 1387 prose romance into one of the most enduring and influential of the German *Kunstmärchen*. *The Golden Pot* was begun the year Hoffmann completed his opera *Undine* (1813) for which Fouqué wrote the libretto, and Hoffmann's Serpentina is clearly a kindred spirit of Melusine/Undine. Fouqué's *Undine* tells the tale of a water spirit who can gain a soul only by marrying a human being and gaining his unconditional love. Undine does indeed capture the heart of the knight Huldbrand and marry him, thus acquiring a soul and with it the capacity to suffer love and to shed tears – a sacred sign of her humanity. Then Bertalda, the adopted daughter of a noble family who was in fact exchanged with Undine at birth, such that the heroine was raised by the humble fisher folk who are Bertalda's true parents, moves in with the newly married couple. Eventually, Huldbrand turns from Undine to Bertalda, alienated and intimidated by Undine's preternatural powers and her familial links with the world of elemental spirits. Huldbrand's betrayal forces Undine to return to her natural element and compels her against her will to wreak vengeance upon him according to the laws of her watery world; on the night of his wedding with Bertalda, she drowns him with her tears. Through his narrator, Fouqué gives us the ostensible message of his novella in his moralizing critique of fairy-tale wish fulfillment: "That treacherous power which lurks, waiting to destroy us, takes pleasure in singing its intended victims to sleep with sweet songs and golden fairy tales. In contrast, the messenger sent from Heaven to save us often knocks loudly and frighteningly at our door" (Fouqué 2000: 113). Perhaps the strongest "message" that Undine conveys to a twenty-first-century reader is the necessity to honor the powers of nature as they are embodied in its heroine. Indeed reader sympathy lies entirely with Undine rather than Huldbrand or Bertalda, implying perhaps unconscious protofeminism on the part of Fouqué who clearly emphasizes the fascination of the woman who transgresses the bounds of culturally constructed femininity in the naturalness of her passion as well as highlighting the tragic consequences of the Christian soul/body split and of the ethic of compulsory female self-sacrifice. Certainly, Germaine de Staël interpreted the undine motif in this feminist fashion, for her *Corinne, or Italy* (1807), the prototypical and enormously influential nineteenth-century novel of the female artist, abandoned by her lover because of her socially transgressive genius, was inspired by an 1804 performance in Weimar of an earlier theatrical version of the legend, the Hensler opera *The Nymph of the Danube* (Balayé 1979: 107).

The Melusine of Letitia Landon's narrative poem *The Fairy of the Fountains* (1835), undoubtedly influenced by Staël's *Corinne*, is also clearly an emblem of female sexual and artistic power. The protofeminism of Landon's Melusine is hardly surprising if we acknowledge in her prefatory remarks to the poem a particularly keen awareness of the historical and cultural specificity of a given variation on a fairy tale motif: "I have allowed myself some license, in my arrangement of the story: but fairy tales have an old-established privilege of change; at least, if we judge by the various shapes which they assume in the progress of time, and by process of translation" (Landon 1997:

225). Along with her mother, Landon's Melusine has been exiled from her rightful kingdom because of her father's transgression of the boundaries of her mother's world; entering her mother's fairy realm without her permission, he sought out her "secret bower" and listened "to the word / Mortal ear hath never heard" (Landon 1997: 228). Avenging her mother's wrong, Melusine employs her own magical powers to bind her father in an enchanted sleep and inter him in a mountain cave. Upon learning of Melusine's deed, her mother banishes her, in a kind of intergenerational repetition compulsion, and curses her such that every seventh day she is transformed into a snake from the waist down. Once she marries, the cycle is repeated, as her husband Raymond breaks the marital taboo, seeks her out in her fountain cave and discovers her serpentine form, dooming them both to separation and despair: "Hope and happiness are o'er, / They can meet on earth no more" (Landon 1997: 241). In Jean d'Arras's original prose poem, it is the secret of women's biological creativity that must be kept from men; the father/husband is forbidden to visit the mother during her lyings-in and her subsequent preparation of her children to enter life. In Landon's poem, Melusine's magical lineage is that of the female poet, for it is the father's eavesdropping on the mother's "more than mortal" *words* that brings doom upon all involved. The mother clearly recognizes her daughter's "fairy power" as the power of the imagination that distinguishes the socially ostracized woman poet:

> And she marked her daughter's eyes
> Fix'd upon the glad sunrise,
> With a sad yet eager look,
> Such as fixes on a book
> Which describes some happy lot,
> Lit with joys that we have not.
> And the thought of what has been,
> And the thought of what might be,
> Makes us crave the fancied scene,
> And despise reality.
> 'Twas a drear and desert plain
> Lay around their sad domain;
> But, far off, a world more fair
> Outlined on the sunny air;
> Hung amid the purple clouds,
> With which early morning shrouds
> All her blushes, brief and bright,
> Waking up from sleep and night. (Landon 1997: 228)

Melusine's serpentine form furthermore links her to the Geraldine of Coleridge's *Christabel* and Keats's Lamia as female embodiments of the seductive and treacherous powers of the imagination.

In the most renowned version of the undine/melusine legend, Hans Christian Andersen's *The Little Mermaid* (1837), the mermaid comes to represent the feminized

Romantic poet who loses his voice and cannot be understood or appreciated by the world of the nineteenth-century bourgeois philistine. In Andersen's version of the tale, both excruciatingly sentimental and searingly brutal, the mermaid once again longs for the chance to marry the handsome prince and gain an immortal soul. Her tail must be cut in two to form human legs, but she will never walk on earth without pain. As the witch who grants her the transformation explains: "every step you take will be like treading on a sharp knife" (Andersen 1983: 60). Similarly, she must give up her beautiful voice when the witch extracts her tongue as payment for her services. Unable to speak, she cannot tell the prince that it is she who has saved his life; he mistakenly believes it is a mortal woman, whom he then marries. Unlike Fouqué's *Undine*, however, Andersen's mermaid transcends the laws of her watery world and refuses to kill the prince, though the act would free her to return to her beautiful ocean realm. In the tale's Christianized conclusion, she is raised to the level of the spirits of the air who do not need the love of a human to become immortal. She will bring relief and healing to humankind with her cooling breezes and, after three hundred years of goodness, will "gain an immortal soul and eternal happiness" (Andersen 1983: 71). In Andersen's little mermaid we recognize the Romantic artist, sympathetic with and in tune with nature, having appropriated its traditionally feminine valence, but out of his element in human society. We also see, as in Andersen's *The Nightingale* (1843) the working-class or peasant poet as voice not just of nature but also of socioeconomic groups marginalized, taken for granted, and even exploited by the bourgeoisie and aristocracy, as Andersen experienced his relations with his patrons, Jonas Collin and his son Edvard (Zipes 1999: 82-5).

The figure of the undine or mermaid is one of the most enduring legacies of the Romantic fairy tale to later literature. The late French Romantic Gérard de Nerval finds her in the heroine of *Octavia* from *Daughters of Fire* (1854). Called away from Paris by "an enchanting voice, a siren's song" (Nerval 1999: 197), the world-weary narrative persona finds Octavia at the bay of Marseilles. This water nymph, "an English girl, her lithe body slicing through the green water at my side" (Nerval 1999: 197), presents him triumphantly with a fish she has caught in her bare white hands. Years later, he meets up with her in Naples, her freedom and beauty sacrificed to the care of a paralytic, insanely jealous husband and an invalid father. Once again we see here a haunting female power trapped or violated by a threatened masculinity. In contemporary culture, the undine figure continues to thrive in modern fairy tales from Jane Yolen's *The River Maid* (1982), a tale of revenge by a water maiden for her imprisonment and rape by an arrogant farmer who dares to move a riverbed, to Disney's *The Little Mermaid*, A. S. Byatt's immensely popular academic fairy tale *Possession* (1990), Carol Goodman's recent murder mystery *The Seduction of Water* (2003), and John Sayles's film *The Secret of Roan Inish* (1994).

Though the *Kunstmärchen* experiences a revival in Victorian and late nineteenth-century Britain and America with the writings of Charles Dickens, Oscar Wilde, Christina Rossetti, and Frances Hodgson Burnett and again in the latter half of the twentieth century in the feminist fairy tales of Angela Carter, Ursula LeGuin, Anne

Sexton, and Olga Broumas who reclaim and rewrite the Romantic association of women, nature, and the nonrational, never again is the genre marked by such a clear effort to celebrate and replicate, at a self-conscious level, the naïve, folkloric voice.[3] Hans Christian Andersen acknowledges the futility of this search for the natural and naïve in his *A Rose from the Grave of Homer*, a brief allegory that serves as a moving and merciless critique of European Romanticism and of his own work in particular. This rose grows from the soil on Homer's grave, soil nourished by the dead bodies of nightingales who die from unrequited love for her, just as the striving, suffering, and melancholy of sentimental poets nurtures the myth of the naïve. Echoing the familiar, indeed by then outworn, classic/Romantic, North/South taxonomy inherited from Staël and A. W. Schlegel, Andersen continues, "a singer from the North, the home of clouds and of the Northern light" (Andersen 1983: 292), plucks this rose growing on Homer's grave and takes it home. "Like a mummy the flower corpse now rests in his *Iliad*, and, as in a dream, she hears him open the book and say, 'Here is a rose from the grave of Homer' " (Andersen 1983: 293). Though Andersen would seem to announce the inevitable sterility of this Romantic search for the "pure" art of storytelling found in the collective voice, Walter Benjamin rekindles this longing in his influential and eloquent essay on "The Storyteller" ([1936] 1969) which opens by proclaiming the death of the art of storytelling. Such nostalgia in one of Europe's most clear-sighted and prescient twentieth-century critics suggests that the legacy of the European *Kunstmärchen* remains a powerful one and that even today the genre is far from extinct.

NOTES

1 Ellis writes, "[T]he Grimms deliberately deceived their public by concealing or actually misstating the facts, in order to give an impression of ancient German folk origin for their material which they knew was utterly false" (Ellis 1983: 36).

2 According to Thalmann, "Brentanos Märchen ist kein Weltanschauungsmärchen mehr, es ist auf das Kasperletheater gestellt..." (Brenta-

no's fairy tales no longer seek to represent a worldview; they are like a Punch and Judy show...; Thalmann 1961: 65, my translation).

3 For a fascinating Romantic precursor to these feminist fairy tales, see Bettine Brentano von Arnim's *Der Königssohn*, written in 1808 but not published until 1913, and English translation (1990).

REFERENCES AND FURTHER READING

Abrams, M. H. (1971). *Natural Supernaturalism – Tradition and Revolution in Romantic Literature*. New York: W. W. Norton.

Andersen, Hans Christian (1983). *The Complete Illustrated Stories*, trans. H. W. Dulcken. London: Chancellor.

Arnim, Achim von (1992). *Schriften. Werke in Sechs Bänden*, ed. Roswitha Burwick, Jürgen Knaack, and Hermann F. Weiss, vol. 6. Frankfurt am Main: Deutscher Klassiker Verlag.

Balayé, Simone (1979). *Madame de Staël: Lumières et liberté*. Paris: Klincksieck.

Benjamin, Walter (1969). "The Storyteller: Reflections on the Works of Nikolai Leskov." In *Illuminations*, ed. Hannah Arendt, trans. Harry Zohn. New York: Schocken, pp. 83-109.

Brentano, Clemens (2000). "Tale of Honest Casper and Fair Annie." In Carol Tully (ed. and trans.), *Romantic Fairy Tales*. London: Penguin, pp. 127-59.

Dai Sijie (2001). *Balzac and the Little Chinese Seamstress*, trans. Ina Rilke. New York: Knopf.

Ellis, John M. (1983). *One Fairy Story Too Many*. Chicago: University of Chicago Press.

Fouqué, Friedrich de la Motte (2000). "Undine." In Carol Tully (ed. and trans.), *Romantic Fairy Tales*. London: Penguin, pp. 53-125.

Goethe, Johann Wolfgang von (2000). "The Fairy Tale." In Carol Tully (ed. and trans.), *Romantic Fairy Tales*. London: Penguin, pp. 1-32.

Heine, Heinrich (1969). *Sämtliche Werke*, ed. Werner Vortriede, 4 vols. München: Winkler Verlag.

Herder, Johann Gottfried (1993). *Schriften zur Ästhetik und Literatur, 1767-1781. Werke*, ed. Gunter E. Grimm, vol. 2. Frankfurt am Main: Deutscher Klassiker Verlag.

Hoffmann, Ernst Theodor Amadeus (1969). *Tales of E .T. A. Hoffmann*, ed. and trans. Leonard J. Kent and Elizabeth C. Knight. Chicago: University of Chicago Press.

Jauss, Hans Robert (1970). *Literaturgeschichte als Provokation*. Frankfurt: Suhrkamp.

Landon, Letitia Elizabeth (1997). *Selected Writings*, ed. Jerome McGann and Daniel Riess. Peterborough, ON: Broadview.

Nerval, Gérard de (1999). *Selected Writings*, ed. and trans. Richard Sieburth. London: Penguin.

Nodier, Charles (1961). *Contes*, ed. Pierre-Georges Castex. Paris: Garnier.

Novalis (Georg Friedrich Philipp von Hardenberg) (1960). *Schriften*, ed. Paul Kluckhohn and Richard Samuel, 4 vols. Stuttgart: W. Kohlhammer Verlag.

Novalis. (1964). *Henry von Ofterdingen*, ed. and trans. Palmer Hilty. New York: Frederick Ungar.

Rousseau, Jean-Jacques (1990). *The First and Second Discourses and Essay on the Origin of Languages*, ed. and trans. Victor Gourevitch. New York: Harper and Row.

Schiller, Friedrich (1966). *Naïve and Sentimental Poetry and On the Sublime*, ed. and trans. Julias Elias. New York: Ungar.

Sychrava, Juliet (1989). *Schiller to Derrida: Idealism in Aesthetics*. Cambridge, UK and New York: Cambridge University Press.

Tatar, Maria (2003). *The Hard Facts of the Grimms' Fairy Tales*. Princeton, NJ: Princeton University Press.

Thalmann, Marianne (1961). *Das Märchen und die Moderne*. Stuttgart: W. Kohlhammer.

Tieck, Ludwig (1985). *Phantasus. Schriften*, ed. Manfred Frank, vol. 6. Frankfurt am Main: Deutscher Klassiker Verlag.

Tieck, Ludwig (2000). "Eckbert the Fair." In Carol Tully (ed. and trans.), *Romantic Fairy Tales*. London: Penguin, pp. 35-51.

von Arnim, Bettina (1913). "Der Königssohn." *Westermanns Monatshefte*, 113: 554-8.

von Arnim, Bettina (1990). "The Queen's Son." In *Bitter Healing: German Women Writers from 1700 to 1830*, ed. and trans. Jeannine Blackwell and Susanne Zantop. Lincoln: University of Nebraska Press, pp. 450-4.

Wackenroder, Wilhelm Heinrich (1983). "A Wondrous Oriental Fairy Tale of a Naked Saint." In Frank G. Ryder and Robert M. Browning (eds.), *German Literary Fairy Tales*, trans. R. M. Browning. New York: Continuum, pp. 47-51.

Zipes, Jack (1999). *When Dreams Came True: Classical Fairy Tales and Their Tradition*. New York and London: Routledge.

9

German Romantic Drama

Frederick Burwick

Although scorned as "sickly and stupid" by William Wordsworth in his Preface (1800) to the *Lyrical Ballads* (Wordsworth 1974, 1: 128), German tragedies attracted huge audiences in London. The influence of German drama on the British stage increased in the 1780s, and by the end of the 1790s, as noted by Allardyce Nicoll, "the enthusiasm for the drama of Kotzebue and his companions" had risen to a height of popularity (Nicoll 1927: 66, quoted in Wordsworth 1974: 172n.). Although many German plays were adapted for the British stage, there was little interest in the "destiny drama" (*Schicksalstragödie*) that enjoyed a decade of popularity in Germany early in the nineteenth century. Best exemplified in Zacharias Werner's *The Twenty-fourth of February* (1806; *Der vierundzwanzigste Februar*), these plays depicted a character compelled by a malignant destiny to commit a horrible crime. The concept of *fate* from classical Greek drama was redefined in terms of contemporary notions of nature, nurture, and familial pathology. Extremely popular, however, were the plays of August von Kotzebue, with more than 20 adaptations performed on the London stage between 1796 and 1801. Kotzebue's *Menschenhass und Reue* (1789), translated by Benjamin Thompson as *The Stranger* (1798), starred Sarah Siddons in the role of Mrs Haller and John Phillip Kemble in the title-role of the Stranger. Sarah Siddons also played Elvira, the conqueror's mistress, opposite Kemble's Rolla, the Peruvian hero in *Pizarro* (1799), adapted by Richard Brinsley Sheridan from Kotzebue's *Die Spanier in Peru*. Among Kotzebue's comedies, *Kind der Liebe* was adapted by Elizabeth Inchbald as *Lovers' Vows* (1798). For Wordsworth, "sickly and stupid" apparently referred to the sentimentalism. William Hazlitt, however, ranked Kemble's performance as the Stranger superior to his Shakespearean roles.[1]

As Charles Shadduck suggests, there may be something underhanded in such high praise: "The cunningest trick available to the theater critic who wants to cut an actor down to size is to bypass his efforts in the great test roles – Macbeth or Hamlet – and praise him unstintingly in some role which is rather less than first-class" (Shattuck 1974, 11: i). On the other hand, the applause of the critics for the performances of

Kotzebue's plays drowns out those who grumble that they are "sickly and stupid." Wordsworth, who read with enthusiasm Friedrich Schiller's *Die Räuber* when Alexander Fraser Tytler's translation appeared in 1797, readily appropriated many of its dramatic elements into the completion of his *The Borderers* (Wordsworth 1982).[2] Wordsworth may well have been introduced to Schiller's play by Samuel Taylor Coleridge, who was drawing from it even more liberally in his composition of *Osorio* (1797), later modified as *Remorse* (1813). In terms of style and complexity of character, one may grant Schiller a literary achievement greater than Kotzebue, but to discriminate between high and low culture does not work well either for the immediate or for the subsequent reception. Kotzebue's plays, especially his comedies, remained popular throughout the nineteenth century; his librettos, set to music by Ludwig van Beethoven, Franz Schubert, and Carl Maria von Weber, continue to enjoy frequent revival.

Storm and Stress, Destiny Drama

When first performed, Schiller's *Die Räuber* (1781) impressed its critics as an assault upon the establishment driven by the rebellious tendencies of the *Sturm und Drang* movement. In leading his renegade band against the tyrannical rule of his brother, Karl Moor finds himself defeated by his own choices, his rebellion doomed to futility. A key word in the play is "despair" (*Verzweiflung*), repeated 17 times in the play, seven times by the old Count Moor in his self-recrimination for having denounced his son. "My curse drove him into death! He fell into despair!" (Mein Fluch ihn gejagt in den Tod! gefallen in Verzweiflung!) The words of the old Count are also echoed by Karl, by his wicked brother Franz, and by the loyal soldier Hermann. It is not the heroic Karl, but the villainous Franz who denounces the value of life and the immortal soul:

> Ich habs immer gelesen, daß unser Wesen nichts ist als Sprung des Geblüts, und mit dem letzten Blutstropfen zerrinnt auch Geist und Gedanke. Er macht alle Schwachheiten des Körpers mit, wird er nicht auch aufhören bei seiner Zerstörung? nicht bei seiner Fäulung verdampfen? Laß einen Wassertropfen in deinem Gehirne verirren, und dein Leben macht eine plötzliche Pause, die zunächst an das Nichtsein grenzt, und ihre Fortdauer ist der Tod. Empfindung ist Schwingung einiger Saiten, und das zerschlagene Klavier tönet nicht mehr.

> (I have always read that our whole body is nothing more than a blood-spring, and that, with its last drop, mind and thought dissolve into nothing. They share all the infirmities of the body; why, then, should they not cease with its dissolution? Why not evaporate in its decomposition? Let a drop of water stray into your brain, and life makes a sudden pause, which borders on nonexistence, and this pause continued is death. Sensation is the vibration of a few chords, which, when the instrument is broken, cease to sound.) (Schiller *Die Räuber*, Act V, scene i)[3]

Pastor Moser tells Franz that this is the "philosophy of your despair," and as the tragedy comes to a close he accuses Franz for have purchased his brief triumph with "infinite despair."

In his historical drama *Götz von Berlichingen* (1773), Johann Wolfgang von Goethe turned to the time of the Peasants' Rebellion (1524-6). Götz may have been an unlikely hero, but Goethe transformed him from the robber-baron who plundered traveling merchants into a defiant champion of freedom and leader of the peasants in the war against oppressive tyrants. Goethe gains sympathy for his hero by contrasting his loyalty to his soldiers with the betrayal and villainy of the former friend of his youth, Adelbert von Weislingen. Weislingen falls in love with Götz's sister Maria and they are engaged. When Weislingen returns to the court of the Bishop of Bamberg, however, he is seduced by Adelheid, who persuades him to abandon Maria, betray Götz, and send the Kaiser's troops against him. The moving forces in this play are oppression versus freedom, betrayal versus loyalty. With their last bottle of wine, Götz proposes a toast, "Long live the Kaiser!" His comrades echo the toast. And what would be their final toast, Götz asks, when their life's blood should flow away and only the last precious drop should remain in their cup. They answer: "Long live freedom!" Götz's very identity is in that freedom. When his wife visits him imprisoned in the tower, he tells her that she seeks him in vain, for Götz is no more: "They have mutilated me piece by piece: my hand, my freedom, my lands, my good name. My head? what does it matter." The betrayer is also betrayed. The final drop in the cup for Weislingen is poison administered by Adelheid, who wants him out of the way so that she can pursue a liaison with the future Kaiser. At the play's end, Götz's dying words are "Freedom! Freedom!"

As Edgar Johnson observed in commenting on Sir Walter Scott's translation of *Götz von Berlichingen*, published in 1799, "the significance of Scott's labor . . . is not what he did for Goethe, but what Goethe did for him" (Johnson 1970, I: 165). Goethe's use of history, a subtle superimposition of the past on the present, anticipated and directed Scott's use of history in the Waverley novels. Even after the initial popularity of the *Sturm und Drang* movement had passed, the theme of revolt against oppression persisted in German drama throughout the Romantic period. Writing at the time of the French occupation of Germany, Schiller's *Wilhelm Tell* (1804) celebrated the oath of the Swiss confederates on the Rütli, swearing to overthrow the Habsburg occupation at the beginning of the fourteenth century. Two historical events in 1803 influenced Schiller's composition of *Wilhelm Tell*: the French troops completed their occupation of Hannover and the Act of Mediation restored independence to the Swiss Cantons. "When will the savior of this land come?" asks the fisherman Ruodi at the close of Act I, scene i. That Tell is the "Savior" (*Retter*) is soon acknowledged by both the Habsburg Bailiff Gessler and the Schwyzer citizen Stauffaucher. Gessler, of course, gives him that title ironically – "Savior, save yourself!" – when he commands Tell to shoot the apple from his son's head. For Schiller, freedom is exemplified through acts of humane kindness and charity, in contrast to the selfish and ruthless acts of the tyrannical despots.

In the 1830s, when liberal factions seeking constitutional reform were caught up in rivalry amongst themselves, Georg Büchner in *Dantons Tod* (1836) dramatized the Gerondist–Jacobin conflict of the 1790s. Writing at the end of the Romantic period, Büchner appropriates and redefines many trends and motifs of the earlier generation. He considered the once popular "destiny" drama (*Schicksalstragödie*) naïve and he parodied its pretensions in the dialogue that closes Act II, scene ii. Two gentlemen are strolling the promenade. One has been expounding the wonders of man's technical genius: "Humanity hastens with giant steps toward its lofty destination." This ecstatic millennialism reminds the other of a new play he has just seen: "A Babylonian tower, a maze of arches, staircases, passages, and all so lightly and boldly blown to bits." He recalls nothing of the human events, only the architectural grandeur and explosive stage effects. The mere recollection of the illusion, however, so overwhelms the speaker that he mistrusts the reality of the terra firma: "One becomes dizzier with every step, the head spins." He staggers and clutches his companion's hand: "Yes, the earth has a thin crust. I always imagine that I could fall through wherever there's a hole. One must walk carefully in order not to break through. But go to the theater, I recommend it" (II. ii). Not merely comic relief, this scene reflects the major motif – "All the world's a stage, / And all the men and women merely players." Büchner does not resort idly to the Shakespearean trope, he uses it to transform *Schicksalstragödie* into an existential impasse. Not just as players upon the stage, as Danton's friend Camille observes in the scene that follows, humanity is condemned to play as wooden marionettes in a puppet theater (II. iii). Büchner argues that the playwright is a historian whose task it is to re-enact with fidelity the events of history, but he also confesses that that his study of the French Revolution left him feeling "destroyed by the terrible fatalism of history," where action is but "a puppet theater, a ridiculous struggle against brazen law, which we might possibly recognize but never command" (Büchner to Minna Jaegle, after 10 March 1834, in Büchner [1813-37] 1992-9, II: 425-6).

In *Dantons Tod*, Büchner radically redefined the earlier "destiny" drama, combining it with the *fiabesque* implications of his puppet metaphor. The fiabesque (from the Italian folk tales, the *fiabe*) had been imported onto the German stage with the revival of the *commedia dell'arte*, and Büchner used its conventions in his comedy, *Leonce und Lena* (1835), and even more profoundly in his grotesque tragedy, *Woyzeck* (1836-7), in which the *commedia dell'arte* characters Capitano and Dottore are given darkly malevolent roles. The hapless and apparently witless Pedrolino character is Woyzeck himself, servant to the Captain, who treats him as a stupid animal. Woyzeck also earns a few pennies by allowing the Doctor to experiment on him. The Doctor feeds him nothing but peas in order to prove some unstated scientific premise. Woyzeck discovers his girlfriend Marie, the Columbina of the play, having an affair with the dandified drum major, the Brighella character. He brings Marie to the side of a pond and slits her throat. Returning to town, Woyzeck gets drunk. Imagining that people are watching him with suspicion, he returns to the pond, throws the bloody knife in, then, trying to throw it into even deeper water, presumably drowns.

Commedia dell'arte, fiabesque

In an effort to establish neoclassical principles on the Italian stage, Carlo Goldoni (1707-93) advocated a ban on *commedia dell'arte*, and he was successful in that he was challenged by Carlo Gozzi (1720-1806), who considered the improvisational tradition too essential a part of the Italian theatrical heritage to be abolished. On his revival of the *commedia dell'arte*, Gozzi gave to the Italian folk players the materials of the Italian *fiabe*. He preserved the stock characters: Pantalone, Capitano, Dottore, Pedrolino, Isabella, Columbina, Arlecchino, Scaramouche, Pulchinella, Truffaldino, Brighella, and for his plots he adapted the popular tales, *Il re cervo* (1762; The King Stag), *La Donna serpente* (1762; The Serpent Woman), *L'amore delle tre melarance* (1763; The Love of Three Oranges), *L'augellino belverde* (1765; The Green Bird). Friedrich von Schlegel, the Romantic critic, praised Gozzi as Italy's leading playwright, and Schiller turned Gozzi's *Turandot* into a serious play, but it was Ludwig Tieck (1773-1853) who recognized the full potential of Gozzi's defiance of neoclassical rule.

With the same rationale as Goldini's, of insuring a more enlightened neoclassical theater, Johann Christoph Gottsched (1700-66) had banned Hanswurst (John Sausage), the impudent and irreverent clown, from the German stage. Tieck was determined to bring him back as Germany's equivalent to the traditional improvisational player; Germany also had its traditional folk tales, the *Märchen*. In 1797, Tieck produced his first folk tale comedies (*Märchenspiele*): *Blue-Beard* (*Ritter Blaubart*), *Puss-in-Boots* (*Der gestiefelte Kater*), followed by *Prinz Zerbino* (1799), *The Topsy-Turvy World* (1800; *Die verkehrte Welt*), and *Little Red Riding Hood* (1800; *Rotkäppchen*). In defying neoclassical principles, Tieck informed his comedies with a relentless disruption of dramatic illusion that exemplified Romantic irony, as defined by Friedrich Schlegel,[4] and was praised by his brother, August Wilhelm Schlegel, as an elaboration of the Shakespearean "play within a play." Tieck had turned that device inside-out with a "play about a play" (A. W. Schlegel 1828).

The disruption of illusion was wrought by "what is not in the play" intruding upon the performance. In *Puss-in-Boots*, one supposedly expects an enactment of the folk tale. The first characters to appear on the stage, however, are the audience, a fictive audience, who begin to criticize the play even before the first act begins. Their dialogue is about the nature of theatrical illusion and the credibility of performance. How can one "enter into a reasonable illusion" when the main character is a talking cat? The audience are the first and most vociferous intruders, but their complaints call forth the playwright and the stage technician; the cat is joined by Hanswurst, and neither is content to play out their roles. The audience rebels, the characters rebel, and in the final scene the performers are upstaged by the stage itself, with Karl Schinkel's opulent decorations imported from *The Magic Flute*.

Introduced by Tieck in the 1790s, *fiabesque* comedy was not always shaped by the same predilection for metadramatic self-reflexivity nor by the same ironic undercutting of its own fantasy. At the outset of his career, Clemens Brentano (1778-1842) sketched over a dozen plays, and brought several to publication: *Gustav Wasa* (1800), *Ponce de Leon* (1801; published 1804), *The Merry Musicians* (1803; *Die lustigen Musikanten*). When Kotzebue ridiculed Friedrich and August Wilhelm Schlegel in his satirical comedy, *The Hyperborean Jackass* (1799; *Der hyperborische Esel*), Brentano came to their defense with a farce in the manner of Tieck's *Puss-in-Boots*. Brentano's *Gustav Wasa* was meant as a counterattack on Kotzebue, who had just written an historical play of the same title. Kotzebue's play was the product of his unfortunate visit to Russia in 1800, where, suspected of Jacobin politics, he was banished to Siberia until he was granted a reprieve after imprisonment for four months. Kotzebue's play celebrates Gustav Wasa as leader of the Swedish liberation following the Danish invasion under Christian II. Following the Massacre of Stockholm, 1520, which culminated with the execution of the leaders of the Swedish national party, Gustav led the people to overthrow the Danish occupation. Gustav was crowned Gustav I in 1523. Henry Brooke had already adapted the subject as historical drama in *Gustavus Vasus, The Deliverer of His Country* (1739), first performed in Dublin in 1744, and revived at Covent Garden, London, in 1805. In his version, Kotzebue's stresses not revolution but nationalism. Satirizing the political ideology of the brothers Schlegel, Kotzebue's *The Hyperborean Jackass* puts their words into the mouth of one of his characters. To make sure that no one misses the point, the published version asserts the fact in introducing the dramatis personae, again in the dedication to the Schlegels as editors of the *Athenäum*, and yet again by underlining all of the verbatim passages in the text.

Brentano seeks to avenge the Schlegels by turning Kotzebue's own method against him. In his parodied version of *Gustav Wasa,* Brentano has his comic character speak Kotzebue's words with the effect that pathos lapses into bathos. The satire may have been addressed against Kotzebue, but Brentano was so adept in mimicking the style of *Puss-in-Boots* that Tieck thought himself the target of a devastating parody.[5] In spite of his appropriation of Tieck's "play about a play" strategy, Brentano develops none of the metadramatic possibilities. When a drunken actor is interviewed in the tavern, or when the fictive audience studies the playbill in the theater, there is no turnabout confusion of what is not "in" the play. Brentano is so completely preoccupied with the intertextual confrontations of parody that he pays no attention to the self-reflexive potential of the dramatic situation.

The Merry Musicians, the only one of Brentano's plays to gain success on the stage, owed its popularity to the combination of melodrama and the antics of *commedia dell'arte*. The music for the melodrama was composed by Peter Ritter (1763-1846), director of the theater orchestra in Mannheim, where he conducted the performances in 1804 and 1805. E. T. A. Hoffmann provided a more elaborate musical setting and produced it as a comic opera at the Warsaw German Theater in 1805. In his appraisal of *The Merry Musicians*, Hoffmann repeats Hamlet's remarks to the players: "The play...pleased not the million; 'twas caviar to the general." Hoffmann liked it – not in spite of but because of its fantastic excesses. Following the example of Tieck's fiabesque comedies, Brentano had appropriated the *commedia dell'arte* masques.

"But! – Holy Gozzi," exclaimed Hoffmann, "what misbegotten creatures have been produced out of the attractive characters of that jovial mischief" (letter to Theodor Hippel, Sept. 26, 1805, Hoffmann 1967-9, I: 193-4; see also Allroggen 1970: 26-7, 43-61).

The *fiabesque* maintained its popularity on the stage throughout the Romantic period. As already acknowledged, as late as 1835 Büchner turned to the *fiabesque* in his *Leonce und Lena*. Tieck's methods are even more obvious in Christian Dietrich Grabbe's *Jest, Satire, Irony, and Deeper Meaning* (1822; *Scherz, Satire, Ironie, und tiefere Bedeutung*). As his title indicates, Grabbe is attentive to metadramatic self-reflexivity. His characters do not step out of their roles, but they call attention to their role-playing and being in a play. Just as Tieck called attention to the staging of Wolfgang Amadeus Mozart's *The Magic Flute* (1791; *Die Zauberflöte*), Grabbe refers to Carl Maria Weber's *The Marksman* (1821; *Der Freischütz*). Weber's opera mingles ingredients well known to German Romanticism: simple peasant virtues threatened by the demonic magic and latent evil of the forest, and a pact with the Devil. Grabbe's play draws upon, but burlesques, the same ingredients. Liddy, the niece and sole heir of Baron von Haldungen, is engaged to Wernthal, who has sought her hand in marriage because he needs her money to pay off his gambling debts. She is also sought after by Freiherr von Mordax who wants her as a sexual plaything; if she continues to resist his overtures he intends to abduct and rape her. She is loved by Mollfels, a longtime friend who, considering himself too ugly and unworthy to court her, has left on an extended journey. Returning just as the play opens, Mollfels seeks out his friends in the village – the schoolmaster and Rattengift (Rat-poison), the poet – to inquire after Liddy's wellbeing. The schoolmaster complains that his talents are wasted on local dunces who have no desire to learn. He is visited by Tobies, a farmer, who pledges victuals and brandy if the schoolmaster will tutor his son, Gottliebchen, and prepare him for the clergy. Although the boy is a complete dullard, the schoolmaster agrees, and plans to take him to Haldungen Hall and seek a further stipend by passing him off as a promising genius. When Mollfels arrives at the schoolhouse, he finds himself in the company of the poet, the dullard, and the schoolmaster. Mollfels is depressed at the news that Liddy is now engaged, and the others attempt to cheer him by getting thoroughly drunk. Almost simultaneous with Mollfels's return, the Devil is ousted from Hell so that the Devil's grandmother can complete her spring cleaning. He is found freezing in the woods by four scientists who transfer him to Haldungen Hall in order to conduct experiments and try to ascertain what species of creature he might be. Once the Devil has thawed out in the Baron's fireplace, he proceeds to work his devilish schemes, bribing Wernthal to buy his claim to Liddy as his bride, and plotting with Mordax to have Liddy delivered to a remote inn where he can abduct her. When Mollfels arrives at the inn to rescue her, Liddy has already managed to rescue herself. The schoolmaster, who has baited his trap with condoms, has caught the Devil. In the grand denouement, Liddy and Mollfels embrace, and the Devil is rescued by a beautiful young woman in Russian furs, who turns out to be his grandmother. The playwright Grabbe arrives, bearing a lantern as did Diogenes in his quest for truth. Although the schoolmaster wants to bar the door to keep him out, Grabbe enters with his lamp: the stage darkens and the curtain falls.

Some practitioners of the *fiabesque* choose not to allow the fantastic elements to be dissolved in ironic exposé. Hoffmann was an author who saw the bourgeois and the imaginative locked in an irresolvable rivalry. For him, the supernatural realm had psychological validity for the imagination. The realm of dreams, desires, fears, and taboos was a safe asylum to poets, dreamers, and visionaries, who were otherwise considered misfits by the practical-minded philistines of bourgeois society. Among his first musical compositions in Berlin was his three-act melodrama, *The Mask* (1799; *Die Maske*), submitted to August Wilhelm Iffland, Director of the National Theater, who declined to produce it. Existing models for melodrama or *Singspiel* adhered to the example of Jean Jacques Rousseau's *Pygmalion* (1770) with an emphasis on the relation between voice, recitatif, and orchestration. Hoffmann gave far more attention to physical movement and dance. He blended elements of the *commedia dell'arte* with those of the *opera buffa*. If he had a particular work in mind, perhaps it was Mozart's *Don Giovanni* (1787), which he made the subject of a tale in 1813. The dramatic action is interwoven with dance – a morris dance, a Turkish march – but also emotional song, as the German artist Treuenfels expresses his love for Manandane, daughter of a wealthy merchant. In addition to his musical setting to Brentano's *The Merry Musicians*, Hoffmann also provided the musical scores for Goethe's *Jest, Cunning, and Revenge* (1801; *Scherz, List und Rache*), Zacharias Werner's *The Cross on the Baltic* (1805; *Das Kreuz an der Ostsee*), C. Macco's *Arlequin* (1808), Franz von Holbein's *Aurora* (1812) and, most successful, Friedrich de la Motte Fouqué's *Undine* (1814), the tragic love story of mermaid and mortal.

Ambiguity and Intuition

Innovator of a completely different style of drama, Heinrich von Kleist depicted characters caught up in situations where intuitive reason (*Vernunft*) is pitted against discursive understanding (*Verstand*). These are, of course, the contrasting modes of thought described by Immanuel Kant in his *Critical Philosophy*. Kleist confessed his Kantian crisis in a letter to Wilhelmina von Zenge on March 22, 1801:

> We can never be certain that what we call truth is really truth, or whether it only seems so. If the latter, the truth that we acquire here isn't truth after we die – and all our efforts to possess ourselves of something which might follow us to the grave are in vain. Oh Wilhelmine, if the point of this thought doesn't pierce you to the heart, don't smile at somebody who feels himself wounded by it in the innermost core of his being. My single, my supreme goal has sunk completely and I have no other... (Kleist 104-5, V: 204-5)

While it might be doubted whether Kant's philosophy alone had brought Kleist to this impasse, the dilemma was certainly fixed in his mind as he wrote his tales and plays. The values of culture and custom are relative, but so too are the truths of perception. Kant not only distinguished sensory phenomena from the actual thing in itself (*Ding an sich*), he declared the impossibility of ever knowing the thing in itself. The mind is thus confined within its own subjectivity incapable of ever knowing a world of objective truth. Plot and character in a Kleistian play turn on the intuitive moment.

Historically known, in the plays of Plautus and Molière, as a salacious comedy of adulterous seduction, *Amphitryon* is transformed by Kleist into a dramatic questioning of identity, loyalty, and fidelity. Jupiter, who took the shape of a swan to seduce Leda, of a white bull to seduce Europa, of a cloud to seduce Io, of a shower of gold to seduce Danae, must assume the identity of her husband, Amphitryon, in order to seduce Alkmene. Jupiter and Mercury appear in Thebes in the shapes of Amphitryon and his servant Sosias. Plautus treated the plot of mistaken identities much as he had in the *Menaechmi*, source for Shakespeare's *Comedy of Errors*. Alkmene and Amphitryon each confronts a difficult test in reconciling their inner experience with their external situation. Although he allows more antic confusion in the parallel subplot involving Sosias and his wife Charis, even here Kleist does not resort to a comic romp with Charis suddenly finding herself with two lovers. The crisis is as much in knowing one's own identity as is in knowing and trusting someone else. The confusion drives the characters almost to desperation and madness before Jupiter reveals his true identity. The question of identity, central to the play, is raised in the opening encounter between Sosias and Mercury as his double:

> MERCURY [in the shape of Sosias, guarding the entrance to Amphitryon's house]:   Halt!
> Who goes there?
> SOSIAS: Me.
> MERCURY/SOSIAS: Me? What me, man?

The all-too-glib declaration of "me" calls for differentiation, not simply in terms of name and occupation, but in terms of personal history, property, and background. All that Sosias can claim as belonging to "me" is immediately usurped by his interrogator, who dismisses the true Sosias as a badly disguised imposter. Having been sent home to Thebes to assure Alkmene that Amphitryon has won the battle against the Athenians and leads his troops on their homeward march, Sosias is informed that Sosias and Amphitryon are already returned. When Sosias endeavors to explain their premature arrival to Amphitryon upon his return on the following morning, Amphitryon accuses him of delusion. However he must soon hear the same report from his beloved Alkmene, who blesses him for his prompt return and for the joy he brought her the previous night. Amphitryon, who cannot believe that his wife would be unfaithful to him, is caught up in agony over her apparent betrayal of his love. Jupiter/Amphitryon, however, can take no satisfaction in having seduced Alkmene, for she recognizes in him only the husband to whom she is devoted. "Wasn't it better last night?" is not a plea that can prompt her to acknowledge a love more bountiful than what she has always felt for Amphitryon. The final act begins with a monologue in which Amphitryon attempts to sort out his public and private predicament: in his social role, he is celebrated for his victory, admired by his troops and his people, at the pinnacle of fame; in his own mind, he is alone, friendless, no longer able to reason or trust his five senses. Nevertheless he trusts Alkmene, knowing that she is incapable of betrayal or deception. The conclusion to the play is a true and not inappropriate *deus ex machina*: by thunder and lightning an eagle descends to reveal the true identity of Jupiter, who gives his blessings to Amphitryon and Alkmene. Informed that she shall bear a child to be named Hercules, Alkmene sinks into the arms of Amphitryon with a final sigh, "Ach!"

The trust that assured the reconciliation at the end of Amphitryon is the missing element that results in the tragic end to *Penthesilea* (1808). Achilles has fallen in love with Penthesilea, Queen of the Amazons, whose love he can court only through the ritual of Amazonian battle. In their first battle, Penthesilea falls unconscious, but Achilles persuades her that she has won, and he is her prisoner. But her Amazons perceive that, in truth, she is his prisoner. They attack Achilles and rescue her. Thinking to win her back by means of another pretended battle, he sends a messenger to deliver the challenge. Penthesilea misunderstands his intention, and takes up the challenge as a love-hate battle to the death. The title character of *Käthchen von Heilbronn* (1808) is guided by intuition and dream, and has no conscious explanation for her devotion to the Baron von Strahl. Similarly, the title character of *Prinz Friedrich von Homburg* (1810) follows an impulsive vision of glory and consequently disobeys his military orders.

The Broken Jug (1808; *Der zerbrochene Krug*), the most often staged of Kleist's plays, is a tale of foiled lechery. Adam, an elderly village judge, has tried to bribe a young girl, Eve, to consent to his sexual advances by promising to release her betrothed, Ruprecht, from his military service in the East Indies. As is revealed at the end of the play, Adam had forged the letter of conscription, for Ruprecht had actually been called to duty at a garrison in the neighboring city. Not willing to barter her body for Ruprecht's release, she rejects the judge's proposal. He grows aggressive; she cries out. Ruprecht breaks in by knocking down the door. Adam manages to escape but breaks a jug in his hasty exit. Kleist forces the distinction between appearance and reality as his frustrated seducer is called to judgment. The evidence against him is gradually unfolded at a trial at which the judge himself presides. His bribe and attempted rape are exposed as the last in the series of incriminating revelations in determining the culprit responsible for the broken jug. The comic effects derive primarily from Adam's lies and evasions, Eve's refusal to expose him for fear that her lover will be sent abroad, and Ruprecht's jealous conviction that his bride-to-be has been untrue. The presence of Walter, the visiting circuit judge, requires Adam to attempt a semblance of integrity, while Licht, his court secretary, uses Adam's desperation to his own advantage.

Although *The Broken Jug* might be named a close match for the sort of domestic comedy that Elizabeth Inchbald, Hannah Cowley, and other women playwrights of the period had made popular on the British stage, there was in fact no similar drama produced during these years in Germany. The comedies of Kotzebue, such as *The Small-town Germans* (1801; *Die deutschen Kleinstädter*) has social not domestic satire as its target. Kotzebue was as deft in ridiculing the groveling German adulation of titles as was Carl Zuckmayer, over a century later, in ridiculing the German fascination with military uniform, rank, and command, in *The Captain of Köpenick* (1931; *Der Hauptmann von Köpenick*). Often dismissed as "trivial drama" or "entertainment piece," the German domestic drama did not advocate any change in the traditional roles for women; it upheld, rather, the status quo and satirized any perceived deviations from it. As actor, playwright, and from 1796, Director of the Berlin National Theater, August Wilhelm Iffland (1759-1814) made domestic drama, the sentimental play of everyday life, a mainstay of the annual repertory. His plays reveal a technical mastery of the stage and effective situations.[6] His best characters are simple and natural, fond of domestic life, given to moralizing platitudes. His best-known plays are *Die Jäger*, *Dienstpflicht*, *Die Advokaten*, *Die Mundel*, and *Die Hagstolzen*.

Actor-manager Playwrights

The women playwrights in Germany did not raise such issues as a woman's right to control her own wealth or women's right to choose her own husband – as in such British plays as Cowley's *Bold Stoke for a Husband* (1783) or Inchbald's *Animal Magnetism* (1788; rev. 1806). Karoline von Günderode (1780-1806), whose "closet" plays *Udohla* (1805), *Magic and Destiny* (1805; *Magie und Schicksal*), and *Nikator* (1806) were published under the pseudonym "Tian," imbued her exotic themes with mythic grandeur and high romance. By contrast, Charlotte Birch-Pfeiffer (1800-68) had a powerful command of theatrical strategy and wrote successfully for the stage. She commenced her career as an actress at the Munich Court Theater, where she assumed leading tragic roles from 1818 to 1826. From 1827 to 1830 she performed at the theater in Vienna, but also accepted guest roles during these years at theaters throughout Europe, with noted accomplishment in the title role of Schiller's *Maria Stuart*. She began writing plays in 1828, including sentimental comedy and historical tragedy. She was especially successful at dramatizing the novels of Victor Hugo, Alexandre Dumas, George Sand, Charles Dickens, and other popular authors. She continued to act even after assuming the management of the Zurich Theater from 1837 to 1843, where she allowed the English playwright Thomas Lovell Beddoes to use her stage for a private performance of Shakespeare's *Henry IV, Part I*. In 1844, she accepted an engagement at the Royal Theater in Berlin, where she remained active until her death in 1868. Her 70 plays, adapted and original, were published in 23 volumes (Birch-Pfeiffer 1863-80).

Birch-Pfeiffer's success, like that of Inchbald in England, owed much to a first-hand knowledge of the theater. An understanding of the development of the drama in Germany requires a familiarity with the leading theaters, their managers, their players, their audiences. Indeed, the distinction between "classic" and "Romantic" on the German stage, no less than between high and low culture, is defined in great part by who, when, and where. Properly celebrated for his transformation of the drama in Germany, Gotthold Ephraim Lessing owed his influence not to just to his plays – *Miss Sara Sampson* (1755), *Minna von Barnhelm* (1763), *Emilia Galotti* (1772), *Nathan the Wise* (1779) – but also to his position as dramaturge and critic at the German National Theater in Hamburg, where he wrote his *Hamburgische Dramaturgie* (1767-9).

Just as one presumes a particular style and manner when referring to Drury Lane under David Garrick or John Philip Kemble, so too the theaters of Berlin, Hamburg, Mannheim, Bamberg, Braunschweig, or Weimar and Lauchstädt, bear the imprint of their managers and players. An idol of playgoers at the Berlin National Theater during the last decades of the eighteenth century was Johann Friedrich Ferdinand Fleck (1757-1801), who tended to rely on instinct and impulse, rather than attempting to control or monitor his actions, with the result that his powerful delivery was sometimes misdirected and lapsed into rant and rave. In 1788, he won accolades for his performance of Othello. For the later generation of the 1820s, Ludwig Devrient (1784-1832), was an actor who thrilled Berlin audiences with his demonic manner in tragedy and his bustling antics in comedy. He gave an individual identity to a broad range of character types and was especially successful in the works of Shakespeare and Schiller.

In 1771 the Hamburg National Theater came under the management of Friedrich Ludwig Schröder (1744-1816). His stepfather, Konrad Ernst Ackermann, and his mother, Sophie Schröder, were both renowned performers, and young Schröder grew up on the stage, playing roles even as a child, learning acrobatics, stage stunts, and tricks of mimicry, from other members of the Ackermann troupe. Schröder became the most celebrated German actor of his day. He founded the Hamburg School of Acting, and was noted for his excellent ensemble productions, introducing historical costume and set design. He translated and produced 11 Shakespearean plays, performing himself in such roles as Hamlet, the ghost of Hamlet's father, Iago, Shylock, Lear, Falstaff, and Macbeth. He also brought to the Hamburg stage the early plays of Goethe – *Götz von Berlichingen*, *Clavigo*, and *Stella*. Schröder left Hamburg in 1780 and spent four years at the Vienna Burgtheater, where he wrote plays and introduced ensemble acting. From 1785 to 1798 he was again director of the Hamburg National Theater.

August Klingemann (1777-1831) was the influential playwright and director who brought the Braunschweig Theater to prominence. He outstripped even Kotzebue as author of the most often produced plays in Germany. In 1797, Klingemann's first play, *The Mask (Die Maske)* was accepted by Goethe for performance by his Weimar troupe in Rudolfstadt. His identity as author of the prose satire, *The Nightwatches* (1804; *Die Nachtwachen*), published under the name Bonaventura, was not established until 1973 (see Schillemeit 1973, Wickman 1974, Flief 1985). He experimented in a full range of genre: *Candid Expressions* (1804; *Freimüthigkeiten*), a satirical comedy; *The Lazzarone, or the Beggar of Naples* (1806; *Der Lazzaroni oder Der Bettler von Neapel*), a sentimental melodrama; *Heinrich von Wolfenschießen* (1806) and *Columbus* (1808), historical drama; *Don Quixote und Sancho Pansa* (1811), comic melodrama. He founded the Braunschweig National Theater, which opened on May 29, 1818, with a production of Schiller's *Braut von Messina*. In 1826 it became the court theater of Duke Carl II. Klingemann personally directed the first public performance of Goethe's *Faust*, opening on January 19, 1829.[7]

That the first public performance of Goethe's *Faust* came relatively late in the period may seem to be a peculiarity in theater history. It had, after all, become known throughout Europe after the publication of Part I in 1808. Goethe had begun the work in 1790 and Part II was not published until shortly before his death in 1832. Faust's dilemma, "two souls dwell, alas, within my breast" ("zwei Seelen wohnen, ach! in meinem Brust"), impressed many as quintessentially Romantic. Germaine de Staël, in *De l'Allemagne*, included a rich sampling of passages in her chapter on Goethe's *Faust* (de Staël [1810] 1985: 35-385). John Murray, de Staël's London publisher, commissioned Coleridge in 1814 to translate *Faust*. Coleridge never finished the translation, but was persuaded by another publisher, Thomas Boosey, to take it up again in 1820. In addition to Coleridge, others who turned their efforts to translating *Faust* were John Anster, George Soane, Percy Bysshe Shelley, and Claire Clairmont. In 1823 Murray was finally able to publish a full translation of Part I by Francis Gower. Coleridge commenced a translation of Schiller's *Wallenstein* (1796-9) during his stay in Göttingen and completed it soon after his return. On the English stage, Schiller found more success than Goethe during the first half of the nineteenth century.

Goethe directed the court theaters in Weimar and Lauchstädt, with performances of Lessing's *Minna von Barnhelm* and *Emilia Galotti*, and Schiller's *Die Räuber*, *Maria Stuart*, and *Don Carlos*. After assuming the theater directorship in January, 1791, he produced his *Egmont* in March. Many of his plays, including his *Torquato Tasso* (published in 1790, first performed in 1806), had their first performance under his direction in Weimar.

The themes of the Romantic drama in Germany were often shaped by the impact of revolutionary issues, the Napoleonic conquest, and the Constitutional movement. Rebellion against oppression was a repeated theme in the drama of the *Sturm und Drang* movement; the vain struggle of free will against inevitable destiny was the theme of the *Schicksalstragödie*. Adultery or loss of fortune provided numerous plots for domestic tragedy. Comedy was strongly influenced by the *commedia dell'arte*, with a consequent engagement of the *fiabesque*. Playwrights also began to emphasize the play as play, with complex turns of self-reflexive metadrama and romantic irony. The melodrama of the period experimented widely with the dramatic uses of song, and corresponded with a growing audience interest in fantasy and the supernatural as somehow copresent or interacting with dramatic realism. In the staging, much attention was given to creating an illusion of the actual time and place both in stage décor and in costuming.

NOTES

1 Mr. Kemble's Stranger is one of his most perfect and characteristic parts.... A deep fixed melancholy sits upon his brow; hope has long left his worn and faded cheek; his still and motionless despair has almost changed him into a statue, but he has not quite "forgot himself to stone". A sigh of involuntary tenderness heaves his stately form, and shows that there is life in it; a tear, "unused to flow", stands ready to start from either eye; a pang of bitter regret quivers on his lip; his tremulous hollow voice, labouring out its irksome way, seems to give back the echo of years departed hope and happiness. He is like sentiment embodied: a long habit of patient suffering, not seen but felt, appears to have subdued his mind, moulded his whole form. We could look at Mr. Kemble in this character, and listen to him, rill we could fancy that every other actor is but harlequin, and that no tones but his have true pathos, sense, or meaning in them. (June 9, 1817, Hazlitt 1930-4, 18: 233-4)

2 "Schiller's *Robbers* appears to have become a direct source for *The Borderers* only in the later stages of the composition, possibly as a result of Wordsworth's visit to Coleridge in March [1797]" (Wordsworth 1982, 6: 11).
3 My translation; all translations are mine unless otherwise indicated.
4 See F. Schlegel (1963: 85) on Romantic irony as "permanent parabasis," as in the illusion-disruption in the comedies of Aristophanes.
5 Carolina Schelling to Friedrich Schleiermacher, June 16, 1800, in *Carolina und Dorothea Schlegel in Briefen*, p. 327, describes Tieck's anger and his ridicule of Brentano in "Der neue Hercules am Scheideweg," in *Poetisches Journal* (Jena, 1800), 81-93; reprinted as "Der Autor, ein Fastnachtsschwank" in Tieck, *Schriften* XIII: 267-79.
6 For criticism of Iffland and his plays, see Iffland (1798-1808, 1807, 1968).
7 On Klingemann's staging see Burwick (1988, 1990).

REFERENCES AND FURTHER READING

Allroggen, Gerhard (1970). *E. T. A. Hoffmanns Kompositionen*. Regensburg: Bosse.
Büchner, Georg ([1813-37] 1992-9). *Sämtliche Werke, Briefe und Dokumente*, ed. Henri Poschmann, 2 vols. Frankfurt am Main: Deutscher Klassiker Verlag.
Burwick, Frederick (1988). "Stage Illusion and the Stage Designs of Goethe and Hugo." *Word and Image*, 4 (3-4): 692-718.
Burwick, Frederick (1990). "Romantic Drama: From Optics to Illusion." In Stuart Peterfreund (ed.), *Literature and Science: Theory and Practice*. Boston: Northeastern University Press, pp. 167-208.
Charlotte Birch-Pfeiffer (1863-80). *Gesammelte dramatische Werke*, 23 vols. Leipzig: Reclam.
Flief, Horst (1985). *Literarischer Vampirismus: Klingemanns "Nachtwachen von Bonaventura."* Tübingen: Niemeyer.
Hazlitt, William (1930-4). *The Complete Works of William Hazlitt*, ed. Percival Presland Howe, 21 vols. London: J. M. Dent and Sons.
Hoffmann, E. T. A. (1967-9). *Briefwechsel*, ed. H. von Müller and F. Schnapp. München: Winkler.
Iffland, August Wilhelm (1798-1808). *Dramatischen Werke*, 17 vols. Leipzig: G. J. Göschen.
Iffland, August Wilhelm (1807). *Almanach für Theater und Theaterfreunde*. Berlin: Bei Wilhelm Oehmigke dem Jüngeren.
Iffland, August Wilhelm ([1798]1968). *Meine theatralische Laufbahn*. Nendeln/Liechtenstein: Kraus Reprint.
Johnson, Edgar (1970). *Sir Walter Scott: The Great Unknown*, 2 vols. New York: Macmillan.
Kleist, Heinrich von (1904-5). *Werke*, ed. Georg Minde-Prouet, Reinhold Steig, and Erich Schmidt, 5 vols. Leipzig: Bibliographisches Institut.

Nicoll, Allardyce (1927). *A History of Late Eighteenth Century Drama, 1750-1800*. Cambridge, UK: Cambridge University Press.

Schillemeit, Jost (1973). *Bonaventura. Der Verfasser der "Nachtwachen."* Munich: Beck.

Schlegel, August Wilhelm (1828). "Review of Tieck's 'Ritterblaubart' and 'Der gestiefelte Kater.' " Reprinted in *Kritische Schriften*, 2 vols. Berlin: Georg Reimer, vol. 1, pp. 311-18.

Schlegel, August Wilhelm (1962-74). *Kritische Schriften und Briefe*, ed. Edgar Lohner. Stuttgart: W. Kohlhammer, 7 vols.

Schlegel, Caroline and Dorothea (1914). *Caroline und Dorothea Schlegel in Briefen*, ed. Ernst Wieneke. Weimar: G. Kiepenheuer.

Schlegel, Friedrich (1963). "Zur Philosophie." Fragment No. 668. In Ernst Behler with Jean Jacques Anstett and Hans Eichner (eds.), *Kritische Friedrich Schlegel Ausgabe*, vol. 18. München, Paderborn: Schöningh.

Shattuck, Charles H. (ed.) (1974). *John Philip Kemble Promptbooks*, 11 vols. Charlottesville: Folger Shakespeare Library/ University Press of Virginia.

Staël, Germaine de ([1810] 1985). *De l'Allemagne*. Frankfurt: Insel Verlag.

Tieck, Ludwig (1828-54). *Schriften,* 28 vols. Berlin: Georg Reimer.

Wordsworth, William (1974). *The Prose Works of William Wordsworth*, ed. W. J. B. Owen and Jane Worthington Smyser, 3 vols. Oxford: Clarendon Press.

Wickman, Dieter (1974). "Zum Bonaventura-Problem: Eine mathematisch-statistische Überprüfung der Klingemann-Hypothese." *Zeitschrift für Literaturwissenschaft und Linguistik*, 4: 13-29.

William Wordsworth (1982). *The Borderers*. In *The Cornell Wordsworth*, ed. Robert Osborn, vol. 6. Ithaca, NY: Cornell University Press.

10

Early French Romanticism

Fabienne Moore

On sent le Romantique, on ne le définit point. Louis-Sébastien Mercier, *Néologie* (1801)

1776: An Epithet is Born

In April 1776, as France eagerly awaited news of the American insurgents' actions, a French insurgent of sorts in the field of letters, the translator Pierre Le Tourneur (1737-88), published the initial two volumes of his *Shakespeare traduit de l'anglois*, the first complete and accurate translation in French prose of Shakespeare's theater. Backed by an unusual coalition of a thousand advance subscribers topped by the French royal family, the King of England, and the Empress of Russia, Le Tourneur ushered in the most powerful counter-example to the theater of Corneille, Racine, and Molière supported by the French literary establishment. The aesthetic battle endured but took a decisive turn when in 1821 there appeared a revision of Le Tourneur's translation whose success prompted Stendhal to announce that finally "a great revolution in theater is brewing in France. Within a few years, we will make prose tragedies and follow Shakespeare's wanderings" (Martino 1925: xciii).

On February 24, 1776, two months before Le Tourneur's launch, a lone figure had sought to catch royal attention and arouse public sympathy by depositing a confessional manuscript on the altar of Notre Dame Cathedral in Paris. Its title announced: *Rousseau juge de Jean-Jacques. Dialogues*. Barred from the sacred choir by an unexpected impassable railing, a desperate Jean-Jacques Rousseau had to turn back, then inward again, resuming his quest for self-introspection and justification. His tell-all autobiographical *Confessions* and accusatory *Dialogues*, although already finished, would appear posthumously, a stunning self-portrait whose sincerity and inner conflicts preempted the moral judgment customary to classic portraiture. In addition, the philosopher dedicated the last two years of his life to composing an unusual diary of musings. Begun in the autumn of 1776, the diary took the form of 10 meditative promenades with the title *Rêveries du promeneur solitaire* (published posthumously in 1782). As he ruminated memories of times past, Rousseau set apart his most serene and happiest recollection, celebrating in the fifth promenade a month-long exile on the tiny Saint-Pierre island on the Swiss lake of Bienne. Still moved by the beauty of the landscape and the protection nature had offered him then, Rousseau reminisced and wrote: "The banks of Lake Bienne are wilder and more romantic that those of Lake Geneva, because the rocks and woods border the water more closely; but they are not less cheerful" (Rousseau 2000: 41).

Thus appeared the French epithet *"romantique."* Where from? Rousseau had very likely recently read Le Tourneur's preface to the *Shakespeare traduit de l'anglois* and its explanation for the neologism *"romantique"* used to qualify a cloudy landscape – a new adjective probably coined by his collaborator Louis-Sébastien Mercier. At the same time, another friend, the Marquis de Girardin, picked up *"romantique"* for his treatise on gardening (1777), whose principles he applied to Ermenonville, the estate where Rousseau was offered a last refuge, becoming his final resting place when he died a few weeks later on July 2, 1778. Ten years later, recounting his sentimental pilgrimage to the site of Rousseau's tomb, set on an islet surrounded by poplars at the heart of Ermenonville, Le Tourneur marveled at the "pleasant vale filled with the most inspiring and romantic beauties" (Le Tourneur 1990a: 41-50, 1990b: 167).[1]

Reborn into French from the English transformation of *romance*, the adjective crystallized around Rousseau and nature. Shakespeare's genius had inspired Le Tourneur and Mercier's provocative statement that "Nature is one and only, like truth; neither one nor the other bears the epithet beautiful."[2] But it took Rousseau's embrace of truth and nature for contemporaries to open themselves to a more hybrid and complex aesthetic, privileging affect over effect, imagination over idealization, the mystery of Romantic nature over the perfection of beautiful artifice.

That two foreigners, Shakespeare and Rousseau, stirred the Republic of letters is not a coincidence. Outsiders bring the shock of the new and unfamiliar, in lieu of conformity and imitation according to pregiven rules. Thus the wave of Anglomania that swept France in mid-century slowly questioned following Greek and Roman models, the hierarchy and separation of genres, and the imitation of beautiful nature, principles now referred to as neo-Classicism. Rousseau did not wage war against ancient times and models – to the contrary he cherished golden age pastorals – but opposed the modern rationalist and materialist worldview. He embraced the freedom to criticize, which Enlightenment philosophers established as a fundamental right, to expose the shortcomings of Enlightenment philosophy as well as the stultifying confines of ancien régime society.

We must be mindful that literary history constructed *a posteriori* the periodization of neo-Classicism, Enlightenment, and early Romanticism to circumscribe movements of thought which, far from separate and consecutive, intersected and bled into one another. Rousseau's oeuvre transcends these partitions.

Jean-Jacques Rousseau (1712-78): Back to Origins

Jean-Jacques Rousseau's writings, character, and mode of existence challenged and permanently altered the French way – manners of thinking and acting framed by national pride and solidified by an absolute monarchy. Although scholars will continually be challenged by the enigma of Rousseau's genius, we can identify two striking features at the source of his nonconformity: the absence of national and educational bounds. Rousseau was born a citizen of Geneva, an independent Swiss Republic offering a unique combination of political and religious freedom for the French outside France. French was written and spoken in a democracy espousing liberal Protestantism. Rousseau's wanderlust drove him to leave Geneva at age 14, beginning a lifelong love/hate relationship, including forgoing then regaining citizenship, converting to Catholicism (1728) then back to Calvinism (1754), living in France with periods of exile in various Swiss counties which, in turn, expelled him, dying in France with his ashes eventually transferred to the Pantheon by French revolutionaries (1794). The vagaries of Rousseau's citizenship (the Swiss, French, and even Prussians could claim him as their own) underscores his nationlessness.

Freed of national identity, Rousseau was also free from the educational confines imposed by family and school: he grew up motherless, given free reign by his father, with no formal schooling and an incomplete apprenticeship as an engraver. Rousseau eventually devised his own idiosyncratic system of learning, with far less exposure to rhetoric than in a traditional education. The singularity of Rousseau's entire oeuvre may derive from this self-education. The absolute freedom of individual conscience despite social pressures, and a natural, "negative" education without walls (institutional or pedagogical), became cornerstones of his philosophy.

To ask "Was Rousseau an early Romantic?" and "Were Romantics all Rousseauists?" is to wonder about the prefiguration in Rousseau's work of themes now associated with Romanticism. Rather than reading forward and backward to find the seeds of Romanticism – with the risk of planting them ourselves – let's focus on how Rousseau's originality distinguished itself from his contemporaries'.

Music, sentiment, nature

Before becoming a man of letters, Rousseau was and remained a man of music. His first publication concerned a new system of musical notation. His career began with two operas *Les Muses galantes* (1744), and *Le Devin du village* (1752). His last years were devoted to composing songs, aptly titled *Les Consolations des misères de ma vie*. He wrote articles on music for Diderot's *Encyclopédie*, and later revised them in a *Dictionnaire de la musique* (1767). He hand-copied musical scores for a living. This passion was a fight as well: in the confrontation between French and Italian music, Rousseau, like most *philosophes*, embraced the melodic freedom and impassioned accents of Italian music and disparaged the French emphasis on instrumental harmony – too mechanical, icy, and "noisy." Transported by the expressivity of Italian music he has just heard, Rousseau's character Saint-Preux will urge his lover Julie to learn this language of the heart: "So abandon forever that boring and lamentable French song that is more like the cries of colic than the transport of passion. Learn to produce those divine sounds inspired by sentiment, the only ones worthy of your voice, the only ones worthy of your heart, and which always carry along with them the charm and fire of sensible temperaments" (Rousseau 1997: 110). Originally developed in the *Essai sur l'origine des langues* (1764), the idea that "Poetry, song, and speech have a common origin" encouraged a return to the original conjunction between music and poetic sentiment, exemplified by Rousseau's own musical prose.

For generations, including his own, only Rousseau has been known on a first-name basis. Whereas Montesquieu, Voltaire, Diderot, or Sade's first names seem inconsequential and are barely remembered, "Jean-Jacques" is substituted for Rousseau in correspondence as well as past and present criticism. Aside from the practical issue of distinction from his namesake, the then-famous poet Jean-Baptiste Rousseau, the public use of Rousseau's Christian name – by himself and others – has a vast symbolic resonance. It lays the private self in the open, it emblazons subjectivity and intimacy. Samuel Richardson's novels of sentiment had illustrated how the heart led to virtue, thus framing the question of sensitivity as a moral quest towards goodness. In his widely successful epistolary novel, *Julie ou la nouvelle Héloïse* (with more than 70 editions from 1761 to 1800) Rousseau opens the tortured heart of Saint-Preux, a young tutor in love with his pupil Julie, who eventually obeys her father's choice of a better match. After her husband knowingly chooses her former lover to become their children's tutor, Julie's virtue struggles until death to turn thwarted love into friendship. In life as in fiction, Rousseau wanted to study individualities and characters: *Émile ou traité sur l'éducation* details an imaginary boy's mental, emotional, and moral development guided by radically new pedagogical principles based on the free discovery of the world of nature and the intellect. When Jean-Jacques turned to himself as subject and object of study in his autobiographical *Confessions*, the story of his life became emblematic of how social forces restrict individual freedom.

Contrary to those who distrusted emotion as misleading and believed reason alone to be reliable, Rousseau maintained that emotions reveal truth, that they tell as much as the mind about how to read the inner and exterior worlds. He honored but did not privilege reason. In the name of truth, therefore, feelings were no longer idealized as in *L'Astrée*, the seventeenth-century pastoral admired by Rousseau, but described in their psychological complexities and piercing force. This liberation of the lyrical self had considerable appeal, particularly among women who turned to sentimental realism to convey their plights in real or imaginary correspondences and novels.

Sentiment and nature had long been wedded in poems and pastorals. Allegories of the seasons, symbolic fruit and flowers, idealized landscapes, an enchanted southern countryside, offered an abstract, eternally pleasing (*riante*) nature severed from reality. As with music and sentiment, Rousseau refused artifice when it came to nature. The wild contrasts of Swiss landscapes beloved since childhood, the rustic pleasures of his various country retreats, and the fascination with plants (stored and classified in herbals) translated into a celebration of nature's spectacles and riches as they affect the soul and penetrate the mind. In lieu of clichéd allegorical deities, Rousseau described nature as an immediate experience, a direct revelation of thoughts and emotions. By subtitling his only novel "Letters of two lovers who live in a small town at the foot of the Alps," Rousseau fused the mountainous locale with his characters' lives. Saint-Preux tries to convey to Julie his awe at the sublime Valais mountains: "the spectacle has something indescribably magical, supernatural about it that ravishes the spirit and the senses; you forget everything, even yourself, and do not even know where you are" (Rousseau 1997: 65). Julie reciprocates by introducing him to her "Elysium," the beautiful private orchard she designed to operate a different magic than the nearby fearsome mountains: a place of delectation through pure illusion, where domesticated nature appears wild. Did Julie's invisible hand follow principles governing English gardens (as opposed to the classic symmetry of French gardening)? Rather, she applied the beloved classical tradition of Virgil's *locus amoenus* (place of delights), a topos of landscape description. Thus Rousseau's approach to nature combined classic poetical reminiscences with a personal affinity for contrasted, soul-stirring landscapes, as well as a passion for botany, the prosaic observation of the vegetal world. This unusual combination gave Rousseau his name as "l'homme de la nature," engraved in the iconography and imagination of the succeeding generation.

The religion of nature became Rousseau's natural religion, based not on revelation, dogma, nor organized churches, but on an intimate, inner sense of God's existence and an innate principle of justice and virtue (conscience). Contemplating the Alps crowning the horizon, a poor ecclesiastic from the mountainous Savoy region confides to the young Émile the essence of natural religion, an unmediated relation to the divine, which means the only essential cult is of the heart. "The Profession of Faith of the Savoyard Vicar" was deemed to be so impious and dangerous by both Paris and Geneva that it caused Rousseau's banishment and the burning of his treatise *Émile*.

Thus Rousseau increasingly experienced nature as a refuge: promenades, reveries, and herborizing excursions provided solace from alienation and persecution. Nature, breathing purity and harmony, freed the writer to follow the meandering streams of consciousness and find his unique rhythm.

1776-1816: A Controversial Period

Rousseau's writings exerted a powerful *gravitas* over the whole European world. A systematic reference point to all aspiring for change (in politics, society, and literature), his work offers a challenge to literary historians in search of Romanticism's beginnings. This is the paradox at the heart of "pre-Romanticism," a convenient though inadequate term applied to a complex period, part eighteenth-century Enlightenment, part nineteenth-century nascent Romanticism, yet not merely transitional. Ever since its coinage around 1910, critics have disagreed on its chronological span, its specificity, or lack thereof, and its relevance. Its prefix implies continuity with the subsequent, recognized Romanticism of Victor Hugo's generation, while its suffix suggests the unity of a movement – a continuity and unity both subject to disputation (see Minski 1998). When a 1972 symposium gathered eminent scholars to ponder the notion of French "pre-Romanticism" they could neither resolve its definition nor jettison the term (Viallaneix 1975). Rather, its ideological underpinnings were clarified. At the beginning of the twentieth century anti-German sentiment drove some French critics to define pre-Romanticism as an evolution internal to French letters, downplaying foreign influences, most notably German, and Germaine de Staël's introduction of them (see e.g., Mornet 1912, Monglond [1930] 1965). To correct the bias of this historical nationalism, comparatists widened the movement to Europe (see e.g., Van Tieghem 1967). Those who struck a balance, acknowledging innovations within a classic framework, nevertheless favored one author over another, diminishing Staël's contribution while heralding Chateaubriand's.[3]

Clearly, pre-Romanticism is a critical construct, not a defined historical period. As Frank Bowman recently put it, the term is "rather suspect since no one ever called himself a pre-Romantic" (Bowman 1999: 77). The challenge therefore consists in adopting a historical perspective that excludes teleological illusions, namely projections of things to come. After structuralism and sociocriticism shaped analysis, recent research has emphasized the overcoming of tradition towards a new, modern vision of literature (see Bénichou 1996, Delon 1998, Fabre 1980, Mortier 1982, Minski 1998). A recent tendency has been to move away from a history of ideas towards a cultural history that establishes "a connection between, on the one hand, the great social and economic transformations that accompanied the passage from the eighteenth to the nineteenth centuries, and on the other hand the upheavals in the modes of thinking and perceiving the world . . . " (Ceserani 1999: 9). In a provoking essay, Bowman (1999) has proposed defining the "specificity of French Romanticism" in terms of "exacerbated polarities," an approach which I would argue also depicts accurately the preceding period, when the Revolution became the ultimate polarizing event for the generation who lived it. Indeed the voices and texts of this period are a study in contrasts, simultaneously original *and* conservative both in form and content. The expression of individual geniuses and the controversy generated by their work speak to sociohistorical unrest and uncertainties born of the Enlightenment's optimistic, forward drive. Rousseau figures prominently in the present chapter to reflect how early this disruption began.

The Specificity of Early French Romanticism

The plight of a generation

Early French Romanticism is first of all the story of one generation who experienced in rapid succession three monumental historical disruptions. This generation lived through the collapse of the monarchy under which they grew up, the capsizing of the

Revolution into the Terror, and the downfall of Napoleon after a 20-year reign. Gains of freedom and equality remained under constant threat, while losses (of lives, fortune, and privileges) mounted. Cycles of nostalgia and expectations, elation and horror, hope and disappointment spread confusion and *mal-être*. Hesitations about women's new status as citizens were reflected in individual fates. While the new Republic chose an allegorical Marianne to represent itself, early French Romanticism wavered between equally compelling and symbolic destinies. Was its Marianne the late Julie de l'Espinasse (1732-76), the philosophes' hostess, a tortured heart who rendered her torment in private correspondence and died of love and tuberculosis? [4] The beheaded martyrs of the Revolution Madame Roland (1754-93) and Olympe de Gouges (1745-93), the author of the *Déclaration des droits de la femme et de la citoyenne* (1791)? The modern thinker Germaine de Staël or her friend Juliette Récamier, the neoclassic icon of beauty and platonic love immortalized by the painter David and hopelessly loved and adulated by her male contemporaries? Muse, medusa, "mistress of an age," women transformed themselves, a change reflected in life and fictional representations where the wish for freedom clashes with knowledge of an unhappy destiny. To women especially but not exclusively, Rousseau became this generation's common reference via his alienation and his drive to respond and generalize it.

Denied freedom of expression by the Terror, then by Napoleon's regime, the early Romantic generation had to continue the political fight of the ancien régime's philosophes, sharing with their forebears the pain of censorship and exile. On the other hand, they gained a renewed appreciation of religious expression when Napoleon reversed the Revolution's religious ban, leading the spiritual dimension to resurface in literature. Three authors stood at the forefront of this chaotic period: Germaine de Staël, Benjamin Constant, and François-René Chateaubriand.

One of the most original and complex features of early French Romanticism remains the role of his generation's best-known member: Napoleon Bonaparte (1769-1821). Not only did the Corsican general turned emperor thrust French politics and history into modernity, but his personality and fate also epitomized the fallen heroism central to Romantic literature. Yet at the same time, his regime's strong reaffirmation of neoclassical values, dubbed the Empire style, and extending from fashion (high-waisted white muslin dresses) to furniture, architecture, and painting, represented a return to antiquity that also left a strong imprint on literature.

A *literature under shock*

This generation called for a new literature to match historical change but this imperative raised questions hard to resolve in the flux of transformations: how to create, what tools to use, what references? Artists could strive for the neoclassical perfection beloved by the French national tradition, or venture imperfect new genres. They could embrace foreign traditions as a process of rejuvenation or fear their lack of taste. The results were hybrid creations, a literature best defined as experimental, partly didactic, partly imaginative.

The poetry of this tumultuous historical period, from the last decade of Louis XVI's reign to the Empire, is a kaleidoscope of themes and styles, a mixture of old and new, with no equivalent figureheads to the central six poets of English Romanticism. Since the mid-eighteenth century theoreticians had studied the origins of language and poetry to advocate a return to musicality and enthusiasm, yet in practice French poets resisted change, and innovations remained circumscribed. Paradoxically and contrary to received opinion, the period stands out for the abundance and variety of its poetic production. But without unity or dominating trend, this poetic profusion does not lend itself to a simple classic/Romantic dichotomy. In search of itself, poetry took various directions. With *Les Jardins* (1782) Jacques Delille (1738-1813) continued the descriptive poetry of nature spearheaded by Jean-François Saint-Lambert (1716-1803) in *Les Saisons* (1769). André Chénier (1762-94) revived classical myths as in "Hermès," and the modern myth of the New World with "L'Amérique," invigorated by American Independence. Creole poets like Évariste Parny (1753-1814) developed exotic, elegiac themes. The theosophist Louis-Claude de Saint-Martin (1743-1803) imagined new rhythms to match spiritual elevation (*L'Homme de désir*, 1790). While the above works are remarkable for their length and scope, there was also an adverse reaction to voluminous, often epic, poems, with the taste for short, "fugitive" poems, symptomatic of the shift towards a new poetics privileging instantaneity over narration (see Delon's 1997 anthology).

The evolution of theater was also incremental although many dramatists broke rules sooner and faster than poets did, and prose was well accepted except for tragedies, the last bastion. A key date in this emancipation is the 1791 law fostered by Beaumarchais (1732-99) establishing authors' rights, which finally broke the actors' despotic control over playwrights. Mercier's polemical treatise on theater (1773) turned against the French classical tradition to advocate the *"drame bourgeois"* composed for the people, who will reach its moral goal through emotion. Like Schiller, Mercier sought to realize dramas about social conditions, not characters. While contemporary actors would not perform Mercier's plays on account of his radical theses, today it is their heavy-handed morality that spoils them for readers and spectators. As will be seen repeatedly, before aesthetics achieved the lyricism called for by early French Romantics, it remained but a doctrinal aesthetic, namely theoretical, wishful thinking. Nevertheless, Mercier, inspired by but more radical than his predecessor Diderot, actively advanced dramatic theory, towards Stendhal's *Racine et Shakespeare* and Victor Hugo's preface to *Cromwell*.

The Three Representatives of Early French Romanticism

Germaine de Staël (1766-1817): The voice of the other

Staël lived only 51 years but pioneered the most progressive and bold ideas. She inaugurated the type of the *"intellectuelle engagée,"* the female intellectual stepping into public debate no matter the cost. In detailing obstacles and hardships, Mary Shelley's essay on Staël's life seemed to invite a reading of the destiny of female genius as the quintessential Romantic quest for freedom and acceptance (Shelley 2002). Born in Paris, she was raised a Swiss Protestant like Rousseau, by parents from the high bourgeoisie who lavished on her the finest education. She learnt from her mother's famed Parisian salon in the presence of luminaries such as Diderot and Grimm, and from the tumultuous political career of her famous father, an agent and victim of the revolutionary cause.[5] French, Swiss, or Swedish according to her needs (she married, *de convenance*, the Swedish Ambassador to Paris from whom she separated in 1797), she breathed cosmopolitanism, inviting an international set of guests to Coppet, her residence by Lake Geneva, and spent her life traveling: first to England (1793) and Germany (where in 1803-4 she met Goethe and Schiller, and hired August Wilhelm Schlegel as her children's tutor); then Italy (1805) and north-eastern Europe (Vienna, Moscow, St Petersburg, Stockholm in 1812-13), back to England, where she met Byron (1813-14),[6] and Italy (1815). Political circumstances repeatedly forced her out of Paris: Coppet became a refuge from the Terror, then her headquarters after Napoleon banished her from the capital in 1803, and his police kept harassing her, prompting her flight to Germany. *Dix années d'exil* (published posthumously in 1820), "the most simple and interesting of her works" according to Mary Shelley, records a decade spent escaping the wrath of him who "oppressed her because she refused to be his tool" (Shelley 2002: 479).

Staël's political independence started early and never swayed: she wrote a plea against the queen's execution, labored for the return of émigrés, including Chateaubriand, then involved herself in parliamentary politics through her friend Constant. Her outspoken letters to Jefferson to press for an American intervention against Napoleon are remarkable examples of her political activism. Napoleon could neither abide her political maneuvering which he deemed dangerous, nor her work, which he read as "anti-French" in its praise of foreigners, or more pointedly in its insulting silence towards the Emperor. The two novels and two major essays that established her reputation as one of Europe's leading *femmes de lettres* provided a response to the continuing historic upheaval reshaping France, as well as an opening towards foreign national traditions and innovations discovered while in exile.

First came *De la littérature considérée dans ses rapports avec les institutions sociales* (1800), an ambitious interpretation of literature as the expression of society, determined by history, geography, and politics. Thus far, traditional criticism appraised beauties and defects according to set rules. Staël still believed taste was not arbitrary even when shaped by national variations, but she invoked genius as the ultimate arbitrator. The essay contrasts Northern and Southern literature, the ancients and moderns, opposing Homer, the father of classical poetry, to Ossian, the origin and representative of the melancholy literature of the North. Northern imagination favors dark imagery, inspiring philosophical self-reflections, reinforced by Christian religion and its emphasis on self-introspection. "In order to characterize the general spirit of each literature," Staël moves from an analysis of Greek and Latin literature to a selection of representative masterpieces from Italian, English, German, and French. Shakespeare rises as a modern who invented a new literature, superior to the classics for its "philosophy of the passions and knowledge of men" although less perfect artistically (Staël 1991: 224). England stands out as a land where freedom has encouraged the sublime meditations of Pope and Milton, and the poetic enthusiasm of Dryden, Gray, Thompson, and Young. "Happy the country where the writers are gloomy, the merchants satisfied, the rich melancholy, and the masses content" (Berger 1964: 205). It is also a land where women are loved and respected, hence the rise of a new genre, novels based not on history or fantasy but imagined characters and their private lives. Staël credits English novelists for being the first to captivate the imagination by painting private affections and moral dilemma (see chap. 15 "De l'imagination des Anglais dans leurs poésies et leurs romans," in Staël 1991: 235-45).

The second part focuses on postrevolutionary France and offers "conjectures" on its future progress, insisting that political freedom and equality are prerequisites for any improvement. In its defense of freedom, *De la littérature* celebrates the philosophy of the eighteenth century as well as Republican liberalism. Against counterrevolutionary conservatives, Staël believed in humankind's "perfectibility," refusing to attribute the crimes of the Revolution to philosophy.

De l'Allemagne applied these principles to Germany, whose language Staël learnt with Wilhelm von Humboldt and whose literature and philosophy she studied in situ. However, Staël's wish to introduce it to France in 1810 met with Napoleon's censorship and order of exile, a reaction to her perceived betrayal of national interest. Regardless, *De l'Allemagne* was published in French in London in 1813 and Paris in 1814, and sold equally well in translation. Tying national character to national literature, Staël inaugurated a new criticism no longer grounded in the rules set by the ancients but in the critic's sympathetic engagement with authors and works under consideration. In this she followed Schlegel's theory of literary criticism based not on the technical details of a literary work but on creative genius. Translated in 1813 by her cousin, Albertine Necker de Saussure, W. Schlegel's *Vorlesungen über dramatische Kunst und Literatur* (1809-11) hailed Shakespeare as an exemplar in the mélange of lyric and dramatic genres, grotesque and serious tones. Besides W. and F. Schlegel's work, Staël presented Germany's greatest philosophers, poets, novelists, historians, and artists (from Goethe to Tieck, Jean Paul, and Mozart among others) drawing comparisons with their French or European counterparts, an original comparative approach not meant to set up models for imitation but rather to foster inspiration and a European union of arts and letters. *De l'Allemagne* also introduced Kant's metaphysics to French readers. His defense of morality and religion went in the same direction as Staël's championing of spiritualism as indispensable to renewal in society, politics, and literature. His was a prime example of the compatibility between faith and reason, which French Enlightenment philosophes had not believed possible. In the final section on "religion and enthusiasm" Staël writes beautifully on the "natural alliance between religion and genius" particularly evident in the contemplation of nature (Staël 1968: II, 272).

Through *De la littérature* and *De l'Allemagne* Staël was channeling into France new sources of inspiration to base a new aesthetic. By contrast, she did not seek to demonstrate new writing principles in her novels, which remain traditional in their form as well as their plot around societal obstacles to love and freedom. Named after their eponymous heroines – in many respects Staël's surrogates – *Delphine* (1802) and *Corinne ou l'Italie* (1807) – put on trial women's condition, at once novels and disquisitions. In her very long, first letter-novel set from 1790 to 1792, a wealthy young widow falls in love with her cousin's fiancé, Léonce, but mothers conspire to separate them. Delphine loses her reputation with impulsive acts of generosity and heedless independence, distressing Léonce who is afflicted by a paralyzing sense of propriety. Manipulators marry him off and trap Delphine into taking religious vows. She escapes to commit suicide rather than survive her lover, who has run away to war after his wife's death. *Delphine*'s perceived immoralism, its views on marriage and the right to divorce or break monastic vows scandalized France and elated Germany. "*Delphine* is a work remarkable as a novel of moral ambiguity written in a tone of moral certitude. [Rousseau's] *La Nouvelle Héloïse* had established this mode, so widely successful with the public" (Gutwirth 1978: 128). Staël reversed the much criticized suicide ending when the book was re-edited in 1820.[7] Permeated by her reading of Rousseau, Goethe, Byron, and Chateaubriand, Staël's tragic tale gives voice to her otherness as a woman artist in the clutches of both oppressive love and repressive society. For the cruel consequence of love as an existential need for women is the purposeful self-abasement of their talents and character (Gutwirth 1978: 102-53). Romanticism and feminism are still anachronisms, held back by the concern for novelistic and moral conventions.

This is true as well of *Corinne ou l'Italie*. This travelogue met with immediate success in France and abroad, including America where Staël sent Jefferson a personal copy. A beautiful female poet, renowned for her eloquent improvisations, living a free-spirited life in her adopted country, Italy, falls in love with a melancholy English lord, Nevil, who eventually leaves her for a paragon of virtue and traditional womanhood, Lucile. The novel gives voice to three nations, calling for a political and ideological reading that got Staël in trouble once again.

The portrayal of female genius, although she meets a tragic fate – the heart-broken Corinne dies – galvanized women authors such as Letitia Landon (L. E. L.) who adapted Staël's plot in *The Improvisatrice* (1824). Byron read *Corinne* as an allegory of the misunderstood genius, of unrewarded creative generosity. He even annotated his lover Teresa's Italian translation of the novel, remarking that Staël "is sometimes right and often wrong about Italy and England – but almost always true in delineating the heart, which is but of one nation and of no country or rather of all" (Byron 1991: 223-4). Mary Shelley agreed but faulted the tragic ending: "For the dignity of womanhood, it were better to teach how one, as highly gifted as Corinne, could find resignation or fortitude enough to endure a too common lot, and rise wiser and better from the trial" (Shelley 2002: 484).

Mary Shelley's main point of contention with the two novels is that "they do not teach the most needful lesson – moral courage" (Shelley 2002: 493). Unlike Richardson's Clarissa and Rousseau's Julie, Staël's unhappy heroines die crushed and diminished, their passions having dominated their reason to the end. In the tradition of Greek and Racinian tragedies, the weight of external forces upon the characters contributes to their downfall.

Published in Italy, Staël's last work, *De l'esprit des traductions* (1816), encouraged Italians to translate English and German poetry to discover new genres and free their art from ancient mythology. She further advocated translation of Shakespeare and Schiller's theater "for theater is really the executive power of literature" (Staël 1861: 296). A. W. Schlegel is the model translator, combining "exactitude with inspiration" in contrast with French habits of adaptation to national taste. This short provocative essay marked the departure point for the Romantic battle in Italy, a fire set by Staël in a final plea for emancipation. To the end "an incorrigible Revolutionary" – in the words of the Milanese governor – she died on Bastille Day, 1817.

Benjamin Constant (1767-1830): Of love and politics

Like Rousseau and Staël, Benjamin Constant was a Swiss Protestant, inheriting a tradition of liberalism of which he would become the most forceful advocate. He received his education in England, Holland, Belgium, and Switzerland, eventually spending two years at Edinburgh, Scotland, where he participated in the exclusive debating club, the Speculative Society.

His passionate and tormented liaison with Staël shaped his literary output as well as his political activism. The enthusiastic articles he wrote for *Le Publiciste* in 1807 defending *Corinne ou l'Italie* had the benefit of insight but also a telling biographical slant, responding to the tragic life of the female genius by justifying the male protagonist's torn character (Balayé 1968). Like Staël, his literary criticism was ahead of practice. When he adapted Schiller's tragedy *Wallenstein* (1809), a preface praised the power of German drama unbound by the French sacrosanct principle of the three unities (time, space, and action), but his tame, abridged, and faulty translation ultimately bowed to French taste, as if the time had not yet come. More successful was the transposition of his unhappy love life into the short novels *Adolphe* (1816) and the unfinished *Cécile*. Constant's prose achieved a piercing exactness in capturing the psychology of characters torn by their prevarication, the author's own failing, so ironically opposed to the constancy implied in his name.

While Staël could never hold an elected office on account of her sex, Constant thrust himself into politics, writing key essays at each turning point (on the Terror, the freedom of the press, elections, bipartisanship, constitutional politics, religion), serving in office when nominated or elected, falling in and out of favor, maintaining in the face of incredible political turmoil and a succession of postrevolutionary authoritarian regimes his opposition to power by force and respect for parliamentarism. He embodied the motto, later used by the ultra-royalists to insult the new generation of poets and critics, that Romanticism is Protestantism in politics, letters and art – the spirit of freedom.

Chateaubriand (1768-1848): Bard of past times

Unlike Staël's childhood, surrounded by a whirlwind of celebrities who inspired and gave free reign to her intellect, Chateaubriand's formative years were pervaded by solitude and gloom, giving free reign to his imagination instead. Chateaubriand grew up in the austere medieval castle of Combourg, surrounded by Brittany's tempestuous ocean, its forlorn marshes and brooding skies, a witness to the comings and goings of ships and the endless wait for the mariners' return. These leitmotivs struck a chord of recognition when discovered in Ossian. Of all French regionalisms, Brittany's Celtic lore was the closest to the Gaelic bard's invocations. Le Tourneur's complete transla- tion of Ossian (1777-84) spurred numerous imitations, including Chateaubriand's. Encouraged by his melancholy sister Lucile, inspired by the English poets Thomas Gray, James Thompson, Edward Young, and by Salomon Gessner's *Idylls*, a morose Chateaubriand tried his hand at poetry, composing from 1784 to 1790 a series of *"Tableaux de la nature"* where nature's beautiful resilience contrasts with the poet's tenuous life. The lyric "I" at the center of these early poems bathes in a Rousseauist reverie.

Outgrowing fugitive poetry, Chateaubriand began to envision an epic narrative, *"l'épopée de l'homme de la nature"* but the ambitious fresco on the North-American Indians would not come to life: " I soon realized I lacked true colors, and if I wanted a faithful picture, I, like Homer, had to visit the people I wanted to paint" (Chateaubriand 1996: 65). To justify his aesthetic project of traveling to America, Chateaubriand conceived of a scientific purpose, namely the discovery of the Northwest passage, itself a journey of epic proportion in keeping with his ambitious dreams and boundless self-assurance. Fraught with contradictions and paradoxes, Chateaubriand's encounter with the New World (April 1791-January 1792) produced a shock that reverberated throughout his life and writing. Although he visited large cities, the traveler followed his exploratory instinct and spent most of his time in the wilderness (*"le désert"*). Instead of the Northwest passage, Chateaubriand discovered a still unspoiled, awe-inspiring nature, home to an indigenous people on the verge of extinction, uprooted and corrupted by settlers and traders – a ruined noble savage.

Following his return from America, Chateaubriand spent seven months in France, hastily married, then joined the royalist army of princes in August 1792. Soon wounded and sick, he fled to his uncle's in Jersey, then moved to England in May 1793. Exile had begun: Chateaubriand would return to France only seven years later, in May 1800.

In 1797 Chateaubriand published his first work in prose, the *Essai sur les révolutions*, an enormous and ambitious comparative history of revolutions as cyclic phenomena. The panoramic essay ends unexpectedly with a lyrical final chapter entitled "Nuit chez les sauvages de l'Amérique" where the author recalls his experience of the sublime. This famous final scene pre-empts the closure of history, by refusing to perceive history as a sealed, apoetical story. Contrary to appearances, the *Essai* is not a farewell to the Muses, an abandonment of poetry for history, but a gesture towards a poetry compatible with the necessity of, and the need for, historical consciousness.

While in exile, Chateaubriand also delved into British literature, commenting on and translating personal favorites, published upon his return to France in a series of articles for the *Mercure de France* (1802) and later grouped in an expanded *Essai sur la littérature anglaise* (1836). In addition to Young and Shakespeare, he selected the lesser-known James Beattie whose *Minstrel, or the Progress of Genius* combined the divine poet and the genius-child in the Scottish shepherd Edwin. Chateaubriand was drawn to other bardic figures. Thomas Gray's defiant bard (*The Bard. A Pindaric Ode,* 1751), the last spokesman of Welsh independence, conveyed the anger, sorrow, and rebellion of those who had fallen victim to history, as many in France's postrevolutionary society. Chateaubriand also translated John Smith, a skillful imitator of Macpherson's *Ossian*. For the 25-year-old Chateaubriand, exiled by the gory aftermath of the Revolution, Ossian's mournful accents, which he so enjoyed as a youth, assumed a powerful immediacy: the importance of history in forging and maintaining one's identity; the crucial role of memory in preserving the past; the threat of erasure by time and death; the survivor's duty to record and testify. Ossian portrayed a devastated landscape of tombs and ruins similar to postrevolutionary France, and expressed similarly painful loss and regret in the wake of an historical trauma. From the fall of the ancien régime to the first-hand discovery of the Indians' tragedy triggered by European conquest, Chateaubriand's early experience of loss was compounded by an exceptionally long yet childless life, which subjected him to witnessing the death of his own generation without begetting a new one, leaving him its sole survivor.

The only voice apt to convey the pervasive sadness of these memories belongs to the elegiac bard, the central archetype of Chateaubriand's life and work. The bard's historical, sociocultural, and mythopoetic role, and the interpretive lyrics and music called for by this role, sums up the origins and destiny of a people. Milton's success in recounting the foundational narrative of Christian religion, Genesis, and his account of the first, the most ineluctable, and most tragic of all prophecies – humankind's subsequent, never-ending Fall – places him at the pinnacle of Chateaubriand's pantheon of bards. Begun in England, his remarkable translation of *Paradise Lost* was eventually completed 35 years later in 1835.

When time came for appeasement, Chateaubriand hoped to repair with the *Génie du christianisme* (1802) the torn link between the French and their traditions, and easily substituted biblical hymns for the Gaelic bard's songs, contrasting David's peaceful lyrics with a violent, haunting past. But the *Génie du christianisme* was also written to atone for the impious, pessimistic *Essai*, which reportedly hastened his mother's death. The *Génie* formulates the essential principles of Chateaubriand's poetics, building a *"théologie poétique"* from the best Christian literature. Christian religion created the conditions for heightened moral conflicts, illustrated in modern epic poems and tragedies; furthermore, Christian religion, by chasing away mythology, revealed nature's true sublime, the source of modern descriptive poetry.

Notwithstanding his celebration of Christianity, Chateaubriand cannot easily be classified as a traditionalist. His deep pessimism is not mere nostalgia but an existential angst in the face of topsy-turvy social and moral values and a weakening of religious faith. In a departure from the Catholic creed, Chateaubriand conceived Christian genius as predominantly the genius of melancholy, without hope or promise of redemption. The yearning for an indefinable ideal causes frustration and loneliness: Chateaubriand identifies this disenchantment as a modern phenomenon, born of the discrepancy between over abundant knowledge and lack of experience. The character René will epitomize *"cet état du vague des passions"* (the vagueness or "unsettled state" of the passions) which consumes the self (Chateaubriand 1976b: 296-8).

Chateaubriand inserted in the *Génie du christianisme* the stories of *Atala* and *René* as "illustrations" of his main thesis, then easily extracted them the better to promote their originality and showcase his talent. *Atala* appeared in 1801, a year earlier than the publication of the *Génie*, and its success paved the way for the enthusiastic reception of the *Génie*. The original framework of the two stories, however, was the unfinished American manuscript of *Les Natchez*, eventually revised 25 years later. This complex genealogy – from two episodes within an epic-like narrative, to illustrations of an aesthetic treatise on religion, then autonomous, albeit unclassifiable, stories – creates ambiguous, multilayered narratives. Atala, a christened Indian, falls in love with the prisoner Chactas captured by her Natchez tribe. They escape into the wilderness, eventually reaching the Catholic mission of Father Aubry. The lovers' initial delight at discovering a common bond (Chactas was adopted by Atala's European father after the latter was forced to leave her mother), is soon burdened by a secret guilt which forbids Atala's union with Chactas. After poisoning herself, Atala confesses that she vowed on her mother's deathbed to remain a virgin. Father Aubry condemns the promise as invalid and the sacrifice misguided, but Atala expires. In the epilogue the narrator encounters the last survivors of the Natchez tribe who inform him that Chactas and Father Aubry perished in the Louisiana massacre perpetrated by the French.

In *René*, an older Chactas is now the sage to whom René, a Frenchman in self-imposed exile, confides his own unhappy story, a confession triggered by a letter announcing his sister Amélie's death. Amélie's soulmate in childhood, René grows apart from her under the pressure of ill-defined feelings and inarticulate longings. Neither traveling abroad nor settling back in France cures his ennui and disgust for life. Amélie returns when her brother's despair puts him on the brink of suicide, but she eventually falls prey to a mysterious ailment, which leads her to withdraw to a convent. The climactic scene occurs as a powerless René watches the ceremony of his sister's religious vow-taking and hears her whisper her criminal passion for her brother.

The twin stories captured the imagination of Europe and met with phenomenal success. Atala and René represented contrasting aspects of the new character later called "Romantic" whose inner torment mirrors a society in the grip of crisis. Set during the corrupted Regency years following Louis XIV's death in 1715, the narrative in effect recalls the traumatic aftermath of the 1789 Revolution. René the European suffers from an agitation without purpose, contradictory impulses that exhaust his wanderlust without achieving peace of mind or heart. For "[t]he heart is a defective instrument, a lyre lacking strings" (Chateaubriand 1980: 80). The half-Indian Atala is alienated like René, she commits suicide like Werther, but she is other, foreign, a modern, split subject, a "*métisse*" (half-caste) who bears the memory of the colonial takeover. This hybridity is embedded in the story's odd style, alternating between the narrator's descriptive prose and the characters' metaphoric language meant to convey their "primitive" voices. Chateaubriand's rhythmic, ternary periods convey the majesty of the wilderness whereas parataxis, namely short, declarative sentences without conjunctions or coordination, transcribes a "*parler sauvage*" that sound paradoxically stilted to our modern ears, and might explain *Atala*'s fall from grace in today's literary cannon. By contrast, René's unbridled expression of vacuity echoes in countless modern dramas.

Catastrophe looms large on Chateaubriand's horizon: struck by the loss of loved ones to the Revolution, obsessed by ruins of literary and political fame (Byron, Napoleon), tormented by history's fateful turns (the downfall of the Indians, the twilight of the Enlightenment), Chateaubriand always contemplated the Fall, the ultimate unhappy ending. The Fall is both the premise and the conclusion of *Les Martyrs* and *Les Natchez*, two epic frescoes in prose, the former opposing pagans and Christians in third-century Gaul, the latter North-American Indians and Europeans. The emotional struggles of their respective protagonists, Eudore and René, their suicidal passivity, their weakening under the burden of exile, their secret wounds, cast them as prototypical antiheroes, and "Romantic" characters. This character assumes yet a different temperament when of the opposite sex: Velléda (Brittany's last bard in *Les Martyrs*) and Mila (René's sister-in-law) are passionate, proud, resolute, active, yet ultimately fall victim to their passion and suffer a similarly tragic fate to their male counterparts.

After the disappointment of *Les Martyrs* in 1809, Chateaubriand officially bade farewell to the muse of poetry and engaged history by becoming a political actor from 1814 until 1830. Even before he recorded his extraordinary life as an epic journey in the autobiographical *Mémoires d'outre-tombe* (1844), a 14-year-old Victor Hugo proclaimed in his 1816 diary: "I want to be Chateaubriand or nothing."

An irreconcilable thematic and stylistic duality at the core of *Les Martyrs* and *Les Natchez* condemned them to a critical purgatory, which has lasted to this day. In each text, the conflict exploded between the epic and the novel, between poetry and prose, Classicism and Romanticism. Indeed *Les Martyrs* and *Les Natchez* are the site of a fundamental hesitation between allegiance to the ancients or to the new Romantic spirit, a hesitation staged as a *mise en abyme*: while relating the decline of Indian tribes and Christian martyrdom, both epic poems seem to ask: is Romanticism a Fall? Is Classicism paradise lost? Chateaubriand's art mirrors his position in letters, poised on the brink of Romanticism, but steeped in Classicism: "mon poème se ressent des lieux qu'il a *fréquenté*: le classique y domine le romantique" (Chateaubriand 1961a: I, 637).[8]

Long outliving Staël and Byron, Chateaubriand wrote his memoirs acutely aware of having begun a "school," but remained divided about his followers.

Senancour (1770-1846): The Invisible Romantic

It seems fitting to end with a case emblematic of the ironies of posterity when it comes to the French early Romantics. When Étienne Pivert de Senancour published his epistolary novel *Oberman* in 1804, the drawn-out, brooding meditations of the lone protagonist failed to capture readers' interests. Thirty years elapsed before the critic Sainte-Beuve and the novelist George Sand wrote articles which turned into prefaces for new editions of *Obermann* in 1833 and 1840, bringing the novel back to life, albeit briefly. It inspired Sainte-Beuve's novel *Volupté* (1834) and Sand's *Lélia* (1833), as well as the composer Liszt,[9] the poet Gérard de Nerval, and Balzac's early novels, in particular *Le Lys dans la Vallée* (*Lily of the Valley*; [1835] 1997). Matthew Arnold wrote two fervent poems in homage to the author of *Obermann*,[10] and also reviewed the book, praising Senancour's "austere and sad sincerity," casting him as the quint-essential Shakespearean tragic character: "as deep as his sense that the time was out of joint, was the feeling of this Hamlet that he had no power to set it right" (Arnold 1960: 157, 160).

With the passage of time, the original confessional, tormented lyricism seemed by then worn on everyone's sleeve, a mere fashion distasteful to its fathers. It provoked Senancour to revise and tone down his one and only novel in 1833, just as Chateau-briand, at exactly the same time, was compulsively footnoting his works in view of their first complete edition. The confrontation of these amended versions has not sufficiently been called upon to understand the conflicted rapport of the early French Romantics with their own creations and the generation who followed them.

NOTES

1 Note that all translations are mine unless otherwise indicated.
2 "La nature est une, comme la vérité: l'une ne comporte pas plus que l'autre, l'épithète de *belle*." ("Discours des Préfaces," in Le Tourneur 1990a: cxxxiii).
3 See Souriau ([1927] 1973), which describes Staël as inferior to Chateaubriand.
4 Her contemporaries never knew this private correspondence. Her *Lettres à M. de Guibert* were published in 1809.
5 Staël's mother, Suzanne Curchod, had been the historian Edmund Gibbon's first and only love but his father prohibited the marriage. Staël's

father, Jacques Necker, was Louis XVI's Finance Minister.
6 See Byron ([1821] 1991). Byron later visited Coppet in 1816, but the Shelleys did not, although they were staying close by in the Villa Diodati on the shores of Lake Geneva where Mary Shelley began *Franken-stein*.
7 Staël had published her *Reflexions sur le suicide* in 1813.
8 This judgment on *Les Martyrs* equally applies to *Les Natchez*.
9 Liszt, "Les Années de pèlerinage: La Vallée d'Oberman" and "Le Mal du pays" (1834).

10 "Stanzas in Memory of the Author of 'Obermann'" (1852), "Obermann Once More" (1867). See Arnold (1986: 66-71, 252-63).

REFERENCES AND FURTHER READING

Primary sources

Arnold, Matthew ([1869] 1960). "Obermann." In *Essays, Letters, and Reviews by Matthew Arnold*, ed. Fraser Neiman. Cambridge, MA: Harvard University Press, pp. 156-63.

Arnold, Matthew (1986). *Poems*. Oxford: Oxford University Press.

Balzac, Honoré de (1997). *Lily of the Valley*, trans. Lucienne Hill. New York: Caroll & Graf.

Byron, George Gordon (1991). "Some recollections of my Acquaintance with Madame de Staël"; "Marginalia in de Staël's *Corinne*." In *The Complete Miscellaneous Prose*, ed. Andrew Nicholson. Oxford: Clarendon Press, pp. 184-6, 222-4.

Chateaubriand, François-René de (1902). *The Memoirs of François-René*, trans. Alexander Teixeira de Mattos, 6 vols. New York: Putnam; London: Freemantle.

Chateaubriand, François-René de (1961a). *Mémoires d'outre-tombe*. 2 vols. Paris: Gallimard.

Chateaubriand, François-René de (1961b). *The Memoirs of Chateaubriand. Selections*, trans. and ed. Robert Baldick. New York: Knopf.

Chateaubriand, François-René de (1969). *Travels in America*, trans. Richard Switzer. Lexington: University of Kentucky Press.

Chateaubriand, François-René de (1976a). *The Genius of Christianity: or, The Spirit and Beauty of the Christian Religion*, trans. Charles I. White. New York: H. Fertig.

Chateaubriand, François-René de (1976b). *The Martyrs*, trans. and ed. O. W. Wight. New York: Howard Fertig.

Chateaubriand, François-René de (1980). *Atala. René*, trans. Irving Putter. Berkeley: University of California Press.

Chateaubriand, François-René de (1996). *Atala. René. Les Aventures du dernier Abencérage*. Paris: Flammarion.

Constant de Rebecque, Henri-Benjamin (1965). *Wallstein, tragédie en 5 actes et en vers*, ed. Jean-René Derré. Paris: Les Belles Lettres.

Constant de Rebecque, Henri-Benjamin (1988). *The Political Writings*, trans. and ed. Biancamaria Fontana. Cambridge, UK and New York: Cambridge University Press.

Constant de Rebecque, Henri-Benjamin (2001). *Adolphe*, ed. Patrick Coleman, trans. Margaret Mauldon. Oxford: Oxford University Press.

Delon, Michel (ed.) (1997). *Anthologie de la poésie française du dix-huitième siècle*. Paris: Gallimard.

Gouges, Olympe de (1986). *Oeuvres*, ed. Benoîte Groult. Paris: Mercure de France.

Lespinasse, Julie de (1997). *Lettres*, ed. Jacques Dupont. Paris: La Table Ronde.

Le Tourneur, Pierre (trans.) (1776-83). *Shakespeare traduit de l'Anglois*, 20 vols. Paris.

Le Tourneur, Pierre (1990a). *Pierre Le Tourneur. Préface du Shakespeare traduit de l'anglois*, ed. Jacques Gury. Geneva: Droz.

Le Tourneur, Pierre (1990b). *Voyage à Ermenonville*. Paris: A l'Ecart.

Macpherson, James. *The Poems of Ossian and Related Works*, ed. Howard Gaskill. Edinburgh: Edinburgh University Press.

Martino, Pierre (1925). *Stendhal. Racine et Shakespeare*, vol. 1. Paris: Champion.

Mercier, Louis-Sébastien (1999). *Du théâtre ou nouvel essai sur l'art dramatique*. In Jean-Claude Bonnet (ed.), *Mon Bonnet de nuit. Suivi de Du théâtre*. Paris: Mercure de France, pp. 1126-478.

Mercier, Louis-Sébastien (1801). *Néologie, ou Vocabulaire de mots nouveaux, à renouveler ou pris dans des acceptions nouvelles*. Paris: Moussard et Maradan.

Rousseau, Jean-Jacques (1990-2001). *The Collected Writings of Rousseau*, ed. Roger D. Masters and Christopher Kelly, 9 vols. Hanover, NH: University Press of New England.

Rousseau, Jean-Jacques (1997). *Julie, or the New Heloise. Letters of two lovers who live in a small town at the foot of the Alps*, ed. and trans. Philip Stewart and Jean Vaché, vol. 6. Hanover, NH: University Press of New England.

Rousseau, Jean-Jacques (2000). *The Reveries of the Solitary Walker*, ed. Christopher Kelly, trans. Charles E. Butterworth, Alexandra Cook, and Terence E. Marshall, vol. 8. Hanover, NH: University Press of New England.

Sainte-Beuve, Charles-Augustin (1995). *Volupté: The Sensual Man*, trans. Marilyn Gaddis Rose. Albany: State University of New York Press.

Sand, George (1978). *Lelia*, ed and trans. Maria Espinosa. Bloomington: Indiana University Press.

Schlegel, August Wilhelm (1965). *Course of Lectures on Dramatic Art and Literature*, trans. John Black. New York: AMS Press.

Sénancour, Étienne-Pivert de (2003). *Obermann*, trans. Arthur Edward Waite. Kila, MT: RA Kessinger Publishing Co.

Shelley, Mary (2002). "Madame de Staël. 1766-1817." In Clarissa Campbell Orr (ed.), *Literary Lives and Other Writings. Vol. 3. French Lives (Molière to Madame de Staël)*. London: Pickering and Chatto, pp. 457-94.

Staël, Anne Louise Germaine de (1861). "De l'esprit des traductions." In *Oeuvres complètes*, vol. 2. Paris: Didot, pp. 294-7.

Staël, Anne Louise Germaine de (1964). *Madame de Staël on Politics, Literature, and National Character*, ed. and trans. Morroe Berger. New York: Doubleday.

Staël, Anne Louise Germaine de (1968). *De l'Allemagne*, 2 vols. Paris: Gallimard.

Staël, Anne Louise Germaine de (1987). *Major Writings of Germaine de Staël*. [originally published as *An Extraordinary Woman. Selected Writings of Germaine de Staël*], trans. and ed. Vivian Folkenflik. New York: Columbia University Press.

Staël, Anne Louise Germaine de (1991). *De la Littérature*. Paris: Gallimard.

Staël, Anne Louise Germaine de (1995). *Delphine*, trans. Avriel Goldberger. De Kalb: Northern Illinois University Press.

Staël, Anne Louise Germaine de (1998). *Corinne, or Italy*, trans. and ed. Sylvia Raphael. Oxford: Oxford University Press.

Staël, Anne Louise Germaine de (2000). *Ten Years of Exile*, trans. Avriel H. Goldberger. De Kalb: Northern Illinois University Press.

Stendhal (Henri Beyle) (1962). *Racine and Shakespeare*, trans. Guy Daniels. New York: Crowell-Collier Press.

Secondary sources

Balayé, Simone (1968). "Benjamin Constant lecteur de Corinne." In Pierre Cordey and Jean-Luc Seylaz (eds.), *Benjamin Constant. Acte du Congrès de Lausanne*. Geneva: Droz, pp. 189-99.

Bénichou, Paul (1996). *Le Sacre de l'écrivain. 1750-1830. Essai sur l'avènement d'un pouvoir spirituel laïque dans la France moderne*. Paris: Gallimard.

Bowman, Frank Paul (1999). "The Specificity of French Romanticism." In Andrea Ciccarelli, John C. Isbell, and Brian Nelson (eds.), *The People's Voice. Essays on European Romanticism*. Clayton, Melbourne: Monash University, pp. 74-88.

Delon, Michel (1988). *L'Idée d'énergie au tournant des Lumières (1770-1820)*. Paris: Presses universitaires de France.

Ceserani, Remo (1999). "The New System of Literary Modes in the Romantic Age." In Andrea Ciccarelli, John C. Isbell, and Brian Nelson (eds.), *The People's Voice. Essays on European Romanticism*. Clayton, Melbourne: Monash University, pp. 7-25.

Fabre, Jean (1980). *Lumières et romantisme. Energie et nostalgie de Rousseau à Mickiewicz*. Paris: Klincksieck.

Finch, M. B. and Peers, E. Allison (1920). *The Origins of French Romanticism*. London: Constable.

Herold, Christopher (2002). *Mistress to an Age. A Life of Madame de Staël*. New York: Grove Press.

Isbell, John C. (1994). *The Birth of European Romanticism: Truth and Propaganda in Staël's "De l'Allemagne."* Cambridge, UK and New York: Cambridge University Press.

King, Everard H. (1984). "Beattie's *The Minstrel* and the French Connection." *Scottish Literary Journal*, II (2): 36-53.

Gutwirth, Madelyn (1978). *Madame de Staël, Novelist. The Emergence of the Artist as Woman*. Urbana: University of Illinois Press.

Gutwirth, Madelyn, Goldberger, Avriel and Szmurlo, Karyna (1991). *Germaine de Staël. Crossing the Borders*. New Brunswick, NJ: Rutgers University Press.

Minski, Alexander (1998). *Le Préromantisme*. Paris: Colin.

Monglond, André (1965). *Le Préromantisme français*. Paris: Corti.

Mornet, Daniel (1912). *Le Romantisme en France au dix-huitième siècle*. Paris: Hachette.

Mortier, Roland (1982). *L'Originalité. Une nouvelle catégorie esthétique au siècle des Lumières*. Paris: Droz.

Souriau, Maurice (1973). *Histoire du romantisme en France*, 2 vols. Geneva: Slatkine Reprints.

Trumpener, Katie (1997). *Bardic Nationalism. The Romantic Novel and the British Empire*. Princeton, NJ: Princeton University Press.

Van Tieghem, Paul (1967). *Ossian en France*, 2 vols. Geneva: Slatkine Reprints.

Van Tieghem, Paul (1973). *Le Préromantisme. Études d'histoire littéraire européenne*. Geneva: Slatkine Reprints.

Viallaneix, Paul (ed.) (1975). *Le Préromantisme: hypothèque ou hypothèse? Colloque Clermont-Ferrand. 20-30 juin 1972*. Paris: Klinckseick.

Viatte, Auguste (1979). *Les Sources occultes du Romantisme. Illuminisme, théosophie. 1770-1820*, 2 vols. Paris: Champion.

11

The Poetry of Loss: Lamartine, Musset, and Nerval

Jonathan Strauss

French Romantic poetry is generally considered to have begun in 1820, with the publication of Alphonse de Lamartine's *Méditations poétiques* (*Poetic Meditations*). This slim collection of 24 poems immediately won a breathtaking commercial success, running through seven editions within its first year, and awakened in the public emotions that until then had not found expression. As Lamartine would later write, "I am the first to have brought poetry down from Parnassus, to have given to what used to be called the muse, instead of a lyre with seven conventional strings, the very fibers of man's heart, touched and shaken by the innumerable shudderings of the soul and of nature" (Lamartine 1968: 303, my translation).[1] Some 12 years later, the young poet Alfred de Musset would recall a friend's reaction: "You struck your brow, on reading Lamartine / Édouard, you blanched like a gambler abandoned by luck" (Musset 1957: 128). In Musset's subsequent commentary on this response, which seems to record more a projection of the poet's own attitudes than a faithful description of his friend Édouard Bocher's, two competing impulses seem forced together: on the one hand the jubilatory discovery that one's most intimate feelings could be the essential matter of poetry and, on the other, a violent sense of rivalry with other poets' expressions of their own interiority. Lamartine himself, however, kept largely aloof from these jealousies and disputes, as well as from the competing parties and *cénacles* that divided the tumultuous Parisian literary scene. Although some of his later poems, especially the lyric novel *Jocelyn*, enjoyed considerable success and he pursued a political career that reached its apogee in 1848, when he effectively, if briefly, became the French head of state, Lamartine's later works never struck the same nerve that his first book had, and his poetry was soon relegated to that dusky realm of literature that is seldom read but will forever be anthologized. In 1871, Arthur Rimbaud would look back and comment, "Lamartine is sometimes visionary, but strangled by the old forms" (Rimbaud 1972: 253). Even Marius-François Guyard, the editor of the authoritative version of Lamartine's poetry wrote, some 40 years ago: "My poet is dreadfully dated" (Lamartine 1963: ix).

It is difficult now to understand the violence of the emotions that Lamartine's poems unleashed, but even a critic like M.-F. Guyard, who denied that they changed anything at all, still recognized, paradoxically, the originality in their "new music."[2] Some of their force undoubtedly came from discovering the value of one's own feelings, from the rush of personal freedom and validation, from the revelation that, unlike Molière's Monsieur Jourdain, in one's soul one had been speaking poetry all along. As the German philosopher G. W. F. Hegel argued, at about the same time that the *Méditations* appeared: "as the center and proper content of lyric poetry there must be placed the poetic concrete person, the poet" (Hegel 1975, II: 1129). Part of the reason for Lamartine's eclipse probably stems from the very success of his poetry: the revolution that he had helped bring about was so quickly complete that there was no need to return to it. Its new aesthetic of individual plenitude had become so normal that even a writer with a sensibility as different as Rimbaud's could argue, some 50 years later, that "the first matter of study for a man who wants to be a poet is knowledge of himself, in his entirety; he looks for his soul . . . it is a matter of making his soul monstrous" (Rimbaud 1972: 251). On the other hand, the very reminder that this plenitude (a word that Rimbaud uses in this passage to describe the goal of poetry) could require a revolution, that it had to be achieved and imposed by another poet, contradicted its very idea by making it contingent on an outside force. To be consistent with himself, Lamartine was obliged, in this sense, to disappear. Conversely, and paradoxically, after his first success, this poet of emotions could only be interesting to a readership that was not emotionally invested in his work, or that did not take its ideological pretensions at face value.

That readership has been long in coming and may not yet have appeared. Hegel had already described the failure of Romanticism – and with it, of art – as an excess of subjective interiority, and this attitude has retained its currency and, indeed, become a cliché (see, e.g., Hegel 1975, I: 586). The entry on French literature in a recent edition of the *World Book Encyclopedia*, for example, states bluntly that "Romantic writers were extremely self-centered" (Brosman 2002: 522). If a certain queasiness, like a sense of shame at their exhibitionism, has attached itself to these authors, such that Rimbaud, for example, can only accept their project if the exposed self becomes monstrous, that queasiness probably also betrays subsequent generations' desire to hide the pleasures of the self and thereby protect them. Precisely because they have attained the status of inaugural work, Lamartine's *Méditations* remind any readers who would take them seriously of both the historical facticity of the individual they portray and the possibility that that individual may exist only as an object of (narcissistic) desire.

But were one to look attentively at the way French Romantic poetry constructs a sense of self, it would soon become apparent that the subject of these works is obsessed by its incompleteness, which takes the specific form of loss. These poems are fixated on death and bereavement. The very first of the *Méditations* is entitled "L'Isolement" (Isolation), but it does not conjure up images of self-fulfillment or subjective wholeness. Instead, it speaks of sadness and dispossession, the feeling that the world has lost its charm and that one lives on in it as if after one's own death. The cause of this dejection, this wound to the solitary self, comes from the absence of another – indeed of a single other, and that specificity is emphasized in one of the most striking lines of French poetry: "Un seul être vous manque, et tout est dépeuplé" (A single being is gone, and all is empty; 1963: 6). The heart of isolation, as this poem depicts it, is the sense of loss, and it is the lost object, rather than the self, that contains within it the plenitude of existence, that envelops in its disappearance the whole of humanity and life. The other contains the completeness of the world. And that other is unique in the sense that he or she cannot be replaced, that there is nothing else in the world that can restore the world.

On the one hand, the loss of the beloved is both catastrophic and inevitable, the tragedy at the core of human existence. As Lamartine writes of "Man": "Il veut aimer toujours, ce qu'il aime est fragile!" (He wants to love forever; what he loves is fragile!; 1963: 6). And yet, on the other hand, the poet seems to be in a strange hurry to reach this catastrophe. He almost never lingers on scenes with his beloved, and on the rare occasions that he does, this human contact is generally depicted as a memory evoked in mourning, which is to say, as an absence rather than a presence. The poem "Le Lac" (The Lake), Lamartine's most famous work and the most certain guarantee of his permanence in the French canon, describes a missed meeting between lovers. It is, as virtually every French schoolchild knows, based on events in the poet's own life – his passion for a young woman named Julie Charles, their intention to meet at Aix-les-Bains, where they had already spent time together at the Le Bourget lake, the illness that prevented her from keeping their appointment, her subsequent death. The poem revisits the site of the lovers' happiness as seen through the eyes of the poet, who has returned alone to the lake. As Barbara Johnson has observed, however, nothing in the elegiac tone of the poem, nothing in its sense of tragedy and finality, would lead one to suspect that Julie Charles, who only died several months *after* the missed rendez-vous, was not already dead at the time (Johnson 1989: 628). In this somewhat unseemly haste to mourn his lover, Lamartine reveals a certain, crucial confusion in the notion of loss. A missed appointment is tantamount to death. Every absence is haunted by the absolute. And the validation, the preciousness of the individual, derives in large part from this fragility, from the constant possibility that he or she could disappear. Indeed, the sense of completeness in a single, other person seems to come, for Lamartine, only when that person is gone.

Similarly, in "Isolement" it is impossible to determine whether the absent one is dead or simply elsewhere. This categorical confusion between the passing and the eternal, between individual and totality, is also evident in the lability with which ostensibly irreplaceable love-objects can stand in for each other, for Lamartine's poetry is caught between mourning for a lost lover and yearning for an absent God. Like "Le Lac," "L'Isolement" appears at first to commemorate the disappearance of a loved person, but the missing "being" it laments is never identified. Instead, it remains the "vague objet de mes vœux," the "bien idéal que toute âme désire, / Et qui n'a pas de nom au terrestre séjour!" (the "vague object of my prayers," the "ideal good that each soul desires / And that has no name on earth!"; 1963: 4). And if what human beings love is fragile, in the poem "L'Homme" (*Man*), it is because

> Tout mortel est semblable à l'exilé d'Eden:
> Lorsque Dieu l'eut banni du céleste jardin,
> Mesurant d'un regard les fatales limites. (Lamartine 1963: 6)

> (Every mortal is like the exile from Eden:
> When God cast him out from the heavenly garden,
> Measuring with a glance the limits of his doom.)

The identity of the unique and absent being has slipped from another person to God, and loss has changed from the disappearance of a lover to a banishment from the divine – a passage that has been facilitated by the transcendence of the beloved, for insofar as she is irreplaceable, she is of an incalculable, an infinite value.

While Lamartine's reputation hangs on a single love elegy, the emphasis of his lyric production as a whole is religious, especially in his subsequent works. And as the object of desire shifts from a perishable person to an immortal God, the value of all that is transient suffers. Increasingly, he uses the word "néant" (nothingness) to designate the material world. At first, the term refers to the opposite of being, the constant threat of irreversible destruction that hangs over natural existence. In the poem "L'Immortalité" (Immortality) Lamartine asks, "Au néant destinés, / Est-ce pour le néant que les êtres sont nés?" (To nothingness sworn / Is it for this nothingness that all creatures are born?; 1963: 18) and in "Stances" (Stanzas) he speaks of "Celui qui du néant a tiré la matière" (He who from nothingness brought forth matter; 1963: 167). In a later poem, "Éternité de la nature" (Eternity of nature), he will write, however, that "Je sens en moi-même mon néant" (I feel my nothingness in me; 1963: 466), indicating that the void is no longer a pure and insensible category or a simple ontological absolute, but has become something a person can feel, like an absence. The subject himself, moreover, identifies with that nonexistence, as if he were not so much a speaking being as a speaking nothing. "Mon âme," he writes a couple of pages later, pursuing this idea, "est une mort qui se sent et se souffre" (My soul is a death that feels and suffers itself; 1963: 481). This emptiness then spreads out beyond the subject: "On trouve au fond de tout le vide et le néant" (At the bottom of everything one finds nothingness and void; 1963: 475), until it poisons existence itself: "Mourir! ah! ce seul mot fait horreur de la vie!" (Dying! ah! the word alone fills life with horror!; 1963: 480).

It is not merely cataclysmic that this subject be lost, it is also unbearable. All that is not God becomes an object of revulsion. But Lamartine was writing in the aftermath of the Enlightenment and the Revolution, from a generation that had witnessed, if only in a spasm of anarchic terror, the institutionalization of God's death. It was against this that Lamartine had to assert his own religious convictions, and as early as the *Méditations* he explicitly rejected the godless, materialist world that discoveries in physics had suggested to many eighteenth-century philosophers. According to the poem "L'Homme," he himself passed through a stage of rationalist atheism, during which "J'étudiai la loi par qui roulent les cieux: / Dans leurs brillants déserts Newton guida mes yeux" (I studied the laws that govern the skies: / In their bright wastes Newton guided my eyes; 1963: 7). These doubts led ultimately to the conviction that those skies were not, in fact, deserted and that their laws did not derive from the soulless combinations of material forces. Still, the fear that God too could die never stopped haunting Lamartine's writings. And sometimes this fear really is like a haunting, an absent utterance that presses, unseen, against what is written and changes it. It can be a single word that slips in fragments through the verses, as in the "Hymne au Christ" (Hymn to Christ):

> Pour moi, soit que ton nom ressuscite ou succombe,
> O Dieu de mon berceau, sois le Dieu de ma tombe!
> Plus la nuit est obscure et plus mes faibles yeux
> S'attachent au flambeau qui pâlit dans les cieux. (Lamartine 1963: 415)

> (For me, whether your name succumbs or relives,
> O God of my cradle, be the God my tomb gives!
> The darker the night, the more my weak eyes
> Seek out the pale torch that illumines the skies.)

The word "tombeau" (tomb) almost always accompanies "flambeau" (torch) in Lamartine's poetry, as if the two terms were necessarily linked in his imagination, like light and dark, loss and restitution, death and resurrection. But there is not a single "tombeau" in this long poem, and instead, its cognate, "tombe" replaces it throughout. Here, in the last lines, however, the longer version of the word is evoked by the return of the "flambeau" two lines after "tombe." Unnecessary for the rhyme, it still lingers in proximity to the remnants of its missing partner, conjuring up an effaced tomb, a lost marker of loss that binds the imagery together in a condensed theogony of despair redeemed.

This poem is marked – literally – by the erasure of an even greater loss. A passage in it of 20 lines contemplates the death of God. Beginning with the question, "Et tu meurs?" (And you die?) addressed to the divinity, it goes on to imagine a world in which the revelations of Christ had become as vacant of meaning as the pagan beliefs they had once replaced. Although it was finally reintegrated into published versions of the poem, this whole section is crossed out in the manuscript. In an anxious, wavering gesture, a doubt is expressed, cancelled out, then let stand: "Et tu meurs?" It is a doubt, moreover, that worries at all of Lamartine's poetry. Had he been convinced of God's immortality, it seems unlikely he would have felt the need to prove it as often as he did, but the alternative is intolerable: the world of absolute dispossession of "L'Isolement," in which pleasures have been emptied of their charm, relations of their meaning, and life reduced to a sort of sentient death.

Paul Bénichou has argued that "in the great French Romantic poetry, *there is no unhappy love*, except with Musset" (Bénichou 1992: 103, emphasis in original). "The death of Elvire," he explains for those who might be puzzled by this statement, "is not, for Lamartine, a misfortune of love: he knows that he has been loved and he believes that he continues to be loved in heaven" (ibid.). Although Lamartine himself does not seem to have shared the great critic's sunny confidence about his love life, Bénichou has put his finger on a crucial element in his poetics: God's existence is a palliative and cure for the loss of a loved one. The only problem, of course, is that God may not exist.

And Bénichou is right that Alfred de Musset's relation to love is different from everything that had preceded it. For all their apparent callowness, Musset's sufferings in love force a rethinking of the question of loss, shifting it away from the problem of God's existence and changing its significance as an ontological category. Born 20 years after Lamartine, he was, even by the standards of his young cohort, remarkable for his precociousness. A frail dandy with fine features, a nervous, embittered sensibility, and a gift for writing sinuous verses, Musset has often struck readers as a superficial and narcissistic poet. Lamartine publicly heaped scorn on him, addressing him in verse as an

> Enfant aux blonds cheveux, jeune homme au cœur de cire,
> Dont la lèvre a le pli des larmes ou du rire,
> Selon que la beauté qui règne sur tes yeux
> Eut un regard hier sévère ou gracieux. (Lamartine 1963: 1209)

> (Blond-haired child, young man with a heart of wax,
> Whose lip bends to the folds of tears or laughs
> According as the beauty who reigns over your eyes
> Had yesterday a severe or a gracious look.)

and then upbraiding him with the stern lesson that "celui qui rit de l'enfance au tombeau / De l'immortalité porte mal le flambeau" (whoever laughs from childhood to the tomb / Bears ill the torch of immortality; p. 1210).

Lamartine was responding to a poem that Musset had addressed to him and in which the young man had tried to reorient the idea of death away from the question of God:

> Qu'est-ce donc qu'oublier si ce n'est pas mourir?
> Ah! c'est plus que mourir; c'est survivre à soi-même.
> L'âme remonte au ciel quand on perd ce qu'on aime.
> Il ne reste de nous qu'un cadavre vivant;
> Le désespoir l'habite, et le néant l'attend. (Musset 1957: 333)

> (What then is forgetting if not to die?
> Ah! more than death, it's surviving oneself.
> The soul returns to heaven when one loses what one loves.
> Nothing is left of us but a living corpse;
> Despair inhabits it and the void awaits it.)

Many of the older poet's terms are in play here: despair and nothingness, the idea of existence as a living death. But the relations of causality have reversed. No longer is loss – or, here, "forgetting" – a result of death, but rather death a result of loss. One is not forgotten because one dies, but instead, one dies in that one is forgotten. This is particularly evident in Musset's description of the "nuit d'horreur et de détresse" (night of horror and distress) in which a lover abandoned him:

> O toi qui sais aimer, réponds, amant d'Elvire,
> Comprends-tu que l'on parte et qu'on se dise adieu?
> Comprends-tu que ce mot, la main puisse l'écrire,
> Et le cœur le signer, et les lèvres le dire
> [...]
> Comprends-tu qu'un lien qui, dans l'âme immortelle,
> Chaque jour plus profond se forme à notre insu;
> [...]
> Un lien tout-puissant dont les nœuds et la trame
> Sont plus durs que la roche et que les diamants;
> Qui ne craint ni le temps, ni le fer, ni la flamme
> Ni la mort elle-même, et qui fait des amants
> Jusque dans le tombeau s'aimer les ossements;
> Comprends-tu que dix ans ce lien nous enlace,
> Qu'il ne fasse dix ans qu'un seul être de deux,
> Puis tout à coup se brise, et, perdu dans l'espace,
> Nous laisse épouvantés d'avoir cru vivre heureux? (Musset 1957: 332)

> (O you who know how to love, respond, Elvire's lover,
> Do you understand how one can part and say adieu?
> Do you understand how this word, the hand can write it,
> And the heart sign it, and the lips speak it
> [...]
> Do you understand how a bond that, in the immortal soul,
> Each day deeper is formed without our knowing –
> [...]
> An all-powerful bond whose knots and weave
> Are harder than rock and diamonds,
> That fears neither time nor iron nor flame
> Nor death itself, and makes lovers
> Even in the tomb love each other's bones –
> Do you understand how for ten years this bond holds us,
> How for ten years it makes one being of two,
> Then suddenly it breaks, and disappearing into space,
> Leaves us horrified to have thought we were living in happiness?)

The single word that made life an object of horror for Lamartine was "mourir" (dying; 1963: 480). But here, death does not really seem to trouble Musset, who imagines, anyway, a love that is stronger. For him, instead, the word of horror is "Adieu," and it drives him to a stunned incomprehension, a stuttering failure even to pose adequately the question of its possibility and significance. "Adieu" emerges from these lines as a nonsense that cannot be integrated into meaningful life but that is nonetheless experienced in that life, like some painful epistemological wound. Even in the term itself, there is a rejection of Lamartine's laborious piety of redeemed loss: to wait until God rejoins the lovers, or to be "à Dieu" (literally "to God") rather than each other, is meaningless.

Musset's reversal reconciles his poetry with what one might call a strong conception of death, or death understood as sheer nonexistence. This was an outlook that had gained ground and then been institutionalized under the Revolution of 1789, when Joseph Fouché, a *député* to the National Convention, had ordered that the gates to all graveyards be inscribed with the words "Death is an eternal sleep" (Kselman 1993: 125-6). True, even unwaking sleep is not quite sheer nonbeing, and the purity of death in Musset's poem is troubled, too, by images of lovers embracing in the tomb. Still, this is infinitely closer than Lamartine to death as an ontological absolute. Nearly a century later, Ludwig Wittgenstein will write that "death is not an event in life," that its nothingness disappears from experience (Wittgenstein 1922: 185, §6.4311). The philosopher Paul Edwards (1978) will argue that it cannot be considered a state, since nothingness does not exist and states are always states of being. And Heidegger will make the certainty of absolute and impending demise the source of human individuality (Heidegger 1962, especially pp. 279-311). But Musset opens the conceptual space for absolute death within his poetry by rejecting its aesthetic and intellectual interest. Unlike a Heidegger or a Lamartine, he does not make nonexistence a foundational category of experience. Instead, the mystery that haunts and horrifies him is an interpersonal and psychological one: the possibility that one can lose another person's love. There is a certain almost Kantian intellectual integrity in this move. For if death is nonexistence and if nonexistence brackets itself out of experience, then what we can know of death can only be derived (or projected) from actual experiences. We can know nothing of death in itself, not because it is heavily guarded and mysterious, but because it is nothing, and what we can know, therefore, is only life. But even that life, Musset argues, is riddled and torn by its own incomprehensibilities. Viewed as superficial for not confronting issues like mortality straight on, for turning instead to the sufferings of love, Musset has, in that very turning, opened the possibility of a far more ontologically rigorous poetic enterprise, and, at the same time, a far more human one. The uniqueness of the other is still expressed in terms of loss, but the absolute value of that loss no longer derives from the absoluteness of nonexistence or *le néant*. Instead it comes from within life. Loss attains its ultimate significance not from the eternity of death but from the irreplaceability of the beloved. And death itself, from this perspective, is revealed to be a derivative, a subcategory of loving separation, a psychological rather than an ontological concept.

The vehemence of Lamartine's response to Musset is less surprising when one considers that the younger poet is redefining loss in almost precisely the terms

Lamartine had tried to avoid or repress: that the notion of absolute absence derives from the loss of the beloved in her specificity and cannot, therefore, be palliated by the presence of another, even if that other is God himself. And Musset offers no solution for this problem: he simply plants himself – and his readers – before its incomprehensibility.

Gérard de Nerval was two years older and much more idiosyncratic a literary figure than Musset. He belonged, early in his career, to a raucous group of young artists and writers that included Théophile Gautier and who were variously known as the Jeunes-France, the Bousingos, or the *petit cénacle* (to distinguish them from the *Cénacle* itself, which was headed by Victor Hugo). Among his contemporaries, Nerval was as famous for the insanity that eventually led to his suicide as he was for his writings. Even his friends tended to treat him with a certain supercilious compassion, because he was genuinely a victim of the madness that many of the rest of them carefully affected. The most enduring of his poetry, written near the end of his life, is hermetic and strange, a dense fabric of complex allusions and references that often seems to fall apart under the very pressure of its own impossible aspirations. His poetic output was slight, a small fraction of his writings, which included stories, novellas, theater, travel narratives, and drama criticism. Because of the opacity of his poetry and because there is so little of it, with Nerval one is almost compelled to read his poems through his other writings. And an abiding, preoriginal sense of loss pervades them.

This is particularly evident in the most famous of Nerval's short stories, "Sylvie," which recounts a series of unhappy love affairs on the part of the narrator. There is a strange picture in the story, much commented on. It is strange because it is not there and yet seems to sum up the whole text, to gather its narrative threads and echoing characters, even its sense of time, into a single figure. "To me this half-dreamt memory explained everything," Nerval writes. "This vague, hopeless love I had conceived for an actress, this love which swept me up every evening when the curtain rose, only to release me when sleep finally descended, had its seed in the memory of Adrienne, a night-flower blooming in the pale effulgence of the moon, a phantom fair and rosy" (Nerval 1999: 150-1). Everything, he promises, is revealed in this return to a hidden memory, to an original encounter, to this visitation by a ghost. There is a key, he says, to his repeated attachments and it will release the meaning of this apparently empty gesture of hopeless love. Then he tries to explain the connections between that first visit and all its revisitings through a comparison: "This resemblance to a figure I had long forgotten was now taking shape with singular vividness; it was a pencil sketch smudged by time that was now turning into a painting, like those studies by the Old Masters that one has admired in some museum, only to discover their dazzling original somewhere else" (1999: 151). But the original, the key to all these insistent returns, disappears under the reader's eyes, for two different similes are being used here, and they do not quite match up. The forgotten image is a faded drawing that turns into a painting, but it is also an old sketch that copies an original. In the first case, the drawing precedes the painting that subsequently repeats it. In the second, the drawing copies the painting. The copy is, in short, indistinguishable from the original – or rather *is* the original – and Nerval thus plunges his story deep into the postmodern logic of the simulacrum, while his inescapable ghost theater transforms itself into a preoriginally alienated society of the spectacle (Newmark 1988: 211-12, 220-1).

These sorts of repetitions repeat themselves throughout his writings. Everywhere, the figures of beloved women fade into one another, and seem to find their emblem in the three Erinyes-like sisters of *Aurélia*, "the contours of whose faces varied like the flame of a lamp, and at each moment something of the one passed into the other" (Nerval 1983-99, III: 708-9). One finds, in this same book, the stuttering creation and recreation of the world, constantly striving and failing to begin. There is also the line of rapacious kings who re-emerged from their own deaths "to be born again in the form of a young child who was later called to empire" (ibid., p. 713). Even the "I" repeats itself in a fantasy of endless, all-consuming reincarnation in the preface to *Les Filles du feu* (The Daughters of Fire): "At bottom, inventing is remembering, said a moralist [...] From the moment I believed I had grasped the series of my previous lives, it was as easy for me to have been a prince, a king, a magus, and even God; the chain was broken and marked the hours as minutes" (Nerval 1984-93, III: 451). The continuity binding the series of "I"s breaks under their uncontrollable proliferation, and in the chaos that ensues even the hours lose their value. How is one to determine an original moment when time itself has given up its self-identity, when hours pass for minutes? And yet this, "au fond" – at the bottom of things – is the moment of invention, the instant of creation, the origin.

There is an anecdote, repeated in several places among Nerval's writings, that would seem to offer some insight into the meaning of all these echoes and returns, if only because the story is about writing itself, about the field in and on which these repetitions take place. As such, it marks a moment when the writing no longer tells but is told, a moment in which the text, this theatre of ghosts, reflects on itself.

The scene appears in fragments and allusions throughout Nerval's publications and correspondence. It concerns the three men who, in the Nervalian cosmogony, are responsible for the invention of printing, men whose ideas blend together to create a miraculous event that none of them alone could have foreseen. But first among equals is Faust, and it is to his name that Nerval most frequently returns when speaking of the origins of typography. In a letter to a friend, two female personages also hover just out of sight: one a "bourgeois woman who does not understand [Faust] and makes him suffer, but who saves him by her religious feelings" and the other "the ideal woman [...] the eternal dream of genius," a Lilith figure who ultimately seeks to frustrate the inventor's work. And Nerval hesitates between two divergent impulses behind the very idea of printing itself, stating at one moment that it had been inspired by Satan and at another by divine providence (Nerval 1984-93, II: 1296).

It took, in short, a very dysfunctional and nonnuclear family to create the printing press, but what the invention itself meant within this dynamic seems at least partially decipherable. One version of the creation story is particularly telling. In it, the young Faust delivers some work to monks in a scriptorium, where he finds them scraping the text from old manuscripts in order to recycle the pages underneath. He is horrified to see one of the men beginning on the *Iliad* and in order to save what might have been the only remaining copy of the poem, he purchases the book. "It was necessary to have a document so that he could leave the monastery with the book. The prior gave it to him graciously and imprinted his seal on the parchment. A ray of light crossed [Faust's] mind. He could shout 'Eureka!' like Archimedes. And must we not see the hand of Providence in the combination of two ideas?" (Nerval 1984-93, III: 50).

The psychoanalyst Piera Aulagnier has argued that myths of origin are collective versions of an attempt to answer a more personal question about the subject's own creation:

> Now, whether it is an individual history or the history of subjects [in general], both share the same requirement [. . .]. The first paragraph cannot show up as a series of blank lines: if such were the case, all of the others would find themselves hanging on the risk that one day a word, by being filled in there, could declare them all to be entirely false. That is why, on the level of the history of subjects, one can say that all myths, which are always the myth of an origin, have the function of guaranteeing the existence of this first paragraph. (Aulagnier 1975: 227)

The subject was not there itself in the moment that, above all, interests it: the moment when it was conceived. So the story must come from elsewhere, must remain from a lost time: it is, in short, a text, like those that are being scraped away in the scriptorium. "Il fallait un écrit" (It was necessary to have a document), as Nerval writes.

Two ideas, long separated, join at last in this jubilant moment that drives an involuntary cry from Faust. *Eureka*: I have found it! And what he has found is, on some level, the psychoanalytic primal scene, the violent encounter when two forces together conceive the new and give a terrifyingly fascinating answer to the question "where did I come from?"

More important than the answer to a nagging mystery, however, is the motivation leading up to this suddenly recovered episode: printing was created to protect against an irreparable loss. This statement can be understood in two different but complementary senses: on the one hand, it means that the story of printing was invented by Nerval to replace another lost origin that he could never recover, an origin more important but forever irrecuperable: some scene involving, say, his mother, who died before he knew her, or a primal scene in the Freudian sense. On the other hand, printing itself is, in the author's understanding, a way to prevent the loss of something unique by copying it and, in that sense, denying its irreplaceability. And so, when in another retelling of the discovery of printing, which pushes its antiquity back to Spartan times, Nerval concludes that "there is nothing new under the sun" (Nerval 1984-93, II: 49), he is also saying that nothing can disappear, since everything is just a repetition. What the origin of printing, of "la lettre mobile" (moveable type), stands in for is perhaps indeterminable, but the choice of proxy argues that that very loss itself does not matter, that printing is just as good, that nothing, therefore, was ever really lost.[3]

The concept of the simulacrum – in other words, the proposition that the original is only a copy of its own copies, like the missing portrait in "Sylvie" – would serve as an argument that nothing was, in fact, lost, and yet it still obliges one to account for the notion of loss itself. We must still explain the need for an – even illusory – origin. We could perhaps contend that as a subject Nerval is constructed to be preoriginally dispossessed or "Desdichado," and that loss consequently precedes the lost. This is essentially Lacan's argument about desire in "The Signification of the Phallus" (Lacan 1977): according to him, desire is a function of the structure of language itself, the residue of the incompatibility between need and its expression. Because I am always another in language, I can never quite say just what I, what just I, need. I am preoriginally designed, in this view, as dispossession. But then, at the risk of naïve positivism, one might argue that something identifiable really is lost, and that this lost object precedes the notion of loss. For although Lacan never states it as such, the primary object of desire, the *objet petit a*, must be the missing I, the one that can never be uttered, rather than any of the other interchangeable objects that devolve from it. Or again, Julia Kristeva, in a variation on the *objet petit a*, sees all loss and dispossession as stemming out of an original separation from the mother's body. That, according to her, was the prelinguistic experience that we have lost in the post-Oedipal world of symbolic language.[4]

One does not have to identify the original lost object, however, to appreciate the value and consequences of dissimulating its loss. By denying the irreplaceability of a missing love object that object becomes the original object not of loss, but of the loss of loss, and all subsequent repetitions – insofar as they foreclose on the possibility of genuine dispossession – serve to reproduce that original loss of loss. This is why the logic must be totalizing – why it is immediately as easy to be God as an insect, and why one must conclude, in a story about origins, that "there is nothing new under the sun." Any genuine singularity, any rupture in the series of repetitions is a recognition of the possibility of the original loss of loss, and therefore of the – now original – loss itself. And the denial of a single loss thus becomes the loss of the singular, the accidental, the unique as such. This is where the logic of the simulacrum leads, at least for Nerval. The "I" is a heartless actress or a printing press.[5]

Nerval's most famous poem, the dark and troubling sonnet "El Desdichado," repeats this logic, slipping easily between the recognition and the denial of loss, as emblematized in the almost effortless movement between the uniqueness of a star and its proliferation.

> Je suis le ténébreux, – le veuf, – l'inconsolé,
> Le prince d'Aquitaine à la tour abolie :
> Ma seule *étoile* est morte, – et mon luth constellé
> Porte le *Soleil noir* de la *Mélancolie*.

Dans la nuit du tombeau, toi qui m'as consolé,
Rends-moi le Pausilippe et la mer d'Italie,
La *fleur* qui plaisait tant à mon cœur désolé,
Et la treille où le pampre à la rose s'allie.

Suis-je Amour ou Phébus ?...Lusignan ou Biron ?
Mon front est rouge encor du baiser de la reine ;
J'ai rêvé dans la grotte où nage la syrène...

Et j'ai deux fois vainqueur traversé l'Achéron :
Modulant tour à tour sur la lyre d'Orphée
Les soupirs de la sainte et les cris de la fée. (Nerval 1984-93, III: 645)

(I am the dark one, – the widowed –, the disconsolate,
The prince of Aquitaine of the abolished tower:
My only *star* is dead, – and my constellated lute
Bears the *black Sun* of *Melancholy.*

In the night of the tomb, thou who hast consoled me,
Give me back Posilipo and the Italian sea,
The *flower* that so pleased my desolate heart,
And the trellis where the vine and rose unite.

Am I Love or Phœbus?...Lusignan or Byron?
My forehead is still red from the queen's kiss;
I have dreamt in the grotto where the siren swims...

And I have twice in victory crossed the Acheron:
Tuning in turn on the Orphic lyre
The sighs of the saint and the fairy's cries.)

"My only *star* is dead, – and my constellated lute / Bears the *black Sun* of *Melancholy*": the constellation covers over the dead *étoile*, obscuring its absence, while what distinguishes it from a simple mass of stars, from the meaningless repetitions of what Hegel called "the bad infinite," is its form. The constellation consequently represents two incompatible ways of denying absolute loss. On the one hand, the multitude of stars contradicts the uniqueness of any single one. On the other, the constellation's very shape displaces the identity of the lost element onto the configuration of the field itself. It is not the individual units themselves that are irreplaceable, according to this thinking, but rather the forms that they together produce.

Generations of scholars have pondered over the references in this poem, unable, except through the most painful contortions, to reconcile the different attributions and self-identifications.[6] But the figure of the constellation suggests that the poem was written precisely to foreclose on any such reconciliation, so that the questions: "Am I Love or Phœbus...Lusignan or Byron?" for instance, should remain eternally unanswered and the "I" flicker indeterminably among a series of alternative and ostensibly mutually exclusive predications.

The poem denies, in this way, the irreplaceable subjectivity of the poet. He, like the star, can never be lost, because he never existed outside an endless proliferation of interchangeable identities. And yet, in a contradictory gesture, in a gesture toward acknowledging the singularity of what is lost, the poet characterizes himself by that very loss, as if it were the finality of his particular being: "the dark one, – the widowed –, the disconsolate" – as if, in fact, there were no consolation possible and that open wound were the identificatory mark of the poet, the key to his subjectivity. The poem makes two divergent arguments, then: nothing is lost and I am nothing but loss. And then it performs a third operation. In the shape itself of the poem – and Nerval's *Chimères* (Chimerae) are almost all sonnets, as if to underscore the importance of their formality – the poem becomes, like the constellation, a substitute for the irreparable loss of the poet, a fetish object to sustain the self-imposed wounds of a discontinuous or eternally absent subject. "Tuning in turn on the Orphic lyre," the poet creates a prosthesis on which to sustain the endless circulation of two noncompossible subject positions, in one of which he denies his singularity and in the other of which he dispossesses himself of it by identifying with an intolerable loss. In the first case there is nothing to lose, in the second it cannot be regained.

As a talisman that protects the subject even in the face of a terrifyingly fragile singularity, the sonnet "El Desdichado" represents not only Nerval's personal attempts to deal with the problem of absolute loss, but also similar struggles on the part of an entire period. For a thread weaves through these three poets and, indeed, through the whole Romantic movement: a belief in the transcendental value of a single person because of his or her singularity. Inseparable from this belief, however, is a new, transcendental fear: that this person, whether it be another (as in the case of Lamartine and Musset) or the self (as with Nerval), can be irretrievably lost. The moment a person – or a star – becomes unique and therefore irreplaceable, his or her loss turns definitive. What distinguishes this period from others that, like the Renaissance, have exalted the individual is the way that the value of a person derives from the notion of absolute loss, the fact that loss precedes the lost. This dispossession takes, as has been seen, various forms. It is the death of a loved one or of God, as in Lamartine. It is the end of a love affair, as in Musset. It is the "lettre mobile," the missing page of self-identity that haunts Nerval. In all of these cases, however, the work of poetry is to express the individual, and that individual is revealed in turn as the product of an absolute and unbearable absence.

This conception of individuality will become even more characteristic of the post-Romantic generations than the idea that the matter of poetry is the poet him- or herself. Mid-twentieth-century philosophers like Martin Heidegger and Alexandre Kojève and the writers they influenced demonstrate how firmly the ideology of death-based subjectivity has taken hold, the extent to which the conceptualization of the individual depends on the notion of his or her disappearance (Strauss 1998: 54-73). But a return to the Romantic period, to the self-designated origin of this absolute valorization of loss, offers a way to rethink the prehistory and presuppositions of the mortal isolation that has passed for intellectual currency during so much of the last two centuries. The individual, as an absolute, need not find its value and uniqueness in its fragility. For although the category of irreplaceability necessarily presupposes that of singularity, the opposite is not true. "There is no one like you" does not mean quite the same as "when you are gone, I will not be able to replace you." "There is no one like you" does not yet contain the notion of loss in it. Separation and difference, yes, but not necessarily loss. And this singularity can itself become an absolute – as in Emmanuel Levinas's idea of the absolute difference between people, or what he calls the "ethical relation" (Levinas 1969: 102-5). The Romantic belief that individuality derives from irreplaceability is a conceptual choice that has passed itself off as a necessity, or, in other words, an ideology. Insofar as it is an ideology that still has not disappeared, in returning to the Romantics, one finds a way to reconsider the limits and facticity of our own sense of personhood.

NOTES

1 All translations are mine unless otherwise indicated.
2 Marius-François Guyard, for example, writes: "nothing is more false than to see in 1820 the beginning date of the Romantic revolution in poetry. But if the *Méditations* in no way caused an upheaval, nonetheless, with the most common words and worn-out figures, Lamartine sounded in them a new music" (Lamartine 1963: xvii-xviii).
3 Nerval uses the expression "lettre mobile" (e.g., 1984-93: 48).

4 See, for instance, Kristeva's analysis of the *chora* (Kristeva 1984: 25-30) and her analysis of poetic "incarnation" in Nerval's "El Desdichado" (Kristeva 1989: 139-72).
5 As the narrator's uncle remarks in "Sylvie," "actresses [are] not women, nature having forgotten to endow them with hearts" (Nerval 1999: 146).
6 For a critical history of scholarship on this poem, see Strauss (1998: 155-205).

REFERENCES AND FURTHER READING

Aulagnier, Piera (1975). *La Violence de l'interprétation: Du pictogramme à l'énoncé.* Paris: Presses Universitaires de France.

Bénichou, Paul (1992). *L'École du désenchantement: Sainte-Beuve, Nodier, Musset, Nerval, Gautier.* Paris: Gallimard.

Bénichou, Paul (1988). *Les Mages romantiques.* Paris: Gallimard.

Brosman, Catharine Savage (2002). "French Literature." In Dale W. Jacobs (ed.), *The World Book Encyclopedia*, vol. VII. Chicago: World Book Inc., pp. 518-24.

Edwards, Paul (1978). "Existentialism and Death: A Survey of Some Confusions and Absurdities." In John Donnelly (ed.), *Language, Metaphysics,* and Death. New York: Fordham University Press, pp. 32-61.

Gautier, Théophile (1907). *A History of Romanticism.* In *The Works of Théophile Gautier*, vol. 16, trans. F. C. de Sumichrast, pp. 3-230.

Hegel, G. W. F. (1975). *Aesthetics: Lectures in Fine Arts*, trans. T. M. Knox, 2 vols. Oxford: Oxford University Press.

Heidegger, Martin (1962). *Being and Time*, trans. John Macquarrie and Edward Robinson. New York: Harper & Row.

Johnson, Barbara (1989). "The Lady in the Lake." In Denis Hollier (ed.), *A New History of French Literature.* Cambridge, MA: Harvard University Press, p. 628, pp. 627-32.

Kristeva, Julia (1984). *Revolution in Poetic Language*. New York: Columbia University Press.

Kristeva, Julia (1989). "Nerval, the Disinherited Poet." In *Black Sun: Depression and Melancholia*, trans. Leon S. Roudiez. New York: Columbia University Press, pp. 139-72.

Kselman, Thomas A. (1993). *Death and the Afterlife in Modern France*. Princeton, NJ: Princeton University Press.

Lacan, Jacques (1977). "The Signification of the Phallus." In *Écrits: A Selection*, trans. Alan Sheridan. New York: W. W. Norton, pp. 280-91.

Lamartine, Alphonse de (1963). *Œuvres poétiques*, ed. Marius-François Guyard. Paris: Gallimard Pléiade.

Lamartine, Alphonse de (1968). *Méditations*, ed. Fernand Letessier. Paris: Garnier Frères.

Lestringant, Frank (1999). *Alfred de Musset*. Paris: Flammarion.

Levinas, Emmanuel (1969). *Totality and Infinity*, trans. Alphonso Lingis. Pittsburgh: Duquesne University Press.

Musset, Alfred de (1957). *Poésies complètes*, ed. Maurice Allem. Paris: Gallimard Pléiade.

Nerval, Gerard de (1984-93). *Œuvres complètes*, ed. Jean Guillaume et al., 3 vols. Paris: Gallimard Pléiade.

Nerval, Gerard de (1999). *Selected Writings*, trans. Richard Sieburth. London: Penguin.

Newmark, Kevin (1988). "The Forgotten Figures of Symbolism: Nerval's *Sylvie*." *Yale French Studies*, 74: 207-29.

Rimbaud, Arthur (1972). *Œuvres complètes*, ed. Antoine Adam. Paris: Gallimard Pléiade.

Strauss, Jonathan (1988). *Subjects of Terror: Nerval, Hegel, and the Modern Self*. Stanford, CA: Stanford University Press.

Tosca, Maurice (1969). *Lamartine ou l'amour de la vie*. Paris: Albin Michel.

Viallaneix, Paul (ed.) (1971). *Lamartine: Le Livre du Centenaire*. Paris: Flammarion.

Wittgenstein, Ludwig (1922). *Tractatus Logico-Philosophicus*, trans. C. K. Ogden. London: Routledge.

12
Victor Hugo's Poetry

E. H. and A. M. Blackmore

Hugo's Poetic Development

Like most writers, Victor-Marie Hugo (1802-85) took some time to find a distinctive voice. The poems published in *Le Conservateur littéraire* (The Literary Conservative, the magazine that he and his brothers edited from 1819 to 1821) and in his first book *Odes et poésies diverses* (Odes and Other Poems, 1822) stood as close to eighteenth-century models as did the early works of Blake or Wordsworth. There were odes in the manner of "the great Rousseau" (not Jean-Jacques the philosopher, but Jean-Baptiste the poet, who was then esteemed as the supreme master of the genre), epigrams in the manner of Voltaire, essays and satires in rhymed couplets. The political and religious beliefs expressed in them were rigidly traditionalistic; their diction, too, consisted largely of stock phrases handed down from the previous century. Line after line was framed with pre-Revolutionary symmetry and balance: "The forest's first song and the day's first fires"; "And the same birds will sing to the same breaking day" ("Le Matin" [Morning], *Odes et ballades* V.viii, ll. 5, 9).[1]

Yet already there were symptoms of unrest. Alongside the poems in *Le Conservateur littéraire* were essays; and the young Hugo's essays commended some decidedly untraditional writings: the poems of André Chénier (first published in 1819), the novels of Walter Scott, the first volumes by Lamartine and Desbordes-Valmore. Voltaire, by comparison, was praised only with severe reservations. The epigraphs in *Odes et poésies diverses* reflected analogous likes and dislikes. They were drawn from Chénier, Schiller (as translated by Madame de Staël), Chateaubriand, Vigny, the Shakespeare of *A Midsummer Night's Dream*, and the Charles Nodier of the macabre tale *Smarra*, as well as from sources admired by conservatives and innovators alike, such as the Scriptures and Virgil – but not from the pillars of French Classicism, such as Voltaire and Racine.

Today Hugo's early *Odes* may seem relatively conventional, but their first readers were struck – indeed disconcerted – by the extent to which they departed from tradition. The young poet was rebuked for varying the rhythm and rhyme-scheme from stanza to stanza ("Les Vierges de Verdun," written in 1818), for "sacrificing grammatical propriety to poetic expressiveness" ("Le Rétablissement de la statue de Henri IV," 1819), for using "low" terms and failing to maintain properly elevated diction ("Moïse sur le Nil," 1820), for writing in a deliberately obscure, "apocalyptic" style ("L'Âme," 1823; "I could make out nothing from it, except that the author is a lunatic," complained Edmond Géraud in May 1824). (See Leuilliot 1985: 1051-8 for further details.) All these audacities remained characteristic of Hugo's work in his maturity. In "Booz endormi" (Boaz Asleep, 1857), for instance, the rhyme-scheme changes in the two stanzas where the narrative takes a dramatic step forward and the mood deepens (ll. 37-40 and 57-60); the style encompasses the conversational ("He'd worked hard on his threshing floor all day," l. 2) as well as the literary ("The gloom was nuptial, solemn, conquering," l. 67); the whole scene is surrounded and invested with deliberate intangibilities, the most celebrated being the mysterious "Jérima-deth" of line 81. There is scarcely any poetic strategy of Hugo's later years that cannot be paralleled somewhere in the volume of 1822.[2]

Yet if it is important to note the continuity between his early and his mature work, it is important to recognize the development too. During the 1820s his political, literary, and religious thought underwent profound changes. By the middle of the century, the former royalist had become a committed opponent of all monarchies; the former Roman Catholic had come to regard the God incarnate in Jesus Christ as incompatible with any human religion; and the former editor of *Le Conservateur littéraire* had become the acknowledged leader of French Romanticism (a label that he himself viewed with characteristic ambivalence).

Hugo was well aware that these three transformations were interrelated. He came to believe that the literary practices of any society are inseparable from its political and religious views. The French poets of the seventeenth and eighteenth centuries had lived in an orderly, stable absolute monarchy – the France of Louis XIV and Louis XV – and their writings had inevitably reflected the society that had shaped them. Such a society would instinctively shun any verbal threat to the established order – any term that might draw too much attention to unpleasant matters, or that might be too closely associated with the underprivileged. So the poets of Louis XIV's reign, and their successors in the following century, confined their vocabulary to words and phrases that were noble, harmonious, and nonthreatening. Anything disreputable or shocking simply could not be said – at least by any person of good breeding.

Till 1789,
The language was the State: words, well or ill born,
Lived in castes, with their own compartments – some,
The noble ones, kept company with Jocastas,
Phèdres, Meropes, and decorum ruled them;
They rode to Versailles in the king's own carriages;
The rest, beggarly rabble, hangdog rascals,

Kept to the provinces: some chained in hulks
Of slang, fond of the lowest kinds of company,
Torn to rags in the marketplace, no wigs,
No stockings; born for prose or farce; stylis-
tic riffraff in the scattered dark; clowns, rustics,
Clodhoppers whom Boss Vaugelas had branded
"Vulg" in the convict Dictionary – expressing
Abject colloquial life, no more: degraded,
Base, sullied, bourgeois.[3] ("Réponse à un acte d'accusation" [Reply to a Bill of
Indictment], *Les Contemplations* I.vii, ll. 40-54)

In the same poem, Hugo proceeds to show how the literary rules of pre-Revolutionary French society prevented any effective criticism of that society. Were there whores on the streets? Were there pigs in power? The language of French Classicism did not allow you to say so, because such words as "pig" (*cochon*) and "whore" (*catin*) were not permitted; the language of French Classicism allowed you to utter your complaint only in terms so mild and roundabout that it was robbed of all its bite.

Hugo argued that he himself belonged to a new, post-Revolutionary era. He could not be confined by the old rules, because he wished to say things that the old rules had forbidden. If you believe in freeing the people, then you must allow them to speak freely. A democratic attitude to the community demands a democratic attitude to its language.

I dressed the old dictionary in liberty's colors:
Away with peasant words and senator words! ...
                        ... "There's no word,"
I said, "where a pure-winged idea can't perch
After flying the azure blue." Disgusting!
Litotes and syllepsis and hypallage
Shuddered. I stood on boundary-stone Aristotle
And declared all words free, adult, and equal....
I had the cow and heifer fraternizing,
One being Betsy, and one Bérénice.[4]
The ode got drunk then, and kissed Rabelais;
The *Marseillaise* was sung on Mount Parnassus;
And the nine Muses tangoed with their breasts bare. ("Réponse à un acte d'accusation,"
ll. 66-7, 71-5, 85-9)

Fundamentally Hugo does not inhabit the same world as the pre-Revolutionary writers. Their universe was tidy, decorous, symmetrical; his is irregular, erratic, unbounded. And his poetry must inevitably express what he sees, not what his predecessors saw.

God – I've said it before – is wide open to criticism.
He knows no restraint. He's wild, unseemly, extravagant:

There giant, here dwarf,
Everything all at the same time; enormous; he doesn't leave out things.
He overdoes chasms and prisms....
How the Academy[5] would tell him a thing or two!
What is the point of the comet? What is the use of the bolide?
To a sturdy, reliable pedant,
Well, the more one is dazzled, the less one is satisfied;
Polonius's saws and Ockham's razors
Suffer God only with some impatience.
God disturbs law and order, works science to death;
As soon as you finish, you have to start it again;
You seem to feel some kind of serpent all scaly with sunrise
Slipping away through your fingers.
Just when you've said "Enough!" he says "In addition!" ("Encore Dieu, mais avec des
restrictions" [More About God, But With Some Reservations], *L'Art d'être grand-père*
IV.v, ll. 29-33, 40-50)

This view of the universe shapes Hugo's poetry at all levels. Like the Creator he
describes, he "disturbs law and order." He will not submit to the authority of an
Academy, any more than he will submit to the authority of a monarchy. He runs
phrases across lines in ways that French critical theory had traditionally forbidden
(Rochette 1911: 223-76): "Litotes and syllepsis and hypallage / Shuddered"; "some
chained in hulks / Of slang." He uses words and images from aspects of human society
that were traditionally regarded as beyond the bounds of poetry, from the most
technical ("syllepsis," "bolide") to the most colloquial ("works . . . to death"). In
matters of overall architecture he is equally unorthodox. His epics, *La Légende des
siècles* (The Legend of the Ages, 1859-83) and *La Fin de Satan* (The End of Satan,
1886), are irregular and fragmented in design; his dramatic poems, from *Cromwell*
(1827) to *Le Pape* (The Pope, 1878) and *Torquemada* (1882), are constructed in
defiance of the traditional unities.

Not that Hugo denies the existence of "order" in the universe. But he believes that
it is not the kind of order depicted by his Classicist predecessors. In the 1826 Preface
to *Odes et ballades* he writes:

Compare the royal garden at Versailles, beautifully leveled, beautifully trimmed,
beautifully kempt, beautifully raked, beautifully sanded; filled everywhere with little
cascades, little pools, little groves, bronze tritons frolicking ceremoniously on oceans
pumped at great expense from the River Seine, marble fauns courting dryads allegor-
ically enclosed in hosts of conical yews, cylindrical laurels, spherical orange trees,
elliptical myrtles, and other trees whose normal shape, being no doubt too trivial, has
been politely corrected by the gardener's knife – compare that much-admired garden to
a primeval forest in the New World, with its gigantic trees, its tall grasses, its dense
vegetation, its myriad birds of myriad hues, its broad avenues where darkness and light
merely play across the greenery, its savage harmonies, its huge rivers sweeping away
islands of flowers, its immense cataracts swaying rainbows! I don't ask which garden has

magnificence, grandeur, beauty, but simply: Which one possesses order, and which one possesses disorder? In the first, waters in captivity or diverted from their course, springing up only to stagnate; gods made of stone; trees transported from their native soil, ripped from their climate, robbed even of their shape, their fruits, and forced to suffer the grotesque whims of cord and pruning knife; everywhere, in short, the natural order contraverted, inverted, overthrown, destroyed. In the second, by contrast, everything obeys an invariable law; a God seems alive in everything. The drops of water follow their inclination and form rivers, which form seas; the seeds choose their soil and produce a forest. Each plant, each shrub, each tree is born in its due season, grows in its own place, yields its own fruit, dies at its due time. Even thorns have beauty there. We ask again: Which one possesses order? Choose between a masterpiece of gardening and the handiwork of nature, between what is beautiful by convention and what is beautiful without the rules, between an artificial literature and an original poetry!

In fact, he maintains that "we mustn't confuse order with regularity. Regularity is only a matter of external form; order arises from the very depths of something, from the intelligent deployment of the fundamental elements of a subject. Regularity is a purely human, material arrangement; order is, so to speak, divine." His favorite philosopher is Kant, not Descartes.

Hugo's poetry – and prose – naturally reflect his conception of the universe. As may be seen from the above examples, they are not totally lacking in order; they are highly ordered, but their order is "wild, unseemly, extravagant," and refuses to be limited by standard human rules. He does not abandon rhyme altogether, for instance; but his use of it is both less orderly and more orderly than the pre-Revolutionary poets'. As we have already observed, he is not afraid to vary the rhyme-scheme from stanza to stanza. Moreover, he sets himself no unbreakable laws about the types of rhyme that may and may not be employed. He is not afraid of the cheapest, most plebeian rhymes; *yeux* (eyes) and *cieux* (skies), *nuit* (night) and *luit* (bright) occur again and again in his verse. When questioned about this, he declared in a letter of November 8, 1855 to Noël Parfait: "There are some words that exist like God in the depths of the language." Yet at the other end of the spectrum, he also employs much more complex rhymes than the Classicist poets had done. He delights in elaborate multisyllabic *rimes riches*.

Hélas! on ne peut être en même temps poëte
Qui s'envole et tribun coudoyant Changarnier,
Aigle dans l'idéal et vautour au charnier. ("Post-scriptum" [Postscript], *Toute la lyre* V.ii, ll. 9-11)

(How can you be both poet in full flight
And tribune swallowing what some Nosy Parker says,
Eagle in the ideal and vulture among carcasses?)

Est-ce le vent de l'ombre obscure?
Ce vent qui sur Jésus passa!

Est-ce le grand Rien d'Épicure,
Ou le grand Tout de Spinosa? ("Pendant une maladie" [During an Illness], *Les Chansons des rues et des bois* II.IV.ii, ll. 16-20)

(Is it a wind that Jesus knows – a
Gale from the shadows that obscure us?
The great Nothing of Epicurus,
Or else the great All of Spinoza?)

He devises intricate stanza-forms that would have seemed lacking in decorum to his predecessors. The arrival and departure of a flight of evil spirits is narrated in lines that gradually increase from two syllables to 12 in length, and then decrease just as gradually back to two ("Les Djinns" [The Djinns], *Les Orientales* XXVIII). A girl swaying in a hammock is presented in verses that playfully enact the motion they describe:

Zara, lovely lazy thing,
   Starts to swing
While her hammock's cords support her
Just above a fountain-spring
   Billowing
Full of the Illysus' water. ("Sara la baigneuse" [Zara Bathing], *Les Orientales* XIX, ll. 1-6.)

There are even rhyme-schemes within rhyme-schemes: in one celebrated passage Hugo embeds 15 three-syllable rhymed lines within four 12-syllable lines, which also rhyme ("Esca," *Les Quatre Vents de l'esprit* II.I.i, ll. 271-4).

The same concept of order may be seen at work on a larger scale in the overall architecture of his poetry collections. In some respects his volumes are more highly organized than his predecessors'; in other respects they are less organized, for their order is that of the Amazonian jungle, not the Versailles garden; it is "wild, unseemly, extravagant, . . . enormous." He seeks to be all-embracing, not homogeneous. The 1822 volume of *Odes et poésies diverses* began with a manifesto on the poet's role in contemporary society, "Le Poëte dans les révolutions" (The Poet in Revolutionary Times), followed by nine odes on recent French political history; then a second manifesto, "La Lyre et la harpe" (The Lyre and the Harp), introduced odes on reflective and metaphysical themes: six on impersonal, remote subjects, followed by six very personal poems addressed to the poet's beloved and a final, equally personal gaze beyond life into eternity, "Le Matin" (Morning). The writer's broad range of interests, and his penchant for arranging his poems into even larger poem-cycles, were already apparent. (By comparison, the most conspicuously innovative collection of the previous decade, Lamartine's *Méditations poétiques*, had been relatively conservative in design: its contents were fairly homogeneous – nearly all of them were, as the book's title announced, meditations – and there was no attempt to make large-scale patterns out of its component poems.) But Hugo's 1822 volume was only the beginning. It eventually grew into an even more intricately structured mass of 72 odes and 15 ballads, with the title *Odes et ballades* (Odes and Ballads, 1828). A poem originally written for the *Odes*, "La Ville prise" (The Captured City), soon seeded a new collection, *Les Orientales* (*Orientalia*, 1829), a series of exercises on Eastern (mainly Greek and Turkish) themes: this too illustrated the Hugolian desire to encompass within a coherent, though not "regular," overall structure (Grant 1979) as diverse a range of material as possible: thus the carefree voyeurist piece already cited, "Sara la baigneuse" (Zara Bathing), was immediately preceded by an urgent political statement, "L'Enfant" (The Child), and immediately followed by a passionate song of probably lost love and presumably hopeless hope:

> Monte, écureuil, monte au grand chêne,
> Sur la branche des cieux prochaine,
> Qui plie et tremble comme un jonc.
> Cigogne, aux vieilles tours fidèle,
> Oh! vole et monte à tire-d'aile
> De l'église à la citadelle,
> Du haut clocher au grand donjon.
>
> Vieux aigle, monte de ton aire
> A la montagne centenaire
> Que blanchit l'hiver éternel.
> Et toi qu'en ta couche inquiète
> Jamais l'aube ne vit muette,
> Monte, monte, vive alouette,
> Vive alouette, monte au ciel!
>
> Et maintenant, du haut de l'arbre,
> Des flèches de la tour de marbre,
> Du grand mont, du ciel enflammé,
> A l'horizon, parmi la brume,
> Voyez-vous flotter une plume,
> Et courir un cheval qui fume,
> Et revenir mon bien-aimé? ("Attente" [Anticipation], *Les Orientales* XX)

> (Rise, squirrel, up the great oak, rise,
> Climb the branch nearest to the skies,
> Which bends and buckles like a reed.
> Stork, ancient towers' sentinel,
> Fly up from spire and parish bell
> To mighty keep and citadel –
> Wing your way with the utmost speed!
>
> Old eagle, from your aerie home
> Soar to the age-old mountain-dome
> Whitened with everlasting snow.
> Lark that, in your unquiet nest,
> No sunrise ever saw at rest,
> Go up, go, zestful lark, go, zest-
> ful lark, go up to heaven, go!

And tell me now, from the tree's height,
From the stone tower's topmost flight,
From bright sky and high bivouac,
On the horizon, through the haze,
O can you see a plume that sways,
A galloping horse that steams and sprays,
And my beloved coming back?)

The *Orientalia* sprang from the impersonal side of the *Odes:* its speakers were captive Greek girls, Turkish military leaders, superstitious Arab peasants, politically tactless European gentry seeing the local sights – figures far removed from Victor-Marie Hugo himself. The more personal, intimate side of the *Odes* gave rise to the tetralogy that followed: *Les Feuilles d'automne* (Autumn Leaves, 1831), *Les Chants du crépuscule* (Songs of the Half-Light, 1835), *Les Voix intérieures* (Inner Voices, 1837), and *Les Rayons et les ombres* (Sunlight and Shadows, 1840). Here the speakers were closely akin to Hugo the man. In "Ce siècle avait deux ans . . ." (This century was two years old . . .) a recent convert to democracy and political liberalism took stock of his heritage; in the central lyrics of the 1835 volume a lover courted his new beloved, while in the later "Tristesse d'Olympio" (The Melancholy of Olympio) he mourned the passage of time and the passing of romance; in "Sur le bal de l'Hôtel de Ville" (A Ball at the Hôtel de Ville) a social reformer attacked the oppression of one class and one sex by another; in "Regardez: les enfants se sont assis en rond . . ." (Look at the children next to one another . . .) a family man contemplated his wife and children; in "Après une lecture de Dante" (After Reading Dante) a controversial poet drew strength from the example of a predecessor. Even when the author was speaking through a fictional persona and discussing the most general of issues, his own personal voice could still be distinctly heard:

La vie, ô gentilhomme, est une comédie
Étrange, folle, gaie, effroyable, hardie,
Taillée au vieux patron des pièces du vieux temps,
Avec des spadassins, avec des capitans.
La morale en est sombre et cependant fort saine.
Tout s'y tient. La vertu, dès la première scène,
Tombe dans une trappe, et la richesse en sort;
Chacun pousse son cri pour se plaindre du sort,
Le savant brait, le roi rugit, le manant beugle;
Le mariage est borgne et l'amour est aveugle,
La justice est boiteuse et l'honneur est manchot;
L'enfer, dont on voit luire en un coin le réchaud
Qui jette au front du riche un reflet écarlate,
De toutes les vertus a fait des culs-de-jatte;
Le bravo quête un duel, l'amoureux un duo;
L'eunuque – c'est l'envie – enrage, crie: "Ah! oh!"
Et jette à tout sultan des regards effroyables;
Toutes les passions, qui sont autant de diables,

Ont leur rôle, tantôt dolent, tantôt pompeux.
C'est beau! Figure-toi la pièce, si tu peux;
Elle a le cœur humain pour scène, et pour parterre
Elle a le genre humain.

A la fin du mystère,

Le rideau tombe. On siffle. – Absurde! tout est mal!
On demande l'auteur et l'acteur principal.
Le riche veut ravoir son argent. Cris, tapage.
– L'auteur! l'auteur! nommez l'auteur! à bas l'ouvrage! –
Alors, apparaissant devant la rampe en feu,
Satan fait trois saluts, et dit: "L'auteur, c'est Dieu." ("La vie, ô gentilhomme, est une
comédie..." [Life, dear sir, is a comedy...], *Dernière Gerbe*, MS 79/121)[6]

(Life, dear sir, is a comedy – wild, daring,
Witty, extravagant, and overbearing,
Done in the style of old-time melodrama,
With thugs in capes and officers in armor.
The moral is severe, but strong and clean.
It's all coherent. In the opening scene
Virtue falls down the trap, and Wealth comes out.
Scholars bleat, peasants moo, and monarchs shout;
Everyone wails and thinks his fate unkind.
Matrimony is one-eyed, Love is blind,
Honor has lost its right arm, Justice limps.
In one corner Hell's gas stove gives a glimpse
Of the rich fellow lit with scarlet ripples.
It turns all of the virtues into cripples.
Bullies seek duels, lovers seek duets;
The eunuch (who is Envy) howls and frets
And gives every last sultan nasty looks.
All of the passions – all of them are crooks –
Play their parts, whining or Olympian.
It's great! Imagine the play if you can:
Onstage the human heart, and in the pit
The human race.

Then, at the end of it,

The curtain falls. Boos. "Lousy, every bit!"
Calls for the author and the leading man.
The rich chap wants his money back. Howls, jeers.
"Down with the work! Who wrote it? Name the clod!" –
At the footlights, in fire, Satan appears.
He bows three times and says: "The author's God.")

A comprehensive survey of Hugo's later poetic achievements would lead us far beyond
the scope of a *Companion to European Romanticism*. Already in the preface to *Les Rayons et*

les ombres he had suggested that his work was deepening: "in this volume . . . the horizon has perhaps broadened, the sky become more azure, the tranquility more profound." Many later readers have had the same impression, and have felt that the poetry collections of the following decade went still further. *Les Châtiments* (The Empire in the Pillory, 1853) was a 7,000-line collection of political satires, *Les Contemplations* (1856) an 11,000-line collection of personal and metaphysical lyrics and meditations. During the same period he began work on his major epic trilogy, much of which remained unpublished for several decades: *La Légende des siècles* (The Legend of the Ages, 1859-83), *La Fin de Satan* (The End of Satan, 1886), and *Dieu* (God, 1891). Perhaps the most original of his subsequent projects were the two that superficially appeared most frivolous: a cycle of playful quatrain-poems on the age-old theme of profane and sacred love, *Les Chansons des rues et des bois* (Songs of Street and Wood, 1865), and a suitably light, though not lightweight, collection devoted to his grandchildren, *L'Art d'être grand-père* (The Art of Being a Grandfather, 1877). As a pendant to his epic trilogy he issued a tetralogy of long philosophical poems, *Le Pape* (The Pope, 1878), *La Pitié suprème* (The Supreme Compassion, 1879), *Religions et religion* (Religions and Religion, 1880), and *L'Âne* (The Donkey, 1880). He also worked on two further collections of political poetry: a never-completed sequel to *Les Châtiments*, much of which was eventually issued as *Les Années funestes* (The Fateful Years, 1898), and a kind of verse diary dealing with the Franco-Prussian War and its aftermath, *L'Année terrible* (The Year of Horrors, 1872). Alongside these volumes devoted to single topics – descendants, in some respects, of the *Orientalia* – he planned two or three collections as variegated as the *Odes and Ballads*; only one of them, *Les Quatre Vents de l'esprit* (The Four Winds of the Spirit, 1881), was completed, but after his death his literary executors gathered most of his miscellaneous unpublished verse into volumes of similar type, which they entitled *Toute la lyre* (The Whole Lyre, 1888-97) and *Dernière Gerbe* (Last Gleanings, 1902).

Hugo's poetry has always elicited exceptionally diverse responses; there is far less agreement about the nature and extent of his literary achievement than there is about (say) Wordsworth's or Goethe's or Pushkin's. The disagreement has existed as long as the poems have been read. As early as the mid-1820s the author of the earliest *Odes* was hailed as a "genius" in some quarters, dismissed as a "lunatic" in others. Today there is still no sign that the conflict is being resolved, or that a general consensus is emerging. One recent author describes Hugo, without qualification or reservation, as "France's greatest writer"; another calls him "a monstrous aberration in literary history." This division of opinion is, of course, due to the very nature of the poems themselves. They were written to provoke – to "disturb law and order" – and they do provoke. Thus it is more than usually difficult to summarize the varying critical attitudes to his work.

Responses to Hugo's Poetry

Nevertheless, three broad phases of Hugo criticism may perhaps be distinguished. During most of his lifetime, and for several decades afterwards, Hugo was the most widely read poet in France – and possibly in the world. (His funeral, in 1885, attracted far larger crowds than the obsequies of any other mere writer have ever done.) No doubt some of his readers were aware only of his prose works, and others only of his verse; but many, at least in France, had some knowledge of both. His successive publications might be revered, or they might be vilified, but they could not be ignored. Everyone with any interest in contemporary literature had to take note of them. Consequently he exerted a vital influence on several generations of his fellow writers, especially in France itself. Often the influence flowed in both directions: the very colleague who drew inspiration from Hugo also provided inspiration for him. Both in points of detail and in its overall architecture, Lamartine's 1832 masterpiece, *Harmonies poétiques et religieuses,* showed that its author had been reading Hugo's 1822-4 *Odes* – which in turn had owed much to Lamartine's 1820 *Méditations poétiques*. A generation later, in 1859, Baudelaire wrote a series of poems deeply influenced by Hugo's *Contemplations* and *Légende des siècles* (as the younger poet himself acknowledged in a letter to Poulet-Malassis on October 1, 1859) – while those Hugo volumes had themselves been influenced by the Baudelaire poems eventually collected in 1857 as *Les Fleurs du mal* (Hugo's "Cerigo," *Les Contemplations* V.xx, is plainly a response to Baudelaire's "Un Voyage à Cythère"). Later still, Hugo's *Chansons des rues et des bois* and some of the *Contemplations* (particularly "La Fête chez Thérèse" (Thérèse's Party, I.xxii)) provided Verlaine with ideas for his *Fêtes galantes* (1869) – while Hugo's love for the jaunty tone and adventurous versification of that little volume may be seen in some parts of his own *Art d'être grand-père*, such as "Fenêtres ouvertes" (Open Windows, I.xi). In those days, therefore, Hugo's verse was not merely an object of study but a living stimulus. The stimulus was not limited to France, nor did it affect only poets. Tolstoy, who seems to have admired Hugo more than any other writer of his century, went to the extent of translating sections of *La Légende des siècles* into Russian prose.

A generation after Hugo's death, there was a reaction against his poetry. This is not an unusual phenomenon: many artists (we might think of Shakespeare and Bach, of Monteverdi and Rembrandt) go through a phase of posthumous neglect before the world regains interest in their work. Few of the most respected twentieth-century writers showed any significant trace of Hugo's influence; few of the leading twentieth-century critics devoted much attention to his verse. Stray lines and phrases had found their way into popular idiom and could be cited half-mockingly in appropriate situations, as they were, for instance, in Marcel Pagnol's *Topaze* (1928), Jean Renoir's *La Règle du jeu* (1939), and Max Ophuls's *Madame de...* (1953). But their author was no longer a living stimulus. As with his near-contemporaries Dickens and Verdi, his very popularity was held against him: he was a "great entertainer" rather than a "creative artist."[7]

In left-wing or radical literary circles there was a partial exception to such views. Hugo's own literary experimentalism and political radicalism appealed to many Dadaist, Surrealist, Marxist, and Anarchist writers, who regarded him with more respect than their more conservative colleagues did. The beginnings of this trend could already be seen during the final decades of the nineteenth century: Rimbaud and Mallarmé, for instance, admired Hugo more unreservedly, and were more profoundly influenced by his work, than the relatively traditionalist post-1880 Verlaine and Leconte de Lisle. Later radical admirers in France included André Breton, Louis Aragon, and Paul Éluard. In Soviet Russia, partly as a legacy of Tolstoy's enthusiasm, Hugo remained an acknowledged classic. Perhaps the best introduction to such views is Aragon's *Avez-vous lu Hugo?* (1952), part critical essay, part anthology, which went through many reprints in spite of its comparatively marginal, nonmainstream circulation.

During the last few decades, Hugo's critical fortunes have paralleled those of other major nineteenth-century artists; again Dickens and Verdi may offer particularly close analogies. He is no longer read by mass audiences, and he exerts no significant influence on contemporary artists; nevertheless, an interest in his work is no longer a sign of bad taste, and in certain circles it has even become a mark of fashion: a character in a "new wave" film (Eric Rohmer's 1992 *Conte d'hiver*) may quote an extended passage from one of Hugo's later philosophical poems and seriously discuss the ideas contained in it, as a character in a film with comparable intellectual pretensions a generation earlier might have discussed a passage of Rimbaud or Donne. At a different level, Hugo's work has become a legitimate object of scholarly study, as seen in the production of major editions (Massin's 1967-71 chronological *Œuvres complètes*; Journet's and Robert's numerous studies of the manuscripts) and major critical monographs (Albouy 1963, Gaudon 1969).

The aspects of the poetry that attract most attention at present are not necessarily those that appealed to readers in Hugo's own day. Here Tennyson's 1877 sonnet "To Victor Hugo" may provide a convenient reference point. Tennyson, like most of his contemporaries, judged Hugo to be the greatest living poet of Europe ("Beyond our strait," 1.6),[8] and his sonnet contains four phrases that may apply primarily to Hugo the poet –

> Cloud-weaver of phantasmal hopes and fears,
> French of the French, and Lord of human tears;
> Child-lover... ("To Victor Hugo," ll. 2-4)

– yet three of those four phrases would probably not satisfy the majority of present-day Hugolian scholars.

Tennyson characterizes the author of *L'Art d'être grand-père* as "Child-lover." That volume is still greatly admired, but recent accounts of it tend to stress not so much the poet's affection for children as his concern with adult political and religious issues (see Millet 1985: 1446-7, who goes so far as to say that the book "is above all a polemic for political clemency," and Ubersfeld 1985: 167-84). We might point, in partial support, to the book's own words: when he listens to the conversation of children, says Hugo, "I find a deep and impressive meaning within it, / Sometimes a severe one." The child, in these poems, is partly a slave oppressed by the tyranny of those in control, partly a willing accomplice in that oppression ("Children, like adults, want to be beasts of burden"), partly a means of escape from the oppression, partly a fresh eye looking at the world without conventional preconceptions, and partly a future tyrant in embryo ("Encore l'Immaculée Conception" [The Immaculate Conception Revisited], *L'Art d'être grand-père* XV.vii, ll. 12-13, 34). "A slave would be a tyrant if he could," Hugo wrote in "La Ville disparue" (The Vanished City, *La Légende des siècles* V, l. 30) at the time when he was working on the *Grand-père* poems.

Tennyson also speaks of Hugo the "Lord of human tears." The funereal elegies in Book IV of the *Contemplations* touched the hearts of so many nineteenth-century readers that Hugo's publisher brought out a special selection of them for the consolation of bereaved mothers. Today those poems continue to speak most strongly to readers who have suffered similar experiences – but such readers are much rarer nowadays, in a culture where comparatively few of our friends and relatives die prematurely. Here many of us must feel that we are gazing dimly back into an alien era when millions could weep inexplicably at the death of Little Nell, and when the queen of England could declare, "Next to the Bible, *In Memoriam* is my comfort." Even for some of Hugo's most sympathetic critics, the effort of imaginative identification that is required may be simply too great, prompting complaints that a poem like "A Villequier" (At Villequier, *Les Contemplations* IV.xv) is "theatrical" and "did a good deal to give Romanticism a bad name for indulgence in the wrong kind of sentiment" (Ireson 1997: 165). *Les Contemplations* is still one of Hugo's most admired collections, but today's readers tend to find its greatness mainly in the reflective and metaphysical poems, or in the structure of the work as a whole (Nash 1976, Frey 1988), and not in the products of "human tears."

Beside "Child-lover" and "Lord of human tears" Tennyson places "French of the French" – a phrase so unspecific that its reference is not immediately apparent. Here, perhaps, we may be seeing a characteristically English and Victorian stance, an attempt to make Hugo's political position more universally acceptable by dissociating it from its distinctive partisan substance (redistribution of wealth, abolition of capital punishment, republican government, etc.) and reducing it to simple patriotism. (Tennyson would of course be thinking mainly about the verse, in *Les Châtiments* and perhaps *L'Année terrible*; little of Hugo's political prose was then in print, apart from his speeches, which were not usually regarded as literature.) Nineteenth-century admirers in other countries (Tolstoy, for instance) were more inclined to maintain that the character and quality of Hugo's work were inseparable from the character and quality of the vision that generated it. If he had been a traditionalist in politics and religion, then, whether for good or ill, his poetry would have been more traditional too; if he had been an anarchist and an atheist, then he might have been more inclined to abandon all pattern and design in his writings. Much recent Hugolian scholarship has followed up these points (which were first made by the poet himself, for instance in the "Réponse à un acte d'accusation" already cited), noting how his writings were partly shaped by the social and political preoccupations of his culture, and partly acted as a criticism of them (Butor 1964: 199-214).

Characteristically Victorian, too, is Tennyson's failure to mention the love poems. Hugo's English contemporaries could not forget that his copious verses on that subject had been addressed largely (and over a period of 30 years, from the 1835 *Chants du crépuscule* to the 1865 *Chansons des rues et des bois*) to a woman other than his wife. In other countries the love poems were often seen as the very best of his work; indeed, François Coppée famously called him "the greatest lyric poet of all ages." Even the severest critics often qualified their disparagement by observing that he could write very pretty love lyrics when he laid aside his more grandiose ambitions (Marzials 1888: 223). Similarly, when nineteenth-century composers wished to display their literary taste and their familiarity with contemporary verse by setting one of Hugo's poems to music, the work they chose was almost always a love poem. Poems of other kinds – even when they were written in the stanzaic forms best suited to nineteenth-century music, and even when Hugo had deliberately designed them to be sung (as with some of the *Châtiments*) – rarely attracted composers, whereas relatively insubstantial pieces of the "I love you" kind were set again and again. In this area, as in the children's poems, current taste tends to notice and prize darker undertones and deeper resonances; uncomplicated love lyrics attract less study than pieces in which love is held in tension against other emotions (Albouy 1964: 1411-13).

Yet Tennyson's other description of Hugo the poet – "Cloud-weaver of prodigious hopes and fears" – reminds us that he was a fellow practitioner with a fellow practitioner's special interests and insights, which may have led him to appreciate aspects of these poems that most of his contemporaries were unable to fathom. Like Baudelaire,[9] he seems to have taken special note of the so-called "visionary" stream of poems running from the early "La Pente de la rêverie" (The Slope of Reverie, *Les Feuilles d'automne* XXIX) through "Puits de l'Inde! tombeaux!..." (Indian caverns! tombs!..., *Les Rayons et les ombres* XIII) and pointing toward masterpieces that still awaited publication, such as the extraordinary Gavarnie fragment of *Dieu*, "Remonte aux premiers jours de ton globe..." (Turn back toward your planet's earliest days..., MS 106/6a-12a). Now that almost the whole of Hugo's poetry is readily available in print, it is relatively easy for us to appreciate that side of his work. Hugo himself repeatedly delayed the publication of *Dieu* because he feared that it would be too challenging for its readers ("the air in that region is a bit too rarefied for them," he wrote); yet nowadays it is perhaps more highly regarded than any other single poem he wrote. John Porter Houston, in his classic introductory survey, called it "to my mind Hugo's most enthralling book" (Houston 1988: 151); and the standard English-language bibliography not only finds "Hugo's poetic masterpiece" here, but also says that the work "contains probably the highest poetry written in French" (Grimaud 1994: 212). In the days of Tennyson and Baudelaire, however, the pattern in the carpet was still invisible to most readers, who tended to spend their time among the simpler love lyrics and elegies for the dead, unconscious of the strange woven clouds that the poet would offer from time to time on the very next page.

Les hommes passeront, la poussière éperdue
Passera, les oiseaux fuiront dans l'étendue,
Les chevaux passeront, les vagues passeront,
Les nuages fuiront et s'évanouiront,
Les chars s'envoleront dans la rumeur des routes;
Mais les obscurités, les questions, les doutes,
Resteront, sans qu'on voie un peu de jour qui point;
Mais les ombres sont là qui ne passeront point;
Mais on aura toujours, quoi qu'on rêve et qu'on fasse,
Devant soi, le prodige et la nuit face à face;
Mais on ne verra rien, jamais, jamais, jamais,
Pas même une blancheur sur de vagues sommets,
Pas même un mouvement de souffles et de bouches,
Dans l'immobilité des ténèbres farouches. ("Les hommes passeront..." [People will
pass...], *Dieu*, MS 106/732.)

(People will pass, dust itself will decay
And pass, horses and waves will pass away,
Birds will fly off into the firmament,
Clouds will be blown away, dispersed, and spent,
Carts will roll by with bustle and congestion –
But mystery, uncertainty, and question
Will remain with no sign of dawn's first glow;
The shadows will be there and never go;
Always, whatever you may dream or do,
Strangeness and darkness will be facing you;
Never – never at all – will you catch sight
Of one white glimmer on a misty height,
Or of one breath or zephyr taking flight
Within the stillness of rebellious night.)

NOTES

1   Poem-numbers in roman numerals conform to those in the *ne varietur* edition (Hugo 1880-5 and 1886-1902); manuscript-numbers in arabic numerals are those by which Hugo's papers were catalogued after his death. Translations in the present chapter are cited from Blackmore (2000, 2001a, 2001b, 2002, 2004).

2   The blend of conservatism and experimentalism in Hugo's early odes has been succinctly analyzed in Venzac (1955: 584-8).

3   Jocasta, Phèdre, and Merope were the aristocratic heroines of tragedies by Voltaire and Racine; the grammarian Claude Favre de Vaugelas (1585-1650) had been influential in ridding French literary style of "vulgarisms."

4   Bérénice, too, was the aristocratic heroine of a tragedy by Racine.

5   The Academy – the Académie française – is the traditional arbiter of French literary taste.

6   Though not published until 1902, the piece was written 60 years earlier and is characteristic of its author's style at the time.

7   This famous (and revealing) formula was first applied to Dickens in Leavis (1948: 19).

8 For obvious reasons, Tennyson would not have wished to include any living English poet in the comparison. His sonnet first appeared in *Nineteenth Century* (June 1877) and was reprinted, slightly revised, in *Ballads and Other Poems* (1880).

9 "Who does not remember 'La Pente de la rêverie,' now already so remote in date? Many of his recent works seem to have arisen, no less naturally than prolifically, from the faculty that presided over the creation of that enthralling poem," Baudelaire wrote in his June 1861 essay "Victor Hugo."

REFERENCES AND FURTHER READING

Albouy, Pierre (1963). *La Création mythologique chez Victor Hugo*. Paris: José Corti.

Albouy, Pierre (ed.) (1964). *Victor Hugo, Œuvres poétiques I*. Paris: Gallimard.

Aragon, Louis (1952). *Avez-vous lu Hugo?* Paris: Éditeurs français réunis.

Baudelaire, Charles (1976). *Œuvres complètes II*, ed. Claude Pichois. Paris: Gallimard.

Blackmore, E. H. and A. M. (eds.) (2000). *Six French Poets of the Nineteenth Century*. Oxford: Oxford University Press.

Blackmore, E. H. and A. M. (eds.) (2001a). *Selected Poems of Victor Hugo: A Bilingual Edition*. Chicago: University of Chicago Press.

Blackmore, E. H. and A. M. (eds.) (2001b). *A Bilingual Edition of the Major Epics of Victor Hugo*, 2 vols. Lewiston, NY: Edwin Mellen Press.

Blackmore, E. H. and A. M. (eds.) (2002). *Contemplations, Lyrics, and Dramatic Monologues by Victor Hugo*. North Charleston, SC: Imprint Books.

Blackmore, E. H. and A. M. (eds.) (2004). *The Essential Victor Hugo*. Oxford: Oxford University Press.

Butor, Michel (1964). *Répertoire II*. Paris: Éditions de minuit.

Frey, John A. (1988). *"Les Contemplations" of Victor Hugo: The Ash Wednesday Liturgy*. Charlottesville: University Press of Virginia.

Gaudon, Jean (1969). *Le Temps de la contemplation*. Paris: Flammarion.

Grant, Richard B. (1979). "Sequence and Theme in Victor Hugo's *Les Orientales*." *PMLA*, 94: 894-908.

Grimaud, Michel, et al. (1994). "Victor Hugo." In David Baguley, ed. *A Critical Bibliography of French Literature 5: The Nineteenth Century*. Syracuse, NY: Syracuse University Press, vol. 1: 208-31.

Houston, John Porter (1988). *Victor Hugo*, 2nd edn. Boston: Twayne.

Hugo, Victor (1880-5). *Œuvres complètes*, 46 vols. Paris: Hetzel.

Hugo, Victor (1886-1902). *Œuvres inédites*, 16 vols. Paris: Hetzel.

Ireson, J. C. (1997). *Victor Hugo: A Companion to his Poetry*. Oxford: Clarendon Press.

Leavis, F. R. (1948). *The Great Tradition*. London: Chatto and Windus.

Leuilliot, Bernard (1985). *"Odes et ballades:* Notice et notes." In Jacques Seebacher and Guy Rosa (gen. eds.), *Victor Hugo, Poésie I*. Paris: Laffont, pp. 1050-64.

Marzials, Frank T. (1888). *Life of Victor Hugo*. London: Walter Scott.

Millet, Claude (1985). *"L'Art d'être grand-père:* Notice et notes." In Jacques Seebacher and Guy Rosa (gen. eds.), *Victor Hugo, Poésie III*. Paris: Laffont, pp. 1446-53.

Nash, Suzanne (1976). *"Les Contemplations" of Victor Hugo: An Allegory of the Creative Process*. Princeton, NJ: Princeton University Press.

Rochette, Auguste (1911). *L'Alexandrin chez Victor Hugo*. Lyons: Emmanuel Vitte.

Ubersfeld, Anne (1985). *Paroles de Victor Hugo*. Paris: Éditions sociales/Messidor.

Venzac, Géraud (1955). *Les Origines religieuses de Victor Hugo*. Paris: Bloud et Gay.

13

French Romantic Drama

Barbara T. Cooper

Contrary to a long-held view, French Romantic drama did not spring fully formed onto the Parisian stage with the premiere of Victor Hugo's *Hernani* in 1830. Perhaps because the controversy surrounding the performance of Hugo's play at the prestigious Comédie-Française was widely reported in the nineteenth-century press, recorded in the memoirs of Hugo's contemporaries, and enshrined in the pages of literary histories and schoolbooks from those times to ours, the work's debut was seen as marking a crucial aesthetic turning point. Modern scholarship has, however, put that contentious event into perspective and has made it clear that the battle generated by the production of *Hernani* was part of an artistic shift that had already begun earlier in the century.

In fact, some of the first signs of the movement away from the formal conventions and traditional subjects of French neoclassical drama were already discernible in Louis-Jean-Népomucène Lemercier's *Pinto, ou La Journée d'une conspiration* (Pinto, or The Day of a Conspiracy; 1800). The piece, which Lemercier saw as exemplifying a new dramatic genre – historical comedy – was written in prose instead of the alexandrine (i.e., 12 syllable) verse French playwrights typically employed in works of serious drama. Also unusual, though not entirely without precedent, was the fact that Lemercier's piece was set in "modern" Portugal (modern designating any era from the Middle Ages on) rather than being drawn from the annals of ancient or biblical history or legend. The play describes the successful efforts of the titular character – a commoner who is secretary to the Duc de Bragance – to liberate his country from Spanish occupation. Designated prime minister at the drama's conclusion, Pinto finds himself in a position to determine the course of the nation's future. This attribution of political agency to a person of ordinary birth was rare outside of the propaganda pieces written during the French Revolution and seems to announce later Romantic dramas such as Hugo's *Ruy Blas* (1838), albeit with a more positive outcome.

Despite *Pinto*'s designation as a comedy, Stendhal – an important theorist of French Romantic drama – would later write, in his essay on *Racine et Shakespeare* (1823-5), that "Notre tragédie nouvelle ressemblera beaucoup à *Pinto*, le chef-d'œuvre de M. Lemercier" (Our new [Romantic] tragedy will be very much like Lemercier's masterpiece, *Pinto*; Stendhal 1970: 75).[1] Lemercier's play appealed to Stendhal as a model for Romantic drama for several reasons. In *Racine et Shakespeare*, Stendhal rejects alexandrine verse as a vehicle for dramatic expression because it calls attention to itself and to the beauty of language rather than allowing for the realistic and straightforward representation of ideas and actions. He contends, moreover, that "[s]i la police laissait jouer *Pinto*, en moins de six mois le public ne pourrait plus supporter les conspirations en vers alexandrins" (if the police allowed *Pinto* to be performed, in less than six months the public would no longer be willing to tolerate conspiracies in alexandrine verse; Stendhal 1970: 97). Stendhal also believed that tragedy must be relevant to the concerns of contemporary audiences, reflecting their historical experiences and worldviews rather than those of previous generations. Racine's plays might have been "modern" in the seventeenth century (suited to the tastes of that day), Stendhal averred, but they were no longer meaningful in the nineteenth century. Neither were more recent tragedies written in line with seventeenth-century aesthetic models. "Je ne vois que *Pinto* qui ait été fait pour des Français modernes" (As far as I can see, *Pinto* is the only work that's been made for modern Frenchmen), he declared (Stendhal 1970: 96-7).

Pinto did not meet another of Stendhal's criteria for modern, Romantic drama, however: the abandonment of the neoclassical unities of time and place. Historical events, Stendhal held, could not be understood in all their complexity if a drama was allowed to show only the final hours before the resolution of a crisis and was limited to a single location. Lemercier was less persuaded of this than Stendhal would be and thus did not abandon the temporal and spatial constraints typical of the French neoclassical dramatic aesthetic until he wrote *Christophe Colomb* (Christopher Columbus, 1809), a three-act verse drama designated a "Shakespearean comedy." Declaring the unities of time and place uniquely incompatible with the story of Columbus's attempt to discover the New World, Lemercier apologized in advance for his break with French neoclassical tradition and cautioned other dramatists not to imitate his formal "irregularities" in their plays. The playwright's repudiation of dramatic innovation and the work's generic label notwithstanding, *Colomb* surely deserves to be seen as a proto-Romantic drama not only because it violates the unities of time and place, moves beyond the usual stylistic and metrical restrictions of French neoclassical drama, and mixes comic and serious elements together, but also because it prefigures the Romantic preoccupation with the isolation and alienation of those individuals whose status or genius sets them apart from society. What is more, if we read Lemercier's account of Columbus's journey as a failed quest – as the temporary frustration of the explorer's dreams of renown and prestige at the end of the piece invites us to do – we can see that Columbus clearly announces "... the Romantic character who must struggle to create himself a hero in opposition to an unheroic world" (Cox 1994: 157). The suicide of the eponymous poet-hero at the conclusion of Alfred de Vigny's *Chatterton* (1834) and the death of the titular character in Musset's

Lorenzaccio (1834) will underscore, with even greater finality than Lemercier suggests here, the inevitable outcome of such an endeavor in Romantic drama.

Lemercier's subjects in *Pinto* and *Colomb* illustrate one of the distinguishing features of French Romantic drama: its preoccupation with moments of social or political tensions and transformations in the creation of national and/or individual destiny. Of course, Lemercier was neither the first nor the only playwright who sought to renew French dramaturgy via the introduction of modern historical subjects. Neither did he fully exploit, as French melodramatists and Romantic dramatists would do, the elements of local color and spectacle inherent in his chosen topics.

Like Lemercier, René-Charles Guilbert de Pixérécourt, the father of French melo-drama, frequently wove modern historical subjects into his plays. *Pizarre, ou La Conquête du Pérou* (Pizarro, or The Conquest of Peru; 1802) is the first melodrama that Pixérécourt seems to have labeled as *historique* (historical), but it is another work so designated, *Tékéli, ou Le Siège de Montgatz* (Tékéli, or The Siege of Montgatz; 1803), that provides a more typical and commercially successful model of the genre. A three-act prose drama enhanced by music, dance, and special effects, *Tékéli* recounts the efforts of a Hungarian nobleman (Count Tékéli) to return home from exile and imprisonment to reclaim his sovereign rights and embrace his beloved wife, Axelina. To do this, he must escape detection by the Austrian forces occupying his country and arrive at the walled city of Montgatz in time to lead a group of besieged patriots in a final battle against the Austrians. Although the play recalls real historical events, Pixérécourt is less concerned with the faithful reproduction of facts than with the representation of a morally unambiguous (Manichean) universe filled with touching emotions and vivid spectacle. The playwright uses picturesque sets and distinctive costumes and customs to bring local color to the incidents showcased in his drama and dazzling stage effects that draw the viewer into sympathetic engagement with the (virtuous) characters in his play. Some of these features, especially those that contribute to the concrete immediacy and *presentness* of time, place, and action in Pixérécourt's work, announce important dimen-sions of Romantic drama rarely, if ever, found in nineteenth-century French neoclassical tragedies whose typical decor was a single, indistinguishable antechamber (*palais à volonté*). The use of plural settings in melodrama and Romantic drama announces more than just an aesthetic shift away from abstract words and locales toward emotionally expressive speech and distinctive physical spaces; it also points to a fundamentally changed perception of story and history and of the role context plays in determining the outcome of all human undertakings and longings. Hugo would later outline his view of the importance of the world in the "Preface" to his play, *Cromwell* (1827), where he wrote that the depiction of the place in which an action occurred made the represen-tation of that action appear more genuine.

There are other early playwrights – Casimir Delavigne, Prosper Mérimée, and Ludovic Vitet among them – whose role in the move toward French Romantic drama likewise deserves recognition. All three of these men used modern history as the basis for some or all of their works and highlighted social or political tensions in their plays. Mérimée and Vitet wrote closet dramas (i.e., works destined to be read rather than performed) and could thus take aesthetic and ideological liberties they might not have otherwise been allowed in the theater. It is also important to acknowledge, however briefly, the significant role played by essayists, translators, and theoreticians such as Germaine de Staël, Benjamin Constant, François Guizot, Alessandro Manzoni, and Stendhal who helped to shape Romantic drama. It is impossible to detail here the arguments they advanced in their pamphlets and prefaces, but each of these writers, in her or his own way, helped to spark discussion and shape the debate over the forms, the subjects, and the significance of tragedy in the modern world. Whether through translation and commentary (Constant adapted and commented on Schiller's *Wallenstein*; Guizot presented Shakespeare) or analysis of foreign dramatic models (Staël wrote about German playwrights and aesthetics in *De l'Allemagne* [On Germany], Stendhal about Shakespeare), each challenged the continuing pertinence and hegemony of French neoclassical dramaturgy and offered suggestions or guidelines for a new type of drama more suited to the times. Their writings, together with the translation of the novels of Walter Scott and the performances of British actors and actresses in Paris in 1822 and 1827, served both as a stimulus to and a justification for change. Indeed, there are many examples of early nineteenth-century French plays derived from the texts of Goethe, Schiller, Shakespeare, and Scott, including Lemercier's *Richard III et Jeanne Shore* (Jane Shore, 1824), Pixérécourt's and Benjamin Antier's *Guillaume Tell* (William Tell, 1828), and Alfred de Vigny's *Le More de Venise* (The Moor of Venice [Othello], 1829). The goal of writers like Staël, Constant, and Stendhal was not to substitute a German or an English model for the traditional French one. Instead, they highlighted the value of "modern" (especially national historical) subjects and proposed a range of politically and aesthetically liberal options (including the freedom to reject the unities of time and place, to ignore the stifling constraints of stage decorum and alexandrine verse, to benefit from the inclusion of local color, etc.).

It was, however, Victor Hugo's "Preface" to *Cromwell* (1827) that most famously sought to redefine tragedy for modern times. Like his predecessors, Hugo wished to free drama from the unities of time and place, from an arbitrary sense of stage decorum, and from past limits on subject matter. Anything that was in nature could be in art, he insisted. Rejecting conventional distinctions between comedy and tragedy, which he deemed incompatible with modern experience and Christianity's vision of human beings' dual nature, Hugo proposed mixing together the (morally and/or physically) sublime and the grotesque to create a drama that offered a richer, more realistic picture of life. Local color, he felt, further contributed to that end. If the times, places, and circumstances that gave rise to events were represented in all their specificity, drama would no longer set forth an abstract image of the past, but would illuminate and explain the relationship between individuals and the world in which they lived. Hugo also believed that verse, provided it was freed from the constraints of lexical and metrical tradition, was fully compatible with modern tragic expression. It could heighten and intensify the theatrical experience rather than stultify it.[2] The (then) unperformable *Cromwell* provided a perfect illustration of his description of modern drama.

Alexandre Dumas

Alexandre Dumas *père* never elaborated a theory on the forms, purpose, or pertinence of French Romantic drama to the modern world. He was, however, the most prolific and popular writer of French Romantic dramas. Influenced by his readings of the works of foreign playwrights and by the performances of the British actors who toured in Paris in the 1820s, Dumas helped to transform serious drama in France by combining the dynamism and spectacle of melodrama with the gravity of tragedy. His plays were generally grounded in "modern" history or treated contemporary social issues.

Dumas's national historical drama, *Henri III et sa cour* (Henri III and his Court, 1829), opened the doors of the Comédie-Française to Romantic drama. Written in prose, the play violated the unities of time and place, made dramaturgically effective use of several different practicable sets, emphasized local color in customs, costumes, props, and decor, disregarded conventional rules of decorum by showing scenes of violence on stage, and took full advantage of the kind of dynamic pacing and emotionally intense dialogue generally associated with melodrama. Indeed, the play's energetic and vivid portrayal of the past must have made the work seem quite unlike any other previously staged at the Comédie.

The plot of Dumas's play highlights the intersection of political passions with amorous ones at a time of civil and religious unrest in France. The seemingly ineffectual King Henri finds his reign challenged by his powerful and ambitious cousin, the Duc de Guise. As a result, the Queen Mother, Catherine de Médicis, long the real power behind the throne, fears losing control over her son and matters of state. Hoping to weaken the influence of both Guise and Saint-Mégrin, one of the king's favorites whom she sees as a rival for Henri's affections, Catherine uses the Duchesse de Guise as a pawn. She arranges an involuntary meeting between the Duchesse and Saint-Mégrin, whose love for one another has gone unspoken and remains unconsummated. This later leads to a confrontation between the duchess and her husband and, at the play's conclusion, to the traitorous assassination of Saint-Mégrin. Meanwhile, Henri manages to undermine his cousin's political ascendancy by declaring himself, rather than Guise, the head of the powerful Holy Catholic League.

This tale of ambition, abuse of power, and the victimization of lovers reveals a world filled with menace and hostility. It is a world governed by human passions and actions rather than by the abstract forces of fate or divine providence. By naming himself head of the League, Henri reclaims his role as head of state and church and thereby reaffirms the existing order. By using violence against his wife and Saint-Mégrin, Guise re-establishes the primacy of patriarchal authority over love. Through deception and manipulation, Catherine eliminates the challenge to her control and restores the *status quo ante*. Saint-Mégrin and the Duchesse de Guise are ultimately caught in the middle of a larger struggle for power they cannot control and from which there is no escape. Our sympathy goes out to them rather than to those who do battle for supremacy over the affairs of state. The unequal contest between personal happiness and political forces set forth in *Henri III* was powerfully portrayed in Dumas's piece but is by no means unique; it would become a frequent subject of French Romantic drama and would be treated in a variety of periods and settings in other works.

Dumas depicted another type of tragic conflict in what is today perhaps his most famous Romantic drama, *Antony* (1831). In that five-act prose piece first performed at the Théâtre de la Porte Saint-Martin (a playhouse that specialized in the production of melodramas), Dumas again violated the unities of time and place and the conventions of neoclassical decorum. (Intent on possessing her, Antony breaks into Adèle d'Her-vey's hotel room in full sight of the audience in Act III; then, at the end of Act V, he kills her on stage, proclaiming that she had resisted his efforts to make her his mistress.) Once again, the playwright displayed a keen sense of modern stagecraft and used emotionally powerful language. But whereas *Henri III* was set in the past (sixteenth century) and focused on characters of unquestioned identity and aristocratic status, *Antony* was set in the present (nineteenth century) and featured a titular character of unknown parentage and uncertain rank.

In Dumas's play, Antony's intense passions and personal superiority cannot erase the stain of his illegitimate birth and consequent lack of social standing, but it is that same marginality which helps us to recognize him as a Romantic hero. Adèle's conflicted emotions, victimization, despair, and death likewise mark her as a Roman-tic heroine. Public condemnation of the lovers' relationship and the play's tragic conclusion emphasize the impossibility of rebelling against society, the frustration of personal ambition and emotional fulfillment in a hypocritical, restrictive world. Indeed, in many of their plays – whether set in the present or in the "recent" past – Dumas and other French Romantic playwrights would regularly insist that the recognition of personal merit and of true love are impossible in the rigidly enforced (but nonheroic) social order that defines the modern world.

If the passions, pessimism, and defeat displayed in *Antony* and *Henri III et sa cour* are representative of much of French Romantic drama, so too is the richly detailed portrait these works offer of the universe their protagonists inhabit. Apposite cos-tumes, props, and set designs lend an aura of authenticity and historical accuracy to the action in their dramas. Such devices serve to abolish distance and to create a feeling of physical and temporal proximity between the audience and the characters on stage. What is more, the multiplication of settings – an astrologer's laboratory, the Louvre, the Duchesse de Guise's oratory in *Henri III*; Adèle's home in Paris, an inn on the route to Strasbourg, the reception rooms in the home of Adèle's friend, the Vicomtesse de Lacy, in *Antony* – brings layers of geographical and social dimension to the action, thereby enhancing its realism. Not only does this scenic diversity allow for the introduction of characters who could not plausibly meet in a single location, it also underscores the significance of the action (e.g., the ostracism of Antony and Adèle takes place in a space whose social character is clearly apparent) and its temporal duration (e.g., Adèle's flight from Paris, the lovers' brief period of withdrawal from society, their return, condemnation, and demise). Emotionally charged language; blocking, gestures, and pacing that emphasize dynamism and heighten dramatic intensity; and scenes of on-stage violence (the Duc de Guise's torture of his wife, Antony's assault on and, later, killing of Adèle) likewise make the fictional universe come alive in a manner totally at odds with the decorous abstraction of neoclassical tragedy.

Like *Antony*, another of Dumas's works, *Kean, ou Désordre et génie* (Kean, or Disorder and Genius, 1836), extols passion and personal fulfillment as important values and suggests that exceptional individuals cannot survive in a world where status and the bounds of acceptable behavior are rigidly (if often hypocritically) defined. *Kean*, a five-act drama in prose written for and performed by the celebrated French Boulevard theater actor, Frédérick Lemaître, offers a fictional account of the life of the English stage star, Edmund Kean. Beguiled by Kean's superior skill in such roles as Romeo and Othello, Éléna de Koefeld, the wife of the Danish ambassador to England, has fallen in love with the actor who loves her in return. What neither of these individuals has yet understood, but what we can already guess, is that their relationship, founded on an illusion, has no future. And indeed, the real-world forces that will separate the aristocratic Éléna from the socially marginalized Kean are made apparent from the beginning of the drama, initially set in the *salon* of the Danish ambassador's London residence. The conversation at a social gathering there makes it clear that Kean, who has been sent an invitation to attend the event, is considered by everyone but Éléna to be a mere entertainer rather than an equal of the upper-class guests (including the Prince of Wales) who are present. Imbued with a sense of his own genius, deluded by the apparent friendship of the Prince – their relationship is based on little more than a shared passion for pleasure and debauchery – and confident of Éléna's affections, Kean sees his position altogether differently. The action in the rest of the play, set in a variety of locations in London ranging from the Drury Lane theater to a low-class bar along the Thames, will serve to dispel his error. In the end, after publicly insulting the Prince and the rest of the theater audience from the stage, Kean will leave for New York (a space of both exile and opportunity) with the young Anna Damby, an orphaned heiress who likewise seeks to flee the constraints London society would impose on her future.

While love is still an important theme in *Kean*, that emotion is neither of the same intensity nor of the same nature as in *Henri III* and *Antony*. Éléna's and Kean's feelings for one another seem less persuasively rooted in the heart than was true in those earlier dramas. What is more, as the subtitle of the play suggests, the true focus of this piece lies elsewhere. At issue is the question of genius or, more specifically, of society's failure to honor genius with the (elevated) status that is its due regardless of an individual's origins, and its unwillingness to accord genius the freedom from the bounds of ordinary rules that it needs to flourish. For some, Kean's exile may not appear as fully tragic as Saint-Mégrin's assassination or Antony's implied execution since there is at least some kind of future for him in (a democratic) New York. However, like Lemercier's Columbus, what Kean most craves, and fails to get, is recognition of his exceptional nature. This makes the actor's involuntary departure from the center of artistic and social distinction (London), the frustration of his amorous and social ambitions just as pitiable as more traditional tragic outcomes.

Alfred de Vigny's *Chatterton* (Comédie-Française, 1835) – the story of a young, impoverished poet who falls victim to English (and, implicitly, French) society's capitalist values and indifference to genius and art – had already told a similar tale on a smaller scale. More formally conservative than most other Romantic dramas, the action in Vigny's piece covers a period of less than 24 hours and is set in the home of a heartless industrialist, John Bell, where Chatterton has taken up temporary lodgings. As the story evolves, the struggling poet's alienation from society is tempered only by the compassion of an elderly Quaker who also lodges at Bell's home and by the furtive assistance of Bell's timid, bullied wife, Kitty – a role played to great effect by Marie Dorval. In the end, unable to pay his debts or to find a place in society that honors his poetic genius, Chatterton commits suicide in his room after burning his manuscripts. Kitty, who has loved the young man without overtly acting on her feelings, dies from shock after finding his inanimate body sprawled on the bed in his room. Dorval's dramatic fall down the staircase shortly before the curtain rings down packed the same kind of emotional punch as her character's death in Dumas's *Antony* where she played Adèle. Both scenes viscerally reinforced their respective drama's philosophical message about the frustration of individual merit or genius by a society whose values (economic worth in *Chatterton*, birth in *Antony*) closed the door to love, ambition, and public recognition and became indelibly fixed in the imagination of audiences who saw the works performed.

Victor Hugo

Despite the popular success and aesthetic innovations found in Dumas's plays and the intellectual and emotional appeal of Vigny's *Chatterton*, it is Victor Hugo's works that are most often held up as examples of French Romantic drama. Hugo's recognized status as a poet and novelist, together with his theoretical pronouncements in the "Preface" to *Cromwell* and the controversy surrounding the form and performance of *Hernani* (Comédie-Française, 1830), no doubt contributed to his designation as the putative head of the Romantic school of drama. As the head of a literary circle known as the *Cénacle* and a vociferous defender of theatrical liberty – he most notably took issue with the censorship of his drama *Le Roi s'amuse* (The King's Jester, 1832) – Hugo further solidified his position as the head of that artistic movement.

With Hugo's *Hernani*, the commingling of political and amorous affairs already seen in *Henri III et sa cour* is once again apparent. In contrast to Dumas's prose piece, however, Hugo's drama, set principally in Spain in the early sixteenth century, was written in alexandrine verse – a traditional form the playwright revolutionized by violating metrical conventions and earlier standards of linguistic propriety. In accord with the views he outlined in his "Preface" to *Cromwell* several years before, Hugo also violated the unities of time and place in *Hernani*. Each act of the drama is set in a different location whose pertinence to the action is clear (e.g., the family portrait gallery where Don Ruy Gomez de Silva invokes his ancestors' honor when refusing to betray the laws of hospitality and surrender his guest, the outlawed Hernani, to Don Carlos, King of Spain; Charlemagne's tomb in Aix-la-Chapelle where Don Carlos, awaiting his election as Holy Roman Emperor, reflects on the role and meaning of power and undergoes a moral change that leads him to pardon Hernani, restore his aristocratic titles, and allow him to marry Doña Sol). Hugo likewise weaves local color into the action, costumes, and settings of the play and combines elements of the comic and the tragic, the sublime and the grotesque. As a result, despite echoes of works ranging from Corneille's *Cinna* and *Le Cid* to Shakespeare's *Romeo and Juliet*, and from comedy to melodrama, the play is distinctively Romantic, tenderly lyrical and darkly dramatic. The clash between partisans of the neoclassical and Romantic aesthetics that took place at the time of the play's premiere, while scarcely the first or the most dramatic of its kind – the battle surrounding Lemercier's *Christophe Colomb* earlier in the century had resulted in injuries and a death – nonetheless seemed to announce the triumph of the Romantic conception of drama.

The love story at the heart of Hugo's play finds three men competing for the hand of the orphaned Doña Sol: her elderly uncle and guardian, Don Ruy Gomez, to whom she is betrothed and who offers her security and profound affection; the young and handsome outlaw, Hernani, who offers her intense passion but no security; and Don Carlos, King of Spain, who offers her the possibility of elevated status and wealth, but whose feelings may well prove less enduring than those of his rivals. The first acts of the play make it clear that the young woman's heart belongs to Hernani. The son of an aristocratic rebel put to death by Don Carlos's father, Hernani lives under an assumed name (he was born Jean d'Aragon) and is himself a political outcast pursued by the authorities. The amorous rivalry that pits the outlaw against the king is thus paired with a political contest that sets the two men at odds with one another at critical moments in the drama (most notably in Acts II-IV). Carlos's transformation in Charlemagne's tomb in Act IV appears to mark the conclusion of the piece. But while Act IV resolves the Hernani–Don Carlos conflict and seems to signal the (political and social) reintegration of the outcast/bandit, it does not settle the debt Hernani owes his other rival for Doña Sol's hand, Don Ruy Gomez. Thus the young lovers' marriage festivities, celebrated with lyrical expansion under the stars at the d'Aragon family castle in Act V, turn tragic when Don Ruy, disguised in a black domino, arrives uninvited and sounds a horn, symbol of the debt of honor that the then-outlawed Hernani had promised to pay him in exchange for his hospitality in Act III. The payment Don Ruy now demands is his rival's death. In the end, both of the newlyweds drink the poison Don Ruy presents to Hernani and the old man is left alone. The couple's on-stage demise, reminiscent of Romeo's and Juliet's tragic deaths, violated the laws of neoclassical propriety which normally banned such unseemly sights from view and highlights once again the substitution of human action for divine intervention.

Politics and passion clash again in Hugo's *Ruy Blas* (1838), a play set in late seventeenth-century Spain and the first work performed at the Théâtre de la Renaissance, an enterprise owned jointly by Hugo and Dumas and intended as a showcase for their works. Disguised and presented at court by his master, Don Salluste, as that nobleman's cousin, Don César, the valet Ruy Blas (played with great success by Frédérick Lemaître) will unwittingly serve Salluste's plan for vengeance against the Spanish Queen who has banished him. Six months later, the valet, long in love with the Queen – he is "un vers de terre amoureux d'une étoile" (an earthworm in love with a star) – has risen in rank on his own merits, but under his assumed name. Now prime minister, he is critical of those aristocrats who would put personal profit above the nation's well-being. After overhearing "Don César"/Ruy Blas's speech condemning the noblemen, the Queen reveals her love for him and asks him to save the state from collapse. The married Queen's feelings, if publicized and/or acted upon, would forever compromise her in the rigid moral and social environment of the Spanish court and that, of course, is exactly what Salluste has hoped all along his plan would accomplish. Returned to Madrid in disguise, Salluste orders Ruy Blas from court and arranges a rendezvous between his valet and the Queen in a mysterious house. After a series of twists and turns, Ruy Blas kills Salluste, drinks the poison the Queen threatened to take when she saw her position and honor endangered, and dies in her arms. In this play, then, as in other Romantic dramas, the present proves impermanent, past actions inescapable, and the future closed to superior individuals who seek personal happiness and other rewards. The political advancement of a member of the lower class, possible only by means of a borrowed identity, is shown to be ephemeral and without long-term effect. The play's emphasis on the constraints imposed by widespread self-interest in maintaining the status quo, eliminating opportunities for reform and meritorious advancement, and frustrating true love no doubt had special resonance for men and women of talent in Louis-Philippe's France.

Indeed, issues of class, power, exclusion, and revenge had already figured in two of Hugo's earlier plays: *Le Roi s'amuse* (The King's Jester, 1832)[3] and *Lucrèce Borgia* (Lucretia Borgia, 1833), both likewise set in the "modern" past. These paired works mixed the "sublime" with the "grotesque" – an aesthetic concept Hugo had already articulated and championed in the "Preface" to *Cromwell*. Triboulet, jester to King François I, is a most unusual tragic figure – a physically deformed and socially inferior individual who, by virtue of his position, is free to make bitingly critical observations on the debauchery and excesses at court. But beneath the clown's trenchant verbal attacks and disgraceful physique beats a heart made transcendent by his love for his daughter, Blanche. Simultaneously grotesque and sublime, Triboulet clearly embodies a central aesthetic and philosophical tenet of Hugo's "Preface" to *Cromwell*, that is, that in the "modern" (Christian) world, human beings are defined by their dual nature (both fallen and redeemed, they are part angel and part devil) and that anything that is in nature is fit for representation on stage. After the virginal Blanche has been seduced by the King, Triboulet seeks revenge. His plans to punish the King go awry, however, and in the end, it is his daughter, not François, who falls victim to his machinations.

Lucrèce was conceived by Hugo as Triboulet's counterpart. Physically beautiful and politically powerful but morally corrupt, she loves her son, Gennaro, who is unaware that Lucrèce is his mother. Again, a desire for vengeance, coupled with secrets and betrayals, unexpectedly bring about the child's death by the parent's own hand. In this case, Lucrèce's past crimes undermine her one good quality – maternal love – and prove her own undoing. While the lubricious, iniquitous woman of power high-lighted in this piece is a somewhat less original tragic protagonist than the court jester, Lucrèce serves the same ideological and artistic purpose in illustrating Hugo's conception of modern, Romantic drama.

Hugo's last Romantic piece, *Les Burgraves* (The Burgraves, 1843), a three-part (*partie*) verse drama, is set at a medieval German court. Its theatrical failure is usually cited as marking the demise of Romanticism, even though some dramas in the Romantic mode continued to be written and performed after that date, especially in boulevard theaters. Crimes of violence and other forms of moral and political corruption lie at the heart of this work that focuses on four generations of the ruling family. Epic in scale and tone, the piece reaches beyond the scope of other historical dramas Hugo had written. It is almost as if the playwright were seeking to combine elements of the story of Cain and Abel with those of the house of Atreus and to suffuse both with the atmospherics of German legend and the "modern" aesthetic of the sublime and the grotesque. Love is present here, as always, as are the themes of injustice and imprisonment which are so frequently found in Hugo's works and in those of other French Romantic dramatists. The conclusion of the play is, however, more optimistic than that of most of Hugo's dramatic writings from this period.

Alfred de Musset

Alfred de Musset's best-known drama, *Lorenzaccio* (1834), also tries to paint a broad tableau, but is far more pessimistic, examining the frustrations of political idealism and reform in a corrupt world. Written as a closet drama (*spectacle dans un fauteuil*), the work, freed from the limits imposed by contemporary stagecraft and censorship, is kaleidoscopic in form and content. Set primarily in Florence during the reign of Alexandre de Médicis, the five-act piece multiplies decors, features a broad range of secondary characters taken from all ranks of society, and entertains discussions on politics and art, morality and religion, ambition and love, purity and degradation. Filled with depravity and violence, the action centers on the titular character whose once-pure being has fused with the mask of debauchery he habitually wears while pursuing his (ultimately quixotic) dream of ridding Florence of tyranny and corrup-tion. Political freedom proves as elusive as personal freedom and in the end, as he had anticipated, Lorenzo's assassination of his cousin Alexandre does nothing to restore liberty to Florence or purity to his own soul. Weighed down by a sense of the hollowness of rhetoric and idealism, seeing no acceptable future for himself or his country, Lorenzo/Lorenzaccio allows himself to be killed by assassins attracted by the monetary reward offered for his death.

The corruption of one's truest, most innocent nature by external forces is set in an altogether different context in Musset's three-act dramatic proverb, *On ne badine pas avec l'amour* (Don't Trifle with Love, 1833-4). There, the affection that the young, orphaned Camille bore her cousin Perdican as a girl is expected to result in their marriage now that the two have completed their studies and grown to adulthood. But Camille's convent education has given her a perverted idea of men and love – an idea that has grown not from Christian doctrine, but from the experience of the betrayed women at her convent school who have filled her mind with their tales of woe. Stung by her refusal of his hand, Perdican soon turns his attentions to Rosette, a young peasant woman and Camille's *sœur de lait* ("sister" because the two were suckled together), whose unschooled trust and innocent affection he uses as a means to prick Camille's ego and spark feelings of jealousy. The naïve Rosette at first believes Perdican's professions of love and proposal of marriage. Later, after overhearing the aristocratic couple confess their true feelings for one another, she dies. Her death creates a permanent obstacle to their nuptials and sends Camille back to the convent with her own bitter story to tell about men and love. Alongside this tragic tale of misprized and misrepresented emotions, Musset has placed "grotesque," one-dimensional secondary characters (*fantoches*) who figure in scenes of comic absurdity that, by contrast, intensify the drama of love lost.

Musset's *Les Caprices de Marianne* (Marianne's Whims, 1833) also treats the subject of love and life lost. A two-act prose piece filled with passages of lyrical beauty and sharp wit, it tells the story of Coelio, an Italian youth passionately and idealistically in love with his elderly cousin's young wife, Marianne, but too timid and inexperienced to overcome her objections to his suit. In a moment of despair, he enlists his friend Octave, a man who seems to live for pleasure and is never at a loss for words, to speak on his behalf. Octave and Marianne engage in several verbal jousts, following which she agrees to an assignation. Believing that his words have won Marianne's heart for Coelio and unaware that the young woman's husband, having overheard their plans, intends to attack her lover, Octave sends his friend to the arranged rendezvous. There Coelio, imagining himself betrayed by Octave, allows himself to be killed. Like *Lorenzaccio* and *Badine*, this play was not written for performance. All three works, however, have been staged with regularity since the twentieth century and have come to be regarded as the finest and most enduring examples of French Romantic drama. Their portrayal of frustrated idealism and innocence, of a world-wariness and world-weariness that leads to an ironically bitter end, today seem to embody most fully the tragic angst of the Romantic generation.

Conclusion

It should be clear by now that French Romantic drama cannot be described solely by means of its formal departures from an earlier neoclassical aesthetic. As important as they were, the liberalization of language and style; the introduction of prose or a metrically freer form of alexandrine verse; the lifting of temporal and spatial limits on action; the promotion of "modern" history, local color, and spectacle; and the rejection of a decorum inherited from earlier times and of generic boundaries that compartmentalized the representation of human existence do not completely explain what makes Romantic drama distinctive. To understand its uniqueness, one must also note the importance of a secularized, purely human causality that, directly or indirectly, grew out of the French Revolution. In the post-Revolutionary, postprovidential era that saw melodrama, Romantic drama, and neoclassical tragedy exist side by side, political, economic, and social forces brought forth new ideas and aspirations, created new opportunities for and obstacles to success, and prompted new means of expression and new definitions of the tragic.

Stendhal, as we have seen, saw literature as an expression of society as it is, not as it was. He believed that if tragedy were to be relevant in the modern world it would have to be human and historical rather than legendary, mythological, or divine; specific rather than universal; national and individual rather than universal. Others – Hugo, Staël, and Constant among them – expressed similar thoughts in different ways. French Romantic drama is thus both the moral and the aesthetic product of its age: an age of uncertainty where past institutions, values, beliefs, and forms no longer won automatic acceptance or held universal appeal. There is often a note of despair, a sense of frustration, and a focus on marginalized individuals in French Romantic dramas. That is because playwrights and audiences understood that they were living at a time when personal and collective aspirations might not be realized, when rewards and forms of public recognition of merit might be withheld, and when passions could be thwarted or traversed by political or social forces beyond an individual's control.

Changed forms, subjects, and performance styles are an important part of the Romantic redefinition of drama in early nineteenth-century France. They signal a new understanding of the forces that shape individual stories and shared histories and as such are deserving of our attention. The energy and despondency that many Romantic heroes display, the ideals they pursue and the respect that they seek but are rarely granted are just as significant. They reflect the struggles and vicissitudes experienced by a generation living in a period of turmoil and transition, of capitalist ambitions and bourgeois values, and offer a key to the *mentalité* of those times.

NOTES

1 My translation; note that all translations in the chapter are mine.
2 See Thomasseau (1999) on the importance of the debate over prose vs. poetry in Romantic drama.
3 This play was the source of Verdi's opera *Rigoletto*.

References and Further Reading

Brooks, Peter (1995). *The Melodramatic Imagination: Balzac, Henry James and the Mode of Excess*. New Haven, CT and London: Yale University Press.

Cooper, Barbara T. (ed.) (1998). *Dictionary of Literary Biography*, vol. 192, *French Dramatists, 1789-1914*. Detroit: Gale Research.

Cox, Jeffrey N. (1987). *In the Shadows of Romance: Romantic Tragic Drama in Germany, England, and France*. Athens, OH: Ohio University Press.

Cox, Jeffrey N. (1994). "Romantic Redefinitions of the Tragic." In Gerald Gillespie (ed.), *Romantic Drama*. Amsterdam and Philadelphia: John Benjamins, pp. 153-65.

Daniels, Barry V. (ed.) (1983). *Revolution in the Theatre: French Romantic Theories of Drama*. Westport, CT: Greenwood Press.

Daniels, Barry V. (2003). *Le Décor de théâtre à l'époque romantique: Catalogue raisonné des décors de la Comédie-Française, 1799-1848*. Paris: Bibliothèque nationale de France.

Dumas, Alexandre (1974-) *Théâtre complet*, ed. Fernande Bassan. Paris: Lettres modernes/Minard.

Gengembre, Gérard (1999). *Le Théâtre français au 19e siècle*. Paris: Armand Colin.

Hugo, Victor (1967-9). *Œuvres complètes, édition chronologique*. Paris: Le Club Français du Livre.

Le Hir, Marie-Pierre (1992). *Le Romantisme aux enchères: Ducange, Pixérécourt, Hugo*. Amsterdam and Philadelphia: John Benjamins.

Lemercier, Louis-Jean-Népomucène (1976). *Pinto*, ed. Norma Perry. Exeter, UK: University of Exeter Press.

Lemercier, Louis-Jean-Népomucène (1809). *Christophe Colomb*. Paris: L. Collin.

Manzoni, Alessandro (2004). "Letter on Romanticism (1823)." *PMLA*, 119 (2): 299-316.

Musset, Alfred de (1990). *Théâtre complet d'Alfred de Musset*, ed. Simon Jeune. Paris: Gallimard.

Naugrette, Florence (2001). *Le Théâtre romantique*. Paris: Seuil.

Pixérécourt, René-Charles Guilbert de (1971). *Théâtre choisi*, ed. Charles Nodier. Genève: Slatkine Reprints.

Staël, Germaine de (1968). *De l'Allemagne*, 2 vols. Paris: Garnier-Flammarion.

Stendhal (Henri Beyle) (1970). *Racine et Shakespeare*. Paris: Garnier-Flammarion.

Rosa, Guy (2000). "Hugo et l'alexandrin de théâtre aux années 30: Une question secondaire." *Cahiers de l'Association Internationale des Études Françaises*, 52: 307-28.

Razgonnikoff, Jacqueline (2004). "Drame ou tragédie: Les Ambiguïtés du répertoire à la Comédie-Française, de 1828 à 1830." In Philippe Baron (ed.), *Le Drame du XVIIIe siècle à nos jours*. Dijon: Éditions Universitaires de Dijon, pp. 85-95.

Thomasseau, Jean-Marie (1995). *Drame et tragédie*. Paris: Hachette.

Thomasseau, Jean-Marie (1999). "Le Vers noble ou les chiens noirs de la prose?" In *Le Drame romantique: Rencontres nationales de dramaturgie du Havre*. Paris: Eds. des Quatre-Vents, pp. 32-40.

Ubersfeld, Anne (1993). *Le Drame romantique*. Paris: Belin.

Vigny, Alfred de (1986). *Œuvres complètes*, ed. François Germain and André Jarry. Paris: Gallimard.

Zaragoza, Georges (ed.) (1999). *Dramaturgies romantiques*. Dijon: Éditions Universitaires de Dijon.

14
Romantic Poetics in an Italian Context

Piero Garofalo

"Italian Romanticism does not exist" declaimed Gina Martegiani (1908), postulating a Voltarian critique that the literary movement was neither Italian nor Romantic. In extrapolating the conclusions of Arturo Graf's and Giuseppe Antonio Borgese's seminal studies, Martegiani argued that nineteenth-century Italian literature was a coherent by-product of Enlightenment culture, devoid of European Romanticism's aesthetics and idealist philosophy. Given its diverse and somewhat contradictory manifestations, the temptation to deny the existence of an Italian Romanticism continues to exert a certain fascination for literary historians. As they reject the solace of grand narratives in favor of discontinuous microhistories, these critics challenge the possibility of establishing a history of "isms" that does not embed political and cultural values into the concepts of periodicity and canonization and thereby marginalize other literary production. To dismiss Romanticism as convenient shorthand for historiographers, however, is to ignore the cultural context of early nineteenth-century literary production. This chapter traces the historical development of Romanticism in Italy as a self-conscious, if not entirely consistent, manifestation of evolving sensibilities while acknowledging both its intellectual debt and its aesthetic innovations with respect to European culture.

Intimations of Romanticism Before 1816

Italian Romanticism's conventional *terminus post quem* is the publication of Madame de Staël's *Sulla maniera e l'utilità delle traduzioni* in 1816, while its generous *terminus ante quem* is the political formation of the Italian nation-state in 1861. The latter provides symbolic closure to a symbiotic relationship with the Risorgimento that uniquely characterizes Italian Romanticism. Given the breadth of the timeframe, literary historians often refer to the 1840-60 period as the "Second Romanticism," to differentiate its prevailing personalities and characteristics. The arbitrariness of these limits also compounds the difficulty of reconstructing a prehistory. Walter Binni (1948), an exponent of pre-Romanticism, stresses Italian cultural continuity and the temporal lag between Romantic manifestations in northern Europe and in Italy. His interpretation claims epistemic coherence for diverse artistic tendencies (individualism, Titanism, pessimism, new empathy toward nature) that since the mid-eighteenth century challenged the Enlightenment's rational Classicism. Marxist critics such as Giuseppe Petronio (1960), however, have dismissed the concept of pre-Romanticism by stressing the rupture and discontinuities in the movement's relationship to the sociopolitical conditions of the period. Less dogmatically, the self-proclaimed Romantics reference both continuity and rupture when they construct their own intellectual genealogy through the articulation of cultural premises.

What their diverse referents share is an iconoclastic willingness to challenge the prevailing mores as in the case of the neglected Giambattista Vico, whose writings the Romantics rediscovered. Vico's insistence on poetry's irrationality, the importance of fantasy, the distinction between logical and poetic activity, and literature's historical and cultural specificity, provided an ideological filter for assimilating German Romantic poetics and stimulated the nineteenth-century search for a *Volksgeist*. Similarly, they revived Saverio Bettinelli, a heavy-handed critic best remembered for taking Dante to task), and Giuseppe Baretti, whose journal *Frusta Letteraria* (1763-5, modeled on Joseph Addison's *Spectator* and Samuel Johnson's *Rambler*) pulled no punches in its critique of the literary status quo. Bettinelli's works introduced Anglo-French sensibility (Shaftesbury, Diderot, and Rousseau) into Italy, and the Romantics admired his *Dell'entusiasmo delle belle arti* (1769), for championing enthusiasm, fantasy, passion, and sentiment. Influential as well was Baretti's *Discours sur Shakespeare et Monsieur de Voltaire* (1777), in which he defends Shakespeare's works from Voltaire's memorable description of being *un énorme fumier* (Voltaire 1975: 232) by affirming the cultural and historical relativism of literary tastes and by challenging Aristotelian tenets of unity. The Romantics also esteemed Pietro Verri's *Il Caffè* (1764-6), which introduced to the peninsula European aesthetic philosophy and which, in its quest for a civil culture, propounded a pragmatic critique of venerated norms, conventions, and traditions. For politically engaged nineteenth-century writers, *Il Caffè* represented a significant manifestation of national identity, and provided an immediate model for the Romantics' premier journal, *Il Conciliatore*, to emulate.

In addition to assimilating the Enlightenment's commitment to the public sphere, the Romantics drew on eighteenth-century theater experimentation to disseminate their aesthetics. The reforms of both Carlo Goldoni, who rejected the classical unities and cast all social classes, and his rival Carlo Gozzi, whose 10 *Fiabe* (1761-5) renounced all pretense to verisimilitude, readily lent themselves to Romantic rereadings. In fact, Goethe, E. T. A. Hoffmann, Lessing, Schiller, A. W. Schlegel, F. Schlegel, Schopenhauer, Staël, and Wagner heartily appreciated Gozzi's representations of the supernatural. If subsequent playwrights failed to achieve a similar impact, it is a tribute to Goldoni's and Gozzi's radical departures from theatrical tradition. While challenging the precepts of dramatic unity, the Romantics privileged historical tragedies, frequently set in the medieval period, which they molded into a new mythology as the cradle of modern Italian civilization. In particular, the tragedies *Il conte di Carmagnola* (1820) and *Adelchi* (1822) by Alessandro Manzoni (1785-1873) established the theoretical and aesthetic foundations for Romantic drama in Italy. Drawing on Shakespeare, Schiller, Goethe, and the Parisian *idéologues*, Manzoni emphasized truth and realism in the articulation of historical narratives that would speak to the present. Also influential were Silvio Pellico (1789-1854) and Giovan Battista Niccolini (1782-1861), both of whom produced modest historical dramas with nationalist undertones. Although Byron and John Hobhouse admired Pellico's *Francesca da Rimini* (1815), and contemporaries hailed Niccolini's *Arnaldo da Brescia* (1843) as an unsurpassable masterpiece, on the stage, Romanticism in Italy found its most congenial expression and diffusion, though late, in the operas of Giuseppe Verdi.

In general, however, Italian Romantics found their immediate literary paradigms in the works of Giuseppe Parini and Vittorio Alfieri, both of whom subsumed poetic strategies that reflected emergent Romantic sensibilities. Parini's poetry, a judicious mélange of Enlightenment and sensist aesthetics, articulated the conviction that literature must perform an elevated moral and civil function. In particular, his satirical *Il giorno* and his civil odes assumed canonical status for the Romantics. From Alfieri, Romantic culture co-opted a sense of Titanist individualism intolerant of social conventions and political proscriptions. His odes to America, the tragedies (*Virginia, Timoleone, La congiura de' Pazzi*, and *Saul*), and the treatises *Della tirannide* and *Del principe e delle lettere* intimated a national political consciousness that left an indelible print on the Risorgimento. Perhaps nowhere more than in his autobiography *Vita di Vittorio Alfieri scritta da esso*, however, did Alfieri display those *Sturm und Drang* qualities that earned him the admiration of the Romantics.

Like Alfieri, the liminal position of Ugo Foscolo (1778-1827) is emblematic of the aesthetic and ideological contradictions that complicate facile categorizations. Although aspects of his literary production evince a thematic and stylistic correspondence with the emerging poetic, his deference to Classicism inhibited Romantic emulation. While Foscolo's epistolary novel *Ultime lettere di Jacopo Ortis* (1802), in contrast to its prototype Goethe's *Die Leiden des jungen Werther*, emphasized the political aspects of social conformity, his odes "A Luigia Pallavicini caduta da cavallo" (1800) and "All'amica risanata" (1802), as well as the unfinished *Le Grazie*, infused a classical impetus into Italian Romanticism. In the oration *Dell'origine e dell'ufficio della letteratura* (1809), Foscolo advanced a new poetic by affirming literature's civil and moral function for the pedagogical edification of the citizenry. Anticipating a central tenet of Italian Romantics, Foscolo argued that literature served a constructive social function and that its quality was correlated to a nation's political freedom. Implicit in this contention was the democratization of literary culture, and the critique of vacuous erudition. In fact, he admonished writers not to neglect "those citizens placed by fortune between the idiot and the literate" (Foscolo 1967: 34)[1] and reminded them in *La letteratura periodica in Italia* (1824) that "vigorous thinking when one writes is more efficacious in developing a style than all the grammars and rhetorical treatises" (Foscolo 1958: 384). Nevertheless, Foscolo maintained an aristocratic attitude toward literature distant from the popularity advocated by Romantics. In *Saggio sulla letteratura contemporanea in Italia* (1818), he described the classic–Romantic controversy as a pedantic debate and displayed little sympathy for Romanticism's Italian manifestations. This attitude is not surprising given Foscolo's conviction, consonant with English and German Romantics, that mythology is a vital poetic element and not a defunct literary relic, as some of his contemporaries had suggested. Nor did the Italian Romantics embrace Foscolo unconditionally: they rejected both his resigned political pessimism and his jaded skepticism as to the value of cultural debates (cf. his views on *Il Conciliatore*). Foscolo's principal statement on Romanticism is his unfinished *Della nuova scuola drammatica italiana* (1825-6) in which he faulted Manzoni's *Conte di Carmagnola* for combining what Foscolo considered to be incompatible elements (history and poetry) – a criticism that Manzoni would tacitly acknowledge 20 years later in *Del romanzo storico*.

The prescient intuitions that these iconoclastic writers articulated reflected the complex crisis that invested the traditional canons of poetics. Expanding literacy and changes in sensitivity and taste produced new relationships between emergent professional writers and the public. As printers become publishers, consumer-oriented packaging displaced patronage-centered production, providing literary producers with increased economic autonomy. Writers contributed translations and prefaces, and served as series editors, thereby assuming responsibility for marketing strategies. For example, in Milan, the *Società tipografica dei classici italiani* (1802) engaged numerous writers in a literary project to promote a notion of civil tradition. Initiatives such as these provided valuable experience for the principal editorial promoters of Romanticism in Italy: Giovanni Silvestri, Antonio Fortunato Stella, Giovanni Resnati, Felice Rusconi, and Vincenzo Ferrario. When Romanticism entered the cultural scene, publishers, writers, and readers were prepared.

Madame de Staël and the Classic–Romantic Controversy

Primarily disseminated through the works of Simonde de Sismondi and Madame de Staël, Romanticism was still poorly understood in 1814, when Davide Bertolotti glossed the adjective "Romantic" as "a bit more extravagant and capricious than *romanesque* [*romanzesco*]" (Bertolotti 1814: 139). Within five years, however, it had entered common usage in Italy. Because the majority of Italian literati lacked access to the source texts, their understanding of Romanticism blurred distinctions between its various expressions, mediated as it was through French translations and commentaries. In particular, Sismondi's *De la littérature du Midi de l'Europe* (1813), Staël's *De l'Allemagne* (1810, Italian translation, 1814), and subsequently A. W. Schlegel's *Vorlesungen über dramatische Kunst und Litteratur* (1809-11) in the shoddy French translation (1814) and even more abysmal French-based Giovanni Gherardini edition

(1817) laid the foundation for Italian (mis)interpretations of European Romanticism. These texts, however, raised issues that were peripheral to the concerns of most writers in Italy. What brought Romanticism to the forefront of the cultural debates was the translation by Pietro Giordani (1774-1848) of Staël's *Sulla maniera e l'utilità delle traduzioni*, which appeared on January 1, 1816, in the Milanese journal *Biblioteca Italiana* (1816-40).

By featuring Staël's reflections in its inaugural issue, *Biblioteca Italiana*, published under the aegis and financing of Lombardy's recently restored Habsburg government, advanced a calculated political agenda. Count Josef Heinrich von Bellegarde had conceived of the journal as a means of enlisting support among those Italian intellectuals who were disillusioned by the Napoleonic experience. He turned to Foscolo, who drafted a program, *Parere sulla istituzione di un giornale letterario*, before realizing that his acquiescence entailed too steep a moral price. The Count's report to Baron Hager, dated March 20, 1815, legitimized Foscolo's anxieties: "[Intellectuals] cannot be neutral. Thus, the government must choose between two means for rendering them innocuous: either annihilate them or conquer them" (Foscolo 1966: 578). With Foscolo's grand refusal, Bellegarde then approached Vincenzo Monti (1754-1828), who politely declined the position, claiming to lack the managerial skills necessary for launching a new periodical. Monti's diplomatic evasiveness led the Count to Giuseppe Acerbi (1773-1826), author of *Travels through Sweden, Finland and Lapland to the North Cape in the Years 1798 and 1799* (London, 1802) and representative at the Congress of Vienna (1815). For the editorial board, Bellegarde enlisted Giordani, Monti, and the geologist Scipione Breislek (1750-1826). The editors extended an invitation to contribute to the journal, which initially downplayed its role as official cultural voice of the regime, to approximately 400 writers. Refusal (e.g., Alessandro Manzoni, Ermes Visconti, Gian Domenico Romagnosi, Melchiore Gioia) or acceptance (e.g., Ippolito Pindemonte, Angelo Mai, Antonio Cesari, Silvio Pellico, Ludovico di Breme, Pietro Borsieri) did not necessarily indicate a partisan political choice, but rather reflected personal preferences and economic necessity – the latter being a haunting specter for professional writers in preindustrial Italy. As the periodical began to shed all pretense of political neutrality, Pellico and Borsieri (1788-1852), both of whom had participated in its preliminary stages, withdrew their support. Borsieri had even penned the inaugural issue's introduction, which called for cultural and political renewal, but the editors chose to relegated it to the dustbin of history, publishing instead Giordani's *Proemio* and Staël's essay. Thus, from its inception, the Romantic controversy in Italy was as much a political as it was a literary contention.

Staël's article ignited a firestorm. In critiquing contemporary Italian literature as a meaningless display of erudition, she invited Italian writers to abandon their slavish imitation of the classics and to familiarize themselves with contemporary European, though primarily German and English, literary production. Exposure to these new currents, she suggested, would modernize Italian letters by inspiring the imagination of writers to produce an authentic literature that would appeal to the public. She laced her relatively innocuous suggestion with severe criticisms, which elicited what could not be an entirely unexpected controversy amongst the readership. While she did not mention the term "Romanticism," it implicitly informed her argument.

Given the geopolitical situation in the peninsula, which was fragmented into eight states and dominated by foreign powers, the negative reactions often assumed political undertones. While the collapse of *ancien régime* society and the Napoleonic campaigns in Italy contributed emotively, if perhaps not in practice, to nationalist aspirations, the restoration of deposed rulers following the Congress of Vienna thwarted both the political and social development of a new sovereign nation-state. Italy remained a geographical expression, which found little correspondence in the diverse languages and customs of its regions beyond a codified literary tradition. In such a climate, the seemingly paternal appeal to foreign models and the wanton dismissal of classically based literary production proved offensive to many readers.

The animosity displayed toward Staël, "the old pythoness" (Bellorini 1975: 11), although couched within the cultural framework of the Romantic controversy, may have had more to do with the messenger than the message. Some within the male-dominated literary establishment, perhaps recognizing, but refusing to acknowledge, the challenges Romanticism's democratization of literary consumption posed to an aristocratic cultural monopoly, preferred to reject her arguments *in toto*. Italian society, however, was not monolithic, and the article also served as a call to arms for those who recognized the opportunities proffered by her proposals.

Staël's argument did betray, however, a lack of familiarity with Italian culture, which had long exhibited a healthy attraction for European literatures. Well prior to 1816, foreign influence had manifested itself through copious translations that introduced pre-Romantic and Romantic motifs: melancholic thought, obsession/fascination with death, defense of spiritualized passions, and predominance of nocturnal and lunar settings. These translations were frequently in verse, even if the source texts were not, to facilitate the cultural assimilation of motifs that might otherwise appear too strident when expressed in prose. Paolo Rolli's 1740 translation of Milton's *Paradise Lost*, predating the Italian editions of both Shakespeare (Domenico Valentini's *Il Giulio Cesare, tragedia istorica di Guglielmo Shakespeare*, 1756) and Goethe (Gaetano Grassi's *Werther: opera di sentimento*, 1782), sparked an early interest in northern literatures. Significant in fostering this interest were Melchiore Cesarotti's *Poesie di Ossian* (1763), a blank verse translation of James Macpherson's "Ossianic" poems, and Aurelio Bertola de' Giorgi's works (e.g., *Idea della poesia alemanna*, 1779; *Idea della letteratura alemanna*, 1784; his translation of Salomon Gessner's *Idyllen*, 1789). In addition, *Robinson Crusoe*, *Gulliver's Travels*, the poetry of Thomas Gray, James Thompson, and Alexander Pope, Klopstock's *Messiah*, and two versions of Edward Young's *The Night Thoughts* (Giovan Giorgio Alberti, 1770, Giuseppe Bottoni, 1775) circulated in the latter eighteenth century. Of course, French translations also provided access to German and English writers. While all these texts stimulated nascent Romantic sensibilities for the melancholic, for idyllic nostalgia, for the nocturnal, and for a new relationship between the poet and nature, the Ossian, Young, and Gessner translations were particularly influential in propagating this new aesthetic.

If authors such as Foscolo and Giacomo Leopardi (1798-1837) translated primarily classical texts, this was due to both personal and social temperament. Philological (Angelo Mai, Luigi Lamberti) and archeological (Ennio Quirino Visconti, Carlo Domenico Fea) discoveries had expanded the classical source texts of late eighteenth-century culture (Ovid, Virgil of the *Bucolics*) with less canonical authors – in particular, Greek. Thus Foscolo, who also translated Sterne, tackled select passages of the *Iliad* and the Catullus version of Callimachus's elegy *Chioma di Berenice*. "Dei sepolcri" (1807), which can be read as an evocation of Greek values, drew upon these exercises in its poetic synthesis of the classical and modern worlds. Leopardi flirted with Homer and Virgil, but dedicated himself to the idylls of the second-century Greek bucolic poet Moschus, to the works of the Roman grammarian Marcus Cornelius Fronto rediscovered by Angelo Mai, and to the *Batracomiomachia*. Nevertheless, Foscolo's and Leopardi's interest in Greek language and culture, in consonance with that of Goethe, Schiller, and Hölderlin, should not belie their attentiveness to contemporary European literature, which is amply documented in their works and notes.

Regardless of the validity of Staël's critique, the culture war that ensued catalyzed the assimilation of Romantic principles into the nineteenth-century's literary sensitivity. Reflecting the evolving social milieu, the protagonists waged their battles in the public forums of journals and periodicals rather than in the private venues of salons and academies traditionally reserved for such pedantic matters. The controversy addressed three principal issues: the use of classical mythology (opposed by the majority of self-proclaimed Italian Romantics who countered with history, modernity, and popular imagination); the opening of Italian literature to contemporary English and German influences (opposed by the Classicists, who countered with a humanist canon); and the utility of Aristotelian precepts of unity (opposed by the Romantics who countered with freedom of inspiration and dynamic movement). While the Italian Romantics' theoretical opposition to mythology would appear at odds with their canonical European counterparts (Blake, Keats, Shelley, Byron, Hölderlin, Schelling) who posited it as a central tenet of their poetics, in practice, the Italians were objecting to the allegorical and decorative recycling of classical myths, especially Romanized ones, and not to mythology *tout court*. They favored revivifying these myths by returning to their Greek sources or creating a new mythology by resuscitating medieval and Christian ones. For example, although Leopardi was critical of Romanticism, his poem "Alla Primavera, o delle favole antiche" (1822) is Romantic in its rejuvenation of mythological material (cf. Schiller's "Die Götter Griechenlands"). Within the context of the polemic, however, the reductive simplification of mythology reflected a rhetorical strategy adopted by advocates of Romanticism in Italy to postulate dialectical oppositions (e.g., modern–ancient, Romantic–classical, historical–mythological) in order to establish their poetics as an instrument for sociocultural modernization. Although both the Romantic and Classicist camps tended to express a need for literary utility, a concern for Italian cultural prestige, and an aspiration for an authentically universal literature, their differences appeared irreconcilable. *Biblioteca Italiana* accentuated this divergence by rapidly evolving from a neutral cultural space into a partisan government forum, which fabricated a problematic nationalism to defend an obscure notion of Italian honor. This political turn stemmed from the questionable premise that maintaining literary order would also preserve the sociopolitical order. Habsburg cultural policy encouraged this polarizing tendency because the heated pedantic debate appeared to distract its participants from engaging in a sociopolitical discussion.

By entrusting to Giordani the first rebuttal in *Biblioteca Italiana*'s April issue, the Classicists proffered an articulate critique of Staël's article. " '*Un italiano' risponde al discorso della Staël*" evinces many of the characteristics and contradictions of Italian Romanticism, which is to say that Giordani's arguments and terminology are themselves, to a degree, Romantic. While he acknowledges the severe limitations of contemporary Italian literary production, he refutes the strategy of foreign imitation advocated by Staël. Sounding rather Romantic, Giordani asserted that Italian culture, by which he meant language, literature, intellectual climate, and imagination, must be the source for any literary renewal. In support of this possibility he indicated the literary treasures unearthed by Mai, Marini, and Ennio Quirino Visconti. Giordani's sensitive response suggested an alternative interpretation of literature from that advanced by Staël. Contending that beauty is the object of art, while truth is the object of science, Giordani argued that the pursuit of beauty necessitates a return to the classics, to which Italian culture is heir. When Staël clarified (in "*Risposta alle critiche mossele*" in *Biblioteca Italiana*, June 1816) that familiarity with foreign literatures did not mean imitation, the ranks had already been divided between Classicists and Romantics.

Giordani also addressed another issue dear to the Romantics: the literary use of dialects. In his negative review (*Biblioteca Italiana*, February 11, 1816) of Domenico Balestrieri's Milanese poems, Giordani argued that dialects, as linguistic manifestations of regional specificity, had to be superseded to promote a common national language. While his dismissal of Balestrieri's poetry incurred the wrath of Carlo Porta (1775-1821), Pietro Borsieri, and Francesco Cherubini (1789-1851), it drew the support of Monti, whose *Dialogo tra Matteo giornalista e Taddeo suo compare* (*Biblioteca Italiana*, June 1, 1816) reiterated Giordani's arguments. Porta retorted creatively (March-September 1816) with 12 ad hominem sonnets in dialect inveighed against Giordani. Although sympathetic to Romanticism, which he considered to be a form of literary pragmatism, Porta remained indifferent to both its celebration of the medieval period and its heroic-tragic vein. He expressed his views on poetic communication in the composition "Il romanticismo" (1819):

> el gran busilles de la poesia
> el consist in de l'arte de piasè,
> e st'arte la sta tutta in la magia
> de moeuv, de messedà, come se voeur,
> tutt i passion che gh'emm sconduu in del coeur (Porta 1975: 180)

(The great enigma of poetry / rests in the art of pleasure, / and this art is all in the magic / of movement, of mixing, as one likes, / all of the passions held hidden in our hearts)

While Porta accused Giordani of linguistic imperialism, Classicists accused Staël of cultural imperialism for exhorting Italians subject to the Habsburgs to abandon their cultural models for Germanic ones. Thus, from the initial stages of the debate, both Romantics and Classicists seized upon national identity as consonant with their respective poetics.

Di Breme's, Borsieri's, and Berchet's Responses to the Classicists

An advocate and architect of Romanticism's nationalist potential, Ludovico di Breme (1780-1820) provided an early response to the Classicist challenge and established the debate's parameters. In his independently published essay *Intorno all'ingiustizia di alcuni giudizi letterari italiani* (June 1816), Di Breme articulated a cultural history founded upon a "Romantic" canon. His argument, indebted to Gian Vincenzo Gravina and Vico, hinges on the premise of cultural relativism: "changing times lead to changes in feelings and thoughts" (Bellorini 1975: 30). Advancing the distinction between ancient poetry and modern poetry, which he drew from Staël's mediation of Schlegel, he stressed a poetic identification between Christianity and Romanticism. In tracing a literary genealogy from Dante to the present, Di Breme emphasized the Italian-Romantic nexus in Italy's cultural development. He evoked these writers, not for imitation, but to inspire original poetic strategies. As an example of innovative poetry he proffered the ode "Le rovine" (1816) by Diodata Saluzzo-Roero (1774-1840), a poet praised by Parini, Foscolo, and Manzoni. From his canon, Di Breme excluded those writers, in particular early modern intellectuals, who in his view advocated the Classicist tradition at the expense of national identity. Denouncing what he perceived as the intellectual indolence of pedants who take refuge in the classics, Di Breme defended poetic creativity and challenged the use of classical mythology, which he considered contrary to a lively spontaneous art.

Pietro Borsieri advanced the second major response to the Classicists. In *Avventure letterarie di un giorno o consigli di un galantuomo a vari scrittori* (1816), Borsieri proposed a socially and politically engaged literature in contrast to the arid erudition of much contemporary literary production. To this end, he argued for the need to construct a new culture based on popular genres that appealed to the emergent bourgeois public. In this respect, Borsieri aligned himself with Porta and against Giordani and Monti, in the dispute over dialects by advocating their use in literature. Borsieri emphasized the enormous cultural abyss that prevented the masses from assimilating refined literary language. He considered the literary use of dialect to be an effective didactic strategy for educating people. Not only did Borsieri promote an interpretation of literature as having to be both educational and popular, but he also argued that studying dialect literature provided a means for both understanding and overcoming the peninsula's significant regional differences.

Following the lead of Di Breme and Borsieri, Giovanni Berchet entered the fray with a disquisition on literature's purpose in contemporary society. The most theoretically articulate of the Romantics' responses even if somewhat derivative, *Sul "Cacciatore feroce" e sulla "Eleonora" di Goffredo Augusto Bürger. Lettera semiseria di Grisostomo al suo figliuolo* (1816) extended a cultural program for establishing a new relationship between culture and society. Influenced by readings in German and English (e.g., Bouterweck's *Ästhetik*, Thomas Gray's "The Bard," which Berchet had translated in 1807) and personal discussions with Byron, Hobhouse, and Stendhal, Berchet developed a veritable Romantic manifesto.

Berchet presented his argument in the guise of a letter sent by the elderly Grisostomo (Greek for "mouth of gold") to his son in response to the latter's request for an Italian translation of Bürger's two ballads. In the letter, the father challenged the classical rules of literature, the need to imitate, and the use of mythology, and he addressed the issue of popular poetry. Grisostomo first explains his decision to translate in prose rather than poetry, thus redirecting the debate on translations to the issues of translation. Prose, he argues, does not pretend to convey the formal qualities of the source text, but instead provides access to its content. In so doing, Grisostomo presents a dynamic interpretation of language of which his letter is itself an example. The father then raises an issue new to Italian Romantics: that poetry be popular. He maintains that Bürger understood the need for a universal, modern, popular, and useful poetry since any other type risked alienating the public. Thus Grisostomo argues for a poetry inspired by popular sources in both form and content, because only then would it satisfy a contemporary public's needs. Appreciating the argument's complexity, he offers to send his son the works of Cesare Beccaria, Bouterweck, Edmund Burke, Vincenzo Cuoco, Lessing, Schiller, A. W. Schlegel, Staël, and Vico so that he might pursue the topic on his own.

From this concept of poetry's popularity, Berchet argues, in the spirit of Vico, that everyone possesses a propensity toward poetry, which may be active (poets) or passive (most people). Amongst the latter, Grisostomo individuates two groups: the Hottentots who are devoid of cultural interests, and the Parisians (derived from Staël's *De l'Allemagne*) who are so overly refined as to have cultivated a purely intellectual poetry devoid of emotion. Between these two extremes are the *popolo*, the emergent bourgeoisie, to whom, the father contends, the poet should address his verse. The *popolo*, however, require a new poetry – one that is relevant to their lives. In delineating this distinction, Grisostomo argues that Classicism is *poesia dei morti* (poetry of the dead) and Romanticism is *poesia dei vivi* (poetry of the living) because the former speaks to the past, while the latter speaks to the future.

Frequently citing the example of German writers, Grisostomo affirms the civil value of popular poetry and incites Italian writers to free themselves from what he considers to be their senseless subjugation to the classics in order to construct a national literature. As the treatise's title suggests, however, the letter advances a semiserious conclusion that retracts the father's arguments in favor of the Classicist position: "My dear son, [. . .] I am sure that you will have realized that my letter to this point has been facetious" (Berchet 1972: 487). Di Breme records in his autobiographical _Grand commentaire_ (1817) that the palinode duped many of their contemporaries.

Despite its tenuous philosophical tenets, Berchet's treatise expanded the scope of the classic–Romantic controversy, thus rejuvenating a debate that had already grown tedious. In his subsequent critical interventions, Berchet elaborated on ideas first developed in _Lettera semiseria_. He condemned the tyranny of the classical rules and the subservient imitation of sterile models; he exalted spontaneous poetry inspired by genuine feelings and the moral, educational, and national impetus of literature. For these same reasons, he rejected both the use of mythology as a literary strategy because in his view it had no relevance to present reality and the use of an archaic literary language because its elitism precluded the expanding literary public from participating in a cultural dialogue. His call for a popular poetry (a frequent refrain among the Romantics), however, remained limited to the idea of making literature accessible to a broader public. Only with Niccolò Tommaseo (1802-74), compiler of the folkloric _Canti popolari toscani, corsi, illirici, greci_ (1841-2) and author of the quasi-Decadent _Fede e bellezza_ (1840), would the concept assume a meaning more consonant with Herder's distinction between _Kunstpoesie_ (art poetry) and _Naturpoesie_ (poetry of nature), as a direct manifestation of _Volksgeist_.

Il Conciliatore

In the wake of Borsieri's, Di Breme's, and Berchet's interventions, and in response to the partisan position assumed by the directorship of _Biblioteca Italiana_, the Romantics launched _Il Conciliatore: foglio scientifico-letterario_ (September 3, 1818 to October 10, 1819), a biweekly periodical modeled on _Il Caffè_. The fruit of Pellico's, Di Breme's, and Borsieri's postprandial discussions in Palazzo Porro, the _foglio azzurro_ (blue sheet), called such because of its color, strove to conciliate, as its motto _Rerum concordia discors_ suggests, the divergent Romantic currents of Di Breme's circle (Pellico, Borsieri) and Manzoni's clique (Berchet, Grossi, Torti, Visconti). Luigi Porro (1780-1860), Federico Confalonieri (1785-1846), Berchet, and Monti also participated in this cultural initiative – though Monti soon distanced himself. Porro and Confalonieri financed the paper, while Di Breme and Pellico served as the principal editors. They divided the journal into four sections: (1) moral sciences; (2) literature and criticism; (3) statistics, economics, manufacturing, agriculture, art, and science; (4) miscellaneous. As opposed to _Il Caffè_ (and all other Italian periodicals), national interest was the defining criteria in determining what to publish.

Il Conciliatore, aspiring to the principles of usefulness, realism, common sense, modernity, morality, cultural relativism, and the dissemination of truth, emerged as the principal forum in the peninsula for the dissemination of Romantic ideals. Reflecting the journal's interregional engagement, its contributors included many non-Milanese. Their express desire to effect sociopolitical change in society produced a conception of literature that subordinated artistic and aesthetic creativity to practical utility. Pellico was particularly explicit in this respect: "Literature is the most useless of the arts if it does not have as its goal the warming of the heart of the nation in which it is cultivated" (Branca 1948-54, 2: 50).

In terms of Romanticism's articulation, Ermes Visconti's two essays "Idee elementari sulla poesia romantica" (November-December 1818) and "Dialogo sulle unità drammatiche di luogo e di tempo" (January 1819) represent the periodical's most enduring contributions. Visconti's theoretical expositions solicited the admiration of Stendhal, who, if imitation is the sincerest form of flattery, proffered an earnest tribute to Visconti with *Racine et Shakespeare*. Goethe also esteemed him, though in a more traditional manner than Stendhal: "We praise in this young man, his great acuity of spirit, perfect clarity of thought, and profound knowledge of both the ancients and the moderns [...] he, we hope, will put an end to the dispute [between Classicists and Romantics] dispensing with those misunderstandings that each day are more confusing" (Bellorini 1975, 2: 477). Visconti shared many of Berchet's views. He reiterated the identification between "Romantic" and "contemporary" while differentiating ancient from modern "classic" poetry. He stressed historical relevance as a dictum for poetic content, arguing that this was the practice of Greek and Roman poets. The ancients, he contended, drew on actual experiences while modern poets who imitated what these classics expressed betrayed the poetic process they professed to defend. In juxtaposition to classical poetry, Visconti suggested that imbuing historical subjects with contemporary ideas defined Romantic poetry. He also forcefully sustained the precept, in marked contrast with German Romanticism, of utility over creativity in the artistic process arguing that "it is appropriate to subordinate verses' aesthetic purpose to the eminent purpose of all studies, the perfection of humanity, the public wellbeing and the private good" (Bellorini 1975: 451). Not all Italian Romantics shared this last opinion. Berchet, for example, while convinced of literature's didactic necessity, maintained in *Lettera semiseria* that it must also serve the public's emotive needs. In *Fanatismo e tolleranza in fatto di lettere* (1820), Giuseppe Nicolini explicitly defended artistic integrity, contending that literature could not be judged on the basis of utility. Similarly, Carlo Tedaldi Fores, representative of a more lugubrious strand of Romanticism, emphasized that "all the fine arts are drawn together by the simple desire to please; because if poetry can at times instruct, this is a praiseworthy, but extrinsic task, which is not necessary" (Tedaldi Fores 1820: 10).

Reactions to *Il Conciliatore*'s periodical's cultural program were swift. Within two months of its inaugural issue, the police commissioner Trussardo Caleppio launched a parodic weekly *L'Accattabrighe ossia Classico-romanticomachia* (November 8, 1818 to March 28, 1819). Printed on pink paper (*carta rosa*) and bearing the antiphrastic motto *Rerum discordia concors*, *L'Accattabrighe* attacked the associates of the *foglio azzurro* as enemies of the state. Even within the not so genteel cultural debates of the period, however, the strident tone of *L'Accattabrighe* drew fierce criticism, so that after a brief run, the Austrian authorities terminated its funding.

With *L'Accattabrighe* now defunct, *Il Conciliatore* came under increased censorial scrutiny. Despite its relatively moderate pronouncements and modest circulation (240 subscriptions – a quantity that is indicative of the limited social participation in the Risorgimento), the journal's dissemination of libertarian and liberal ideals and anti-Austrian leanings concerned Habsburg officials. While initially opting to exercise a vigilant censorship over *Il Conciliatore*'s contents, they moved ultimately to proscribe its publication. Its suppression, however, only served to feed the self-fashioning myth that identified Romanticism with the nationalist movement. In a letter to his brother dated August 1819, Pellico asserted that the classic–Romantic controversy was just a manifestation of the irreconcilable differences between liberals and reactionaries: "The persecutions that we have suffered, the publication delays placed on *Il Conciliatore*, the continuous rumors that we were on the verge of being shut down, opened the eyes of even the most blind, and Romantic was recognized as a synonym for liberal, and no one dared call himself Classicist, except extremists and spies" (Pellico 1963: 171).[2] This reductive political and cultural equivalency of Romantics as liberal and Classicists as reactionary belies the historical complexities. Both Giordani and Leopardi rejected Romanticism, but the former was exiled by the Austrian authorities, while the latter was the object of oppressive political persecution. Both Giordani and Monti opposed the use of dialect, but they did so to promote the development of a national language. Nevertheless, the Romantics' conception of the nation as a dynamic reality often led them to political engagement and to concrete action, which is not surprising given their view of literature as a moral and civil praxis. Indeed subsequent to the failed coups of 1820-1, many of Romanticism's proponents were subject to forceful government repression and detention. For participating in nationalist secret societies such as *Carboneria* (and its more militant *Federati* branch), many of *Il Conciliatore*'s contributors were either incarcerated (Pellico, Borsieri, Gioia) or exiled (Berchet, Porro).

Political displacement constitutes an important aspect of Romanticism's development in Italy because it produced a transcultural exchange among writers already actively engaged in constructing a new poetics. Paris and London tended to be the refuges of choice. For example, Berchet went to Paris where he met Claude Fauriel, Victor Cousin, Madame Cabanis, and Sophie de Condorcet. Fauriel, an admirer of *Lettera semiseria*, became Berchet's French translator for the first edition of the patriotic poem "I profughi di Parga" (1823). Forced to depart under threat of extradition, Berchet went to London (1822-9) where he produced some of his most critically acclaimed verse: *Le romanze* (1822-4) and *Le fantasie* (1829). Gaesbeek Castle (the inheritance of Giuseppe Arconati and his wife Costanza Trotti) near Brussels provided a third mecca for Berchet and others during these turbulent years.

Leopardi's and Manzoni's Reactions to Romanticism

The turmoil of 1820 marked the close of the classic–Romantic controversy's most fervid period although the debate attracted renewed critical attention with Vincenzo

Monti's "Sermone sulla mitologia" (July 1825), in which he lamented the influence of German Romanticism's "arid truths" and advocated the use of mythology in poetry. Monti's sermon appeared in the Florentine journal *Antologia* (1821-33), *Il Concilia-tore*'s cultural heir. Launched by Giovan Pietro Vieusseux (1779-1863), founder of the reading-room *Gabinetto scientifico e letterario* (1820), *Antologia* served as a forum for significant European articles and review. Although less overtly political than *Il Conciliatore*, the Grand Duchy suppressed *Antologia* for its perceived anti-Austrian leanings on March 26, 1833.

Giacomo Leopardi frequented the *Gabinetto* in 1827, but his engagement in the controversy dates back to its origins. His two earliest views on Romanticism (the July 18, 1816 response *Lettera ai sigg. compilatori della "Biblioteca Italiana" in risposta a quella di mad. la baronessa di Staël Holstein ai medesimi* to Staël's clarifications and the 1818 *Discorso di un italiano intorno alla poesia romantica*), although published posthumously, represent significant statements on Leopardi's cultural development. While he remained committed to the classical tradition and vigorously opposed Di Breme's views on the sentimental in poetry, his reflections transcend facile literary categorizations. In these writings, Leopardi argued against the use of any models and advocated the construction of new literary forms. His proposal that literature seek an unmediated inspiration from nature (intended in a broad sense that included human society) redirected the argument from an academic textual exercise to a socially engaged cultural debate. In essence, he suggested that the question to ask was not whom to imitate but what to say. This poetic strategy represented a qualitative shift, which found little resonance in the pages of *Biblioteca Italiana*.

Leopardi was explicit in his rejection of several Romantic tenets. Although he considered poetry to be both an imitation and a gift of nature (the criterion he used for evaluating Romanticism), he did not interpret imitation as a representation of reality. His dismissal of realism had to do with poetic creativity, which he considered a product of the imagination, and with poetic pleasure, which he saw as the aim of poetry (not social and moral usefulness as the Romantics maintained). He argued that truth and realism were contrary to poetry because they limited both the imagination and the sense of wonder (the source of poetic pleasure). Leopardi was also critical of what he discerned as the Romantics' tendency to shift poetry from a sensory to an intellectual activity – an aspiration that he found to be in contradiction with their stated goal of producing a popular literature.

Despite these reservations, Leopardi shared many affinities with Romanticism. His poetry's contemplation of the inner life, of the infinite, of nature (even if his nature tends to be unfeeling, indifferent to humans, even hostile, unlike the maternal nature of Wordsworth or the consoling nature of the German forests), its privileging of a certain social Titanism, its celebration of poetic autonomy, and its construction of a new poetic language constituted a radical manifestation of Romanticism. Perhaps nowhere is this more evident than in the *Zibaldone*, Leopardi's posthumously published intellectual diary, which is both a seminal document and comment on Romanticism in Italy.

Like Leopardi's, Alessandro Manzoni's poetics resist reductive classifications. Despite Mario Pieri's description of him as "the coryphaeus of Italian Romanticism [...] Too bad that he is overcome by Romanticomania" (Pieri 1827: iv), Manzoni assumed a subdued approach to Romanticism, refusing invitations to contribute to either *Biblioteca Italiana* or *Il Conciliatore*. His first significant statement on the issue appeared in the *Conte di Carmagnola*'s preface where he defended his decision not to respect the unities of time and space in the play. He argued that these rules, extrapolated from Greek theater and Aristotle, lacked universal validity and suggested that instead of blind obeisance to preconceived norms, each work of art should be judged on its own merits. Manzoni qualified this assertion by proposing a new set of criteria based on a work's reasonableness and purpose. These moral and rational elements characterize Manzoni's Romanticism, which tends to place a didactic emphasis on the relationship between art and truth.

This pre-emptive defense did not still criticisms so Manzoni clarified his views in *Lettre a M. Chauvet sur l'unité de temps et de lieu dans la tragédie* (written in 1820, but published in 1823). The poet, like the historian, he argued, must remain faithful to history; however, unlike the historian who superficially records past events, the poet brings to life the feelings and passions of history's protagonists. In a sense, then, Manzoni rejects poetic creativity in favor of the truth, of which history is the ultimate source. The poet's task is to extract stories from history and to restore the human dimension neglected by historians. While this process may entail the invention of characters and situations, these creative contributions must be consonant with and in the service of reality. Manzoni also drew a distinction between dramatic poetry and the novel in which the former analyzes characters based on historical facts while the latter must invent verisimilar stories consonant with the personalities of the characters. Precisely because the novelist has more creative freedom than the dramatist, Manzoni considered the genre to be the more difficult of the two. Implicit in this argument is the suggestion that the historical novel is most apt to avoid potential vagaries. In *I Promessi sposi* (1840), he applied these theories by constructing a realistic historical narrative with an evident didactic intent and by using a diction that bridged to a certain extent the gap between the written and spoken language.

Manzoni's *Lettera sul romanticismo al Marchese Cesare Taparelli d'Azeglio* (written in 1823, but published in 1870) engaged directly in the classic–Romantic debate emphasizing those elements of Romanticism most consonant with his literary poetics. He propounded truth and moral utilitarianism as the aims of literature, which, in turn, had to become more democratic. In these affirmations, Manzoni infused Romanticism with Christian morality. He praised it for freeing literature from pagan traditions and, to the usual Romantic rejections of mythology, he added, "the use of the fable is idolatry" (Manzoni 1943: 606) because it sustained pagan practices that would otherwise have been forgotten. In this letter, however, Manzoni also advanced Romanticism's limitations and assessed its influence as ultimately more negative than positive.

Manzoni later renounced the historical novel, including his own efforts, in *Del romanzo storico e, in genere, de' componimenti misti di storia e invenzione* (1845), arguing that all narratives containing creative elements are false because poetry and history are heterogeneous activities. This conclusion left little space for literary creativity and also underscored Romanticism's diverse manifestations in Italy. In fact, writers such as Tedaldi Fores, Francesco Domenico Guerrazzi, and several from the south (Pasquale De Virgilii of Abruzzo, and the Calabrians Domenico Mauro and Vincenzo Padula) expressed those darker aspects of Romanticism that aspired to the passions of Alfieri, Foscolo, and Byron rather than to the moral and aesthetic ideals of Manzoni. Nevertheless, Manzoni's moral and intellectual rigor left an indelible imprint on Romantic culture in Italy.

Sentimentalism dominates the poetry of the much maligned "Second Romanticism." The designation refers to the superficial imitation/exaggeration of typically Romantic motifs (cult of history, popularity, sentiment, patriotism, religion, originality) in the period 1840-61. Two writers subsumed under this rubric, Aleardo Aleardi (1812-78) and Giovanni Prati (1814-84), retained a degree of artistic integrity. Fame came to the former with *Lettere a Maria* (1846), aimed at a female public, and acclaim in his poetic historical meditations (e.g., *Monte Circello*). Prati found success with his scandalous *Edmengarda* (1841), which recounted the adultery of Daniele Manin's sister Ildegarde, and with his poetry, influenced by Byron and Hugo. Second Romanticism languishes in a tedious aesthetic qualified by an inability to articulate a new cultural poetic. While Romanticism in Italy arrived with a bang, it left with a whimper.

Let us return to Martegiani's claim. Does Italian Romanticism exist? To the extent that any cultural movement can be defined within geopolitical parameters, Romanticism achieves theoretical and artistic expression in Italy. With respect to the main branches of European Romanticism, Italian Romanticism is a moderate and cautious offshoot whose aspirations and characteristics tend to be culturally specific. The preponderance of the classical tradition, the boon and burden of Italian intellectual development, inhibits the grafting of the more radical outgrowths exhibited by much of European Romantic culture. Nationalism and historicism characterize Italian Romanticism as do the privileging of affinities with the Enlightenment (albeit with an initial distancing from its more antireligious and materialist aspects), and the imbuing of a civil, political, and moral purpose in art. These didactic attributions convey the concomitant responsibility of an art capable of communicating to a broader, bourgeois public and engaging in modern life. Perhaps its legacy lies less in its literary patrimony than in its demystification of cultural production, which for the Italian Romantics is inherently political.

NOTES

1 My translation. Note that all translations are mine, unless otherwise indicated.
2 Like "Romanticism," the use of the term "Classicism" with reference to literature is relatively new. It first appears in Italy in the pages of *Il Conciliatore* and Ermes Visconti's "Idee elementari sulla poesia romantica" (1818). Stendhal picks it up from Visconti and uses it in *Racine et Shakespeare* (1823), while its English debut is in Thomas Carlyle's "Essay on Schiller" (1831). Only in Italy, however, was the term widely used in the nineteenth century.

REFERENCES AND FURTHER READING

Primary sources

Alfieri, Vittorio (1977). *Opere. Vittorio Alfieri*, ed. Arnaldo Di Benedetto. Milan and Naples: Ricciardi.

Allevi, Febo (1960). *Testi di poetica romantica (1803-1826)*. Milan: Marzorati.

Bellorini, Egidio (ed.) (1975). *Discussioni e polemiche sul romanticismo (1816 1826)*, ed. Anco Marzio Mutterle, 2 vols. Rome and Bari: Laterza.

Berchet, Giovanni (1972). *Opere*, ed. Marcello Turchi. Naples: Rossi.

Bertolotti, Davide (1814). "Cronaca letteraria e morale." *Lo Spettatore* 1 (3): 139.

Binni, Walter (1948). *Preromanticismo italiano*. Naples: Edizioni scientifiche italiane.

Borgese, Giuseppe Antonio (1905). *Storia della critica romantica in Italia*. Naples: Edizioni della Critica.

Branca, Vittore (ed.) (1948-54). *Il Conciliatore: foglio scientifico-letterario*, 3 vols. Florence: Le Monnier.

Breme, Ludovico di (1817). *Grand commentaire sur un petit article*. Geneva: J. J. Paschoud.

Calcaterra, Carlo (ed.) (1979). *Manifesti romantici e altri scritti della polemica classico-romantica*, revised Mario Scotti. Turin: UTET.

Foscolo, Ugo (1958). *Saggi di letteratura italiana*, ed. Cesare Foligno. Florence: Le Monnier.

Foscolo, Ugo (1966). *Epistolario 6 (1 Aprile 1815– 7 Settembre 1816)*, ed. Giovanni Gambarin and Francesco Tropeano. Florence: Le Monnier.

Foscolo, Ugo (1967). *Lezioni, articoli di critica e di polemica: 1809-1811*, ed. Emilio Santini. Florence: Le Monnier.

Giordani, Pietro (1961). *Scritti*, ed. Giuseppe Chiarini. Florence: Sansoni.

Graf, Arturo (1898). *Foscolo, Manzoni, Leopardi: saggi; aggiuntovi preraffaeliti, simbolisti ed esteti e letteratura dell'avvenire*. Turin: Loescher.

Leopardi, Giacomo (1981). *Canti*, ed. Emilio Peruzzi, 2 vols. Milan: Rizzoli.

Leopardi, Giacomo (1991). *Zibaldone di pensieri. Edizione critica e annotata*, ed. Giuseppe Pacella, 3 vols. Milan: Garzanti.

Leopardi, Giacomo (2003). *The Canti with a Selection of His Prose*, trans. John Gordon Nichols. New York: Routledge.

Manzoni, Alessandro (1943). *Opere varie*, ed. Michele Barbi and Fausto Ghisalberti. Milan: Casa del Manzoni.

Manzoni, Alessandro (1957-74). *Tutte le opere di Alessandro Manzoni*, ed. Alberto Chiari and Fausto Ghisalberti, 10 vols. Milan: Mondadori.

Manzoni, Alessandro (2004). *The Count of Carmagnola and Adelchis*, trans. Federica Brunori Deigan. Baltimore: Johns Hopkins University Press.

Martegiani, Gina (1908). *Il romanticismo italiano non esiste. Saggio di letteratura comparata*. Florence: B. Seeber.

Monti, Vincenzo (1953). *Opere. Vincenzo Monti*, ed. Manara Valgimigli and Carlo Muscetta. Milan and Naples: Ricciardi.

Pellico, Silvio (1963). *Lettere milanesi (1815-21)*, ed. Mario Scotti. Turin: Loescher.

Petronio, Giuseppe (1960). *Il romanticismo*. Palermo: G.B. Palumbo.

Pieri, Mario (1827). *Memorie inedite*. Florence: Gabinetto Vieusseux.

Porta, Carlo (1975). *Poesie*, ed. Dante Isella. Milan: Mondadori.

Pullini, Giorgio (ed.) (1959). *Le poetiche dell'Ottocento. Antologia critica*. Padua: Liviana.

Tedaldi Fores, Carlo (1820). *Romanzi poetici di C. Tedaldi-Fores*. Cremona: Feraboli.

Visconti, Ermes (1979). *Saggi sul bello, sulla poesia e sullo stile*, ed. Anco Marzio Mutterle. Bari: Laterza.

Voltaire (1975). *Les Œuvres complètes de Voltaire. Vol. 127. Correspondence and Related Documents. Vol 43. March-October 1776. Letters D19962-D20376*, ed. Theodore Besterman. Banbury, UK: The Voltaire Foundation.

Secondary sources

Avitabile, Grazia (1959). *The Controversy on Romanticism in Italy. First Phase, 1816-1823*. New York: S. F. Vanni.

Betti, Franco (1997). "Key Aspects of Romantic Poetics in Italian Literature." *Italica*, 74 (2): 185-200.

Binetti, Vincenzo (2002). "Between Romanticism and Realism: The Poetics of Engagement and the *Romanzo sociale* during the Italian Risorgimento." *Forum for Modern Language Study*, 38 (2): 126-39.

Carlson, Marvin (1994). "The Italian Romantic Drama in Its European Context." In Gerald Gillespie (ed.), *Romantic Drama*. Amsterdam: Benjamins, pp. 233-47.

Carsaniga, Giovanni. "The Age of Romanticism." In Peter Brand and Lino Pertile (eds.), *The Cambridge History of Italian Literature*. Cambridge, UK and New York: Cambridge University Press, pp. 399-449.

Chandler, S. Bernard (1978-9). "Manzoni and the European Romantics." *Italian Culture* 1: 77-98.

Corrigan, Beatrice (1966). "Neapolitan Romanticism and the Social Conscience." *Studies in Romanticism* 5: 113-20.

Dombroski, Robert S. (1981). "The Ideological Question in Manzoni." *Studies in Romanticism*, 20 (4): 497-524.

Drake, Richard (1982). "Decadence, Decadentism and Decadent Romanticism in Italy: Toward a Theory of Decadence." *Journal of Contemporary History*, 17 (1): 69-92.

Ferrucci, Franco (1983). "Italian Romanticism: Myth vs History." *Modern Language Notes*, 98 (1): 111-17.

Isbell, John Claiborne (1997). "The Italian Romantics and Madame de Staël: Art, Society and Nationhood." *Rivista di Letterature Moderne e Comparate*, 50 (4): 355-60.

Kimbell, David R. B. (1981). *Verdi in the Age of Italian Romanticism*. Cambridge, UK: Cambridge University Press.

King, Martha (1976). "Early Italian Romanticism and *The Giaour*." *The Byron Journal* 4: 7-19.

Kostka, Edmund (1997). *Schiller in Italy: Schiller's Reception in Italy: 19th and 20th Centuries*. New York: Peter Lang.

Kroeber, Karl (1964). *The Artifice of Reality: Poetic Style in Wordsworth, Foscolo, Keats, and Leopardi*. Madison: University of Wisconsin Press.

Matteo, Sante (1998). "Ossian and Risorgimento. The Poetics of Nationalism." In Larry H. Peer (ed.), *Romanticism across the Disciplines*. Lanham, MD: University Press of America, pp. 27-40.

McKenzie, Kenneth (1940). "Romanticism in Italy." *PMLA*, 55 (1): 27-35.

Rossi, Joseph (1955). "The Distinctive Character of Italian Romanticism." *The Modern Language Journal*, 39 (2): 59-63.

Springer, Carolyn (1987). *The Marble Wilderness: Ruins and Representation in Italian Romanticism. 1775-1850*. Cambridge, UK: Cambridge University Press.

15

Ugo Foscolo and Giacomo Leopardi: Italy's Classical Romantics

Margaret Brose

Traditionally, Italian Romanticism has been relegated to a minor role in the history of European Romanticism. Italy entered the European debate over Romanticism only in 1816 when Mme de Staël published her essay "Sulla maniera e l'utilità delle traduzioni" (On the Manner and Utility of Translations) in the journal *Biblioteca Italiana*. Her essay attacked "modern" Italian literature, and urged Italians to translate and study the new European writers of the North. The essay inspired the foundation of a new journal, the *Conciliatore* (1818-19) under the direction of Silvio Pellico (1789-1854)[1] which supported the tenets of Mme de Staël's essay. Even before this date, however, several Italian writers had published pamphlets which stressed many of the principles of German Romanticism: national unity as the premise of linguistic unity, the discovery of a popular literature, the importance of the "pathetic" and the sentimental over the eighteenth-century predilection for a poetry of the "marvelous."

There are several reasons why Italian Romanticism has been seen as secondary in comparison to the English, French, and German traditions. First, Italian Romanticism quickly fused with the patriotic Risorgimental fervor of the times, and was consequently less interested in the debates about strictly literary Romanticism. Second, Italian Romanticism remained more closely allied to the classical tradition than its northern counterparts. Italian poets adhered more rigorously to the norms of classical meter and prosody, and to classical themes. We may attribute this to the deep and uninterrupted tradition of Latin literature in Italy; indeed, the Italian language may be seen to be a modern version of Latin. The foremost Romantic poets in Italy, Ugo Foscolo and Giacomo Leopardi, described themselves as Classicists, and in fact were philologists who were fluent in Greek and Latin. We might say that Italy's Romantics remained more "Mediterranean" than their German or French or English counterparts. Finally, it may also be true that the other Romanticisms needed to marginalize Italy and its writers, to keep Italy as an imaginary site of the origins of

Western Culture, passionate yet pure. Along with Greece, Italy was every Romantic's ideal place of ruins and fragments. It was to this primordial Italy that poets such as Byron, Keats, and Shelley would flee.

How Romantic were the Italian Romantics? Ugo Foscolo may be considered a melodramatic Romantic whose highest aesthetic ideals were Hellenic; Leopardi as a Romantic shot through with a materialist skepticism. Alessandro Manzoni (1785-1873), the author of one of the finest historical novels, *I promessi sposi* (The Betrothed, 1827) spent his life scrupulously rewriting the novel in the hopes of perfecting his ideal of "historical verisimilitude," that is, of exorcizing every trace of the "fantastic" and the imaginary. This impossible goal is deeply un-Romantic at heart. However, many of the tenets of the German Jena group (the Schlegel brothers, Schelling, Novalis, and Tieck) characterize the work of Foscolo and Leopardi. René Welleck's three traits or norms of Romanticism, discussed in the introduction to this volume – imagination for the view of poetry, nature for the view of the world, and symbol and myth for poetic style – would apply to both Foscolo and Leopardi. Thus, in Leopardi's idyllic poems, the theme of childhood's imaginative power prevails; Imagination is valorized over Reason; he privileges nighttime, the moon, and the village country setting. The Leopardian sublime is intimate rather than overpowering, not the Kantian negative sublime. Foscolo on the other hand casts himself as a tragic victim of civilization and its discontents; a fierce patriotic fervor inspires him; he longs for the classical Greek ideals of love and female beauty; art and literature are seen as redemptive; death is welcomed over any possible compromise. So, too, both Foscolo and Leopardi are outcast poets, Foscolo out of political and idealistic commitments, and Leopardi out of an inability to forge human relationships; the former an extrovert, and the latter an introvert. Despite their materialistic convictions, both sought consolation in nature and in the poetic imagination.

Ugo Foscolo

Niccolò Ugo Foscolo (known as Ugo) was born on February 6, 1778, on the Ionian island of Zante. His father was Andrea Foscolo, an impoverished Venetian nobleman, and his mother Diamantina Spathis, a Greek peasant. At the time of his birth, the island of Zante was under the control of Venice, the *Serenissima*. In 1784 Foscolo's father, who worked as physician, moved to Split in Dalmatia, which was also under Venetian rule. Diamantina and her four children (Ugo, Rubina, Giovanni Dionigi, and Costantino Angelo) followed in 1785. After the death of Ugo's father in 1788 Diamantina left her children with her sisters and mother on the Ionian islands, and went to Venice to stabilize her financial affairs. The four children joined her in Venice in 1792.

The Greek origins of Ugo Foscolo mark his every endeavor, literary and political. He defined his Hellenic island birth in sacred terms. In his sonnet "A Zacinto" (To Zante), written between 1802 and 1803, Foscolo linked his birth to that of the goddess "Venus, who with her first smile, made those islands fecund," ll. 5-6).[2] The sonnet opens:

> Né più mai toccherò le sacre sponde
> ove il mio corpo fanciulletto giacque,
> Zacinto mia, che te specchi nell'onde
> del Greco mar da cui vergine nacque
> Venere [. . .] (ll. 1-5)

(Never more shall I touch the sacred shores where my infant body lay, O my Zante, you who mirror yourself in the waves of the Greek sea from which the virgin Venus was born.)

The nexus of filial adoration for his lost motherland develops into a cult of the dead, a thanatology, where the exiled poet dreams of a material return of his body to the amniotic protection of the womb. Such an attitude will also mark his autobiographical epistolary novel of 1802, the *Ultime lettere di Jacopo Ortis* (*Last Letters of Jacopo Ortis*) in which a triangle develops between the hero's passion for Teresa, an unattainable young woman, and his need to return to his mother and to protect his lost motherland.

Foscolo never subscribed to the tenets of literary Romanticism. Indeed, most of his literary production came well before the debate over Romanticism began in 1814. Instead of a literary controversy, it was the political upheavals in Venice and Northern Italy at the end of the eighteenth century that galvanized his fierce sensibility. Foscolo was later considered by many to be the "prophet" of the nineteenth-century Risorgimento movement that culminated in the creation of the Italian nation in 1860. He was a fervent citizen of Venice and believed in taking up arms and risking death to protect national liberty. Like Dante, Foscolo was an exilic writer. In fact, Foscolo's tumultuous political life was marked by a triple exile: from his native Hellenic-Venetian island of Zante, from the Republic of Venice, and finally from Italy itself. He died, still in exile, in London in 1827.

As a young man, Foscolo attended the Venetian literary salon of Isabella Teotochi Albrizzi, with whom he fell in love. He also made the acquaintance of Melchiorre Cesarotti (1730-1808), the translator into Italian of the *Songs of Ossian*, one of the most influential literary texts of European Romanticism. Foscolo even attended some of the classes taught by Cesarotti at the University of Padua. From early on, Foscolo manifested a melancholic and yet volatile personality, and these years were marked by numerous literary, political, and amorous adventures. His early writing demonstrated his vast knowledge of several linguistic and poetic traditions and literary forms – Greek, Latin, Italian, French, and English.

In the spring of 1797 Venice replaced its rule by the city's decadent patricians with a provisional government made up of citizens. French soldiers entered Venice and were greeted with enthusiasm by the Venetians. Following the model of the great

Italian tragedian Vittorio Alfieri (1749-1803), Foscolo composed a political tragedy in 1796 entitled *Tieste* (Thyestes), marked by its controversial antityrannical theme. In 1797 he penned two odes "A Bonaparte liberatore" (To Bonaparte the Liberator) and "Ai novelli repubblicani" (To the New Republicans) in praise of the French conqueror, and the newly resurrected ideal of Liberty. But Italian freedom was already being threatened by Napoleon who, in the Treaty of Campoformio of October 17, 1797, handed over Venice to the Austrians in return for control of Lombardy. Foscolo was forced to leave his beloved Venice in 1797, just before the Austrians took control, and moved to Milan, the capital of the newly formed Cisalpine republic. Foscolo lived his entire life under the shadow of the betrayal of Campoformio, in a commotion of frenzy, pain, desperate hope, and anger, forever torn between loves and hatreds, political optimism and bitter disillusionment. His attitude towards Napoleon was ambivalent, filled with praise and admiration and at the same time admonitory and critical. In April 1799 Foscolo joined the troops of the Cisalpine Legion and French soldiers in battle against the Austrian-Russian troops who sought to undo whatever order had been established in Italy. Foscolo took part in the siege of Genoa, on April 30, 1800, and was injured twice.

While in Genoa in 1799 he composed his first ode "A Luigia Pallavicini caduta da cavallo" (To Luigia Pallavicini Fallen from a Horse) a hymn to feminine beauty and grace. Two years later, in 1802 in Milan, he composed another ode, "All'amica risanata" (To his Lady-friend on her Recovery), also in praise of the classical beauties of the female. These two odes belong to the neoclassical tradition of the Arcadian movement in Italy, and established Foscolo's fame. The women are represented as elegant mythological figures who inhabit the pantheon of the Greek female gods, their contingent historical realities transposed into the ideality of eternal Beauty in its absolute purity. The odes appeared to some early readers as too controlled, distanced, perhaps even cold. Certainly the odes contain none of the quivering, perfectly balanced lyricism and political passion of Foscolo's three great masterpieces: his epistolary novel of 1802 the *Ultime lettere di Jacopo Ortis* (Last Letters of Jacopo Ortis), his elegant but tortured sonnets, and his poetic masterpiece *Dei sepolcri* (Of Tombs) of 1807.

In 1803 Foscolo published together his two odes and 12 sonnets. The 12 sonnets (1802-3) are gemlike masterpieces that excel at fusing classical control with Romantic emotion. The sonnet structure strains to contain the unresolved passions of the exiled Foscolo: nostalgia for his lost motherland, an almost erotic attraction to night and death, and grief for his dead brother Giovanni. We have already mentioned his sonnet to his island birthplace "A Zacinto." Another sonnet "Alla sera" (To the Evening) sings a love song to the evening, whose coming is cherished by the poet because the evening is the image of the "fatal quiet of death."

Two of the sonnets are self-portraits, and present the poet as a turbulent Romantic hero, "rich in virtues and vices," who praises Reason yet follows wherever his pleasure leads, and who will find peace only in death ("Solcata ho fronte" [Furrowed is my brow]). The sonnet to his brother Giovanni, upon his youthful suicide, is deeply moving: Foscolo imagines that one day he "will sit at the side of his tomb" on Zante where their mother lives, to "mourn the lost flower of his youthful years" (.... me vedrai seduto / su la tua pietra, o fratel mio, gemendo /il fior de' tuoi gentili anni caduto, ll. 2-4). The cult of the tomb and death finds its origin here in these passionate sonnets.

In 1803 Foscolo published a commentary to Catullus's *The Lock of Berenice* (*La chioma di Berenice*). Although the work was intended to satirize the pedantry of the philological style of editing then in vogue in Italy, the volume is most notable for demonstrating Foscolo's own considerable philological gifts. In this work Foscolo holds that poetry arises from the encounter between contemporary passions and the timeless dimension of myth. This is indeed the distinguishing feature of Foscolo's greatest works, which are imprinted with the immediacy of contemporary historical and political exigencies yet presented in the suspended light of myth.

Foscolo's next works forever changed the course of Italian literature. In these same years, 1798-1802, he wrote and published the first version of the *Last Letters of Jacopo Ortis*, a passionate autobiographical epistolary novel. In 1807 Foscolo published his brilliant long poem *Of Tombs*. These works show a sublime blend of the personal, the historical, and the fantastic. Thematically, they are based on an idealized form of Classicism, but the fervor and mode of expression are undeniably Romantic. And although they bear traces of specific influences, they appeared on the Italian literary scene with unprecedented novelty and force.

The *Last Letters of Jacopo Ortis* is a novel that defies categorization. It represented a new genre in Italy even though its epistolary structure can be traced back to eighteenth-century novels such as Richardson's *Pamela*. The mixture of autobiographical data, historical vicissitudes, literary borrowings, and a nature wholly wild and fantastic, lend an almost Gothic tone to the work. There were two obvious European precedents, *La Nouvelle Héloïse* by Jean-Jacques Rousseau (1761), with its disdain for corrupt society; and more especially, *The Sorrows of Young Werther* by Johann Wolfgang von Goethe (1774), which created the mold for the artistic hero, with his hopeless passion, intense communion with nature, isolation from society as a whole, and eventual suicide.

Yet the autobiographical dimension of the *Last Letters of Jacopo Ortis* prevails, and the fictional frame of the epistolary novel allows the author to present confused, fragmentary, contradictory, and confessional information to his interlocutor, his best friend (and eventual editor of the novel), Lorenzo. In the figure of Teresa, Jacopo's beloved, Foscolo has melded features and attributes of three of his loves. The novel was first planned while Foscolo was still in Venice. In its inception, it was to be a love story inspired by Petrarch. Indeed, the original title was *Letters to Laura*; the Petrarchan influence remains in one of the sections of the novel entitled "Fragment of the Story of Lauretta." Yet the aftermath of the Treaty of Campoformio inspired Foscolo to reconceptualize the novel primarily in terms of political disappointment, with the love interest assuming a secondary importance. Once Foscolo read *The Sorrows of Young Werther*, he made other changes as well. Foscolo decided to have Jacopo address the majority of the letters to his best friend Lorenzo, just as Werther writes his letters to his friend Wilhelm in Goethe's novel. Both works will portray a restless passionate young man driven to suicide as the society around him collapses.

The novel recounts the bitter disappointments of the hero Jacopo, Foscolo's alter ego, in love, in politics, and in his melancholic attachment to his motherland, and to his mother. Indeed this nexus of female figures – cradle, womb, mother, nation, and beloved – will be developed into the single erotic force which motivates all of Foscolo's work, and will be ultimately identified with the cult of death. The underlying tensions of the novel reflect the existential crisis of the author, who is torn between believing in the mechanistic laws of nature and his enthrallment to his individual subjectivity; torn, that is, between the precepts of Rationalism and Romanticism.

The first line of the *Last Letters of Jacopo Ortis* foreshadows its conclusion: "The sacrifice of our homeland is complete. All is lost, and life remains to us – if indeed we are allowed to live – only so that we may lament our misfortunes, and our shame" (Foscolo 2002). The ideals of love, liberty, beauty, and art will, one by one, be destroyed by the harsh realities of the contemporary society. The Treaty of Campoformio exiles the eponymous hero Jacopo from his homeland. He falls in love with Teresa, and despite the fact that she returns Jacopo's feelings, she has been promised to another man (Edoardo) in an arranged marriage, which suits her father's financial exigencies. Upon his first meeting with Teresa, Jacopo hyperbolically writes to his friend: "I have seen her, Lorenzo, 'the divine maiden' [. . .] I went home with my heart full of joy. What can I say? Is the sight of beauty enough to lay to rest all the suffering of us sad mortals?"(2002: 10). Teresa's father, Signor T., and Edoardo are the villains of the story, men who live according to conventional morality and economic exigencies, men without hope, illusions, or passion. Jacopo is unable to accept conventional morality or to compromise with it. Suicide becomes the only and the necessary solution.

In this sense, the *Last Letters of Jacopo Ortis* is a pre-eminently Romantic work, even though it was written before the Romantic controversy officially developed in Italy. While the fierce classical and biblical heroes of the dramatist Vittorio Alfieri may be the ancestors of Jacopo, the novel is clearly grounded in contemporary Italy. Beyond this, it bears the unique Italian Romantic stamp of being deeply classical in its appreciation of the cult of beauty and female grace. Yet the *Last Letters of Jacopo Ortis* remains an astute psychological portrait of the sensitive soul of a young person faced with the loss of all illusion, of all faith. In this way it is also a sociologically accurate portrait of a society undergoing tremendous change, awash in a sea of conflicting political and moral models. The *Last Letters of Jacopo Ortis* is certainly Italy's first novel, and perhaps its first historical novel. Whether Jacopo is a fully realized character, logically and artistically homogeneous – a question posed even the by the first critics – can remain undecided. The mutability, complexity, and hyperbolic nature of the character, and the fragmentary nature of the narrative, confer upon it an undeniable authenticity. In one of the last fragments that Jacopo writes to his friend Lorenzo, he invokes Death in terms consonant with his love sonnet to the evening, the image of death ("Alla sera"): "O Death [. . .] You are a necessary part of Nature. By now you hold no more terror for me. To me you are like a sleep in the evening, rest after labour" (Foscolo 2002: 124). The novel was published in subsequent editions in Zurich in 1816, and in London in 1817.

The astonishing innovation of the *Last Letters of Jacopo Ortis* is matched by *Of Tombs*, published in 1807, a brilliant political poem responding to the historical situation of Foscolo's day (in this same year he brought out his translation of the first book of Homer's *Iliad*). *Of Tombs* has a political purpose, and the opening contemplation of the sepulchre moves quickly to a catalogue of the great Italian men buried in the Florentine church of Santa Croce, to finally, Greek battlefields and tombs. It is a call to action. As such, it follows no clear line of thought. The poem charts the inner debate of Foscolo who does not believe in an afterlife, who follows the precepts of eighteenth-century mechanistic materialism, but who understands that political unity can only be engendered by mourning the dead.

Foscolo's poem is a response to the 1804 Napoleonic Edict of Saint Cloud, which forbade the burial of the dead in marked graves and within the city limits. Against Napoleon's prohibition to name the dead, Foscolo's constructs a poem in which naming the dead becomes the primal sacred act of community building. Here Foscolo elaborates his own *ars poetica*, conceptualizing the grave as the place that most nourishes human memory, the tie that binds the dead to the living. The grave is the custodian of the past, and bestows eternal life upon human and civic values against the erosion of time. *Of Tombs*, written in unrhymed verses of 11 syllables (*endecasillabi sciolti*), opens as a voice eerily questions life within the tomb:

> All'ombra de' cipressi e dentro l'urne
> confortate di pianto è forse il sonno
> della morte men duro? [. . .] (ll.1-3)

(In the shadow of the cypress trees and kept within funerary urns comforted by weeping, is the sleep of death perhaps less bitter?)

The poem continues for 295 verses to answer this rhetorical question in the affirmative. All thing pass into nothingness; but the memory of great deeds and great men, nourished by the tears of mourning, will keep civilization alive, and will engender new acts of heroism. The poem praises the work of women, traditionally the mourners of the dead, as the guardians of the tombs and of the stories we tell about the virtuous. "Only those who leave no legacy of human affection have little joy in funerary urns." Foscolo will describe this loving bond between the living and the dead as heavenly. "Heavenly is this correspondence of loving feelings, a heavenly gift to humans" (". . . . Celeste è questa / corrispondenza d'amorosi sensi, / celeste dote è negli umani," ll. 29-31). Following the philosophy of the early eighteenth-century Neapolitan writer Giambattista Vico (in his *New Science* of 1725), Foscolo posits that the burial of the dead, along with the institution of marriage, is one of the constitutive elements of human civilization. "The urns of the strong fire the strong soul to excellent deeds." As Foscolo had written elsewhere, his subject was "the resurrection of nations," and "not the resurrection of bodies."

Then, in a rapid transition from the Italian tombs to the world of universalizing Greek mythology, Foscolo describes the Muses guarding Greek sepulchres, and singing; their "harmony overcomes the silence of a thousand centuries." This stirring political poem closes with the words of Cassandra who foresees the wandering poet Homer as he enters the tombs, embraces the funerary urns, and interrogates them for their tales of heroism. "The secret caves will moan, and the tombs will narrate all." Homer's song will soothe the tormented souls, and blood shed for one's motherland will thus be immortalized "as long as the Sun shines upon human sorrows" ("...finchè il Sole / risplenderà su le sciagure umane," ll. 294-5).

If we were to isolate the astounding originality of Foscolo's conception of poetry, we would have to highlight the interconnection between death, poetry, and a secular eternity. Foscolo understood that poetry was the source of human creativity and of the human fantasy. Poetry's capacity to give shape to the fleetingness of human life can bestow a form of immortality upon the contingency of human existence. His aesthetic belief in the transcendent universal value of Myth and Beauty was at war with his Enlightenment, rationalistic rigor and skepticism, his materialism, as well as with his idiosyncratic autobiographical obsessions, with his desire to make a myth of his own life. It may be that these tensions and oppositions created the catalytic passion of Foscolo's works; it may also be that they gave rise as well to what has been perceived as the difficulty of his poetic style. Foscolian syntax is characterized by its extreme elasticity and tension; the lyrics move from epigraphic, aphoristic brevity to deeply embedded long Latinate phrases. The poetic verse may be abruptly interrupted by semicolons or dashes; or may overflow the metric line with complex *enjambements* for many verses. As Lord Byron acutely noted, at this point in time Foscolo had "proved his genius but not fixed its fame, nor done his utmost."

In 1808 Foscolo was appointed to the Chair of *Eloquenza* (Italian and Latin Literature) at the University of Pavia. In January of the following year he delivered his inaugural speech on the "Origin and Role of Literature," which posits the origins of literature and those of civilization as one with allegory and augury. But the French government decided that eloquence was no longer to be taught at the university, and the Chair was withdrawn. Foscolo had difficult relations with Milanese society because of his anti-Napoleonic sentiments. This attitude informs his second tragedy, *Ajace* (Ajax) written in 1811. Foscolo left Lombardy for Florence; here he began the long neoclassical poem *Le Grazie* (The Graces) which he never completed. The three hymns, dedicated to the sculptor Antonio Canova, were inspired by his neoclassical sculptures. While the Canova sculptures actually represent three classical goddesses, Venus, Vesta, and Pallas, to whom the hymns are dedicated, Foscolo chose to entitle his poem *Le Grazie* (the three Graces, who bring civilization and comfort to the human race, were Aglaia, Euphrosyne, and Thalia). Once again, Foscolo posits that

poetry and its sublime ideality of beauty is the constitutive force of human civilization and the only refuge from the chaos of the contemporary world. In 1813, the poet
published his brilliant translation into Italian of Laurence Sterne's (1713-68) *Sentimental Journey Through France and Italy*. Foscolo's third tragedy, the *Ricciarda* (1813)
was staged at this time, but when the Regno Italico fell to Austrian powers in 1814,
Foscolo decided not to swear allegiance to the new political authorities and fled to
Switzerland. There he published an edition of the *Last Letters of Jacopo Ortis*, and
Ipercalisse (under the pseudonym of Didimo Chierico), a prose Latin satire condemning
all manner of political and literary movements.

In flight from the Austrian government, the poet moved to England in 1816.
Foscolo's London life was marked by the same tensions and ambivalence as before. He
was initially warmly welcomed by the intellectuals of the country (they called him the
Italian Byron), and contributed to many literary reviews. Soon, however, his melancholy and excessive personality alienated people and caused him to fall heavily in
debt. From 1822 on he lived with his daughter Floriana (born in 1805, fruit of his
affair with Fanny Emerytt), falling into destitution, yet never ceasing his prodigious
activity as a writer and literary critic. Among these numerous publications, his essays
on Petrarch, on the *Divine Comedy*, and on Italian narrative and drama, remain
extremely important contributions to the history of literary criticism. In 1818 he
wrote an "Essay on the Present Literature of Italy" in which he spoke of the
contemporary Italian debate between "classical" and "Romantic" as "an idle question."
The Romanticists in Italy were in favor of rejecting the use of classical mythology in
literature; in contradistinction, the recovery of social, political, and aesthetic virtues
from the ancients was Fosolo's persistent dream.

Ugo Foscolo died completely forgotten, in Turnham Green, England, on September
10, 1827. He was 49. He was buried in the cemetery of Chiswick; in 1871 his remains
were taken to Florence, and laid to rest in the church of Santa Croce, in the very site
and among the very tombs that he had elegized in his superb poem *Of Tombs*.

Giacomo Leopardi

Giacomo Leopardi is one of the most powerful poets of the Romantic sublime, one of
the great innovators of poetic style and of critical writing on poetic language.
Leopardi thought deeply about the principles of poetry, and about the human
conditions that motivate our need to read poetry; these thoughts led him into
considerations about the ontology of happiness, boredom, hope, and memory. Leopardi's letters and notebooks, the *Zibaldone* (Miscellany), give us insight into a
vigorous and sensitive mind, and into a psyche that had to bear the effects of a
disabled body and depressed spirit. In his melancholy isolation, his affective affinity
with nature, his failed amorous relationships, and his early death at not quite 39,
Leopardi seems to incarnate the archetype of the Romantic poet. That is to say, he
fulfills the archetype of the sensitive, reclusive poet, whose life was sublimated into

his art. Foscolo, as we have seen, represents another archetype, the exuberant, politically and erotically extroverted poet, whose life was turned into an art object.

Conte Giacomo Leopardi was the oldest child of Conte Monaldo Leopardi and Adelaide Antici, both of noble families. Born on June 29, 1798, in the town of Recanati in the Marche, the young poet lived a stifling provincial life. In 1799 his brother Carlo was born, and one year later his sister Paolina. The bond between these three siblings, almost triplets, was intense; there were two more siblings born at a later date who did not participate in the close relationship of the three. In some ways, Giacomo's childhood was happy, for while the political upheavals occurring in Italy in the wake of the French Revolution had repercussions on the life of the parents, the children of the family were by and large left to entertain themselves.

Giacomo's father had provided the family with an excellent library for those times. The library was to become Leopardi's prison and salvation. Giacomo was educated privately at home by his father and by ecclesiastical tutors, but at a very young age he began his own self-education, utilizing the volumes in the paternal library. He was a prodigy, gifted with a rare intelligence; he taught himself to read and write Greek, Hebrew, and several modern languages while still an adolescent. Between 1808 and 1816, the young poet penned some remarkably erudite works and translations from Horace, Homer, and Hesiod, among others. By 1813 he had composed his first poetical works, sermons, and even two tragedies, *La virtù indiana* (Indian Virtue) and *Pompeo in Egitto* (Pompey in Egypt). He translated the idylls of the Alexandrian poet Moschus, which influenced his own poetic style and his choice of the *idillio* as his privileged poetic form. In 1815 Leopardi composed a philosophical "Essay on the Popular Errors of the Ancients" ("Saggio sopra gli errori popolari degli antichi"), which demonstrated both his Enlightenment and religious training, and showed a growing interest in the creative role of myth, fable, and fantasy. These latter interests were developed in the more than 4,650 pages of the *Zibaldone* (composed between 1817 and 1832, but most intensely between 1820 and 1826), and in his brilliant series of ironic dialogues *Le operette morali* (Little Moral Works) of 1827. The years spent in the paternal library, in total isolation, engaged in what the poet himself called "seven years of mad and desperate study"[3] were profoundly detrimental to his health, physical and psychological. He suffered from neurological, skeletal, and respiratory disorders, as well as poor vision, which eventually caused near blindness.

1816 marks a turning point in the poet's life, what Leopardi himself called his "literary conversion" that is, "the passage from erudition to the beautiful." In 1816 Leopardi composed "Inno a Nettuno" (Hymn to Neptune) which purported to be a translation from the Greek (and which fooled even the best philologists of Leopardi's day), and also his first original poems, "Le rimembranze" (Memories), an idyll, and "L'appressamento della morte" (The Approach of Death). These poems already touch on the hallmark Leopardian theme of one's lost youth. Giacomo harbored a secret love for his married cousin Geltrude Cassi Lazzari, and in 1817 the young poet composed a love poem inspired by her, "Il primo amore" (The First Love). By this time, Giacomo was recording all manner of thoughts in his notebooks, which were to become an idiosyncratic encyclopedia containing both autobiographical reminiscences and a series of philosophical, linguistic, literary, and anthropological essays.

1819 marks another turning point, which Leopardi called his "conversion from poetry to philosophy." This conversion was in some sense a conversion away from his religious upbringing, and towards an atheistic, materialistic worldview. Mme de Staël had an enormous influence on his thought, and Leopardi writes that until he read certain of her works he did not think he could be a philosopher. Her work demonstrated to the Italian poet that there was no real incompatibility between nature, source of the imagination and the emotions, on the one hand, and the faculties of reason and abstract thought, on the other.

There has been considerable debate about whether or not Leopardi was a true "philosopher," whether or not there is a system to his thought. In many ways, the answer must surely be yes; there are remarkable consistencies between his discussions of the development of languages, cultures, human happiness, the function of pleasure or boredom, and the poetic sublime. But we should consider Leopardi's rich philosophical thinking not so much a system of pessimism as a laboratory – the fertile ground for disseminating and exploring ideas that will come to fruition in his poetry. While many of Leopardi's philosophical ideas were current in his time, and thus not original to him, his poetry is at all times thoroughly innovative and unique.

In his early years, Leopardi contrasted nature with human civilization: nature was beneficent and beautiful; Nature, our Mother, intended us for happiness. But civilization, with its valorization of Reason and its belief in the myth of progress, made humankind ever more unhappy. Human desires grew more complex, and consequently, produced greater disappointments. Later, Leopardi would view nature as inimical to humanity, not as a benign mother but as an evil stepmother (*matrigna*), and he considered all dreams of progress as folly. "We are fully alienated from Nature," he wrote. Leopardi viewed reason as the enemy of the ideals of beauty, love, happiness, and heroism. These were, as we have seen, the incandescent ideals that illuminated the works of Ugo Foscolo. Thus for Leopardi, the conversion to philosophy did not mark the abandonment of poetry, but rather the point at which his philosophical understanding of the interrelationship between reason and nature was transmuted into perfect lyric verse.

The fundamental theme of Leopardi's lyrics and prose is the opposition between the human desire for infinite happiness and the limited, fragmented, and delusory nature of reality. This contrast is born of the opposition between the experience of every present moment as necessarily *finite* and our innate desire for a feeling of *infinitude*. Leopardi felt that the experience of happiness could only be elicited by the imagination: by poetic images that refigure the past as memory (*rimembranza*), and the future as hope (*speranza*). It is for this reason that as a theoretician of poetry, Leopardi felt that his own "modern" age could no longer produce poetry based on the creation of new images (*una poesia immaginativa* – an imaginative poetry), but only poetry based on the analysis of interior states of feelings (*una poesia sentimentale* – a sentimental poetry). Indeed, Leopardi joined the then current literary debate between proponents of Classicism and Romanticism, writing two anti-Romantic polemical essays, the more interesting being *Discorso di un italiano intorno alla poesia romantica* (Discourse of an Italian on Romantic Poetry, 1818).

In his *Discourse* Leopardi explicitly supports the Classicist position, all the while actually espousing views consonant with what we call Romanticism. The poet, according to Leopardi, must always strive for naturalness and simplicity, qualities he admired in his beloved Greeks. Like Samuel Taylor Coleridge, John Keats, and Edgar Allan Poe, Leopardi sought to use the kind of words and sounds that through their very indefiniteness tend to activate the imagination. Leopardi likens the ancient poets to children, filled with "the infinite workings of the imagination." Leopardi, like William Wordsworth (whose work Leopardi does not appear to have known) conceived of the poetic sublime as arising from our experiences of childhood's "first affections / Those shadowy recollections" ("Ode: Intimations of Mortality," ll. 152-3, in Wordsworth 1950: 461). The memory of the past is always a memory of a childhood experience. In a famous passage of the *Zibaldone*, Leopardi writes that "the world and its objects are in a certain sense doubled."[4] Things exist to the extent that they can be remembered in poetic images. Things seen with the eyes are necessarily finite, limited; things reseen with the imagination can be represented as infinite. Thus Leopardi stressed repeatedly that the present "could never be poetic": "il presente, qual egli sia, non può esser poetico." "Remembrance," Leopardi states, is the "essential and principle" component of the poetic sentiment. Both hope and memory are spatially and temporally distant, therefore creating images and sentiments that are indefinite and indeterminate. Poetic language, similar to "the wandering imagination we experienced in our childhood," dispels the delusory clarity that modern language and thought impose upon our experience of the world.

Leopardi's poems are collected in the volume he entitled *Canti* (Songs), an allusion to Petrarch's (1304-74) *Canzoniere* (Songbook); in fact, in 1826 Leopardi published a commentary on Petrarch's *Canzoniere*. The *Canti* contains 41 poems, comprising several distinct groups: a number of civic odes and several occasional *canzoni*; his first group of idylls of 1819-21, known as *i piccoli idilli* (the little idylls); and his five "great idylls," *i grandi idilli*, of 1826-8; a group of five poems know as "the cycle of Aspasia," dedicated to an unrequited love; and his last poems written in Naples, in the years before his death in 1837.

In 1818 he composed several patriotic *canzoni* "All'Italia" (To Italy) and "Sopra il monumento di Dante" (On the Monument to Dante). Between 1820 and 1822 he wrote two *canzoni* with classical themes: "Bruto minore" (Brutus the Younger) and "Ultimo canto di Saffo" (Sappho's Last Song). The most salient feature of many of these is Leopardi's agonistic heroic stance against the tyranny of destiny and its destructive laws, and an acceptance of suicide. The political *canzoni* were written between 1820 and 1821, at the time of the revolutionary movements organized by the *Carbonari* in Naples, Milan, and Turin. Yet at the same time, 1819-21, Leopardi was beginning his innovative and tender idyll poems, *i piccoli idilli*.

The poet returns to the scene of his childhood in Recanati. The poems are replete with visions of the gentle landscape, the hills and valleys where the young Leopardi would go to gaze at the horizon and imagine the infinite: the church bells ringing, the moon rising, the village fair, an artisan returning home from the fields, the village maiden working at her loom. The earliest idylls are sentimental as well as descriptive lyrics, and they usually open with some reference to or account of the landscape near Recanati. The actual geography and objects described are just the pretext for the evocation of the emotions of childhood, primarily the remembrance of the many hopes he had then, and the sentiment of the infinite and the indefinite which informs our infantile dreams. The pain of the present moment, its disappointments and finitude, will be sublimated into the contemplation of the vastness of nature. Stylistically, the idyllic poems mark Leopardi's progressive distancing from traditional metric systems, especially closed forms.

The 1819 lyric, "L'infinito" (The Infinite) is perhaps Leopardi's most famous poem and a model of his idylls. The poem has 15 verses, resembling somewhat the form of the sonnet (14 lines), but without any fixed rhyme scheme. The poem opens with a description of Mt Tabor, the hill in Recanati where the young Leopardi often went to seek solace.

> Sempre caro mi fu quest'ermo colle,
> E questa siepe, che da tanta parte
> Dell'ultimo orizzonte il guardo esclude. (ll. 1-3)

(Always dear to me was this solitary hill, and this hedge, which block the gaze from so vast a part of the farthest horizon.)

The poet concentrates not on Mt Tabor but on what is blocked from view. Leopardi writes that he is "gazing" beyond the landscape, imagining "boundless spaces" and "superhuman silences," and the "profoundest quiet" ("Ma sedendo e mirando, interminati / Spazi di là da quella, e sovrumani / Silenzi, e profondissima quiete," ll. 4-6). This mental imaging ("Io nel pensier mi fingo," "I in my mind create," l. 7) takes the poet out of the present and into the boundless rhetorical figures of his imagination. The wind he hears in the present is compared to the infinite silence he imagines. The poem closes with the poet virtually drowning in the spaces of his imagination, as he gives into the sublimity of their vastness:

> ... Così tra questa
> Immensità s'annega il pensier mio:
> E il naufragar m'è dolce in questo mare. (ll. 13-15)

(Thus in this immensity my thought is drowned: and the shipwreck in this sea is sweet to me.)

Two years after writing "L'infinito" Leopardi described it as a poem that demonstrates the production of the experience of the sublime by means of contrasts between the finite and the indefinite. This contrastive principle underlies both sequences of idylls, those of 1819 and of 1828. Contrast and blockage, as Longinus and Burke and other theorists of the sublime had also recognized, were at the heart of the poetical sublime. The concept of indefiniteness is correlative to this notion of blockage, as the great German Romantic painter Caspar David Friedrich (1774-1840) wrote about one of his paintings: "When a scene is shrouded in mist, it seems greater, nobler, and heightens the viewers' imaginative powers, increasing expectation – like a veiled girl. Generally the eye and the imagination are more readily drawn by nebulous distance than by what is perfectly plain for all to see" (cited in Maaz 2001: 21).

"La sera del dì di festa" (The Evening of the Holiday, 1820), another early idyll, is also structured by a series of contrasts. The poet hears the song of an artisan returning home after the holiday festivities, which he contrasts both to the clamor of the now defunct Roman Empire and to an experience in childhood, when he would lie in bed and listen to a similar sad song. The two songs are described in parallel syntax: "fieramente mi si stringe il core" (l. 28) and "già similmente mi stringeva il core" (l. 46): "fiercely grips the heart" and "similarly gripped the heart." The return of that childhood auditory sensation removes the poet from his present unhappiness, and from the recognition of life's transience, and returns him to his childhood, a time of hope and sublime indefinite sentiments.

In 1822 Leopardi finally received his family's permission to travel and spent several months in Rome, but the capital city was a bitter disappointment for the poet, who returned to Recanati to once again bury himself in work. During the next two years he wrote the majority of the entries of the *Zibaldone*. He also composed most of the ironic prose dialogues of the *Operette morali*, in which he adheres to sensationalist epistemological principles and develops his ideas about pleasure. During this time, Leopardi ceased to write poetry but deepened his belief in a materialistic conception of the universe, viewing the world as nothing more than a perpetual transformation of its molecules and physical matter. The materialistic base of the universe necessarily renders false all idealistic conceptions of beauty, imagination, youth, glory, virtue, and of the infinite. Leopardi concludes that humankind must open their eyes to the mediocrity and misery of human life. We must look directly into the void, the nothingness (*il nulla*) that is existence.

After a third brief stay at Recanati, Leopardi moved to Florence in 1827, and then to Pisa. Here in 1828 he began to write poetry again and once again he revisited the scene of his childhood in Recanati. This second idyllic sequence (1828-30) – *i grandi idilli* – also moves between the poles of hope and remembrance, yet with a more disillusioned sense of the possibilities of love and fantasy. Here Leopardi's youthful memories are described as error or illusion (*errori, illusioni*). The poems of *i grandi idilli* return to the childhood landscapes and emotions of his first idylls, which are now at an even farther remove. In "A Silvia" (To Sylvia) the poet addresses a young village maiden, who died young of tuberculosis.

> Silvia, remembri ancora
> Quel tempo della tua vita mortale,
> Quando beltà splendea
> Negli occhi tuoi ridenti e fuggitivi,
> E tu, lieta e pensosa, il limitare
> Di gioventù salivi? (ll. 1-6)

(Silvia, do you still remember that time in your mortal life when beauty shone in your laughing and fugitive eyes; and you, happy and thoughtful, were climbing up to the threshold of youth?)

Silvia, the symbol of the poet's youthful hopes, died before reaching maturity. Is this, the poet queries, the fate of all humankind ("Questa la sorte dell'umane genti?" l. 56). The poem closes with an answer in the affirmative, and an evocation of the tomb of his wept-for hope (*mia lacrimata speme*) and metaphorically, of Silvia herself:

> All'apparir del vero
> Tu, misera, cadesti: e con la mano
> La fredda morte ed una tomba ignuda
> Mostravi da lontano. (ll. 60-3)

(At the appearance of Truth you miserable one [hope], fell; and with your hand / from a distance you pointed to both cold Death and the nude Tomb.)

"Le ricordanze" (Memories), the longest of the *grandi idilli*, explicitly problematizes memory, and the contrasts between past and present. The poet returns to his father's house to remember his childhood happiness. The objects described (rooms, garden, star-studded sky, bells tolling in the village church) elicit the return of memories.

> ...Qui non è cosa
> Ch'io vegga o senta, onde un'immaginar dentro
> Non torni, e un dolce rimembrar non sorga. (ll. 55-7)

(There is nothing here that I see and hear that does bring back an image and from which a sweet remembrance does not rise up.)

In "Le ricordanze", the poet addresses his lost hope:

> O speranze, speranze; ameni inganni
> Della mia prima età; sempre, parlando,
> Ritorno a voi; che per l'andar del tempo,
> Per variar d'affetti e di pensieri,
> Obbliarvi non so. Fantasmi, intendo
> Son la gloria e l'onor...(ll. 78-83)

(Oh hopes, hopes, you dear deceits of my young years; always, when speaking, I return to you; despite the passing of time and my changing affections and thoughts, I do not know how to forget you. Glory and Honor are but Phantasms, I now see ...)

The illusion and its deconstruction cohabit the lyric. In another of the *grandi idilli*, "Canto notturno di un pastore errante dell'Asia" (The Night Song of a Wandering Shepherd from Asia) an innocent shepherd gazes up at the moon and interrogates it. Surely the moon understands the movements of the heavens, and the misery of human life, says the shepherd. The moon is silent but the shepherd confides to it what little he does know, that is, the universal condemnation of human life. The poem closes with lapidary and oxymoronic concision: "è funesto a chi nasce il dì natale" (the day of birth is funereal to whomever is born, l. 143). Cosmic pain and the cosmic beauty of the starry night sky meld.

1830 marks another turning point in Leopardi's life, although not one that he himself would label a conversion. With the help of friends, Leopardi was able to return to Florence, where he met and fell in love with Fanny Targioni Tozzetti. While it is clear that the two did share a friendship, the poet experienced this relationship as a bitter and unrequited love. The passion for Fanny, whom Leopardi called Aspasia, after the famous mistress of Pericles, inspired a cycle of five poems (called "the cycle of Aspasia") which describe love, along with death, as the supreme experiences for humankind. At this time Leopardi also struck up a friendship with an exiled Neapolitan writer, Antonio Ranieri; Fanny, Leopardi, and Ranieri became friends. Leopardi's letters to Ranieri in 1832-3, when he was temporarily away from Florence, resemble love letters. Fanny, in fact, spoke of Ranieri and Leopardi as "eterni legittimi compagni" (eternal legitimate companions; quoted in Carsaniga 1977: 99). Ranieri, a mediocre writer himself, certainly admired Leopardi's brilliance. In 1833 Leopardi, already quite ill, moved to Naples, where he lived with Ranieri until his death in 1837.

The rejection of Leopardi by Fanny was felt by the poet as a mortal blow, as "A se stesso" (To Himself), the briefest poem of the Aspasia cycle reveals. The poem opens with the poet's command to his heart to stop beating:

> Or poserai per sempre,
> Stanco mio cor. Perì l'inganno estremo,
> Ch'eterno io mi credei. Perì. (ll. 1-3)

(Now you shall rest forever, my tired heart. The last illusion has perished, which I had believed eternal. Perished.)

The poet avers that not only is hope dead, but even the desire for hope has died. "Life is bitterness and boredom, nothing more. And the world is filth." ("...Amaro e noia/ La vita, altro mai nulla; e fango è il mondo," ll. 9-10). Nature, no longer beneficent, rules for the common destruction of all humankind, and for "the infinite vanity of all" ("E l'infinita vanità del tutto," l. 16). It may be that the Aspasia poems and the loss of Leopardi's last illusion, that of love, functioned as a form of exorcism, clearing the imaginative space for his last and incomparably masterful poems.

During the Neapolitan period, 1833-7, Leopardi wrote the last of the *Operette morali*, several canzoni, an ironic heroic-comic epic poem, and his last two lyrical poems "Il tramonto della luna" (The Setting of the Moon) and "La ginestra" (The Broom Flower). In these last poems Leopardi arrives at what has been seen by several critics as his political phase of "Titanism," in which he urges people to repudiate all consolatory myths, and to unite together in the face of the materialistic powers of nature. In these last two poems, Leopardi brilliantly places his materialist ideology within a Romantic landscape.

"Il tramonto della luna" is in fact a palinode to his idyllic universe. Leopardi's beloved hills are delicately described at the *incipit* of the poem: illuminated by the moon at dusk, filled with shadow, swathed in silvery color; the wind and the lonely song of a workman fill the auditory scene. These hills will be whitened with the return of dawn after the bleakness of night. In comparison, human life will see no return of dawn or dusk. For humankind, the Gods have placed the sepulchre as the sign of eternal night: ". . . ed alla notte / Che l'altre etadi oscura, / Segno poser gli Dei la sepoltura," ll. 65-8).

"La ginestra" may be considered an anti-idyllic poem, in that it resists the evocation of memory or hope, of the indefinite and the infinite, and remains rooted in the bleakness of the present. The poem can be profitably situated within the context of the poetry of ruins and graveyards that flourished in Europe in the eighteenth and nineteenth centuries. Leopardi's poem resounds from the burnt lava slopes of Mt Vesuvius where, in 79 AD volcanic eruption buried the city of Pompeii. In his attempt to understand the cataclysmic nature of this event, Leopardi refuses the consolation of any theism, which would seek meaning in some transcendental order. Instead he exalts humankind's materialistic destiny, which at least does not seek refuge in illusions. The volcanic wasteland of Vesuvius, inimical to life, gives birth only to the humble broom flower that is seen as the sign of the sepulchre of a lost civilization. Leopardi creates here a radically new contextualization for the graveyard poem, moving far beyond both the pastoral country churchyard of Thomas Gray's "Elegy" and the urban environment of Foscolo's *Sepolcri*.

"La ginestra" presents a denaturalized skeletal landscape, within which the ruins of Pompeii and the broom flower are markers of nonrecoverable absence. Foscolo's *Sepolcri* had mapped the development of the funerary inscription from its mythic origin, cypresses watered by female tears, to the stone inscriptions that replace that earlier language of plants. Leopardi pushes this chain of substitutions further, beyond the mythic and the elegiac, and posits the broom flower as a vegetal sign outlasting stone inscriptions precisely because of its willingness to bend to nature. The poem opens with an insistence on rootedness in a bleak burnt-out present:

> Qui su l'arida schiena
> Del formidabile monte
> Sterminator Vesevo (ll. 1-3)

(Here on the arid back of the formidable exterminator Mt Vesuvius)

Juxtaposed to the exterminating mountain is the "sweet-smelling broom flower, happy in the wasteland" ("odorata ginestra / Contenta dei deserti," ll. 6-7). The landscape has become mineral: "Questi campi cosparsi / Di ceneri infeconde, e ricoperti/ Dell'impietrata lava" (These slopes strewn with sterile ashes, sealed down with lava turned hard as stone, ll. 17-19). But these mineral slopes give birth to a vegetal sepulchral marker:

> ...Or tutto intorno
> Una ruina involve,
> Dove tu siedi, o fior gentile, e quasi
> I danni altrui commiserando, al cielo
> Di dolcissimo odor mandi un profumo
> Che il deserta consola. (ll. 32-7)

(Now all around a ruin stretches where you sit, oh gentle flower, and almost as if you were commiserating the sorrows of others, you send to the sky a perfume of the sweetest scent which consoles the desert.)

The poet ironically summons to these burnt-out slopes anyone who believes that the human race is in the care of "loving Nature." Against the facile belief in progress, Leopardi asks his foolish century "to mirror itself" in these blackened slopes. Leopardi passionately exhorts humankind to unity and brotherhood in the common war against nature. While we continue to arrogate to ourselves the boast of eternity, the humble broom flower perfumes the air. Of course, the flower too will succumb to the killing fires of Vesuvius, but it will do so without struggling, and without vain and cowardly supplication before a future oppressor. The poet eulogizes the *ginestra* at the close of the poem as wiser and stronger than humankind, who incorrectly considers itself immortal. That there was a critical political message in all of Leopardi's works was certainly recognized: by 1836, the year before his death, the Austrian, Papal, Neapolitan, and Florentine governments had all prohibited the publication of the *Operette morali* and the *Canti*.

Leopardi's poetry, encompassing what critics have called his idyllic and his anti-idyllic modes, does not present a uniform or static position. Philosophical meditation and poetic remembrance may be the two poles of Leopardi's expressive universe; yet they are in a reciprocal and mutually constitutive relationship. Although one must recognize the truth of the illusory nature of ideals and hopes, and of the search for meaning in nature, one must first resuscitate these chimeras, experience their beauty and their appeal, and then negate them. The poems are not merely mimetic of nature; they constitute an interior landscape of emotions and pathos. It is the affective movements of the human heart that are portrayed, even as Leopardi proclaims the pure materiality of the world.

NOTES

1 Silvio Pellico, Italian writer and patriot, was best known for his memoir *Le mie prigioni* (*My Prisons*) of 1832.
2 All citations from Foscolo's poetry are from Foscolo (1995).

3 Translations from Leopardi prose and poetry are mine.
4 All citations from Leopardi's works are from Leopardi (1967). This edition comprises five volumes: *Le poesie e le prose*, 2 vols.; *Zibaldone*, 2 vols.; *Le lettere*, 1 vol.

REFERENCES AND FURTHER READING

Primary sources

Foscolo, Ugo (1995). *Opere*, ed. Franco Gavazzeni. Milan: Riccardo Ricciardi Editore.
Foscolo, Ugo (1974). *Ultime lettere di Jacopo Ortis*. Milan: Garzanti.
Foscolo, Ugo (2002). *Last Letters of Jacopo Ortis* and *Of Tombs*, trans. J. G. Nichols. London: Hesperus Press.
Leopardi, Giacomo (1967). *Tutte le opere di Giacomo Leopardi*, ed. Francesco Flora. Milan: Mondadori Editori.
Leopardi, Giacomo (1992). *Zibaldone. A Selection*, ed. and trans. Martha King and Daniela Bini. New York: Peter Lang.

Secondary sources

Bigongiari, Piero (1976). *Leopardi*. Florence: La Nuova Italia.
Bini, Daniela (1983). *A Fragrance from the Desert: Poetry and Philosophy in Giacomo Leopardi*. Saratoga, CA: Anma Libri.
Binni, Walter (1973). *La nuova poetica leopardiana*. Florence: Sansoni.
Brose, Margaret (1983). "Leopardi's 'L'Infinito' and the Language of the Romantic Sublime." *Poetics Today*, 4 (1): 47-71.

Brose, Margaret (1989). "The Politics of Mourning in Foscolo's *Dei sepolcri*." *European Romantic Review* 9 (1). 1-34.
Brose, Margaret (1998). *Leopardi sublime: la poetica della temporalità*. Bologna: Re Enzo.
Cambon, Glauco (1980). *Ugo Foscolo, Poet of Exile*. Princeton, NJ: Princeton University Press.
Carsaniga, Giovanni (1977). *Leopardi: The Unheeded Voice*. Edinburgh, UK: Edinburgh University Press.
Casale, Ottavio Mark (ed. and trans.) (1981). *A Leopardi Reader*. Urbana and Chicago: University of Illinois Press.
Damiani, Rolando (1998). *All'apparir del vero. Vita di Giacomo Leopardi*. Milan: Mondadori.
Flores, Angel (ed.) (1966). *Leopardi: Poems and Prose*. Bloomington: University of Indiana Press.
Fubini, Mario (1978). *Ugo Foscolo: saggi, studi, note*. Florence: La nuova Italia.
Kroeber, Karl (1964). *The Artifice of Reality: Poetic Style in Wordsworth, Foscolo, Keats, and Leopardi*. Madison: University of Wisconsin Press.
Leopardi, Giacomo (1982). *Operette morali: Essays and Dialogues*, trans. Giovanni Cecchetti. Berkeley: University of California Press.

Maaz, Bernhard (ed.) (2001). *Alte Nationalgalerie Berlin: Museum Guide*. Munich, London, and New York: Prestel.

Manacorda, Giorgio (1973). *Materialismo e Masochismo: il "Werther," Foscolo e Leopardi*. Florence: La Nuova Italia.

Matteo, Sante (1985). *Textual Exile: The Reader in Sterne and Foscolo*. New York: P. Lang.

O'Neill, Tom (1981). *Of Virgin Muses and of Love: A Study of Foscolo's Dei sepolcrii*. Dublin: Irish Academic Press.

Origo, Iris (1935). *Leopardi. A Study in Solitude*. Oxford: Oxford University Press.

Perella, Nicholas James (1970). *Night and the Sublime in Giacomo Leopardi*. Berkeley: University of California Press.

Radcliff-Umstead, Douglas (1970). *Ugo Foscolo*. New York: Twayne.

Singh, G. (1964). *Leopardi and the Theory of Poetry*. Lexington: University of Kentucky Press.

Whitfield, J. H. (1954). *Giacomo Leopardi*. Oxford: Basil Blackwell.

Wordsworth, William (1950). *The Poetical Works*, ed. Thomas Hutchinson. London: Oxford University Press.

16
Spanish Romanticism

Derek Flitter

Spanish Romanticism has, self-reflexively throughout its own gestation and as mediated by successive generations of literary criticism, proved a form of cultural production acutely susceptible to what Iris M. Zavala has designated "interpretaciones antagónicas" (antagonistic interpretations), figuring in Spanish literary history beneath the sign of the paradox (Zavala 1994: 25). Contemporary overviews provide two larger definitions. On the one hand, as a broad consensus position for the bulk of the period between 1814 and the mid-century, there is the perception of a cohesive movement founded upon medievalism, cultural nationalism, and Christian spirituality and directed towards the restoration of a characteristically Spanish collective imagination against the unwarranted intrusions of a universalizing, rationalistic, and neoclassical Enlightenment. Opposed to this is a critical reaction occurring principally in the 1830s, one often of censure rather than of affirmation, that depicts Romanticism as an anarchical and subversive literature profoundly questioning those certainties upon which society had been traditionally based. Among the multifarious assessments generated since, there may be numbered some equally conflictive formulations. First is an essentialist view of Romanticism as cultural phenomenon that emphasizes the revival of typically Spanish imaginative practices inherited from the country's own medieval literature and its seventeenth-century Golden Age and a concomitant protest against neoclassical formalism. Secondly, there is an approach that seeks a metanarrative in the course of contemporary political events and underlines the significance, to the evolution of the movement, of the return to Spain in the 1830s of many of those writers exiled under the previous Absolutist order. Alternatively, we find a metaphysically orientated response that privileges that cluster of important works perceived as articulating a form of religious skepticism or cosmic rebellion. Emerging in the 1970s, meanwhile, came an identifiably Marxist interpretation, in which the literary works are the expression of states of mind commensurate with the conscious consolidation of a bourgeois revolution. Other commentators have concentrated on the determining presence of cultural coordinates at work interdependently in several related areas of intellectual history, identifying an integrated and constructive pattern of predominantly conservative and neo-Catholic thought at the nucleus of Spanish Romantic discourse. The reference list offered here provides for all of these mutually contradictory explications of Romanticism in Spain. My narrative of events, while endeavoring to communicate to the nonspecialist a thorough review of such divergent approaches, will at the same time postulate my own latest thinking, rooted in an apprehension of the symbology commonly found in the major creative works of the period.

The reception of Romantic aesthetics in Spain occurred in a relatively piecemeal fashion between 1814 and 1834, something not exactly surprising given the abrupt and occasionally violent changes marking the course of Spanish political history. The historical prelude to that process was the Peninsular War. The progressive Cadiz Constitution of 1812, debated at a time when that city, at the end of a long and narrow causeway, had been the only part of the Spanish mainland not subject to occupation by the French, had formalized aspirations towards representative freedoms and constitutional liberty, most controversially enshrining in its codification the sovereignty of the people. Such aspirations had been rapidly suppressed at the end of hostilities in 1814 by a young king previously incarcerated in France, Ferdinand VII, insistent upon a return to Absolutist forms of government. The "Cadiz liberals" as much as the pro-French intelligentsia (known as the *afrancesados* or "frenchified"), thus found themselves either exiled or imprisoned. An army-led rising in 1820 had ushered in a further three-year experiment in constitutional democracy, abruptly terminated by forces of the Holy Alliance. From 1823 until the death of Ferdinand 10 years later, Spain endured a period of trenchant Absolutism and political repression labeled the "ominous decade," exemplified by the policy of authoritarian control regulated by Calomarde, notorious Minister of the Interior. It was perhaps inevitable, within such a climate, that Romanticism should acquire a specifiable ideological dimension, and almost equally as inevitable that, in the wake of both the Napoleonic campaigns and the traditionalist tenor of Romantic theory as systematized in Germany, its entailments should come to be perceived as staunchly conservative.

Romanticism was, prior to 1833, a term generally understood as referring exclusively to that set of perspectives on literary history articulated by the brothers August Wilhelm and Friedrich Schlegel in their respective courses of lectures delivered in Vienna between 1808 and 1812 and rapidly disseminated across Europe. Literary works were classified as either ancient or modern, classical or Romantic, with other accompanying dualistic coordinates firmly attached: pagan and Christian respectively when it came to religious orientation, sensual and spiritual in terms of sentimental expression, collective and individual as divergent primary emphases of purpose and direction. Crucially in the Spanish case, a fundamental component of this pattern was the revival of interest in and acclaim for the work of Pedro Calderón de la Barca (1600-81), a dramatist viewed as comparable to Shakespeare and quintessential imaginative mediator of a precious Christian and Romantic tradition unfairly maligned by an uncomprehending neo-Classicism. It was a patriotic stimulus reinforced by the Schlegels' similarly positive reappraisal of Spain's ballad tradition, discarded by the Age of Reason as rude and imperfectly formed examples of popular superstition. Add to this the notion that the neoclassical mindset that had spurned Calderón and restored the prescriptive models of antiquity had come to be exemplified by a French Enlightenment culture which, in enthroning human reason and scientific inquiry, had more or less professed itself to be at best heterodox or, more likely, openly atheistic – one has but to read Friedrich Schlegel's own denunciation of Voltaire to be acutely aware of this – and the result was, within the Spain of the immediate postwar period, a righteous-minded affirmation of Romanticism as a salutary moral doctrine as much as a set of aesthetic principles. It was viewed as such by the expatriate German businessman and bibliophile who introduced Schlegelian theory to Spain, Johann Nikolaus Böhl von Faber, whose campaign to reinstate Calderón in the face of that dramatist's "frenchified" and unpatriotic detractors was launched in Cadiz itself in 1814. The set of attitudes obtaining in the 1820s are encapsulated in words of José Joaquín de Mora, the German's occasional sparring-partner in the long-running literary dispute carried on in the Cadiz and Madrid press, who, writing in the newspaper *El Constitucional* in 1820, affirmed that Liberalism was, within the range of political opinions, the equivalent of classical taste in that of literary ideas.

It was a formulation of "Romantic" that remained consistent and coherent, if limited in scope, throughout the decade of the 1820s, in the pages of the short-lived but influential Barcelona journal *El Europeo* in 1823-4, and, more notably still, in Agustín Durán's defining pronouncements on the theater in his *Discurso* of 1828, which made detailed and specific application of the ideas of those Durán designated erudite German critics (Flitter 1992: 34-8). Bearing in mind this degree of system-atization, it was next to impossible for Spanish critical opinion to comprehend the phenomenon of a "Romantic" writer who derived inspiration from the classics: Eugenio de Ochoa, in providing respective portraits of Classicist (designated by the pejorative Spanish word *clasiquista*) and Romantic for the literary journal *El Artista* in 1835, would still cling to the basic dualistic principle, contrasting the necessarily aged and decrepit Classicist who stuck to Aristotle and Boileau with the young and sensitive Romantic whose heart was set aflame by the Christian Middle Ages, gothic cathedrals, El Cid, and Calderón (Navas-Ruiz 1971: 129-31). Ultimately of far greater import is that it would be a long time before Spanish critical opinion and Spanish literary readers could countenance the idea that Romanticism might contain profound religious questioning or articulate a despairing and pessimistic outlook on life and the world. The Schlegelian Romantic doctrine – and *"doctrina"* was a word commonly used, usually in the plural, to describe Romantic ideas during the period in question – had become so broadly accepted and understood in the course of two decades that Romantic radicalism, when it made its appearance in Spain, and particularly on the Spanish stage under the influence of the new plays of Hugo and Dumas, was regarded as an adulteration, an unwarranted distortion of the movement's true meaning. Joaquín Roca y Cornet, a militant neo-Catholic, was to observe that the fault lay not with the literary school but in the abuses to which it had been subjected (Juretschke 1989: 56).

A new and more progressive approach to the ongoing literary debate was undoubtedly dynamized by the potential for significant political change after Ferdinand's death in 1833 and the renewed presence within the country of some of its liberal elder statesmen and intellectual heavyweights. Much has been made of the contribution of the returning political exiles to the literary and intellectual life of mid-1830s Spain, as men like Antonio Alcalá Galiano, Francisco Martínez de la Rosa (at one and the same time Prime Minister of Spain and author of the first genuinely Romantic drama to be performed in Madrid) and Angel Saavedra, Duque de Rivas, all resumed active roles in the public life of the country they had been forced to abandon under the régime of Ferdinand VII. Alcalá Galiano would contribute the preface to Rivas's 1834 narrative poem *El moro expósito,* a document that entirely eschewed "doctrinal" aesthetic positions, while Rivas's 1835 play *Don Álvaro, o la fuerza del sino,* would also, as we shall see, go some way towards breaking any perceived Romantic mold. A tendency towards more eclectic and less formulaic thinking is exemplified by the declaration of the influential journalist and political critic Mariano José de Larra in 1834 that the age itself demanded the profound spiritual questioning of a Byron or Lamartine (Larra 1960, I: 274). Larra, like Alcalá Galiano, desired a framework of literary ideas that would dispense with polarizing prescriptions such as the classical–Romantic dichotomy and produce instead a modern and forward-looking literature capable of engaging with contemporary problems in a bold and adventurous way whatever its formal or stylistic content.

Larra's own historical drama *Macías,* first performed on the Madrid stage in the autumn of 1834 although written two years earlier, is demonstrably the practical expression of its author's conceptual and structural independence of spirit. The play, while centering on the figure of the lovelorn eponymous troubadour customarily assigned the epithet of "*el enamorado*" (the man in love) in Spanish literary history, is clearly not intended to effect the diffuse poetic idealization of the Middle Ages that was so commonly a feature of Romantic aesthetics and increasingly a pre-eminent component part of creative literature. The Macías of Larra's drama is figured instead as a passionate lover who makes strident and insistent emotional demands entirely inconsonant with the poetic mystique of a courtly love that thrives without the aid of reciprocity. More than this, he incarnates an uncompromising form of social rebellion, audacious and genuinely revolutionary in its intensity and scope, that brooks no concessions to traditional morality and countenances no deviation from its own unswerving purpose. Like so many of his Romantic counterparts, Macías is definitively separated from his beloved Elvira on earth due to the selfish and cynical intriguing of others. What differentiates Larra's play is not so much its lack of a posited metaphysical solution so much as its robust discarding of any traditional discourse of the sacred and transcendent. Unpersuaded of the sufficiency of any putative eventual reward – reunion with Elvira in eternal life – Macías explicitly forswears the validity of her nuptial obligations to another man, the self-serving

Fernán Pérez; he then articulates a hugely energetic and forceful vision of love as the only valid life-principle that owes much to Rousseau in its figuration of natural law and at the same time reinforces his characterization as dauntless but inexorably doomed social rebel.

In terms of its stagecraft, too, *Macías* breaks with the parameters of Romantic theater as envisaged by the theorists. It is the only play commonly allocated a place within the canon of Spanish Romantic drama to observe quite rigorously the unities of time, place, and action: the plot encompasses a single day of January, 1406, beginning at dawn and closing at dusk; all of its scenes are enacted within the confines of the castle of Enrique de Villena, Grand Master of the Order of Calatrava; and dramatic interest focuses relentlessly upon the struggles of Macías himself against a social and moral order that inevitably destroys him. It is noteworthy also that in its settings the play invests little in the forms of metaphorical transposition that were to become such a hallmark of Romantic dramaturgy, the location of the action so often no more than the expression of evident corollaries of place and mood. In Larra's play, the emphasis is on more elusive but arguably more potent forms of symbolic suggestion, in the narrowly obsessive range of the protagonist's view of his own situation and in the various analogues of restriction and confinement to be found in his physical imprisonment and social marginalization.

In the crucial years between 1834 and 1837, it was to be the theater, and especially the Madrid stage, that was to be the crucible of aesthetic, ideological, and spiritual controversy. Indeed it would not be unfair to suggest that the fortunes and future direction of Spanish Romanticism were definitively resolved by the reception and interpretation of a handful of key texts, some original creations and others translations of the French dramas of Hugo and Dumas. What is increasingly plain is that concerted critical positioning as much as audience reaction seems to have exerted a determining effect.

The Spanish Romantic play which, more than any other, and almost since the time of its first performance in March 1835, has customarily been taken to embody the spirit of rebellion – both formal, in its dramatic structure, and metaphysical, in its despairing outlook – is the Duque de Rivas's *Don Álvaro, o la fuerza del sino*. The hero, son of a Spanish viceroy and an Inca princess, is widely admired in eighteenth-century Seville both for his personal qualities and for his glamorous accomplishments in areas such as bullfighting and swordplay; he is in love with and loved by Leonor, daughter of the Marqués de Calatrava, but his uncertain origins debar him as a respectable suitor. He believes that his *sino* or predestination to suffering thwarts him at every step. Surprised by Leonor's father when the couple are about to elope, Álvaro throws to the ground his pistol only for it to fire and mortally wound the Marqués. Fighting with the Spanish armies in Italy under an assumed name, he saves the life of Don Carlos, brother to Leonor, who has gone to Italy to track down his father's killer; when Carlos discovers Álvaro's true identity he insists upon a duel in which Álvaro unwillingly fights and kills his opponent. Álvaro then becomes a monk, only to be located by a second brother, Alfonso, whom Álvaro likewise reluctantly engages and fatally wounds in single combat. The hermit summoned from a nearby cave to administer the last rites to the dying Alfonso turns out to be none other than Leonor herself; Alfonso, in his final moments, kills his sister in cold blood, believing her still to be guilty of sinful love, while Álvaro, utterly desperate, hurls himself to his death from a crag in the midst of a terrific storm. The hair-raising finale, it should be noted, is heavily mitigated in this drama's more familiar form of Verdi's opera, where Álvaro simply exclaims "Morta!" at Leonora's death, the Guardiano seemingly correcting him with the phrase "Salita a Dio" (Gone on to God) before the curtain falls, and where Leonora's earlier words reprise those of Ravenswood in *Lucia di Lammermoor* in their anticipation of an uncomplicated heavenly reunion: "Lieta or poss'io precederti / alla promessa terra. La cesserà la guerra, / santo l'amor sarà' (I can happily go before you to that promised land, where warfare shall be at an end and love shall be ever holy).

Two moments in particular provide potent textual markers for the play's alleged cosmic rebellion: Álvaro's tremendous protest against God in Act III, scene iii, where he figures himself as a prisoner constantly tormented in life by a malignant jailer-God who delights in the suffering inflicted upon his hapless victim; and the climactic final scene, in which he figures himself as an anti-Christ, an emissary from Hell. Little wonder, then, that the play's protagonist has come to be seen as the archetype of the Romantic Revolution, an emblem of protest against a social order that has margin-alized him and a supernatural order that has relentlessly and mercilessly persecuted him. *Don Álvaro* rapidly came to be viewed as the most dangerously nihilistic product of the Spanish Romantic stage, the vehicle for a despairing personal philosophy that ruled out any possibility of religious consolation.

While *Don Álvaro* initially bewildered audiences unprepared for the audacity of its stagecraft and the intensity of its expression, much greater popular success was achieved by a young Spanish playwright with a drama that was his first to be staged: *El trovador*, by Antonio García Gutiérrez, is far better known for its adaptation to Italian grand opera, but its favorable reception from the time of its première in March 1836 was unparalleled in Spanish Romantic theater. Manrique, the eponymous troubadour, is represented, unlike Larra's Macías, with all of the mystique reserved in the Romantic mind for the medieval chivalric lover, the lute upon which he accompanies his own songs being an inseparable component of his dramatic persona. Even more so than his predecessor, however, Manrique makes implacable emotional demands upon his lover Leonor, urging and eventually persuading her to break her religious vows and flee with him from the convent where she has sought refuge. Believing herself to be irreparably damned for this action, she takes poison as a deliberate stratagem to bring about his later release from prison, promising herself in return to the rival suitor who has imprisoned the troubadour. This man, Nuño, has no intention of keeping his own side of the bargain, however, and has Manrique executed. Only as the axe falls is the troubadour's real identity finally disclosed: Manrique is brother to Nuño, snatched from his cradle by the gipsy woman Azucena and brought up as her own son; with Manrique's death Azucena's mother, burned at the stake as a witch on the orders of Nuño's father, is finally avenged.

Last in the triumvirate of plays generally seen as the foremost contributions to original Spanish drama of this turbulent period is Juan Eugenio Hartzenbusch's *Los amantes de Teruel*, a work based upon one of medieval Spain's best-known legends. The story of Diego Marsilla and Isabel Segura has much in common with that invented by Walter Scott for Edgar Ravenswood and Lucy Ashton in *The Bride of Lammermoor*, and even more so with Donizetti's operatic version, *Lucia di Lammermoor*, premièred in Naples in 1835. Marsilla is born into a family of impeccable pedigree that has fallen upon hard times; in order to win the hand of Isabel, he is given six years to make his fortune. In his absence, Isabel is falsely told of his desertion and death and, in order to protect the reputation of her mother, threatened with the release of compromising letters, she agrees to marry the blackmailer, Rodrigo Azagra. When Azagra desists, Isabel nonetheless goes through with the wedding, feeling herself bereft after what she believes to be the loss of Marsilla; he, however, returns to Teruel to claim her, just minutes too late to prevent the ceremony. Marsilla, unable to accept that Isabel is definitively bound to another, dies on stage of a broken heart, while Isabel swiftly follows him in the play's final moments.

In all of these plays a decisive dramatic feature, it is often claimed, is the profound connection between love and death, one that posits love as the true existential principle and which, when that love is doomed, consigns the lovers to necessary despair and destruction. Nevertheless, the shared symbological framework of these plays might be seen to lead us in a markedly different direction. For example, nothing definitively discounts an interpretation of Rivas's play as a dramatization of the consequences, albeit disproportionate in their catastrophic effect, of a specifiable weakness or moral deficiency on the part of its protagonist. Rivas was, for the first 15 years of his writing career, an author of neoclassical tastes, and not without reason have critics drawn attention to the Aristotelian entailments of this play. The force of destiny of the title may function as an allusion, as then exemplified by the action, to the psychological disposition of a given individual to believe in astrology, in the predestination of human lives by the stars, and thus to ascribe the reverses of fortune habitually suffered in the course of an individual life to an agency of fate outside the control of the human will rather than to any human frailty, whatever the degree to which personal choice has informed a given outcome. One of the literary discourses most acutely possessed of symbolic content and resonance, a discourse that relies upon the efficacy of symbolic loading to project a desired immediacy and for which the phenomenological distance that inevitably accompanies metaphysical abstraction is a particular danger, is the eschatological discourse of Revelation. Clandestinely entering the Calatrava family mansion, Álvaro asks whether the sacred heavens are at last to reward his trials with an eternal crown (Rivas 1994: 96), foreseeing eternal happiness thanks to the beneficent intervention of a providential God. What he in effect does, in characteristically Romantic fashion, is to effect a transposition of the language of eschatology out of the discourse of religion and into that of love. He attributes to love a dimension not just habitually corresponding to religious discourse but also customarily reserved, within that discourse, for Last Things; what Don Álvaro designates a "corona eterna" is a crown of human love bestowed upon him by marriage with Leonor, a sacralization of Romantic passion, whereas in Revelation the crown is gained as recompense for enduring with unswerving faith the tribulations of this world (Revelation 2: 10). Don Álvaro perceives a final judgment to result either in the attainment of Romantic love in its reciprocity (salvation) or else in its lack (damnation). When, in Act IV, he reaches the point of lamenting his having ever known Leonor, his "-Hora de maldición, aciaga hora!" (What accursed day, what bitter hour!; Rivas 1994: 164) inevitably calls to mind the penitential text of the *Dies irae, dies illa* that foresees the terrors of the hour of Apocalypse, reinforcing the rhetorical connection between Don Álvaro's professed love for Leonor and his eventual death.

Even the death of the Marqués may be read in this light. Álvaro has previously charged and cocked his gun, so that we are not dealing unequivocally with a tragic accident but an unforeseen consequence of an act of free will. Álvaro's later metaphorization of life in the world and its vicissitudes as a preordained imprisonment is also present in the mystic discourse of the monk of Patmos, but now Álvaro, prisoner to the belief that he is ill-starred and persecuted, leads us to imagine a lifelong sentence from which a merciless guardian will countenance no release. Unable to bear his pain, his period of trial, with Christian resignation, Don Álvaro protests against a malign God who treats him as a mere plaything. Leonor's reaction to the tragedy is very different. She reaches the Convento de los Ángeles as a place of ultimate refuge, professing remorse and a desire to atone for her previous conduct. Leonor's language reveals a profound piety, irresistibly calling to mind the informing paradigm of Job. In her dialogue with the Padre Guardián in Act II, Scene vii, he assures her that all the tribulations of this passing world are fleeting and always end in release (Rivas 1994: 119-20).

In the profound questioning of Don Álvaro, there are glimpses of the ultimate consequences of rebellion against this system on the part of humanity. The only remedy left to Don Álvaro, sunk in despair, is suicide, enacted as one final theatrical gesture in which he curses the whole of the created world and calls down its apocalyptic destruction. The choir of monks, meanwhile, implores divine mercy to the accompaniment of the offstage chanting of the *Miserere*. This last, the penitential Psalm 51, articulates utter human dependency upon God and an acknowledgement on the part of the individual sinner that the only response to suffering is to trust in the deity's ultimate goodness. What alternative was left to a generation like that of the Duque de Rivas, seemingly born to instability and prone to disaster in an age increasingly imprinted with the erosion of faith, and experiencing social, political, and metaphysical turmoil? What was one to do if one was not persuaded that historical events responded to a providential plan, to an ultimately beneficent and meaningful divinely ordained pattern? The answer, in the Spanish context, was memorably enunciated in Larra's much quoted review of Dumas's *Antony*: this play, he wrote, was the cry uttered by the forefront of humanity, a cry of despair upon finding only chaos and nothingness at the end of its journey (Larra 1960, II: 247). This is the cry voiced by Don Álvaro in Rivas's drama of the previous year: "¡Húndase el cielo! ¡Perezca la raza humana! ¡Exterminio! ¡Destrucción!" (Let the heavens collapse! Let the human race perish! Extermination! Destruction!; Rivas 1994: 189). He heralds Armageddon, figuring himself as the beast that emerges from the pit at the end of all things. After the first Spanish performance of *Antony*, *Don Álvaro* itself became the object of increasingly negative criticism; Enrique Gil y Carrasco, for example, made reference to the play's despairing and skeptical philosophy, asserting that it lacked any constructive social purpose (Gil y Carrasco 1954: 479). What is not in dispute is that *Don Álvaro* provides us with a terrifying intimation of the moral incoherence of the world as it comes to be conceived by the play's protagonist. Nonetheless, the eschatological components present in the symbolic framework allow us at least to suspect that the work was conceived as a cautionary drama, counseling against the promptings of despair, and that its spectacular theatricality was calculated to intensify both the effectiveness and the immediacy of its warning; this, after all, is how Rivas's close friend Alcalá Galiano saw it and explained it at the time of its first performance.

A similar symbolic framework dominates the important monologue of Isabel Segura in Act V of Hartzenbusch's play. While Marsilla has attributed his unhappiness to divine malevolence in lines that more or less precisely recreate the furious protest of Rivas's Don Álvaro, Isabel enters into a compassionate inner dialogue with a merciful God, her rhetoric belonging unquestionably to the discourse of Christian Stoicism: "fenecido/ el tiempo de prueba/[. . .] nos luce la aurora/de la recompensa" (our time of trial now ended, there dawns the light of our reward; Hartzenbusch 1971: 142). The speech contains a veritable roll-call of the salient components of Stoicism as applied to the Christian faith: suffering in life as a trial, a period of tribulation that may be overcome by faith so that the soul attains its divine reward. In the case of Hartzenbusch's play, it is hardly surprising that a thirteenth-century woman of gentle birth should reveal an intimate reliance on religious faith at such a critical moment in her life. On an historical plane, meanwhile, it was the conscious application of just such a philosophy which, according to the Enlightenment-entailed emphases of nineteenth-century Spanish liberalism, had enabled the Catholic church to perpetuate the moral enslavement of the people. We ought not to forget that Rivas's play has as its historical setting the middle of the eighteenth century, the historical moment of the preparation of the great *Encyclopédie* of Diderot and D'Alembert.

Perhaps unexpectedly so, it is in *El trovador* that the transposition of key symbols from the discourse of eschatology into that of human love reaches its furthest consequences. Act III, scene iv, in which the stage set irresistibly suggests a religious painting with Leonor at the prayer-desk in her simple convent cell, sees the heroine explicitly renounce her role as bride of Christ in favor of her love for the troubadour Manrique, confessing the falseness of her religious vows and their displacement; her mind, she says in this crucial monologue, "se extasiaba/ en la imagen de un mortal" (found ecstasy in the image of a mortal man; García Gutiérrez 1997: 150). Manrique, on his arrival, insists that Leonor had been unfaithful to him rather than to God, using the emphatic adjective *"perjura,"* and, at the end of a tense dialogue, Leonor abandons herself to this Romantic passion in the full realization of its ultimate consequences. Recreating the same metaphor used by Don Álvaro immediately prior to his suicide, she protests: "mira el abismo/bajo mis pies abierto; no pretendas/ precipitarme en él" (look at the abyss that lies open beneath my feet; do not strive to hurl me into it; García Gutiérrez 1997: 155). While, in Act IV, scene v, Leonor professes a definitive view of this perspective on recognizing that her bond with Manrique is a "nudo de maldición que allá en su trono/enojado maldice un Dios terrible" (accursed bond for which yonder, on His throne, a terrible God will curse us; García Gutiérrez 1997: 167). This sacrilization of human love is best emblematized, meanwhile, in Act V, scene vii, in Manrique's lament for Leonor's death, its iconography unmistakable as the troubadour asks for a crown of flowers to place on her brow: "será aureola luciente, / será diadema de amores" (it shall be a gleaming halo, a diadem of love; García Gutiérrez 1997: 195). Manrique invests the dead Leonor with the visual characteristics of an image of the Blessed Virgin, in what is possibly the pivotal moment in Spanish Romantic theatre.

Yet, unfortunately as far as the possible realization of Larra's vision of a new literature was concerned, his consistent demands for a fresh kind of writing coincided with the appearance within Spain of the French Romantic drama of Hugo and Dumas. The plays of Dumas in particular had been briefed against even before their first Spanish staging, and by figures as commanding of respect as the Catholic priest and political moderate Alberto Lista. Early in 1834 Lista had launched a furious attack upon the French dramatists, in which he distinguished between two distinct Romantic currents: on the one hand, Schlegelian historical Romanticism, with its reassuring medieval and Christian associations; on the other, a newly emergent "monstrous" literature: dramatic spectacle reduced to a series of unconnected sketches, moral decency trodden underfoot in descriptions of adulterous love and wickedness which the author attempted by all means to make interesting; frenzied language; in short, the natural order of things entirely unhinged. That, according to Lista, was what was now being called Romanticism (Flitter 1992: 77-8). As far as *Antony* was concerned, Larra himself would go a long way towards concurring in Lista's judgment; aghast at the spectacle of social disorder personified in *Antony*, in both literary and philosophical terms, he shuddered at the "great immorality" of a piece that possessed too many morbid attractions (Larra 1960, II: 248).

We should not find it surprising that the vogue of a new and radical brand of Romanticism was short-lived, particularly in the theater, where the emphasis swiftly came to be upon the adaptation of Spain's existing Golden-Age themes and situations to the demands of the nineteenth-century stage; and negative judgments of Romantic radicalism usually ascribed "subversive" tendencies to the nefarious inspiration of France. As David Gies has pointedly reminded us in summing up the conflicts, literary and otherwise, of the 1830s, it was no longer a question to be decided between neo-Classicism and Romanticism but of one between "el romanticismo benévolo" (a benevolent Romanticism) and a profoundly different "romanticismo exagerado, degradado, execrado" (exaggerated, degraded, execrated Romanticism; Gies 1989: 15). Leonardo Romero Tobar has likewise drawn attention to the rejection of "la tendencia fatalista" (the fatalistic tendency) detected in French Romanticism by a range of critics – Lista, Juan Donoso Cortés, José María Quadrado, and others – who nevertheless adopted the essential postulates of Schlegelian historical Romanticism (Romero Tobar 1994: 34). So far as Spanish Romanticism had an ideology, as I have painstakingly sought to show elsewhere (Flitter 1992, 2000), it was a traditionalist, restorative, and Catholic ideology. The neo-Catholic philosopher and theologian Jaime Balmes is a case in point: commenting on his 1842 essay "De la originalidad," Hans Juretschke states that the piece reproduces in its essence the entire Romantic aesthetic; as he concludes: "En su credo estético, Balmes es romántico" (In his aesthetic credo, Balmes is a Romantic; Juretschke 1989: 194).

So what are we to make of the critical commonplace that the returning political exiles brought Romanticism to Spain as part of their baggage? This last metaphor, it should be noted, was employed by Frederick Courtney Tarr as long ago as 1939 in his argument against just such a supposition; the idea has, however, continued to enjoy common currency thanks to the longevity of the assumption, most memorably voiced by Victor Hugo, that "true" Romanticism is by definition liberal and/or revolutionary. Critics favoring this definition, and especially those identified by Philip Silver (1997) as engaging in a transferential or politically committed narrative of the period, have then been able to emplot their respective accounts as romance. Within this scenario, those liberals forced into exile during the "ominous decade" of Absolutist rule return from more enlightened climes with a bright new literary and political vision to restore hope to a sadly benighted nation. Hence even an account as recent as that of Diego Martínez Torrón is founded upon a transparent metanarrative or "magnífica novela" (magnificent novel; Martínez Torrón 1993). Its application involves of course a calculated downplaying of the role of those literary men responsible for the introduction into Spain of German theories of Romanticism in the 1820s. These writers are customarily either vilified or excluded: Vicente Llorens' captious treatment of Böhl, for whom, he states, the Holy Inquisition would have seemed dangerously subversive, is a case in point (Llorens 1979: 354).

The future direction of Romanticism in Spain, by any objective criteria, was to depend more upon the reception, albeit in a changed intellectual climate, of new philosophical and aesthetic prescriptions by those Spanish writers who had either continued to reside in Spain during the "ominous decade" or else who had been too young actively to participate in or even to remember the events of the Peninsular War or the earlier constitutional parliament of 1820-3. Ultimately, the case for a new and definitive orientation of Spanish Romanticism provided by the returning exiled liberals rests upon the transforming impact of the plays by Martínez de la Rosa and the Duque de Rivas, premièred respectively in 1834 and 1835; of the poetry of José de Espronceda; and, in terms of ideas, of Alcalá Galiano's prologue to *El moro expósito*. Concerning the theater, Ermanno Caldera and David Gies have cautioned against any notion of an abrupt change in dramatic practice fueled by the French experience.

Caldera argues that Romanticism was not for Spain merely an injection of foreign motifs, or at least that such foreign-inspired features were no more than a catalyst which had energized a process initiated some time before (Caldera 1988: 450). Gies, approvingly citing this passage, sums up by stating that "Romantic drama in Spain remains incomprehensible if we ignore its immediate indigenous history" (Gies 1994: 97). It might be added that neither Martínez de la Rosa nor Rivas wrote anything of the kind again, that *Don Álvaro* aroused principally bewilderment and was not frequently performed, and that the French Romantic drama that is often taken to have inspired the two plays, a form of drama lambasted by Lista before any such works had appeared on the Spanish stage, was virulently rejected by a large body of critical opinion and its vogue short-lived. In contrast, native-inspired Romantic drama in the hands of Hartzenbusch, José Zorrilla, Antonio Gil y Zárate, and others proved popular and successful with critics and audiences alike well into the 1840s. In poetry, the tide too turned against lurid excess in favor of the kind of restorative, nationalistic verse exemplified by Zorrilla (Flitter 1993); in literary criticism, Alcalá Galiano's position gained little currency, never achieving anything approaching the status and influence of Durán's much earlier *Discurso*, a work that, if we pay attention to period preferences and literary orientation, might much more aptly be regarded as the definitive manifesto of Spanish Romanticism. Alonso Seoane recapitulates in the following way: although there is room for considerable nuancing, what was a passing phase was the defining impact of a radical Romanticism containing a worldview of religious skepticism; it was the earlier Schlegelian model that came to be considered "único y auténtico 'romanticismo' " (the only authentic Romanticism; Alonso Seoane 1993: 75-6).

After Larra's death in February 1837, Romantic radicalism was associated most potently with the poetry of Espronceda, who has always been closely linked with Byron. For Enrique Piñeyro, an early historian of Spanish Romanticism, Espronceda's poetry of combative protest went to the very heart of the new art in its unrelenting and eloquent struggle against both the privations and the violent reactions of its age (Churchman 1909: 17). Espronceda's "Canción del pirata" irresistibly reminds us of Byron's corsair, and generally embodies Churchman's description of Byronic heroes as men freed from all law, human or divine, as noble rebels who "personify anarchic individualism, unchained natural forces" (Churchman 1909: 60). Not just in its narrative extent, however, but also in the sheer ferocity of its lyricism and in the strength of its air of existential rebellion, it is *El estudiante de Salamanca* that, amongst Espronceda's works, comes closest of all to recreating Byronic protest. The student himself, Félix de Montemar, undoubtedly possesses the requisite *frisson* of evil and there is too the suggestion of his having committed some mysterious heinous crime. As Cardwell shrewdly notes, however, Montemar's violent death is all the more striking inasmuch as a common theme of Espronceda's sources had been renunciation of a life of debauchery and sin for one of penitence and contrition; all of those stories upon which the poem is founded are moral in tone and designed to warn and edify (Cardwell 1991: 12). The blackguard student who nonchalantly fights duels and heartlessly seduces and abandons women, seemingly destined for final repentance if the source texts are to be respected, in Espronceda's radical rewriting refuses to the last to renounce his titanic activity, something which locates him with Faust, Manfred, or Cain rather than with his Spanish antecedents (Cardwell 1991: 13, 17).

This lack of a shaping religious context means that Espronceda's political rebellion is in essence a metaphysical revolt. He writes against the arguments of Christian revelation and moral example "not by refuting them but by turning them inside out or inverting them. He is working against the ideologies (and the authority invested in those ideologies) of Christian teaching and Catholic society whose structures are rooted in revealed religion and moral precept" (Cardwell 1988; Cardwell 1991: 27). Within such a frame, Montemar's death is underwritten by none of the eschatology of the Counter-Reformation, it contains no charge of mortal sin and the lack of spiritual preparedness, no assertion of purgation and ultimate justice, no presupposition of an ultimately benevolent God. In the face of loss of faith, we cannot but assert our rebellious individuality, and henceforth move from passive acceptance to active revolt (Cardwell 1991: 27-8). This places Espronceda's poem at a significant remove even from some of those more contentious examples of original Spanish Romantic drama.

The lack of concerted critical outrage at what must have been the acutely apparent nihilism of *El estudiante de Salamanca* can be explained by a number of significant factors. First, the narrative description of the poem, its settings, could very evidently have been read as the product of the poetic sublime as long practiced and understood in Spain. Secondly, it was transparently the case that, whatever the force of its radically altered ending, Espronceda's text was manifestly using recognizable Spanish sources: almost all charges of unwarrantable radicalism leveled against Romantic texts presupposed the unwary imitation, by a Spanish writer, of a foreign original (*Don Álvaro*, for example, had been conceived and drafted during its author's political exile in France). Thirdly, in a society that was very predominantly devout, Montemar's death might appear as merely the justifiable retribution meted out to a notorious wrongdoer: most Spanish literary readers would surely have recalled the employment by Calderón of a skeleton clothed as a mysterious and promisingly attractive woman in *El mágico prodigioso*, complete with the textually explicit moral that all the pleasures of this mortal world are transient. We might add that the elusiveness of its temporal setting and its *capa y espada*, or cloak and dagger, features would almost certainly have placed the events of the poem at a reassuring phenomenological distance, stripping it of the potency of contemporary immediacy, which is what seems to have been most feared of all. The recreation of a legendary story rooted in past tradition was never likely to shock Spanish susceptibilities as profoundly as an *Antony*.

Nevertheless, by the time Espronceda's close friend Enrique Gil y Carrasco came to review his collected volume of poetry in the weekly *Semanario Pintoresco Español* in 1840, times had changed incalculably from the last years of the 1820s. What could be figured as sublimely passionate and mysterious had, a decade later, assumed a far more threatening outlook: boundless doubt, uncertainty, and sorrow had clouded the mirror of the soul, resulting in violent inner conflict and upheaval. Out of all this stemmed the vacillating, ill-defined, and, to a degree, contradictory nature of contemporary imaginative writing; the "religious sadness" of Milton and Luis de León had been replaced by the "inconsolable skepticism" of Childe Harold and the frenzied, permanently unsatisfied passion of Chateaubriand's René (Navas-Ruiz 1971: 226-7). Gil looked at Espronceda's Ossianic poem "Oscar y Malvina" and saw an admirable recreation of the dreamlike impassioned melancholy that underpinned the work of the Celtic bard (Navas-Ruiz 1971: 229). The "Canciones" inevitably fare less well: the Spanish poet's hangman and condemned criminal belonged, as Gil expressed it, to the bitter, sardonic, and disconsolate school of Byron; they were products of a sorrowful and solitary muse that despised all consolation and wallowed in its own suffering (Navas-Ruiz 1971: 233). "A Jarifa" he regards as a quintessential example of a skeptical and macabre verse, bereft of faith, stripped of all hope but rich in disillusion and sorrow, verse that rends the heart asunder rather than move it to feeling (Navas-Ruiz 1971: 237).

It is both illuminating and instructive to counterpoint some of this surprisingly sharp critique – Enrique Gil was a dear friend of Espronceda and would give an emotional address at the latter's graveside in 1842 – with the approbation that Gil had accorded in the previous year to the early poetry of Zorrilla. Although drawing attention to what he regarded as significant defects of style and construction, Enrique Gil lauded the "philosophical intention" of the young Zorrilla, which he summarized as the aim of raising up and rejuvenating Spain's poetic nationhood, of plucking traditions out of the dust, and of restoring, to all possible degree, that elevated knightly spirit which the nation had lost together with the glories that sustained it but whose seed still rested in sensitive hearts (Navas-Ruiz 1971: 224).

Zorrilla, who acquired celebrity overnight after reading out one of his earliest compositions at Larra's graveside to an enthralled audience of the literary men of the day, readily committed himself to this emotional and reassuring appeal to national traditions (Flitter 1993), which represented the best if not only real guarantor of public success, something that most certainly did not reside in any air of doubt and mocking speculation. Nicomedes-Pastor Díaz's words in prefacing Zorrilla's first published volume of poetry are intimately revealing of the imprint that the latter's work rapidly acquired. His poems, wrote Díaz, captured a medieval grandeur lost to the present age, and effectively contrasted the cold, ignoble, and ridiculous qualities of the present era with the magnificence, solemnity, and sublimity inherent in recollections of the age of religion and chivalry (Díaz 1969, I: 112). In the preface to his second volume of poems, published in 1838, we find Zorrilla's own celebrated proclamation of "la patria en que nací y la religión en que vivo. Español, he buscado en nuestro suelo mis inspiraciones. Cristiano, he creído que mi religión encierra más poesía que el paganismo" (the country into which I was born and the religion that I live and breathe. As a Spaniard, I have sought my inspiration in our own soil. As a Christian, I have always believed my own religion to contain more poetry than paganism; Alonso Cortés 1943: 204). Summoned to the stage after the first performance of his early play *Cada cual con su razón*, Zorrilla would make his oft-quoted scathing reference to the "monstruosos abortos de la elegante corte de Francia" (monstrous abortions of the elegant French court) and declare his preference for models nearer to the native Spanish tradition than to Hernani or Lucrezia Borgia (Zorrilla 1943, II: 2207). Finally, the verse prologue to his *Cantos del trovador* of 1840-1 professed: "Lejos de mí la historia tentadora / de ajena tierra y religión profana. / Mi voz, mi corazón, mi fantasía, / la gloria cantan de la patria mía" (Away, away, alluring tales of strange realms and pagan faith. My voice, my heart and my poetic fantasy shall sing the glories of my own land; Alonso Cortés 1943: 258). The imaginative vision of Zorrilla's verse narratives and historical dramas, like the comparable literary creations of so many of his contemporaries, tallies with the Romantic prescriptions of the broader medieval revival, while his *Don Juan Tenorio* exemplifies Spain's fundamentally conservative Romanticism in its sources, traditions, outlook, and conceptual pattern.

Zorrilla's Romantic version of the story of Don Juan, brought to the stage in 1844, sets the seal upon the trajectory of Spanish Romanticism away from radical questioning and towards essential processes of reassurance. Unlike his predecessors, Zorrilla has the notorious seducer redeemed and saved by the love of the innocent and virtuous Doña Inés, in some of the most famous scenes in the history of the Spanish stage. There is a parallel with some of the earlier texts, particularly with *Don Álvaro*, in Zorrilla's development of the idea of personal responsibility. In the first part of the play, Don Juan reacts in the face of provocation and kills both his principal adversary and the father of the woman he wishes to marry, the latter in cold blood, unable to maintain the new-found goodness and humility that have been inspired in him by Romantic love for Doña Inés. He first attempts to justify his actions, declaiming "Llamé al cielo y no me oyó" (I called out to Heaven and Heaven did not hear me). When Don Juan then seeks to blame God for his actions in professing "de mis pasos en la tierra / responda el cielo y no yo" (let Heaven, not I, answer for my steps on earth; Zorrilla 1988: 179), it is hard not to think of a connection between Zorrilla's play and the earlier one by Rivas; a common factor here lies in their protagonists' refusal to take responsibility for the results of their actions. In Act IV of Rivas's drama Don Álvaro reiterates the point in referring to "la desgracia inevitable de que no fui yo culpable" (the inevitable tragedy for which I was not responsible; Rivas 1994: 152). In order for the *deus ex machina* resolution of Zorrilla's play to function (the spirit of the dead Inés appears at the very last moment, so that Don Juan can repent when one last grain of sand is left in the hourglass that represents his life draining away, and as the statue of the dead Comendador famously takes him by the hand to lead him to Hell), it is indispensable that Don Juan first admit personal responsibility: hence when he returns to Seville five years later in the second part of the play and sees the funerary statue of Inés he rebukes himself with the words "por mi mal no respira" (on account of my wickedness she breathes no more; Zorrilla 1988: 191). The uncomplicated metaphysical sublimation of love is figured at the very end of Zorrilla's drama, albeit in the most mawkish terms, in a way that is reminiscent of Wagner's *The Flying*

Dutchman of the previous year, in a process of transfiguration in the sky: Inés redeems Juan just as Senta redeems the Dutchman.

As Jean-Louis Picoche has averred, the salient constant features of Spanish Romanticism were thus its supernatural emphasis and its dynamically intense patriotism (Picoche 1978: 156). Indeed, across an enormously wide area of intellectual enquiry, historical Romanticism as first formulated in Germany enjoyed almost unchallenged pre-eminence in the Spain of the first half of the nineteenth century (Herrero 1978: 354). Philip Silver inclines even to extend the mandate into the second half of the century, tracing the dissemination of a conservative literary Romanticism as "a nationalistic politico-literary ideology throughout the nineteenth century" (Silver 1997: 3). This last phrase is indicative of the calculated uses of Romantic theory in works that often sought, as José Escobar put it, to displace contemporary sociopolitical concerns onto a transcendent imaginative plane (Escobar 1989: 322). Spanish Romanticism therefore contains, at its core, a series of mediated reflections upon the ideological and existential concerns of nineteenth-century humanity, albeit those concerns are customarily transposed onto national themes, legends, and traditions of an earlier age. It is perhaps ironic that a nation should forge its own imaginative paradigm out of a vision that is translated from abroad, but Spanish writers expressly adapted that vision to the demands of their own situation at a conflictive and pivotal moment in their country's history.

REFERENCES AND FURTHER READING

Alonso Cortés, Narciso (1943). *Zorrilla, su vida y sus obras.* Valladolid: Diputación.

Alonso Seoane, María José (1993). "Introducción." In Francisco Martínez de la Rosa, *La conjuración de Venecia, año de 1310.* Madrid: Cátedra.

Caldera, Ermanno (1988). "El teatro en el siglo XIX." In José María Díez Borque (ed.), *Historia del teatro en España. II. Siglos XVIII y XIX.* Madrid: Taurus, pp. 377-624.

Cardwell, Richard (1988). "Byron: Text and Counter Text." *Byron and Europe,* Special issue *Renaissance and Modern Studies,* 32: 6-23.

Cardwell, Richard (1991). "Introduction." In *José de Espronceda, The Student of Salamanca/El estudiante de Salamanca,* trans. C. K. Davies. Warminster, UK: Aris & Phillips.

Churchman, Philip (1909). "Byron and Espronceda." *Revue Hispanique,* 20: 5-210.

Díaz, Nicomedes-Pastor (1969). *Obras completas de don Nicomedes-Pastor Díaz,* ed. José María Castro y Calvo, 3 vols. Madrid: Rivadeneyra.

Escobar, José (1989). "Romanticismo y revolución." In David T. Gies (ed.), *El romanticismo.* Madrid: Taurus, pp. 320-35.

Flitter, Derek (1992). *Spanish Romantic Literary Theory and Criticism.* Cambridge, UK: Cambridge University Press.

Flitter, Derek (1993). "Zorrilla, the Critics and the Direction of Spanish Romanticism." In Richard A. Cardwell and Ricardo Landeira (eds.), *José Zorrilla: 1893-1993. Centennial Readings.* Nottingham, UK: University of Nottingham Monographs in the Humanities, 1-15.

Flitter, Derek (2000). "Ideological Uses of Romantic Theory in Spain." In Carol Tully (ed.), *Romantik and Romance: Cultural Interanimation in European Romanticism.* Glasgow: Strathclyde Modern Language Studies 4, pp. 79-107.

García Gutiérrez, Antonio (1997). *El trovador,* ed. Carlos Ruiz Silva. Madrid: Cátedra.

Gies, David T. (ed.) (1989). *El romanticismo.* Madrid: Taurus.

Gies, David T. (1994). *The Theatre in Nineteenth-Century Spain*. Cambridge, UK: Cambridge University Press.

Gil y Carrasco, Enrique (1954). *Obras completas de don Enrique Gil y Carrasco*, ed. Jorge Campos. Madrid: Rivadeneyra.

Hartzenbusch, Juan Eugenio (1971). *Los amantes de Teruel*, ed. Salvador García Castañeda. Madrid: Castalia.

Herrero, Javier (1978). "El naranjo romántico: esencia del costumbrismo." *Hispanic Review*, 46: 343-54.

Juretschke, Hans (1989). "El problema de los orígenes del romanticismo español." In Hans Juretschke (ed.), *Historia de España Menéndez Pidal. XXXV: La época del romanticismo (1808-1874). Vol. I: Orígenes, religión, filosofía, ciencia*. Madrid: Espasa-Calpe.

Larra, Mariano José de (1960). *Obras de D. Mariano José de Larra (Fígaro)*, ed. Carlos Seco Serrano, 5 vols. Madrid: Rivadeneyra.

Llorens, Vicente (1979). *El romanticismo español*. Madrid: Castalia.

Martínez Torrón, Diego (1993). *El alba del romanticismo español*. Seville: Alfar/Universidad de Córdoba.

Navas-Ruiz, Ricardo (1971). *El romanticismo español. Documentos*. Salamanca: Anaya.

Picoche, Jean Louis (1978). *Un romántico español: Enrique Gil y Carrasco*. Madrid: Gredos.

Rivas, Angel Saavedra, duque de (1994). *Don Álvaro o la fuerza del sino*, ed. Miguel Ángel Lama, introduction Ermanno Caldera. Barcelona: Crítica.

Romero Tobar, Leonardo (1994). *Panorama crítico del romanticismo español*. Madrid: Castalia.

Silver, Philip (1997). *Ruin and Restitution. Reinterpreting Romanticism in Spain*. Liverpool: Liverpool University Press.

Tarr, Frederick Courtney (1939). "Romanticism in Spain and Spanish Romanticism: A Critical Survey." *Bulletin of Spanish Studies* 16: 3-37.

Zavala, Iris M. (ed.) (1994). *Romanticismo y realismo. Primer suplemento*, vol. 5/1 of *Historia y crítica de la literatura española*, ed. Francisco Rico. Barcelona: Crítica.

Zorrilla, José (1943). *Obras completas*, ed. Narciso Alonso Cortés, 2 vols. Valladolid: Diputación.

Zorrilla, José (1988). *Don Juan Tenorio*, ed. Aniano Peña, Madrid: Cátedra.

17

Pushkin and Romanticism

Michael Basker

Aleksandr Sergeevich Pushkin (1799-1837) enjoys an unassailable reputation, not only as the greatest writer of the Romantic era in Russia (the "Pushkin period," as it is often known), but as Russia's greatest national poet and the protean source of virtually everything of significance in the Russian literature to follow. His first, precocious success in 1820 coincided with the eventual and thorough consolidation of Romanticism – which, like literary movements before and since, had come to Russia late: after a protracted period of Sentimentalism (pre-Romanticism) that had coexisted alongside neo-Classicism since the 1770s, it had been slowly established over the previous decade and a half, primarily thorough the meditative elegies and epistles, literary ballads and songs of V. A. Zhukovksii and the elegies of Konstantin Batiushkov. It reached its peak in the 1820s, and came to an effective end with the premature deaths of Pushkin and, four years later, a second figure of unquestionable genius, Mikhail Lermontov. By a curious – or symptomatic – coincidence, both were killed in duels, in which ill-founded rumor has persistently sought to implicate imperial authority, in 1837 and 1841, at the respective ages of 37 and 26. The early 1840s saw such major vestiges of Romantic writing in Russia as F. I. Tiutchev's continuing metaphysical lyricism, V. F. Odoevskii's *Russian Nights* (1844), and N. V. Gogol's evocations of the phantasmagoric metropolis in *The Portrait* and *The Overcoat*. It is notable, however, that these last of Gogol's five "Petersburg tales" appeared in the same year as Part I of his *Dead Souls* (1842). This was the period of the rise of Russian Realism, the prelude to the golden age of the Russian novel.

Despite Pushkin's centrality to a period which is labeled the Age of Pushkin as readily as the Age of Romanticism, his own allegiance to Romantic precepts was rarely and only briefly unalloyed. Particularly in Russian criticism, his artistic evolution is typically represented as a path from neo-Classicism through Romanticism to Realism. In truth, though, the progression is far from clear. Pushkin, as we shall see, was perennially capable of blurring distinctions and transcending lines of demarcation. He had an ability to entertain contrarieties which may seem

Romantic in origin, but is ultimately subversive of all fixed points of view, all single outlooks, including the Romantic. He is simultaneously Romantic and not Romantic, and elements of all three modes (Classicist, Realist, Romantic) often coexist and interact.

In one respect, Pushkin's credentials as Romantic are apparent from the very range of his writing, which at least from the time he graduated from the Lyceum at Tsarskoe Selo in 1817 had the character of incessant experimentation. He produced elegies and "Byronic" verse narratives, Ossianic poems and gothic ballads, graveyard poetry and nocturnal meditations, not only some half-dozen "fairy tales" but also, in *Evgenii Onegin*, an entire novel in verse, which drew initial impetus from Byron's *Beppo* and has been frequently compared to the latter's *Don Juan*, but is essentially and gloriously *sui generis*. In drama, Pushkin spurned prevalent neoclassical conventions for what he discerned as the model of Shakespeare ("free and broad portrayal of character," "verisimilitude of situation and truth of dialogue," "art" untrammeled by "Rules"; Pushkin 1956-8, VII: 164, X: 162, VII: 38).[1] In conjunction with his reading of N. M. Karamzin's *History of the Russian State*, this led in *Boris Godunov* (1824-5, published 1831) to another startlingly unprecedented generic hybrid that he himself thought of as a "truly Romantic tragedy" (Pushkin, 1956-8, VII: 73). Shakespearian plotlines have also been discerned behind the four no less startlingly innovative "Little Tragedies" – condensedly fragmentary studies in extremes either of passion (avarice in *The Covetous Knight*, envy in *Mozart and Salieri*, the erotic imperative in *The Stone Guest*) or situation (*The Feast in the Time of the Plague*; all 1830). The prose to which Pushkin turned increasingly over his last decade included a cycle of parodic short stories with a relatively complex series of embedded narrators (*The Tales of Belkin*, 1830), a consummate tale of the supernatural (*The Queen of Spades*, 1833, published 1834), and a "historical romance" somewhat superficially à la Walter Scott (*The Captain's Daughter*, 1835-6). Biographically, too, there is much to consolidate Pushkin's Romantic image. Above all, he had the aura of exile. Pushkin was banished from St Petersburg in 1820 at the direct behest of Alexander I, as the result of a handful of vicious epigrams on prominent government figures and some liberal verses critical of serfdom and (more mildly) autocracy: dispatched first to the south (travels through the Caucasus, Kishinev, Odessa); then, after further misdemeanors – insubordination, injudicious amorous pursuits, an incautious avowal of atheism in a letter intercepted by the authorities – to the monotonous Russian rural isolation of his parents' small provincial estate of Mikhailovskoe (1824-6). The theme and the pose of exile, as well as a sense of his own marginality – as the descendant of Peter the Great's black protégé, on the fringe of "society," the court, and the aristocracy – were of lasting significance to him. Other traits of the Romantic personality seem manifest in Pushkin's avid womanizing (there exists an encrypted and somewhat disputed "Don Juan's" list, the significance of which is perhaps easily exaggerated), in his inveterate dueling (upwards of 30 duels, according to some calculations), or, say, in the near-obsessive gambling which betrays an abiding, superstitious fascination with the workings of fate.

Yet for all Pushkin's espousal of Romantic norms, caveats are almost invariably required. Stylistically, with rare exceptions (*Boris Godunov?*), there is a Classicist's striving for lightness and elegance, symmetry and harmony of form (from overall structure to metrical and stanzaic pattern and the texture of sound), economy, clarity, and precision of expression. Behaviorally, too, the author who avowed to Alexander's successor, Nicholas I, his sympathy for the Decembrist insurrectionists of 1825, became increasingly conservative (or, it could be argued, realistically fatalistic) in his appraisal of the autocracy, a supporter of the status quo whose intolerance of the Polish unrest of the 1830s, for instance, shocked liberal colleagues. After much anxious soul-searching he also became a family man, who sought – though never quite found – an ideal of family happiness and peace, and whose religious faith certainly deepened in his last years. Above all, however, it would seem that Pushkin simply did not share the intense self-absorption of the full-fledged Romantic ("I am not cut out to be the hero of a Romantic poem," he admitted apropos of *The Prisoner of the Caucasus* in a letter of 1822; Pushkin 1956-8, X: 49). He maintained an intellectual fascination not so much with Romantic philosophy (he never shared his Russian contemporaries' widespread enthusiasm for Schelling and German Idealism) as with the Romantic typology that dominated the age; but he also almost unfailingly displayed a subversively rationalist skepticism, a playful detachment, an awareness of others and openness to multiplicity of perspective, and, in the final analysis, a sheer curiosity and zest for life, that set him apart from the tortured introversion of the archetypally Romantic being. This distinction becomes particularly apparent by contrast with Lermontov – one of whose finest "late" lyrics, constitutes the nighttime meditation of a solitary lyric self on a metaphorical open road (<Выхожу один я на дорогу> – "I come out alone upon the road," 1841, Lermontov 1964: 127-8). The poem dwells on alienation from the natural and divine order and the incomprehensible pain of individual existence, accepts that the past is unworthy of regret and that life has nothing more to offer, and moves on, predictably enough, to a yearning for easeful death, "oblivion and sleep." Pushkin, in <Безумных лет угасшее веселье> ("The burnt-out joy of reckless years," 1830), a scarcely less pivotal elegiac contemplation of an extinguished past and the gloomy (унылый - a key epithet in the Russian Romantic code) present path to a future of toil and grief, nevertheless makes a tellingly different appraisal of a comparable predicament. The past remains a source of attachment, not alienation ("the sorrow of former days becomes stronger, the older it is"), and solution is sought not in death but in a graciously accepting openness to life and the (classicizing?) hope that harmony, pleasure, and even love will be renewed:

> Но не хочу, о друти, умирать;
> Я жить хоуу, чтоб мыслить страдать,
> И ведаю, мне будут наслажденья
> Меж горестей, забот и гревлненья:
> Порой опять гармонией упьюсь,

Над вымыслом слезами обольюсь,
И может быть -- на мой закат печальный
Блеснет любовь улыбкою прошальной (Pushkin, 1956-58, III: 178)

(But I do not want, my friends, to die; / I want to live, to think and suffer, / And I know
that I will have pleasures / Amidst sorrows, troubles, and tribulations; / At times I will
again be intoxicated with harmony, / And shall shed tears over my creative invention, /
And perhaps, at my sad sunset, / Love will shine with a farewell smile.)

The temperamental contrast and specificity might be amplified by a lengthy series of
similar examples. Pushkin's own espousal of, and distancing from, Romanticism is
manifest in various ways almost constantly throughout his career: this essay will
concentrate on some key literary works of his most Romantic period of Southern exile,
of 1820-4, culminating in his "problematization" of the Romantic aesthetic in
The Gypsies, and look briefly thereafter at his continuing ruminations on Romantic
themes in a small selection of major works: *Eugene Onegin*, *Mozart and Salieri*, and *The
Bronze Horseman*.

First Success and Southern Exile: Pushkin's Byronic Phase

Pushkin began his poetic career in prolific fashion as a pupil at the newly opened and
remarkably enlightened Imperial Lyceum (1811-17). His more important verse of the
period, such as "Recollections in Tsarskoe Selo" (1814), betrays an odic quality
stemming directly from neo-Classicism, and a rationalistic didacticism which is
equally of no account in the present context. A different matter is the first and
longest of his narrative poems, *Ruslan and Liudmila*, the almost 3,000 lines and six
cantos of which were completed over the three years to 1820 and brought the young
author immediate celebrity. This exuberant mock-heroic epic tells of Liudmila's
wedding-night abduction by the dwarf-magician, Chernomor, and the quest for her
recovery by Ruslan and three envious rival suitors (Rogdai, Ratmir, and Farlaf). After
many fanciful episodes, enabling protracted evocations of a wicked witch and 12
seductive maidens in their enchanted castle, of a magic hat that confers invisibility,
and a martial encounter with a severed head, Ruslan engages in an epic struggle with
Chernomor – whose power is in his beard, which raises him and Ruslan hundreds of
feet into the air. When the hero hacks off the beard the tale promises to conclude with
his success; but Ruslan is then killed by the cowardly Farlaf, who abducts the sleeping
Liudmila. Unsurprisingly, Ruslan is nevertheless revived at last, by the magical
"living and dead water" of Russian folk tradition, to relieve the besieged city of
Kiev and awaken his bride for the ritual happy ending. Critics have concurred in
finding no profound meaning here. *Ruslan and Liudmila* is a virtuoso piece in which
plot matters less than the manner of its telling; and if there is much ingenious
invention, there is also much scarcely concealed borrowing, in a playful amalgam of

Ossianic and Russian folk-heroic motifs (traditional heroic narrative *bylina* epic and fairy tale), elegant eroticism in the manner of Bogdanovich, and elements appropriated from Ariosto, Voltaire (*La Pucelle*), Parny, and others besides. Above all, it would seem, the poem constitutes a complex parodic game with the lyric forms of Pushkin's immediate predecessors, Zhukovskii and Batiushkov. Parody and the eclectic combination of seemingly uncombinable elements was – and would long remain – Pushkin's path to the affirmation of his own poetic voice. The poetic procedure, in its unconstrained neglect of accepted rules, also reflected what he himself then thought of as "Romanticism."

Pushkin's most intensive Romantic phase, in the more conventionally accepted sense of the term, began however with his banishment from the capital in the weeks that saw *Ruslan and Liudmila* into print. His fresh departure, literary as well as literal, was heralded by the impressive elegy "Extinguished is the orb of day" (<Погасло дневное светило>; Pushkin, 1956-8, II: 7-8), written on board the ship that took him from Feodosiia to Gurzuf in August 1820. An atmospheric seascape is the background to a melancholic meditation on unhappy love and parting, the loss of youth, the treachery of friends and confidantes, and the cooling of the heart; but it is the poetic persona's very shift to self-analysis that is of greatest moment. Evidently seeking to forestall the imputations of his readers, Pushkin retrospectively subtitled his poem "An Imitation of Byron." In reality, it was a reworking of the elegiac conventions of Batiushkov: another piece of experimental appropriation, which incidentally anticipated the already quoted "The burnt-out joy of reckless years" in its ungeneric insistence on the possibility of "new adventures" ahead.

Over the next months, Pushkin did indeed become an avid reader of Byron. The fruits of his enthusiasm are particularly apparent in four narrative poems – *The Prisoner of the Caucasus* (1820-1, published 1822), the never completed *The Robber Brothers* (1821-2, extant fragment published 1825), *The Fountain of Bakhchisarai* (1821-3, published 1824), and *The Gypsies* (1824, published 1827). Collectively, these exotic tales of alienation and passion are habitually referred to as Pushkin's "Southern" or (more especially by Western critics) his "Byronic" poems.

There is some critical debate as to how far *The Prisoner of the Caucasus* is indeed beholden to Byron, about whom Pushkin, on his own admission, now "raved" (Pushkin, 1956-8, VII: 170). Its plot has been likened to Chateaubriand's *Atala*, and there are palpable borrowings from the native Russian elegy and descriptive narrative poem. It seems clear enough, however, that *The Prisoner* could not have been conceived without the "Eastern" precedent of *The Bride of Abydos*, *The Giaour*, and particularly *The Corsair*. Its Russian hero has left his native land in search of freedom and, as he confesses to the silently attentive Circassian maid who falls in love with him, he is weary of his world, having rejected the "conditions of society" and left behind an unhappy love in a shadowy past. But there are multiple ironies – indubitably more Pushkinian than Byronic. The hero seeks freedom, but spends the entirety of the poem in chains – a "slave," as the narrator repeatedly puts it, held captive in a remote village by indifferent, bellicose Caucasian tribesmen. When the latter are again called away to arms, the "strong" hero is released by the young girl, to whom he pledges his affection as she proffers the saw that will cut away his shackles. But she is more fiercely constant in emotional commitment than he. He has previously spurned her advances, on the grounds that past experience of unrequited passion prevents him from loving again; rejected, the Circassian mirrors his sentiment, but differs in her unwavering refusal to relent. The price of his freedom is her wonderfully, un-Byronically understated suicide; she dies wordlessly, fading almost imperceptibly into the river he has just crossed so that, with scarcely a backward glance in her direction, he is "free" to return to the Russian army from whence he came.

The poem is, in Byronic fashion, episodic, beginning *in medias res*, with little detail of past events (Pushkin even excised from the final version the description of the hero's capture). "Plot" is punctuated by grandiose descriptions of Caucasian nature – and more prosaic ones of Circassian daily life – which together make up more than a quarter of the text. These are, however, markedly more precise, and laconic, than in Byron, while characters are depicted through speech and action, with little interiority. The narrative is restrainedly undigressive, and the entire poem, though longer than those which follow, runs to a modest 777 lines of iambic tetrameter. Its tacit ironies are unsettlingly compounded in the Epilogue, which unexpectedly praises not the freedom of the local tribesmen and exhilarating natural scene, but Russian military conquest of the savage Caucasian lands.

A less satisfactory extension of the Byronic manner was *The Fountain of Bakhchisarai*. The merits of this poem – which Pushkin later dismissed out of hand ("Between you and me," he confided to his friend Viazemskii, "*The Fountain of Bakhchisarai* is rubbish . . . "; Pushkin, 1956-8, X: 67) – are in the static, sensual description of the harem at Bakhchisarai and the enveloping sense of nostalgia for days and grandiloquent deeds long past. The poem offers considerably more than *The Prisoner* in the way of lyrical interpolation and apostrophe, simile and subjectivism; it is more atmospheric and altogether more "decorative," but plot and intellectual substance suffer accordingly. It tells how, some centuries ago, the fierce Crimean Khan Girei fell for the latest addition to his harem, a beautiful Polish maiden whose princely father he had slaughtered on a raid of conquest. The captive Mariia understandably spurns Girei's advances. Girei is distraught and abandons the harem – thus paving the way for his former favorite, Zarema, desperate to reassert her place in her beloved's affections, to confront Mariia in an impassioned monologue. Pushkin's recourse to "disconnected fragments" – as he put it in another letter to Viazemskii and repeated in a letter to A. A. Del'vig a few days later (Pushkin, 1956-8, X: 69, 71) – allows him to sidestep narration of the dramatic consequences of this encounter (a procedure he would repeat, tongue-in-cheek, in Chapter 3 of *Onegin*, and in earnest at the close of *Mozart and Salieri*). Mariia, it transpires, "passed suddenly away," and Zarema, "whatever her guilt," was put to death the same night – drowned by "mute" guards whose silence explains nothing. Girei continues thereafter his despondently bloodthirsty rampage through distant lands.

It is striking that the reticence and concision of exposition which in Pushkin are perennial strengths and sources of complexity, prove less than effective in this overcharged Romantic context. The Khan's character, in particular, is depicted entirely from without, through gesture and deed. We see the responses of the Byronic hero, but the inner turmoil they reflect is nowhere explicitly disclosed, and he seems hopelessly stereotypical as a result. Even the more interesting juxtaposition of the passionate, sensual, eloquent, Muslim-convert Zarema to the appropriately named Mariia, palely virginal, pious, passive, and silent, is in this instance too inflexibly schematic to persuade.

Romanticism Declined: The Significance of *The Gypsies*

By the time of *The Gypsies*, Pushkin's artistic and intellectual divergence from the Byronic model crystallizes into a more general expression of disenchantment with Romanticism. The poem can be read as a subversive rejection both of Byronic-Romantic individualism and of the Rousseauesque concept of the noble savage. Not surprisingly, there is a concomitant shift in poetic. *The Gypsies* is the shortest and densest of the Southern poems, arranged into 11 unnumbered dramatic episodes. Characters' speech, interspersed with laconic "stage directions," is paramount. Narrative interventions are brief, and limited description notably takes the form of ethnographically precise, saturated cataloguing. Two short lyrical digressions – on Ovid's exile, and the "little bird of God" which knows neither tribulation nor toil and can winter insouciantly in the West – are thematically pointed; and in contrast to the previous works, which feature set-piece Circassian and Tatar "songs" divorced from plot, a gypsy song performed here by Zemfira ("Old husband, Dread husband, Cut me, Burn me"; Pushkin 1956-8, IV: 218) is directly provocative of the tragic denouement. A further departure from Romantic prolixity is seen in the elegant structural symmetries in the disposition of scenes and characters, particularly in opening and closing episodes.

The basic story is the already familiar one of the educated European who flees his society in search of freedom and fulfillment in exotic otherness, amidst a more primitive people: in this case, a nomadic gypsy band, wandering the Bessarabian steppe. Although Aleko (Pushkin's namesake, as is routinely indicated) is "pursued by the law" (Pushkin 1956-8, IV: 208), his invective against "the unfreedom of stifling cities, / Where people trade their liberty / And bow their heads before idols" (p. 213) lends this deliberately vague formulation a glamorously political connotation. It might, however, also be noted that Aleko seemingly falls in with the gypsies more by accident than exercise of will – led almost ignominiously to their encampment by his lover Zemfira. She has found him, inauspiciously, "behind the burial mound," and at once asserts a startlingly confident, proprietorial assurance ("He is ready to follow me anywhere . . . He will be mine"; p. 208).

For two years Aleko leads a life of ease with Zemfira – by whom he fathers a child – and the larger gypsy community. But Zemfira tires of him, and he has bad dreams. He admits to her father, who recounts how Zemfira's mother, Mariula, abandoned him for another, that he, Aleko, could not behave in the same way as the father had: <От прав моих не откажусь> ("I shall not renounce my rights"; Pushkin 1956-8, IV: 227). Not only would he assert his claim to curtail the woman's freedom, but he would not hesitate to exact vengeance on his rival, whom he would kick viciously from a cliff top even while he slumbered, and find sweet pleasure in the sound of his fall. When Zemfira arranges another graveyard rendezvous with another gypsy, the prognostication is borne out: Aleko murders both Zemfira and her new lover. Directionless, no longer in possession of himself, he is left behind by the gypsies on the following day like a wounded crane in autumn.

Unlike that of the previous poems, the moral of this tale is explicitly pointed by Zemfira's anonymous father, the "Old Man":

> Ты не рожден для дикой доли,
> Ты для себя лишь хочешь воли (Pushkin 1956-8, IV: 234)

("You are not born for a savage lot, / You want freedom for yourself alone")

The Western individualist's Romantic quest for freedom is narrowly egocentric. It is also ruinous to others. The Byronic cult of willful passion and bloody vengeance is exposed, in ordinary human terms, as shockingly vicious and shabbily self-indulgent (the Byronic overtone is incidentally made emphatic by a parodic echo of *The Corsair* in the cliff-top episode just referred to), and the very motive for fleeing society might seem suspect. (One begins to wonder whether Aleko in his urban past had not already committed some comparable criminal act – not of political protest, but of spiteful violence.) In any case, the prejudices and assumptions of that society cannot be shaken off: Aleko cannot but think in terms of "rights" (a conspicuously "civilized," legalistic concept), of ownership and the ungypsy-like convention of monogamy, if not actual marriage; of what is "mine." He was indeed "not born" for a wild lot (the rhyming of *dolia* and *volia*, "lot" and "freedom," will persist in Pushkin), for as always, "freedom" of choice and action are inevitably compromised from the outset by the contingency of origin.

By contrast to Aleko, the "savage (gypsy) lot," as presented by the chorus-like figure of the unindividualistic "Old Man," seems admirably noble. Its superiority is most poignantly apparent in the words with which, without a trace of vengefulness, he dismisses the proud selfhood and societal norms of his own daughter's killer:

> Оставь нас, гордый человек!
> Мы дики, нет у нас законов,
> Мы не терзаем, не казним --

Не нужно крови нам и стонов --
Но жить с убийцей не хотим...
... Мы робки и добры душою,
Ты зол и смел -- оставь же нас... (Pushkin 1956-8, IV: 233-4)

("Leave us, proud man! / We are savage, we have no laws, / We do not torture, do not execute, / We do not need blood and groans, / But we do not wish to live with a murderer.... / We are timid and good of soul, / You are wicked and bold – leave us...")

It is, however, entirely characteristic of the maturing Pushkin's skeptical relativism that this seeming apotheosis of "noble savagery" proves more provisional than its dignified rhetoric and final position in the narrative might initially intimate.

In the first place, the Gypsies' day-to-day existence is in truth scarcely more attractive than the aspirations of the freedom-seeking individualist. On the very first morning in the Gypsy camp, the Old Man, with a stylistic incongruity that may reinforce the point, calls on Zemfira and Aleko to leave their "bed of luxury" (Pushkin 1956-8, IV: 210): life henceforth will be a matter of humdrum toil. Aleko must choose a trade – and leads a tamed, suggestively shackled bear around the villages for cash. Even gypsies, it is wryly implied, are not free to ignore basic economic needs; while a passing reference to "unreaped millet" (p. 217) suggests that Aleko and his adoptive family supplement their meager income by some petty thieving from the peasants' fields. The Romantic myth is deflated by some "ignoble" realism.

There are other reservations of a different order. If Aleko's violence is reprehensible, so, paradoxically, may be the fatalistic passivity by which the Old Man resigned himself to Mariula's desertion. Since then he has cared for Zemfira but never looked at another woman; his own existence has become woefully limited, so narrowly circumscribed that his very renunciation has perhaps made him prematurely "old" (Zemfira is not yet 20). This is mirrored in leitmotifs of coldness that characterize him from the first scene; but it is his failure to do anything to prevent the final bloody debacle that that makes his unassuming "nobility" positively reprehensible. His wisdom, perspicacity, and lengthy private conversations with both Aleko and Zemfira equip him to foresee disaster; but, as with Mariula, and in stark contrast to Aleko, he does not react. He allows "fate" to take its very predictable course.

From yet another point of view, however, the Old Man's "golden age" depiction of the Gypsies as timid and innately good is in itself erroneously untenable. Eloquent proofs are his own daughter's bold passion and aggressive individualism, and the "traditional" Gypsy song of vengeance and pain with which she exultingly goads her husband. Love (erotic passion) and Death seem as inextricably intertwined here as in the sophisticated world of the Byronic-Romantic; and this chimes with the assertion of the narrator, who is suddenly personalized in a brief (and once more militaristic) epilogue, to conclude:

> Но счастья нет и между вами,
> Природы бедные сыны!
> ...И всюду страсти роковые,
> И от судеб защиты нет. (Pushkin 1956-8, IV: 235-6)

(But there is no happiness even with you, / Poor sons of nature! / ... And everywhere are fateful passions, / And from the fates there is no defense.)

Put another way, this is to dismiss as misconceived and ultimately illusory the juxtaposition of gypsy and urban-European, "savage" and "civilized" around which much of the poem (and a major strand of Romanticism) has ostensibly been structured.

More fundamental to *The Gypsies*, it finally appears, is an underlying contrast of recurrent character types that cut across distinctions of ethnicity, ideology, and cultural trend: between active and passive temperaments, the proclivity either to rebel against the vicissitudes of fate, to resist or reject the way things are (to kick the sleeping body over the cliff, however futile the gesture) which, for the sake of convenience, might be labeled Romantic, or, by contrast, to accept whatever tribulations life may serve up, in a conservative acquiescence in the universal status quo. The difficulty here is that neither is satisfactory: the one leads to death and destruction, the other to limitation and denial of life. The pivotal significance of *The Gypsies* in Pushkin's oeuvre lies, however, in the articulation of the problem. The poem presages a transition, an end to exclusive concentration on the Romantic mindset toward a broader, and more broadly realist, examination of how best to understand and accommodate to the dilemma of living – not beyond societal norms, but within the social, historical, and even biological spheres by which every individual, weak or strong, is in reality inescapably constrained. The issue will be perennially restated by Pushkin through various recontextualizations of the polarities just outlined. And for all the apparent wrong-headedness and insubstantiality of Aleko, the Romantic vision and the powerful man of will continue to figure almost obsessively in Pushkin's thinking, as a fascinating component within a set of competing alternatives.

Romanticism Recontextualized

The most obvious and indisputably important embodiment of this change is the novel in verse *Evgenii Onegin*, which Pushkin began in 1823 and completed in 1831. Work on the second chapter was contemporaneous with *The Gypsies*. In plot terms, Pushkin now places the Byronic hero not in the exotic elsewhere of the literary imagination, but firmly within a contemporary Russian society evoked with such a wealth of detail that the most important and influential of all Russian nineteenth-century critics, Vissarion Belinskii, was famously prompted to describe the work as an "encyclopedia" of Russian life (Belinskii 1953-9, VII: 503). Not surprisingly, Onegin fares no better than his "Southern" predecessors. Moreover, one of the profound issues Pushkin now addresses is the sincerity of the Romantic pose, the relationship of fashionable attitudinizing to authentic being: what is the "true" self, and how far – if at all – can individual personality be realized independently of, or even through the medium of, the assumptions of the day.

Onegin, after a frivolous upbringing, becomes splenetically disenchanted with the privileged but seemingly vacuous world of high society to which he was born, but flees (not least to escape his debts) no further than his dying uncle's modest provincial estate. From this initial high-point of lofty-minded independence, he falls steadily in the estimation of both narrator and reader. In contrast to the garrulous narrator, this Romantic hero becomes habitually bored after just three days in the country, and like the *Prisoner of the Caucasus*, soon spurns the advances of a local maid, similarly protesting that he is "not intended for happiness," that his elevated soul is ill-suited to conjugal bliss. In this case, however, the response is tinged with a banal ordinariness. Although Onegin cannot fail to distress "poor Tatiana," he behaves better than he might: he neither cynically seduces her nor discloses her indiscretion to others, and in the speech he delivers in the (un-Romantic) kitchen garden, with its patronizing and ultimately ironic injunction to the young interlocutor to learn greater self-control, is guilty of little more than slightly pompous moralizing. His blinkered egotism will nevertheless soon do more serious harm to others, and rebound upon himself. His underestimation of Tatiana's resilience and consequent petty irritation during her nameday party leads him, in unedifying pique (more deflationary banality!), to manufacture a situation in which his impetuous younger friend, Lenskii, is almost bound to challenge him to a duel. Onegin duly if inadvertently murders him, through a double failure both to exercise the self-control he had counseled to Tatiana and to transcend a concern for social opinion (what might be thought of him if he calls off the fight) which ill accords with his pose of cynical superiority. Lenskii's death is, in broader terms, an epitaph on the defunct Sentimentalist elegiac posturing he espouses, and which Pushkin revisits with some echoes of his own early work and self. But the weakness – and ordinariness – of the Byronic hero are almost as fatal. The narrator parts company with him for a while, then abandons him in ignominious posture at the novel's inconclusive "end," lovelorn (if he is capable of sincere emotion) at the feet of an unresponsive Tatiana, the Romantic muddle in his head an obstacle to timely maturation.

The point is reinforced by the contrasting growth of the heroine, from the thought-patterns of European pre-Romantic novels by "Richardson and Rousseau," and a contrary, concurrent immersion in the customs and superstitions of the Russian folk, toward greater analytical acumen and increasing understanding of self and world. Unlike earlier, suicidal heroines – or even the Old Man of *The Gypsies* – Tatiana does not perish as a result of rejection, but determines to learn the truth about "the one for whom she sighed." Gradually disabused, she exercises what modicum of choice she can within the limiting conventions of her society, rejecting unsuitable suitors to attain to a notable element of inner freedom in the marriage she finally contracts. This takes her beyond the limitations and delusions of the various forms of self-indulgent Romanticism the novel has examined, to a self-possessed control and intellectually clear-sighted acuity which are nevertheless not devoid of "poetic" sensibility. In this she is put forward as the narrator's "Ideal."

However, this "storyline" constitutes only one facet of the "novel in verse," the quintessentially Pushkinian, hybrid form of which, it might be argued, neatly reflects the polarities of the heroine's (and narrator's) progression. The prosaic and poetic, "novel" and "verse," effusive Romanticism and illusion-dispelling "realism," are thematized in a series of incessant contrasts and judgmental evaluations between sets of ideas and inclinations – on the one hand, for instance, youth, love, springtime, glamorous foreign importations, inspiration, dreams, and illusion; on the other, the caution of age, analytical reason, self and self-interest, winter, the unexotically Russian, analytical reason, cynicism, and disillusion (see Woodward 1982). Such contrarieties not only frame and encompass the actions and motives of characters, but constantly engender temperamentally contrastive appraisals of even the most everyday objects ("pale Diana"; "the stupid moon on the stupid horizon"). In all this, the narrative procedures of the "free novel" – so replete with digression and overt narratorial play that the entire work has sometimes been deemed a parodic game, enacted around the shadowy semblance of a plot – are notably offset by the strict form of the idiosyncratically contrived, endlessly flexible but impeccably observed 14-line "Onegin stanza." Whatever the implications of the characters' fates, "Romantic" unconstraint and "classical" precision seem equally and inextricably manifest in the very fabric of the work.

While these differing strands continue to find varied formal and thematic reflection in many subsequent works, Pushkin's most challenging and complex reappraisal of the particular problem of the Romantic rebel is surely to be found in *Mozart and Salieri*. Like Aleko and Onegin, Salieri, too, is driven to murder. But the act he commits – the poisoning of the world's greatest musician, calculated, in a sense, over a period of 18 years – is anything but impulsive. In consequence, his stature seems immeasurably greater.

Salieri is himself a formidable musician, who has risen to success by dint of hard work and talent, the archetypally brooding Romantic artist's lifetime of single-minded dedication to his art. Mozart, however, has been born with an unrivaled, unsurpassable genius, a gift of which – in Salieri's jaundiced view – he is unaware and utterly unworthy, and which is detrimental to the smooth evolution of the musical art Salieri loves. It is the complex, double-edged emotion of envy – simultaneous antipathy and adoration – which ostensibly prompts him to kill. But it emerges from the powerfully eloquent, paradoxically rational analyses of this condition – which occupy the two soliloquies at the heart of Pushkin's maximally condensed, two-scene drama – that the underlying cause is a resentment at the very order of life that can allow such gross injustice. As much might be gleaned from the play's startling opening words (the musical simile, incidentally, constituting the unobtrusive first sign of monomaniacal obsession):

Все говорят: нет правды на земле.
Но правды нет – и выше. Для меня
Так это ясно, как простая гамма. (Pushkin, 1956-8, V: 357)

(All say there is no truth[2] on earth. / But there is no truth on high. / That is as clear to me as a simple scale.)

Salieri, in going beyond the opinion of the crowd ("All say"), implicitly aligns himself here with the grandest of all Romantic rebels against God's providence – and his Satanic quality is tacitly underscored by imagery of fire and the serpent, of the poison he has carried for many loveless years at his breast, even, it might be argued, by a punning on the Russian word for poison (*iad*) that implicates both hell (*ad*) and overweening selfhood (*ia*: I).[3] It is one of the play's many paradoxes that this rebel wants greater order, progress, justice, and control than life can offer: his is a Romantic rebellion in the name of classical clarity, that would exclude all that is random. Its articulation includes a "justification" of killing in the name of a noble ideal – the greater good (*pol'za*) – that has a sinister resonance with utilitarian political philosophies and points an unnervingly direct continuum between Romantic disaffection and High Stalinism. Not inconsistently with this, it also becomes apparent that what lies beneath the Satanic pride (an echo of the Old Man's valediction to Aleko?) that prompts Salieri to challenge the disposition of the universe is self-contempt and a hatred of life itself which, in his single-minded exclusiveness of purpose, he perhaps never really loved. The message, as before, is that Romantic rebellion is a sterile impasse; but its representation in this relatively late work seems curiously more profound, agonized, and perversely ennobled than anything Pushkin had depicted previously.

Mozart provides a potential counterbalance. His classicizing temperament enables a light-hearted openness to the incongruous and unexpected, while in his artistic creation, with a paradoxically Romantic prescience, he is capable of intuiting profoundly haunting visions of mortality alongside frivolous insouciance. Ultimately, however, his life-affirming "acceptance" is unsettlingly naïve and self-deceiving, and it is emblematic of this that he leaves the stage for home after unwittingly drinking poisoned wine, never suspecting that his sudden indisposition is terminal. The world these characters inhabit is one of bleakness and chance, unavenged murder, and sudden death without the redeeming catharsis of awareness. Divine providence, if it exists at all, is incomprehensible in human terms.

Profound issues of Romanticism are reconsidered in such other later works as the *Queen of Spades* and the *Captain's Daughter*, with their common interest in the nature of fate and respective examinations of supernatural forces and the laws of history; but a final word on Pushkin's Romanticism might be offered here with reference to his greatest masterpiece, *The Bronze Horseman*. As is evident once more from its structure, this poem is both Romantic and not Romantic. The "Introduction" is a classicizing paean to the neoclassical city of St Petersburg, which draws heavily on the odic tradition, while polemicizing with the Polish Romantic Mickiewicz. The man of will – in this case Peter the Great – is here cast not as rebellious outcast, but as the grand constructive genius, the bringer of order, light, and progress (those things Salieri craved!) where previously there was unenlightened, formless, ahistorical darkness. But, of course, there is a downside; and the "Introduction" is, with minimal comment, juxtaposed to the gloomily autumnal tale of Evgenii, a poor denizen of the modern city, that constitutes the main body of the poem. Unlike his previous namesake, Onegin, this is a most unassuming individual, moved by a dream of social conformity and the ambition for a contented marriage and happy home that is more petty bourgeois than pastoral-idyllic. Early, submerged allusions to *Melmoth* or *The Giaour* seem merely parodic, but when Evgenii's hopes are dashed upon losing his fiancée Parasha in the catastrophic flood of 1824 (God's vengeance on Peter's hubristic creation?), high Romantic ingredients come to the fore: a battle with the elements, descent into madness and a shadowy nether kingdom, restless wandering, loss of self, and a single gesture of rebellion against the "creator" – Peter, or his equestrian emblem in bronze – culminating in a phatasmagoric pursuit through nocturnal city streets. Though it might remain uncertain whether Peter's galloping statue is the embodiment of some supernatural force or a mere product of the diseased mind, the Romantic resistance of the alienated outsider, as so often in Pushkin, leads inexorably to death.

The Bronze Horseman, shorter and denser than any other of Pushkin's narrative poems including *The Gypsies*, raises a plethora of far-reaching issues – on the nature of identity and the forces of history; the incompatible needs of state and individual; the nature of Russia, poised between East and West; the rights or wrongs of military and economic progress; the pitfalls of revolution and the need for autocracy. One of the most profound stems from the familiar polarities of acceptance and rebellion. Evgenii fails to accept that life cannot offer fixity, a humble haven (*priiut*) of peace and certainty as the reward for honest toil, so that the "little man," rather than the grand hero, here becomes a reluctant rebel in consequence. This then chimes with *Mozart and Salieri* in prompting speculation on the nature of life itself. Typically enough for the mature Pushkin, the issue becomes most urgent, though never quite explicit, after Evgenii's death. His body is found on a small island in the Neva estuary, on the threshold of a crumbling wooden hut washed up by last year's flood and naturally assumed by the vast majority of commentators to be that of his drowned (once more!) Parasha. The poem might thus seem to end on a note of cathartic reconciliation – a promise of harmonious restitution of thwarted lovers beyond the grave, notably sanctioned by oblique references to God and resurrection. Another reading, however, might suggest the mockery of a cruel divinity: Evgenii has reached the threshold, where he is tantalizingly doomed to die (to quote an earlier, despairingly Romantic passage of the poem: "Or is the whole of our life / Nothing but an empty dream, / Heaven's mockery of the earth?"; Pushkin, 1956-8, IV: 388). But this view, too, may be undercut by another. The hut is empty, all identifying features obliterated: it is, perhaps, an entirely "random" remnant of the flood, and it would be the raving of a "madman" to see it as anything more, to "read in" a connection with Parasha. There is in other words no significant patterning of events – benevolent or mocking – no providential logic in the apportioning of happiness or disaster. The universe is not (classically) ordered but (Romantically) chaotic.

It may be argued that the uncertainty of the ending – which, for good measure, also points full circle to the beginning, back to the wasteland where Peter planned to construct life to his own design – is of itself profoundly Romantic. It might also be construed as unblinkered, skeptical realism. It is at least certain that the Romantic worldview continues to figure in Pushkin's most searching exploration of the nature of life.

NOTES

1 All translations are mine.
2 Or "right," or "justice": the Russian word is laden with implication.

3 Cf. the illuminating discussion by Robert Louis Jackson (1973).

REFERENCES AND FURTHER READING

Primary sources

Belinskii, Vissarion G. (1953-9). *Polnoe sobranie sochinenii*, 13 vols. Moscow: Akademiia Nauk.

Lermontov, Mikhail Iu. (1964). *Sobranie sochinenii*, 4 vols. Moscow: Khudozhestvennaia literatura, vol. 1.

Pushkin, Aleksandr Sergeevich (1956-8). *Polnoe sobranie sochinenii*, 10 vols. Moscow: Akademiia Nauk.

Pushkin, Aleksandr Sergeevich (1971). *Pushkin on Literature*, ed. and trans. Tatiana Wolff. London: Methuen; New York: Barnes and Noble.

Pushkin, Aleksandr Sergeevich (1975). *Eugene Onegin: A Novel in Verse*, trans. with commentary Vladimir Nabokov, 4 vols. London: Routledge & Kegan Paul.

Pushkin, Aleksandr Sergeevich (1982). *Mozart and Salieri: The Little Tragedies*, trans. Antony Wood. London: Angel.

Pushkin, Aleksandr Sergeevich (1984). *Collected Narrative and Lyrical Poetry of Alexander Pushkin*, trans. Walter Arndt. Ann Arbor, MI: Ardis.

Pushkin, Aleksandr Sergeevich (1999). *The Collected Stories*, trans. Paul Debreczeny, introduction John Bayley. London: Campbell.

Pushkin, Aleksandr Sergeevich (2002-3). *The Complete Works of Alexander Pushkin*, ed. I. Sproat, 15 vols., Downham Market, UK: Milner.

Pushkin, Aleksandr Sergeevich (2003). *Eugene Onegin: A Novel in Verse*, trans. Charles Johnston, preface John Bayley, introduction and notes Michael Basker. London: Penguin.

Pushkin, Aleksandr Sergeevich and Lermontov, Mikhail (1984). *Narrative Poems by Alexander Pushkin and by Michael Lermontov*, trans. Charles Johnston. London: The Bodley Head.

Secondary sources

Bayley, John (1971). *Pushkin: A Comparative Commentary*. Cambridge, UK: Cambridge University Press.

Bethea, David M. (1998). *Realizing Metaphors: Alexander Pushkin and the Life of the Poet*. Madison and London: University of Wisconsin Press.

Binyon, T. J. (2002). *Pushkin: A Biography*. London, HarperCollins.

Briggs, A. D. P. (1983). *Alexander Pushkin: A Critical Study*. London: Croom Helm.

Brown, William Edward (1986). *A History of Russian Literature of the Romantic Period*, vol. 3. Ann Arbor, MI: Ardis.

Debreczeny, Paul (1983). *The Other Pushkin: A Study of Alexander Pushkin's Prose Fiction*. Stanford, CA: Stanford University Press.

Greenleaf, Monika (1994). *Pushkin and Romantic Fashion: Fragment, Elegy, Orient, Irony*. Stanford, CA: Stanford University Press.

Jackson, Robert Louis (1973). "Miltonic Imagery and Design in Puškin's Mozart and Salieri: The Russian Satan." In V. Terras (ed.), *American Contributions to the Seventh International Congress of Slavists, Warsaw, August 21-27, 1973, Volume II: Literature and Folklore*. The Hague: Mouton, pp. 261-9.

Leighton, Lauren, G. (1999). *A Bibliography of Alexander Pushkin in English: Studies and Translations*. Lewiston, NY, Queenston, ONT, and Lampeter, UK: Edwin Mellen Press.

Sandler, Stephanie (1989). *Distant Pleasures: Alexander Pushkin and the Writing of Exile*. Stanford, CA: Stanford University Press.

Vickery, Walter N. (1992). *Alexander Pushkin*, revised edn. New York: Twayne.

Woodward, James (1982). "The 'Principle of Contradictions' in Yevgeniy Onegin." *Slavonic and East European Review*, 60: 25-43.

18

Lermontov: Romanticism on the Brink of Realism

Robert Reid

Russian Romanticism: Problems of Definition

Russian Romanticism has traditionally been an area of heightened critical attention for several reasons. First, the Romantic period as a whole coincides with the coming of age of Russian literature and it is arguable that its future trajectory was in large measure determined by the pioneering works of national literature which were produced between, say, 1800 and 1840. Secondly, the most influential writers of the period – Pushkin (1799-1837), Lermontov (1814-41), and Gogol (1809-52) – while exhibiting in their works much that was Romantic in form and content, also subscribed to the realist aesthetic which, according to traditional periodization, begins to supplant Romanticism in the 1840s. If this chronology is applied rigorously it might appear that only Gogol qualifies as a realist, and indeed Pushkin's and Lermontov's contributions to realism arguably lie in the influence of their works on later realist writers. A third area which gives scope for critical debate is the perceived ideological orientation of Romanticism. It has long been noted that attempts to define Romanticism end with a list of topoi which defy integration into a single organic whole: individualism, idealism, flight from reality, love of nature, nationalism, revolution, and so on. This famously led Lovejoy ([1924] 1948) to propose that there was not one, but there were many Romanticisms. However, this plurality has made it relatively easy for a particular attribute to be foregrounded with paradoxical results. Thus, with the rise of critical realism in the 1840s and 1850s, and its promotion by radical critics of the Belinskii school, Romantic works were elevated to the canonical status once enjoyed by their classical antecedents.[1] The officially sanctioned canon which found its way into educational institutions during the 1840s, 1850s, and 1860s emphasized *narodnost'* – national character or nationalism – a feature, certainly, to be found in much Romantic writing, but a conveniently conservative one.[2]

Soviet literary critics confronted a problem of a quite different order. As part of the enormous revisionist project to ensure that citizens of the Soviet state could safely handle its now politically incorrect pre-Revolutionary literary heritage, Romanticism came under close critical scrutiny. Since the mid-1930s a state-sanctioned realist aesthetic – Socialist Realism – had been elevated to canonical status and Romanticism inevitably attracted official suspicion, a situation again facilitated by a judicious choice of definitions: in this case individualism, idealism, and flight from reality. By the same token, however, the more politically acceptable attributes of nineteenth-century Romanticism – its anticonventionalism and revolutionary themes – were emphasized *per se* rather than as characteristics of Romanticism. The 1930s also saw the emergence of the pragmatic term *romantika* to characterize those Romantic motifs which could be deemed acceptable in a Socialist Realist work. The last significant critical debate relating to Romanticism took place in the 1960s in the form of a dispute around the rival merits of Lovejoyan pluralism and the more traditional notions of periodization and movement. The aesthetic details of this debate are less important than its political implications. It has to be seen within the context of Khrushchev's reforming policies: the general relaxation of political control of culture permitted the ideologically suspect concept of Romanticism to be discussed more (though not completely) openly, and moreover with some reference to foreign scholarship.

If we are to draw any lesson from the fluctuations in official perception to which Russian Romanticism has been subject over the last two hundred years, it is that, however the concept is defined, it is profoundly ideological in its implications. Moreover, its ideological content can be construed as conservative or progressive depending on the regnant political context. Some of Romanticism's ideological coloration derives from the political soil in which it was nurtured: national conscious-ness from eighteenth-century Germany, revolutionary orientation from Revolutionary France, Byronic individualism from England. At the same time, however, nineteenth-century Romanticism can be seen as an attempt to address the revealed inadequacies of eighteenth-century rationalism and by implication the classical aesthetic that articulated it: a project of "creative renewal" (Furst 1969). This has been traditionally expressed in terms of an opposition between two movements – Classicism and Romanticism (the latter ousting the former) – but it is possible, if controversial, to view Romanticism as the natural heir to Classicism, not merely in terms of a reinvigoration of artistic tropes, but also in its restoration of an aesthetic which was essentially elitist, despite the new preoccupations with revolutionary and nationalist themes.[3] The true opponent of Romanticism, according to this view, would indeed be realism, because in Russia, particularly, it was viewed as a fundamentally democratic medium with correspondingly distinct resources in language, plot, and characteriza-tion. It is certainly true that in the distinctive features of Russian realism – democ-ratization of character ("the little man") and setting (the city), mimetic description, social typicality – one can perceive Romantic aesthetics in reverse. However, it is equally true that the mimetic principle which underlies realism, and was preached in its extreme form by Chernyshevskii, limits artistic scope. What we in fact perceive in the greatest Russian realists is the appropriation of techniques from their Romantic predecessors: a unique synthesis of realist mimesis and Romantic psychologism. In my examination of Romanticism in Lermontov's works, then, I shall attempt to emphasize their strong ideological engagement, their protorealism, and the ways in which the themes they broached passed into the mainstream of Russian literature.

Lermontov: The Semiotics of Romantic Behavior

Lermontov's life confronts us with a complex instance of behavioral semiotics. On one level he may be viewed as Russia's quintessentially Romantic poet, ever in pursuit of situations which enhanced and projected his Romantic self-image. Among these are such experiences as love affairs, duels, exile, delight in the exotic, personal unhappiness, and social isolation. In terms of Romanticism's grand plot, Lermontov may be said to move from creative precocity (he was writing works of literary significance at the age of 16), through rebellious nonconformity, to exile and an early, self-predicted death. However, it is also the case that for Lermontov, as for other Russian literary contemporaries and successors, the Romantic paradigm was not merely aesthetic but existential. As a young aristocrat living under the stifling reign of Nicholas I, Lermontov experienced a very real kind of frustration and lack of fulfillment, and was in many ways a typical representative of the so-called "superfluous man" produced by the social and political atmosphere in Russia during the first half of the nineteenth century. This lent an authenticity to the more personal manifestations of his alienation and a social accuracy to his literary projections of his own condition. Lermontov's two spells of Caucasian exile (1837 and 1840) likewise represent a sociopolitical animation of a Romantic topos. The Caucasus, while it could easily be made to embody Orientalism, exoticism, and Rousseauistic primitiveness, was in Lermontov's time, as now, the site of bloody conflict between rival nationalisms, as well as a religious interface. It was also, along with Siberia, a frequent destination for political exiles (for Pushkin, for instance, and some of the Decembrists) and Lermontov was following in this tradition.[4] To this extent Lermontov was influenced creatively by the penal experience which has historically been a prominent inspirational component of Russian literature both in the nineteenth and twentieth centuries. Indeed, if we include in this poems which reflect his periods of confinement preceding his exile we will find that a great deal of his creative work falls into this penal ambit. A major feature of Lermontov's Romanticism is his struggle to use Romantic forms to reflect real-life experience. At the same time, though, the stereotypical nature of these forms resists the representation of real life in mimetic detail, leading at times to the impressionism which some commentators have detected in his work (Liberman 1983). This aesthetic tension in much of Lermontov's work reminds us that Romanticism in its later period could be as prescriptive as Classicism, and that in this context the rise of realism was a creative release.[5]

In view of what has been said so far, it is probably correct to view Lermontov as a poet who was progressively politicized by his experiences. However, this was essentially a process of accretion rather than supersession. We do indeed find many poems of a subjective or solipsistic nature early in his career, but later too he continued to produce such works alongside others which reflected his mature and politically honed ideology. Typical of the first type of poem is "The Sail" ("Parus," 1832) and "Earth and Heaven" ("Zemlia i nebo," 1830-1).[6] In "The Sail" the poet contemplates a solitary white sail out at sea which, functioning as both metonym and metaphor – steersman and the Romantic self – motivates the hypophoric questioning which forms the body of the poem: why has the boat left its native shores; what is it seeking in foreign climes? The paradoxical answer is that it is "wishing for a storm / As though in storms to find some peace" (I, 488).[7] "Earth and Heaven" is more generalized still, lacking even a pictorial core. Again, however, an initial question is posed – "How can we fail to love earth more than heaven?" (I, 344) – and answered in terms of earth's greater proximity and affinity to humankind. Lermontov was still writing uncompromisingly subjective Romantic lyrics in his mature period: "I look at the future with fear" ("Gliazhu na budushchnost' s boiazn'iu," 1838) and the well-known "It is tedious and sad" ("I skuchno i grustno," 1840). Lyrics such as these are striking for their lack of defined sociopolitical context, but this is not Romanticism by default: closer structural scrutiny of such works shows an engagement with the Kantian premises which underlay the Romantic worldview, in particular the conceptualization of time and space as conditions rather than objects of cognition.

Lermontov's Romantic Symbolism

Apart from these overarching Romantic preoccupations, we can also detect in Lermontov's oeuvre recurrent symbols and motifs which exemplify not only his own personalization of the Romantic repertory, but also a technique which would be developed more fully by Blok and the Symbolists some 60 years later: the use of semantically rich images as points of convergence for complex abstractions. Thus the dagger features in several poems as a polysemantic image capable of drawing together otherwise disparate subjects into the poet's creative ambit. In "The Dagger" ("Kinzhal," 1838) the dagger's provenance and ownership are carefully detailed: "A brooding Georgian forged you for revenge, / A free Circassian whetted you for fearful battle" (I, 38). Now it belongs to the poet, having been given to him as a valedictory love token: "I received you from a lily-white hand / For remembrance, at the moment of parting . . . " (I, 38). Georgian, Circassian, and Russian, the chief ethnic participants in the Caucasian drama of Lermontov's time, are here inferentially inducted into a poem which is ostensibly an Orientalized love lyric. In "Your heavenly gaze gleams / Like blue enamel" ("Kak nebesa, tvoi vzor blistaet," 1838) the lyric hero's infatuation is such that "For a single sound of your magic voice, / For a single glance / I am ready to part with my *Sech*'s pride, / My Georgian dagger" (I, 41). Dagger and woman here confront the hero with an either/or of masculinity, found elsewhere in Lermontov: the choice between love and warfare. "The Dagger" also broaches this dilemma via secondary symbolism: the poet receives the parting gift from his beloved and "For the first time it was not blood which dripped from you [the dagger] / but a bright tear – a pearl of suffering" (I, 38). These two images are suggestive of a conflict widely addressed by Lermontov in his works with an explicitly Caucasian setting: the disjunction between feelings and passion, particularly in the form of human weakness, and the uncompromising demands of an authoritarian martial ethos. In "Your heavenly gaze gleams" reference to the *Sech* – a fortified Cossack encampment – identifies the lyric voice as that of a Cossack, a member of the most ambiguous socioethnic group of the region, synonymous with professional militarism, and paradoxically representative both of assimilation (to many of the Asiatic mores of the region) and of Russian imperial expansion (staunch Orthodoxy, loyalty to the Tsar).

"The Poet" ("Poet," 1838) represents Lermontov's fullest exploitation of the symbolic potential of the dagger image. Here the dagger itself is made to embody two extremes: the violent and heroic activity for which it was made and later an enforced and shameful idleness. First used by a Caucasian tribesman, it passed to the Cossack who killed him and thence to an Armenian shopkeeper in whose care it languished until bought by the poet and hung, for decoration, on his wall where "It gleams like a golden toy... / Alas, inglorious and innocuous..." (I, 48). In this poem the dagger becomes an eloquent symbol of decadence and disempowerment, the more so because the weapon itself is shown to possess no inherent virtues: fate and circumstance determine whether it will be put to its designated use, lie idle, or become a mere ornament, and indeed the poem effectively emplots the dagger's fall into indignity. Rather as an afterthought, Lermontov uses the rest of the poem to explicate his image in terms of the supine condition of the modern poet ("In our pampered age, poet, have you not also / Lost your avocation...?" I, 49) and while this part of the text is relevant to Lermontov's view of the role of the artist, it is the dagger itself which most clearly defines the parameters of Lermontov's creative world. Lermontov transforms a Romantic prop into the metonymic focalizer for a series of ideologically fraught topoi: the Caucasus and its multiethnicity; Russia's role in the region; primitive notions of martial valor in Romantic theory and imperial practice; the impossibility of an autonomous, individual ethos unfettered by social determinants.[8]

The natural world also supplies Lermontov with recurrent symbols which he invests with anthropomorphic connotations similar to those of the dagger. Leaves and trees, while they may be found throughout his work as an inevitable descriptive backdrop, are foregrounded in certain works to particular effect. In some poems, for instance "The Reed" ("Trostnik," 1832), this manifests itself in an orthodoxly Romantic use of pastoral and folkloric motifs. In "The Reed" a fisherman makes a pipe out of a reed beneath which, unbeknown to him, a young maiden has been buried. Her lamenting voice speaks out when he plays the pipe. The ballad also contains the stock folk motifs of the cruel stepmother and the treacherous – in this case murderous – lover. "The Leaf" ("Listok," 1841) too conforms to established

Romantic repertory, but displays Lermontov's characteristic focalizing technique: a leaf torn from an oak tree is blown aimlessly about the steppe until it lodges against the root of a plane tree where it seeks shelter. The leaf's description of itself figuratively represents the rootless protagonist found in a number of Lermontov's works: "I have matured too early and grown up in a harsh country... / Alone and aimless I have long wandered the earth, / I have withered for want of shade; sleepless and without rest have I wilted./ Take this stranger into your leaves of emerald green, / I have a fund of strange and wonderful stories" (I, 124). The leaf's overtures are rejected by the plane tree, whose reply also reinforces the theme of society's rejection of the poet: "You have seen much – but why do I need your stories? / Even the birds of paradise itself are tedious to me" (I, 124). Though the poem lacks clear geographical parameters, the trees are subtly chosen: the oak (masculine in Russian) suggesting Russia and the North, the feminine plane tree (as evinced by Lermontov's frequent use of it in this regional context) the Caucasus and the South. Thus while as Andronikov (I, 597) suggests "The image of the storm-driven leaf is a widespread symbol of the fate of the political exile" (in Russian and European literature of the Romantic period), Lermontov biases the poem gently in the direction of his own situation, exiled to the Caucasus for the second time, and the plane tree itself can be read additionally as an emblem of the region ("Move on wanderer! I know you not! / I am loved by the sun, for him I flower, for him I shine," I, 125). The juxtaposition of natural beauty to individual suffering, and the indifference of the former to the latter, were themes intensified by Lermontov's sojourns in the Caucasus, and they feature prominently in his mature narrative works *The Demon* (*Demon*, 1839), *The Novice* (*Mtsyri*, 1839), and *A Hero of Our Time* (*Geroi nashego vremeni*, 1840) in all of which individual tragedy is played out against a stunning Caucasian landscape.

Other poems which employ tree or leaf symbolism also exploit exotic provenance: a desiccated piece of palm brought back from the Holy Land is the occasion for religious musings in "The Branch from Palestine" ("Vetka Palestiny," 1837); In "Three Palms" ("Tri pal'my," 1839) a group of Arabian nomads cut down three isolated palms and thus destroy a tiny desert oasis. The common setting suggests the Middle East as a location for primal moral events which are fundamental to Lermontov's philosophical and religious views. The principle of symbolic focalization is found in a range of other forms too. Rocks, mountains, and rivers are made to perform this function and several of them make explicit reference to the Caucasus: "The Cross on the Rock" ("Krest na skale," 1839), "Hurrying to the North from afar" ("Spesha na sever iz daleka," 1837), "The Terek's Gifts" ("Dary Tereka," 1839), "The Argument" ("Spor," 1841). While we can find examples of these same natural features not topographized in this way ("The Cliff" ["Utes," 1841], for instance) it is precisely this investment of traditional Romantic staples with Lermontov's real-life experience which gives the majority of them their force and uniqueness. Key here is an early work – "The Caucasus" ("Kavkaz," 1830) – written when Lermontov was 16, recalling his first visit to the Caucasus as a boy: "Though early separated from you by fate, / O southern mountains / You need only be seen once to be eternally remembered / Like a sweet song from one's homeland / I love the Caucasus...I was happy with your mountain ravines; / Five years have passed and still I pine..." (I, 202). This primal insight evolves into ever more complex forms throughout Lermontov's life under the experiential impact of the region to which he would be twice exiled, serve as a frontline soldier, and die in a duel.

Thus far we have dealt with texts which, while identifiably belonging to the Romantic repertory, are subtly infused with references to Lermontov's life and experience. We now move on to examine three sources of cultural influence on the poet which together illustrate the degree to which Lermontov was both receptive to the broader themes of Romantic culture and creatively resourceful enough to resist enslavement by them. The first of these relates to Lermontov's special relationship to Scotland; the others to the impact on him of two major figures of the Romantic period: Byron and Pushkin.

The Scottish Dimension

Lermontov was of Scottish ancestry. His forebear, George Learmonth, originally from Fife, was a Scottish mercenary serving with the Polish army who was captured by the Russians in 1613, changed sides, settled in Russia and received a grant of land and gentry status for his military service to the state. Lermontov knew his family history and would have read the ballad *Thomas the Rhymer* in Scott's *Minstrelsy of the Scottish Border* and the copious scholarly notes which Scott provides about its author/hero Thomas Learmonth – "The Rhymer." Thomas Learmonth was the semilegendary progenitor of Lermontov's family, a bard and soothsayer and, according to some accounts, a supporter of William Wallace. Scott, and Scottish Romanticism more generally, played a powerful role in determining Russian literary consciousness in the first half of the nineteenth century. As a geographical and cultural interface between ancient (Highland) and modern (Lowland) values Scotland had clear affinities with the Caucasus of Pushkin, Marlinskii, and Lermontov himself. There are a number of Scottish echoes in Lermontov and two youthful poems which seem to be inspired directly by his Scottish descent: "Ossian's Grave" ("Grob Ossiana," 1830) and "Long-ing" ("Zhelanie," 1831). In the first of these, only eight lines long, the poet's imagination transports him to Ossian's grave. The poem is double-layered: it is a homage to Scotland, a Northern homeland for Romantic poets, but also the personal homeland of a Lermontov, exiled from : "...the hills of my Scotland" (I, 247). Equally however, there is no concrete basis for the poet's musings: since Ossian himself is a fictional creation he can have no grave, and its imaginary location "in the steppe" underlines Lermontov's ignorance of Scottish geography. Even so the poem has a totemic flavor to it: the poet wishes to "breathe his native breezes" and "live afresh" in Scotland (I, 247).

"Longing" has a broadly similar theme but is related far more specifically to Lermontov's own ancestry. In it we can detect the influence of Scott's own sequel to

Thomas the Rhymer which he included, along with the ballad itself, in *Minstrelsy of the Scottish Border*. Scott describes Thomas Learmonth, the Rhymer, feasting, reciting, and harping for his noble guests "In Learmonth's high and ancient hall" (Scott 1932: 128). It is to this ancestral seat, now crumbling and empty, that Lermontov imagines himself returning, in the form of a raven. Common to both Scott's ballad and Lermontov's poem is the image of the bardic harp. In Scott's ballad, Thomas, aware that he must depart for Elfland, cuts short his recitation: "There paused the harp; its lingering sound / Died slowly on the ear…" (Scott 1932: 132). And as he departs, "the dying accents" of the harp, hanging round his neck, sound in the wind. In his imaginary visitation Lermontov imagines himself touching a Scottish harp in the deserted castle: "The sound would soar about the vaulted ceiling; / I would listen alone, and awoken alone, / It would fall silent as suddenly as it had sounded" (I, 368). The harp, symbol of Thomas Learmonth's bardic inspiration, is recovered by his Russian descendant. Just as Learmonth's departure is marked by the aeolian plaint of his harp strings, so Lermontov, returning to his hereditary castle in the guise of a raven, reanimates the harp with a brush of his wing: an occult return to match an occult departure. However, where Scott has Thomas Learmonth's harp play to an audience, Lermontov offers a solipsistic semiotics: both the harp and its player are alone. It is a purely personal encounter with his poetical forebear, or rather with an aspect of his forebear with which he identifies. Thomas Learmonth was also, according to tradition, an aristocrat and a soldier, the originator of a martial family tradition which survived transplantation to Russia: Lermontov therefore styles himself "The last descendant of bold warriors" (I, 369). Though these Scottish motifs in Lermontov's work are sparse they are highly significant and confirm a specific pattern of alienation and affiliation in the writer's socioethnic consciousness. In one sense Lermontov appeals to his distant Scottish descent as a way of emphasizing his Romantic alienation from Russian society. In another, however, his family myth serves to underline his Russianness since it is a story of his family's honorable acclimatization over two hundred years: Lermontov is a Russian aristocrat and soldier and to that extent unavoidably of the establishment. Even so, the "Russian / not Russian" binary is fundamental to Lermontov's creative consciousness and manifests itself also in his feelings about the Caucasus and his attitude to Western cultural influences. Of the latter the most significant is that of Byron.

Romantic Influences: Byron and Pushkin

Both Pushkin and Lermontov were keenly aware of Byronism in the sense of a lived experience as much as a literary style: Pushkin famously characterizes the dandified hero of *Eugene Onegin* as "a Childe Harold in a Muscovite's cloak" (*Eugene Onegin* ch. VII, stanza 24). However it was Lermontov rather than Pushkin whom literary history has come to regard as the embodiment of the Byronic. It can be argued that Byron's work was the single most significant influence on Lermontov's poetry;

alternatively, however, Pushkin can be seen in this role, although many of his works too, particularly those with southern themes, are themselves influenced by Byron. Two of Lermontov's early poems offer apparently contradictory insights into the poet's own view of his relationship to Byron. At first glance the earlier of them ("K..." ["To...," 1830]) seems to suggest the young poet's desire to closely emulate his elder, while the later and better known one ("No, I am not Byron, but another" ["Net, ia ne Bairon, ia drugoi," 1832]) appears to reject any identification. However in the first poem Byron is introduced only in the second verse by way of a prolonged illustration of why the reader should not "sympathize [with the poet], / Although my words are for the moment sad..." (I, 255). Byron is made to exemplify, perhaps ideally, the complex of emotional and moral attitudes which the poet attributes to himself. The second poem begins with a forthright rejection of identification with Byron, and moves on, by way of a brief concessive statement ("Like him I am a wanderer pursued by the world," I, 459) to an enumeration of the principal differentia: (1) unlike Byron I have a "Russian soul"; (2) I have a different destiny ("I started earlier and I will finish sooner; / My mind will not accomplish much," I, 459). The concessive statement can be seen as a compression of the Byronic qualities explicated in the first poem, so that to some extent it is superseded by the second. Moreover the structure of the second poem inverts that of its predecessor: whereas the latter talks briefly about Lermontov and moves on to Byron; the former soon puts Byron aside in favor of the poet himself.[9] What is important, however, is that in neither of these poems is there any hint of artistic debt to Byron. Instead what is stressed is the poet's uncompromising individualism in the face of a hostile society. It is this typically Russian adaptation of a Western idea to native conditions which explains the attraction of Byron for Lermontov and his contemporaries.[10] In fact by far the most interesting section of "I am not Byron..." is the poet's own enigmatic characterization of himself with which the poem concludes: "Who will tell my thoughts to the crowd?" (I, 459). This links him closely to another powerful influence for whom this theme was a constant preoccupation – Alexander Pushkin.

It is impossible to overestimate the importance of Pushkin's significance for Lermontov. Pushkin was at the height of his creative powers when Lermontov began to write and, although the older poet was far less wedded to Romanticism than his successor, Pushkin's evocations of the Caucasus, as well as his concept of the status and avocation of the poet become subjects of central importance for Lermontov. When Pushkin was killed in a duel in 1837 Lermontov effectively declared himself his heir by immediately writing and circulating "The Death of a Poet" ("Smert' poeta"), a poem expressing outrage at Pushkin's death. Pushkin's fatal duel with Georges Danthès, the adopted son of the Dutch Ambassador in St Petersburg, was ostensibly about the latter's pursuit of Pushkin's wife, but it was widely felt that Pushkin had been hounded to his death by a vindictive and unsympathetic establishment.[11] By this time Pushkin was no longer at the height of his popularity, and was obliged to occupy a demeaning palace sinecure by a suspicious Tsar who personally vetted his literary work. He was the embodiment of the alienated poet described in his own verse ("The Poet and the Crowd" ["Poet i tolpa," 1828]), a theme which also appealed to Lermontov. Thus a European Romantic stereotype became tragic reality on Russian soil: thousands of common people attended the funeral of the poet who, as Lermontov puts it in "Death of a Poet": "Rose up against society's opinions, / Alone, as ever...and was killed" (I, 21). This ideological commitment to art – whereby a poet's death in a duel becomes a significant political event – is characteristically Russian and is explicable by various historical and cultural factors. It is certain, however, that Romanticism's stress on the special calling of the artist was an important catalyst in determining Russian attitudes to writers and writing during the nineteenth century and for most of the twentieth.

As well as its political import "The Death of a Poet" sets the keynote for Lermontov's view of poetical inspiration. In Pushkin Lermontov believed he had witnessed the poet/crowd opposition, the pedigree of which goes back to Horace ("Odi profanum vulgus et arceo...") enacted in its most extreme form: "And removing his wonted crown – they placed a crown of thorns on him / With laurels intertwined: / But the secret spines cruelly / Tormented his glorious head" (I, 22).[12] Elsewhere in Lermontov we will find this motif repeated: the poet's divine gifts are superfluous or ridiculed by the ignorant multitude (in "The Poet" for instance). In part we can attribute this to an innate aristocratism which Lermontov shared with Pushkin: the inflammatory last verse of "Death of a Poet" is merely an explicit reformulation of an idea implied by Pushkin himself in poems like *The Bronze Horseman* (*Mednyi vsadnik*, 1834) and "My Genealogy" ("Moia rodoslovnaia," 1830): that his own kind, the ancient hereditary gentry, had been eclipsed by vulgar upstarts whose parents were ennobled for their political support by Catherine the Great. These, writes Lermontov, in "Death of a Poet": "Surround the throne in a rabid crowd, / The executioners of freedom, Genius and Glory" (I, 23). Equally, however, this outlook defines the limits, and signals the twilight of Romanticism in Russia. The personal isolation which becomes so frequent a refrain in the later Lermontov, while formulating itself in terms of the futility of verbal communication and the dangers of frank self-expression, conceals beneath it the loss of a socially and culturally sympathetic addressee. Works by Lermontov which particularly exhibit this are "No, I am not Byron" (the two last lines), "There are words / With dark meaning..." ("Est' rechi- znachen'e / Temno...," 1840), "Do not trust, do not trust yourself, young dreamer" ("Ne ver', ne ver' sebe, mechtatel' molodoi," 1839); and one can also find the same idea expressed in *The Novice*: "Can one narrate one's soul" (II, 53) and Pechorin's description of his youth in *Princess Mary*, one of the story-chapters in *A Hero of Our Time* ("Fearing ridicule, I buried my best feelings in the depths of my heart and there they died," IV, 89).

The most explicit elaboration of this theme by Lermontov is in his "Journalist, Reader and Writer" ("Zhurnalist, chitatel' i pisatel'," 1840), a short dramatic poem written, significantly, while Lermontov was under arrest following his duel with the son of the French Ambassador for which he was soon to be exiled. A poet (the "writer") is sick and is being visited by a literary critic (the "journalist") and a member of the reading public (the "reader"). In the journalist's view, the writer's sickness is a boon because it keeps him from social distractions which are inimical to "mature creation": whereas misfortune, which includes "exile and confinement" (Lermontov's current vicissitudes) will produce "a sweet song" (I, 77-8). The writer, however, confesses that his present condition has not produced the desired effect: he has nothing to write because all the traditional (Romantic) topics are written out: "What is there to write about? The East and South / Have been dealt with long ago; / Abusing the crowd has been tried by every poet; They've all praised married life, / Soared in spirit heavenwards, / Prayed silently / To an unknown beauty / And bored everyone to tears" (I, 78). The reader has his turn next. He initially gives the impression of a philistine whose first concern is for the physical appearance of literary journals and their abundance of misprints. He dismisses contemporary poetry as rubbish, while prose, if it is not translation, consists of short stories which "Make fun of Moscow / And denigrate civil servants. / On whom do they base these portraits? / Where do they hear these dialogues? And even if *they* have heard them / *We* don't want to..." (I, 79). In conclusion, however, he wonders when "barren Russia" will cast aside "false tinsel": "When will thought find simple language? / When will passions find a noble voice?" (I, 79). There then follows an exchange about literary criticism between the reader and the journalist and both conclude by lamenting the nonproductiveness of the "sick" writer, thus giving him the pretext for a concluding riposte.

The writer describes two kinds of inspiration to which he is subject, both recognizably within the paradigm of Romantic creativity: the first joyful and ecstatic; the second bitter and full of regret. He declines to show the products of either kind of creative process to the public – for fear of ridicule in the first instance and, in the second, of disturbing the reader and exciting censure. "Tell me," he begs, "What shall I write?" (I, 82). The writer's confession of his creative solipsism is the culminating moment in the threefold debate between the principal agents in the text-producing process and asserts the primacy of authorship in that process. At the same time the device of the writer's "illness" deconstructs itself on closer examination: ironically, the writer's description of his own creative block, of his nonproduction of text, is itself a text, in a distinctly Romantic idiom, delivered by a lyric voice which nevertheless asks in desperation "Tell me, what shall I write?" It is the reader who inadvertently supplies the answer and also provides a clue to the direction Russian literature will take (though he himself would clearly not approve of it) when he alludes to literature which denigrates civil servants. Six years later Dostoevskii makes the civil service clerk Devushkin (in *Poor Folk*) take similar umbrage on reading what he believes to be a portrait of himself in the clerical protagonist of Gogol's great realist landmark *The Overcoat*: "And what is the point of writing things like that? What use do they serve?...one's entire public and private life is held up for inspection in the form of literature...it will be impossible for me to go out on the street...everything has been described in such detail that I will now be instantly recognized by my walk alone" (Dostoyevsky 1988: 68). Of course Romanticism had traditionally held up the *poet's* "entire public and private life" for inspection; the outraged reaction of a *reader* compelled to identify an unflattering fictional creation with himself is something new and symptomatic of the mimetic and socially typifying techniques of the new critical realism.

The Major Narrative Works: *The Demon, The Novice,* and *A Hero of Our Time*

Lermontov's reputation by no means rests solely on his lyric poetry. He wrote narrative poems – including *The Demon* and *The Novice* – both set in the Caucasus. His novel, *A Hero of Our Time*, was one of the classic texts (the others being Pushkin's *Eugene Onegin* and Gogol's *Dead Souls*) which laid out the creative parameters for the great novelists of the latter part of the nineteenth century. It is to these narrative works, produced late in Lermontov's short career, that we now turn: these are the texts in which Lermontov most clearly confronts, and ultimately transcends, the problematics of Romanticism.

The Demon and *The Novice* explore in narrative form many of the preoccupations broached severally by the lyrics. *The Novice* is based on the true story of a Circassian boy captured by Russian soldiers in a raid on a mountain village and handed into the care of Georgian monks. In Lermontov's poem the boy, preparing for holy orders, escapes from the remote Georgian monastery under cover of a thunderstorm and attempts to return to his home in the distant hills which he can see from his monastery cell. After vainly wandering for three days, in the course of which he is mauled by a mountain lion, he ends up where he started and dies after telling the story of his escape to an old monk by way of confession. In one sense the poem is quintessentially Romantic: the young escapee attempts to assert his identity, only to become tragically disoriented. There is a vain attempt by the exile to recover his true home, and nature is encountered as a sublime mixture of beauty, indifference, and danger. On closer scrutiny, however, we discover, as so often in Lermontov's works, a political subtext for which the Romantic *sujet* is a convenient vehicle. The triangulation of Russian, Circassian, and Georgian cultures locates the tale on the fault line of the Russian imperium, precisely the position occupied by Lermontov himself in the latter part of his life. The forcible abduction of a Muslim (Circassian) child to a Christian country (Georgia) and his subsequent induction into the holy orders of an alien religion is a potent metaphor of imperial intervention. The poem also plays in an original way with the traditional Romantic binary opposition of civilization/savagery and culture/nature. The novice finds himself unable to survive in the world outside the monastery walls precisely because of the success with which he has acclimatized himself to the monastic life. His cherished dream of returning to his homeland is utterly inefficacious against environmental reality. There are no hereditary advantages to be drawn upon in his struggle with the harsh mountainous landscape and natural hazards; indeed in lines later excised by Lermontov the novice in his delirium imagines a Circassian war party riding past him: "With a wild whistle, like a storm, / They rushed by close to me. / And each one, leaning over from his mount, / Threw a scornful glance / At my monkish garb...? I could scarcely breathe, tormented by shame" (II, 563).

Lermontov seems here to be problematizing ethnicity and, in his insistence on the role of environment in determining character, is, despite the Romantic idiom, anticipative of realist assumptions: the hero is estranged both from his racial origins and from the natural world, two key areas of engagement for Romantic aesthetics. Most significant, however, is the poem's Russocentricity. Russian ethnicity, while not represented explicitly in the poem, is all the more powerful for its being embedded in its semiotic mechanisms. The introductory stanza of the poem describes the monastery and its graveyard: the gravestones tell "Of past glory and of / A King, weary of his crown / Who in a certain year / Entrusted his people to Russia. / And God's blessing descended / On Georgia! She has flourished / Ever since... / Not fearing enemies / From beyond the friendly bayonets" (II, 52). This is the hegemonic context of the poem and one in which Russian writer and Russian reader would broadly concur. It is reminiscent of Pushkin's odic celebration of Peter the Great's metropolis in *The Bronze Horseman* as an ironic prelude to describing the wretched story of one of its humble inhabitants. In both poems two distinct forms of discourse embody two competing perspectives on Russian reality: the autocratic and the democratic; the imperial and the autochthonous.

It is this sensitivity to the ethno-imperial interface which identifies *The Novice* as close in theme and ideology to the culminating work of Lermontov's career, the novel *A Hero of Our Time*. Yet it is his narrative poem *The Demon* which is most often cited as the novel's direct precursor.[13] This is because the hero of *The Demon* can be shown to have an obvious affinity with the hero of the novel, who also possesses, if only figuratively, a "demonic" character. *The Demon*, however, was a long-term project of Lermontov's, first drafted at a time when he was still very much in thrall to Romantic paradigms. Even so the seven successive redraftings of the poem produced a work which managed, on a philosophical level, to address the moral dilemmas of the post-Kantian universe, while at the same time functioning as an allegory of the Russian imperial condition. Significantly, it is the Romantic impressionism of *The Demon* which enables it to sustain these different layers of meaning. Indeed an examination of the successive drafts shows a move away from, rather than towards, greater concretization of the hero and his motivations. Lermontov's critique of Kantianism uses the Demon figure much as it was used by Laplace, and before him Descartes, as a kind of extreme instance of human consciousness. Kantian ethics rests on the universalization of individual moral obligation, but what if we imagine an individual who is either wholly evil or, as in the case of the Demon, one whose God-ordained obligation is "to sow evil" (II, 85)? *The Demon* also debates a related topic: the rival merits of voluntarism, and consequentialism as mainsprings of human behavior. It is thus very much a philosophical work — more so perhaps than any other by Lermontov — but equally one which evinces considerable skepticism about some of the fundamental assumptions of Romantic axiology. Thematically *The Demon* owes a good deal to Miltonic and Byronic sources as well as to Goethe and Vigny. The Demon (it is never made clear whether he is *the* Devil or *a* devil) joylessly wanders the world spreading evil, until he catches sight of a young Georgian woman on the eve of her wedding. He falls in love with her and there instantly rekindles in him a longing to recover the paradise he has lost. Having engineered the death of her bridegroom, he persistently woos her, pursuing her even into the convent where she has attempted to take refuge from his visitations. When she dies in his fiery embrace an angel intervenes to pilot her soul to heaven, leaving the Demon to continue his hopeless wanderings.

A line of criticism particularly favored by Soviet critics interpreted this plot both as an allegory of Lermontov's own experiences and, more broadly, those of his generation: young highly educated aristocrats who felt themselves progressively marginalized in the Russia of Nicholas I, who, after the Decembrist revolt of 1825, came to mistrust the aristocratic elite to which its instigators belonged, preferring instead to govern through bureaucratic institutions. Lermontov has traditionally been thought to epitomize the embittered, disillusioned young "superfluous man" of this era and it is certainly possible to trace the psychological contours of this type beneath the Romantic representation of the poem's protagonist. The damnation of the Demon by an implacable God can be seen as a figurative representation of the relationship between subject and autocrat; the longing for a pre-Fall state is nostalgia for the former relationship between Tsar and aristocrat; the reconnection with things earthly which the Demon's love for the heroine briefly resurrects is the possibility of an authentic social existence which political conditions deny, and the coupling of the Caucasian context with the theme of exile suggests Lermontov's own inscription into the plot. Interpreted in this way *The Demon* confirms a use of Romantic aesthetics with which we are by now familiar: pre-existing Romantic paradigms are subtly infused with ideological and political parallelism – Romantic exile with real political exile, divine proscription with royal proscription.

Despite the undoubted ideological efficacy of this aesthetic, the culminating achievement of Lermontov's literary career – *A Hero of Our Time* – suggests that it was ultimately unable to fully articulate the social, political, and cultural issues which faced Russia towards the middle of the nineteenth century. Albeit in oversimplified terms, we may say that *A Hero of Our Time* is a realist novel produced by a writer whose literary and personal career were quintessentially Romantic. In effect Lermontov achieves with the novel a kind of Copernican inversion of the creative processes which we have examined so far. Instead of realist subtextual content beneath an overtly Romantic form, we have an innovative use of a variety of structural devices to give the vivid illusion of reality. (One early translator of the novel thought that it was a documentary account of military life in the Caucasus, rather than a work of fiction.) However, on closer inspection the novel preserves many important Romantic motifs. The novel consists of five chapters, interlinking stories which chronicle the exploits of a young army officer, Grigorii Pechorin, who has been posted to the Caucasus, probably for some misdemeanor. Three of the constituent stories purport to be extracts from Pechorin's journal; of the other two one is an account by the fictitious editor of Pechorin's journal of his acquisition of it while traveling in the Caucasus (including his brief meeting with Pechorin himself); the other is an oral account of one of Pechorin's exploits collected by the editor from an army officer who knew him. The realism of the work is enhanced by the plurality of narrative voices and by the apparently disparate agendas of the narrators themselves. The editor is concerned mainly to record the scenery and customs of the Caucasus; the army officer who tells him about Pechorin is largely motivated by his admiration for Pechorin's exploits and baffled fascination with his unfathomable character. The overall and avowed purpose of the novel is to explicate the enigmatic psychology of the hero by approaching it from a variety of perspectives. One of these, of course, is the hero's own and in the three stories narrated by himself he emerges as a disillusioned, cynical, and manipulative figure, whose antisocial machinations bring heartbreak and sometimes death to those with whom he comes into contact. In this sense he can be seen as a realist incarnation of the Romantic Demon and more generally as a kind of narrative concretization of the fragmented Byronic lyric hero present throughout Lermontov's poetry.[14]

Despite Lermontov's attempts to objectivize Pechorin, reviewers were quick to identify the novel as a self-portrait. Stung by this interpretation Lermontov wrote a Preface to its second edition in which he sought to explain his purpose. He argued that Pechorin was not the portrait of a single man but of the vices of a whole generation in their extreme form. Of course, his justification here is not dissimilar in intention from his poem of some years before, dissociating himself from Byron. It was a plea for his hero (in the earlier case his lyric hero) to be considered objectively rather than subjectively: as a social portrait rather than a personal portrait. It is a plea in effect for Realism: for the acceptance of the fictional protagonist as typologically valid.

In *A Hero of Our Time* Lermontov attempted to estrange or lay bare the traditions of Romantic plot and psychology, while not dissociating himself from their existential validity. Had he survived, he might well have passed effortlessly into the developing mainstream of Russian realism. Instead he bequeathed to a still young literature a novel which was both influential and contradictory. Successive writers held it up as the benchmark for realistic multifaceted psychological portrayal. At the same time, along with other works by Pushkin and Gogol, it was in part responsible for preserving and developing Romantic motifs in the characterization techniques employed by subsequent generations of realist novelists.[15] Indeed one can say that it is this Romantic core which is the defining feature of Russian realism; and that, however paradoxically, Russia's greatest exponent of Romanticism was one of the principal founders of Russian realism.

324 *Robert Reid*

NOTES

1 On this see Lanu (2001: 48ff).
2 Even so it is not correct to characterize Russian Romanticism as inherently "conservative" or to assume that "Russianness" was invariably a conservative theme as is sometimes implied. See Cranston (1994: 142).
3 See the discussion of D. S. Likhachev's theory of periodization in Weststeijn (2004).
4 Exile, particularly in a Romanticized form, is a key component of the traditional Russian image of the Caucasus, since Romantic writers who had undergone that experience were largely responsible for creating the image. On this see Ram (1995).
5 Interestingly Lermontov's poetical language can be shown to move progressively away from the conventional archaisms favored by his immediate predecessors towards linguistic forms more in line with the standard speech of his time. See Motina (1997).
6 Transliteration of the titles of Lermontov's works uses the Library of Congress system without diacritics. Wherever possible conventional translations of titles and first lines have been used. Where there is no conventional version, I have aimed at literal accuracy.
7 All translations are my own unless otherwise stated. References are to the Andronikov and Oksman (1964) four-volume edition of Lermontov's works by volume and page.
8 Not all commentators would necessarily endorse the case for Lermontov's broadly ideological use of symbols. Smirnov, for instance,

stresses their Romantic expressionism: as an artist Lermontov expresses himself "not via the direct articulation of his thoughts, but through aspects of the external form of the symbol" (Smirnov 1989: 7).
9 Andronikov (1964, I: 360) speculates that the poem is a riposte to comparisons of the poet with Byron, which were current among his circle.
10 On this see Kuhiwczak (1997).
11 Lermontov's poem was the first among many verse commemorations. For a discussion of these see Fedorov (1964). See also Tynianov and Nikitina (1964).
12 For a full analysis of this aspect of the poem see Nedzvetskii (1972).
13 For a comparison of *The Demon* and *The Novice* see Lotman (1997: 61-9).
14 A compatible Bakhtinian view of the transition described here stresses Lermontov's increasing emphasis on dialogism. See Waszink (1993).
15 All of Lermontov's narrative protagonists – the novice, the Demon, and Pechorin – embody the conflict between strong personal autonomy and a restraining external or higher force which is a recurrent feature of Romantic characterization. (On this see Mart'ianova 1997.) Arguably this is the fundamental psychological predicament which Romanticism bequeaths to later writers like Dostoevskii and Tolstoy.

REFERENCES AND FURTHER READING

Andronikov, I. L. and Oksman, Iu. G. (eds). (1964). *Lermontov, M. Iu. Sobranie sochinenii v chetyrekh tomakh.* Moscow: Khudozhestvennaia literatura.
Cranston, M. (1994). *The Romantic Movement.* Oxford: Blackwell.
Dostoyevsky, F. (1988). *Poor Folk*, trans. David McDuff. Harmondsworth, UK: Penguin.
Federov, A. (1964). "*Smert' poeta* sredi drugikh otlikov na gibel' Pushkina." *Russkaia literatura*, VII (3): 32-45.
Furst, L. (1969). *Romanticism in Perspective.* London: Macmillan.
Fusso, S. (1998). "The Romantic Tradition." In M. V. Jones and R. Feuer Miller (eds.), *The Cambridge Companion to the Classic Russian Novel.*

Cambridge, UK: Cambridge University Press, pp. 171-89.

Golstein, V. (1998). *Lermontov's Narratives of Heroism*. Evanston, IL: Northwestern University Press.

Kelly, L. (1977). *Lermontov: Tragedy in the Caucasus*. London: Constable.

Kuhiwczak, P. (1997). "Translation and National Canons: Slav Perceptions of English Romanticism." *Essays and Studies*, 50: 80-94.

Lanu, A. (2001). "Formirovanie literaturnogo kanona russkogo romantizma: Na materiale uchebnikov i istorii literatury (1822-62)." *Novoe literaturnoe obozrenie*, 51: 35-67.

Liberman, A. (1983). *Mikhail Lermontov: Major Poetical Works*. London and Canberra: Croom Helm.

Lotman, Iu. (1997). *O russkoi literature: Stat'i i issledovaniia (1958-1993)*. St Petersburg: Iskusstvo-SPB.

Lovejoy, A. O. ([1924] 1948). "On the Discrimination of Romanticisms." In *Essays in the History of Ideas*. Baltimore: Johns Hopkins University Press, pp. 228-53.

Mart'ianova, S. A. (1997). "Personazhi russkoi klassiki I khristianskaia antropologiia." In V. B. Kataev et al. (eds.), *Russkaia literatura XIX veka I khristianstvo*. Moscow: Izdatel'stvo Moskovskogo universiteta, pp. 25-31.

Mersereau J. (1962). *Mikhail Lermontov*. Carbondale: South Illinois University Press.

Mersereau, J. (1989). "The Nineteenth Century: Romanticism 1820-40." In C. A. Moser (ed.), *The Cambridge History of Russian Literature*. Cambridge, UK: Cambridge University Press, pp. 136-88.

Motina, I.V. (1997). "Ob odnoi poeticheskoi traditsii v poezii M. Iu. Lermontova." *Russkii iazyk v shkole: metodicheskii zhurnal*, IV: 60-4.

Nedzvetskii, V. A. (1972). "Poet, tolpa, sud'ba (*Smert' Poeta* M. Iu. Lermontova)." *Izvestiia Akademii nauk SSSR: Seriia literatury i iazyka*, XXXI: 239-47.

Ram, H. (1995). "Translating Space: Russia's Poets in the Wake of Empire." In A. Dinwaney and C. Maier (eds.), *Between Languages and Cultures: Translation and Cross-Cultural Texts*. Pittsburg, PA and London: University of Pittsburg Press, pp. 199-222.

Reid, R. (1997). *Lermontov's "A Hero of Our Time."* London: Bristol Classical Press.

Scott, W. (1932). *Minstrelsy of the Scottish Border*, vol. IV, ed. T. F. Henderson. Edinburgh and London: Oliver and Boyd.

Smirnov, A. A. (1989). "Romanticheskii simvol v lirike Lermontova." *Vestnik Moskovskogo universiteta: Seriia 9, Filologiia*, 5: 3-9.

Tynianov, Iu and Nikitina, Z. (1964). "Literaturnyi istochnik *Smerti poeta*." *Voprosy literatury*, VIII (10): 98-106.

Waszink, P. (1993). "Not Mine but the Poet's Heart: Vygotskij's Concept of Katharsis and Dialogical Speech in Album-Lines by Byron and Lermontov." In W. G. Weststeijn (ed.), *Dutch Contributions to the Eleventh International Congress of Slavists: Bratislava 30/8/93-9/9/93*. Amsterdam: Rodopi, pp. 315-30.

Weststeijn, W. (2004). "Pushkin between Classicism, Romanticism and Realism." In R. Reid and J. Andrew (eds.), *Two Hundred Years of Pushkin. III: Pushkin's Legacy*. Amsterdam. Rodopi, pp. 47-56.

19

Adam Mickiewicz and the Shape of Polish Romanticism

Roman Koropeckyj

Upon hearing of the death of Adam Mickiewicz in 1855, his poetic and ideological rival Zygmunt Krasiński (1812-59) proclaimed, "We are all descended from him" (Krasiński 1970: 617). For three generations of Polish Romantics Mickiewicz's presence as "the first and the greatest" was ineluctable, as it would be for every subsequent generation of Poles, down to the rapper who could claim that "if Mickiewicz was alive today, he'd be a good rhymer" (Green 2002). The appearance of Mickiewicz's first collection of poetry in 1822 reconfigured Polish literature programmatically and irreversibly. With practically every work that followed – individual poems, poetic cycles, tales, dramas, and an epic, which in the most recent edition of his works amounts to no more than 1,500 pages of large print – Mickiewicz pushed the limits of this reconfiguration, transforming not only the literary sensibility of his contemporaries, but the very discourse of his nation at a critical moment of its existence. And like his beloved Byron, Mickiewicz sought to incorporate his poetic vision in the real, to create a poetry of praxis that would bring freedom to his compatriots and, ultimately, redeem the world.

Childhood

Adam Mickiewicz was born in 1798 on a homestead in what is now Belarus but was then referred to as Lithuania. After the final partition of the Polish-Lithuanian Commonwealth in 1795, this European backwater, with its overwhelmingly Polish, mostly impecunious gentry, East Slavic peasantry, and Jewish towns, had been absorbed by the Russian Empire, which at first lightly and then ever more heavy-handedly began imposing its own order on a largely traditional society. But memories of the old way of life were still very much alive, as were hopes for an independent, reunified Commonwealth. Napoleon reignited these hopes briefly, and the sight of the Grande Armée as it passed through Lithuania in 1811-12 fixed itself indelibly in

Mickiewicz's mind. To the end of his days he would retain an almost mystical attachment to the figure of Bonaparte.

The future poet came of petty gentry stock. His father, a somewhat fractious sort, was a lawyer in the small town of Navahrudak (Nowogródek). His mother too was from the petty gentry, although it is not unlikely that she was descended from converted Jews. Mickiewicz's life-long fascination with Jewishness would seem to bear this out.

Youth

After eight years of a traditional elementary education, Mickiewicz enrolled in the University of Vilnius, which he attended until 1819 as a student of classical philology. The university was very much a product of Lithuania's belated Enlightenment. His professors were for the most part devout rationalists and judicious patriots, their aesthetic horizon shaped by eighteenth-century neo-Classicism. But then so too was Mickiewicz's, whose earliest efforts at poetry were conventional exercises in Classicist poetics. That the poet would go on to be at one point himself a professor of classical literature is indication enough of the kind of education he received in Vilnius. The robustness and lucidity of his poetry, even at its most Romantic, bespeaks the degree to which he internalized the Greeks and the Latins.

Yet as decisive as Mickiewicz's academic training was for his intellectual development, the university provided him with something incalculably more valuable: a cohort of like-minded youths, like himself products of the petty gentry, whose only hope for a livelihood was education. They formed a semisecret fraternity, akin somewhat to Prussian *Tugendbunden*, that was devoted to self-improvement and the cult of friendship. Calling themselves the Society of Philomaths, the young men shared their elders' Enlightenment ideals: that the nation's survival depended on civic responsibility, which, in turn, was a function of education. What set them apart was not so much the impatient confidence of youth, but rather a conscious sense of youth, which in their eyes itself legitimated their aspirations. Over the course of some six years, the Philomaths adumbrated their program in countless meetings and carefully choreographed festivities. It took Mickiewicz to articulate fully its implications.

His 1820 "Oda do młodości" (Ode to youth), unabashedly Schillerian in inspiration, deftly exploits neo-Classicist poetics in order to subvert the discourse that engendered them:

> Bereft of heart, bereft of spirit, these are but skeletons of men;
> Youth! give me wings!
> So I can soar above this lifeless world
> Into illusion's edenic realm:
> Where ardor miracles creates [...].

> Together, youthful friends! . . .
> The happiness of all is everybody's aim;
> Strong in unity, wise in madness,
> Together, youthful friends! [. . .]
>
> Reach where vision reaches not;
> Force what reason will not force;
> Youth! your power is your eagles' flight,
> Like thunder is your arm. (Mickiewicz 1993-, 1: 42-3)[1]

The poem asserts, in no uncertain axiological terms, the potential of a new generation, juxtaposing its vitality and idealism with the smug calcification of its elders. But it does so in an altogether radical way. In its appeal to the "wisdom of folly" and summons to "overcome what reason cannot overcome," "Oda do młodości" is nothing less than a manifesto of a new, explicitly anti-Classicist, antirationalist sensibility, one, moreover, that in the charged atmosphere of the time was immediately understood by his contemporaries as "conjoining revolutionary aspirations in literature with aspirations for patriotic revolution" (Koźmian 1973: 425). Its concluding lines, "Welcome, morning star of liberty, / The sun of salvation is next" (Mickiewicz 1993-, 1: 44), would become a rallying cry for Polish insurgents in 1830.

But it was precisely this conjunction that guaranteed its resonance. Although not published until 1827, "Oda do młodości" coursed in manuscript as the hymn of a new generation. Practically every line entered the language as so many slogans, while the poem itself underwent countless permutations at the hands of succeeding generations, who adapted its imagery and rhetoric to the circumstances of the moment. When, after the failure of the 1863 uprising, Polish society began to reassess the political consequences of Romanticism, it was in the irrational, maximalist exuberance of "Oda do młodości" that it recognized the kernel of its predicament.

Mickiewicz wrote "Oda do młodości" in Kaunas (Kowno), a bleak provincial town where he had been sent to teach school in 1819 and where, with the exception of summers spent exploring the Lithuanian countryside and a year-long sabbatical among his cohort in Vilnius, he would remain until 1823. Although he found some solace in an affair with a married woman, it was above all continuous contact with his Philomath brethren, chronicled in a voluminous correspondence, that alleviated the poet's misery. It was here that he began reading his European contemporaries intensely, first Schiller, Goethe, and the German Idealists, then Byron, who came to share the same space in Mickiewicz's pantheon as Napoleon, that other great "poet" of life. The upshot of his reading was a cycle of "ballads and romances," which together with several miscellaneous poems comprised Mickiewicz's debut volume.

Titled simply *Poezje* (Poems), volume 1, it appeared in Vilnius in 1822, just as a polemic between proponents of the Romantic "style" and the neo-Classicist establishment was beginning to intensify. Mickiewicz's collection changed the nature and direction of the debate irrevocably. The introduction to the volume, which weighed in on the side of the new sensibility, is unremarkable, just as the "romances" are unexceptionable sentimentalist idylls. The "ballad" "Romantyczność" (Romanticity), however, is a forceful manifesto of a specifically Mickiewiczian Romanticism. In depicting a raving girl who insists to an empathetic crowd that she can see her dead lover's ghost, the narrator records his own empathy; to a scholarly sage who berates them all for "blaspheming against reason," he responds:

> "Affect and faith speak more strongly to me
> Than the lens and the eye of a wise man.
>
> You know but dead truths, unknown to the folk,
> You observe the world in speckles of dust, in every flash of a star.
> You can't grasp living truths, you'll not a miracle behold!
> Have a heart and gaze into that heart!" (Mickiewicz 1993-, 1: 57)

Mickiewicz was not the first to write ballads in Polish, but he was the first to use the form programmatically, as a challenge not only to the aesthetics of neo-Classicism, but to its very epistemology. The remaining ballads in the collection evoke a world – more literary, to be sure, than folkloric – in which the rational and the irrational, the mundane and the supernatural, continually intersect: a gentryman fishes a nymph out of a lake concealing a sunken city; the ghost of a murdered husband returns to punish his duplicitous wife; a medieval necromancer outwits the Devil. But no less challenging, especially to the neo-Classicists who dominated literary life in Poland's cultural capital Warsaw, was Mickiewicz's gesture of situating this world in local Lithuanian realities, its particularism underscored by his provocative use of provincialisms.

Poezje, volume 1, transformed Polish literature. Even those who decried his ballads as fit only for "dirty Lithuanian scullery maids" (Billip 1962: 334-5) could not deny Mickiewicz talent. Its appearance guaranteed the triumph of Romantic sensibility in Poland. Aspiring young poets from every corner of Poland began, for better or worse, pumping out ballads as a manifestation of both literary rebellion and sophistication. In the eyes of Mickiewicz's contemporaries, the ballad all but came to define the Polish Romantic "school." At the same time, it impelled poets to explore medieval chronicles, local geography, and above all the songs and legends of the former Commonwealth's various folk. Polish Romanticism was in this respect very much a product of the provinces, erupting from areas that for the most part were ethnically mixed, be it Mickiewicz's Lithuania, with its Belarusan peasantry and memories of the medieval Lithuanian state, or Ukraine, where such poets as Antoni Malczewski (1793-1826), Seweryn Goszczyński (1801-76), Józef Bohdan Zaleski (1802-86), and Juliusz Słowacki (1809-49) drew on Ukrainian folklore as well as a history marked by the bloody conflict between Cossacks and Poles.

Less than a year after the appearance of *Poezje,* volume 1, Mickiewicz published volume 2. It contained works of a very different character. The epic poem "Grażyna" is set in the Romantically requisite Middle Ages, when still pagan Lithuanians were struggling against the encroachment of the Teutonic Knights. Unable to dissuade her husband, a Lithuanian prince, from allying himself with their enemy, the eponymous heroine decides to act on her own. As her husband sleeps, she puts on her husband's armor and herself leads his soldiers against the Germans. She is mortally wounded. Shamed, her spouse joins her on the funeral pyre.

Aside from the medieval setting and the nocturnal atmosphere, "Grażyna" is not all that innovative. Where it is novel is in its depiction of the heroine, "by her charm a woman, by her spirit a hero" (Mickiewicz 1993-, 2: 46). She is one of a series of several female figures in Mickiewicz's work who reject their traditional role in acts of individual sacrifice for the sake of a national cause.

With the remaining work in the volume, Mickiewicz once again revolutionized Polish literature by creating its first modern drama. *Dziady* (Forefathers' Eve) (usually called the Kaunas-Vilnius *Dziady* in order to distinguish it from the later "Dresden" *Dziady*) is a *Lesedrama,* generically unstable: it is subtitled "A Poem" and the whole opens with a ballad ("Upior" [The Ghoul]). Adding to this sense of instability is the numbering of the drama's two parts – 2 and 4, respectively – suggesting fragmentariness. The two parts are in fact quite dissimilar, in style as well as content; part 2, moreover, is prefaced by a prose introduction. What unifies the whole is the notion of living death, articulated in the opening ballad in the image of a ghoul, "still on this earth but no longer of it" (Mickiewicz 1993-, 3: 9), and then explored as if in variations in the two parts of the drama.

Part 2, which gives the work its title, evokes a purportedly Belarusan pre-Christian rite of the dead held on All Saints' Eve. As his prose introduction suggests, Mickiewicz set out to (re)create a specifically Slavic ritual that has its analogies among "all pagan peoples" (Mickiewicz 1993-, 3: 13). In ancient Greece it ostensibly gave rise to tragedy; in the hands of the Polish Romantic it takes the shape of something without precedent. Presiding over the ritual is a shaman-like figure, who conjures up a series of spirits: two children who never tasted bitterness; a cruel landlord who had no compassion toward his serfs; and a young maiden who rejected love – all of them barred from heaven on account of some lack. However, with the uninvited appearance of a fourth figure, a young man with a bleeding wound on his breast who, unlike the others, remains mute, Mickiewicz introduces a distinctly Romantic note that serves as a tenuous link between parts 2 and 4, and at the same time shifts the drama from the Romantically ethnographic to the Romantically autobiographical.

In the spring of 1821, Mickiewicz fell in love with Maria Puttkamer, the young bride of a relatively wealthy acquaintance. Although he was loved as much as he loved, circumstances doomed the affair, but not before much torment and even an attempted suicide on Maria's part. The lovers had read Rousseau and *Werther* and Madame Krüdner carefully and with engagement. Now Mickiewicz set about transforming his feelings into his own poetic fiction, and the poetic fiction into a kind of hyperbolized simulacrum for genuine emotions, which it, in turn, stoked.

Part 4 also takes place on All Saints' Eve, but in the house of a Uniate priest and his children. Their supper is interrupted by a disheveled young man in whom the priest soon recognizes his former student Gustaw. Gustaw launches into a disjointed monologue, punctuated by an occasional comment from the priest, in which he raves about his own life and view of the world, but all refracted through the story of his unfortunate love for a girl who was forced to marry someone richer. By turns passionate and tender, sarcastic and pleading, rebellious and resigned, his rant is an eruption of pure affect. When the clock strikes 11, Gustaw stabs himself in the heart but does not die. His ontological status, neither dead nor alive and mad to boot, is the measure of a despair that transforms the pain of frustrated love into an existential howl:

> A lover of delusions seen only in dreams.
> Unable to bear the dull round of things earthly,
> I, who scorned commonplace, everyday beings,
> I sought, oh! I sought that lover divine,
> Who never existed here under the sun [. . .]
> [. . .]
> Then I finally found her!
> By my side I finally found her,
> I found her! . . . only to lose her forever! (Mickiewicz 1993-, 3: 49-50)

Dziady, part 4, is the first and most powerful articulation of Romantic love in Polish literature. So powerful, in fact, and so credibly did it deploy a lover's discourse, that readers assumed it to be nothing less than a versified chronicle of the poet's own affair. And in a sense it was, but only insofar as it constituted the first chapter of Mickiewicz's symbolic autobiography, inscribed now in each successive work he produced. Yet few in the poet's audience took to heart Gustaw's own condemnation of "brigand books" – Goethe's, Madame Krüdner's, Rousseau's, Schiller's, and now, presumably, Mickiewicz's own – that could "warp" a young reader's mind with fantastic "delusions" (Mickiewicz 1993-, 3: 49). On the contrary, for many Polish Romantics, particularly during the years of repressive miasma that followed the 1830 uprising, a lover's madness came to serve as a vehicle not so much for expressing the pain of ill-starred romance as for registering a protest against the pain of existence. And herein lies the paradox of *Dziady,* part 4: as an exploration of Romantic love *qua* love, it remains in Polish Romanticism a largely isolated phenomenon, its implications unrealized. Its appearance was possible only before the November uprising; for subsequent generations, consumed by the discourse of national struggle, Romantic love was "somehow too much of a luxury" (Piwińska 1984: 518).

In this respect, Mickiewicz's own biography constituted something of a template. In October 1823, the poet, together with his Philomath friends, was arrested on charges of belonging to a secret organization that purportedly "sought to spread ill-advised Polish nationalism by means of education" (Borowczyk 2003: 717). The arrests were part of a broader Russian assault on Polish institutions by Nikolai Novisiltsov, the tsar's administrator in Warsaw. As a secret society, the Philomaths proved a tempting target, although there was nothing conspiratorial in their activities. After some months of internment and interrogation, Mickiewicz and a few others were sentenced to exile in "provinces far from Poland" (ibid.), where they were to seek employment according to their respective specialties. In November 1824 Mickiewicz set out for St Petersburg, never to see Lithuania again.

Exile

The poet arrived in the imperial capital just as it was recovering from a devastating flood. During his short stay there he befriended a circle of Russian writers, including Konrad Ryleev, who would soon be implicated in the Decembrist uprising. The Ministry of Education assigned Mickiewicz to teach in Odessa, but the tsar changed his mind shortly after the poet set out for the south. Mickiewicz thus spent nine months in Odessa unemployed, living on a government stipend, until another assignment materialized.

Mickiewicz's reputation as Poland's poetic star preceded him; his status as a political victim of the tsarist regime added luster to it. But then too, the poet had extraordinary charisma; he was intelligent, charming, and, of course, appropriately moody. The ladies of Odessa's salons, Polish and Russian alike, could not get enough of him, nor he of them. "Like a pasha" (Mickiewicz 1993-, 14: 346), he found himself surrounded by a harem of adoring women, who schooled the young teacher from the provinces in the social and erotic arts. Among them was Karolina Sobańska, the mistress of the tsar's administrator in the south and herself an informer. It was in her company that Mickiewicz took an excursion to the Crimea, where amidst Tatar palaces, mosques, and sublime nature he "saw the orient in miniature" (Mickiewicz 1993-, 14: 392).

Mickiewicz learned of his new assignment, a sinecure in the chancery of the governor-general of Moscow, in the fall of 1825. He left Odessa with a notebook full of elegies and a cycle of erotic sonnets engendered by his experiences in the city's salons and boudoirs, as well as another cycle inspired by the Crimea.

The first cycle is an exploration of love, very different, however, from the ravings of Gustaw. The experiences depicted in the 22 sonnets are explicitly sensual yet highly conventionalized, a reflection of the rococo eroticism of aristocratic salons, where flirtation and the well-turned *pointe* were at a premium. The form of the sonnet, as well as the occasional mention of Laura (i.e., Maria Puttkamer), only underscores this effect. By the same token, the poems are evidence of an eroticism that is at once passionate and playful, physical and intellectual. Near the end of the cycle, however, there surfaces a note of resentful dissatisfaction on the poet's part with the price he is paying for these blandishments, a realization that "the bard" is pandering to his "listener" ("Ekskuza" [Excuses], Mickiewicz 1993-, 1: 232), trading his art for love.

The cycle of Crimean sonnets, is, on the one hand, in some ways no less conventional. With its excessive Oriental stylization, lifted primarily from French and German translations of Middle Eastern poetry, the work Polonizes Europe's fascination with the exotic, sharing with it the blindness and insight of Romantic

Orientalism. For a Polish audience, however, as yet largely unfamiliar with Byron, Moore, or even Goethe, Mickiewicz's "Allah, dragoman, minaret, namaz, and izan" (Mickiewicz 1993-, 5: 184) were as provocative as his earlier Lithuanian provincialisms. On another level, the cycle chronicles a journey of self-discovery. In a series of encounters with a Tatar nobleman (*mirza*), the khan's palace in Bahçesaray, dizzying mountain scenery and seascapes, and the ruins of Balaklava, Oriental otherness and the sublime of nature combine to inscribe a chronicle of passage that concludes with the emergence of a triumphant artist, supremely confident in "the immortality of [his] songs [...] from which the ages will weave adornment for [his] brow" ("Ajudah," Mickiewicz 1993-, 1: 252). It was this, the final sonnet of the cycle, that inspired the most famous contemporary depiction of Mickiewicz: dressed in stylish striped trousers, white Byronic shirt, red scarf, and fur burka, the poet "leans on Judah's crag" (ibid.) staring dreamily into the ethereal distance with one hand tucked under his chin, the other into his shirt à la Napoleon – the quintessential Romantic.

The two cycles appeared together in 1826 in a volume entitled *Sonety* (Sonnets), published, appropriately enough, in Moscow. Dealing as they do with a recently acquired jewel in the Russian crown, the Crimean sonnets fit neatly into the empire's Orientalist discourse. That their author was himself the inhabitant of a land recently absorbed into that empire made his gesture all the more salient. Translated almost immediately into Russian, *Sonety* guaranteed Mickiewicz's entry into Moscow's literary circles. His talent was quickly acknowledged by his Russian contemporaries, among whom Pushkin was the most prominent. The relationship of the two poets was not particularly close. It was based, rather, on a mutual respect for each other's talent and on the recognition that each was "the beloved poet" of his respective people. This recognition survived even the 1830 uprising, which found the two poets on irreconcilable sides of the Polish–Russian conflict. They continued to appear in each other's work both polemically and empathetically: in Pushkin's *Bronze Horseman* (1833) and his unfinished poetic portrait of Mickiewicz, "He lived among us..." (1834); in Mickiewicz's "Digression" to *Dziady*, part 3 (1832), and then in his 1837 obituary of the Russian poet as well as in his lectures at the Collège de France.

Russian society lionized Mickiewicz, first in Moscow and then in St Petersburg, where the poet effectively settled in the winter of 1827. The recognition bestowed by the imperial center on one of its provincial own served to validate Mickiewicz in the eyes of his own compatriots, for whom his star now burned with unequaled brightness. What added to his cachet, among Poles and Russians alike, was his extraordinary gift for improvisation. In the company of Polish expatriates Mickiewicz improvised in Polish verse – on one occasion, some two thousand lines of a historical tragedy! – for his Russian friends, in French prose. For both audiences it was, by all accounts, an uncanny experience, as if, as Pushkin put it, "he had been inspired from above" (1995: 331).

Mickiewicz's move to St Petersburg was also connected with tending to the publication of something he had been working on since his sojourn in Odessa. It was a poetic tale, Byronic in its opacity, Scottian in its antiquarianism, entitled

Konrad Wallenrod. Once again the setting is medieval Lithuania, with its struggle against the Teutonic Knights. Now, however, this struggle was projected – in effect allegorized – through the prism of Mickiewicz's three years in Russia (including his brush with the Decembrist conspiracy), as well as the escalating tensions between Poland and Russia.

The tale recounts the story of Konrad Wallenrod, who is elected grand master of the Teutonic Knights as they are about to conduct yet another campaign against the Lithuanians. As the reader learns in retrospect, Wallenrod is himself a Lithuanian, who had been kidnapped by the Germans, together with his mentor Halban. The two had eventually made their way back to Lithuania, where Konrad, his national identity kept alive over the years by Halban, married Aldona. But while battling the Germans he had realized that in open combat the Lithuanians were no match for their more powerful foe. "Unable to find happiness at home, because there was none in his land" (Mickiewicz 1993-, 2: 109), he had decided to abandon his beloved wife and assume the identity of a Teutonic Knight in a treacherous scheme to destroy the order from within. In this he now succeeds. He leads the knights in a winter campaign against the Lithuanians that proves disastrous. All this, however, comes at the cost of love, his own conscience, and, ultimately, his life. Discovered for what he is, Wallenrod commits suicide, broken, tragically, by a life of deceit. "I cannot go on any longer," he says at one point,

> I am a human, after all!
> In ignoble duplicity my youth have I spent,
> In bloodshed and plunder – now stooping with age,
> Treacheries bore me, I'm unable to fight,
> Enough of revenge – even Germans are humans. (Mickiewicz 1993-, 2: 128-9)

But Halban, who had disguised himself as Wallenrod's minstrel, survives his pupil in order to preserve the memory of his deed in song, "the ark of the covenant / Between ages gone by and the present," which guards "the nation's cathedral of memories, / With an archangel's wings and an archangel's voice – / Wielding, at times, an archangel's sword" (Mickiewicz 1993-, 2: 101).

Konrad Wallenrod is perhaps Mickiewicz's most complex, as well as confusing, work: confusing, because it evinces the compositional compromises the poet was forced to make in order to get the poem through the censor (that it made it through at all is astonishing); complex, because of its place in Mickiewicz's symbolic autobiography. For, more than just a story in which treacherous means are justified by patriotic ends, *Konrad Wallenrod* is also a narrative about two poets, or, rather, about just one, symbolically bifurcated. If, for his part, Halban is a Tyrtean poet, whose songs are an inspirational call to arms, the eponymous hero is depicted as an elegiac poet, "Chasing after his youth in the depths of the past [. . .] in the land of his memories" (Mickiewicz 1993-, 2: 76). Konrad's fateful decision to save his people thus requires nothing less than his death *qua* poet. In writing a work that addressed directly his nation's predicament and by the same token assuming the role of a national bard, Mickiewicz was in effect killing the poet he had heretofore been, a gesture no less tragic than his hero's own self-destruction (cf. Grabowicz 2000: 57). Juliusz Kleiner (1948), one of Mickiewicz's better biographers, dotted this "i" when he subtitled the first volume of his study *The History of Gustaw* and the second *The History of Konrad.*

Arguably no other work by Mickiewicz had such immediate consequences, and led to so many misunderstandings. His nemesis Novosiltsov, in a private report to the tsar that was, however, ignored, saw through it immediately; Mickiewicz's Classicist critics condemned the work's moral implications; Poland's youth, for its part, read it as a call to arms, blithely ignoring its tragic dimension. Upon the outbreak of the 1830 uprising, news of the insurgents' attack on the Russian viceroy's residence in Warsaw prompted one Pole to exclaim that "the word has become flesh, and Wallenrod – the Belvedere Palace." Tyrtean poetry, inspired by the example of Halban, evolved into a staple of Polish Romanticism, the agitprop of its day. More egregiously, *Konrad Wallenrod* came to be perceived not only as a blueprint for conspiratorial activity, but as legitimating the belief that the nation's good justified even the most despicable means. Indeed, the term "Wallenrodism," denoting a strategy of deception by the weak against the strong, was soon used to characterize an ostensible mode of Polish behavior, praised by some, reviled by others, exploited by patriot and scoundrel alike.

Ever since settling in St Petersburg, Mickiewicz had been seeking permission to go abroad. Thanks to influential friends, he finally obtained it. Shortly before his departure, he published a two-volume collection of his works, some previously published – including *Konrad Wallenrod* – others new. Among the latter was a poem entitled "Farys" (The Faris; i.e., an Arab horseman), Mickiewicz's own Romantic take on an Arab qasida. It is the first-person story of a lone horseman's ecstatic ride through the desert as he overcomes a series of personified natural obstacles through the sheer force of vital energy, "piercing the heavens first with thought then with soul" (Mickiewicz 1993-, 1: 314). Like "Oda do młodości," the poem was soon reconfigured by numerous epigones as an articulation of "the romantic feeling of boundless power" (Kleiner 1948, 2, part 1: 178). By the same token, to post-1863 critics "Farys" became an exemplum of Romanticism's worst excesses, a misguided apotheosis of "extreme individualism, adventurism, and idleness" (quoted in Janion 2001: 127).

The Grand Tour

Mickiewicz left Russia for Germany in May 1829. The four and a half years of exile had transformed him, as one of his Russian admirers put it, from a "strong" poet into a "powerful" one, mentioned now alongside Byron, Scott, Goethe, and Moore. As he began his Grand Tour – Germany, Bohemia, Switzerland, Italy – his reputation opened doors to some of Europe's most prominent artistic and aristocratic salons. In

Prague he was greeted warmly by the Czech revivalists; in Weimar he paid his respects to Goethe; in Bonn he visited August Wilhelm von Schlegel; and in Rome, where he settled until 1831, he moved among the city's cosmopolitan elite, meeting painters from the French Academy, James Fenimore Cooper, the Bonapartes, as well as some of Russia's leading intellectuals. He also fell in love with 21-year-old Henrietta Ewa Ankwicz, the daughter of a Polish count, but any illusions he may have had about a deeper commitment were soon dispelled.

As rich as it was in experiences, travel was not conducive to writing. In the two years after leaving Russia Mickiewicz produced only a handful of poems. Two were inspired by Henrietta (including a paraphrase of Goethe's "Mignon") and one, an elegiac meditation on the insistence of memory written in the Alps in Splügen, by Maria Puttkamer. Perhaps the most remarkable was "Do matki Polki" (To a Polish mother), which Mickiewicz wrote in 1830 on the eve of the Polish uprising. An unremittingly dark evocation of Poland's predicament, it envisions a land whose mothers must teach their sons to deceive and conspire in "a war without glory / And [. . .] a martyrdom . . . without resurrection":

> Once he is vanquished, the dry wood of a scaffold
>   Will remain as his grave's only marker,
> All his glory will be but a woman's brief sobs
>   And the converse of kinsmen long into the night. (Mickiewicz 1993-, 1: 320-1)

The poet's vision proved prescient. But rather than dissuade, it fueled what became a Romantic cult of martyrdom that culminated in the disastrous uprising of 1863, "the converse of kinsmen" seemingly reward enough for self-annihilation in the name of the national cause.

News of the November 1830 uprising caught Mickiewicz in Rome. As the author of *Konrad Wallenrod*, he was hailed as one of the uprising's progenitors, but he himself had little faith in its success. The decisions he was forced to make in this regard only deepened a growing depression, which he sought to allay, ever so tentatively at first, through religion. His conversion can be traced in a series of six religious poems that focus on the struggle between pride and humility informed, characteristically, by an emphatic confrontation with reason.

Crisis and Revitalization

Mickiewicz tarried in Rome for several months. On hearing that the uprising had spread to Lithuania, he finally decided to participate. He traveled first to Paris and then to the Grand Duchy of Poznań, the Prussian region of Poland, unaffected by the fighting. By the time he attempted to cross the border into Russian-controlled Poland in the fall of 1831, the uprising was drawing to its inevitable conclusion. Mickiewicz spent the next seven months on the estates of Poznań's Polish gentry, socializing, hunting, and making love, trying to hush the guilt he now felt for his failure to take part in the most decisive experience of his generation. This sense of guilt, a measure of the gap between expectations and deeds, effectively conditioned the remainder of his life.

In the early spring of 1832, the poet settled in Dresden, where every day he witnessed the movement of defeated Polish fighters as well as the country's political and cultural elite traveling west to seek refuge in France, the so-called Great Emigration. It was here that Mickiewicz one day "felt as if suddenly above him there burst a sphere of poetry" (quoted in Koropeckyj 2001: 13). In the space of a month he wrote most of *Dziady*, part 3 – over 2,500 lines! More than just a drama of extraordinary vision, it is also the chronicle of Mickiewicz's transformation from poet into a prophet of national revitalization, the culmination of a process that had begun in St Petersburg.

Only loosely connected to parts 2 and 4, part 3 consists of nine scenes and a prologue. On one, the "historical," level, it focuses on the persecution of Vilnius youth at the hands of Novosiltsov in 1823-4. Real dates (November 1, 1823), real names, as well as allusions to actual places and events – a prison cell in a Vilnius monastery (scene 1), a house near Lviv (scene 4), a Warsaw salon (scene 7), a soirée at Novosiltsov's (scene 8) – but also versified dialogues written in the most colloquial of speech imbue this level with a sense of authenticity. On another level, and in this reminiscent of a medieval mystery play, the historical events function as *figurae*, the fate of the persecuted Lithuanian youths at once inscribing and inscribed by not only the martyrdom of the entire nation, but the eternal struggle between good and evil – symbolized by the presence of right and left angels – for human souls. These levels intersect in the figure of the drama's central character, who in the prologue undergoes a metamorphosis from Gustaw to Konrad, a moody, rebellious poet. His "improvisation" (scene 2), an ecstatic trance akin to the flight of a shaman, constitutes the central scene of part 3. Armed with the powers, and pride, of poetic genius, Konrad demands that God grant him also the prophetic power "to rule souls" (Mickiewicz 1993-, 3: 161) so that, in view of God's ostensible indifference, he, the poet, who "is million" because he "suffers for millions" (ibid., p. 164), can make his nation happy. Konrad is subsequently possessed by the devil and then, in the course of an exorcism, seems to be replaced by the figure of a humble monk, Father Peter (scene 3). It is given to the latter to experience a prophetic vision of Poland's future (scene 5): although crucified now by the three partitioning powers, the nation is promised a savior, "born of a foreign mother, his blood that of ancient heroes / And his name is forty-four" (ibid., p. 191).

When asked on several occasions whom he envisioned here, Mickiewicz gave different answers. It is nonetheless clear that in the course of writing the drama the poet underwent a personal transformation, which in turn served as a template for a messianist vision of national regeneration. Precisely because of its defeat and martyrdom Poland was now not only guaranteed salvation, but a special place in the divine order of things as the Christ of nations. No less central in this respect was the role of the divinely inspired poet as the bearer of these tidings. In the face of the combined traumas of defeat and dislocation, the compensatory vision of the poet-prophet effectively sanctioned his claim to the spiritual leadership of his people – and by the same token, the privileged role of literature in the service of the national cause. Quite simply, Mickiewicz viewed his work "as a continuation of the war, which, now that swords have been put away, one must continue waging with the pen" (Mickiewicz 1993-, 15: 156). Soon enough, other poets – above all, Juliusz Słowacki and Zygmunt Krasiński – strove to position themselves as Poland's spiritual leaders, offering alternative visions of national salvation, while a host of epigones sought legitimization in Konrad's apotheosis of the Romantic poet. That in 1968 a ban on performances of *Dziady* in Warsaw triggered violent demonstrations against the communist government is testament to the work's enduring hold on Poland's national psyche.

To the nine scenes of the drama Mickiewicz appended six short epic poems that are meant to chronicle the progress of Konrad, now called The Pilgrim, in Russian exile. There is good reason to believe that in this "Ustęp" (Digression) Mickiewicz recreated from memory something he had conceived while still in Russia. However this may be, what the cycle offers is an outsider's estranged, largely satiric, perspective on the Russian empire as embodied in its northern capital – its origins, winters, architecture, military displays, monuments (Falconet's statue of Peter I), poets (Pushkin/Ryleev), and, finally, the flood of 1824, a divine omen of the empire's eventual demise. The cycle concludes with a poetic epistle addressed "Do przyjaciół Moskali" (To my Russian friends), which, while acknowledging the martyrdom of the Decembrists, expresses bitter disappointment with poets like Pushkin who rejoiced in the defeat of the Polish uprising.

Emigration

Mickiewicz took his vision in Dresden to be a divine revelation. Shortly after settling in Paris in the summer of 1832, he published, anonymously, a pamphlet entitled *Księgi narodu polskiego i pielgrzymstwa polskiego* (The Books of the Polish Nation and Polish Pilgrimage), in which he sought to project his personal metanoia into an explicitly millenarist doctrine aimed at transforming the Polish emigration and through it Europe itself. The first part, written in biblically stylized prose, conceptualizes the history of humankind as a struggle between tyranny and liberty across successive epochs, each figuring the next. Just as Christ was crucified by a tyrannical Rome, so too Poland, a state that had remained true to the principles of Christian liberty, was crucified by the satanic trio of Russia, Prussia, and Austria, with the help of the French; and just as Christ's resurrection ushered in the golden age of medieval Christianity, so too Poland's resurrection will usher in a European polity based on Christian principles of equality and liberty.

In the second part of *Księgi*, Mickiewicz addresses the Polish émigrés, the "Pilgrimage," as the nucleus of the new order. In a series of gospel-like parables, he adumbrates an entire system of behavior, down to dress and modes of speech, to which they must adhere in order to hasten the resurrection of Poland and with it the emergence of a new Christian era. To Mickiewicz's disappointment, the emigration expressed little patience with his brand of mystical politics. Not so the homeland, where the contraband *Księgi* became a "gospel" for Polish patriots. And not so Mickiewicz's foreign admirers. Translated into French, the work made a deep impression on Lamennais, Sainte-Beuve, Mazzini, and Carlyle, and helped inspire the nascent Ukrainian national movement.

As Mickiewicz was elaborating his vision in a series of articles in the émigré newspaper *Pielgrzym polski* (The Polish Pilgrim), he was at the same time writing a work that on the surface seems radically different from the hyper-Romantic prophetism of *Dziady,* part 3. On a deeper level, however, the epic poem *Pan Tadeusz, czyli Ostatni zajazd na Litwie* (Pan Tadeusz, or the Last Foray in Lithuania) is as much a reflex of the symbolic paradigm crystallized in *Dziady* as the messianic *Księgi.* Subtitled "A Gentry Tale from the Years 1811 and 1812 in Twelve Books in Verse," the poem appeared in 1834, although Mickiewicz had been working on it with interruptions since 1832.

Inspired, in part, by the novels of Walter Scott and Goethe's *Hermann und Dorothea*, *Pan Tadeusz* is only superficially the story of the eponymous hero, Master Tadeusz Soplica, the adopted scion of a Lithuanian landowner who finds himself embroiled in love intrigues upon his return to the family estate in the summer of 1811. Rather, the tale narrates the transformation of a traditional gentry community into a modern national collective on the eve of Napoleon's invasion of Russia. In what is essentially a processual drama consisting of breach, crisis, redress, and reintegration, the eruption of the conflict between two families, the Soplicas and the Horeszkos, over ownership of a ruined castle brings into relief a set of multilayered tensions – personal, socioeconomic, ethnic – that had been eroding the traditional order for several generations. The conflict culminates in an armed foray by the last living Horeszko and his allies from the Dobrzycki clan onto the Soplica estate. However, when a Russian battalion arrives to restore order, threatening the very existence of this fractious collective, the quarreling sides unite against their common foe. Thanks to the intervention of a sympathetic Russian officer, a number of the Lithuanian combatants are asked simply to emigrate for a time, which allows them to slip over the border and join Napoleon's Polish Legions. The community, at once redefined and regenerated by the crisis, is reintegrated the following spring as the Legions enter the world of *Pan Tadeusz*, integrating it, in turn, into history and the larger national collective. The moment is celebrated in an improvised concert on the dulcimer by a Jewish tavern-keeper that recapitulates the tragedies and triumphs of recent Polish history.

The drama of the collective is itself refracted through the story of a single individual, the monk Father Robak, who in his earlier life as Jacek Soplica – yet another of Mickiewicz's (autobiographical) protagonists who undergoes a change of name/identity (cf. Borowy 1951) – was largely responsible for the originary breach in the collective. A proud troublemaker in his youth, he had killed the no less haughty

340 *Roman Koropeckyj*

magnate Horeszko after being refused his daughter's hand, a crime all the more heinous in that it was committed while Horeszko was defending his castle against Russian troops. Accused (wrongly) of collaboration, Jacek becomes a monk and dedicates his life to the national cause. His deathbed confession after the foray serves as that necessary moment of redress through which his collective reassesses its ethos and undergoes transformation.

As an allegorical narrative that seeks to resolve Poland's postinsurrectionary predicament in the subjunctive of poetic fiction, *Pan Tadeusz* is salient enough. But that it attained the status of Poland's national epic is above all a testament to Mickiewicz's capacity to integrate that narrative into a seamless tapestry wherein nature is the woof to society's warp. Armed with a remarkable memory that nostalgia only intensified, the poet recreates a universe of sights and sounds and smells, of sunsets and storms, hunter's stews and vegetable patches, repasts and mushroom gathering, one that is mundane rather than lofty, but by the same token imbued with an ineffable "noumenal" shimmer (Witkowska 1998: 186). It is a supremely well-ordered universe, where, as in an idyll that *Pan Tadeusz* ultimately is, everything has its place: master and servant, people and nature, strife and reconciliation, humor and pathos. And spinning it all is a narrator whose gentle irony evinces the distance of this universe from the harsh émigré reality of "the Paris sidewalks" (Mickiewicz 1993-, 4: 383).

For his Romantic readers, *Pan Tadeusz* was something of a disappointment. Many felt that he had squandered an opportunity to depict a heroic Polish past, having chosen instead to focus – mockingly, even – on the mundane and the trivial. It was left to post-Romantic readers, already sensitized to the conventions of realism, to ensure the work's greatness, recognizing as they did in the poet's evocation of the quotidian the very essence of a Polishness that had been erased, it seemed, by partition and modernity.

Pan Tadeusz was Mickiewicz's last major poetic work. Although in 1836 he published a collection entitled *Zdania i uwagi* (Apothegms and Sayings), containing over a hundred epigrams paraphrased from the works of Jakob Boehme, Angelus Silesius, and Saint-Martin, these were largely an exercise in personal meditation collected over the previous few years. To be sure, he continued to write, or at least attempted to write – lyrics, fables, mystical ruminations, even sequels to both *Dziady* and *Pan Tadeusz* – but he published none of these nor, for that matter, did he finish many. The most remarkable is a series of crystalline poems written in 1839-40 that read like autoepitaphs:

> When my corpse sits down among you,
> Looks in your eyes and loudly speaks,
> My soul is then so distant, oh, so distant,
> It wanders and as it does it keens, oh, keens. (Mickiewicz 1993-, 1: 412)

Mickiewicz was never one to write according to a regular schedule. He produced in explosive bursts, often between long lulls. The lull this time lasted some six years, and the renewal of creative energy would not be articulated in verse. It was as if with the valedictory evocation of "the land of childhood years" (Mickiewicz 1993-, 4: 385) in *Pan Tadeusz* he had bid farewell to poetry, as if Father Robak's death signified his own death as a poet. He compensated by striving to fulfill his prophetic mission in deed rather than art.

By the time *Pan Tadeusz* was published, Mickiewicz had largely withdrawn from émigré life, his attention directed inward in a quest for spiritual perfection. In the summer of 1834, the poet married Celina Szymanowska, a descendant of Jewish converts; she turned out to be mentally unstable. As the family grew, its financial situation worsened. Mickiewicz's attempts to earn money by writing dramas in French proved misguided, despite the encouragement of George Sand and Madame d'Argoult. To make ends meet, he accepted a professorship in the classics at the University of Lausanne in 1839, but his tenure there was cut short by an invitation to become the first professor of Slavic Literature (!) at the Collège de France. Mickiewicz could not resist this opportunity for informing Europe about the historical mission of the Slavs in general and the Poles in particular. Delivered in French over the course of four academic years (1840-4), with practically no notes, Mickiewicz's lectures proved to be his most sustained improvisation.

For all his erudition, Mickiewicz was not a scholar; he was a Romantic who valued affect over learning. This said, his attempt to survey not only the literatures of the Slavic peoples – their folklore, language, and history – but also their relations among themselves and with Europe in order to articulate the "idea" of Slavdom, was beyond his capacities. The lectures are disorganized, full of misquotations, factual errors, and flights of fantasy. There are, nonetheless, moments of acute critical insight, especially in his discussions of Russian literature and Polish–Russian relations. But Mickiewicz made up for his shortcomings as a scholar with his enthusiasm, concerned as he was more with moving his audience than inculcating knowledge. And for at least the first two years, his listeners – including his colleagues at the Collège Michelet and Quinet – seemed impressed. Near the end of the second year, however, the tone of the lectures changed.

Sectarianism and Politics

In the summer of 1841, with his wife in an asylum, Mickiewicz was approached by Andrzej Towiański (1799-1878), a mystic from Lithuania, who claimed he could cure Celina. He did so (temporarily), and at the same time succeeded in converting the poet to what he termed "God's Cause." Like all such sects, it was not so much the doctrine – a murky mélange of quietist adventism, metempsychosis, spiritism, and Bonapartism – but rather the "Master's" charisma that drew followers from among the émigrés. Mickiewicz became Towiański's most prominent disciple, something of a Paul to the latter's Christ. He used his lectures at the Collège as a pulpit for codifying and spreading the Master's teachings, which included a blistering critique of the official church akin in some respects to modern liberation theology. Away from the rostrum, the poet's life revolved around his circle of adepts, in an atmosphere at once of ecstasy, manipulation, and rifts, while his domestic life was disrupted by an affair with a fellow Towianist, with whom he had at least one illegitimate child.

As Mickiewicz's lectures took on the air of revival meetings, the French authorities suspended them. This notwithstanding, the lectures soon appeared in print, first the last two years in 1845 under the title *L'Église officielle et le messianisme,* then four years later in their entirety under the title *Les Slaves.* By 1846, however, Mickiewicz had broken with Towiański, although he never renounced his teachings as such. Indeed, the relationship may be described as resembling therapy. After five years with the Master, the transference was successful. Mickiewicz was ready to act.

His opportunity came with the outbreak of European unrest in 1848. With Italy in rebellion against the Hapsburgs, the poet decided to join the struggle "for your freedom and ours" by creating a "legion." Armed with a manifesto for Poland's future proclaiming, among other things, full equality for women and Jews, the legion consisted of only a handful of men, but it was greeted enthusiastically in the Italian cities through which it marched. In an audience at the Vatican, the poet impertinently reminded the pope that "God's spirit [was] now inside the smocks of the people of Paris" (Kostenicz 1969: 98). On his return to Paris, he founded *La Tribune des peuples,* a short-lived newspaper that became Mickiewicz's mouthpiece for his brand of Christian socialism and Bonapartism. Ironically, it was Louis Napoleon who shut it down and then three years later, in 1852, dismissed the poet from the Collège. In compensation, Mickiewicz, following the footsteps of Charles Nodier, was made a librarian at the Bibliothèque de l'Arsenal.

Senescence and Rebirth

Although seemingly broken at the relatively early age of 53, Mickiewicz nonetheless longed for action. With the West's declaration of war against Russia in 1854 and the concomitant revival of hopes on the part of Polish émigrés, the poet convinced one of the leaders of the emigration to dispatch him to Turkey, where he was to help in the formation of Polish-Cossack detachments. He also hoped to create a Jewish legion that would fight in the war against Russia. Although his wife had recently died, he apparently felt no compunction about leaving behind his six children. After several months of feverish activity in Istanbul and Bulgaria, Mickiewicz succumbed to what was probably food poisoning. He died in Istanbul on November 26, 1855. His body was taken to France, where it was buried in Montmorency outside of Paris.

In 1890 Mickiewicz's remains were transferred to Cracow. Escorted by multitudes, they were interred in the royal cathedral of Wawel, to lie side by side with the bodies of Polish kings. Perhaps nothing bespeaks more of the place the poet occupies in Poland's collective psyche.

NOTE

1   All translations are my own.

REFERENCES AND FURTHER READING

"Adam Mickiewicz Bicentennial, 1798-1998" (1998). Special issue, *The Polish Review* 43 (4): 387–73.

Billip, Witold (ed.) (1962). *Mickiewicz w oczach współczesnych. Dzieje recepcji na ziemiach polskich w latach 1818–1830. Antologia.* Wrocław, Warsaw, and Cracow: Ossolineum.

Coquin, François-Xavier, and Maslowski, Michel (eds.) (2002). *Le Verbe et l'histoire: Mickiewicz, France et l'Europe.* Paris: Maison des sciences de l'homme: Institut d'études slaves.

Borowczyk, Jerzy (2003). *Rekonstrukcja procesu Filomatów i Filaretów 1823–1824. Historia śledztwa przeciw uczestnikom konspiracji studenckich i młodzieżowych w Wilnie oraz w Wileńskim Okręgu Naukowym.* Poznań: Wydawnictwo Naukowe UAM.

Borowy, Wacław (1951). "Poet of Transformation." In Manfred Kridl (ed.), *Adam Mickiewicz: Poet of Poland.* New York: Columbia University Press, pp. 35-56.

Fieguth, Rolf (ed.) (1999). *Adam Mickiewicz: Kontext und Wirkung. Materialen der Mickiewicz Konferenz in Freiburg/Schweiz, 14.-17. Januar 1998.* Freiburg: Universitätsverlag.

Gille-Maisani, Jean-Charles (1988). *Adam Mickiewicz, poète national de la Pologne. Étude psychanalytique et caractérologique.* Montreal: Bellarmin.

Grabowicz, George G. (Hrabovych, Hryhorii) (2000). "Symvolichna avtobiohrafiia u Mitskevycha i Shevchenka." In *Shevchenko iakoho ne znaiemo (Z problematyky symvolichnoï avtobiohrafiï ta suchasnoï retseptsiï poeta.* Kiev: Krytyka, pp. 52-67.

Green, Peter S. (2002). "Polish Hip-Hop Rocks the Homies on the Blok." *New York Times*, April 5, late edn.: A4.

Grudzinska-Gross, Irena (1995). "Adam Mickiewicz: A European from Nowogródek." *East European Politics and Societies*, 9 (2): 295-316.

Janion, Maria (2001). *Purpurowy płaszcz Mickiewicza. Studium z historii poezji i mentalności.* Gdansk: Slowo/obraz terytoria.

Kleiner, Juliusz (1948). *Mickiewicz*, 2 vols. Lublin: Towarzystwo Naukowe KUL.

Koropeckyj, Roman (2001). *The Poetics of Revitalization: Adam Mickiewicz between Forefathers' Eve, part 3 and Pan Tadeusz.* Boulder, CO: East European Monographs.

Kostenicz, Ksenia (1969). *Legion włoski i "Trybuna Ludów." Styczeń 1848–grudzień 1849.* Kronika życia i twórczości Mickiewicza. Warsaw: PIW.

Kozmian, Kajetan (1972). *Pamiętniki*, ed. Marian Kaczmarek and Kazimierz Pecold, vol. 3. Wrocław, Warsaw, Cracow, and Gdańsk: Ossolineum.

Krasiński, Zygmunt (1970). *Listy do Adama Sołtana*, ed. Zbigniew Sudolski. Warsaw: PIW.

Krzyżanowski, Julian ([1931] 1968). *Polish Romantic Literature.* Freeport, NY: Books for Libraries Press.

Kridl, Manfred (ed.) (1951). *Adam Mickiewicz: Poet of Poland.* New York: Columbia University Press.

Lednicki, Wacław (ed.) (1956) *Adam Mickiewicz in World Literature: A Symposium.* Berkeley: University of California Press.

Masing-Delic, Irene (ed.) (2001). "Mickiewicz: 'East' and 'West.'" Special issue, *Slavic and East European Journal*, 45 (4): 605-731.

Mickiewicz, Adam (1993-). *Dzieła*, 17 vols. Warsaw: Czytelnik.

Milosz, Czeslaw (1983). *The History of Polish Literature*, 2nd edn. Berkeley: University of California Press.

Piwińska, Marta (1984). *Miłość romantyczna.* Cracow and Wrocław: WL.

Pushkin, Aleksandr (1995). *Połnoe sobranie sochinenii*, vol. 3, part 1. Moscow: Voskresen'e.

Walicki, Andrzej (1982). *Philosophy and Romantic Nationalism: The Case of Poland.* Oxford: Clarendon Press.

Weintraub, Wiktor (1954). *The Poetry of Adam Mickiewicz*. The Hague: Mouton.

Weintraub, Wiktor (1959). *Literature as Prophecy: Scholarship and Martinist Poetics in Mickiewicz's Parisian Lectures*. The Hague: Mouton.

Weintraub, Wiktor (1985). "Adam Mickiewicz (1798-1855)." In Jacques Barzun (ed.), *European Writers: The Romantic Century*, vol. 5. New York: Scribners, pp. 607-34.

Welsh, David (1966). *Adam Mickiewicz*. New York: Twayne.

Witkowska, Alina (1998). *Mickiewicz. Słowo i czyn*, 2nd edn. Warsaw: PWN.

20

The Revival of the Ode

John Hamilton

Revolution

Revivals do well by revolutions. For legitimacy, persuasiveness, and sheer force, movements of political or cultural innovation wisely turn to the distant past in order to move behind the present state of affairs and its oppressive hold on the popular imagination. It is unsurprising, therefore, but no less striking, that one of the primary literary proponents of the Terror and the quasi-official poet of the National Convention, Ponce-Denis Écouchard-Lebrun, was referred to publicly as Lebrun-Pindare. The intention, no doubt, was to ascribe to the modern poet's *chants républicains* all the freedom, abruptness, and even violence associated with the archaic Greek dithyrambs. "The name of Pindar," as Diderot had defined it for the *Encyclopédie*, "is nothing more than . . . the name for enthusiasm itself" (Diderot 1876: 293). Nonetheless, as a writer of odes, Lebrun was adopting a form that had come to represent, especially in France, the most academically overburdened and politically conservative of literary genres. Indeed, to revive the ode at this point in history required a resuscitation of that which ostensibly had been dead for quite some time. The difficulty of the task proved to be proportionate to the splendor of the accomplishment, whose consequences would move far beyond the immediate political application. Over the course of this stunning project, together with analogous developments from across Europe, the ode would be transformed from a particular sort of poetic expression into the very paradigm of modern lyric.

In France, with rare exceptions, after its brilliant emergence in the Renaissance with the poetry of the Pléiade, the ode tended to be chosen by second-rate poets eager to promulgate a sublime style, replete with tiresome figures, overwrought conceits, and ridiculous periphrases, usually in the service of the monarchy and the aristocracy. The ceremonious tone and heightened diction of the form readily proved to be the appropriate vehicle for the glorification of the *ancien régime*, as the majority of French odes from the seventeenth and eighteenth centuries attests. Not lawlessness, Boileau had declared, but a "beau désordre," wherein all disparate elements, all mythic digressions and obscure allusions, were reined in and reigned over by an overriding sovereign principle. In short, according to neoclassical precepts, then, the Pindaric mode was simply synonymous with encomium, with the praise of all that is noble.

When, in critical response to this tradition, Voltaire turned to the ode form, he took advantage of Pindar's notorious difficulty – a quality that has always complicated any straightforward program of praise – and produced a lighter, satiric verse. His entertaining octosyllables are opposed to any effects of sublimity:

> Sors du tombeau, divin Pindare,
> Toi qui célébras autrefois
> Les chevaux de quelques bourgeois
> Ou de Corinthe ou de Mégare;
> Toi qui possédas le talent
> De parler beaucoup sans rien dire;
> Toi qui modulas savamment
> Des vers que persone n'entend
> Et qu'il faut toujours qu'on admire. (*Ode 17, To Catherine II of Russia*, 1766, ll. 1-9, in
> Voltaire 1877, 8: 486)

> (Come out of your tomb, divine Pindar,
> You who celebrated in the past
> Horses and a few bourgeois
> Either from Corinth or from Megara;
> You who possessed the talent
> To speak a lot without saying anything;
> You who skillfully modulated
> Verses that no one understands
> And that always must be admired.)[1]

Although a parody of what Charles Batteux identified as the "heroic" or "Pindaric" ode (in his *Cours de belles-lettres*, 1740–50), Voltaire's work nonetheless situates itself along the lines of traditional odic genres, for example the moral or "Horatian" ode and the "festive" odes associated with Anacreon.[2] The effect is one of exposure or debunking. In this regard, it continues the tendency popularized by Charles Perrault and sustained by figures like Élie Catherine Fréron and Antoine Houdar de La Harpe, that Pindar's verse was not sublime at all, but rather sheer nonsense – *galimatias*.

With his self-styled "audacious" verse, Lebrun-Pindare strives against both the classical justifications of Boileau as well as the wicked delectation of enlightened moderns. His poetic approach aligns itself with the style of the "sacred ode," modeled on the Psalms and informed by tropes of regeneration. Lebrun thereby pursues Ronsard's proto-Romantic dream of initiating a new epoch of poetry, bursting with innovation, emotion, and provocative ideas. Just as Ronsard followed the twin streams back to their Pindaric and Horatian sources, so Lebrun characterized his poetry as a return to mythic origins, radical enough to constitute a poetic revolution that would correspond to the current milieu of political upheaval. To this end, Lebrun adopted contemporary notions of genius:

> Tel éclate un libre génie,
> Quand il lance aux tyrans les foudres de sa voix.
> Telle à flots indomptés sa brûlante harmonie
> > Entraîne les scepters des rois. ("Ode sur le Vaisseau Le Vengeur," 1793, ll.
> 17-20, in Allem 1966: 263)

> (Thus bursts a free genius
> When he hurls at the tyrants the bolts of his voice.
> Thus with indomitable waves his burning harmony
> > Sweeps away the scepters of kings.)

A prevalent construct of the last decades of the eighteenth century, the discourse of genius saturates this ode with themes of freedom, continuity, immediacy, and usurping power – in a word, with the character of an absolute beginning. In appropriating both the thunderbolt of Jupiter and the flood of original song, the verse participates in the force of the origin, from which it suffers no gaps, no disruptions, no breaks in efficacy. Here, lawlessness is more specifically being before the law, at the origin of laws, and therefore bound to none (*indomptés*). The Romantic ode is so frequently vocational, precisely because, as here, it places the poet at the very site of sovereignty. Eschewing all derivation, the ode, at its most hopeful – and perhaps, at its most naïve – works to give birth to itself. In the name of Pindar, who strove to salvage the present by reanimating the past, freedom is denied to latecomers and reserved only for those capable of experiencing the new dawn. The gesture of identification, which produces a Lebrun-Pindare, is itself emblematic of the time's ecstatic, but short-lived, exuberance – a story wholly bound up with the Romantic recuperation of, and subsequent disillusionment with, the ode form.

Decades before, across the Rhine, German court poets had already discovered how to exploit Pindar's famed digressiveness as a way to circumvent their commissions. On a simply formal level, the unruliness of Pindaric metrics, which Horace had codified as "free from law" (*lege solutis*), had been arrogated by Friedrich Klopstock to produce the "free rhythms" of his hymns of the 1750s. Poems like "Dem Allgegenwärtigen" (To the Omnipresent One, 1758) again combined elements of Hebrew psalmody with Pindaric fervor. The blend had already enjoyed a formidable tradition, for instance in the work of Jean-Baptiste Rousseau, who freely adapted the Psalms for his first book of *Odes* (1723), and in the early work of John Milton, who composed one of the first and finest examples of the English Pindaric ode, *On the Morning of Christ's Nativity* (1629). Klopstock's odes formulate their own program of liberation specifically along the lines of Pietism, of a deeply religious commitment to maintaining an immediate relation with the divine. This desire to evoke the presence of the godhead inscribes

Klopstock's practice in the grand hymnal tradition, which refers back to the Homeric Hymns and to the Hymns of Callimachus, where the poetic act of calling (*klêsis*) effects the god's appearance before the community.

The conception of poetry's invocative or "kletic" capacity was underwritten by the theories espoused by Bishop Robert Lowth, whose lectures at Oxford, *On the Sacred Poetry of the Hebrews* (1753), would motivate generations of poets across Europe to consider their work as an inspired reconnection with the fount of all poetry. In French literature this tradition, best represented by J.-B. Rousseau's religious odes, was maintained uninterrupted straight into the nineteenth century, for example in Lamartine's dithyramb *La Poésie sacrée* (in *Méditations poétiques*, 1820). For Lowth, the ancient poets were explicitly "ambassadors of Heaven, men favored with an immediate intercourse and familiarity with the Gods." Clearly a description of sublimity, this expression of enjoying a relation of immediacy with the origin readily developed into the Prometheanism that would soon intoxicate a later age with fantasies of usurping the position of the divine creator. In his notes for a *Treatise on the Ode* (1765), Johann Gottfried Herder borrows liberally from Lowth's work, when he identifies the ode as "the firstborn child of sensibility, the fountainhead of poetic art, and the germ cell of its life" (Herder 1992: 36). In terms that explicitly anticipate Lebrun's tyrannicidal furor, Herder describes the ode as "a fire of the Lord . . . which shakes the living to the core of their nerves, a current that rips away everything movable in its swirl" (ibid.). Herder's own experiment in the ode form, *Der Genius der Zukunft* (1769) coalesces the Pindaric, Horatian, and biblical strands as it conjures the image of the thundering poet:

> Mit Flammenzügen glänzt
> in der Seelen Abgründen der Vorwelt Bild
> und schießt weitüber weißagend starkes Geschoß
> in das Herz der Zukunft! Siehe! da steigen
> der Mitternacht Gestalten empor! wie Götter aus Gräbern empor
> aus Asche der Tugendglut die Seher! Sie zerreißen
> mit Schwerterblitzen das Gewölk! Sie wehn
> im Blick durch die Sieben der Himmel, und schwingen sich herab!
> Denn liest der Geist in seines Meers
> Zauberspiegel die Ewigkeit. – – (ll. 19-28, in Herder 1889: 322-3)

> (With flaming traits there gleams
> in the soul's abyss an image of the former world
> and it shoots far out a prophetically strong shot
> into the heart of the future! Look! there rise up
> midnight's forms! like gods out of graves up
> out of the ash of virtue's glow there rise the seers! They sunder
> the clouds with sword-bolts! They drift
> in a glance through the heaven's Pleiade, and swing down!
> Then the Spirit reads in the magic mirror
> of his sea eternity. – –)

Johann Wolfgang Goethe, who fell under Herder's influence when he met him in Strasbourg as a 21-year-old student of law, was quick to take up the suggestion to read Pindar. In the following year, the young poet confessed to his mentor, "I am now living in Pindar" – an experience that led to his first experiments in odic profusion:

> Wenn die Räder rasselten
> Rad an Rad, rasch ums Ziel weg
> Hoch flog
> Siegdurchglühter
> Jünglinge Peitschenknall,
> Und sich Staub wälzt'
> Wie vom Gebürg herab
> Kieselwetter ins Tal,
> Glühte deine Seel' Gefahren, Pindar,
> Mut. – Glühte? – (*Wandrers Sturmlied*, 1772, ll. 101-10, Goethe 1998: 36)

> (When the wheels rattled,
> Wheel upon wheel, rushing to the finish,
> High flew
> The cracking whips
> Of the boys who glowed with victory,
> And dust was stirred,
> Downward, as from the mountaintop,
> Like a hailstorm into the valley,
> Before dangers, Pindar, did your soul glow
> Courage. – Did it glow? –)

In addition to evoking the ancient Olympic games that were the occasion of Pindar's victory songs, Goethe's free verse, its bold rhythmic effects and striking compounds ("Siegdurchglühter," "Peitschenknall"), contribute to the general characterization of the ode as a vehicle for the sublime or grand style. The diction belongs to Klopstock, who was considered the best representative of the dithyrambic style ascribed to Pindar. As for Goethe's main image, it alludes to Horace's famous description of the Theban's poetics in his fourth book of *Odes*:

> Monte decurrens velut amnis, imbres
> quem super notas aluere ripas,
> fervet immensusque ruit profundo
> Pindarus ore (*Odes* 4. 2. ll. 5-8, in Wickham 1986: 27)

> (From the mount descending like a river, which
> the rain has fed over the well-known limits,
> he boils and boundless crashes at the mouth
> profound, Pindarus)

Horace's representation of this vertical movement, which carries the flood from a high source and sends it crashing to the earth, comprises a structure that persists throughout Goethe's "genius" period. It occurs, for example, in the creative-destructive flood images that pervade the *Werther* novella and also in the resounding incipit to his ode, *Mahomets Gesang* – "Seht den Felsenquell / Freudehell" ("See the cliff spring / joy bright").[3] Hölderlin's *Der Rhein* and Shelley's *Mont Blanc* contain still further developments of this fundamental motif. In a single, compact image, the Pindaric flood affirms the more optimistic or celebratory strand in Romantic poetry: an assertion that a link to some originating and therefore legitimizing force can be made and upheld. This hope is entirely grounded in the Pindaric tradition of public, encomiastic poetry, which ostensibly aimed to establish for the community a bond with its mythic past. As in the case of the Progress Poems of Thomas Gray and William Collins, the Pindaric ode continued to be used in a wishful attempt, however qualified, to reinsert the present into the continuum that flows from mythic antiquity.

The Swan and the Bee

This kind of optimism seems to be inherent in the Pindaric tripartite structure itself, which traditionally organized the ode into strophe, antistrophe, and epode, and thereby nearly guaranteed a dialectical process toward synthesis. On the level of form, the Horatian strand is distinguished from this complex architectonic structure, insofar as it utilizes shorter stanzas, often isometric, of four to six lines, for example in Sapphic or Asclepiad strophes. In terms of content, one could even consider the quieter, reflective tone of the Horatian ode as a destabilizing element that would upset any harmonizing scheme. Indeed, Horace's Pindar-Ode, which so effectively institutes the exemplary image of this desire, in fact follows the conventions of the Latin *recusatio* or refusal poem. *Odes* 4.2 reasserts that Pindar is the greatest of public poets, one capable of celebrating great figures, like Augustus, one equipped with the poetic means for uniting today's occasion with the glorious stories of the distant past. And Horace, precisely because he represents his lyric art as private rather than public, moral rather than celebratory, meditative rather than solemn, cannot adopt Pindar's grand style. To do so would be to fail, just as Icarus – the paradigmatic epigone – failed. In contrast to the sublimity of the Pindaric flood, in opposition to the Pindaric swan, Horace prefers to work like a bee, hovering above the banks of his native Tiber. The selfsame dynamism lies beneath many Romantic odes. It is constituted by the tension between the confident hope to act as a prophet-priest and the less sanguine realization of one's inability to perform such feats. Derived from the models of both Pindar and Horace, the modern ode reflects the conflicting claims of what Stuart Curran, in his discussion of the English ode, has called its "intrinsic paradox," namely that "almost from the first, an Horatian voice was invested with a Pindaric form" (Curran 1986: 71).

The "ontological and vocational doubt," which Paul Fry sees as the fundamental trait of all modern odes, is surely grounded in this twofold tendency. The remarkably dramatic quality of many Romantic odes seems to consist in the persistence of this private insecurity, ultimately traceable to Horace's famous refusal, as it attempts to question the order that the triadic format tries to impose. For Fry, this problem generally differentiates the ode from the hymn: "Like the hymn, the ode...longs for participation in the divine, but ,it never participates communally, never willingly supplies a congregation with common prayer because it is bent on recovering a priestly role that is not pastoral but hermetic" (Fry 1980: 7). To be sure, two great examples of the English Romantic ode, Wordsworth's *Intimations of Immortality* (1802-4, published in 1807) and Coleridge's *Dejection: An Ode* (1802), reflect this fundamental tension – a phenomenon of "flux and reflux." Wordsworth's poem, with its notorious (and self-confessed) confusion, furnishes the classic statement of disillusionment: "It is not now as it hath been of yore / .../ The things which I have seen I now can see no more" (ll. 6, 9). Composed in irregular Pindaric stanzas, the poem gives voice to the poet's "obstinate questionings" (l. 141), to the profoundest epistemological and metaphysical doubts ("Blank misgivings of a Creature," l. 144) – in short, to "thoughts that do often lie too deep for tears" (l. 203). In a highly compressed fashion, the poem's epigraph itself offers evidence – intimations? – of the poet's Pindaric dreams of continuity and Horatian disenchantment:

> The Child is father of the Man;
> And I could wish my days to be
> Bound each to each by natural piety. (from "My Heart Leaps Up," Wordsworth 1932: 353-6)

Wordsworth has removed his original epigraph from Virgil and instead, quite unconventionally, cites his own work – a telling gesture of autonomy that underscores the wish for an easy flow from past to present identity. Expressed in a contrafactual condition ("could"), however, that possibility is severely disrupted. As a writer of a modern ode, Wordsworth is far removed from the hymnist's confident encounter with the divine, from Lowth's Oriental source of enthusiasm. Emphatically mortal, the poet is a man "who daily farther from the east / Must travel" (ll. 71-2). Still, with the autocitation of the epigraph, he clearly has usurped the position of divine source: he has fathered himself, however dubiously. The ode, which had always been Pindarically sanctioned to make the most abrupt of transitions, is practically unique in being capable of accommodating the entire spectrum of lyrical thought. Both transcendent trust and vocational insecurity are served by the form, both the uneasy intimacy of the *Intimations* and the quiet resignation of the "Ode to Duty" (1805) or the "Vernal Ode" (1817). A note attached to *Tintern Abbey* (1800) already alludes to this versatility: "I have ventured not to call this Poem an Ode; but it was written with a hope that in the transitions, and the impassioned music of the versification would be found the principal requisites of that species of composition" (Wordsworth 1952: 517). Coleridge, who, while studying at Cambridge, happened to win the prize for best Greek ode (on the slave trade in the West Indies), clearly appreciated the form's adaptability.

He readily applied it to represent the entire range of his politics, from the Jacobin fervor of the *Ode to the Departing Year* (1796) to the self-styled recantation of *France: An Ode* (1798), which expresses the repulsion felt on the occasion of Napoleon's invasion of Switzerland ("Forgive me, Freedom! O forgive those dreams!" l. 64). As it follows, nothing less than the ode's rigorously dialectical structure could contain the high drama of the *Dejection Ode*. Here, strophe collides with storm-tossed antistrophe, simultaneously undermining any tendency to harmonize. The notorious Pindaric leap from one theme to the next (the *saltus dithyrambus*) now gives expression to the profoundest vacillations of the confessing soul:

> There was a time when, though my path was rough,
> This joy within me dallied with distress,
> And all misfortunes were but as the stuff
> Whence Fancy made me dreams of happiness:
> For hope grew round me, like the twining vine,
> And fruits, and foliage, not my own, seemed mine.
> But now afflictions bow me down to earth:
> Nor care I that they rob me of my mirth;
> But oh! each visitation
> Suspends what nature gave me at my birth,
> My shaping spirit of Imagination. (ll. 76–86, Coleridge 1996: 181)

As a response to Wordsworth's *Intimations*, *Dejection* perpetuates and then modifies the "conversational" mode: what began as an epistle becomes an ode the moment Sara Hutchinson is transformed into "Lady." Irregularly Pindaric in form, with stanzas of varying lengths, the ode nonetheless puts into question the very idea of encomium. Significantly, it is not an "Ode on Dejection"; rather, it is as though Coleridge would emphasize the melancholy that lies at the core of all celebration, the dark side of all imaginative power.

The great hymns of Friedrich Hölderlin share in this troubled vision. The poet's first attempt at a Pindaric ode, *Wie wenn am Feiertage...* (As on a Holiday..., 1799), planned out in triads with strophic response, begins optimistically as a formulation of poetry's vatic role, but fragments towards the end in impotent despair:

> Des Vaters Stral, der reine versengt es nicht
> Und tieferschüttert, die Leiden des Stärkeren
> Mitleidend, bleibt in den hochherstürzenden Stürmen
> Des Gottes, wenn er nahet, das Herz doch fest.
> Doch weh mir! wenn von
>
> Weh mir!
> Und sag ich gleich,
>
> Ich sei genaht, die Himmlischen zu schauen,
> Sie selbst, sie werfen mich tief unter die Lebenden
> Den falschen Priester, ins Dunkel, daß ich

Das warnende Lied den Gelehrigen singe.
Dort (ll. 63-74, Hölderlin 1951: 120)

(The Father's ray, the pure, will not sear our hearts
And, deeply convulsed, and sharing his sufferings
Who is stronger than we are, yet in the far-flung down-rushing storms
Of the God, when he draws near, will the heart stand fast.
But woe is me! when of

Woe is me!

And I say at once,

I approached to see the Heavenly,
And they themselves cast me down, deep down
Below the living, into the dark cast down
The false priest that I am, to sing,
For those who have ears to hear, the warning song.
There) (Translation by Michael Hamburger, slightly modified)

Hölderlin inherits the high hymnal style of Klopstock and the exuberance of Goethe's *Sturm und Drang*, but can uphold neither. The failure, of course, analogous to Coleridge's "stifled, drowsy, unimpassioned grief" (*Dejection*, l. 22) is absolute brilliance. As in the case of Wordsworth, Hölderlin turned to the ode form after an experience of disillusionment, in his particular case not only with the promises of the French Revolution, but with the claims of the idealism which had informed his earlier hymns in rhyming quatrains. The turn to the larger, varied format, which coincided with an intense occupation with translating Pindar, can be read as a symptom of the poet's overall loss of trust in easy systematization or synthesis. Again, reminiscent of Wordsworth, if Hölderlin *could*, he would affirm continuities, but – "weh mir!" – he could not. The more accomplished hymns of the subsequent period, for example, *Der Rhein* (1801), *Friedensfeier* (1801-02), and *Patmos* (1802), exploit the dialectical energy of the ode's triadic structure, but still resist resolution. Hölderlin's notoriously literal translations of Pindar are evidence enough of his refusal to sublimate the sensuousness and materiality of poetry's language.

Mourning and Melancholia

For those struggling to assert some kind of national identity, this love for the concrete particularities of one's language is altogether crucial. Ugo Foscolo, who not only was in exile from his Hellenic home, the island of Zante, and from Venice, but also endured the French occupation in Milan, had recourse to the ode form for his most political and most powerful poem, *Dei Sepolcri* (1807). Written in protest against the 1804 Napoleonic Edict of Saint Cloud, which prohibited the marking of graves within the city limits, *Dei Sepolcri* proclaims the necessity of burial and mourning.

For Foscolo, such rites are not held to serve some religious idea of immortality, but rather are aimed at maintaining a lasting public memory, by the community and for the community (Brose 1998: 2).

> Celeste è questa
> Corrispondenza d'amorosi sensi,
> Celeste dote è negli umani; e spesso
> Per lei si vive con l'amico estinto
> E l'estinto con noi, se pia la terra
> Che lo raccolse infante e lo nutriva,
> Nel suo grembo materno ultimo asilo
> Porgendo, sacre le reliquie renda
> Dall'insultar de' nembi e dal profano
> Piede del vulgo, e serbi un sasso il nome,
> E di fiori odorata arbore amica
> Le ceneri di molli ombre consoli. (ll. 29-40, Foscolo 1994: 24)

> (Heavenly, this
> Corresponding tenderness of feeling,
> Heavenly this gift to humans; by its means
> We often live with the departed friend
> And the friend with us – if the reverent earth,
> Which welcomed him in infancy and fed him,
> By granting him now in its motherly lap
> A last asylum, keeps his relics sacred
> From the weather's insults and the profane feet
> Of the crowd, and a stone preserves his name,
> And a friendly tree fragrant with flowers
> Solaces his ashes with soft shade.) (Translation by Michael Ferber)

As the ode progresses, Foscolo imagines his addressee seeking in vain the resting place of satirical poet Giuseppe Parini, who lies hidden and unattended in some common grave, with neither marker nor epitaph ("non pietra non parola," l. 75). This kind of negligence lies at the root of Italian homelessness: "I sit among these plants and sigh / for my mother's house" ("io siedo e sospiro / il mio tetto materno," ll. 64f). The poet therefore summons the Pindaric capacity of encomium and applies it to ground cultural identity – "Alas! above the dead / no flower can grow where no one honors it / with human praises and with the tears of love" ("Ahi su gli estinti / non sorge fiore, ove non sia d'umane, / lodi ornato e d'amoroso pianto," ll. 88f). Praise (*lodi*) redeems, as well as mourning. By way of metaphors of resurgence and efflorescence (*sorge fiore*), Foscolo redirects the ode's elegiac tone (*amoroso pianto*) to serve as the foundation and the condition for social history and nationhood.

Hölderlin's great Pindaric, *Der Rhein*, partakes of an analogous program of poetic nationalism. In a note appended to the poem, he outlines how the descriptive sensuousness or introspective sensitivity – *Empfindsamkeit* – of the lyric mode has been channeled through the epic mode's narrative expression of action, in order to arrive at the reflective ideal associated with the poet's conception of drama. In this way, within a clear, triadic structure, the poem elicits or performs the bridal feast that reunites mortals and immortals.[4] In other words, the ode becomes the privileged medium for revealing the indispensability of culture heroes, like Hölderlin's Rousseau, like Foscolo's Parini, and their contribution, through death, to the birth of community. Accordingly, both *Der Rhein* and *Dei Sepolcri* begin in the shadow of mourning – "In the dark ivy," "In the shade of cypresses" ("Im dunkeln Epheu," "All'ombra de' cipressi") – only to politicize it.

It is a scheme that carries on with Foscolo's poetic heir, Giacomo Leopardi who, in odes imbued with the recognition of human suffering, happens upon that which alone is capable of binding humankind together. *La Ginestra, o il fiore del deserto* (The Broom, or The Flower in the Desert), from Leopardi's book of *Canti* (1836), posits Nature as humankind's cruelest enemy, a fundamental antagonist who restrains us to a material, merely biological existence, and therefore to death: "quell'orror che primo / ... / strinse i mortali in social catena" ("that horror which first forced mortals into social bonds," ll. 147-9, Leopardi 1984: 255). Although Nature is presented in a more benign light in the ode, *Alla Primavera* (To Spring), it is merely a gesture to instill in the poet the capacity to heal a mortal existence that forever remains bereft of the gods:

> Tu le cure infelici e i fati indegni
> Tu de' mortali ascolta,
> Vaga natura, e a favilla antica
> Rendi a l'ingegno mio (ll. 88-91, Leopardi 1984: 69)

> (Listen to the unhappy cares and the undeserved fate
> Of mortals, listen,
> Kind nature, and rekindle the ancient flame
> In my mind.)

Broadly speaking, Leopardi's narrative schemes, which move – albeit impossibly – from mourning to renewal, reflect a trend in the Romantic ode to deploy the emotional power of elegy away from personal devastation toward more positive ends. Again Horace served as an important model for defining lyric in contradistinction to the elegiac mode. In *Odes* 1.33, for example, he urges the elegist Tibullus "not to grieve more than too much" (*ne doleas plus nimio*, l. 1, Wickham 1986: 27). Elsewhere, Horace admonishes the poet Valgius for pursuing a lost love incessantly and, with particular programmatic intent, suggests a corrective that would redeem lyric as he conceives it:

> desine mollium
> tandem querellarum, et potius nova
> cantemus Augusti tropaea
> Caesaris (*Odes* 2.9 ll. 17-20, in Wickham 1986: 41)

> (Stop your soft
> laments at last, and rather
> let us sing the new trophies of Augustus
> Caesar)

Collective song (*cantemus*) corrects personal sorrow; political themes (*Augusti tropaea Caesaris*) prevent the poem from dissolution into private pain. With its resilient capacity to synthesize extremes, the ode's tripartite structure readily suits the desire to temper the constitutive poles of elegy and encomium. Conventionally, strophe and antistrophe collide like thesis and antithesis, only to resolve in the synthesis of the epode. Often the syllogistic arrangement was made to appear quite explicit, as in Gottsched's translations of Pindar, which he marks with the terms "Satz," "Gegensatz," and "Schlußsatz" (thesis, antithesis, and conclusion). In Romantic practice, this synthesizing capacity may be utilized to reconcile personal grief and private pain by way of a sublimation that is, if not ideal, than ideally social – hence, Leopardi's "social catena."

Odic lamentation, therefore, takes many shapes and is rarely performed for its own sake, but rather presents itself as a moment in the overcoming of disillusionment and the grounding of fresh utopian visions. Shelley's famous "Ode to the West Wind" (1820) expresses loss by relinquishing his potency, only to become a more fit channel for the winds of revolution and social change. In this poem, composed in Foscolo's Italy, "attended by that magnificent thunder and lightning peculiar to the Cisalpine regions" (Shelley 1977: 221), Shelley abandoned both the Pindaric strophe and the Horatian stanza. Instead, he chose a striking "mixed mode" – sonnets in *terza rima* – which had the effect of alluding both to Dante and Shakespeare, while invoking the political tone of Wyatt's satires and the prophetic energy of Milton's paraphrases of the Psalms. Shelley's poem thereby embodies most of the chief aspects of the European ode tradition, directing poetry's hierophantic potential to effectuate liberty among humankind ("Be thou, Spirit fierce, / My spirit! Be thou me, impetuous one!" ll. 61-2). In this sense, the optimism responds both to Godwin's cold empiricism as well as Coleridge's darker recognition of the epoch's false promises ("In mad game / They burst their manacles in the name / Of Freedom, graven on a heavier chain," *France: An Ode*, ll. 86-8). Just as Pindar served as the paradigm of the Sublime for Longinus, so the ode provided Shelley with a poetics of pure imagination, of deep feeling (*Mont Blanc*) capable of liberating humankind from the tyranny of what is empirically given.

In a related key, for his *Ode to Napoleon Buonaparte* (1814), Byron turns from the emperor's political and moral failings toward a more hopeful scenario of freedom. Whereas the poem sets out by meditating ironically on the extreme reversals of Napoleon's fortune ("The Desolator desolate! / The Victor overthrown!"), it concludes with a look westward, perfectly analogous to the Progress tradition of Collins and Gray, now across the Atlantic, where an honest future may emerge and redeem humankind from Europe's political exhaustion:

Where may the wearied eye repose
　　When gazing on the Great;
Where neither guilty glory glows,
　　Nor despicable state?
Yes – one – the first – the last – the best –
The Cincinnatus of the West,

　　　　Whom envy dared not hate,
Bequeath'd the name of Washington,
To make man blush there was but one! (ll. 163-71, Byron 1975: 180-2)

With Byron the ode constitutes the most appropriate form for transforming the
impractical political optatives of Wordsworth, for responding to the suspicions of
Coleridge, for "desublimating," as it were, the imaginative constructs of Shelley, by
introducing an empirically sound, declarative mood, for example in *Venice: An Ode*:

　　　　Still one great clime, in full and free defiance,
　　　　Yet rears her crest, unconquer'd and sublime,
　　　　Above the far Atlantic! (Stanza IV, Byron 1975: 454)

Certainly, it was this potential to arrive at an emphatically particular political voice that
led the young Victor Hugo to assume the ode form for his own anti-Bonapartist (and
pro-Bourbon) program. To this end, his *Odes et poésies diverses* (1822) rely a good deal on
the form's dual tendencies, toward public encomium in the Pindaric mode and private
contemplation in the Horatian. In either case, as Hugo himself defines it in the preface
to the 1823 edition, in language altogether reminiscent of Boileau, the ode should
present a "fundamental idea" through a single event. The French Restoration hereby
found its genre. Although the king himself was notoriously reported to have found the
first, rather cheaply produced edition of Hugo's odes as "badly dressed" ("mal fagoté")
he was apparently quite pleased with his portrait in the brilliant ode on *La Mort du duc
de Berry*, written on the occasion of the sovereign's visit to his dying nephew:

　　　　Monarque en cheveux blancs, hâte-toi, le temps presse;
　　　　Un Bourbon va rentrer au sein de ses aïeux;
　　　　Viens, accours vers ce fils, l'espoir de ta vieillesse;
　　　　Car ta main doit fermer ses yeux! (ll. 81-4, Hugo 1964: 315)

　　　　(Monarch in white hair, hurry, time is at hand;
　　　　A Bourbon is to return to the bosom of his ancestors;
　　　　Come, rush to the side of your son, the hope of your old age;
　　　　For your hand must close his eyes!)

Here one may glimpse the remarkable harmonization of Pindaric praise and Horatian
meditation. Nobility is animated by a pain familiar to all. The crucial, classical

allusion is to the early death of Augustus's nephew, Marcellus, whose mournful portrayal in the *Aeneid* reportedly caused his mother, Octavia, to collapse. Even at this early stage in his career, Hugo is capable of the high, Virgilian role. His poetic persona, for example in the programmatic headpiece, *Le Poète dans les revolutions*, confidently provides the subjective ground for societal reflection. In this manner, without abandoning the political, Hugo's odes consistently strive toward a Romantic ideal adopted from Lamartine, namely to give voice to the deepest and most private human sentiments – "toutes les fibres du cœur humain."[5]

This quintessentially Romantic desire for deep psychological investigation finds particularly strong expression in the complex design and subtle rhythms of the odes of John Keats (published in 1820). Innovations in form correspond to innovations in content, as in the famous opening lines to the "Ode on Melancholy," where in a nearly Horatian *recusatio*, the poet rejects the conventions inherited from Edward Young's Gothic epoch:

> No, no, go not to Lethe, neither twist
> Wolf's-bane, tight-rooted, for its poisonous wine;
> Not suffer thy pale forehead to be kiss'd
> By nightshade, ruby grape of Proserpine;
> Make not your rosary of yew-berries,
> Nor let the beetle, nor the death-moth be
> Your mournful Psyche, nor the downy owl
> A partner in your sorrow's mysteries;
> For shade to shade will come too drowsily,
> And drown the wakeful anguish of the soul. (Keats 1994: 194)

The series of renunciations is unified throughout by means of the ode's emblematic and expressly oral vowel, the open-mouthed /o/. It is a nearly musical practice, entirely characteristic of Keats, but also recalling the kletic or "calling" qualities of Klopstock's and Hölderlin's hymns as well as the ascetic, meditative tone of Leopardi. The fact that Keats was able to sustain a high degree of poetic perfection together with the sincerest sentiments of one pained by the conditions of human existence is a testament to the splendid refinement but sheer honesty of the ode form, a remarkably broad and inclusive genre that "dwells with Beauty – Beauty that must die" (l. 21).

This stunning quality of Keats's work depends in no small measure on a richly diverse European tradition, one that is nonetheless strikingly coherent. Whether public or private, celebratory, meditative, or religious, odists' persistent self-repre-sentations as singers – as open mouths – lend unity to the manifold of poetic experience. As Théodore de Banville remarked with hindsight in *Petit Traité de poésie française*: "The Ode absorbed all poetic genres, as it became modern poetry in its entirety" (cited in Ireson 1997: 326). It is precisely in this sense that the Romantic revival of the ode marks a rejuvenation of lyric, grounded in a deep commitment to source and origin, while remaining wholly engaged in the hopeful project and despairing realizations of the modern.

NOTES

1 My translation; note that all translations are mine unless otherwise indicated.

2 On eighteenth-century genre theories in connection with the ode, see Curran (1986: 56-84).

3 David Wellbery's translation; see his analysis of this ode in relation to the Horatian tradition of genial liquidity (Wellbery 1996: 121-83).

4 The note, in Christopher Middleton's translation, along with a brief explication, can be found in Hölderlin (1951: 142-8). On the broader implications of Hölderlin's plan in relation to trends within European Romanticism, see De Man (1984).

5 Lamartine returned to this formulation to define his poetics in the first preface to his *Méditations* (1849): "Je suis le premier qui ait fait descendre la poésie du Parnasse, et qui ait donné à ce qu'on nommait la Muse, au lieu d'une lyre à sept cordes de convention, les fibres memes du cœur de l'homme" (cited in Ireson 1997: 29).

REFERENCES AND FURTHER READING

Allem, Maurice (ed.) (1966). *Anthologie poétique française: XVIIIe siècle*. Paris: Garnier, 1966.

Brose, Margaret (1998). "The Politics of Mourning in Foscolo's Dei Sepolcri," *European Romantic Review*, 9 (1): 1-34.

Byron, Lord (1975). *The Poetical Works of Byron*, ed. Robert Gleckner. Boston: Houghton Mifflin.

Coleridge, Samuel Taylor (1996). *Selected Poems*, ed. Richard Holmes. London: HarperCollins.

Curran, Stuart (1986). *Poetic Form and British Romanticism*. Oxford: Oxford University Press.

Diderot, Denis (1876). *Encyclopédie*. In *Œuvres complètes*. Paris: Garnier.

De Man, Paul (1984). "The Image of Rousseau in the Poetry of Hölderlin." In *The Rhetoric of Romanticism*. New York: Columbia University Press, pp. 19-45.

Fayolle, Roger (1982). "La Dépindarisation de Ponce-Denis Écouchard-Lebrun dit Le Brun-Pindare." *Œuvres et critiques*, 7 (1): 87-99.

Foscolo, Ugo (1994). *Opere: Poesie e tragedie*, ed. Franco Gavazzeni. Turin: Einaudi-Gallimard.

Fry, Paul (1980). *The Poet's Calling in the English Ode*. New Haven, CT: Yale University Press.

Goethe, J. W. (1998). *Gedichte und Epen I*, ed. Erich Trunz. In *Werke*, 14 vols. Munich: Deutscher Taschenbuch, vol. 1.

Heath-Stubbs, John (1969). *The Ode*. Oxford: Oxford University Press.

Herder, Johann Gottfried (1889). *Poetische Werke*, ed. Carl Redlich. In *Sämmtliche Werke*, ed. Bernhard Suphan, 33 vols. Berlin: Weidmann, vol. 29.

Herder, Johann Gottfried (1992). *Selected Early Works: 1764-1767*, trans. Ernst Menze. University Park: Pennsylvania State University Press.

Hölderlin, F. (1951). *Gedichte nach 1800*. In *Sämtliche Werke*, ed. Friedrich Beißner, 8 vols. Stuttgart: Kohlhammer, vol. 2.1.

Hugo, Victor (1964). *Œuvres poétiques I*, ed. Pierre Albouy. Paris: Gallimard.

Ireson, J. C. (1997). *Victor Hugo: A Companion to his Poetry*. Oxford: Clarendon Press.

Keats, John (1994). *The Complete Poems*. New York: Modern Library.

Leopardi, G. (1984). *Canti*, ed. Domenico de Robertis. Milan: Edizioni Il Polifilo.

Shelley, Percy Bysshe (1977). *Poetry and Prose*, ed. Donald Reiman. New York: Norton.

Viëtor, Karl (1923). *Geschichte der deutschen Ode*. Munich: Drei Masken.

Voltaire (1877). *Œuvres complètes*, ed. Adrien Beuchot, 52 vols. Paris: Garnier.

Wellbery, David (1996). *The Specular Moment: Goethe's Early Lyric and the Beginnings of Romanticism*. Stanford, CA: Stanford University Press.

Wickham, Edward (ed.) (1986). *Q. Horatius Flaccus, Opera*. Oxford: Oxford University Press.

Wordsworth, William (1932). *The Complete Poetical Works*, ed. Andrew George. Boston: Houghton Mifflin.

Wordsworth, William (1952). *Poetical Works*, ed. E. de Selincourt. Oxford: Clarendon Press.

21

"Unfinish'd Sentences": The Romantic Fragment

Elizabeth Wanning Harries

Love-songs and scatter'd rhymes
Unfinish'd sentences, or half erased,
And rhapsodies like this, were sometimes found – (Charlotte Smith, "Beachy Head")

The phrase "Romantic fragment" calls up two quite different sets of associations. On the one hand, we tend to think of poems (and sometimes other texts) that seem unfinished, often called fragments, written between, say, 1790 and 1830. On the other hand, it is almost impossible not to think of the cult of ruins and of fragmentary relics of earlier times that has been part of European thought since the Renaissance and was assimilated into British thought as inherently "Romantic" in the eighteenth century. In his "Preface to *Adonais*" (1821), Shelley juxtaposes the two contrasting ideas:

> I consider the fragment of Hyperion, as second to nothing that was ever produced by a writer of the same years.
>
> John Keats died at Rome of a consumption, in his twenty-fourth year, on the – of – 1821, and was buried in the romantic and lonely cemetery of the protestants in that city, under the pyramid that is the tomb of Cestius, and the massy walls and towers, now mouldering and desolate, which formed the circuit of ancient Rome. The cemetery is an open space among the ruins covered in winter with violets and daisies. It might make one in love with death, to think that one should be buried in so sweet a place. (Shelley 1967: 73)

Shelley begins with his judgment of Keats's first "Hyperion" poem. The poem was published in 1820 as "Hyperion: A Fragment" and abruptly breaks off in Book III, as Apollo painfully becomes one of the Olympian gods, with a series of asterisks:

At length
Apollo shriek'd; – and lo! from all his limbs
Celestial * * * * * * * * * * *
* * * * * * * * * * * * * * (Keats 1978: 356)

This shattered ending has become an icon of the Romantic fragment, the poem that cannot reach a resolution. And yet Shelley sees it as the poem that has placed Keats "among the writers of the highest genius who have adorned our age" (Shelley 1967: 73).

Shelley moves from this high praise to the bleak statement of Keats's early death and then, without warning or much transition, to a description of the Protestant cemetery in Rome where Keats had been buried that winter. His evocation of that "romantic and lonely" place, surrounded with desolation and yet so "sweet," echoes the descriptions of ruined landscapes that were conventional throughout the eighteenth century and continue to be conventional today. The violets and daisies that cover the "open space" suggest the equally conventional trope of life within the ruins, of life persisting in the context of lost civilizations and death.

In her essay "Garden Agon," Susan Stewart distinguishes between the "cult of order" and the "cult of ruin," as two differing habits of mind that have their roots in historical moments but continue into the present:

A garden involves composition with living things; it can also involve composition with inert matter – walls, rocks, stones, bricks, gravel, walkways, statues, urns, and other material artifacts. But such inert matter is thereby made meaningful by its juxtaposition to living forms. When we find the encroachment of moss on a brick or thyme on a rock appealing, we are pleased by the fixity of the inert and the mutability of its natural frame. When we find an obelisk in a field of weeds or, as with Wallace Stevens's jar in Tennessee, we place a fixed form in a wilderness, an analogous pleasure arises from the opposite relation of figure to ground. Stone will endure; the sundial will orient us in time and space – this is the sensibility of the Enlightenment and the cult of order. Water will wear stone away; all the fixed world will decay – this is the sensibility of the Romantic and the cult of ruin. (Stewart 1998: 111-12)

Stewart's description of these opposed "sensibilities" depends on a historical distinction that is perhaps too simple – many bright lights of the Enlightenment responded to the pleasures of both order and decay; many Romantics were obsessed with the possibilities of order amid apparent disorder. But her interest in the way we "frame" gardens and in the relationship of "figure to ground" can help us understand not only Shelley's love of the Roman cemetery, but also our continuing interest in literary fragments. Part of the "sweetness" of the cemetery for Shelley is the juxtaposition of the Roman ruins and the tiny flowers, the crumbling artifacts and the signs of continuing life. Part of our interest in the "ruin" comes from its mutability but also the suggestion of a vanished whole. Part of our interest in the literary fragment comes from the interplay between the suggestiveness of the words actually on the page and the shadowy "ground" of the possible "finished" work.

Or, to put this another way, Stewart (as usual) has put the whole constellation –
fragments, ruins, suggestions of the past and of the whole – in a particularly fruitful
formal and historical context. Though the cult of the ruin and of the literary fragment
are not inventions of the Romantic period at all, it seems impossible to disentangle
them. The repeated association of the word "fragment" with "Romantic" is in fact
misleading, since many European writers in the eighteenth century and earlier (from
Petrarch on) considered and often called their texts fragments. But it is certainly true
that many poems labeled "fragment" appeared during the Romantic period. Some
were so called by their authors, like Keats's "Hyperion"; some were posthumously
collected and labeled by editors. The early deaths of so many of the canonical
Romantics made this particularly likely, of course. Many poems not so labeled also
appear to be fragmentary, or to celebrate the fragmentary. Shelley's "Ozymandias" and
Keats's "On Seeing the Elgin Marbles," both written in 1817 and both "finished" or
"perfect" sonnets, are only two well-known examples of the tendency to dwell on the
suggestive power of the fragmentary in what seems to be an achieved and final form.

Many critics have focused on the kind of fragment that seems to have appeared
involuntarily in what we now call the Romantic period. John Beer stresses this possible
meaning. He says, for example, that in the Romantic period "fragmentariness was not
designed by but forced upon its author," or "the Romantic poetic fragment will end up
as such not in accordance with the artist's intentions but in spite of them" (Beer 1995:
241, 242).[1] This seems to be true of "Hyperion" and of many other Romantic poems.
But, at least as often, British Romantic poets and their European contemporaries fixed
upon the fragment as an existing, even fashionable form that could express their
particular anxieties and sense of historical belatedness. The *Athenaeum* group in Germany deliberately generated many aphoristic fragments; Friedrich Schlegel, Novalis,
and Schleiermacher all experimented with fragmentary forms, following their recent
predecessors Hamann and Herder. Both Byron and Pushkin found the construction of
fragments, or deliberate fragmentation, a source of continual ironic energy and invention (see Greenleaf 1994, chapter 1). To put this more succinctly, I believe that there are
at least two kinds of literary fragments in the Romantic period: one the *involuntary*
fragment, cut off by death or by the writer's inability to finish the poem; one the
deliberate or *planned* fragment, designed from the beginning as partial and apparently
incomplete.[2] To treat all fragments as examples of Romantic longing for totality or
grasping for the ungraspable seems to me a mistake, and a mistake still generated by
what Jerome McGann (1983) has taught us to see as the "Romantic ideology."

The coexistence of these radically different kinds of fragment makes it difficult to
talk about the Romantic fragment as a distinctive genre or as a period form. Rather,
what I want to do here is to work intensively with several examples of fragmentation,
written between 1790 and 1830, that show the complexity of the term and of the
ways it has been understood, both in the period and later.[3] My examples must
necessarily be arbitrary. I've chosen them because I think they at least begin to
suggest the range of fragmentary practices and gestures – and the range of writers
who could be seen as "fragmentists."

An Involuntary Fragment: Hölderlin's "Wie wenn am Feiertage..."

In 1799-1800 the German poet Friedrich Hölderlin began writing his great series of late hymns, many based loosely on the Pindaric odes he had been translating. One of the earliest of these hymns was "Wie wenn am Feiertage...," known to us in two versions: a prose draft and the fuller but still fragmentary hymn.[4] The first seven stanzas, apparently complete though syntactically complex, move from a description of a morning after a clearing thunderstorm to praise of Nature herself and of the gods who have revealed themselves to the poet through their own lightning. Like Semele, the poets must bare their heads and risk destruction in order to receive and to pass on the signs from the gods:

> Doch uns gebührt es, unter Gottes Gewittern,
> Ihr Dichter! mit entblösstem Haupte zu stehen,
> Des Vaters Strahl, ihn selbst, mit eigner Hand
> Zu fassen, und dem Volk ins Lied
> Gehüllt die himmlische Gabe zu reichen. (Hölderlin 1992: 240)

(Yet, fellow poets, it behooves us to stand bare-headed beneath God's thunderstorms, to grasp the Father's ray, no less, with our own hand, and, wrapping the heavenly gift in song, to offer it to the people.)[5]

Hölderlin suggests the danger of the poets' knowledge and the necessity of wrapping or insulating the gift of the gods in poetry to communicate it. Poets must become pure enough, their hands guiltless enough, to receive the lightning without being singed or destroyed.

What appear to be the next and last two stanzas are full of incomplete and broken-off lines:

> Doch weh mir! wenn von
>
> Weh mir!
>
> Und sag ich gleich,
> Ich sei genaht, die Himmlischen zu schauen,
> Sie selbst, sie werfen mich tief unter die Lebenden
> Den falschen Priester, ins Dunkel, daß ich
> Das warnende Lied den Gelehrigen singe.
> Dort (Hölderlin 1992: 241)

(But alas! when from ... alas! ... and I say at once ... I approached to see the heavenly gods, and they themselves cast me down, deep down under the living, false priest that I am, into the dark, to sing, for those who have ears to hear, the warning song. There ...)

After the stanzas of confidence in the poets' ability to withstand and interpret the gods' unmediated lightning , the "I" of the poem suddenly sees himself as a sinner, as unclean, as unworthy of any communication with them. To approach or move near to the gods is a perilous undertaking. Like Tantalus, he is thrown deep under the earth, where his song of praise becomes a song of warning. The ruptures in the manuscript, like the rupture in Keats's *Hyperion*, come precisely at the moment when the poet-figure must "die into life" like Apollo (*Hyperion*, III, l. 130, Keats 1978: 356) or become like one of the Immortals.

The draft of part of Hölderlin's hymn is on the reverse of the manuscript of another unfinished poem, "Rousseau," that ends (if it ends) with a stanza beginning "Kennt er im ersten Zeichen Vollendetes schon" (He recognizes in the first sign the whole, the finished . . .). Both poems are about the possibility of consummation, of full knowledge and communication with the gods, but also about its dangers.[6] The gods speak aphoristically, in gestures and in signs, that only the poet can interpret: "Dem Sehnenden war / Der Wink genug, und Winke sind / Von Alters her die Sprache der Götter" (To the one who yearned the hint was enough, and hints have always been the language of the gods; "Rousseau," ll. 30-2, Hölderlin 1992: 238). Hölderlin's fragmentary lines reveal the crushing difficulty of becoming their interpreter. Keats's Apollo says, "Knowledge enormous makes a God of me" (*Hyperion* III, l. 113, Keats 1978: 355), but a few lines later the poem breaks off.[7] In much the same way, Hölderlin asserts the right and duty of the poet to receive the signs the gods give us – through lightning and other symbolic and cryptic "hints" – but the poet's inability to withstand their fiery message is then reflected in the broken lines that end the poem.

Such "involuntary" fragment poems, then, do reflect an inability to complete, an intellectual and poetic impasse. They suggest a whole that they cannot create, a wished-for situation that they find it impossible to imagine completely. Keats published his poem as "A Fragment"; Hölderlin left "Wie wenn am Feiertage . . ." unfinished and untitled, in manuscript like almost all of his other work. Editors have performed acts of archaeology and of reconstruction on both poems, bringing earlier, half-erased versions to light, asserting continuities with later work, sometimes suggesting as certainties questions that the text itself does not answer.[8] Our conception of the poem as fragment seems to include the possibility of filling in the gaps – sometimes reflected in an insistence on the reader's role in dealing with the poem. These gaps, however, are *aporiae*, moments in which the poets can only mark their own failure to create a whole.

Many critics see such poems as particularly Romantic – often citing Friedrich Schlegel's aphorism from the *Athenaeum* (1798) as support: "Viele Werke der Alten sind Fragmente geworden. Viele Werke der Neuern sind es gleich bei der Enstehung" (Many works of the ancients have become fragments. Many works of the moderns are fragments at the time of their origin).[9] These poems, however, were not imagined or constructed *as fragments*; rather, they *became* fragments in the process of composition and despair. One could argue, I suppose, that fragments like "Hyperion" and "Wie wenn am Feiertage . . ." have become particularly Romantic because we have reproduced them and placed them at the center of our literary histories of Romanticism (McGann 1994: 211-12). But in their breaking-off we can see instances of what Marjorie Levinson calls the "accidental" fragment, the fragment that does not reflect authorial "intention." Another of Schlegel's aphorisms might be more relevant here: "Es gibt so viel Poesie, und doch ist nichts seltener als ein Poem! Das macht die Menge von poetischen Skizzen, Studien, Fragmenten, Tendenzen, Ruinen, und Materialen" (There is so much poetry, and yet nothing is rarer than a Poem! That comes from the huge number of poetical sketches, studies, fragments, tendencies, ruins, and raw materials; *Kritische Fragmente* 4, in Schlegel 1967: 147).

Deliberate Fragments: Hoffmann and Byron

In these fragments, published in 1797 and 1798, I think Friedrich Schlegel was describing what he saw around him – the welter of published fragments in Europe in the later eighteenth century – not predicting the future of poetry to come. Like his contemporaries, he was certainly aware of Sterne's fragmentary novels and the many shattered texts that had followed them, not only in English but in French and German as well. Rousseau's *Rêveries d'un promeneur solitaire* – written on scraps of paper and the backs of playing cards from 1776 to 1778, the year of his death – were collected and published in 1782 with the first six books of the *Confessions*. Denis Diderot's comic masterpiece, *Jacques le fataliste et son maître*, had just been published in German (though it had circulated in Grimm's manuscript *Correspondance littéraire* since before 1780); its gaps and *lacunae,* as well as its central episode, reflect Sterne's formal freedom and inventiveness. Sébastien-Roch-Nicolas Chamfort's *Oeuvres* (including many individual "maxims" and thoughts) had been published in 1795, just after his death; his editor Guingené had collected all the bits and pieces he had written on little scraps of paper and put them together in four volumes. André Chénier's poems – some simply fragmentary, some left unfinished at his execution in 1793 – had also just been collected and published. Schlegel came of age in a literary world that both published and celebrated the incomplete, the unfinished, the suggestive, the interrupted. His *Lyceumsfragmente* (1797), *Athenaeumsfragmente* (1798), and *Ideen* (1800), as well as Novalis's *Blütenstaub* (Grains of Pollen, 1798), are responses not only to a time of European political crisis but also to a literary trend, a fashion that demanded a new approach to the literary.

As Lacoue-Labarthe and Nancy have argued, we should see Schlegel's and Novalis's fragments as deliberate:

> a confusion is maintained, and sometimes exploited, between a piece that is struck by incompletion, let us say, and another that aims at fragmentation for its own sake. A propitious shadow is thus allowed to obscure what this genre essentially implies: the fragment as a determinate and deliberate statement, assuming or transfiguring the accidental and involuntary aspects of fragmentation. (Lacoue-Labarthe and Nancy 1988: 41)

In their terms, Keats's "Hyperion" and Hölderlin's "Wie wenn am Feiertage..." are "struck by incompletion"; neither could be brought to a full and finished form. The "shadow" of such poems always lies behind deliberate fragments (just as the crumbling of classical artifacts lies behind both torsos and the artificial ruins built in eighteenth-century gardens), giving them a penumbra of death, lack, and loss. According to Lacoue-Labarthe and Nancy, the deliberate fragment both mimics and transforms or "transfigures" the involuntary fragment, exploiting its resonance to inform the textual and generic choices the authors have made.

In other words, when Romantic writers wrote deliberate fragments, they were aware both of the history and of the paradoxes of their undertaking. No one was more so than Friedrich Schlegel, who alternated between describing his aphorisms as "hedgehogs," finished and complete in themselves (*Athenaeumsfragment* 206 in Schlegel 1967: 197) and as "Randglossen zu dem Text des Zeitalters" (marginal notes to the text of the times; *Athenaeumsfragment* 259, p. 209).

This interplay between the finished and the unfinished, the perfect and the imperfect, gives novels like E. T. A. Hoffmann's *Lebens-Ansichten des Katers Murr* (*The Life and Opinions of Tomcat Murr*, 1819-21) part of their point and power. Hoffmann's subtitle, *Nebst fragmentarischer Biographie des Kapellmeisters Johannes Kreisler in zufälligen Makulaturblättern* (Together with a Fragmentary Biography of the Conductor Johannes Kreisler on Random Sheets of Waste Paper), while appropriately Sternean, fails to convey the full fragmentary nature of the text. The tomcat's *Opinions* are almost as fragmentary as the conductor's biography; both are constantly interrupted midsentence by a section of the other "text" or by an editor's note:

> −Hier hat, wie der Herausgeber es dem geneignten Leser bemerklich machen muß, der Kater wieder ein Paar Makulaturblätter ganz weggerissen, wodurch in dieser Geschichte voller Lücke wiederum eine Lücke entstanden. Nach der Seitenzahl fehlen aber nur acht Kolumnen, die eben nichts besonders wichtiges enthalten zu haben scheinen, da das Folgende sich im ganzen so ziemlich an das Vorhergegangene reiht. Also weiter heißt es: − − − nicht erwarten durfte. (Hoffman 1992: 405)

> At this point the editor is obliged to inform his gentle reader that the cat has torn a few more sheets of paper out entirely, leaving yet another gap in a history full enough of gaps already. Judging by the page numbering, however, only eight columns of print are missing, and they do not seem to have contained anything of special importance, since on the whole what comes next follows on quite well from the previous passages. The text then continues:... could not expect. (Hoffman 1999: 286)

Hoffmann continuously accentuates the manuscript fiction, inserting a fragment of a fragmentary episode from Sterne's fragmentary *Sentimental Journey*, ending with the pretended promise of another chapter, or perhaps even a volume.[10] The friction between the two torn narratives − the tomcat's autobiography full of humor and bravado, the conductor's biography full of mock sentimental passages and Romantic celebrations of the artistic – makes the novel a particularly telling example of the play with the fragmentary in the period.

But not all deliberate fragments were in prose. I've argued elsewhere that Coleridge's "Kubla Khan," often described as *the* most Romantically "unfinished" poem, is in fact an example of a deliberate fragment, deeply influenced by Sterne's fragmentary practices (see Harries 1994: chapter 6). And one of our difficulties in reading Byron as a Romantic poet is that he constantly refuses to draw that imaginary circle that would make his work *seem* to be complete. His *Don Juan* (1818-24), "never intended to be serious," spins out a series of stops, false starts, and deliberate gaps; as he wrote to his publisher in 1819, "you ask me for the plan of Donny Johnny: I *have* no plan – I *had* no plan; but I had or have materials" (Byron 1972: 310). His comic epic has deep roots in earlier fragmentary practices like Ariosto's, for example, as his stanza form, *ottava rima*, also suggests. His burlesque of narrative contingencies recalls Fielding's comic chapter titles and transitions like "in which place, we think proper to leave him, some time, to his repose, and shall here, therefore, put an end to this chapter" (*Tom Jones*, Book VII, ch. 12). Throughout the 16 cantos Byron "completed" – sometimes talking of 12, sometimes of a hundred – he plays with the possibilities of an open, unfinished form.[11]

One stanza will have to do as an example of Byron's fragmentary verve, a stanza from Canto IV, just after the lingering death of Haidée:

> But let me change this theme, which grows too sad,
>   And lay this sheet of sorrows on the shelf.
> I don't much like describing people mad,
>   For fear of seeming rather touched myself.
> Besides I've no more on this head to add;
>   And as my Muse is a capricious elf,
> We'll put about and try another tack
> With Juan, left half-killed some stanzas back. (Canto IV, Stanza 74, Byron 1973: 207)

Byron moves abruptly from the "sheet of sorrows" that describes Haidée's death to his characteristic self-referential humor, claiming successively that madness is too touchy a subject, that he's run out of material, and that his "Muse" can't stick to one topic for long. He plays with the problem of narrative continuity, returning to the hero he has "left / half-killed some stanzas back." The nautical imagery – "put about" and "tack," both sailing terms that indicate a change of direction – may obliquely continue the theme of the sea that has dominated Cantos II-IV, but also suggests the veering course of the poem itself. Each narrative strand has its own mood and trajectory; the poet can only pretend to bring them into some sort of unity. His art is an art of juxtaposition and improvisation. Throughout the poem, the narrator's comic backing and filling always permits us to think of alternative narratives, alternative choices, other possible outcomes:

> Let us ramble on.
> I mean to make this poem very short,
> But now I can't tell where it may not run. (Canto XV, 22, Byron 1973: 502)

Don Juan is, of course, also an involuntary fragment, since Byron left 14 stanzas of a 17th Canto at his death – and clearly intended to write more. But in its additive and rambling form, what remains is an excellent example of the fragmentary narrative, both in prose and in poetry, that characterizes the Romantic period. Hoffmann, Byron, and many of their contemporaries were deeply committed to the fragment as an existing form that could suggest the untidiness of life and the multiple fictions involved in coming to an ending.[12] Closure in their work characteristically depends on an ironic move that undermines its own finality; Romantic narrative typically is full of *disjecta membra* and interruptions. (Even the Romantic habit of inserting poems in a prose narrative could be seen as an attempt to interrupt and question the narrative flow.) Their deliberate fragments both continue earlier traditions and give those traditions a new intensity and ironic subtlety.

Charlotte Smith's "Beachy Head"

I want to end with a controversial poem of the period that has been characterized as both fragmentary and complete: Charlotte Smith's "Beachy Head" (published in 1807, the year after she died). Her first editor (perhaps her sister, perhaps the bookseller, Joseph Johnson, himself) presents the poem as an involuntary fragment, unfinished because of her illness and death: "The Poem entitled BEACHY HEAD is not completed according to its original design. That the increasing debility of its author has been the cause of its being left in an imperfect state, will it is hoped be a sufficient apology" (Smith 1993: 215). This early opinion has recently been echoed by John Anderson, who claims that the poem is "a majestic fragment, like Shelley's 'The Triumph of Life' left enticingly unfinished" (Anderson 2000: 547).

On the other hand, Smith's most reliable recent editor, Stuart Curran, has argued that the poem has a complete and satisfying shape:

> From a modern experience of Romanticism, nurtured by the sometimes oblique narrative strategies of its major poets, a work that begins atop a massive feature of the landscape and ends immured within it bears a remarkable coherence, the more so since in no poem of the period can one find so powerful an impulse to resolve the self into nature. (Smith 1993: xxvii)

For Curran, the poem's imaginative movement from the top of Beachy Head itself at sunrise to a cave in the base of the cliff, from a wide view of the sea and the surrounding landscape to the confined caves and sepulchres at the end, suggests a carefully planned itinerary and formal closure. Unlike the editor of the 1807 volume, Curran sees the poem as complete, though he also notes that the "textual problems may be unsolvable" (1993: xxvii).

We will probably never know whether Smith herself thought of the poem as complete or as a fragment.[13] But what does this disagreement show us, and how can we understand it? What features of the poem might explain it? Unlike "The Triumph of Life," the poem has no missing feet or half-finished lines. Smith's sinuous blank verse proceeds almost undisturbed from the beginning through 731 lines, interrupted only by a couple of poems in stanza form attributed to one of the hermits of the poem.

But, as Curran and Anderson both note, the poem itself is full of images of ruin and decay. One of the lonely men who haunt the poem has made his home in an old castle or fortress

> where hard by
> In rude disorder fallen, and hid with brushwood
> Lay fragments gray of towers and buttresses,
> Among the ruins, often he would muse – (ll. 507-10, Smith 1993: 239)

In one of her many notes to the poem, Smith comments that many of the fortresses built by Stephen of Blois "are now converted into farm houses" (Smith 1993: 238). Domesticated ruins – ruins like Tintern Abbey used as walls by farmers and the poor or "houseless" – were a common feature of the landscape in Britain at the time. But Smith emphasizes the solitary wandering of her "stranger" among the ruins, rather than the refuge he finds within the crumbling walls. The hermit Darby lives in a deep cave, "mined by wintry tides" (l. 673, p. 245) at the base of Beachy Head itself. A wanderer like the "stranger," he lives among natural ruins and fragments; in the storm that ends his life (and the poem)

> – the bellowing cliffs were shook
> Even to their stony base, and fragments fell
> Flashing and thundering on the angry flood. (ll. 718-20, Smith 1993: 243)

As in Coleridge's "Kubla Khan," these fragments are natural, energetic, and dangerous.[14] In "Beachy Head," Smith melds the traditional imagery of ruin – the crumbling castles, churches, and turrets that were part of the European landscape – with the natural history of decay and decomposition. Smith's references to natural history, particularly geological speculation, form a powerful substratum for the poem. Her many discursive notes about everything from birds to British history may seem strange and unnecessary to us, but they are all part of Smith's attempt to situate the poem in a deeply historicized "speaking" landscape.

This landscape is also a poetic space. We eventually learn that the "stranger" is also a poet, who has left some lines as evidence of his fleeting presence:

> But near one ancient tree, whose wreathed roots
> Form'd a rude couch, love-songs and scatter'd rhymes
> Unfinish'd sentences, or half erased,
> And rhapsodies like this, were sometimes found – (ll. 573-6, Smith 1993: 241-2)

Here Smith calls up all the imagery of the deliberate fragment: "scatter'd rhymes," "unfinish'd sentences," "half erased." Though her poem itself may seem complete, she invokes the possibility of the unfinished.[15]

In the "stranger's" verses, she repeats the theme of natural shelters like the "rude couch": a "sylvan room" (l. 613, p. 243) that shields from the heat of summer, a "sand rock cave" (l. 621, p. 243) that protects from the frost. She speaks of the possibility that he may one day live in a "cane-constructed bower" (l. 664, p. 245) on a South Sea island. All this leads to the final figure of the poem – the hermit Darby and his "cavern mined by wintry tides" (l. 673, p. 245) at the base of Beachy Head. Withdrawn from the world, he seems to wait for storms so that he can save the sailors who are wrecked, the opposite of the "wreckers" who throughout the poem wait for the loot the storms can bring in their "commerce of destruction" (l. 190, p. 225). The hermit's cave is doubled and redoubled in the last lines, as he digs a "sepulchre" for sailors he has been unable to save and then as his cave becomes his own grave and gravestone:

>   his drowned cor'se
> By the waves wafted, near his former home
> Receiv'd the rites of burial. Those who read
> Chisel'd within the rock, these mournful lines,
> Memorials of his sufferings, did not grieve . . . (ll. 724-8, Smith 1993: 247)

Here shelter, the grave, and poetry (as epitaph) come together. Though it remains unclear what "lines" are "chisel'd within the rock" – his own verses? something the mountain shepherds have written? Smith's lines themselves? – the poem ends with a buried inscription that seems indelible and permanent. (Our momentary hesitation between the past and the present tense in reading the "read" of line 726 suggests this permanence.) At the end of the poem, poetry becomes a lasting part of the British landscape that Smith has so movingly invoked.[16]

But poetry, like the landscape itself, can also be ruinous and fragmentary. The stranger's "unfinish'd sentences" are left near the shattered towers and fallen walls of a ruined fortress. Even the hermit's epitaph is engraved in a chalk cliff that is endangered and constantly changed by storms, fragments falling.[17] Throughout the poem, Smith suggests a reciprocal relationship between the features of the landscape and poetry, not only her own. Like Shelley in the "Preface to *Adonais*," she sees decay and ruin, both natural and cultural, as an eloquent setting for the poetry of death and loss. ("Beachy Head" is clearly part of what Susan Stewart calls "the cult of ruin.") Though debate about the poem's form will undoubtedly continue, to place it in the context of

Romantic fragments, both involuntary and deliberate, helps us see some of its most salient features, features that are often overlooked. It is certainly a "mosaic" or collage of quotations and allusions, to other poets and to her own work, as John Anderson has shown. But it is also a meditation on the expressive power of the ruined and the unfinished. For Smith, fragments – natural, geological, architectural, and poetic – form a system of signs that always point to meanings beyond themselves. In Hölderlin's terms, one might say that they are like the "Zeichen" (signs) of the gods, meaningful though partial gestures that must be interpreted. In Friedrich Schlegel's terms, one might say that "Beachy Head" is "a system of fragments" that, taken together, work to suggest a whole.[18] Smith builds her last long poem on the metonymic principle of the fragment. In doing so, she shows the power of the fragment – whether involuntary or deliberate, whether formal or thematic – to suggest buried connections and the outlines of a whole.

Fragmentary Coda

In other words, there is really no such thing as a uniquely Romantic fragment. The Romantics inherited ideas about and examples of planned and unplanned fragments from their predecessors, as I have tried to suggest. And both kinds of fragment continue throughout the nineteenth century and beyond. Carlyle, in some ways the first "eminent Victorian," obviously follows the tradition of *Tristram Shandy* and *Kater Murr* as mutilated manuscript in his *Sartor Resartus: The Life and Opinions of Herr Teufelsdröckh* (1833-4). But there are many other, later examples. Lewis Carroll published the first stanza of "Jabberwocky" as a "Stanza of Anglo-Saxon Poetry," written in rune-like letters, in a family periodical *Mischmasch* in 1855. In his mock-exegesis of the nonsense lines, he calls it "an obscure, but yet deeply affecting, relic of ancient Poetry."[19] Henri Frédéric Amiel's *Fragments d'un journal intime* were published after his death (in 1883-4); they are literally fragments or extracts from the 14 thousand pages he had written, but they also are improvisatory, full of erasures and false starts. Hawthorne includes a chapter called "Fragmentary Sentences" in *The Marble Faun*; Melville speaks of *Moby Dick* as "a draught – nay, but the draught of a draught." These examples could be multiplied many times over, and continued into the twenty-first century. The fragment is always with us, not least in the preoccupations of postmodern aesthetics.

The fragments I've dwelt on here are certainly not all examples of the "diasparactive" mode of longing and failed quest that McFarland and Beer emphasize. They may be desperate or playful, deeply personal or ironic. We may disagree about their status as fragment, as critics have about "Beachy Head," or about their indebtedness to earlier traditions. We may also become more and more suspicious of our own reading practices, since to read a fragment also means to attempt to "read" what isn't there.[20] But we should try to read Romantic fragments in two different ways: in the formal continuum of a mixed genre that goes back at least to Petrarch and Rabelais and against the elegiac cultural ground of ruin, epitaphs, and loss.[21]

NOTES

1 In *Romanticism and the Forms of Ruin*, McFarland concentrates almost exclusively on fragment as reflecting what he sees as the "diasparactive modality" of the period life: "the pervasive longing of the Romantics was at the same time an index to the prevailing sense of incompleteness, fragmentation, and ruin" (McFarland 1981: 11).

2 In her book *The Romantic Fragment Poem*, Marjorie Levinson (1986) outlines four types of fragment: "true," "completed, " "deliberate," and "dependent." I've found, however, that her ingenious categories often make it hard to see the basic distinctions I've outlined above.

3 Not that the definition of the "period" is simple, either. For a wide-ranging and excellent discussion of some of the anomalies that become evident when we try to talk about a European Romantic period, see Drummond Bone "The Question of a European Romanticism," particularly footnote 3 (1995: 284-5). French Romanticism, like Romantic music, comes significantly later than in other national literatures.

4 We have the handwritten manuscripts, but Hölderlin never oversaw the publication of a volume of his poetry. A first volume came out in 1826, edited by Ludwig Uhland and Gustave Schwab, but at that point he had been mad and living in a tower near Tübingen under the care of a keeper for 20 years. "Wie wenn am Feiertage" was first published in 1910. It wasn't until the early twentieth century that Hölderlin's poetry became well-known and widely influential. His life (1770-1843), ending in nearly 40 years of madness, became tangled up in interpretations of his fragmentary work – much as Keats's early death influenced reactions to poems like "Hyperion."

5 Translation mine. I have consulted translations by Michael Hamburger and by Christopher Middleton.

6 See Lawrence Kramer for a discussion of the invocation of the gods in Romantic and post-Romantic poetry; as he points out, "to name them, to fix them as a poetic image, is already to have lost them" (Kramer 1978: 485). See also Paul de Man, "Intentional Structure of the Romantic Image" and "Images of Rousseau in Hölderlin" in *The Rhetoric of Romanticism*.

7 Here it would be interesting to explore the parallels between Keats's treatment of Apollo and Hölderlin's well-known lines in his 1802 letter to his friend Casimir Ulrich Böhlendorff: "as one says of heroes, I can well say of myself that Apollo has struck me."

8 For a brief but searching meditation on such editorial practices, see Paul de Man's comments on the editorial history of Shelley's "The Triumph of Life" in *The Rhetoric of Romanticism*: "What relationship do we have to such a text that allows us to call it a fragment that we are then entitled to reconstruct, to identify, and implicitly to complete?" (de Man 1984: 94).

9 *Athenaeumsfragment* 24 (in Schlegel 1967: 169, translation mine). See my *Unfinished Manner* for a rereading of this aphorism in terms of the many deliberately unfinished texts that were written in the last half of the eighteenth century (Harries 1994: 2).

10 Here I obviously must disagree with Jeremy Adler, who wrote the introduction to the Penguin translation: "the last Kreisler fragment elaborately stage-manages the plot, as if anticipating a lengthy denouement. Such stage-setting contradicts the old critical view that the novel was an intended fragment, in the Romantic style, or that it was unfinishable, though how the novel would conclude must remain pure speculation" (Hoffmann 1999: xxx). As my colleague Jocelyne Kolb points out, the tomcat's narrative is continuous, though interrupted, and the Kreisler

pages end where they began. But the reader's experience of the novel is discontinuous, underlined by the supposed death of Murr himself at the end that, as the editor mock-mournfully says, has made his autobiography remain a fragment.

11 Though Marjorie Levinson says that Byron's "wry and witty ... practice [in *Don Juan*] is better explored in the context of modernist poetics" (Levinson 1986: 130), I think it is crucial to see the poem as a Romantic fragment deeply involved in the many contradictory currents of the time. Neither a throwback to the eighteenth century nor a sister poem to Pound's *Cantos* or *The Wasteland*, *Don Juan* is part of its era. If what we think of as "Romantic" poetics can't include the poem, we need to rethink them.

12 See Levinson for a discussion of "irresolution" in Byron's *The Giaour: A Fragment of a Turkish Tale* (Levinson 1986: 115-18, 126-8). She claims that the poem's "formal failure" is a result of Byron's faulty historical method, completely missing the function (and the literary tradition) of the supposed Turkish manuscript that motivates the poem's circling narratives.

13 In her letters of 1804-6 Smith often speaks of what she calls her "local poem" (i.e., "Beachy Head") and of her difficulties in completing it; in July 1806 she says that "the close of the local poem I have not yet sent up" to her publisher in London, implying that it was finished. She also sketches the final story of the poem, "The extraordinary story of Parson Darby," in the next letter, to Joseph Johnson. See Smith's *Collected Letters* (2003: 739-42).

14 Smith could not have known Coleridge's poem, first published with "Christabel" and "The Pains of Sleep" in 1816. But her fragments, falling with such force from Beachy Head, have something of the same disruptive vitality (see Harries 1994: 160).

15 As Anderson points out, Smith echoes lines and themes from William Cowper's *The Task* throughout the poem. This "rude couch"

may be an oblique homage reference to the "sofa" of which Cowper sings.

16 "Beachy Head" belongs in part to the genre Geoffrey Hartman meditates on in his essay "Wordsworth, Inscriptions, and Romantic Nature Poetry": "The poet *reads* landscape as if it were a monument or grave" (Hartman 1970: 223).

17 Beachy Head is still crumbling, and is still a place to watch migratory birds (as Smith seems to have). Bodies still wash up on its base from the Channel. It has also become a well-known place for suicides.

18 As Friedrich Schlegel wrote to his brother August Wilhelm in 1797, "Ich kann nur von mir, von meinem ganzen Ich gar kein andres Echantillon geben, als so ein System von Fragmenten, weil ich selbst dergleichen bin." (I can only give you of myself, of my whole self no other tiny sample but a system of fragments, because I myself am like that; quoted in Eichner's introduction to the *Charakteristiken* I, Schlegel 1967: xl, n. 3).

19 See Martin Gardner's marginal notes in *The Annotated Alice* (Carroll 2000: 148-9). Carroll is obviously playing on the eighteenth-century tradition of the recovery of ancient manuscripts, both genuine (Percy) and fake ("Ossian" and Chatterton).

20 For comments on reading fragments, see Hans-Jost Frey (1996: 48-9): "The fragment is unreadable: it has not been read when one takes notice of what is there nor can one read more than what is there.... In the face of the fragment a basic methodological rule for rigor in speaking about texts fails: the rule that what is said must be corroborated by the text, must withstand its test." Julian Wolfreys (2000: 63) brought this passage to my attention.

21 Thanks to my colleagues Jocelyne Kolb and William Oram for their careful and thoughtful readings of an early version of this article at a very busy time. They not only found many omissions and stupidities (though the ones that remain are not their fault), but also helped me rethink its shape and argument.

REFERENCES AND FURTHER READING

Primary sources

Byron, George Gordon, Lord (1972). *Selected Prose*, ed. Peter Gunn. Harmondsworth, UK: Penguin.

Byron, George Gordon, Lord (1973). *Don Juan*, ed. T. G. Steffan, E. Steffan, and W. W. Pratt. Harmondsworth, UK: Penguin.

Carroll, Lewis (2000). *The Annotated Alice: The Definitive Edition*, ed. Martin Gardner. New York: W. W. Norton.

Hoffmann, E. T. A. (1992). *Lebens-Ansichten des Katers Murr; Werke 1820-21*, ed. Hartmut Steinecke. In *Sämtliche Werke*, 5. Frankfurt am Main: Deutscher Klassiker Verlag.

Hoffmann, E. T. A. (1999). *The Life and Opinions of the Tomcat Murr*, trans. Anthea Bell. Harmondsworth, UK: Penguin Books.

Hölderlin, Friedrich (1992). *Gedichte*, ed. Jochen Schmidt. In *Sämtliche Werke und Briefe*, I. Frankfurt am Main: Deutscher Klassiker Verlag.

Keats, John (1978). *The Poems of John Keats*, ed. Jack Stillinger. Cambridge, MA: The Belknap Press of Harvard University Press.

Schlegel, Friedrich (1967). *Charakteristiken und Kritiken I (1796-1801)*, ed. Hans Eichner. In *Kritische Friedrich-Schlegel-Ausgabe*, II, ed. Ernst Behler. München: Schöningh.

Schlegel, Friedrich (1971). *Friedrich Schlegel's Lucinde and the Fragments*, ed. and trans. Peter Firchow. Minneapolis: University of Minnesota Press.

Shelley, Percy Bysshe (1967). *Shelley's Critical Prose*, ed. Bruce R. McElderry, Jr. Lincoln: University of Nebraska Press.

Smith, Charlotte (1993). *The Poems of Charlotte Smith*, ed. Stuart Curran. New York: Oxford University Press.

Smith, Charlotte (2003). *The Collected Letters of Charlotte Smith*, ed. Judith Phillips Stanton. Bloomington: Indiana University Press.

Secondary sources

Anderson, John (2000). "*Beachy Head*: The Romantic Fragment Poem as Mosaic." *Huntington Library Quarterly* 63 (4): 547-73.

Beer, John (1995). "Fragmentations and Ironies." In John Beer (ed.), *Questioning Romanticism*. Baltimore and London: Johns Hopkins University Press, pp. 234-64.

Blanchot, Maurice (1969). *L'Etretien infini*. Paris: Gallimard.

Bone, Drummond (1995). "The Question of a European Romanticism." In John Beer (ed.), *Questioning Romanticism*. Baltimore and London: Johns Hopkins University Press, pp. 123-32.

de Man, Paul (1984). *The Rhetoric of Romanticism*. New York: Columbia University Press.

Frey, Hans-Jost (1996). *Interruptions*, trans. Georgia Albert. Albany: State University of New York.

Greenleaf, Monika (1994). *Pushkin and Romantic Fashion: Fragment, Elegy, Orient, Irony*. Stanford, CA: Stanford University Press.

Harries, Elizabeth Wanning (1994). *The Unfinished Manner: Essays on the Fragment in the Later Eighteenth Century*. Charlottesville: University Press of Virginia.

Hartman, Geoffrey H. (1970). "Wordsworth, Inscriptions, and Romantic Nature Poetry." In *Beyond Formalism: Literary Essays 1958-1970*. New Haven, CT: Yale University Press, pp. 206-30.

Kramer, Lawrence (1978). "The Return of the Gods: Keats to Rilke." *Studies in Romanticism*, 17: 483-500.

Kritzman, Lawrence (ed.) (1981). *Fragments: Incompletion and Discontinuity*. New York: New York Literary Forum.

Lacoue-Labarthe, Philippe and Nancy, Jean-Luc (1988). *The Literary Absolute: The Theory of Literature in German Romanticism*, trans. Philip Barnard and Cheryl Lester. Albany: State University of New York Press.

Levinson, Marjorie (1986). *The Romantic Fragment Poem: A Critique of a Form*. Chapel Hill and London: University of North Carolina Press.

McFarland, Thomas (1981). *Romanticism and the Forms of Ruin: Wordsworth, Coleridge, and the Modalities of Fragmentation*. Princeton, NJ: Princeton University Press.

McGann, Jerome (1983). *The Romantic Ideology: A Critical Investigation*. Chicago: University of Chicago Press.

McGann, Jerome (1994). "Literary History, Romanticism, and Felicia Hemans." In *Re-Visioning Romanticism: British Women Writers, 1776-1837*, ed. Carol Shiner Wilson and Joel Haefner. Philadelphia: University of Pennsylvania Press.

Newlyn, Lucy (1995). "'Questionable Shape': The Aesthetics of Indeterminacy." In John Beer (ed.), *Questioning Romanticism*. Baltimore and London: Johns Hopkins University Press, pp. 209-33.

Stewart, Susan (1998). "Garden Agon." *Representations*, 62 (Spring): 111-43.

Wolfreys, Julian (2000). *Readings: Acts of Close Reading in Literary Theory*. Edinburgh: Edinburgh University Press.

Zinn, Ernst (1959). "Fragmente über Fragmente." In J. A. Schmoll gen. Eisenwerth, *Das Unvollendete als Künstlerische Form: Ein Symposion.* Bern: Francke, pp. 161-9.

22

Romantic Irony

Jocelyne Kolb

It is equally deadening for the mind to have a system – and to have none. One must therefore determine to have both.

(Es ist gleich tödlich für den Geist, ein System zu haben und keins zu haben. Er wird sich also wohl entschließen müssen, beides zu verbinden.) (Friedrich Schlegel, *Athenäum* Fragment 53)

Any successful attempt to define romantic irony must fail. This is exactly the kind of sentence – epigrammatic, paradoxical, polemical – for which Friedrich Schlegel is famous. Schlegel (1772-1829) is the original theorist of what now is called romantic irony, and it is a tribute to his lasting influence that those who cite and use him have often been infected by his style. By his early style, that is, for Schlegel is remembered mostly for the essays and aphorisms (which he called "fragments") that he wrote during the intense early phase of German Romanticism, in the waning years of the eighteenth century. There are 35 volumes in the critical edition of Schlegel's works, including his correspondence and the writings and translations signed by him but sometimes written by his wife Dorothea Mendelssohn Veit Schlegel, the eldest daughter of the philosopher Moses Mendelssohn; but it is only the second volume of the edition, the *Charakteristiken und Kritiken I* (1796-1801), that scholars consult with regularity and rigor. A glance at the edition on the shelves of any university library will prove as much: whereas the second volume is either absent or dog-eared, the other volumes look pristine, regardless of whether they appeared in the late 1950s and early 1960s or in the 1980s and 1990s.[1]

Schlegel is again in vogue, thanks largely to Behler's magisterial edition and thanks also to the currency of Schlegel's ideas. His incessant and unsettling questions, his mistrust of anything fixed, and his preoccupation with the act of writing anticipate postmodernism and the tenets and close readings of deconstruction (Muecke 1969, Behler and Hörnisch 1987, Garber 1988b, Behler 1990, 1997, Beer 1995). Romantic irony encapsulates such thinking, and the term is used with increasing frequency and assurance by Anglo-American critics. It trips off the tongue as easily as words like *Angst* or *Bildungsroman*, sometimes with the same estranged results, putting one in mind of Schlegel's *Athenäum* Fragment 19: "The best way to be unintelligible or, rather, misunderstood is to use words in their original meaning" ("Das sicherste Mittel unverständlich oder vielmehr mißverständlich zu sein, ist, wenn man die Worte in ihrem ursprünglichen Sinne braucht," Schlegel 1967: 168).[2] Sometimes the meaning of romantic irony is oversimplified, and usually it is in dispute. Some critics are distressed by the difficulty of defining it with precision, like Lilian Furst, who has examined its origin and usage with her characteristic thoroughness (Furst 1984). Raymond Immerwahr would reserve the term "romantic irony" for the authors Schlegel specifically links with irony and designates as "romantic," such as Cervantes and Shakespeare, Petrarch and Ariosto. Immerwahr prefers the term "poetic irony" (Immerwahr 1985: 142), while other critics refer to "literary irony" (Schnell 1989).[3] A simple solution, and one with a noble critical parentage, is to speak of "Schlegel's irony," as Novalis does in *Blütenstaub* ([1798] 1960, 2: 425, Wheeler 1984: 88-9), or of "Schlegelian irony," as Kierkegaard does in *The Concept of Irony* (Kierkegaard [1841] 1965: 282). For Novalis, Schlegel's irony "seems...to be true humor" ("scheint . . . echter Humor zu sein"), and he concludes that "one idea benefits from having several names" ("mehre [sic] Namen sind einer Idee vorteilhaft"). His conclusion is more comforting than Schlegel's own wry characterization of aesthetic definitions in *Athenäum* Fragment 82 as a form of legitimization and a display of virtuosity reminiscent of singers' bravura arias and philologists' Latin (Schlegel 1967: 177).

Yet the term "romantic irony" is useful as a way of distinguishing this irony from other kinds (for instance Socratic, dramatic, rhetorical, tragic) and more useful still as a way of fixing it in an aesthetic context (Allemann 1970). Ingrid Strohschneider-Kohrs, whose book remains the gold standard for work on romantic irony (Strohschneider-Kohrs [1960] 2000), does not fret about the name but uses "romantic irony" almost interchangeably with "artistic irony" ("künstlerische Ironie"), a designation introduced in the early nineteenth century by two theorists of irony, Adam Müller (1779-1829) and Karl Solger (1780-1819).[4] The term "artistic irony" is less tainted by polemics and chronological misassociations than "romantic irony" and has the added advantage of suggesting works that are not literary, such as Berlioz's *Symphonie fantastique*, Schumann's song cycle *Dichterliebe*, operas like Richard Strauss's *Ariadne auf Naxos* and *Capriccio*, Caspar David Friedrich's paintings, or Manet's "Le Déjeuner sur l'herbe" ("Picnic on the Grass").

History of Romantic Irony

René Wellek credits Schlegel with having "introduced the term irony into modern literary discussion" (Wellek 1955: 16), and Frederick Garber calls Schlegel "the paramount theorist, the one with whom we have to begin and who always stands as the point of reference" (Garber 1988a: 8).[5] Behler speaks of the near identity between irony and early Romantic theory and says that the theory of irony "is almost exclusively Friedrich Schlegel's work" (Behler 1993: 141), and Gary Handwerk says that "As nearly as any idea can be, Romantic irony was the progeny of a single person, Friedrich Schlegel, whose work has been a touchstone for almost every recent theoretical discussion of irony" (Handwerk 2000: 207). As a term, however, "romantic irony" was not a part of Schlegel's critical vocabulary. It occurs a few times in early notebooks that were not meant for publication (Strohschneider-Kohrs [1960] 2000: 1), and its meaning is complicated rather than clarified by the knowledge that Hans Eichner has identified six different ways in which Schlegel uses the word "romantic" (Schlegel 1967: liii-lvi). For Eichner to have found so many shades of meaning is even more striking than the meanings themselves, and one stumbles – and should stumble – over the word "romantic" as much as over the word "irony" in approaching the subject of romantic irony. Garber mentions the term's "curious anomalies, not least of which is the adjective" and adds that the "anomaly is often an anachronism, one which has a good deal to tell, though we ought to be cautious about what we think it is telling" (Garber 1988a: 358). When the word "Romantic" is capitalized, the irony often is limited to the Romantic period and understood as a technique rather than an aesthetic – as the destroying of an illusion. In the article on "irony" from the enlarged edition of the *Princeton Encyclopedia of Poetry and Poetics* (Preminger 1974: 407-8), for example, romantic irony is called "a special form of irony described by Tieck and practiced most notably by Jean Paul Richter and Heinrich Heine: the writer creates an illusion, especially of beauty, and suddenly destroys it by a change of tone, a personal comment, or a violently contradictory sentiment." What is defined here is not so much romantic irony as *Stimmungsbrechung* in its simplest form, literally the breaking of a mood, which is a manifestation of romantic irony but not identical with it. *Stimmungsbrechung* reminds the reader of a philosophy acutely conscious of the disjunction between pairs such as illusion and reality, theory and practice, or tragedy and comedy. Duality is the watchword of this philosophy, tension its *raison d'être*.

The flaw in the definition from the *Princeton Encyclopedia of Poetry and Poetics* is that it is severed from the succinct and serviceable characterization of irony that directly precedes it: "To the German romantics (Schlegel, Tieck, Solger) irony was a means of expressing the paradoxical nature of reality. Since it exposed two meanings, simultaneously it could suggest the polarities (e.g., absolute v. relative; Subjective vs. Objective; mental categories vs. *Ding an sich*) which post-Kantian philosophy found everywhere in experience" (Preminger 1974). This is Schlegelian territory. Schlegel repeatedly and insistently intertwines philosophy and literature, for example in the concluding sentence of *Lyceum* Fragment 115, where he announces that "Poetry and philosophy shall be united" ("Poesie und Philosophie sollen vereinigt sein," Schlegel 1967: 161). Furthermore, romantic irony has been the purview of philosophers as much as of literary critics, with Kant, Fichte, and Schelling present at its birth and Hegel vociferously against it (Handwerk 2000). As a child of philosophy, romantic irony is expressive of forms and ideas rather than the name for a technique; as a child of the early German Romantic movement, romantic irony is associated with yearnings and the striving for something perceived but out of grasp. Critics often evoke the intangible and self-conscious quality of romantic irony with chapter titles such as "Towards a Definition of Romantic Irony" (in Sperry 1977), or "A Conclusion in Which Nothing Is Concluded" (in Mellor 1980), or "In Search of a Theory" (in Furst 1984), or, more recently, "In Search of Romantic Irony" (in Gurewitch 2002).

Intangibility and self-consciousness are not limited to the Romantic period, however, and Schlegel's examples of irony extend well into the past, just as those of the critics cited here range from the eighteenth to the twentieth centuries – even when, as in the case of Strohschneider-Kohrs, Mellor, or Gurewitch, the focus is on works of European Romanticism. Schlegel's examples and those of his successors belong to the uncapitalized romanticism that designates a kind rather than a period of art. His irony, as Furst says, "must be accorded archetypal as well as historical status" (Furst 1984: 237). Capitalizing or not capitalizing the word "romantic" effects a shift in thinking aptly reflective of the thing itself, of its double and willfully vacillating nature.

Keeping in mind the association of romantic irony with the Romantic Movement yet thinking beyond the period is a form of mental gymnastics that Schlegel himself practiced with enviable agility. As a critic of immense learning and imagination, Schlegel thought beyond the confines of specific periods but with a complete knowledge and awareness of them. His adoption of the aphorism is a case in point: he writes openly to Novalis about his debt to Chamfort's aphorisms, calling his fragments "eine kritische Chamfortiade."[6] When he equates irony with paradox in *Lyceum* Fragment 48, for example, his form is reminiscent of the eighteenth century, both in epigrammatic style and in his favoring of the paradox: "Irony is the form of paradox. Paradox is everything both good and great" ("Ironie ist die Form des Paradoxen. Paradox ist alles, was zugleich gut und gross ist," Schlegel 1967: 153). But this is an estranged eighteenth century. Schlegel does not adopt the clarity and rationalism or even, as Michel Chaouli points out, the "right sort of pleasure" associated with the aphorism (Chaouli 2002: 56-7).[7] Schlegel also varies the length of his fragments so that their rhythm is unpredictable, with terse ones like this put into relief by others as long as a page – Chaouli speaks felicitously of "interruptions" (Chaouli 2002: 57) – the most famous being his programmatic hymn to modern literature in *Athenäum* Fragment 116. Schlegel orders his thoughts and *aperçus* so that they echo and complement and contradict each other and do honor to the name of fragment, with the paradoxical effect that together they lose their fragmentary quality. His equation of irony and paradox is one of 127 fragments that touch on topics as varied as irony, genius, criticism, poetic technique, and politics and that contain flashes of the famous or infamous *Frechheit* (impertinence or insolence) that has been so provoking to some readers (Schiller and Goethe among them) and delightful to others. His unorthodox shaping of contrasts is itself an example of what romantic irony does.[8]

Schlegel's Irony and Beyond

Despite the disputes and frustrations over defining romantic irony and the variety of examples chosen to illustrate it, critics and scholars agree on a number of matters: that the thing itself is essential to our understanding both of Romanticism and of a modern aesthetic; that its roots are philosophical as well as literary; and that Friedrich Schlegel is its original theorist. Some would take Schlegel out of the foreground, like Gurewitch, who sardonically names one chapter "The Beatification of Friedrich Schlegel" (Gurewitch 2002), or Furst, who faults Strohschneider-Kohrs (1960) and Mellor (1980) for relying too heavily on Schlegel. But even the skeptics must and do begin by considering what Schlegel says; and both skeptics and groupies refer to the same handful of fragments and passages – *Lyceum* Fragment 48 being one of them – in which Schlegel approaches irony in an allusive and often witty way, more suggestive than definite, as befits his subject.

Most important among these passages is *Athenäum* Fragment 116, which has the same resonance for the criticism of German Romanticism that the blue flower of Novalis does for German Romantic literature. It is not that Schlegel defines or speaks directly of irony here but that the fragment contains his fervent, even ecstatic, program for the literature that incorporates his ideas about irony, the kind of writing that Schlegel calls "romantic poetry" ("romantische Poesie"). *Athenäum* Fragment 116 derives its name from the journal *Athenäum*, which Schlegel edited between 1798 and 1800 with his brother, the critic August Wilhelm Schlegel (1767-1845), and which Wellek calls the "crucial document" of the early Romantic movement, the equivalent in Germany to the *Lyrical Ballads* of Coleridge and Wordsworth in England (Wellek 1955: 1). The 116th is the most famous of the 451 fragments that were written mostly by Schlegel but with contributions from Schleiermacher, Novalis, and Caroline Schlegel. A handful of fragments were written by all together in the spirit of *Sympoesie* and *Symphilosophie* – the fusing of minds that Schlegel imagined and at times even achieved during this early period and of which the journal *Athenäum* provides an eloquent manifestation.[9]

Schlegel begins with a short declarative sentence that, like the equation of irony and paradox in *Lyceum*- Fragment 48, at first glance seems lucid but upon reflection is less so: "Romantic poesy is a progressive universal poesy" ("Die romantische Poesie ist eine progressive Universalpoesie," Schlegel 1967: 182). Schlegel's usage is both definite and idiosyncratic, as it is for the word "irony." The word *Poesie* can mean "lyric poetry," but when Schlegel continues by saying that "romantische Poesie" must combine poetry and prose, it is obvious that *Poesie* means more than verse:

> Romantic poesy is a progressive, universal poesy. Its aim isn't merely to reunite all the separate species of poetry and put poetry in touch with philosophy and rhetoric. It tries to and should mix and fuse poetry and prose, inspiration and criticism, the poetry of art and the poetry of nature; and make poetry lively and sociable, and life and society

poetical; poeticize wit and fill and saturate the forms of art with every kind of good solid matter for instruction, and animate them with the pulsations of humor.

(Die romantische Poesie ist eine progressive Universalpoesie. Ihre Bestimmung ist nicht bloß, alle getrennte Gattungen der Poesie wieder zu vereinigen, und die Poesie mit der Philosophie und Rhetorik in Berührung zu setzten. Sie will, und soll auch Poesie und Prosa, Genialität und Kritik, Kunstpoesie und Naturpoesie bald mischen, bald verschmelzen, die Poesie lebendig und gesellig, und das Leben und die Gesellschaft poetisch machen, den Witz poetisieren, und die Formen der Kunst mit gediegenem Bildungsstoff jeder Art anfüllen und sättigen, und durch die Schwingungen des Humors beseelen.) (Schlegel 1971: 175, 1967: 182)

To the initiated – those who have been reading the fragments and making the necessary associations from one to the other – Schlegel's double meanings are clear. Just two fragments earlier, for example, he has defined *Poesie*, decidedly if teasingly, by avoiding a definition:

A definition of poetry can only determine what poetry should be, not what it really was and is; otherwise the shortest definition would be that poetry is whatever has at any time and at any place been called poetry.

(Eine Definition der Poesie kann nur bestimmen, was sie sein soll, nicht was sie in der Wirklichkeit war und ist; sonst würde sie am kürzesten so lauten: Poesie ist, was man zu irgendeiner Zeit, an irgendeinem Orte so genannt hat.) (Schlegel 1971: 174, 1967: 181)

Initiated and attentive readers know, too, that *romantisch* contains the word "*Roman*" or "novel" (Eichner 1956). For the uninitiated or inattentive, however, Schlegel refers specifically to the novel a few lines later so that they cannot miss his point, and in the last sentence of the fragment he replaces the word *Poesie* with the words *Dichtart* and *Dichtkunst* to speak of *romantische Dichtkunst*. Literally *Dichtart* denotes a kind of writing and *Dichtkunst* the art of writing it. He has therefore clarified his meaning while emphasizing (and demonstrating) both the practice of writing and the "progressive" rather than finished nature of "romantic poetry." The fragment concludes with a return to the original phrase *romantische Poesie* in slightly varied form when Schlegel says that "in a certain sense all poetry is or should be romantic" ("in einem gewissen Sinn ist oder soll alle Poesie romantisch sein") (Schlegel 1971: 176, 1967: 183). The literature he envisions is one for which words like "poetry" and "novel" no longer mean what they did before and that also contains a "poetics" not unlike the one displayed in his fragments.

It is against the background of *Athenäum* Fragment 116 that one must read what Schlegel says elsewhere about irony. When he equates irony and paradox in *Lyceum* Fragment 48, for example, it is consistent with his image in *Athenäum* Fragment 116 of romantic poetry as a mirror of the world that reflects the age but also reflects back on itself in an endless series of mirrors, "hovering on the wings of poetic reflection" between the work and its creator. This in turn recalls *Athenäum* Fragment 51, where irony is identified as the "constant alternation between self-creation and self-destruction," a mobile state anticipating Byron's "*mobilité*," the term that, as Paul Fry reminds us, "Keats called negative capability and Hazlitt gusto – and that Friedrich Schlegel 20 years earlier called irony" (Fry 2000: 16). Schlegel's usage in Fragment 51 reflects the association of irony with "mobility," because he shows irony to be something attained rather than set when he uses the phrase "to the point of irony": "Naïve is what is or seems to be natural, individual, or classical *to the point of irony*, or else to the point of continuously fluctuating between self-creation and self-destruction" ("Naiv ist, was *bis zur Ironie oder bis zum* steten Wechsel von Selbstschöpfung und Selbstverichtung") (Schlegel 1971: 167, 1967: 172, emphasis added). Schlegel's definition of "naïve" in this fragment is a response to Schiller's terminology in the essay "On Naïve and Sentimental Poetry" (1794-5). In Schiller's classification, "naïve" poetry – that of Homer and Goethe, for example – does not have the same self-consciousness as "sentimental" poetry like that of Shakespeare and Sterne. As usual, Schlegel revises his source rather than mimicking it, most noticeably by replacing the word "sentimental" with the word "irony."

Two further passages are regularly and rightly cited by students of Schlegel's irony. In *Lyceum* Fragment 42 Schlegel speaks of philosophy as the "home of irony" ("Heimat der Ironie") and lists different kinds of irony in order of importance and complexity, from rhetorical to Socratic and culminating in poems that "breathe the divine spirit of irony" ("den göttlichen Hauch der Ironie atmen"). In his elaboration he uses the image of clowning, again with a literary allusion – this time to the commedia dell' arte – and again with the aid of paradox, which transfigures the image into "transcendental buffoonery":

> There are ancient and modern poems that are pervaded by the divine breath of irony throughout and informed by a truly transcendental buffoonery. Internally: the mood that surveys everything and rises infinitely above all limitations, even above its own art, virtue, or genius; externally, in its execution: the mimic style of an averagely gifted Italian *buffo*.

> (Es gibt alte und moderne Gedichte, die durchgängig im Ganzen und überall den göttlichen Hauch der Ironie atmen. Es lebt in ihnen eine wirklich transcendentale Buffonerie. Im Innern, die Stimmung, welche alles übersieht, und sich über alles Bedingte unendlich erhebt, auch über eigne Kunst, Tugend, oder Genialität: im Äußern, in der Ausführung die mimische Manier eines gewöhnlichen guten italienischen Buffo.) (Schlegel 1971: 148, 1967: 152)

Finally there is Schlegel's memorable characterization of irony as a "permanent parabasis" ("permanente Parekbase," Schlegel 1963: 85). The term "parabasis" designates the interruptions in Greek comedy during which the chorus speaks directly to the audience, and Strohschneider-Kohrs remarks that Schlegel has chosen the best possible literary technical term to convey his idea of irony (Strohschneider-Kohrs [1960] 2000: 37, Chaouli 2002: 198-207). Once again the choice exemplifies Schlegel's practice of adopting terms inherited from literary criticism and estranging their meaning, in this case a term from comedy applied to literature that suspends the idea of genre altogether.

Each of these allusions to irony exemplifies Schlegel's critical precept of evoking a subject through style, as if to salvage for criticism some of the neoclassical decorum that he and the other Romantics discard. His paradoxes, wit, and images are essential to his idea of irony and expressive of its dual perspective, of the "hovering" between different tones and between a work and its creator – an "implicit analogy," as M. H. Abrams puts it, "between God's creation of the world and the artist's making of a poem," giving "new application to the Renaissance metaphor of the poet as creator" (Abrams 1971: 239, Muecke 1969: 190-2, 223-4).

The Practice and Psychology of Romantic Irony

Examples of romantic irony always come in a double form, but it is not the balanced, symmetrical form of Classicism or neo-Classicism. Like Schlegel's aphoristic style and predilection for paradox, the doubleness of romantic irony cites and alters a neoclassical model – and the Classicism from which that model derives (Wellek 1955, Fry 2000). The roots of romantic irony are to be found in the doubleness of the rhetorical irony that Booth calls "stable" (Booth 1974); but its dualism remains unresolved and does not produce a Hegelian synthesis. It is a dualism evident in authors' irrepressible and often irreverent humor as well as in the clash of their wit and wistfulness. Psychology also plays its part (Robertson 1985, Schanze 1994: 590-604). Schlegel's "compulsive introspection" as a very young man – which Eichner rightly calls "a frequent phenomenon in gifted adolescents" – can be transferred to his ideas about irony and about literature. Eichner explains the introspective habit as "a state of mind in which a person cannot do or say anything without, at the same time, watching himself do or say it" (Eichner 1970: 14). From a literary point of view, this state of mind often takes the form of "permanent parabasis," the regular interruptions that show how authors reflect on their creations and distance themselves from them, the affectionate yet critical god-like stance of which Abrams speaks.

Certain works have long been identified with romantic irony, prompting Handwerk to speak of "ironic canonization" (Handwerk 1993: 281). Among Schlegel's own models are works by Cervantes, Sterne, Diderot, and Goethe; other works have acquired their canonical status more recently, foremost among them Byron's *Don Juan* (Garber 1998b, Gurewitch 2002). For purposes of illustration, and to bring into focus traits of romantic irony and its reception, there is an obvious if not a canonical choice: Heine's *Doppelgänger* poem (as it has come to be called, although the word Heine himself uses is *Doppeltgänger*), the 20th poem in the *Heimkehr* (*Homecoming*) section of *Buch der Lieder* (Book of Songs, 1827), where Heine offers his most definite and well-known treatment of a motif that, as Prawer remarks, is "more adequate than any other to convey [Heine's] recurrent experience" (Prawer 1961: 263-9, quotation p. 265). In this central poem from the collection that made Heine famous (the poem itself having received special billing because of Schubert's equally famous setting), the poet stands outside his beloved's former house by moonlight. He is forlorn, self-pitying, and nostalgic – until he observes his double making fun of him, "aping him" ("nachäffen") for wringing his hands in anguish (Heine uses the neologism "Schmer-zensgewalt," literally "the power of pain"):

> Still ist die Nacht, es ruhen die Gassen,
> In diesem Hause wohnte mein Schatz;
> Sie hat schon längst die Stadt verlassen,
> Doch steht noch das Haus auf demselben Platz.
>
> Da steht auch ein Mensch und starrt in die Höhe,
> Und ringt die Hände, vor Schmerzensgewalt;
> Mir graust es, wenn ich sein Antlitz sehe –
> Der Mond zeigt mir meine eigne Gestalt.
>
> Du Doppeltgänger! Du bleicher Geselle!
> Was äffst du nach mein Liebesleid,
> Das mich gequält auf dieser Stelle,
> So manche Nacht, in alter Zeit? (Heine 1975: 231)

> (The night is still, the streets are dumb,
> This is the house where dwelt my dear;
> Long since she's left the city's hum
> But the house stands in the same place here.
>
> Another man stands where the moonbeams lace,
> He wrings his hands, eyes turned to the sky.
> A shudder runs through me – I see his face:
> The man who stands in the moonlight is I.
>
> Pale ghost, twin phantom, hell-begot!
> Why do you ape the pain and woe
> That racked my heart on this same spot
> So many nights, so long ago? (Heine 1982: 85)

Heine welds psychology and aesthetics through the contrast of moods, of subjective and objective, of sentiment and wit; he juxtaposes inherited Romantic images with a bittersweet and longing mockery of them; and he undermines the simplicity of the folk-like form he uses. But his contrasts are not resolved, and the motif of the *Doppelgänger* allows for two contrasting perspectives to remain distinct. The poem ends with a question rather than an answer, because for Heine, as Sammons says, there is "no mediation between these contraries in the situation. The resolution is the poetry itself" (Sammons 1979: 62).

As much as Heine's treatment of the *Doppelgänger* motif, it is his placement of the poem – and indeed the placement of all poems in the cycle – that qualifies him as a romantic ironist. On a heightened level, he orders his poems much as Schlegel orders his fragments, so that a poem's mood and meaning shift and deepen, depending on its placement in the cycle. Consequently, the double and contradictory stance of the *Doppelgänger* is present from one poem to the next as well as within a single poem. Heine is known to have ordered his poems carefully and, as he himself emphasizes, artfully (Altenhofer [1982] 1993). His ordering is what makes the *Stimmungsbrechung* an "aesthetic of contrasts," in Höhn's phrase, rather than a coy or calculating technique (Höhn 1997). In some poems the element of surprise or the contrast of mood and diction is altogether absent, for instance in the poems from *Lyrisches Intermezzo* that Schumann chose to set for *Dichterliebe*. When these poems are read with the others in the cycle, however, as they are meant to be, or when one considers the effect of the piano as well the voice in Schumann's cycle, the duality is palpable.

One of the *North Sea* (*Nordsee*) poems from the *Book of Songs*, "Seegespenst" (Sea Ghost), is famous for its *Stimmungsbrechung* and illustrates the claim that the destroying of an illusion, like romantic irony, is more than a technique or a trick. The poet leans over the railing of a ship and loses himself in a daydream; his vision of the beloved at the bottom of the sea seems so real that he starts to jump overboard and join her – until he is pulled back in the nick of time by the contrasting mood, sound, and diction of the captain, who says "with an angry laugh" ("ärgerlich lachend"): "Doctor, what the devil's got in you?" ("Doktor, sind Sie des Teufels?") (Heine 1975: 389, 1982: 143). That the poet can be seduced by his own vision is a sign of his power in creating it, and the example from "Seegespenst" fits Schlegel's *Selbstschöpfung* ("self-creation"), which precedes the *Selbstvernichtung* ("self-destruction") in Schlegel's characterization of irony from *Lyceum* Fragment 42. But Heine does more than break a mood. He breaks likewise with a literary tradition by echoing and altering Goethe's poem "Der Fischer," where the fisherman succumbs to his vision and half jumps and half is pulled into the water (Goethe is expressly ambiguous: "Halb zog sie ihn, halb sank er hin" ["She half pulled him, he half sank in"]), and where the woman is separate from the fisherman rather than a creation of his imagination. The "ghost" in the title is not only an "apparition" (in Draper's rendering), but also the ghost of Goethe. Another ghost in the poem intensifies both the poet's self-consciousness and his readers' consciousness of what he is doing: it is the ghost of Heine's own "Lorelei" poem in *Buch der Lieder*, where the fisherman meets the same fate as Goethe's and is "swallowed by the waves," but in a doubling frame that separates the poet from the fisherman and allows the poet to reflect and consequently to survive. More than Goethe's poem "Der Fischer," the "Lorelei" poem resembles Goethe's *The Sufferings of Young Werther* (*Die Leiden des jungen Werther*, 1774), with its editor's frame and the move from a solipsistic first-person epistolary narrative to a distanced third-person perspective, a novel that can be counted among works noted for their romantic irony (Garber 1988b).

In German literary criticism, it is not customary to associate Heine with romantic irony. For some critics he is not enough of a philosopher and not enough of a

Romantic; for others his irony is rhetorical rather than Schlegelian, and he does not write novels. Even those who do associate Heine with romantic irony often modify the term; he has been called a "postromantic ironist" (Garber 1998b: 249) and a "defrocked romantic ironist" in imitation of the phrase *"romantique défroqué"* that was coined for Heine by Blaze de Bury and adopted by Heine in the *Geständnisse* (Kolb 1987: 403, 419). A recent study considers him a romantic ironist but speaks of his "modern romantic irony" (Kerschbaumer 2000), and Jeffrey Sammons distances Heine from the concept by speaking cleverly of his "anti-Romantic irony" (Sammons 1979: 62). Heine scholars who reject the association do so for reasons that have more to do with literary history than with Heine. They object – and with good reason – to the notion that Heine's aesthetic consists of no more than *Stimmungsbrechung* and that *Stimmungsbrechung* is identical with romantic irony (Allemann 1970, Preisendanz 1970). But their objections can be countered by reasoning that *Stimmungsbrechung* is emblematic of Heine's breaks with tradition and of his ambivalence in all things and that it therefore represents more than waking from a dream or breaking an illusion. Some critics consider Heine too much of a realist, too close to politics to qualify as a romantic ironist, the argument being that Romantic illusions are escapist and that Heine, while attracted to a world of poetry and a world of illusions – for example in early poems from *Buch der Lieder* like "Die Lorelei" or "Gespräch auf der Paderborner Heide" or "Seegespenst" and late poems from *Romanzero* like "Böses Geträume" or "Rückschau" or "Frau Sorge" – perceives its dangers too vividly to yield to them. There is also the irreverence of Heine's humor, which to some is frivolously incompatible with the loftiness of romantic irony. But Heine's humor derives largely from the dual perspective of which the *Doppelgänger* is the paradigm, and humor is more often a characteristic of the romantic ironist than a disqualifying trait (Kolb 1987, Gurewitch 2002). Some of Schlegel's main examples of irony – Shakespeare, Cervantes, Sterne, and Diderot – are humorists, often bawdily so, and they are authors to whom Heine shows a resemblance, as he does to Byron (Bourke 1980, Garber 1988b, Kolb 1995).

Hegel is also to blame. Having condemned romantic irony, he has made it off limits for those – and they are not a few – who consider Heine a Hegelian. But romantic irony need not "breed a capricious aestheticism," as Handwerk points out when he calls Kierkegaard and Hegel mistaken for deriding its negativity and subjectivity (Handwerk 1993: 282). Heine's satire proves as much, and to those who reject the connection of satire and romantic irony (like Strohschneider-Kohrs [1960] 2000: 244-5), one can counter that Heine is a satirist of a particular stripe – a "tragic satirist," as Prawer puts it (Prawer 1961). Heine combines lyricism and satire in his *Doppelgänger* aesthetics, and he holds allegiances to opposites rather than to one idea, the "puzzle" about him being, as Prawer puts it, "that he could feel so strongly attracted where he felt equally strongly repelled" (Prawer 1961: 53). This is the pose that Sammons has called "elusive" (Sammons 1969), and it is the pose of the romantic ironist.

Heine's *Doppelgänger* owes much to E. T. A. Hoffmann, but the dualistic psyche of Hoffmann's characters does not yield as readily to an aesthetic form as it does in Heine's practice. Hoffmann's doubles have more to do with horror than humor, and the two figures of the *Doppelgänger* lead the separate existence of a Doctor Jekyll and Mr Hyde. Their awareness of each other is generally not a self-awareness, as it is in the *Doppelgänger* poem, but rather an expression of how one self is tormented by the presence of another. It is in other ways that Hoffmann shows himself to be a romantic ironist, for example in his late novel *Kater Murr* (1821), as critics note with increasing frequency (Robertson 1985, Garber 1988b, Furst 1988, Schnell 1989, Handwerk 2000, Gurewitch 2002). Already in the title Hoffmann introduces the different perspectives of a first- and third-person narrative as well as the doubleness, self-consciousness, and playfulness central to romantic irony: in its long entirety the title is *Opinions of the Tomcat Murr together with a fragmentary Biography of Kapellmeister Johannes Kreisler on Random Sheets of Waste Paper* (*Lebensansichten des Katers Murr nebst fragmentarischer Biographie des Kapellmeisters Johannes Kreisler in zufälligen Makulaturblättern*). This is amusing, but it is the serious amusement of *A Sentimental Journey*, the kind Goethe invokes in his legendary characterization of *Faust* as "these very serious jests" ("diese sehr ernsten Scherze").

Formally *Kater Murr* resembles the *Doppelgänger* motif, with each half of the narrative side by side as separate parts of a whole: the tomcat Murr writes his self-congratulatory autobiography in deliberate and orderly fashion on the back of scrap paper containing a biography of Kreisler in fragmentary disorder. His procedure recalls Schlegel's memorable phrase "artfully ordered confusion" from the *Conversation about Poetry* (*Gespräch über die Poesie*). Schlegel, in speaking of romantic poetry, wit, and irony, cites the examples of Cervantes and Shakespeare, whose writing he admires for its "artfully ordered confusion, this charming symmetry of contradictions, this wonderful alternation between enthusiasm and irony that lives even in its smallest parts of the whole" ("künstlich geordnete Verwirrung, diese reizende Symmetrie von Widersprüchen, dieser wunderbare Wechsel von Enthusiasmus und Ironie, der selbst in den kleinsten Gliedern des Ganzen lebt," Schlegel 1967: 318-19). Despite the contrasting tone between Murr's autobiography and Kreisler's biography, the parts are linked by the humor that derives from the disjunction between Murr's perceptions with the reader's, and from the clash of one part with the other. Some characters appear in both parts, which has the effect of making it seem as if one part of the novel were observing and imitating, even mocking, the other, rather like the figure in Heine's *Doppelgänger* poem. The dazzling play with prefaces proclaims the work's romantic irony from the start, with Murr's contrasting "real" and "false" prefaces framed by Hoffmann's preface and by the editor's apologetic injunction that the reader disregard all three. Hoffmann's paradoxical mixture of control and powerlessness, cast in humorous form, shows what a romantic ironist can do, particularly when these traits are combined with the unresolvable questions about the willed or unwilled nature of fragmentariness in *Kater Murr*.[10]

Hoffmann and Heine thought of themselves as heirs to Sterne, whose narrative experiments in *Tristram Shandy* and emotional self-awareness and aesthetic control in *A Sentimental Journey* have always exemplified what is understood by romantic irony. Another kindred spirit is Diderot, not only in *Jacques le fataliste et son maître* (*Jacques the Fatalist and His Master*), the canonized cousin of *Tristram Shandy*, but also in the more radically experimental *Le Neveu de Rameau* (*Rameau's Nephew*), where a battle of wits and perspectives takes place between "He" ("Lui") and "Myself" ("Moi") against a background of chess playing (Simpson 1979: 182-3). Works like these are harbingers of modernism, and it is not uncommon for studies of romantic irony in the eighteenth and early nineteenth centuries to conclude with examples of romantic irony in the twentieth. Romanticism is unthinkable without romantic irony, which lives on throughout the nineteenth and twentieth centuries in works of such authors as Pushkin, George Eliot, Tolstoy, and Thomas Mann – and into the present. Literature, and literary criticism, would be much the poorer without it.

NOTES

1 The history of this edition is related by Ernst Behler, its principal editor and one of the world's foremost experts on Schlegel, in Behler (1998).

2 My translation; note that all translations are mine unless otherwise indicated.

3 Immerwahr's essay, like Eichner's (1956), is a touchstone of Schlegel criticism; it originally appeared in 1951 in English but was reprinted in German with an afterword in which Eichner takes into account the documents that had not yet appeared when he wrote his article and responds to later Schlegel criticism.

4 That Strohschneider-Kohrs's study has not been superseded, despite the immense amount of criticism on romantic irony since its appearance in 1960, is evident from its publication history. In the reprinted version of 1977, Strohschneider-Kohrs added a detailed afterword and responded to new publications, both of Schlegel's works and of Schlegel scholarship, but she did not find it necessary to alter her findings or her argument; in 2002 the edition of 1977 was reprinted without changes and only a brief introduction. Even those who disagree with Strohschneider-Kohrs's historical frame (Romanticism) and her emphasis on the destroying of illusion (*Illusionszerstörung*) do so with great respect. Muecke (1969, 1970,

1982), who with Booth (1974) sets the standard for work on irony in English, calls her study of romantic irony "definitive" (Muecke 1970: 87, 1982: 106).

5 Wellek speaks simply of "irony," sparing his energy for the larger debate about the meaning of Romanticism (Fry 2000, Ferber in the Introduction to this volume); one of the great merits of Garber's collection of essays is to demonstrate the range of the topic with respect to chronology and artistic medium.

6 Letter to Novalis of September 26, 1797, quoted by Eichner (Schlegel 1967: xli), who discusses Schlegel's use of the aphorism generally and his acknowledgment of Chamfort, citing also Rühle-Gerstel (1922).

7 Chaouli's distinction between aphorism and fragment is one source of his original and persuasive reading of Schlegel's poetics. On the form of the fragment, see, too, Harries (1994).

8 For a catalogue of the topics Schlegel touches on in his collections of fragments, see the subject index in Schlegel 1967: 425-43 and the appendix to Lacoue-Labarthe and Nancy (1988, 155-64).

9 In *Athenäum* Fragment 125, for example, Schlegel invokes *Symphilosophie and Sympoesie* as the fundament of a "new epoch of the sci-

ences and the arts." See, too, *Lyceum* Fragment 112 and the *Athenäum* Fragments 82, 112, 125, and 264 (Schlegel 1967: 161, 177, 181, 185, 210). Eichner's table of contributors to the Fragments does not list Caroline Schlegel (Schlegel 1967: cxiii), but Behler and Peter both name her (Behler 1978: 72 and 1983: 30, Peter 1978: 38).

10 See Steinecke's masterful commentary to *Kater Murr* (Hoffmann 1992), where the novel's fragmentariness is only one of the many topics he treats.

References and Further Reading

Primary sources

Byron, Lord (1982). *Lord Byron: Don Juan*, ed. T. G. Steffan, E. Steffan, and W. W. Pratt. New Haven: Yale University Press.

Diderot, Denis (1956). *Rameau's Nephew and Other Works*, trans. Jacques Barzun and Ralph H. Bowen. Garden City, NY: Doubleday.

Diderot, Denis (1977). *Le Neveu de Rameau*, ed. Jean Fabre. Geneva: Droz.

Goethe, Johann Wolfgang (1985). *Der junge Goethe, 1757-1775*, ed. Gerhard Sauder. In Karl Richter et al. (eds.), *Sämtliche Werke nach Epochen seines Schaffens. Münchner Ausgabe*, vols. 1 and 2. Munich: Hanser.

Goethe, Johann Wolfgang (1990). *The Sufferings of Young Werther and Elective Affinities*, ed. and trans. Victor Lange. New York: Continuum.

Heine, Heinrich (1975). *Buch der Lieder*, ed. Pierre Grappin. In Manfred Windfuhr et al. (eds.), *Historisch-kritische Gesamtausgabe der Werke, Düsseldorfer Ausgabe*, vol. 1. Hamburg: Hoffmann und Campe.

Heine, Heinrich (1983). *The Complete Poems of Heinrich Heine: A Modern English Version*, trans. Hal Draper. Boston: Suhrkamp/Insel.

Hoffmann, E. T. A. (1992). *Lebens-Ansichten des Katers Murr*, ed. Hartmut Steinecke. Frankfurt am Main: Deutscher Klassiker Verlag.

Hoffmann, E. T. A. (1999). *The Life and Opinions of The Tomcat Murr*, trans. Anthea Bell. London and New York: Penguin.

Novalis (Friedrich von Hardenberg) (1960). *Das philosophische Werk I*, ed. Richard Samuel. In Paul Kluckhohn and Richard Samuel (eds.), *Schriften: Die Werke Friedrich von Hardenbergs/ Novalis*, vol. 2. Stuttgart: W. Kohlhammer.

Novalis (1997). *Philosophical writings*, ed. and trans. Margaret Mahony Stoljar. Albany: State University of New York Press.

Schlegel, Friedrich (1963). "Zur Philosophie." In Ernst Behler with Jean Jacques Anstett and Hans Eichner (eds.), *Kritische Friedrich Schlegel Ausgabe*, vol. 18. München, Paderborn: Schöningh.

Schlegel, Friedrich (1967). *Charakteristiken und Kritiken I (1796-1801)*, ed. Hans Eichner. In Ernst Behler et. al. (eds.), *Kritische Friedrich-Schlegel-Ausgabe*, vol. 2. Paderborn: Schöningh.

Schlegel, Friedrich (1957). *Literary Notebooks*, ed. Hans Eichner. London: University of London, Athlone Press.

Schlegel, Friedrich (1968). *Dialogue on Poetry and Literary Aphorisms*, trans. Ernst Behler and Roman Struc. University Park and London: Pennsylvania State University Press.

Schlegel, Friedrich (1971). *"Lucinde" and the Fragments*, ed. and trans. Peter Firchow. Minneapolis: University of Minnesota Press.

Schlegel, Friedrich (2001). *On the Study of Greek Poetry*, ed. and trans. Stuart Barnett. Albany: State University of New York Press.

Solie, Ruth (ed.) (1998). *The Nineteenth Century*. In Oliver Strunk (ed.), *Source Readings in Music History*, vol. 6. New York and London: W. W. Norton.

Sterne, Laurence (1978-2002). *The Florida Edition of the Works of Sterne*, ed. Melvyn New and Joan New. Gainesville: University Press of Florida.

Wheeler, Kathleen M. (ed.) (1984). *German Aesthetic and Literary Criticism, vol. 1: The Romantic Ironists and Goethe*. Cambridge: Cambridge University Press.

Secondary sources

Abrams, M. H. (1971). *The Mirror and the Lamp: Romantic Theory and the Critical Tradition*. Oxford: Oxford University Press.

Allemann, Beda (1970). "Ironie als literarisches Prinzip." In Albert Schaefer (ed.), *Ironie und Dichtung*. Munich: C. H. Beck, pp. 11-37.

Altenhofer, Norbert ([1982] 1993). "Ästhetik des Arrangements. Zu Heines 'Buch der Lieder.'" In Volker Bohn (ed.), *Die verlorene Augensprache*. Frankfurt am Main and Leipzig: Insel, pp. 154-73.

Barricelli, Jean-Pierre (1988). "Musical Forms of Romantic Irony." In Frederick Garber (ed.), *Romantic Irony*. Budapest: Akadémiai Kiadó, pp. 310-21.

Beer, John (1995). "Fragmentations and Ironies." In John Beer (ed.), *Questioning Romanticism*. Baltimore and London: Johns Hopkins University Press, pp. 234-64.

Behler, Ernst (1972). *Klassische Ironie, Romantische Ironie, Tragische Ironie. Zum Ursprung dieser Begriffe*, 2nd edn. Darmstadt: Wissenschaftliche Buchgesellschaft.

Behler, Ernst (1978). *Friedrich Schlegel in Selbstzeugnissen und Bilddokumenten*. Reinbek bei Hamburg: Rowohlt.

Behler, Ernst (1990). *Irony and the Discourse of Modernity*. Seattle: Washington University Press.

Behler, Ernst (1993). *German Romantic Literary Theory*. Cambridge, UK and New York: Cambridge University Press.

Behler, Ernst (1997). *Ironie und literarische Moderne*. Paderborn: Schöningh.

Behler, Ernst (1998). "Die Geschichte der Friedrich Schlegel Ausgabe," *Athenäum*, 8: 211-29.

Behler, Ernst and Hörnisch, Jochen (eds.) (1987). *Die Aktualität der Frühromantik*. Paderborn: Schöningh.

Bishop, Lloyd (1989). *Romantic Irony in French Literature from Diderot to Beckett*. Nashville, TN: Vanderbilt University Press.

Booth, Wayne (1974). *A Rhetoric of Irony*. Chicago: University of Chicago Press.

Bourke, Thomas (1980). *Stilbruch als Stilmittel*. Peter Lang.

Brown, Marshall (1979). *The Shape of Romanticism*. Ithaca, NY: Cornell University Press.

Brown, Marshall (ed.) (2000). *The Cambridge History of Literary Criticism, vol 5: Romanticism*. Cambridge, UK and New York: Cambridge University Press.

Chaouli, Michel (2002). *The Laboratory of Poetry: Chemistry and Poetics in the Work of Friedrich Schlegel*. Baltimore and London: Johns Hopkins University Press.

Comstock, Cathy (1985). "'Transcendental Buffoonery': Irony as Process in Schlegel's "Über die Unverständlichkeit."' *Studies in Romanticism*, 26: 445-64.

Conrad, Peter (1978). *Shandyism: The Character of Romantic Irony*. New York: Barnes and Noble.

Eichner, Hans (1956). "Friedrich Schlegel's Theory of Romantic Poetry." *PMLA*, 71: 1018-41.

Eichner, Hans (1970). *Friedrich Schlegel*. New York: Twayne Publishers.

Fetzer, John (1990). "Romantic Irony." In Gerhard Hoffmeister (ed.), *European Romanticism: Literary Cross-Currents, Modes, and Models*. Detroit: Wayne State University Press, pp. 19-36.

Frank, Manfred (2003). "'Romantische Ironie' als musikalisches Verfahren am Beispiel von Tieck, Brahms, Wagner und Weber." *Athenäum: Jahrbuch für Romantik*, 13: 163-90.

Fry, Paul (2000). "Classical Standards in the Period." In Marshall Brown (ed.), *The Cambridge History of Literary Criticism, vol 5: Romanticism*. Cambridge, UK and New York: Cambridge University Press, pp. 7-28.

Furst, Lilian R. (1984). *Fictions of Romantic Irony*. Cambridge, MA: Harvard University Press.

Furst, Lilian R. (1988). "Romantic Irony and Narrative Stance." In Frederick Garber (ed.), *Romantic Irony*. Budapest: Akadémiai Kiadó, pp. 293-309.

Garber, Frederick (ed.) (1988a). *Romantic Irony*. Budapest: Akadémiai Kiadó.

Garber, Frederick (1988b). *Self, Text, and Romantic Irony: The Example of Byron*. Princeton, NJ: Princeton University Press.

Gurewitch, Marvin (2002). *The Comedy of Romantic Irony*. Lanham, MD: University Press of America.

Handwerk, Gary (1993). "*Review of Romantic Irony: The Comparative History of European Literature.*" *Comparative Criticism* 15: 279-83.

Handwerk, Gary (2000). "Romantic Irony." In Marshall Brown (ed.), *The Cambridge History of Literary Criticism, vol 5: Romanticism*. Cambridge, UK and New York: Cambridge University Press, pp. 203-25.

Harries, Elizabeth Wanning (1994). *The Unfinished Manner: Essays on the Fragment in the Later Eighteenth Century*. Charlottesville: University of Virginia Press.

Hinton, Stephen (2002). "Romantische Ironie in der Musik?" *Beiträge zur Kleist-Forschung*, 16: 21-35.

Höhn Gerhard (1997). *Heine-Handbuch: Zeit, Person, Werk*, revised edn. Stuttgart and Weimar: Metzler.

Immerwahr, Raymond ([1951] 1985). "Die Subjektivität oder Objektivität von Friedrich Schlegels poetischer Ironie." In Helmut Schanze (ed.), *Friedrich Schlegel und die Kunsttheorie seiner Zeit*. Darmstadt: Wissenschaftliche Buchgesellschaft, pp. 112-42.

Kerschbaumer, Sandra (2000). *Heines moderne Romantik*. Paderborn: Schöningh.

Kierkegaard, Søren ([1841] 1965). *The Concept of Irony, with Constant Reference to Socrates*, trans. Lee M. Capel. Bloomington: Indiana University Press.

Kolb, Jocelyne (1987). "'Die Puppenspiele meines Humors': Heine and Romantic Irony." *Studies in Romanticism*, 26: 399-419.

Kolb, Jocelyne (1995). *The Ambiguity of Taste: Freedom and Food in European Romanticism*. Ann Arbor: University of Michigan Press.

Kortländer, Bernd (2003). *Heinrich Heine*. Stuttgart: Reclam.

Lacoue-Labarthe, Philippe and Nancy, Jean-Luc ([1978] 1988). *The Literary Absolute: The Theory of Literature in German Romanticism*, trans. Philip Barnard and Cheryl Lester. Albany: State University of New York Press.

Lussky, Alfred Edwin (1932). *Tieck's Romantic Irony, with Special Emphasis upon the Influence of Cervantes, Sterne, and Goethe*. Chapel Hill: University of North Carolina Press.

Mellor, Anne (1980). *English Romantic Irony*. Cambridge, MA: Harvard University Press.

Muecke, D. C. (1969). *The Compass of Irony*. London: Methuen.

Muecke, D. C. (1970). *Irony*. London: Methuen.

Muecke, D. C. (1982). *Irony and the Ironic*. London: Methuen.

Peter, Klaus (1978). *Friedrich Schlegel*. Stuttgart: Metzler.

Perrey, Beate Julia (2002). *Schumann's Dichterliebe and Early Romantic Poetics: Fragmentation of Desire*. Cambridge, UK: Cambridge University Press.

Prang, Helmut (ed.) (1972). *Die romantische Ironie*. Darmstadt: Wissenschaftliche Buchgesellschaft.

Prawer, S. S. (1961). *Heine, the Tragic Satirist: A Study of the Later Poetry 1827-1856*. Cambridge, UK: Cambridge University Press.

Preisendanz, Wolfgang (1970). "Ironie bei Heine." In Albert Schaefer (ed.), *Ironie und Dichtung*. Munich: C. H. Beck, pp. 85-112.

Preisendanz, Wolfgang (1983). "Die umgebuchte Schreibart. Heines literarischer Humor im Spannungsfeld von Begriffs-, Form- und Rezeptionsgeschichte." In *Heinrich Heine. Werkstrukturen und Epochenbezüge*. Munich: Fink, pp. 131-57.

Preisendanz, Wolfgang (1991). "Der Ironiker Heine: Ambivalenzerfahrung und kommunikative Ambiguität." In Gerhard Höhn (ed.), *Heinrich Heine: Ästhetisch-politische Profile*. Frankfurt am Main: Suhrkamp, pp. 101-15.

Preminger, Alex (ed.) (1974). *Princeton Encyclopedia of Poetry and Poetics: Enlarged Edition*. Princeton, NJ: Princeton University Press.

Robertson, Ritchie (1985). "Shakespearean Comedy and Romantic Psychology in Hoffmann's *Kater Murr*." *Studies in Romanticism*, 24: 21-46.

Rosen, Charles 1998. *Romantic Poets, Critics, and Other Madmen*. Cambridge, MA: Harvard University Press.

Rühle-Gerstel, A. (1922). "Friedrich Schlegel und Chamfort." *Euphorion*, 24: 809-60.

Ryals, Clyde de L. (1990). *A World of Possibilities: Romantic Irony in Victorian Literature*. Columbus: Ohio State University Press.

Sammons, Jeffrey L. (1969). *Heinrich Heine: The Elusive Poet*. New Haven, CT: Yale University Press.

Sammons, Jeffrey L. (1979). *Heinrich Heine: A Modern Biography*. Princeton, NJ: Princeton University Press.

Schanze, Helmut (ed.) (1985). *Friedrich Schlegel und die Kunsttheorie seiner Zeit*. Darmstadt: Wissenschaftliche Buchgesellschaft.

Schanze, Helmut (ed.) (1994). *Romantik-Handbuch*. Tübingen: Alfred Körner.

Schnell, Ralf (1989). *Die verkehrte Welt: Literarische Ironie im 19. Jahrhundert*. Stuttgart: Metzler.

Simpson, David (1979). *Irony and Authority in Romantic Poetry*. Totowa, NJ: Rowman and Littlefield.

Sperry, Stuart M. (1977). "Toward a Definition of Romantic Irony in English Literature." In George Bornstein (ed.), *Romantic and Modern:*

Revaluations of Literary Tradition. Pittsburgh, PA: University of Pittsburgh Press, pp. 3-28.

Strohschneider-Kohrs, Ingrid (1960 [2002]). *Die romantische Ironie in Theorie und Gestaltung*. Tübingen: Niemeyer.

Wellek, René (1955). *A History of Modern Criticism: 1750-1950, vol. 2: The Romantic Age*. New Haven: Yale University Press.

23

Sacrality and the Aesthetic in the Early Nineteenth Century

Virgil Nemoianu

The negotiations between sacrality and/or religion on the one hand and literature and/ or art and aesthetics on the other are complex ones in any age, and they were even more so at the beginning of the nineteenth century. Therefore it would be most practical to begin by a brief review of the critical judgments on the issue, to continue by pointing to some historical and intellectual aspects, and finally to speak about literature itself, as well as some of the ways in which theoreticians of the age engaged in intellectual dialectics at the interface of these two areas.

I

A number of significant scholars (among them Meyer Abrams and Harold Bloom) highlighted decades ago that the Romantic enterprise as a whole was from the very beginning combined with religious intentions in different ways.

Bloom wrote several times about the connection between gnosticism and some of the main Romantic visions (e.g., Bloom 1963). Indeed, it is not absurd to argue that the image of divinity during the period in which Romanticism flourished was one in which divinity no longer enjoyed the image of a rational, dry Creator ("the Great Clockmaker"), but rather a much more disorderly ("wild and wooly") Being; a movement from Deism to Pantheism was noticed by other observers before and after Bloom suggested it.

In turn, Abrams (1971) posited that Romanticism as a whole had a large subtext (a "plot") that was but a secularization of the biblical plot of Genesis-Fall-Redemption. Of course, at least for the early ("core") Romantics, this was usually an *implicit* combination, not one loudly or visibly articulated. The equivalent of the biblical Garden of Eden was placed in different historical epochs (the Middle Ages, classical antiquity, prehistoric times, etc.) or geographical latitudes (the Pacific Islands, ancient India, pre-Colombian America, the remote Scandinavian or Celtic North, and others). The "Fall" was in this sense the whole of history, and the future could well be some utopian moment to be expected immediately or at some other stage in time.

These contemporary critics had their foundations and their predecessors in the Romantic age itself, that is to say with actions and directions with which newer theories do not stand in contradiction, but are rather in a situation of convergence. In fact religious discourses found a new place inside the larger field of the intellectual discourses of the West for a variety of reasons. Thus we know that the biological sciences of the early nineteenth century (zoology, paleontology, botany, and the like), as well as many of the social sciences (anthropology, early sociology) or indeed even history and linguistics, had chosen a comparatist slant as their favorite methodology. Likewise, many of the earliest scholars in religious studies used comparative lines of analysis to broaden their insights, enthusiastically including non-European (or ancient) religions and myth-systems in their studies. The rise of this "science of religion" (the pioneering efforts toward which had of course started much earlier, centuries earlier, in fact) is nevertheless anchored by contemporary research in France most specifically during the "second" Restoration, the Orleans regime of the 1830s and 1840s (see Despland 1999) and, I would add, also in Germany, and to a lesser extent, in Britain and the rest of Europe. The process seems to have been developed as follows: scholars first set up systems of religious comparatism. The names and works of luminaries like Benjamin Constant, Josef Görres, and Georg Friedrich Creuzer come immediately to mind. Their theories were based on the Renaissance and post-Renaissance doctrine of the "double revelation," which granted some dignity to other, non-Christian religions, as either precursors or as simplified forms of Christianity. In turn such comparisons could lead to general theories of symbols. The interesting thing is that such theories of symbols (still closely connected with comparative religion and much visited by literary writers) in turn gave birth to frameworks of the "civil religion" that loomed so large in the French Third Republic, as well as to theories of natural religion, the latter in Michelet and Quinet in particular (Despland 1999: 284-99). This was largely due to Catholic initiatives (the names of Montalambert, Ozanam, Lacordaire, Lamennais, and the Abbé Migne figure among the most prominent), although Protestant and Jewish contributions were essential. These "frameworks" descended from comparative religion were as often as not revolutionary, pantheist, or atheist. We may venture the argument that, despite enormous ideological differences, there are structural similarities, for instance, between Saint-Simon and Joseph de Maistre, growing out of their common (and diametrically opposed) utopian aspirations (see also Despland 1999: 46-9). Such intellective processes may be said to have laid the foundations of much later modern conceptions of history (and the philosophy of history) as secularized versions of religious thinking, as discussed in Karl Löwith's *Weltgeschichte und Heilsgeschehen* and in Eric Voegelin's *Order and History* among others.

One short note may be in order here. I would not like to leave the impression that I consider Romanticism as the *exclusive* vehicle or environment for all these changes.

Preparatory signs, sometimes important intellectually and culturally, can be recognized early on, in the eighteenth and even in the seventeenth century. Among these I would mention the tradition of Jansenism and Quietism in France (Van Kley has recently argued that Jansenism is the unacknowledged source of the French Revolution); the explosive emergence of Methodism in England; the "Pietist" movement, mostly in German-speaking lands; the revival of occult preoccupations in the eighteenth century (Swedenborg, Rosicrucianism, and many others); activities in Eastern Orthodox Christianity and in Judaism. These all represent the appropriate context for the evolution of the nineteenth century, even when the immediate trigger was provided by the events of 1789-1815, as a culmination of the systematic eighteenth-century persecution.

II

This brings us to the sociohistorical background of these deep-rooted changes in religious discourse. Indeed, we may ask ourselves *why* such changes became necessary.

The answer is rather obvious. In the years preceding and immediately following the French Revolution organized religion in continental Europe was threatened in its very being in ways that had never been equaled before, nor were they to be paralleled in quite the same way during the next 200 years. Thus the Jesuit order (a major crutch of Catholicism during the Counter-Reformation) was banned in virtually all European countries between 1773 and 1814, indeed abolished by the Vatican itself, surviving precariously and in conditions of dubious legal and canonical validity in Russia and in America. In France any practice of religion was virtually forbidden for approximately a decade, and the persecution of the clergy was nothing short of brutal. The head of the Roman Catholic Church was physically compelled to officiate at the nuptial rites of the new French tyrant; Pope Pius VII was later (1809) dispossessed, arrested, dragged as a political prisoner across Italy and France, and kept in captivity until the collapse of the Napoleonic dictatorial regime. Between 1789 and 1815 the number of priests dropped by half in France, the number of annual ordinations by about 90 percent. In England Catholics continued to be severely confined, while Anglicanism too was in much disarray. In country after European country, for many decades religious orders were dismantled in the name of social relevance, holidays scrapped, the state control of religious institutions (a control dating from the sixteenth and seventeenth centuries) ruthlessly reaffirmed (Bavaria, Portugal, and the Habsburg possessions, primarily Austria, might be good examples), and church property was confiscated. Only 30 of 1,500 Benedictine abbeys survived in all of Europe (among the victims were Cluny, Cîteaux, and Clairvaux); likewise the number of Dominican houses dropped from 500 to 80 (and the number of friars dropped from about 25,000 to 3,000). Trappists were transported in chains to French Guiana; the Carthusians were particularly hard hit in that by 1803 they had lost all their 68 houses in France and 18 in Germany; while in Portugal all 50 Augustinian monasteries were suppressed. Joseph II of Austria, while not as brutal as the rulers of Bavaria and the French revolutionaries (who roundly declared that somebody choosing a monastic life was thereby forfeiting all civil and citizenship rights), was nevertheless one of the most relentless persecutors of monastic life. Moreover "Josephinism" imposed the rule that sermons should limit themselves to matters of social morality, and allowed religious orders to function only if they served practical purposes. Joseph II tried "to make the Austrian Church as thoroughly independent of the Holy See as a Church could be without ceasing to be Catholic" and "Preaching was reduced to moral instruction in which little reference was made to the Christian mysteries" (McCool 1977: 22). I would also argue, without going into details, that the often-praised "Josephinist" policy towards the Jews in the empire was ambiguous and perhaps hypocritical.

It is therefore small wonder that in 1815, when normality and the rule of law were re-established in Europe after decades of violence and upheaval, religiously minded people should have tried to reassess the function of religion in society. It might even be argued that the period 1815-65 was one of the greatest ages of religious apologetics ever known, at least in the modern age. The sovereigns themselves changed their style. No more Joseph II, no more Friedrich II, no more Catherine the Great. Perhaps the most typical monarch of the post-1815 period was not the much-maligned Charles X of France, but Friedrich Wilhelm IV of Prussia who reigned between 1840 and 1861. He was deeply influenced in his youth by Pietism, thought ultimately of the state as a *Gesamtkunstwerk*, and had advisers who combined conservatism with religion, and sometimes with the beautiful (see Barclay 1995: 24-9, 32-4, 55, 66-8, 76, 78, 80, 85, 94). Ludwig I of Bavaria and other contemporaries might serve as confirmations and analogies (see Gottfried 1979: 73-92). Simultaneously Christian-Democrat and Christian-Socialist movements began to crystallize and to influence society, often in a moderate left direction. It is often forgotten that Christianity had a key role in the emergence of industrial workers' trade unions (Sauvigny 1955: 252, Sevillia 2003: 225-46), or that decisive impulses for the abolition of the slave trade came from both Protestant and Catholic churches.

In Anglo-American societies this process had begun even earlier. Suffice it to mention here the name of the great Hannah More (1745-1833) who, at the prodding of John Newton, the evangelical minister and hymn-writer, turned toward the publication of ethical and religious tracts and studies. She became the first person in world history to sell over a million copies of any single work: her novel *Coelebs in Search of a Wife* (1809) appeared in 41 editions (11 in Britain, 30 in the United States) within months; her collected works appeared in four different editions during her lifetime, and it has been said that she set a pattern not only for popular religious discourses henceforth, but even for the political propaganda of the nineteenth century. The popular success of Hannah More and of others like her indicates the tremendous thirst for restoring a more complete understanding of human nature (one that would take into account the transcendent horizons inherent in it) after the relentless pressures of the Enlightenment intellectual and political elites (see Jones 1952,

Johnson 1991: 381-3 for a short assessment). In fact it has been convincingly argued (Mellor 2000: 13-38) that More may have single-handedly counteracted the revolutionary tendencies in England and may have strengthened thus the cause of moderate reform. This would make her, in our terminology, a typical Biedermeier figure (see Nemoianu 1984). What ensued in 1815 was therefore not primarily "reaction," as the clichés of conventional history would have it, but rather an enormously expanded public debate as to the most practical ways in which the religious impulses and needs of humankind can be accommodated in a world that, by common agreement, was in the process of accelerated, unstoppable movement toward modernizing changes. This fascinating debate (in which, as is all-too-often forgotten in all quarters, women usually played a much more decisive part than in *any* other area of public manifestation) had as its theme not domination, but inclusiveness.

Within this continent-wide conversation – one that, more than cultural trends, and at least as much as political discourses, went far beyond the social or intellectual upper strata and quite deeply into the masses of the population – there were in fact very few who clamored for a full restoration of church privileges, or for a framework in which religion should have powers of cognitive arbitration. Where such positions could gain a political foothold, they did more harm than good to their stated aims and may well have contributed to the failure of the Restoration, at least in France and in Spain (Sauvigny 1955: 81-2, 87, 300-5, 414-17) . Such was the case with those inspired in France by the doctrines of Louis de Bonald.[1] Other positions can be recognized in other countries with varying effects. A good example in the Austria of Metternich was that of the zealous orthodox Catholic, Clemens Maria Hofbauer (1751-1820), Bishop of Vienna, later declared a saint and the second patron of the city. Hofbauer, though a man of modest education, had the knack of inspiring intellectuals and he grouped around himself for a few years an astounding number of intellectuals interested in a Catholic revival, beginning with Friedrich and Dorothea Schlegel. Although he carefully avoided political involvements, he was under constant police supervision and suffered interrogations and house searches because of his religious views and influence (Fleischmann 1988). In France Prosper Guéranger refounded Benedictine monasticism, starting with the abandoned priory of Solesmes (famous even today). In fact, France witnessed after 1815 a spectacular revival of monasteries, seminaries, and priestly vocations (Sauvigny 1955: 308, 312) and of reinfiltration of ecclesiastics in schools, universities, and public life (Sauvigny 1955: 318).

An example somewhat similar to that of the intellectuals of the "Hofbauer circle" is that of Samuel Taylor Coleridge, who proposed in *The Constitution of Church and State* (1829) an "organic" concept of social organization, with a certain entanglement of the religious and intellectual classes which, together, would act in a filtering and advisory capacity to society as a whole. Coleridge (and to greater extent than recognized, Southey) exerted influence not on a wider public, but certainly on select intellectuals. This is particularly true of the Tractarians of the Oxford Movement, some of whom went all the way to becoming Roman Catholics (Newman and Manning in particular) while others (Keble, Froude, Pusey) considerably reformed the intellectual and cultural foundations of Anglicanism by reclaiming its century-old traditions and encouraging it to become involved again in the values of art and architecture, literature and music. They all drew sustenance from Coleridge's and Southey's doctrines. (See, e.g., Dawson [1933] 2001; even earlier, Church [1891] 1970 had described in detail how members of the movement had been connected with contemporary French religious authors.) In fact it is not wrong to say that even a quintessential Victorian liberal like Gladstone drew on Coleridge and even Burke.

At the other end of the spectrum, social utopians and mystics from Owen, Saint-Simon, and Fourier to Mme de Krudener, Ballanche, and Saint-Martin, as well as the Poles Towiañski and Skarga clamored for a kind of translation of religious hope into terrestrial paradises, or else for discovering direct (almost mechanical or magical) channels of connection and influence between spiritual transcendence and earthly affairs. It is worth insisting that not only the socialist utopians, but also (in their comprehensive schemes) figures like Auguste Comte and Victor Cousin (the first very clearly, the second only to some extent) as well as Jules Michelet and Edgar Quinet, were in effect endeavoring to secularize the aspirations of Christianity without entirely losing the values and substances of spiritual transcendence.[2] This was also the purpose (sometimes avowed, sometimes tacit) of German Idealism (Nipperdey 1991: 404, 429).

III

Of course between these two extremes we find, as is to be expected, a wide intermediate area in which the imaginary and the fictional combine in rich and unexpected ways with earnest examination and passionate searchings. The literary (and the aesthetic more generally) combines with and mutually engages in substitutions with religious discourses. One must first mention the large number of Romantic poets or prose writers who found literary empowerment in religion, whether early in their career or later: Wordsworth, Coleridge, Shelley, Friedrich Schlegel, Tieck, Eichendorff, Lamartine, Mickiewicz, Gogol, Hugo, and dozens of others.

To turn first to more theoretical kinds of writing, let us say that there were many who tried to find a network of relations between all known religions, and thus sketch out the deep structure of human dealings with transcendence. A significant example of this kind is provided by Benjamin Constant's *De la religion considéré dans sa source, sa forme et ses développements*, published in five volumes (1824-31). A true liberal (indeed, one of the doctrinal originators of liberalism in Europe), Constant tried to indicate the overall ramifications of any religious idiom with all the others. In Germany slightly earlier Friedrich Creuzer in *Symbolik und Mythologie der alten Völker* (1810-12) laid the foundation of a science of myth and religion (dealing with the distinction between allegory and symbol that was so central for Goethe's theorizing also) that was to flourish later under the auspices of Sir James Frazer and Jessie Weston, as well as of Kérenyi, Eliade, Campbell, and other outstanding figures of a full-fledged discipline.

Even more complex are the cases of those who, like Creuzer and Constant, engaged in the same pursuits, but also wanted to hang on to traditional Christianity, as well as to respond to the political works and acts of the day. A typical example among others is Joseph Görres (1776-1848) in his *Mythengeschichte der alten Welt* (1810); Görres at the same time moved from left to right and back again while still arguing for both a Catholic conservative framework and one conspicuously inclusive of Eastern religions; as a matter of fact he thought that *all* religions derived from *one* common trunk rooted in India, "the land of the world's youth" (Munk 1994: 575). These views are expressed quite well particularly in *Glauben und Wissen* (1805) and then, more methodically, in *Mythengeschichte der asiatischen Welt* (1810). He was influenced by Friedrich Schlegel and in turn tried to provide support for Brentano and the Grimm brothers in their rediscovery of fairy tales. In 1827 Görres was hired by the University of Munich as professor of general and literary history and wrote his *Christliche Mystik* in which among other things he outlined some principles of Catholic social doctrine that were later developed by Bishop von Ketteler. Görres may also have exerted some indirect influence on Bachofen and Nietzsche.

An even more interesting zig-zagging can be observed in the case of Félicité de Lamennais (1782-1854) who moved from hard-line Catholic apologetics (perhaps partly under the influence of Ballanche) to Christian liberal populism and finally to a kind of nondenominational democratic radicalism, working out evangelical values and teachings toward their sociopolitical implications (Bowman 1990: 78). His *Paroles d'un croyant* (1834) marked the turning point toward independent leftism for Lamennais. His style and ideological stance influenced many later French thinkers, including Victor Hugo and Edgar Quinet.

Even a cursory and incomplete overview such as the present chapter cannot overlook the important figure of the Protestant Friedrich Schleiermacher (1768-1834), who developed a theory of religion founded on sentiment, intuition, and empathy, while at the time resorting to the judicious use of hermeneutics in order to bolster these faculties. Schleiermacher dispensed with dogmatics and, more generally, with religious theorizing or even the history of religion and favored reliance on the intuitive feeling of religious emotions, a kind of transfer of mystical spirituality; the next step would be thereafter, according to him, a process of detailed hermeneutic "unpacking" of all these results of pure religious experience. Schleiermacher's theories (both in the field of hermeneutics, and in that of immediate, untheorized experience) influenced considerably both religious and literary-cultural criticism and built bridges between them. Likewise Antonio Rosmini-Serbati (1797-1855), who was the friend and adviser of Manzoni, Cavour, and a good number of popes and cardinals, and founder of a powerful Institute of Charity, though his life was plagued by controversy. Rosmini was an incredibly prolific author.[3] He is a highly interesting figure, even though he is poorly known outside Italy; his intention was to create a system on Augustinian foundations that would answer the Kantian system and at the same time assimilate it: finding a modern, contemporary idiom for age-old Christian truths.

In Eastern Europe at the same time two or three events stand out. One is the interest in a mixture of Christianity, pre-Christian mythologies, and folklore seen as a chief source of national memory. Prominent figures engaged in these endeavors are numerous: the towering folklorist researcher Vuk Karadzić (1787-1864) in Serbia; the philologist Bogdan P. Hasdeu (1838-1907) with his *Cuvente den betrani* (1878) in Romania; in Hungary Férenc Kazinczy (1759-1831) and a number of his followers including Istvan Horvat (1784-1846) or Férenc Kölcsey (1790-1838); in Poland the so-called "Ukrainian School of poetry" – Antoni Malczewsk (1793-1826), Severyn Goszcznski (1801-76), Jozef Bohdan Zaleski (1802-86) – and even more than these the thinkers August Ciezkowski (1814-94), Bronislaw Trentowski (1808-96), and J. M. Hoene-Wronski (1778-1853). To make a long story short, this process was general throughout the early nineteenth century all over Eastern Europe.

It must also be strongly underlined that many of the developments in Western Christianity on which we have dwelt (specifically the new forms of spiritual revival) find their counterparts in Eastern Christianity. Some of these were purely religious, as is the case with the outstanding figure of Paissy Velitchikovsky (1722-94). Of Ukrainian and Jewish ethnic background, he soon left home and traveled widely in Eastern Europe, being stationed for a while at Mount Athos. Most of his life was spent, however, in Western and Northern Moldavia, where he reformed the monastic system and wrote in Romanian; his emphasis was Christocentric, prayerful, and spiritual. Simultaneously, in 1782 the *Philokalia* was published in Greek at Venice, followed promptly (in 1792) by a Russian variant under the title *Dobrolubya* at Moscow. This was a collection of traditionally transmitted (sometimes apocryphal) texts of Patristic origin (as well as medieval and later texts) that contained advice on spirituality and on the beauty of the good; it contributed in decisive ways to altering Eastern Orthodox modes of religion. Meanwhile in Montenegro the ruler and archbishop Petar Njegoš (like his contemporary, the Croat Catholic nobleman Mazuranić) contributed in important ways to the revival of both religiosity and literature among South Slavs.

This combination of the religious with the aesthetic can be clearly seen, strongly and openly, in the Hungarian *Aurora* circle and other Romantics, for instance Mihály Vörösmarty (1800-55) or Janos Arány (1817-82), as it can be recognized in the late works of Adam Mickiewicz (1798-1855; I have in mind specifically *The Books of the Polish Nation and its Pilgrimage* [1832], written in biblical prose, but also the early *Forefathers' Eve* [1823]); in the Romanian works of Fr. Eufrosin Poteca (1786-1859), the critic and poet Heliade Rădulescu (1802-72), as well as Alecu Russo (1819-59); in the works of Lithuanian Bishops Valancius and Barnauskas, or of the Estonian poets Kristjan Peterson and Reinhold Kreutzwald. Again, the process was widespread over the whole of Eastern Europe, and sometimes preceded or was richer than similar activities in Western Europe.

Judaism coexisting, usually uncomfortably, in that part of the world, can also be recognized as a powerful player in the ferment of the whole of Europe. From an almost secularized version of Enlightenment Judaism as illustrated by Moses Mendelssohn and others (who had been bolstering the "Reform Judaism" which emerged soon after the Lutheran Reform), the two chief directions in the first half of the nineteenth century went toward the setting up of "conservative Judaism" (the "Historical School" as it was called for a while) and, perhaps even more important, Hasidism, which had already emerged by the middle of the eighteenth century and (in emphasizing joy and community) had great cultural impact and connections. The name of Rabbi Nahman of Bratslav (1772-1811) is important here in so far as he represents the "Romantic" counterpart to the more rationalist, "classical," and Enlightenment teachings of Moses Mendelssohn. What is common to many of these of these movements (Christian and Judaic alike) is that they turned toward nature, culture, faith, and interiority rather than dwelling primarily upon strict ethical principles and dogmatic epistemology.

IV

For the intellectuals of the time, as well as for a rather broad section of the general audience, perhaps the most stimulating and exciting works were those that endeavored to vindicate God through his works, above all through the experience of the *beauty* of creation. I will mention a few of the most innovative, ambitious, and prestigious among these works, not forgetting the turning point represented by Chateaubriand's *Le Génie du christianisme* (1802). These include the almost forgotten *Die heilige Kunst* by Alois Gügler, a Swiss high-school teacher of Lucerne, along with the contrastive example of Jaime Balmés, the fiery and erudite Catalan preacher.

Chateaubriand's historical novel *Les Martyrs* is historically important in so far as it was the forerunner of a whole subgenre of sentimental, melodramatic, and apologetic works in the nineteenth and the twentieth centuries, although it is aesthetically rather modest. *Le Génie du christianisme* played an overwhelming political and ideological role in its own time and for at least a hundred years later, in changing the mode of arguing for Christianity. This influence was due to the work's intellectual substance but also to sheer weight of circulation. Chateaubriand was deliberately trying to remove the debate about Christianity from under the sovereignty of analytical rationalism. Of the essentials signaling divinity in its fullness, it is beauty, at least as much as, and perhaps more than, truth or goodness that is the most accessible and reliable. The preverbal forces of sense-impression and emotion provide more convincing testimony to the nature of the Creation and of God than rational debate and analysis.

It ought to be mentioned here that Chateaubriand's position differs nevertheless from the one that we encounter in the later nineteenth century when aesthetics, the arts, and literature become virtually replacements of religious experience, as in the writings of Schopenhauer, Matthew Arnold, the Pre-Raphaelites, and many others on the Continent. Chateaubriand, in contrast to these, understands beauty as diverse abundance and harmony (what would now be called the ecological or the homeostatic). Chateaubriand's *leitmotif* is that of fertility and abundance of the concrete.

He also emphasizes the continuity and close relationship between nature and culture. In *Le Génie du christianisme* we find numerous examples in which nature's creatures and events support human activity, while arguments in favor of the validity and worth of religion are drawn from cultural occurrences in an almost seamless way.

Like his direct predecessors Fénelon (see Richardt 1993), Malebranche, and many other divines in other centuries and countries, Chateaubriand thinks that we should speak about two successive acts of creation, the first of physical nature, as depicted in Genesis, as well as observed by our own senses and examination, the second of the spirit, as sketched out in the Gospels: the psychological, ethical, and spiritual teachings of Jesus Christ. This explains the correspondence between the cultural and the natural realms. The *Gestalt* of a struggling humanity in the face of God could qualify and soften the impact of pure linearity and progress. The historical spectacle as "vanity of vanities" is but the theatrical scenery required by the beauty of absence.

Alois Gügler's unfinished work *Die heilige Kunst, oder Die Kunst der Hebräer*, appeared in five small volumes between 1814 and 1836 and has remained virtually unresearched, marginalized, and ignored even by Catholic theology or thinking.[4] Gügler seems to have influenced a few later, better known philosophers, such as Mohler. His emphasis on biblical poetry coincides with Chateaubriand's positions in *Le Génie du christianisme*.

Its first volume, the only one to which I will refer here, deals with the author's general assumptions, while two each of the subsequent volumes deal in some detail with the books of the Old Testament and those of the New Testament. It is not clear to me to what extent Gügler consciously draws on Romantic philosophers and poets, or simply works along parallel lines with them. In any case, the similarities are stark. Like Herder, Gügler believes in a "national creative spirit" and in a Genesis-oriented philosophy of history that we could describe as protological. The somewhat pantheistic or theosophical touches in the later (exegetical) volumes remind us of Fichte's style and thought, and even more of Schelling and Baader. The exalted and flowery style seems learned from Jean Paul. Like Hölderlin, Gügler sees Ancient Greece as being somehow part of Asia, or of a broadly understood mystical-paradisal East, a universe of pure, unadulterated humanity, still united with the divine and the natural. Like Novalis, Gügler privileges "the holiness of the night," attributing to it the creative features inherited from divine parenthood. It is not impossible to conceive that Gügler acted as a gleaner and synthesizer of all these ideas and sources. Still, Gügler embodies better than many others what, as M. H. Abrams and others have argued, was the very core of Romanticism: the paradigm of Edenic innocence-Fall-Redemption inscribed in the secularized (and yet spiritual) form of cultural (and particularly poetic) achievement.

According to Gügler's theory, the world should be regarded as God's beautiful craftsmanship. As a consequence, it is only natural that it is precisely in the aesthetic creativity of all races and climes that the divine and the religious will gain maximum transparency. Nevertheless, in the different local and national mythologies the experience of the divine is either splintered, diffuse, or blocked. The chief exception is provided by the history and art of Ancient Hebrew culture. There we have, according to Gügler, an exemplary relationship between the divine steering of history and its narrative expression. The art-like unfolding of the Old Testament provides the durable model for any human history whatsoever, as well as being a measuring rod for it. By contrast, the New Testament narratives and the ecclesial time are less historical and less individually focused since, again, according to Gügler, their salvational theme provides for less tension (or rupture) between the two fundamental levels of human existence. However, the mediation between the transcendent and the secular needs is brought about by aesthetic activity which ultimately brings the universe to peaceful completion.

Gügler, though little known, even inside his own country and religion, represented brilliantly a widespread trend. How attractive the aesthetic argument was for all those desirous to rehabilitate Christianity and to find a new, secure, place for it in the radically modified world after 1815, can be seen by looking at the contrastive example of Jaime Balmés who lived between 1810 and 1848. He became a priest in 1834, and received a doctorate in theology in 1835. He did not hold positions on university faculties, but was elected a member of numerous academies, for instance in Barcelona, Madrid, and Rome, on the strength of his publication record. Prominent among these publications is a parallel of Catholic and Protestant civilization (directed against the theories of François Guizot), a massive volume immediately translated into French and English (in 1842); he also published treatises on metaphysics, ethics, and the history of philosophy, started several journals, wrote volumes of Christian apologetics, and engaged in political writings and activity.

One interesting thing about Balmés from the point of view of this chapter is that he ostensibly did not pay much attention to aesthetic issues. He seems to have been unaware of the work of Alexander Baumgarten (let us remember that his 1750 *Aesthetica* had after all coined the very term and launched the domain's career in Germany, and eventually throughout Europe), who is never mentioned in his short *Historía de la filosofía* (part IV of a comprehensive philosophical handbook published in 1840). He liked Chateaubriand and wrote on him, though not without some critical notes. Balmés understood by "aesthetics" only the theory of perception, and he placed his opinions on this merely as a kind of introductory section to the metaphysics chapter of his 1840 work; there he dealt with the senses and reserved just one dull page to the imagination. That is precisely the reason why it is so significant to discover that in the books of one so seemingly distanced from the aesthetic argument it manages nevertheless to break through at key points of his demonstrations.

Thus in *Cartás a un escéptico* ([1840-43] 1846) Balmés generally confines himself to the usual areas of reason and morality as he defends faith against religious indifference. Nevertheless, late in his text (letters 22, 24, and 25, out of a total of 25) he turns energetically toward aesthetic points, some of which seem borrowed from the Kantian philosophy that Balmés usually criticizes. For him, the beauty of Catholic religious services, the postulation of saints as intermediaries, and various rituals, are justified because they provide sensorial props to the frailty of human nature in its effort to reach the infinite and the sublime; concrete sense perception expresses the ideal and the spiritual (letter 22). The point is picked up again, even more explicitly, in letter 24, when Balmés tackles the practical usefulness of the imagination: it places objects on the terrain of virtue to attract and captivate intense passions (such as those of Teresa of Avila, Bernard de Clairvaux, or St Jerome) which otherwise would have been inevitably engulfed by the intensity of sin.

Finally, in letter 25, Balmés roundly admits that religion chimes with poetry and fantasy more than with prosaic philosophy. In any case, he explains, language itself must be seen as a divine gift, the origin and existence of the universe is exceptional and unusual, and ultimately there is at the very heart of being mystery and the miraculous. Given these circumstances, it is perfectly normal that the accounts provided by religion should be poetical.

V

Unquestionably, we can note a stubborn persistence of Catholic imagery and thought traditions inside the most various (and often adversarial) discourses, from the political to the aesthetic. To a certain extent this was due to the desire of Restoration scholars to find a kind of middle ground between the aggressive secularization of the Jacobins and the inertia of the devout ultramontanist factions; these scholars in religious studies tried to bridge the apparent gaps between a much more assertive scientific worldview and the religious traditions of society. Another aspect is the connection between French literary aesthetics and Romantic religion described also as an "erased code" or a "reprise littéraire" of the later by the former (Despland 1999: 489-502, see also Despland 1994) .

The persistence of Christian imagery in French writing in the early nineteenth century is formidable. It is not limited to occasional literary passages such as those we encounter in Nerval's *Aurélia* or in Lamartine's poems, or even in Victor Hugo's prose and poetry (Bowman 1990: 167-81). It moves on to insistent parallels between Jesus and Socrates, or even Napoleon (Bowman 1990: 3-13, 34-60) to be found in both literary and paraliterary writings. It has been correctly pointed out that during the French eighteenth century, starkly and staunchly religious titles were no less numerous than those of deists or atheists, even though less prominent (Sevillia 2003: 195, Viguerie 1995). Likewise, after 1815 there is a profusion of the imagery of "religious blood" to be found in ecclesiastical writings (Jean-Baptiste Lasausse, Cardinal Thomas Gousset, and scores of others), in poetry (Victor Hugo, Musset, and other French and English Romantics), even in scientific writings (Alfred Maury, Imbert-Goubeyre) (see the excellent detailed analysis of Bowman 1990: 81-105). Thus Victor Hugo famously exclaimed in one of his odes (written in 1853, but published in 1870 in *Châtiments*): "Souffrons comme Jésus, souffrons comme Socrate" (Let us suffer like Jesus, let us suffer like Socrate) while in the same volume in "A un martyr" Hugo writes "Et de l'adieu du Christ au suprême moment: / – Ô vivants, aimez-vous! aimez. En vous aimant, / Frères, vous fermerez mes plaies.–" (And Christ's adieu in his supreme last moment / Oh living creatures, love each other! Love. By loving / you, my brothers will heal my wounds). The "Les Mémorables" section of Nerval's *Aurélia* depicts in some detail the reconciliation of history, the re-establishment of cosmic harmony, the proclamation of divine glory by the whole of nature and of the universe; the playful and frivolous Musset himself deals with "L'Espoir de Dieu" and "A la mi-Carême," to say nothing about Lamartine whose poetry is imbued with Christian imagery and thematics as in "Témoignons pour le Christ, mais surtout pour nos vies; / Notre moindre vertu confondra plus d'impies / Que le sang d'un martyr" (Let us bear witness for Christ, but mostly through our lives / the least of our virtues will defeat more unbelievers / Than the blood of a martyr; "Aux chrétiens" in "Harmonies poétiques et religieuses," Book I) or "Voilà, voilà le Dieu que tout esprit adore, / qu'Abraham a servi, que rêvait Pythagore, / ... Ce Dieu que l'univers révèle la raison, / Que la justice attend, que l'infortune espère, / Et que le Christ enfin vint montrer à la terre!" (Watch, watch the God that is adored by any spirit / who was served by Abraham, the one of whom Pythagoras was dreaming / ... /This God who is revealed to us by reason / who is expected by justice, for him misfortune keeps hoping / And whom Christ finally showed to the whole earth; in "Dieu," no. 28 in *Méditations poétiques*). However, to me the best example remains that of Shelley's *Prometheus Unbound* where the avowedly atheist poet turns the figure of the God- and cosmos-shattering revolutionary (almost unwillingly) into a Christ-like figure. It is also true that many revolutionaries of the age (in 1848, during the antislavery campaign and on other occasions) resorted to Christ-like imagery, ideals, and modeling.

We can add here a few words about the mode in which writers themselves adapted the new discourses on religion and theology and used them. As I said at the beginning, literature throughout the West felt itself responsible for and involved with a revamping of religion and the injection of more emotional dimensions over and above the somewhat rationalistic or even dry ways in which religion was taught, preached, or practiced throughout the West.

The nineteenth century provides fascinating examples of combinations between philosophy, literature, and religion. It should be said that Gügler, for instance, was caught in a wide circle active in southern Germany, Switzerland, and Austria. He himself was the direct "descendant" of Johann Michael Sailer (1751-1832), who along with the medical specialist Johann Nepomuk Ringeis (1785-1880) and others represented the ideological core of the University of Landshut and later Munich (see Gottfried 1979: 56-69, Munk 1994). This is just one example among the many modes of networking that characterized this area in terms of the religion/literature interface. It is precisely during the highpoint of this activity that Clemens Brentano, a Catholic, but not conspicuously so in his earlier literary work, dedicated several years (1819-24) to the recording of the visions of the stigmatized nun Katharina Emerick – the multivolume lives of Jesus and of the Holy Virgin are the result of this recording; its written form probably owed much to Brentano himself.

This is not the place to review the amazing abundance of valuable theological works that emerged during this period. Nevertheless it is appropriate to say that *some* of these apologists either actively sought an alliance with literary art, or simply found themselves inserted in the literary world and exerting some influence on it. Cardinal Newman would be an excellent example: he had learned much from Coleridge, his style of writing was exquisitely literary, and he was easily accepted as a serious and distinguished essayist at the time, as well as later (cf. also Alexander 1935: 21-4 among innumerable other judgments). In France, Chateaubriand could be mentioned again, even though he was not more than an occasional apologist, and certainly no theologian at all. On the other hand, Félicité de Lamennais was clearly endowed with a good theological mind, albeit with an explosive and fickle temperament. He was soon adopted by the literary world as one of its legitimate members and interacted with his colleagues in interesting ways. Rosmini was not only perhaps the greatest Catholic philosopher of the age, but he deeply influenced Manzoni. Georg Hermes, Anton Günther, and Johann Sebastian von Drey were absorbed by intellectuals or writers either directly or indirectly (McCool 1977: 31, 61, 67-9, 88-109, 119-24, see also Munk 1994). Of particular significance in German-speaking lands and elsewhere were the "circles" of religious intellectuals which acted as a link between literary intellectuals and theologians. The names of Cardinal Hofbauer and of Sailer in Landshut and Munich have already been mentioned. It is indispensable to add here particularly the scintillating Countess Amalie von Gallitzin (1748-1806), along with Franz von Fürstenberg (1729-1810), who in Münster acted as a kind of clearing-house, connecting different wings of (especially) Roman Catholics. One of the Münster circle's most imposing achievements was bringing about the conversion of Count Friedrich Leopold zu Stolberg (1750-1819), who ultimately managed to write a 15-volume *Geschichte der Religion Jesu Christi* (1806-18) a kind of world history from a Christian perspective, meant to counteract the Enlightenment. Although the work remained unfinished it is fair to say that it had in German-educated circles an influence almost comparable to that of Chateaubriand's *Génie* (e.g., Munk 1994: 569-70)

It is quite true that the "reawakening" of German literature had been from the beginning involved with religious thematics; it is enough to think of Klopstock's *Messias* for instance, but the names of Jung-Stilling, Hamann, or Matthias Claudius (even Lessing and Goethe to some extent) also come to mind. On the other hand what German Romanticism in its different shapes brought was a much deeper processing and an almost systematic harvesting of the field. It is also true that in parallel with literature in its narrow sense (or preceding it in time) a number of first-rate thinkers strove to (re)activate the religion/literature interface. Hagiography, aphoristic nuggets, and pious legends on the Christian side, parabolic stories on the Jewish one, had flourished for hundreds, not to say thousands, of years either on the surface or in more subterranean ways. Prominent thinkers like St Bonaventure, or even earlier Pseudo-Dionysus the Areopagite, had loudly proclaimed the aesthetic as an indispensable facet of the divine and as a mode of communication thereof. However, it may be said that the period we are discussing was particularly abundant in efforts of this type. Friedrich Wilhelm Schelling (1775-1854), one of the half-dozen of prominent Romantic Idealist philosophers, concentrated, particularly in the second half of his career, on the way in which reason connects to faith primarily by means of the beautiful. Earlier, Johann Gottfried Herder (1744-1803) set up, along with Johann Georg Hamann (1730-88), a very prompt reaction to what they perceived as Kant's unrelenting and abstract rationalism. The first of them was more moderate in that he relativized Kantianism from a historical point of view and might well be regarded as the remote ancestor of "multiculturalism" through a philosophy of history; the second was both stylistically and content-wise more cryptical and radical, and glorified emotional irrationality and the priority of poetic instincts over any judgment and rational argument. Just slightly later, Franz von Baader (1765-1841) represented the German equivalent of Ballanche and Saint-Martin by combining the subconscious and natural organic values with a mystic, unstructured religiousness. These and others sometimes influenced writers directly, or, if not, provided a kind of theoretical validation and bolstering for the poets.

The *démarche* of the philosophers and theologians of the time (particularly the Catholic ones) is best summarized by McCool (1977): refuting the rationalists either by demonstrating that "human reason was intrinsically incapable of reaching any true or certain conclusions about religious or moral issues" (a more traditionalist standpoint) or else adapting "one of the prevailing contemporary philosophies to Catholic apologetics and systematic theology." The advantages of the latter approach were clear. Christian faith was provided with a framework through which its revealed mysteries could be presented to the educated classes in a rigorous intellectual system, while at the same time undermining the habitual rationalist objections against religion (McCool 1977: 18). In fact this line of argument could attract major thinkers, or "bring them back into the fold." Probably the most spectacular example is that of Schelling who, throughout the second half of his life, concentrated on searching for the best rationalist framework inside which the religious and the aesthetic could be merged. Again the names of Görres and Creuzer could be adduced.

Among the writers who allowed their personal or biographical choices to overflow and sometimes imbue their literary production one may mention, in Germany, Novalis, Gotthelf, Annette Freiin von Droste-Hülshoff, Mörike, Grillparzer (despite his accesses of political bitterness), and later Stifter, as well as numerous others. In France perhaps Lamartine and Balzac are among the most outstanding cases. In England Felicia Hemans, the later Wordsworth, and a number of women novelists (including, arguably, Jane Austen) might be enumerated. The situation is somewhat more complicated in Eastern Europe where the enthusiastic adoption of Western views sometimes blocked the open expression of religious views in literature. However it is precisely in this area of Europe where a "deep structure" of religious views is the most fertile area of exploratory research and where an aesthetic religiosity became most powerfully entrenched until well after 1900. I must re-emphasize that, in most of these *literary* cases, sooner rather than later the aesthetic comes to substitute for the religious, almost against the wishes of the authors.

One interesting episode of the post-1815 evolution in Germany at least was the outright struggle of a number of otherwise nonpolemical writers against the "Vormärz" and "Junges Deutschland" groups: not necessarily or primarily from a political and ideological point of view but because of the opposition of the latter to religion. Examples might be the long review by Wolfgang Menzel, perhaps the leading critic of the time, of Karl Gutzkow's novel *Wally, die Zweiflerin* (1835), the arguments of which had wide echoes and were in fact adopted by others. The Swiss Protestant parson and distinguished writer Jeremias Gotthelf, otherwise fairly left-wing in his views, lambasted "Junges Deutschland" for having corrupted traditional liberalism and dragged it toward radical and socialist positions, not least through its utilitarian and antireligious standpoint. (This can be well seen in his two short stories *Doktor Dorbach der Wühler* and *Ein deutscher Flüchtling*, as well as in his prominent novel *Jakobs des Handwerksgesellen Wanderungen* of 1846, in which Georg Herwegh is the main target.) A rather timid and retiring figure, Annette Freiin von Droste-Hülshoff wrote poems such as *Mein Beruf* or *Warnung an die Weltverbesserer* in which she expressed worry and anguish against a potential de-Christianization of the world.[5]

I am not sure whether the captivating story of the destiny of "village bells" (Corbin 1998) in nineteenth-century France may serve as a kind of explanatory analogy to the switches and combinations between literary art and religion during the same period. Let us see. Despite various grumblings and setbacks from the Middle Ages on, the church bells had served as an absolutely decisive marker for the sensory culture not only in France, but throughout Europe. They had sacralized time and its organization and had defined the "sound landscape" for centuries. The French Revolution, aiming to regenerate the human race, saw from the very beginning that it ought to annihilate this particular mode of sense perception. The respect and veneration toward the deceased (a foundation of all traditional societies all over the globe), the ritual solemnization of human rites of passage, the auditory certification of human emotions and time divisions, became objects of destruction. Step by step, throughout a decade, the revolutionary movement with all its power first successfully limited the usage of bells and later literally dismantled them and melted the bells into coins or weapons, while also legislatively reducing or forbidding their use. This was done against sullen passive opposition (and only occasional outbreaks of exasperated violence) on the side of a population that in France until close to the middle of the nineteenth century was still 80 percent rural. The decision of the imperial administration after 1802 to allow again the sounding of bells was received with joy, as a liberation. (Napoleon himself enjoyed considerably this particular harmony as different sources tell us; see, e.g., Corbin 1998: 384, nn. 10 and 11) .

The whole of the nineteenth century was thereafter marked by a long and highly interesting battle between the secular and the religious forces of society as to the ownership and uses of bells. Issues such as the length of pealing, the particular hours when they could be used, the secular purposes of the bells, access to bell towers, noise disturbance, and a score of others were debated at a local and even at a national level. Early French Romantic literature tended to eulogize nostalgically the sensorial culture dominated by bell sounds, while later in the nineteenth century the emphasis was often on the mournful and the sinister connotations of bells. Ultimately the victory was won by the dogmatically laicized society. In the later twentieth century, while bells were not completely banished or abolished, we see them firmly restrained and marginalized. The sound landscape is dominated by sirens, motor and mechanical noises, radio and stereo blasters, and various cacophonies. Most important, bells were and are subordinated to practical uses, such as announcing time. There is thus a kind of coexistence with the religious as a minor partner and its substitution by secular, de-Christianized practices (see Corbin 1998, especially pp. ix-xii, 3-44, 218-53, 287-308).

Different as all this may be from literary activity, it can nevertheless serve as a convenient referential background. (On a sociopolitical level the number of former clerics now laicized is notable: Talleyrand, Baron Louis, and others). Like the bells, literature in the nineteenth century tended toward a conjunction of the aesthetic and the religious. Similarly, as I have stressed earlier, the aesthetic becomes the *senior* partner by the end of the century, but here our parallel ceases to be useful in as far as in literature the pairings, conjunctions, and dialectics continue in a much greater variety of shapes.

VI

What I hope to have demonstrated in this chapter is the following. The eighteenth century and even the nineteenth century were engaged in the secularization of the religious horizon and *Weltanschauung*. These were turned into a diversity of messianisms: philosophical, ideological, literary, political, ethical. The response of religion to this expropriating activity was an expropriation of its own, namely the conquest of the aesthetic, of vast realms of the feelings and of the emotions, in a word, of the "expansions" of this modernizing, Romantic-responsive world. There can be no doubt that the early nineteenth century witnessed throughout the West a marked reappraisal of religion. Governmental hostility toward organized religion subsided gradually. Largely because of pressures from below, the opinion that societies are difficult or impossible to conceive in the absence of some kind of religious dimension was generally accepted.

At the same time, however, serious efforts can be noted on the religious side to revamp, renew, or modernize a whole range of its own forms, images, and positions. Perhaps the emergence and success of "Conservative" Judaism is a most prominent example here: retrieval of the sacral beauties of traditional ritual, but not radical return to strictly Orthodox disciplines. Anglican procedure was rather similar. The change in attitudes by Roman Catholics was, though slower, even more profound, in the sense that the Church's repositioning itself in a minority role was for the first time acknowledged along with the need to vindicate the utility of religion inside the body social and in front of it.

The connection of the religious dimension to the realm of the beautiful was an extremely important part of this repositioning strategy. Religion began to claim for itself the role of a guardian of the emotional, imaginative, and symbolic resources of humanity. While not entirely relinquishing its ties to the good and the true, there were numerous cases in which the beautiful was placed over and above them; at any rate, the beautiful was no longer relegated to a mere auxiliary role. While these initiatives came sometimes from institutional ecclesiastic sources and can therefore be interpreted as conscious and "constructed," they often arose among writers and artists, in largely spontaneous gestures. The examples I have presented are quite early in the century, but it is fair to say that the mutual (and multiple) engagements of cultural work and religious faith were to become a prominent and highly characteristic feature of the nineteenth century as a whole. These events certainly had a stabilizing role and gave new life to religion(s) throughout the West.

The other side, however, was the growing and earnest conviction that the arts and literature could in fact somehow replace religion.[6] Thus in some fundamental ways nineteenth- and twentieth-century "aestheticism" could be seen as an offspring of the entanglement between sacrality and the beautiful. The entanglement between the two was not devoid of dangers for both. The humanistic realm began to be suspected of being just a mask, or alibi, or cover-up for reasons of religious proselytizing. Meanwhile religion could see itself occasionally subverted or vulgarized as being "merely" aesthetic or fictional. This set of issues was highlighted particularly by the end of the nineteenth century and the beginning of the twentieth century. It is still present and continues to deserve our full attention.[7]

NOTES

1　There is a shrewd analysis in Dru (1967).

2　See Bowman (1990: 155-66). This whole exceptional work is a true mine of information, intelligent reflection, and of discovery of the lines of connection between the religious field and other areas of symbolization in early nineteenth-century France.

3　The definitive critical edition of his works was started in 1934 by Castelli and is intended eventually to reach 100 volumes (there are 49 as of this writing); a similarly ambitious undertaking is the edition of translations into English started around 10 years ago by British Benedictines at Durham.

4　There is a short biographical work by J. L. Schiffmann, *Lebensgeschichte A. Güglers*

(1833). The most serious study is included in Balthasar (1961, I: 89-97) and I draw on its conclusions. See also Hardelin (1967) and Klinger (1975).

5　I follow here mostly the informative judgments of Bauer (1980-90).

6　Beethoven had already argued in favor of art substituting religion. See Johnson (1991: 120-1).

7　This chapter deals specifically with the varieties of intermeshing between the aesthetic and the religious. It is not intended as a comprehensive survey of the treatment and functioning of religion in Europe and North America during the early nineteenth century. I would like to emphasize here that in my opinion a perfectly good argument can be made in favor of a Europe that was being de-Christianized apace during these decades. We know very well that for instance the works of Voltaire and Rousseau were more widely read and circulated during this period than the sum of their adversaries' writings. Major studies contributing to the dismantling of Christianity and/or the Bible appeared simultaneously with those mentioned above: not only scholarly works, but also productions of wider intellectual appeal, such as those of David Strauss, Ludwig Feuerbach, and soon Renan, Darwin, and Marx, to list just a few prominent names. My purpose was merely and precisely to explain *why*, in the face of this formidable social and intellectual activity, society maintained its stability and its allegiance to Christian traditions.

References and Further Reading

Abrams, Meyer H. (1971). *Natural Supernaturalism: Tradition and Revolution in Romantic Literature*. New York: Norton.

Alexander, Calvert, S. J. (1935). *The Catholic Literary Revival*. Milwaukee: Bruce.

Balmés, Jaime (1844). *El protestantismo comparado con el catolicísmo, en sus relaciones con la civilización europea*, 4 vols. Barcelona: Jose Taulo.

Balmés, Jaime (1846). *Cartas á un escéptico en materiá de la religión*. Barcelona: Brusi.

Balthasar, Hans Urs von (1961). *Herrlichkeit*, 7 vols. Einsiedeln: Johannes Verlag.

Barclay, David E. (1995). *Friedrich Wilhelm IV and the Prussian Monarchy 1840-1861*. Oxford: Clarendon Press.

Bauer, Winfred (1980-90). "Geistliche Restauration versus Junges Deutschland und Vormärz-Literaten." In Horst Glaser (ed.), *Deutsche Literatur. Eine Sozialgeschichte*, vol. 6. Hamburg: Rowohlt, pp. 97-111.

Bloom, Harold (1963). *The Visionary Company: A Reading of English Romantic Poetry*. Garden City, NY: Doubleday.

Bowman, Frank Paul (1990). *French Romanticism. Intertextual and Interdisciplinary Readings*. Baltimore and London: Johns Hopkins University Press.

Chateaubriand, François-René, vicomte de (1978). *Génie du christianisme*. In *Essai sur les révolutions. Génie du christianisme*. Paris: Gallimard, Pléiade.

Church, R. W. ([1891] 1970). *The Oxford Movement 1832-1845*. Chicago: University of Chicago Press.

Corbin, Alain (1998). *Village Bells. Sound and Meaning in the Nineteenth-Century French Countryside*, trans. Martin Thom. New York: Columbia University Press.

Dawson, Christopher ([1933] 2001). *The Spirit of the Oxford Movement*. London: St Austin Press.

Despland, Michel (1994). *Reading an Erased Code. French Literary Aesthetics and Romantic Religion*. Toronto: University of Toronto Press.

Despland, Michel (1999). *L'Émergence des sciences de la réligion. La Monarchie de Juillet: un moment fondateur*. Paris: L'Harmattan.

Dru, Alexandre (1967). *Erneuerung und Reaktion. Die Restauration in Frankreich 1800-1830*. Munich: Kösel.

Fleischmann, Kornelius (1988). *Klemens Maria Hofbauer. Sein Leben und seine Zeit*. Graz: Styria.

Gottfried, Paul (1979). *Conservative Millenarians. The Romantic Experience in Bavaria*. New York: Fordham University Press.

Hardelin, Alf (1967). "Kirche und Kult in der Luzerner theologischen Romantik (Alois Gügler und Josef Widmer)." *Zeitschrift für katholische Theologie*, 80: 139-75.

Johnson, Paul (1991). *The Birth of the Modern. World Society 1815-1830*. New York: Harper Collins.

Jones, Mary Gwladys (1952). *Hannah More*. Cambridge: Cambridge University Press.

Klinger, Elmar (1975). "Alois Gügler (1782-1827)." In Heinrich Friesch and Georg Schwaiger (eds.), *Katholische Theologen Deutschlands im 19ten Jahrhundert*, vol. 1. Munich: Kösel, pp. 274-302.

Löwith, Karl (1967). *Weltgeschichte und Heilsgeschehen*. Stuttgart: Kohlhammer.

McCool, Gerald A. (1977). *Catholic Theology in the Nineteenth Century. The Quest for a Unitary Method*. New York: Seabury.

Mellor, Ann K. (2000). *Mother of the Nation*. Bloomington: Indiana University Press.

Munk, Hans (1994). "Die deutsche Romantik in Religion und Theologie." In Helmut Schanze (ed.), *Romantik-Handbuch*. Stuttgart: Kroner, pp. 556-89.

Nemoianu, Virgil (1984). *The Taming of Romanticism. European Literature and the Age of Biedermeier*. Cambridge, MA: Harvard University Press.

Nipperdey, Thomas (1991). *Deutsche Geschichte 1800-1866. Bürgerwelt und starker Staat*. Munich: Beck.

Richardt, Aimé (1993). *Fénelon*. Ozoir-la-Ferrière: Editions In Fine.

Sauvigny, Guillaume de Bertier de (1955). *La Restauration*. Paris: Flammarion.

Sevillia, Jean (2003). *Historiquement correct. Pour en finir avec le passé unique*. Paris: Perrin.

Van Kley, Dale (1996). *The Religious Origins of the French Revolution*. New Haven, CT: Yale University Press.

Viguerie, Jean de (1995). *Histoire et dictionnaire du temps des Lumières*. Paris: Laffont.

Voegelin, Eric (1956-87). *Order and History*, 5 vols. Baton Rouge: Louisiana State University Press.

24

Nature

James C. McKusick

Concepts of Nature in European Romanticism

One of the defining characteristics of the Romantic movement in Europe is its enduring engagement with the natural world. Throughout the Romantic period, imagery and ideas drawn from nature are omnipresent in the work of poets and novelists, painters and musicians, philosophers and political theorists. For many European Romantic writers, the natural world is more than just a backdrop or setting for human activity. Rather, the representation of nature and the exploration of the human relationship to nature permeates all aspects of literary art from genre and form to plot and character. The relationship of literature and nature is explored not only in works that are explicitly *about* nature (such as Chateaubriand's *Travels in America* or Eichendorff's "Moonlit Night"); nature is also present in different manners and with differing effects throughout the course of European Romanticism. It appears as the antagonist in Vigny's "The Death of the Wolf" and Goethe's "Elf-King." It provides the metaphors for articulating complex philosophical and theological concepts, as in Rousseau's *Discourse on the Origin of Inequality* or Coleridge's "The Eolian Harp." It is the vehicle for human self-understanding and for the articulation of the most profound emotions of love and grief, as can be seen in Goethe's *The Sorrows of Young Werther* or Lamartine's "The Lake." Moreover, examining nature *in* literature can also provide a helpful means of interrogating the nature *of* literature. The creative and dynamic processes of the natural world have often served as a model for writers to understand their own artistic creativity, as in Keats's "Ode to a Nightingale" or in any number of poems by Hölderlin.

Of course, the definition of the term *nature*, and the historical shifts of the word's meaning, have helped to encourage these multiple literary manifestations. The term *nature* meant something quite different to the rationalist philosophers of the Enlightenment than it did to the poets and novelists of the Romantic period. From the Latin verb *nasci*, meaning "to be born," the first and earliest usage of the word *nature* denotes the inherent qualities of a thing – that which gives something its distinctive features and makes it unique. With respect to persons, this might mean their dominant disposition or what might otherwise be called their "character." *Nature* can also refer to the sum total of things in the universe and the aggregate of their respective innate characteristics. In this definition, *nature* is something static and unchanging. The second, more recent, use of the term refers not to the sum total of attributes, but rather the sum total of forces and powers at work in the universe. This definition presents nature as dynamic, subject to change and causing changes. Yet these are not the only explanations of this broad concept. Because of the scope of its various connotations, *nature* is often explained in relationship to its conceptual opposites, such as spirituality, art, or civilization. These oppositions are themselves tied to larger intellectual discourses in which the term is used. For the rationalist philosophers and scientists of the Enlightenment, nature is a well-regulated machine, best studied through direct observation and experience. For the writers of the Romantic period, nature is often more inscrutable, a dynamic flux of vital energies, best engaged by an intuitive process of colloquy and sympathetic identification. Both the rationalist and the Romantic discourses of nature, and the conflicts between them, have had a profound effect on the literary expressions of what nature is, where humankind fits into the natural scheme, and what our relationship to nature can or should be.

The clash between rationalist and Romantic discourses, and the confrontation between the respective notions that nature is either static or dynamic, takes an important turn precisely at the dawn of the Romantic period. Part of the new usage and the new concept of nature as a vital, dynamic process derives not just from the shifts brought on by the critique of rationalism advanced by Hume and Rousseau, or the *Naturphilosophie* proposed by Fichte and Schelling. The idea of nature was also profoundly affected by the many voyages of discovery and exploration in the Americas, Africa, and the Pacific Ocean. The use of the word *nature* is indelibly altered by the European awareness of remote and "primitive" peoples who dwell far from conventional society. To talk about the expression of nature in European literature from 1750 through 1830, then, one must of necessity consider the vast amount of travel writing published in the same period. The physical and geographical expansion of European awareness coincided with a complementary intellectual, spiritual, and cultural expansion. The representation of American Indians, South Sea Islanders, and other indigenous peoples, either as noble savages or as hostile and barbarous "natives," shaped a great deal of European writing about nature in the Romantic period. Nowhere is this more apparent than in the works of Jean-Jacques Rousseau (1712-78) and François-René de Chateaubriand (1768-1848).

Rousseau and the State of Nature

In 1755, Jean-Jacques Rousseau published his *Discourse on the Origin and Foundations of Inequality,* an enormously influential essay that seeks to describe the prehistoric origins of modern society. Rousseau explains at the outset that his description of the "state of nature" is purely hypothetical; it is "a state which no longer exists, perhaps never did exist, and probably never will exist; and of which, it is, nevertheless, necessary to have true ideas, in order to form a proper judgment of our present state" (Rousseau [1755] 1913: 169). The state of nature is evidently a myth or enabling fiction that allows Rousseau to advance a critique of contemporary society, and of the rationalist philosophy upon which it is based. At the core of this conception, the "state of nature" offers a vision of an ideal human existence in harmony with the natural world. Drawing extensively upon published accounts of exploration and discovery in the Americas, Africa, and the South Seas, Rousseau argues that humankind in its original state of nature lived a simple, peaceful, happy life, with none of the miseries and diseases that attend life in a civilized society. In the state of nature, humans lived alone, without any need for language, tools, or houses; there were no families, tribes, or interpersonal relationships of any kind. Although such a solitary life might appear terribly lonely and emotionally impoverished, Rousseau nevertheless regards it as far happier than our own, since humans in the state of nature do not suffer from any of the dissensions and conflicts that necessarily accompany a more civilized existence. Jealousy, for example, cannot occur in the state of nature, since there are no exclusive or permanent relationships between men and women. Nor can slavery occur, since no man can bind another to his will. And there can be no disagreements over personal property, since property does not exist in the state of nature.

Rousseau goes on to envision the unfortunate process by which humankind relinquished its original state of nature and acquired all the features of a civilized society. Over a span of many centuries, humans invented tools for fishing and hunting, devised clothing, and learned to control fire:

> On the seashore and the banks of rivers, they invented the hook and line, and became fishermen and eaters of fish. In the forests they made bows and arrows, and became huntsmen and warriors. In cold countries they clothed themselves with the skins of the beasts they had slain. The lightning, a volcano, or some lucky chance acquainted them with fire, a new resource against the rigours of winter: they next learned how to preserve this element, then how to reproduce it, and finally how to prepare with it the flesh of animals which before they had eaten raw. (Rousseau [1755] 1913: 208)

In Rousseau's view, the invention of tools and the discovery of fire are very mixed blessings. Tools intended for hunting will inevitably become weapons of war, and by eating cooked meat, he argues, humans will become prey to disease. Further inventions are in store: humans invent language, by which they are enabled to form organized societies, and they invent agriculture, which leads to deforestation, erosion, and the creation of barren deserts in formerly fertile terrain. In a discursive footnote, Rousseau (quoting Georges-Louis Leclerc, Comte de Buffon) evokes the environmental catastrophe that must follow upon the heels of a technologically advanced civilization:

As men consume enormous quantities of wood and plants for fire and other uses, it follows that the layer of vegetative earth in an inhabited country must always diminish and finally become like the terrain of Arabia Petraea, and like that of so many other provinces of the East – which is in fact the region of most ancient habitation – where only salt and sand are found. (Rousseau [1755] 1992: 70)

Clearly, for Rousseau, the development of technology, despite its immediate benefits to individuals, in the long run will threaten the very existence of humankind. In this respect, the *Discourse on the Origin of Inequality* foreshadows some of the essential ideas of present-day environmentalism and the Green movement in modern European politics.

Rousseau's evocation of the state of nature, and his extended critique of civilized society, served as a powerful inspiration for writers and artists all over Europe. Especially in France, a younger generation of poets, novelists, intellectuals, and politicians took Rousseau's ideas quite literally and endeavored to put them into practice. Rousseau's political ideas, as further adumbrated in *The Social Contract* (1762), had a direct influence upon the formation of a revolutionary ideology that led to the fall of the Bastille in 1789. As a symbol of tyranny, the Bastille stood for all that was corrupt, depraved, and unnatural in contemporary French society. Meanwhile, younger writers were seeking out wild, scenic, and remote landscapes in which to witness and record the state of nature at first hand. In 1791, for example, François-René de Chateaubriand, an aristocrat exiled by the French Revolution, embarked for an extended trip through North America. Chateaubriand's *Travels in America* (first published in 1827) vividly describes his first encounter with the American wilderness: he travels from New York City up the Hudson River, along the Mohawk Trail, past the last outposts of civilization, and onward to the Great Lakes. He observes daily life among the Huron and Iroquois, and he offers detailed descriptions of plants and animals. He encounters hunters, planters, ospreys, and rattlesnakes; he is inspired by the deafening roar of Niagara Falls; he falls down a "frightful abyss," breaks his arm, almost drowns, and is finally rescued by "savages." An eventful journey! Throughout his travels, Chateaubriand shows great respect and admiration for all Native American people, especially the Iroquois, whom he idealizes as noble savages:

The big round eyes of the Iroquois sparkled with independence, and his entire appearance was that of a hero; there shone upon his forehead the intricate combinations of thoughts and the elevated emotions of the soul. This intrepid man was not at all surprised by firearms when they were used against him for the first time; he stood firm under the whistling of the balls and the noise of the cannon, as if he had heard them all his life.... Such was the Iroquois before the shadow and the destruction of European civilization were extended over him. (Chateaubriand [1827] 1969: 172-3)

Such an evocation of the intrinsic goodness of humankind, and the corrupting influence of European civilization, owes a great deal to Rousseau's conception of the state of nature.

After he returned to France, Chateaubriand published several novels dealing with life among remote and "savage" peoples; one of the best-known of these novels is *Atala* (1801), a tale of romance set in the remote wilderness of the Louisiana Territory (soon to be explored by Lewis and Clark). Chateaubriand describes this setting as a "New Eden" full of frolicking wildlife:

> Life and enchantment are spread there by a multitude of animals, placed in these retreats by the Creator. Across a clearing may be seen bears drunk on wild grapes, swaying on elm branches; caribou bathe in the lakes; grey squirrels sport amid thick foliage; mocking birds and tiny Virginia doves as small as sparrows alight on lawns red with wild strawberries; green parakeets with yellow head, empurpled woodpeckers, fiery cardinal birds, climb and fly around the cypress trunks; humming birds flash on the Florida jasmine, and bird-catching serpents hiss in the tree-tops, hanging there like creeping plants. (Chateaubriand [1801] 1963: 5)

Within this idyllic setting, the novel's Indian heroine (Atala) falls passionately in love with Chactas, a brave of the Natchez tribe. But, due to the malign influence of Christian missionaries, Atala has taken a vow of eternal chastity, and so she cannot marry Chactas. As this unhappy plot unfolds to a fatal conclusion, its underlying premise becomes quite evident: European civilization is very bad for you. Stay in the woods!

German Nature Writers: Flying Home

The influence of Rousseau is also apparent among many German writers of the Romantic period. This is particularly true of Johann Wolfgang von Goethe (1749-1832), whose first novel, *The Sorrows of Young Werther* (1774), evinces a passionate enthusiasm for wild and scenic landscapes, "primitive" people living in a state of nature, and young lovers untrammeled by social conventions. The youthful protagonist of this epistolary novel has retired to the German countryside for some much-needed rest and recreation. (The stress of city life, and the unexpected death of his fiancée, have been hard on him.) Gamboling through meadows, reposing on the greensward, reading Homer in the original Greek, and opening his senses to the pure mountain air and sunshine, Werther finds his imagination rekindled and his heart rejuvenated:

> A wonderful serenity has taken possession of my entire soul, like these sweet mornings of spring which I enjoy with my whole heart.... When, while the lovely valley teems with vapour around me, and the meridian sun strikes the upper surface of the impenetrable foliage of my trees, and but a few stray gleams steal into the inner sanctuary, I throw myself down among the tall grass by the trickling stream; and, as I lie close to the earth, a thousand unknown plants are noticed by me: when I hear the buzz of the little world among the stalks, and grow familiar with the countless indescribable forms

of the insects and flies, then I feel the presence of the Almighty, who formed us in his
own image, and the breath of that universal love which bears and sustains us, as it floats
around us in an eternity of bliss. (Goethe [1774] 1917: 2-3)

With its boundless exuberance, its affection for even the humblest of God's creatures,
and its evident pantheism (that is, the belief that God's love is manifested everywhere
in Creation), this passage exemplifies the vigor and keen sensibility, as well as the
naïveté, of the young Werther.

Living among unlettered "peasants" who lead a simple, happy life, Werther might
well believe that he has arrived in a second Eden, a true state of nature:

Happy is it, indeed, for me that my heart is capable of feeling the same simple and
innocent pleasure as the peasant whose table is covered with food of his own rearing, and
who not only enjoys his meal, but remembers with delight the happy days and sunny
mornings when he planted it, the soft evenings when he watered it, and the pleasure he
experienced in watching its daily growth. (Goethe [1774] 1917: 22)

This solitary, self-sufficient lifestyle is disturbed, however, when Werther meets a
local girl named Lotte; she is sweet, innocent, playful, and flirtatious, and he
immediately falls in love with her. But it turns out that Lotte is already engaged to
Albert, a man of high social status who is in many ways the opposite of Werther:
mature, responsible, genteel, and utterly conventional. Although Lotte feels genuinely attracted to Werther, and even seems to welcome his boyish advances, she still
marries Albert, and the novel proceeds to a tragic conclusion. The influence of modern
society proves fatal to Werther, who partakes of a primal innocence, an innate
goodness, like Rousseau's natural man.

The Sorrows of Young Werther was an immediate bestseller throughout Europe, and it
proved to be an enduring landmark in the development of European Romanticism.
Young men everywhere, and especially young poets, imitated Werther's dress, his
mannerisms, his boundless affection for nature, and even his unfortunate penchant for
suicide. A good deal of German Romantic poetry, including much of Goethe's own
lyric poetry, reads as if it were written by the young Werther: it is suffused with
natural imagery, it exudes a vaguely pantheistic sensibility, and it evokes a solitary
wanderer who pines after lost love. One such poem is Goethe's "Nähe des Geliebten"
(Presence of the Beloved), excerpted here:

> Ich denke dein, wenn mir der Sonne Schimmer
> Vom Meere strahlt;
> Ich denke dein, wenn sich des Mondes Flimmer
> In Quellen malt.
>
> Ich sehe dein, wenn auf dem fernen Wege
> Der Staub sich hebt,
> In tiefer Nacht, wenn auf dem schmalen Stege
> Der Wandrer bebt.

(I think of you when the shimmer of the sun gleams from the sea; I think of you when the glimmering light of the moon is reflected in the springs.

I see you when the dust rises on the distant road; in deep night, when the wanderer trembles on the narrow bridge.) (Forster 1957: 222-3, translation modified)

These dreamy, evocative images convey the intensity of the speaker's desire and longing for his beloved, while also evoking a luminous, windswept landscape that is almost entirely devoid of human presence. This poem is entitled "Presence of the Beloved," but where is the beloved? In a certain sense, she *is* the landscape: the absent beloved becomes present in the mind of the wanderer through his ability to perceive and appreciate the beautiful, ever-changing appearances of nature.

A somewhat similar sensibility is apparent in Joseph von Eichendorff (1788-1857), another German writer whose lyric poetry evinces a deep affection for the natural world. Like Goethe, Eichendorff has an almost uncanny ability to make simple images express a profound depth of meaning, as in the following poem, "Mondnacht" (Moonlit Night):

> Es war, als hätt' der Himmel
> Die Erde still geküßt,
> Daß sie im Blütenschimmer
> Von ihm nun träumen müßt.
>
> Die Luft ging durch die Felder,
> Die Ähren wogten sacht,
> Es rauschten leis die Wälder,
> So sternklar war die Nacht.
>
> Und meine Seele spannte
> Weit ihre Flügel aus,
> Flog durch die stillen Lande,
> Als flöge sie nach Haus. (Forster 1957: 316)

> (It seemed as if the heaven
> In silence kissed the earth.
> That she would have to see him
> In blossom-shimmer dream.
>
> The breeze went through the meadows
> The grain-ears gently waved,
> The forest rustled softly,
> So star-clear was the night.
>
> And now my soul expanded,
> Spreading its wide wings;
> It flew through silent farmlands
> As if it flew toward home.) (translation by Michael Ferber)

Everything in this poem is understated, yet clear-cut and quietly expressive. Beginning with a merely hypothetical supposition – "it *seemed as if* the heaven . . . kissed the earth" – the poem explores the consequences of that supposition, seeing the earth in a new way, as if for the first time. With growing confidence in its own imagery, the poem ends with a compelling assertion of human engagement in this silent, moonlit landscape. Once again, the speaker is a wanderer who pines after something that is lost, but in this poem the wanderer does truly find what he is looking for – what all travelers long for. He is flying home.

Friedrich Hölderlin (1770-1843) takes a somewhat different approach to the poetic representation of the natural world. Throughout his poetry, Hölderlin seeks to express a vision of lost perfection, an ideal that he finds most fully embodied in the poetry and mythology of ancient Greece. No one living in the modern world can hope to recapture the living presence of the pagan gods, but even in their absence, some remnant of their ancient glory may be discerned in the appearances of nature. Such an outlook is evident in the brief lyric poem "Sonnenuntergang" (Sunset):

> Wo bist du? Trunken dämmert die Seele mir
> Von aller deiner Wonne; denn eben ist's,
>   Daß ich gelauscht, wie, goldner Töne
>   Voll, der entzückende Sonnenjüngling
> Sein Abendlied auf himmlischer Leier spielt';
> Es tönten rings die Wälder und Hügel nach,
>   Doch fern ist er zu frommen Völkern,
>   Die ihn noch ehren, hinweggegangen.

(Where are you? My soul looms drunken with all your joy, for it is just this moment that I was listening to the entrancing youthful sun-god
Playing his evening chant on a heavenly lyre; the woods and hills re-echoed it. But he has gone, far away to pious peoples who still revere him.) (Forster 1957: 292)

In the opening question, the poet addresses his beloved, using the familiar "du" form of the pronoun, as if she were present right here, at this very moment. But of course, she is not here, even though the light of the setting sun has fired the poet's imagination with joyful exultation – as if the ancient Greek sun-god, Apollo himself, were actually present, playing his music on a heavenly lyre. As the poem proceeds without pause into its second stanza, the poet becomes more calm, reserved, and even bitter in his sense of irrevocable loss. The gods have all departed, gone away forever from this land to a place where they are still revered – a place that is not of this world. Our world has become silent and dead, emptied of divine presence. And the poem's opening question still hangs unanswered: "Where are you?" – as if to suggest that the beloved has also departed, never to return.

In Hölderlin's poetry, the natural world may reveal traces, or remnants, of the ancient gods, but only when the poet is himself transformed by the power of ecstatic vision. At other times – indeed, most of the time – the world is empty and silent, devoid of divine presence. Like Rousseau, who believed that the innate goodness of human nature was imperiled by the corrupting influence of society and the growing sophistication of modern technology, so too Hölderlin regards modern society as fallen, destroyed by the progress of reason and science. Hölderlin's poetic outlook seems quite pessimistic, since there is nowhere on Earth where the ancient gods are still revered. In his view, the ancient Greek way of life, in harmony with divine presences in nature, has been lost forever.

German Romantic poetry often uses dynamic imagery of landscapes transformed by light – morning and evening, sunset and moonrise – to represent the transformation of human relationships with the natural world. The poet who initially pines over the absence of his beloved is gradually moved by the beautiful appearances of nature to aspire toward healing and spiritual growth. In such poems, nature provides more than merely a passive backdrop for human drama; it is an actor in the drama, holding the potential to transform human experience. The English Romantic writers were profoundly affected by their reading of German literature, and the emergence of English Romanticism in the late eighteenth century was directly influenced by contemporary developments in Germany. Among English poets, none were more directly engaged with German literature and culture than William Wordsworth (1770-1850) and Samuel Taylor Coleridge (1772-1834).

English Nature Writers: Spots of Time

During the 1790s, William Wordsworth and Samuel Taylor Coleridge collaboratively pioneered new ways of seeing and responding to the natural world. Both were fascinated by recent developments in German literature, and Coleridge was especially impressed by the innovations of Goethe and Schiller in poetry, fiction, and drama. In 1794 Coleridge addressed a sonnet to Schiller, whose play *The Robbers* had kept him awake past midnight, trembling with "wild ecstasy." In 1798, Coleridge and Wordsworth traveled together to Germany, where they steeped themselves in the language, explored the literature, and made a pilgrimage to visit the elderly poet Klopstock, known as the "German Milton" for his religious epic poetry. After learning to speak the German language, Coleridge enrolled for a year of study at the University of Göttingen, while Wordsworth and his sister Dorothy led a more reclusive existence in Goslar, where Wordsworth wrote the first draft of his great autobiographical poem, later to be known as *The Prelude*. The influence of German Romanticism is broadly apparent in the poetry of Wordsworth and Coleridge, especially in their collaborative volume of poems, *Lyrical Ballads*, first published in 1798. *Lyrical Ballads* marks a bold new departure in English verse, heralding the advent of Romanticism as a literary movement. Some of its most distinctive features are the revival of ballad stanza, reliance upon the language of everyday life, and extensive use of natural imagery drawn from direct personal observation. To be sure, none of these features is unprecedented in literary history; the innovative character of *Lyrical Ballads* lies rather in its seamless integration of pre-existing parts. Indeed, many of the distinctive features of *Lyrical Ballads* can be traced to literary developments in Germany: both Goethe and Herder were fascinated by the ballad stanzas used in *Volkslieder* (folk songs), while Goethe led the development of a new kind of nature poetry, concrete, vernacular, and yet expressive of deep emotion.

Coleridge's preface to his first collection of poems, *Sonnets from Various Authors* (1796), articulates a new and distinctively Romantic approach to the representation of nature in poetry:

> Those Sonnets appear to me the most exquisite, in which moral Sentiments, Affections, or Feelings, are deduced from, and associated with, the scenery of Nature. Such compositions generate a habit of thought highly favorable to delicacy of character. They create a sweet and indissoluble union between the intellectual and the material world. (Coleridge 1912, 2: 1139)

For Coleridge, it is not enough for the poet to be a detached observer of picturesque scenery; rather, the poet must seek a "sweet and indissoluble union" with the natural world. But how can such union be accomplished? Coleridge most memorably addresses the relationship between human consciousness and the natural world in "The Eolian Harp," a poem addressed to his wife, Sara, in 1795. Coleridge speculates that his own mental activity resembles the music generated by an Aeolian harp, an instrument placed in an open window to catch the breeze:

> Full many a thought uncall'd and undetain'd,
> And many idle flitting Phantasies,
> Traverse my indolent and passive brain,
> As wild and various as the random gales
> That swell and flutter on this subject lute! ("The Eolian Harp," ll. 39-43, Coleridge 1912, 1: 101-2)

Just as the Aeolian harp generates random, yet strangely expressive notes in response to the wind that moves its strings, so too the human mind, even in moments of indolence, generates thoughts and "idle flitting Phantasies" in response to perceptual stimuli. By implication, the activity of thinking is less purposeful than we suppose, since all mental activity must occur in response to some outward stimulus. Coleridge pursues this line of speculation in the following lines of "The Eolian Harp":

> And what if all of animated nature
> Be but organic Harps diversely fram'd,
> That tremble into thought, as o'er them sweeps
> Plastic and vast, one intellectual breeze,
> At once the Soul of each, and God of all? (ll. 44-8, Coleridge 1912, 1: 102)

Coleridge evokes the harmony and interconnectedness of all living things, each one impelled to activity by the "intellectual breeze" of divine energy that sweeps through the universe. The underlying conception here is pantheistic, but the passage is intended less as a statement of religious belief than as a metaphysical speculation. What if all creatures on Earth, from aardvarks to zebras, along with human beings, partake of the same life force, and possess the same freedom of thought and action? Because it encompasses "all of animated nature," this passage makes explicit the ecological implications of the Aeolian harp metaphor. Coleridge bears witness to the cosmic harmonies that prevail among all living things.

Coleridge's engagement with the natural world is apparent in many of his poems, especially during the 1790s, when he was collaborating closely with Wordsworth. In *The Rime of the Ancient Mariner*, for example, Coleridge conveys a sense of the sheer mystery and wonder of the natural world, and he advocates an unconditional love for "all things both great and small" (l. 615, Coleridge 1912, 1: 209). In "This Lime-Tree Bower My Prison," Coleridge attests that natural beauty can be found anywhere, even in the most humble of surroundings. He discovers beauty in commonplace objects, not scenery on a grand scale, and he finds pleasure in the gentle "dappling" of sunshine made by leaves waving in a soft summer breeze (ll. 43-51, Coleridge 1912, 1: 180). Like many of the German Romantic poets, Coleridge is fascinated by the transformative potential of light, as he observes in the *Biographia Literaria* (1817):

During the first year that Mr. Wordsworth and I were neighbours, our conversations turned frequently on the two cardinal points of poetry, the power of exciting the sympathy of the reader by a faithful adherence to the truth of nature, and the power of giving the interest of novelty by the modifying colours of imagination. The sudden charm, which accidents of light and shade, which moon-light or sun-set diffused over a known and familiar landscape, appeared to present the practicability of combining both. These are the poetry of nature. (Coleridge [1817] 1983, 2: 5)

For Coleridge, then, the "poetry of nature" emerges from two main sources: fidelity to the "truth of nature," and the "modifying colours of imagination." Just as "accidents of light and shade" have the power to transform a "known and familiar landscape," so too the poetic imagination can transform ordinary experience into something extraordinary.

One of Wordsworth's most distinctive contributions to the development of Romantic nature poetry is his exploration of the role of human memory in the construction of meaning. For Wordsworth, the remembered experience can be even more powerful, more deeply laden with significance, than the original experience. Such an attitude is apparent in his poem, "I wandered lonely as a cloud" (1807), where he records his impression of "a host of golden daffodils" that he observed on a lakeshore near Grasmere. The flowers have an immediate effect upon his mood, making him feel "gay" to see "such a jocund company." Yet the real impact of the scene does not dawn upon him until much later. Lying on his couch "in vacant or in pensive mood," his mind recalls the glad motion of the daffodils, fluttering and dancing in the breeze:

> They flash upon that inward eye
> Which is the bliss of solitude;
> And then my heart with pleasure fills,
> And dances with the daffodils. (ll. 21-4, Wordsworth 1940-9, 2: 217)

For Wordsworth, the remembered daffodils have a much greater meaning, and leave a more profound impression, than the real ones ever did. In his view, a remembered experience gains value simply by virtue of becoming an integral part of the self, and its positive affect contributes to the inward self-awareness that constitutes personal identity.

The first draft of Wordsworth's autobiographical poem, *The Prelude*, was composed at Goslar in the winter of 1798-9, and the bleakness of his surroundings may well have contributed to the warmth and richness of the remembered experiences that are encapsulated in this poem. The earliest version of the poem, dating from 1799, displays a much greater simplicity, concreteness, and immediacy than any of the later versions, and for this reason the 1799 version is well worthy of critical attention. It is here that Wordsworth first articulates his concept of "spots of time," which are moments of experience (often from childhood) that carry special intensity in recollection. Such "spots of time" provide focal points of meaning, and remain for many readers the center of interest in the much longer poem that developed out of this 1799 version of *The Prelude*.

As his first example of such a "spot of time," Wordsworth offers an episode from his early childhood, when he rode on horseback across a desolate landscape. Along the way, he passed the location "where in former times / A man, the murderer of his wife, was hung / In irons" (ll. 309-11). The only visible trace of this dreadful scene is a long green ridge of turf, shaped like a grave. Turning away from this ominous memento of human mortality, the young boy departs, only to encounter another dreary scene as he climbs upward:

> And reascending the bare slope I saw
> A naked pool that lay beneath the hills,
> The beacon on the summit, and more near
> A girl who bore a pitcher on her head
> And seemed with difficult steps to force her way
> Against the blowing wind.... (*Prelude*, 1799 version, part 1, ll. 314-19, Wordsworth 1979: 9)

Wordsworth struggles to express the meaning of this encounter, commonplace in itself, but still somehow fraught with hidden significance:

> ...It was in truth
> An ordinary sight, but I should need
> Colours and words that are unknown to man
> To paint the visionary dreariness

Which, while I looked round for my lost guide,
Did at that time invest the naked pool,
The beacon on the lonely eminence,
The woman and her garments vexed and tossed
By the strong wind. (part 1, ll. 319-27, Wordsworth 1979: 9)

There is something about the "visionary dreariness" of this scene that imprints it upon the awareness of the young poet, who was perhaps only five years old at the time of the incident. Recollected many years later, it compels the attention of the poet (and the reader) by virtue of its enigmatic quality, its subtle suggestiveness.

Part of the meaning of this "spot of time" inheres in what is *not* there. The boy has lost his guide, and evidently missing too is any sense of paternal protection, or of divine presence – the boy is deprived of any comfort, either real or spiritual, in the barren landscape. The "bare pool" is unreflective, the girl with the pitcher pays him no heed, and the "lonely eminence" carries a "beacon" that may give guidance to sailors, but not to those who travel on land. Evidently the boy feels himself utterly alone, cast out into an empty world, without any friends or family to give him a reassuring sense of identity and purpose. And yet – paradoxically – Wordsworth presents this experience as a primary instance of a "spot of time" by which the mind is "nourished and invisibly repaired." So, despite the young boy's feelings of disorientation and abandonment, in retrospect the scene must have provided some spiritual sustenance to the future poet that was struggling to be born within Wordsworth.

Such existential bleakness is not typical of Wordsworth's nature poetry; indeed, his poetry almost always endeavors to reach an affirmative statement concerning the way that nature contributes to the formation of human character. Such is the larger message of *The Prelude*, most succinctly expressed by the title of Book 8 (in the final published version of 1850): "Retrospect: Love of Nature Leading to Love of Man." And yet, for Wordsworth, the "love of nature" is not merely instrumental. Nature is valuable in itself, and by living in proximity to wild and rustic landscapes, humans can reach their full potential, and become more truly themselves. This is the fundamental assertion of Wordsworth's "Preface to *Lyrical Ballads*" (1800), which offers a number of arguments in defense of the representation of "humble and rustic life" in poetry. This essay offers a classic statement of the central role of nature in Romantic poetry:

Humble and rustic life was generally chosen, because, in that condition, the essential passions of the heart find a better soil in which they can attain their maturity, are less under restraint, and speak a plainer and more emphatic language; because in that condition of life our elementary feelings co-exist in a state of greater simplicity, and consequently, may be more accurately contemplated, and more forcibly communicated; because the manners of rural life germinate from those elementary feelings, and from the necessary character of rural occupations, are more easily comprehended, and are more durable; and, lastly, because in that condition the passions of men are incorporated with the beautiful and permanent forms of nature. (Wordsworth 1940-9, 2: 386-7)

Poetry can represent the "beautiful and permanent forms of nature" only through an adequate medium: "a plainer and more emphatic language," of the sort really spoken by farmers and shepherds, beggars and leech-gatherers, in remote and rural places. The neoclassical ideal of urbanity is here replaced by its opposite, an ideal of rusticity.

The transformation of human awareness through contact with nature is the main theme of "Lines Written a Few Miles Above Tintern Abbey," the last poem published in *Lyrical Ballads*. In this poem, Wordsworth describes how he returned to the banks of the Wye River in 1798, after a five-year absence. Wordsworth mentions the "wreathes of smoke, / Sent up, in silence, from among the trees" (ll. 18-19), evidence of itinerant charcoal-burners engaged in converting wood into charcoal for use in local iron foundries. Yet Wordsworth does not dwell upon such harmful changes in the land; rather, he focuses upon those aspects of the landscape that have retained their wildness, presenting the appearance of a "wild secluded scene" (l. 6) even in the midst of human habitation:

> The day is come when I again repose
> Here, under this dark sycamore, and view
> These plots of cottage-ground, these orchard-tufts,
> Which, at this season, with their unripe fruits,
> Among the woods and copses lose themselves,
> Nor, with their green and simple hue, disturb
> The wild green landscape. ("Tintern Abbey," 1798 version, ll. 9-15, Wordsworth 1940-9, 2: 259)

These lines stress the fecundity, greenery, and wildness of the landscape on the banks of the Wye, even though it is inhabited by people engaged in farming, livestock raising, and cottage industry. It retains its wild character, yet it is not a wilderness.

In the closing section of "Tintern Abbey," Wordsworth turns to his sister Dorothy, who has evidently been standing silently by his side the whole time. He notices "the shooting lights / Of thy wild eyes" (lines 119-20) and exhorts her to sustain the immediacy of her response to the natural world. The word "wild" occurs three times in this final verse paragraph, always in connection with Dorothy's "wild eyes" and "wild ecstasies" in the presence of Nature. Although the poet himself can no longer feel such "ecstasies," the poem clearly places great value upon such a fierce and passionate response to the natural world.

Dorothy Wordsworth (1771-1855) was herself a nature writer of impressive ability, and her distinctive vision of the natural world is preserved in her remarkable manuscript journals. Her Alfoxden Journal, composed in 1797, describes three eventful months in which her brother and Coleridge were collaborating on the production of *Lyrical Ballads*. Dorothy was just then discovering her own voice as a writer, and her journal entries reveal her fascination with the precise appearances of the natural world. As she records the daily events of her household, the comings and goings of their visitors, and the progress of the seasons, Dorothy frequently pauses to examine unique details in the surrounding landscape: a single strawberry blossom, a mass of straggling clouds, and the spinning motion of insects in the sun.

Dorothy Wordsworth continued to discover her voice in the Grasmere Journals, composed from May 1800 to January 1803. These journals, written amid the awe-inspiring scenery of the English Lake District, reveal even more of her personality, and of her deep intellectual and emotional response to the natural world, while they continue to record a rich variety of daily events. Not intended for publication, these notebooks have a relaxed informality and an emotional frankness that is exceptional in any published writing of this period. Unpublished until 1897, Dorothy's journals were known only to her brother William and perhaps a few other close friends and relatives. Nevertheless, her journals mark an important step forward in the development of a Romantic response to nature, since they articulate new ways of perceiving and knowing the self in relation to the natural world.

French Nature Writers: Toward New Shores

In France, the development of a distinctively Romantic literature was delayed until after the fall of Napoleon and the return of those writers, such as Chateaubriand, who had left France and opposed the Revolution. In the meantime, many French readers had been exposed to Romantic literature from other nations, particularly from England and Germany, due largely to the influential writings of Madame de Staël and Benjamin Constant. Accordingly, under the restored Bourbon monarchy, a new generation of French writers found British and German literary models ready at hand. The development of a distinctive French Romantic literature was carried forward by a group of young men associated with the literary journal *La Muse française*, among whom the central figures were Alphonse de Lamartine (1790-1869), Alfred de Vigny (1797-1863), and Victor Hugo (1802-85). Each of these writers shows the influence of German poetic precursors, especially in their use of natural imagery to express deep and complex feelings; but each finds a personal voice and makes an original contribution to the formal and expressive qualities of French lyric poetry.

Alphonse de Lamartine was the first of these poets to gain widespread attention with the publication of his *Méditations* in 1820. This collection of poems was inspired by the death of his beloved, and the pervasive tone of the collection is one of suffering and grief. Like his German contemporaries, Lamartine tends to express emotion indirectly, by presenting it through clear and simple images drawn from the natural world. The following excerpt from the "Le Lac" (The Lake) demonstrates this technique:

> Ainsi, toujours poussés vers de nouveaux rivages,
> Dans la nuit éternelle emportés sans retour,
> Ne pourrons-nous jamais sur l'océan des âges
> Jeter l'ancre un seul jour?

Ô lac! l'année à peine a fini sa carrière,
Et, près des flots chéris qu'elle devait revoir,
Regarde! Je viens seul m'asseoir sur cette pierre
Où tu la vis s'asseoir! (ll. 1-8, Lamartine 1968: 48)

(Thus, endlessly driven toward new coasts,
Into night eternal borne away,
Will we never, on the sea of time,
Cast anchor for one day?

O lake! the year has scarcely run its course.
Near the waves she hoped to see once more,
Look! I come alone to sit where she sat
On this stone, by this shore.) (translation Michael Ferber)

Lamartine recalls the tender and affectionate moments that he once experienced with his beloved, Julie Charles, on the placid waters of this lake. At present, forever bereft of her company, he ponders the meaning of her loss, and larger questions concerning the nature of time and human destiny. If time is like a body of water – a lake, or an ocean – can anyone find a moment of stasis, a place to cast anchor? Or does time flow on relentlessly? This question hangs unanswered in the first two stanzas, and indeed the entire poem offers no resolution, no consolation, but only deepens the initial question. For Lamartine, it seems that no resting place may be found, nor will memory endure; no anchor will hold in time's ocean. All humans are impelled forward in time, toward new shores.

Alfred de Vigny was the next major poet to advance the Romantic agenda with the publication of his *Poèmes* in 1822. Vigny is best known for his long narrative poems that explore moral, patriotic, and religious themes, such as "Le Cor" (The Horn), which describes the death of Roland, or "Le Mont des Oliviers" (The Mount of Olives), which recounts an episode from the life of Jesus. In such narrative poems, his use of natural imagery, while lush and detailed, is largely incidental to the main thread of events.

In several of his poems, however, Vigny directs central attention to the life of wild animals and explores their relationship with humankind. In "La Mort du loup" (The Death of the Wolf), for example, Vigny presents a first-person narrative, told in the voice of a hunter who enters a remote wilderness to track and kill a wolf. After following its tracks through a dark forest, the hunter and his companions find the wolf, accompanied by a female and four wolf-pups. Without mercy, they kill the wolf, shooting him with many bullets and brutally stabbing him with their knives. Before he dies, however, the wolf displays great courage, and the hunter is led to reflect upon the moral superiority of animals over men:

Hélas, ai-je pensé, malgré ce grand nom d'Hommes,
Que j'ai honte de nous, débiles que nous sommes!
Comment on doit quitter la vie et tous ses maux,
C'est vous qui le savez, sublimes animaux. (ll. 73-6, Vigny 1914: 217)

(Alas! I thought, despite this great name "Man,"
How shameful we are in our feebleness!
How to quit this life and all its ills
You already know, sublime animals!) (translation Michael Ferber)

The hunter must admit that the wolf is a supremely strong and noble creature; men, in comparison, are selfish, lazy, and weak. Indeed, in this final stanza, the poem takes an unexpected turn: the wolf, in its last dying breath, gives the hunter a stern lecture on value of accepting one's fate:

Il disait: "Si tu peux, fais que ton âme arrive,
A force de rester studieuse et pensive,
Jusqu'à ce haut degré de stoïque fierté
Où, naissant dans les bois, j'ai tout d'abord monté." (ll. 81-4, Vigny 1914: 218)

(It said: "If you can, make your soul arrive,
By strength of study and clear thought,
At that high degree of stoic pride
Which I, born in the woods, have long achieved.") (translation Michael Ferber)

It is very rare in European literature to see the wolf idealized to this extent; traditionally the wolf has been regarded as an embodiment of evil, and by the end of the eighteenth century it had been hunted to the verge of extinction throughout Western Europe. But in this poem Vigny reverses the traditional hierarchy of man and beast, and in so doing, he intimates that the wolf has much to teach humankind. Instead of killing wild animals without remorse, we should learn from them.

Victor Hugo's poetry represents the culmination of the Romantic movement in French literature, and he is also a leading proponent of Romantic aesthetic theory. In the 1826 preface to his *Odes et ballades*, Hugo compares the traditional poetic forms and tightly controlled language of neo-Classicism to the tidy geometric layout of a formal garden; Romanticism, in contrast, offers a bold departure from these norms: "Thought is a virgin soil, whose fertile productions seek to grow free and at random, without classification, without alignment into linear beds like the flowers in a classical garden, or like the flowers of language in a rhetorical treatise" (Hugo 1964, 1: 280, translation mine). According to Hugo, poetry demands absolute freedom of expression, and each poem must find its own form organically, without regard to rules. He advocates a poetics of "savage harmony":

Compare this [formal] garden to a primitive forest of the New World, with its giant trees, its thick fronds, its dense vegetation, its thousands of birds and thousands of colors; its broad avenues where light and darkness mingle in the foliage, its savage harmonies, its great rivers that carry islands of flowers, its immense cataracts that give off rainbows! (Hugo 1964, 1: 280, translation mine)

Hugo seeks to import the wild abundance of the South American jungle into the formal garden of French poetry. Drawing upon contemporary narratives of exploration and discovery, and following in the footsteps of Rousseau and Chateaubriand, Hugo uses wilderness as more than just a metaphor for the uncontrolled fecundity of poetic language. In his view, poetry should *embody* wild nature in both form and content.

As a writer, Hugo was extremely versatile and enormously prolific; for over 60 years, poems, plays, novels, satires, and much else poured forth from his pen. He was not primarily a nature writer, but nonetheless he displayed an effortless facility in composing short, richly textured lyrics that evoke the natural world in all of its varying moods. In "Nuits de Juin" (June Nights), for example, Hugo portrays a dark, yet wakeful landscape that is pervaded by "an intoxicating scent":

> L'été, lorsque le jour a fui, de fleurs couverte
> La plaine verse au loin un parfum enivrant;
> Les yeux fermés, l'oreille aux rumeurs entr'ouverte,
> On ne dort qu'à demi d'un sommeil transparent.
>
> Les astres sont plus purs, l'ombre paraît meilleure;
> Un vague demi-jour teint le dôme éternel;
> Et l'aube douce et pâle, en attendant son heure,
> Semble toute la nuit errer au bas du ciel.

(In summer, when day has fled, the plain covered with flowers pours out far away an intoxicating scent; eyes shut, ears half open to noises, one only half-sleeps in a transparent slumber.

The stars are purer, the shade seems pleasanter; a hazy half-day colours the eternal dome; and the sweet pale dawn awaiting her hour seems to wander all night at the bottom of the sky.) (Hartley 1957: 54, translation modified)

This poem evokes the breathless intensity of summer nights in the countryside, redolent with strange scents, sounds, and half-lights, while it remains entirely impersonal, deliberately leaving aside any human drama. Perhaps the poem is telling us that humans need not be the center of attention; nature can speak for itself. Indeed, Nature is subtly personified here, especially in the figure of dawn, who wanders invisibly beneath the horizon until her hour arrives. Without much thematic development, this poem is especially memorable for the richness of its language and the subtle suggestiveness of its imagery.

Conclusion

All of the authors discussed here were engaged in a fundamental re-examination of the human relationship with the natural world. The idea of nature, and indeed the very meaning of the word "nature," underwent a significant transformation over the course of the Romantic period. Throughout Europe, writers were rediscovering the simple pleasures of a life lived far from urban areas, amid placid rural landscapes. The eternal human desire to return to the garden of Eden is expressed in this historical moment as a longing or nostalgia for a state of nature that (according to Rousseau) may never have existed, but which still proves to be necessary as a myth, or enabling fiction, to get the work of imagination done.

Following in the footsteps of Rousseau, young writers all over Europe were seeking out wild, scenic, and remote landscapes in which to witness and record the state of nature at first hand. Chateaubriand explored the American wilderness, Wordsworth wandered through the Alps, and Goethe traveled to Italy, where he discovered the pagan simplicity and naturalness of rural folk-life under a sultry Mediterranean sky. Poets and painters everywhere discovered the expressive potential of landscapes transformed by light, the glimmering colors of moonshine and the shadow-play of clouds moving over fields and forests. Like many contemporary poets, the English painter J. M. W. Turner (1775-1851) was fascinated by the subtle atmospheric qualities of color observed through rain and mist, and the German painter Caspar David Friedrich (1774-1840) was likewise drawn to the spectral gleam of light upon the hard reflecting surfaces of alpine and arctic landscapes. In painting as in poetry, these shifting colors serve to represent the transformation of human relationships with the natural world. In the view of many Romantic artists and writers, humans are transformed by their proximity to the natural world: the senses are unfolded, the imagination is kindled, and the heart is awakened.

It became fashionable in the early twentieth century to debunk and ridicule such high Romantic aspirations. The classic exponent of such criticism is Irving Babbitt, whose book, *Rousseau and Romanticism* (1919) roundly rebukes Rousseau and all of his Romantic progeny for their allegedly naïve, egotistical, and antihumanistic worldview. In a fairly typical utterance, Babbitt contrasts the hard-nosed attitude of the "man of science" with the childish, irresponsible outlook of the "Rousseauist": "If the man of science and the utilitarian do not learn what nature is in herself they learn at least to adjust themselves to forces outside themselves. The Rousseauist, on the other hand, does not in his 'communion' with nature adjust to anything. He is simply communing with his own mood" (Babbitt 1919: 302). For Babbitt, the Romantic fascination with nature is merely a trap, a diversion from the serious business of life.

After two centuries of rapid industrialization, environmental pollution, extinction of species, and destruction of habitat, such a "utilitarian" view of nature has itself become untenable. Nature must be more than just a source of raw materials and a handy receptacle for human waste. At the dawn of the third millennium, we are only too aware that the life and death of humankind is inherently linked to the life and death of our planetary ecosystem. For this reason, the Romantic response to nature should not be dismissed out of hand, even if it may at times seem immature or self-indulgent. In their best work, the European Romantic writers offer a strikingly prescient vision of humankind living in peaceful coexistence with the natural world. Their work is a legacy to our own troubled moment in the history of the Earth.

REFERENCES AND FURTHER READING

Abrams, M. H. (1984). *The Correspondent Breeze: Essays on English Romanticism.* New York: Norton.

Babbitt, Irving (1919). *Rousseau and Romanticism.* Boston and New York: Houghton Mifflin.

Bate, Jonathan (1991). *Romantic Ecology: Wordsworth and the Environmental Tradition.* London: Routledge.

Bate, Jonathan (2000). *The Song of the Earth.* Cambridge, MA: Harvard University Press.

Chateaubriand, François-René de ([1801, 1802] 1963). *Atala* and *René.* London: Oxford University Press.

Chateaubriand, François-René de ([1827] 1969). *Travels in America*, trans. Richard Switzer. Lexington: University of Kentucky Press.

Coleridge, Samuel Taylor (1912). *The Complete Poetical Works of Samuel Taylor Coleridge*, ed. Ernest Hartley Coleridge. Oxford: Clarendon Press.

Coleridge, Samuel Taylor ([1817] 1983). *Biographia Literaria*, ed. James Engell and W. Jackson Bate, 2 vols. Princeton, NJ: Princeton University Press.

Cranston, Maurice (1994). *The Romantic Movement.* Oxford: Blackwell.

Forster, Leonard (ed. and trans.) (1957). *The Penguin Book of German Verse.* Baltimore, MD: Penguin Books.

Fulford, Tim, Lee, Debbie and Kitson, Peter J. (2004). *Literature, Science and Exploration in the Romantic Era: Bodies of Knowledge.* Cambridge, UK: Cambridge University Press.

Goethe, Johann Wolfgang von ([1774] 1917). *The Sorrows of Werther.* The Harvard Classics Shelf of Fiction, vol. XV, selected by Charles W. Eliot, notes and introductions by William Allan Neilson, trans. Bayard Taylor. New York: P. F. Collier & Son.

Harrison, Robert Pogue (1993). *Forests: The Shadow of Civilization.* Chicago: University of Chicago Press.

Hartley, Anthony (ed. and trans.) (1957). *The Penguin Book of French Verse.* Baltimore, MD: Penguin Books.

Hugo, Victor (1964). *Oeuvres poétiques.* Paris: Gallimard.

Keegan, Bridget and McKusick, James C. (eds.) (2001). *Literature and Nature: Four Centuries of Nature Writing.* Upper Saddle River, NJ: Prentice Hall.

Kroeber, Karl (1994). *Ecological Literary Criticism: Romantic Imagining and the Biology of Mind.* New York: Columbia University Press.

Lamartine, Alphonse de (1968). *Méditations*, ed. Fernand Letessier. Paris: Garnier.

McKusick, James, C. (2000). *Green Writing: Romanticism and Ecology.* New York: St. Martin's Press.

Oelschlaeger, Max (1991). *The Idea of Wilderness: From Prehistory to the Age of Ecology.* New Haven, CT: Yale University Press.

Oerlemans, Onno (2002). *Romanticism and the Materiality of Nature.* Toronto: University of Toronto Press.

Roe, Nicholas (2002). *The Politics of Nature: Wordsworth and Some Contemporaries*, 2nd edn. London: Palgrave.

Rousseau, Jean-Jacques ([1762, 1755] 1913). *The Social Contract and Discourses* (includes *A Discourse on the Origin of Inequality*), trans. G. D. H. Cole. London: J. M. Dent.

Rousseau, Jean-Jacques ([1755] 1992). *Discourse on the Origins of Inequality (Second Discourse); Polemics; and, Political Economy.* In *The Collected Writings of Rousseau*, vol. 3, ed. Roger D. Masters and Christopher Kelly; trans. Judith R. Bush, Roger D. Masters, Christopher Kelly, and Terence Marshall. Hanover, NH: University Press of New England.

Schama, Simon (1995). *Landscape and Memory.* New York: A. A. Knopf.

Thomas, Keith V. (1983). *Man and the Natural World: A History of the Modern Sensibility.* New York: Pantheon Books.

Vigny, Alfred de (1914). *Poèmes*, ed. Fernand Baldersperger. Paris: L. Conrad.

Wordsworth, William (1940-9). *The Poetical Works of William Wordsworth*, ed. Ernest de Selincourt and Helen Darbishire, 5 vols. Oxford: Clarendon Press.

Wordsworth, William (1979). *The Prelude, 1799, 1805, 1850*, ed. Jonathan Wordsworth, M. H. Abrams, and Stephen Gill. New York: Norton.

Worster, Donald (1994). *Nature's Economy: A History of Ecological Ideas*, 2nd edn. Cambridge, UK: Cambridge University Press.

25

Romanticism and Capitalism

Robert Sayre and Michael Löwy

This chapter is an attempt to propose a new concept of Romanticism. Far from being consensual this new interpretation goes against the grain of much Romanticism scholarship, which is based on the apparently obvious assumption that we are dealing with a literary movement of the early nineteenth century. In our view this assumption is doubly wrong: Romanticism is much more than a literary phenomenon – although of course it has an important literary component – and it did not come to an end either in 1830 or in 1848. For us Romanticism, as a cultural protest against modern industrial/capitalist civilization, is one of the main forms of modern culture, and it extends from Rousseau – to mention the name of a founding father – to the present, that is, from the second half of the eighteenth to the beginning of the twenty-first century. Our thesis is based on a Marxist approach to cultural phenomena, albeit a heterodox one, which attempts to link literature, art, religion, and political ideas to social and historical contexts.

The dominant trend in Romanticism scholarship perceives it as composed only of literary and aesthetic phenomena, defined by some common traits. This is the approach adopted by the three most famous North American specialists in the history of Romanticism: M. H. Abrams, René Wellek, and Morse Peckham. For Abrams (1973), their diversity notwithstanding, the Romantics share certain *values*, such as life, love, liberty, hope, and joy. Wellek ([1949] 1989) asserts that the Romantic movements form a unified whole and possess a coherent set of ideas, each of which implies the others: imagination, nature, symbol, and myth. Peckham ([1951] 1989) proposes to define Romanticism as a revolution of the European mind against static/ mechanistic thought and in favor of dynamic organicism. In this version, its common values are change, growth, diversity, and the creative imagination.

These attempts at definition – like numerous other, similar ones – no doubt designate significant features that are present in the work of many Romantic writers. However, they appear completely arbitrary. Why are certain features selected and not others? Individual authors makes their own choices, and sometimes revise their earlier decisions in favor of a new, equally arbitrary list. The chief methodological weakness of this sort of approach, based on an inventory of features, is its *empiricism*. It does not go below the surface of the phenomenon. As a descriptive overview of the Romantic cultural universe it can be useful, but its cognitive value is limited. Composite lists of elements leave the principal questions unanswered. What holds everything together? Why are these particular elements associated? What is the unifying force behind them that can explain Romanticism's various empirical features? How can we account for the contradictions of Romanticism, a movement that can take both realist and nonrealist, mystical and sensual, revolutionary and counterrevolutionary, democratic and aristocratic, retrograde and utopian forms?

The eminent specialist A. O. Lovejoy, despairing of explaining these contradictions, regretted that the "only really radical remedy – namely that we should all cease talking about Romanticism," would certainly not be adopted (Lovejoy 1965: 39). This approach strikes us as sterile. There are many terms in literature ("realism") or politics ("freedom") that are polysemic. Once purged of all such ambiguous concepts language would be perhaps more rigorous but considerably impoverished!

Most literary studies ignore the other dimensions of Romanticism, its political forms in particular. Conversely – and following the narrow logic of academic disciplines – political scientists often have an equally regrettable tendency to neglect the properly literary aspects of Romanticism. How do they approach the movement's political diversity? Specialists of political Romanticism such as the German scholar Fritz Stern or the French historian Jacques Droz often sidestep the difficulty by focusing exclusively on its conservative, reactionary, and counterrevolutionary aspect while simply ignoring the revolutionary Romantic authors.

A certain number of Marxist thinkers have a different approach. They see the common axis, the unifying element of the Romantic movement, in its *opposition to the modern bourgeois world*. This hypothesis appears to us by far the most interesting and productive. However, the bulk of the research inspired by Marxism suffers from a serious disadvantage. Like many of the non-Marxist writings mentioned above, Marxist analysts often perceive in Romanticism's antibourgeois critique only its reactionary, conservative, retrograde aspects. This applies to the great Hungarian social philosophers, Karl Mannheim and Georg Lukács, and their numerous followers. The Austrian art historian Ernst Fischer and the British sociologist of culture Raymond Williams are among the few exceptions.

What seems to be missing in past discussions of Romanticism, then, is an overall analysis of the phenomenon that takes its full extent and multiplicity into account, while providing a sociohistorical grounding for it. The concept that we propose is an attempt to do that, by positing a definition of Romanticism as a contextually specific worldview, or collective mental structure. The notion of worldview (*vision du monde*), developed by the French cultural sociologist Lucien Goldmann, expanding on a long tradition in German thought (the theory of *Weltanschauung*), does not designate a vague list of themes but rather a coherent totality organized around an axis. Romanticism as a worldview constitutes a specific form of criticism of "modernity," which we would define as the encompassing, multifaceted civilization that develops in conjunction with capitalism. The specificity of the Romantic critique resides in its being made in the name of values and ideals drawn from the precapitalist, premodern past, whereas other critiques can be made in the name of "progress," considering that modernity has not gone far enough in directions already initiated.

The Romantic sensibility is bound up with an experience of loss, the painful conviction that in modern capitalist reality something precious has been lost, at the level of both individuals and humanity at large. Certain essential human values have been alienated – qualitative values as opposed to the purely quantitative exchange value that prodominates in modernity. This alienation, keenly sensed, is often experienced as exile: in defining the Romantic spirit, Friedrich Schlegel speaks of the soul "under the willows of exile" (*unter den Trauerweiden der Verbannung*; quoted in Furst 1980: 34). Nostalgia, then, is at the heart of the Romantic attitude. What is lacking in the present existed in a more or less distant past, real or imaginary/mythical, often idealized when real. The defining characteristic of that past is its difference from the present – a period in which the various modern alienations did not yet exist. Romantic nostalgia, then, looks to a precapitalist past, or at least to a past in which the modern socioeconomic system was not yet fully developed.

Nostalgia for this lost paradise is generally accompanied by a quest for what has been lost, an attempt to recreate, to bring to life again, the ideal past state, although there is often no desire to literally reproduce the past and there also exists a "resigned" form of Romanticism. The paths that the Romantic quest can follow are extraordinarily diverse. They can be enacted in many different cultural fields or disciplines beyond those of literature and the arts. They can be carried out on the level of the imaginary/intellectual (fictional/poetic representations, historical reconstructions, theorical explorations) or on that of the real and the concrete (individual behavior patterns or collective movements, large and small), and they can be focused on immediately transforming the present or laying the groundwork for the future. They can work on the environment in which one lives or escape to an exotic "elsewhere" (in reality or in imagination). Some ways in which Romantics have sought to transform the degraded here and now are dandyism, and aestheticism more generally, the utopian experiment and the cult/cultivation of love or childhood. The future-oriented aspirations of other Romantics, in which recollection of the past serves as a weapon in the struggle for the not-yet-existing is most memorably exemplified in Blake's famous lines from the preface to *Milton*. Here the poet wonders whether the divine presence manifested itself in England "in ancient time," before its hills were covered by "these dark Satanic mills." And he commits himself to a "spiritual struggle" that will end only when "we have built Jerusalem / in England's green and pleasant land" (Blake 1982: 95-6).

The Romantic Critique of Modernity

The Romantic opposition to capitalist/industrial modernity does not always challenge the system as a whole, but rather reacts to a certain number of features of modernity that are experienced as inhuman or esteemed to be particularly pernicious. The following are thematic constellations that most frequently appear in Romantic works.

The disenchantment of the world

In a famous passage of the *Communist Manifesto*, Marx and Engels observed that "the most heavenly ecstasies of religious fervor, of chivalrous enthusiasm, of philistine sentimentalism" of the past had been killed by the bourgeoisie, "drowned . . . in the icy water of egotistical calculation" (Marx and Engels 1975: 487). Seventy years later, Max Weber noted in a celebrated talk, "Science as a Vocation" (1919): "The fate of our times is characterized by rationalization and intellectualization and, above all, by the 'disenchantment of the world.' Precisely the ultimate and most sublime values have retreated from public life either into the transcendent realm of mystic life or into the brotherliness of direct and personal human relations" (Weber 1994: 302). Romanticism may be viewed as being to a large extent a reaction on the part of "chivalrous enthusiasm" against the "icy water" of rational calculation and against the *Entzauberung der Welt* – leading to an often desperate attempt to *re-enchant the world*. From this standpoint, the well-known image *"die mondbeglanzte Zaubernacht"* (the moonlit-enchanted night) from the German Romantic poet Ludwig Tieck can almost be read as the philosophical and spiritual program of Romanticism.

Religion – both in its traditional forms and in its mystical or heretical manifestations – is an important means of "re-enchantment" chosen by the Romantics. But they also turned to *magic*, the esoteric arts, sorcery, alchemy, and astrology; they rediscovered Christian and pagan myths, legends, fairy tales, "Gothic" narratives; they explored the hidden realms of dreams and the fantastic – not only in literature and poetry, but also in the visual arts, from Füssli and Blake in the nineteenth century to Max Klinger and Max Ernst in the twentieth.

The Romantic fascination with *night* must be interpreted in the same context; for darkness can be seen as a place of spells, mystery, and magic, opposed to *light*, the classic emblem of rationalism. In one of his *Hymns to the Night* (1800) Novalis poses a strange and paradoxically plaintive question: "Must ever the morning return? / Endeth never the empire of Earth? / Harmful activities delay / The heavenly flight of the Night" (Novalis 1924: 12).

Among the Romantics' strategies for re-enchanting the world, the recourse to *myth* holds a special place. At the magic intersection between religion, history, poetry, language, and philosophy, it offers an inexhaustible reservoir of symbols and allegories, phantasms and demons, gods and serpents. There are several ways to delve into this treasure trove: poetic or literary reference to ancient, Oriental, or popular myths;

"scholarly" – historical, theological, philosophical – study of mythology; and attempts, such as the Surrealists', to create new myths. In all three cases, the loss of the religious substance of myth – the result of modern secularization – makes it a secular figure of enchantment, or rather a nonreligious one.

The quantification of the world

As Max Weber sees it, capitalism was born with the spread of merchants' account books, that is, with the rational calculation of credits and debits. The *ethos* of modern industrial capitalism is *Rechenhaftigkeit,* the spirit of rational calculation. Many Romantics felt intuitively that all the negative characteristics of modern society – the religion of the god Money (Carlyle called it Mammonism), the decline of all qualitative, social, and religious values, as well as of the imagination and the poetic spirit, the tedious uniformity of life, the purely "utilitarian" relations of human beings among themselves and with nature – stem from the same source of corruption: market quantification. The poisoning of social life by money and the poisoning of the air by industrial smoke are understood by several Romantics as parallel phenomena, stemming from the same perverse root.

Charles Dickens offers an illustrative example of the Romantic charge against capitalist modernity. Dickens was one of Marx's favorite authors, although the former was in no way given to socialist ideas. His *Hard Times*, a novel published in 1854, contains an exceptionally well-articulated expression of the Romantic critique of industrial society. In it, the cold, quantifying spirit of the industrial age is personified by a utilitarian ideologue and member of Parliament, Mr Thomas Gradgrind. This is a man "with a rule and a pair of scales, and the multiplication table always in his pocket," always "ready to weigh and measure any parcel of human nature, and tell you exactly what it comes to" (Dickens 1965: 4). For Gradgrind everything in the universe is "a mere question of figures, a case of simple arithmetic" (ibid.) and he organizes the education of children strictly according to the salutary principle that "what you couldn't state in figures, or show to be purchaseable in the cheapest market and saleable in the dearest, was not, and never should be" (pp. 22-3). Gradgrind's philosophy – the harsh and pitiless doctrine of political economy, strict utilitarianism, and classic laissez-faire ideology – is based on the principle that "everything was to be paid for. Nobody was ever on any account to give anybody anything, or render anybody help without purchase. Gratitude was to be abolished, and the virtues springing from it were not to be. Every inch of the existence of mankind, from birth to death, was to be a bargain across a counter" (p. 274).

The mechanization of the world

In the name of the natural, the organic, the living, and the "dynamic," the Romantics often manifested a deep hostility to everything mechanical, artificial, or constructed. Nostalgic for the lost harmony between humankind and nature, enshrining nature as the object of a mystical cult, they observed with melancholy and despair the progress of mechanization and industrialization, the modern conquest of the environment. They saw the capitalist factory as a hellish place and the workers as damned souls, not because they were exploited but because, as Dickens put it in a gripping image in *Hard Times*, they were enslaved to the machine, to the mechanical movements, the uniform rhythm of the steam-engine's piston, which "worked monotonously up and down like the head of an elephant in a state of melancholy madness" (Dickens 1965: 22).

The Romantics were also haunted by the terrifying prospect that human beings themselves could be mechanized, as in E. T. A. Hoffmann's famous tale "The Sandman," where the beautiful woman Olympia is in fact an automatic puppet, whose movements "seem to stem from some kind of clockwork" and whose singing is "unpleasantly perfect" (Hoffmann 1969: 161). In a commentary on Hoffmann, Walter Benjamin observed that his tales are based on an identification of the automatic with the satanic, the life of modern people being "the product of a foul artificial mechanism governed by Satan from within" (Benjamin 1977: 644, our translation). One of the most important dimensions of this protest is the Romantic critique of *modern politics* as a *mechanical* system – that is, "inorganic" and "geometrical," artificial, lifeless, and soulless. This critique can even go so far as to challenge the state as such. For example, in an anonymous document from 1796-7 discovered by Franz Rosenzweig and published under the title *Das älteste System des deutschen Idealismus* (The oldest system of German idealism), probably written by the young Schelling, we find this appeal: "We must go beyond the State! For every State necessarily treats free human beings like a mechanical system of gears [*mechanisches Räderwerk*]" (Schelling 1975: 110, our translation). Without going that far, many Romantics considered the modern state, based on legal contracts, and a rational bureaucratic administration, to be as mechanical, cold, and impersonal a system as the factory.

Rationalist abstraction

According to Marx, the capitalist economy is based on a system of abstract categories: abstract work, abstract exchange value, money. For Max Weber, rationalization is at the heart of modern bourgeois civilization, which organizes all economic, social, and political life according to the requirements of goal-oriented-rationality (*Zweckrationalität*, or instrumental rationality) and bureaucratic rationality. Finally, Karl Mannheim shows the connection between rationalization, disenchantment, and quantification in the modern capitalist world. According to him, "this 'rationalizing' and 'quantifying' thinking is embedded in a psychic attitude and form of experience with regard to things and the world which may itself be described as 'abstract' . . . [This] rationalism . . . has its parallel in the new economic system" oriented toward exchange value (Mannheim 1986: 62).

The Romantics' ideological struggle against abstraction often takes the form of a return to the *concrete*. In German political Romanticism, the concrete, historical, traditional laws of every country or region are opposed to abstract natural laws; the concrete "freedoms" of each social state are opposed to "Freedom" in the abstract; national or local traditions are opposed to universalist doctrines, and the concrete, particular, specific aspects of reality are opposed to general rules or principles. One of the most important forms of this "concrete thinking" is *historicism*. Confronting a reason that wants to be seen as atemporal and abstract/human, the Romantics rediscover and rehabilitate history. The historical school of law (Savigny, Gustav Hugo), the conservative German historiography (Ranke, Droysen), the surge of historical novels (the works of Walter Scott, Victor Hugo's *Notre-Dame de Paris*, Alexandre Dumas's many novels), the relativist historicism in the social sciences of the late nineteenth century (Dilthey, Simmel) – these are all manifestations of the Romantic historicization of culture as a whole.

The Romantic opposition to rational abstraction can also be expressed as a rehabilitation of *nonrational* and/or *nonrationalizable* behaviors. This applies in particular to *the* classic theme of Romantic literature: *love* as a pure emotion, a spontaneous attraction that cannot be reduced to any calculation and that is in contradiction with all rationalist strategies of marriage – marriage for money, marriage "for good reasons." There is also a positive revaluation of intuitions, premonitions, instincts, feelings – terms that are intimately associated with the usual image of "Romanticism."

The dissolution of social bonds

The Romantics are painfully aware of the alienation of human relationships, the destruction of the old "organic" and communitarian forms of social life, the isolation of the individual in his or her egoistic self, which taken together constitute an important dimension of capitalist civilization, centered on urban life. Saint-Preux in Rousseau's *Julie, or The New Héloïse* is only the first in a long line of Romantic heroes who feel lonely, misunderstood, unable to communicate in a meaningful way with their fellow human beings, and this often occurs at the very center of modern social life, in the "urban desert."

In literary representations of this theme, isolation, or "solitude in society," is experienced in the early stages of Romanticism above all by privileged souls – poets, artists, thinkers; but starting with Flaubert (his *Sentimental Education* in particular), a large number of novels show and analyze the failure of communication as being the universal – and tragic – condition of all human beings in modern society. We see reflections of this preoccupation not only at the thematic level but also in literary forms, such as internal monologues or nonomniscient narration – that is, narration in which the narrators find themselves enclosed within their own consciousness and manage only partially, or not at all, to penetrate the subjectivity of others. Modern literature offers various attempts to rediscover the lost community and bring it into the imaginary universe: the circle of pure souls gathered around Daniel d'Arthez in Balzac's *Lost Illusions*, the bands of adventurers, soldiers, and revolutionaries in Malraux's novels, to mention just a few examples.

Genesis

Concerning the historical starting point, or genesis, of the Romantic movement, the tendency to take at face value the labels applied either by contemporaries or by the later tradition, in short to conflate words and things, has resulted in the origins of Romanticism rarely being situated prior to the French Revolution. Everything from earlier periods that resembles more or less closely what came to be called Romanticism is usually labeled "pre-Romantic."[1] In the context of our approach, the movement's genesis must be located in the course of what has been customarily called "the century of Enlightenment," more specifically around the middle of that century. On this point we share the perspective of Jacques Bousquet, who has edited an anthology of eighteenth-century Romanticism. As Bousquet notes, "no culture has an absolute beginning or end. But it is still not impossible to see in what period, if not at what moment, one cultural tendency predominates over the others." Whereas in the seventeenth and the first half of the eighteenth century only "anticipatory signs" that "remained secondary" can be noted, in the second half of the eighteenth century a "reversal" comes about (Bousquet 1972: 18, 118). Like its antithesis, capitalism, Romanticism evolved over a prolonged historical period. But the two antagonists truly came into being as fully developed structures only in the late eighteenth century.

Before that, elements of the worldview are expressed within the framework of other, older forms of thought and sensibility. Romanticism properly speaking, as an overall cultural response to a generalized socioeconomic system, is specifically *modern* and corresponds to a "qualitative leap" in the historical development of societies, the advent of a radically new order that contrasts decisively with everything that has gone before. In *The Great Transformation* (1944), the well-known Austro-Hungarian economist Karl Polanyi rightly stresses the unprecedented character of this mutation. For him, what is happening is the "metamorphosis of the caterpillar" (p. 71), in which the economic realm, in the form of the self-regulating market, for the first time in human history becomes autonomous and dominant with respect to the entirety of society. Late eighteenth-century Romanticism arose as a protest against this phenomenon — against the various effects of the advent of a market economy with its broad penetration of cultural life, and also against certain ideological facets of the spirit of the Enlightenment, those most closely bound up with the new "reification" of life that reduced human motivation to egoistic calculation.[2]

The origin of the phenomenon can be situated in three countries: France, England, and Germany. For it is in these relatively "developed" countries that Romanticism occurred earliest and most intensely. Later on these countries also exercised a massive influence over the development and expansion of the various other national currents of Romanticism. In his anthology of eighteenth-century Romanticism, Jacques Bousquet convincingly refutes the idea that France was considerably behind the others. He recalls that some major French texts, for example Rousseau's *Julie, or The New Héloïse*, appeared before their counterparts in the other countries, but also shows that in late eighteenth-century France a strong Romantic dimension characterized many second-ary works and authors now unknown except to specialists. At this time in France, as in Germany and England, there was in fact *a dense Romantic cultural fabric*, not just a few outstanding works. Romanticism emerged on more or less equal terms, independently and simultaneously in the three countries in question, the ones that were relatively most "advanced" in the process of modernization and the development of capitalism.

Typology

Looking at the vast cultural field of Romanticism as we have defined it, we might ask whether certain typical forms can be identified within it. Though many typologies are doubtless possible, in the framework of our concept the most relevant one would concern the specific attitudes or positions adopted with respect to the problem of modern capitalist society – the various *politics* of Romanticism, not in any narrow sense but rather one that brings together the economic, the social, and the political. A set of categories along those lines, though, should be seen only as Weberian "*ideal types*"; for often a given cultural expression does not correspond entirely to any of them, or combines several, and a given author may move from one position to another, sometimes several times in the course of a career. Some of the astonishing political metamorphoses of Romantic writers can precisely be best understood as typological shifts *within* the same fundamental matrix.

This having been said, we can distinguish the following general types of Roman-ticism:

Restitutionist: In a sense the closest to the essence of the overall phenomenon, since it is defined as aspiring to the literal restitution – the restoration or the recreation – of some precapitalist past, often though not always in the medieval period.

Conservative: Here the aim is not so much to re-establish a lost past but to maintain traditional elements of society (and government) such as they have managed to persist into the present, or to restore the status quo that obtained before the French Revolution. Social configurations are defended that are already well along on the road toward capitalist development, but they are valued precisely for what they *preserve* of ancient, premodern forms.

Fascist: The rejection of capitalism is blended with a violent condemnation of parliamentary democracy as well as of communism. Its anticapitalism is also often tinged with anti-Semitism: capitalists, the wealthy, and those who represent the spirit of cities and modern life are depicted as Jews. The Romantic critique of rationality is taken to its outer limits, becoming a glorification of the irrational and of raw instinct in their most aggressive forms.

Resigned: This form arises most notably starting in the second half of the nineteenth century, when capitalist industrialization appears more and more to be an irreversible process and when the hope for a restoration of precapitalist social relations tends to fade away. Romantics of this type are led to conclude, with deep regret, that modernity is a fact to which one has to resign oneself.

Reformist: In this case we find a conviction that the old values can be reinstated, but the measures advocated to reach that goal are limited to reforms: legal reforms, the evolution of consciousness and so on. There is often a striking contrast between the radicalism of the critique and the timidity of the solutions imagined.

Revolutionary and/or utopian: This form projects the nostalgia for a precapitalist past into the hope for a radically new future. Rejecting both the illusion of a pure and simple return to the organic communities of the past and the resigned acceptance of the bourgeois present or its amelioration via reforms, revolutionary or utopian Romanticism aspires – in a way that may be more or less radical, more or less contradictory – to the abolition of capitalism and to an egalitarian utopia in which certain features or values of earlier societies would reappear. Within this type, one can distinguish several distinct currents, which may be designated as follows: Jacobin-democratic, populist, utopian-humanist socialist, libertarian, Marxist.[3]

Another question which must be addressed in a sociohistorical interpretation of Romanticism, is whether a sociological profile can be identified for producers and receptive publics of Romantic culture. We would argue that the producers – creators and transmitters – of Romanticism may originate from many different social groups but usually have in common their belonging to the "classical" or traditional intelligentsia (as distinguished from a more "modern" one made up of scientists, technicians, engineers, etc.). For the way of life and culture of these intellectuals can be said to be fundamentally hostile to bourgeois industrial civilization. Their mental universe is governed by qualitative values – ethical, aesthetic, religious, political, and so on – that constitute their very *raison d'être* as intellectuals. The audience of Romanticism – its social base in the fullest sense – is, however, larger, being made up potentially of all classes or social categories for whom the development of modern capitalism can provoke a decline or a crisis in their status, and/or threaten their way of life and values. This would include the aristocracy, the lower middle class, the clergy, and a range of "traditional" intellectuals, including students. We should add that *women*, independently of class origin, maintain a privileged relation with Romanticism from the outset. For women have historically been excluded from the creation of the principal values of modernity (by scientists, businessmen, industrialists, politicians), and their social role has been defined as centered on qualitative values: family, feelings, love, culture.[4]

But we must recognize that in the contemporary world the sociological base of Romanticism appears to be wider still, for both producers and publics. It is as if capitalist-industrial civilization had reached a stage in its development in which destructive effects on the social fabric and the natural environment have taken on such proportions that certain Romantic themes – and certain forms of nostalgia – exercise a diffuse influence going well beyond the groups with which they were once primarily associated.

To illustrate the breadth and depth of the Romantic critique of modernity beyond the traditionally assigned boundaries of Romanticism, we will focus on two examples not commonly associated with the latter: Ruskin in the mid-to-late nineteenth century, and Surrealism in the twentieth century.

Ruskin

Art critic, professor of drawing and art history, essayist, and lecturer on the most diverse subjects, one of the great Victorian "sages," John Ruskin (1819-1900) is arguably a key figure in British Romanticism. At a particularly significant moment in the development of modernity, he was an exemplary witness and a mediator not only among several generations, but also between cultural and economic criticism, aesthetics, and social protest. His literary career stands at almost equal distance from the inception of Romanticism and our own day, and corresponds to the period in which the capitalist system triumphed in the country where it had developed earliest and most powerfully. Ruskin's thought became a crossroads of influences in the English Romantic tradition, for while he thoroughly assimilated the earlier developments, particularly via Thomas Carlyle, his work and life played a crucial role for many contemporary artists, writers, and movements, especially the "Pre-Raphaelites," a literary and artistic group characterized by a focus on Nature and a return to styles, themes, atmospheres, and religious sentiments of the Middle Ages and early Renaissance. Ruskin's influence eventually extended forward strongly into the twentieth century, partly through his impact on William Morris.

The basic problem that Ruskin consistently raised, throughout his career and in many different forms of writing, involved the attainment of true human value and the conditions of possibility of that attainment. This true value, the locus of the sacred for Ruskin, might be characterized as "humanity-in-Nature." Simultaneously aesthetic, moral, and social, this nexus of value is seen to have been respected in the past, to be desecrated in the present, but potentially recoverable in the future. By Ruskin's account the fall from grace took place in stages, the beginning of the end being the waning of the Middle Ages. The evil that was eating away at the old world was the seed of what was to come, for "it was the *selling* of absolution that ended the Medieval faith" (Ruskin 1905-12, XVIII: 447, emphasis added). The Renaissance saw the harmful development of individual luxury and vanity,[5] but it is only in the modern world that the nadir was reached. In *Unto this Last*, a particularly influential work of socioeconomic analysis and criticism published in 1860, Ruskin denounces the era of "political economy founded on self-interest" (Ruskin 1905-12, XVII: 105).

The radically degenerate modern era, which involves at the same time the disenchantment of the world by science, the desiccating rule of money, and the destruction of the natural environment by industrialism, nevertheless offers the possibility of redemption, and this provides the theme of the tale *The King of the Golden River* (1841), an early work of fantasy which already contains the germ of Ruskin's later social commentary. As a result of the sins of selfishness and avarice, three brothers find themselves expelled from a valley that resembles the Garden of Eden but is reduced, through the fault of two of them, to a desert. The purity of the third brother nevertheless ends up bringing it back into flower: "And thus the Treasure Valley became a garden again, and the inheritance, which had been lost by cruelty, was regained by love" (Ruskin 1905-12, I: 347).

Ruskin is impossible to locate within the typology of the politics of Romanticism, and indeed illustrates perfectly something demonstrated by the typology as a whole, namely that Romanticism is a political hermaphrodite, manifesting itself at the two extremes and all across the ideological gamut. We find the same ambivalence and multiplicity in Ruskin himself, who at different times identified himself as a Tory, a communist ("the reddest of the red"), or simply as someone who always swam against the current. And the irony is patent, but quite characteristic of Romanticism, that this disciple of the archreactionary Carlyle should have been a spiritual father to the anarchist/socialist William Morris and to a significant sector of the left in the twentieth century.[6]

Surrealism

Of all the cultural movements of the twentieth century, Surrealism is probably the one that brought the Romantic aspiration to re-enchant the world to its highest expression, and that most radically embodied Romanticism's revolutionary dimension. Intellectual rebellion and social revolution, the transformation of life (Rimbaud) and the changing of the world (Marx): these two polestars have oriented the Surrealist movement since its origin, pulling it toward a perpetual search for subversive cultural and political practices. The movement founded by André Breton never abandoned its intransigent rejection of the established social, moral, and political order – nor its jealous autonomy, despite its commitment to various tendencies of the revolutionary left: first communism, then Trotskyism, and finally anarchism.

In one of its earliest documents, "La Révolution d'abord et toujours" (The revolution first and always; 1925), the Surrealist movement proclaimed its irreducible opposition to capitalist civilization: "Wherever Western civilization reigns, all human bonds have given way, except those based on interest, 'payment in hard cash.' For more than a century, human dignity has been reduced to the level of exchange value . . . We do not accept the laws of economy and exchange, we do not accept the slavery of labor . . . ."[7] Much later, in his essay "Tower of Light" (1951), recalling the movement's first stirrings, Breton observed: "At this point, surrealism rejects everything: no political movement could harness its energies. All the institutions on which the modern world is resting and that have led to the First World War we deem aberrant and scandalous" (Breton 1995: 265).

The privileged targets of the Surrealist attack on Western civilization are abstract – blinkered rationalism, shallow realism, and positivism in all its forms. Starting with the *First Manifesto of Surrealism* (1924), Breton denounced the attitude that would banish the chimerical, that is, imaginary, dimension of life, "under the pretense of civilization and progress"; confronted with this sterile cultural horizon, he asserted his belief in "the omnipotence of dream" (Breton 1972: 10, 26).

Breton and his friends never hid their deep attachment to the German Romantic tradition of the nineteenth century (Novalis, Achim von Arnim) as well as that of the English (especially the Gothic novel) or the French. To be sure, the Surrealists' reading of the Romantic legacy is highly selective. What attracted them to "Hugo's gigantic façades," to certain texts by Musset, Aloysius Bertrand, Xavier Forneret, and Nerval, as Breton wrote in "Marvelous versus Mystery" (1936), was the "original impetus to emancipate man *totally*" (Breton 1995: 1-2). Moreover, according to Breton (in "The Political Position of Surrealism"), "a good number of Romantic or post-Romantic writers . . . such as Pétrus Borel, Flaubert, Baudelaire, Daumier, and Courbet" are moved by a "completely spontaneous hatred of the typical bourgeois" and share "a common will not to compromise in any way with the reigning class," whose domination they consider as a sort of pestilence "against which [. . .] it will some day be necessary to apply a red-hot iron" (Breton 1972: 217).

The use of premodern cultural traditions and forms was also selective. The Surrealists drew unhesitatingly on alchemy, occultism, the Kabbala, magic, and the so-called primitive arts of Oceania, Africa, and America. In all their activities, their goal was to go beyond the limits of "art" – as a separate, institutionalized, ornamental activity – and embark upon the limitless adventure of re-enchanting the world. However, as revolutionaries inspired by the spirit of 1789, by Hegel, and especially by Marx, they were intransigent adversaries of the values that lie at the heart of reactionary-Romantic culture: religion and nationalism. As the *Second Manifesto* (1930) declares: "Everything remains to be done, every means must be worth trying, in order to lay waste to the ideas of *family, fatherland, religion*" (Breton 1972: 128). At the entrance to the Surrealists' lost paradise, a well-known libertarian inscription is written in flaming letters: "neither God nor Master!"

E. P. Thompson

To illustrate the contemporary Romantic critique of modernity, we will focus on two important British authors, E. P. Thompson (1924-93) and Raymond Williams (1921-88). Their contributions, broad in scope, have played a crucial role not only in their chosen fields but in British intellectual and political life in general. Furthermore, each one embodies the revolutionary form of the Romantic vision in a particularly coherent and fruitful way.

The critique of modern capitalist civilization runs like a red thread throughout E. P. Thompson's political, theoretical, and historiographical works. The originality, subversive power, and coherence of his historical works are intimately connected with his capacity to rediscover, restore, and reformulate in (heterodox) Marxist terms the

Romantic tradition of protest against capitalist-industrial society. This is true of *William Morris: From Romantic to Revolutionary* ([1955] 1977), *The Making of the English Working Class* (1963), and *Customs in Common* (1991). It is no accident that Thompson's last two books are devoted to Romanticism: *Witness against the Beast: William Blake and the Moral Law* (1993) and *The Romantics: England in a Revolutionary Age* (1997, published posthumously). We shall restrict ourselves here to his great work on the formation of the English working class, a book that has profoundly marked English-language historiography over the last 35 years.

Rejecting the conformist views – the "conventional wisdom" – of many economic historians who identify human progress with economic growth, Thompson does not hesitate in *The Making of the English Working Class* to evoke "the truly catastrophic nature of the Industrial Revolution" (Thompson 1963: 198). In this context, he seeks to understand – rather than to condemn out of hand as "regressive" – the reaction of popular strata in nineteenth-century British society against machines (as in the "Luddite" movement) and their nostalgia for a style of work and leisure that preceded the pitiless disciplines of industrialism. A similar sentiment inspired the disappointed Romantic authors who turned toward the past while denouncing the "manufacturing system" in their texts. Refusing to label them reactionaries, Thompson brings to light the subversive potential of their critique: "this current of traditionalist social radicalism, which moves from Wordsworth and Southey through to Carlyle and beyond, seems, in its origin, to contain a dialectic by which it is continually prompting revolutionary conclusions" (1963: 343).

Raymond Williams

Raymond Williams's work extends from the late 1940s to the late 1980s. It addresses a multiplicity of themes – literature, theater, the media, and culture in its multiple senses – and relates these diverse fields to society, history, and politics. While his thinking unquestionably evolved over the years, Williams never renounced its Romantic underpinnings. In the 1970s, like others of the "New Left," he moved somewhat closer to orthodox Marxism with structuralist leanings, and *Marxism and Literature* (1977) is probably the least Romantic of his works. But in the 1980s he reacted more and more energetically against structuralism and post-structuralism, and once again put the revolutionary Romantic perspective at the center of his reflection while developing it further.

In *Culture and Society* (1958), the book that made Williams famous, he studies a tradition of English writing that extends from the late eighteenth century to the present and that corresponds largely to the Romantic movement we have been discussing, in an attempt to save it from appropriation by the right (he began the research and reflection that led to the book in 1948, at the beginning of the Cold War). *The Country and the City* (1973), written at a time when Williams had already moved perceptibly closer to Marxism, explores a tendency in English literature that partially overlaps with the one discussed in *Culture and Society*, analyzing the often complex relations between literary images and actual history in the country/city dichotomy. Its distinctive contribution lies in going beyond the strong present-and-future orientation of much Marxist writing, showing the effective presence of pre-capitalist values in the modern emancipatory project, through the historical becoming of the Romantic vision.

In *The Country and the City*, Williams's affinity with the Romantic critical tradition takes on a highly personal inflection. More than in *Culture and Society*, he develops his own positions and evokes his own experience. He refers to his youth in a rural region of Wales and to the united character of his community, having to do in part with its small size (it is a "knowable community"). From his youth he retains a deep attachment to the earth, and the manipulation of that theme by the conservative right makes him angry. But Williams also highlights the possibilities for self-development offered by the city, and what he aspires to, finally, is the *transcendence* of the very opposition between city and country, in a postcapitalist society rooted in precapitalist values. In fact, as he points out in one passage, this transcendence of the city/country division, a division that contains all the others, had already been evoked by Blake when he sought to build "Jerusalem / In England's green and pleasant land" (Williams 1973: 149).[8]

Conclusion

We hope to have suggested how Romanticism can be seen as a broad, variegated, and long-lasting movement constituting itself as a pitiless critic, through many means and media, against the blindness of the ideologies of progress. The Romantic critics have touched – sometimes intuitively or only partially – on what was the unthought for the apologists of the modern capitalist status quo. They have *seen* what was outside the scope of the liberal individualist worldview: reification, quantification, the solitude of individuals, uprootedness, alienation via merchandise, the uncontrollable dynamic of machines and technology, temporality reduced to the instantaneous, the degradation of nature. In short, they have described the *facies hippocratica* of modern civilization. The fact that they have at times presented this diagnosis in the name of an elitist aestheticism, a retrograde religion, or a reactionary political ideology should not detract from the force of its acuity.

Disturbed by the progression of the malady we call capitalist modernity, the nineteenth- and early twentieth-century Romantics were often melancholic and pessimistic in their outlook. Moved by a tragic sentiment of the world and by terrible premonitions, they presented the future under the darkest possible colors. Yet they fell far short of anticipating the extent to which reality would outstrip their worst nightmares in the course of the twentieth century. It remains to be seen how future inheritors of the Romantic cultural tradition will respond to the challenges to come, and try to imagine utopian alternatives to the present civilization.

Notes

1   Paul Van Tieghem played the most important role in spreading this notion in France, especially in *Le Préromantisme* (1924-30).

2   The relationship between Romanticism and the Enlightenment in the eighteenth century and thereafter is a complex one. The opposition is far from total between the two movements, and many Romantic writings can be seen as radicalizations or extensions of the problematics of the Enlightenment.

3   See the collection of essays by Max Blechman, *Revolutionary Romanticism* (1999). One would probably have to add also ecological Romanticism, an interesting example of which is the recent work of Joel Kovel, an ecosocialist critic of capitalism inspired by William Blake and William Morris. See his *The Enemy of Nature* (2002).

4   It is interesting to note that among the characters of Alfred de Vigny's *Chatterton* who are opposed to the capitalist John Bell, in addition to workers we find a poet (Chatterton), a religious figure (the Quaker), and also a woman (Kitty Bell), all of whom thus represent groups that are particularly sensitive to Romanticism.

5   See the passages on the Renaissance in the third volume of Ruskin's *Modern Painters (1843-60)*, vol. 5 of Ruskin (1905-12).

6   George Bernard Shaw once commented, "I have met in my lifetime some extremely revolutionary characters; and quite a large number of them, when I have asked, 'Who put you on to this revolutionary line? Was it Karl Marx?' have answered, 'No, it was Ruskin'" (Shaw 1961: 132).

7   In the review *La Révolution surréaliste*, 5 (1925), our translation. The text is signed by a large number of artists and intellectuals from the group, including Breton, Aragon, Eluard, Leiris, Desnos, Péret, Soupault, and Queneau.

8   Raymond William's influence is visible in some of the most interesting recent essays on Romanticism, such as J. David Black, *The Politics of Enchantment* (2002).

References and Further Reading

Abrams, M. H. (1973). *Natural Supernaturalism. Tradition and Revolution in Romantic Literature*. New York: Norton.

Barbéris, Pierre (1969). "'Mal du siècle,' ou d'un romantisme de droite à un romantisme de gauche." In *Romantisme et politique (1815-1851)*. Paris: Armand Colin, pp. 164-82.

Benjamin, Walter (1977). "E. T. A. Hoffmann und O. Panizza," vol. 2, *Gesammelte Schriften*. Frankfurt: Suhrkamp.

Black, David J. (2002). *The Politics of Enchantment: Romanticism, Media and Cultural Studies*. Waterloo, ON: Wilfried Laurier Press.

Blake, William (1982). *The Complete Poetry and Prose of William Blake*, ed. David Erdman. Berkeley: University of California Press.

Blechman, Max (1999). *Revolutionary Romanticism*. San Francisco: City Lights.

Bousquet, Jacques (1972). *Anthologie du XVIIIe romantique*. Paris: Pauvert.

Breton, André (1972). *Manifestoes of Surrealism*, trans. R. Seaver and H. R. Lane. Ann Arbor: University of Michigan Press.

Breton, André (1995). *Free Rein*, trans. M. Parmentier and J. d'Amboise. Lincoln and London: University of Nebraska Press.

Dickens, Charles (1965). *Hard Times*. New York: Harper and Row.

Droz, Jacques (1966). *Le Romantisme allemand et l'État: Résistance et collaboration en Allemagne napoléonienne*. Paris: Payot.

Fischer, Ernst (1986). *Ursprung und Wesen der Romantik*. Frankfurt: Sendler Verlag.

Furst, Lilian R. (1980). *European Romanticism: Self-Definition*. London: Methuen.

Hobsbawm, Eric (1962). *The Age of Revolution, 1789-1848*. New York: New American Library.

Hoffmann, E. T. A. (1969). *The Tales*, vol. 1 *Selected Writings of E .T. A. Hoffmann*, ed. and trans. L. J. Kent and E. C. Knight. Chicago and London: University of Chicago Press.

Kovel, Joel (2002). *The Enemy of Nature: The End of Capitalism or the End of the World?* New York: Zed Books.

Lovejoy, Arthur O. (1965). "The Need to Distinguish Romanticisms." In J. B. Halsted (ed.), *Romanticism: Problems of Definition, Explanation, and Evaluation.* Boston: D. C. Heath, pp. 37–44.

Löwy, Michael (1979). *George Lukacs – From Romanticism to Bolshevism*, trans. P. Camiller. London: NLB.

Löwy, Michael and Sayre, Robert (2001). *Romanticism Against the Tide of Modernity*, trans. C. Porter. Durham and London: Duke University Press.

Mannheim, Karl (1986). *Conservatism: A Contribution to the Sociology of Knowledge*, ed. D. Kettler, V. Meja, N. Stehr. London: Routledge and Kegan Paul.

Marx, Karl and Engels, Friedrich (1975). *Manifesto of the Communist Party.* In Karl Marx and Friedrich Engels, *Collected Works*, vol. 6, trans. R. Dixon et al., 47 vols. New York: International Publishers.

Novalis (1924). *Werke.* Stuttgart: Walter Hädecke Verlag.

Peckham, Morse ([1951] 1989) "Toward a Theory of Romanticism." In R. F. Gleckner and G. E. Enscoe (eds.) *Romanticism: Points of View.* Detroit: Wayne State University Press, pp. 231–57.

Polanyi, Karl (1957). *The Great Transformation.* Boston: Beacon Press.

Ruskin, John (1905-12). *The Library Edition of the Works of John Ruskin*, ed. E. T. Cook and A. Wedderburn. London: George Allen.

Sayre, Robert (1978). *Solitude in Society: A Sociological Study in French Literature.* Cambridge, MA and London: Harvard University Press.

Schelling, F. W. J. von (1975). *Materialen zu Schellings philosophische Anfänge*, ed. M. Frank and G. Kurz. Frankfurt: Suhrkamp.

Shaw, George Bernard (1961). "Ruskin's Politics." In D. Laurence (ed.), *Platform and Pulpit.* New York: Hill and Wang, pp. 130–44.

Thompson, E. P. (1963). *The Making of the English Working Class.* New York: Pantheon Books.

Thompson, E. P. (1977). *William Morris: Romantic to Revolutionary.* London: Merlin Press.

Van Tieghem, Paul. (1924-30). *Le Préromantisme*, 2 vols. Paris: Rieder-Alcan.

Weber, Max (1994). "Science as a Vocation". In *Sociological Writings*, ed. W. Heydebrand, trans. H. H. Gerth and C. W. Mills. New York: Continuum, pp. 276-303.

Wellek, René ([1951] 1989). "The Concept of Romanticism in Literary History." In R. F. Gleckner and G. E. Enscoe (eds.) *Romanticism: Points of View.* Detroit: Wayne State University Press, pp. 286-301.

Williams, Raymond (1958). *Culture and Society, 1780-1950.* New York: Harper and Row.

Williams, Raymond (1973). *The Country and the City.* New York: Oxford University Press.

26

Napoleon and European Romanticism

Simon Bainbridge

The Romantic Icon

The figure of Napoleon presided over much of the writing of European Romanticism, casting a shadow across the lives and works of many of the poets, novelists, dramatists, and thinkers of the period. Honoré de Balzac kept a statue of Bonaparte in his study, to which he attached a slip of paper on which was written, "What he failed to achieve by the sword, I shall accomplish by the pen" (quoted in O'Flaherty 1969: 263). Goethe, who commented after meeting the French Emperor at Erfurt in 1808 that "nothing higher and more pleasing could have happened to me in all my life" (quoted in Martin 2000: 132), gave a prominent place in his study to his statue of the man whose life he would describe as "the stride of a demigod from battle to battle and from victory to victory" (quoted in Ziolkowski 1960: 101). In Britain, both Byron and Hazlitt were proud possessors of busts of the figure who for them represented the only remaining hope for the political dreams of the French Revolution. Imperial icons also came to assume an important role in the writing of the period: in Hazlitt's *Liber Amoris* (1823) the narrator H. gives a "small bronze figure" of "the God of my idolatry" to Sarah as a token of his love (Hazlitt 1930-4, IX: 112); Julien Sorel, the Napoleon-obsessed hero of Stendhal's *The Red and the Black* ([1830] 2002), keeps a portrait of Napoleon hidden in the mattress of his bed; while Pushkin's eponymous hero Eugene Onegin is characterized by the twin symbols of Romanticism that are found in his room:

> Lord Byron's portrait on the wall,
> the iron figure on the table,
> the hat, the scowling brow, the chest
> where folded arms are tightly pressed. (Pushkin 1979: 186)

What the narratives of such factual and fictional acts of idolatry frequently reveal is how intense, personal, controversial, and often rather fragile the relationship with

Napoleon was: Byron fought to defend his bust of Napoleon at Harrow "against the rascally time-servers" but he saw his defeat in 1814 in iconoclastic terms, describing how his "poor little pagod" had been "pushed off his pedestal" (Byron 1973-82, III: 256); Sorel's attachment to his portrait leads Mme de Rênal to mistake it for that of the woman he loves and he is forced to burn it to preserve his reputation in Restoration society; Sarah's rejection of H.'s love culminates in his own act of iconoclasm as he destroys the gift that had been the symbol of his total devotion: "I then dashed the little Buonaparte on the ground, and stamped upon it, as one of her instruments of mockery" (Hazlitt, 1930-4, IX: 145). (The continuing power of the trope of Napoleonic iconoclasm would be further testified to later in the century when Conan Doyle made the serial shattering of statues of the Emperor the subject of the Sherlock Holmes mystery, *The Case of the Six Napoleons*).

Napoleon's elevation to iconic status by many European writers of the Romantic period, as well as the attempts by others to shatter the imperial idol, should come as no surprise given the extent to which he dominated the European political and cultural scene in the first half of the nineteenth century. His extraordinary career combined the roles of soldier and politician and saw him rise from relative obscurity during the revolutionary decade of the 1790s to become Emperor of France in 1804, controlling most of Europe until his final defeat at Waterloo in 1815 and exile to St Helena where he died in 1821. Napoleon's significance and meaning was the central political debate of the period, particularly among those who fought to establish him as the champion or the destroyer of the French Revolution, and his career contributed directly to new formulations of the historical process, such as those of Friedrich Hegel who responded enthusiastically to Napoleon's victory at Jena in 1806, declaring him "this world-soul" (see Plant 1983: 120). Even to contemporaries, the dramatic events of Napoleon's life appeared the stuff of epic, romance, or tragedy. As Bishop Richard Whately wrote in his satire of Humean skepticism, *Historic Doubts Relative to Napoleon Bonaparte* (1819), Bonaparte's career carried with it "an air of fiction and romance":

> All the events are great, and splendid, and marvellous: great armies, great victories, great frosts, great reverses, "hair breadth 'scapes", empires subverted in a few days . . . everything upon that grand scale, so common in Epic Poetry, so rare in real life, and thus calculated to strike the imagination of the vulgar and to remind the sober-thinking few of the Arabian Nights. (Whately 1985: 24-5)

In much of the writing of the period from across Europe, Napoleon was transformed into a mythical figure, an equivalent to those other Romantic archetypes of transgression and seemingly limitless desire: Faust, Satan, Prometheus, and Don Juan. He also became the focus for examinations and projections of qualities which have been seen as central to Romanticism, such as genius, imagination, and creativity. This chapter will begin by looking at the challenges Napoleon posed to writers, in terms of both their representations of him and their conceptions of their own roles, before moving on to consider the evolving responses to his career and the literary shaping of his legend.

The "Poet in Action" and the Napoleons of Literature

In Balzac's novel *Autre Etude de Femme*, the poet Canalis asks the question "Who will ever succeed in explaining, in depicting, or in understanding Napoleon?" (quoted in Marceau 1976: 467). Canalis rather grandly conceives of himself as one of the great writers of the age, an equivalent to Byron, Lamartine, Hugo, Delavigne, and Béranger, and his question was one that obsessed his real-life counterparts. While Napoleon's personality and career stimulated no end of explanation, depiction, or attempts at understanding, it seemed impossible to achieve a final or fixed version. Napoleon appeared too grand, too multifarious, and too sublime to be fully comprehended. To many he seemed an unprecedented phenomenon, as Whately commented, "in vain will [the judicious man] seek in history for something similar to this wonderful Bonaparte; 'nought but himself can be his parallel' " (Whately 1985: 25). Of course, historical parallels were sought for Napoleon (who conceived of himself in historical terms), but the power of his image seemed to defeat rational or objective explanation, as Chateaubriand observed: "Such is the difficulty caused by dazzling fame to the impartial writer; he thrusts it aside as far as possible, so that truth may be seen in all its nakedness, but the glory returns like a radiant mist and immediately suffuses the picture" (quoted in O'Flaherty 1969: 259). Similarly, in his political journalism written when Napoleon was at the height of his power, Coleridge argued that it was precisely in his domination of the public's imagination that Bonaparte's danger lay, the "brilliance" and "splendour" of his image "dazzled and blinded" the observer, preventing any real judgment of his political qualities (see Bainbridge 1995: 125). A virulent opponent of Napoleon from approximately 1802 onwards, Coleridge argued that the French dictator possessed "those daring and dazzling qualities that too often make a tyrant pass for a hero" and he dedicated himself to trying to strip Napoleon of his imaginative appeal, presenting him as a monster and base-born usurper engaged in a career of petty crime (Coleridge 1978, II: 150). In opposite fashion, Napoleon's imaginative appeal led his biographer, the radical journalist William Hazlitt, to adopt him as "the child and champion of the revolution," converting Napoleon into an object of popular appeal, an "idol that the world adore... that dazzles the senses, haunts the imagination" but that still represented an "abstract idea" – the cause of the people (Hazlitt 1930-4, VII: 149, XVII: 34).

The contest over Napoleon's meaning during his lifetime, as well as the polarized terms in which it was conducted, were such that Whately could joke in 1819 that he could not have existed: it was not possible that one individual could have performed so many wonderful achievements or have so many different characters assigned to him. As Whately's emphasis on the conflicting and contradictory nature of writing suggests, representations of Napoleon perhaps tell us more about the author or the position from which he or she is writing than they do about their subject. This was certainly Goethe's sense of Scott's biography of Napoleon (1827), of which he argued that it "will in no way be a document for the history of France, but it will be one for the history of England" (quoted in Ziolkowski 1960: 102). For Goethe, it was this sense of debate that was more important than arriving at any essential truth: "In any case, it is a voice that cannot be absent in this crucial historical process. In general, I like to hear the most conflicting opinions concerning Napoleon" (ibid.).

If one reason for the difficulty in understanding Napoleon's career can be put down to the conflicting versions and assessments of him, others in the period saw the interpretative challenge as generated by the conflicts, contradictions, and instabilities of his own career and personality. In seeking to answer his own question, Balzac's Canalis stresses not only the extraordinariness of the Napoleonic adventure but also the antithetical nature of his character:

> The noblest power ever known, the most concentrated power, the most corrosive, the most acid power that ever was; a singular genius who marched a civilization in arms far and wide over the earth without ever finding it a resting place ... Hypocritical and generous, a lover of both glitter and simplicity, without taste yet a patron of the arts; but despite these antitheses, whether by instinct or constitution, great in everything.
> (quoted in Marceau 1976: 467)

Antithesis became one of the key figures through which Napoleon was understood in the period, seen most famously in Byron's passage on Waterloo in *Childe Harold's Pilgrimage* III (1816) in which it provides not only the basis of his character but also motivates and determines his career:

> There sunk the greatest, nor the worst of men,
> Whose spirit antithetically mixt
> One moment of the mightiest, and again
> On little objects with like firmness fixt,
> Extreme in all things! hadst thou been betwixt,
> Thy throne had still been thine, or never been;
> For daring made thy rise as fall: thou seek'st
> Even now to re-assume the imperial mien,
> And shake again the world, the Thunderer of the scene! (Byron 1980-93, II: 89)

Antithesis comes to structure many of the literary accounts of Napoleon, as in Victor Hugo's poetic juxtaposition of the global (even cosmic) scale of Napoleon's career with the tiny islands of Corsica and St Helena where he began and ended his life ("The Two Islands," 1825) or in Pushkin's attempt to assess the larger meaning of Napoleon in a poetic sketch of 1824:

> Why were you sent and who sent you?
> Of what, good or evil, were you the faithful executor? (quoted in Wesling 2001: 44)

If Napoleon represented a representational challenge to writers throughout Europe, he could also be seen to challenge their sense of their own roles. Balzac specifically conceived of himself as a Napoleon of literature, comparing his creative process to Napoleonic battles (an "Austerlitz of creation") and seeking to gain an equivalent status as the figure who dominated his age (see Besser 1969: 129-35). However, for other writers Napoleon's achievements threatened to overshadow and potentially render irrelevant their own ambitions. According to Hazlitt, this was the reason for the Lake poets' (Wordsworth, Coleridge, and Southey) hatred of Bonaparte: "They had no great objection to what he was doing – but they could not bear to think that he had done more than they had ever dreamt of. While they were building castles in the air, he gave law to Europe. He carved out with the sword, what they had only traced with the pen" (Hazlitt 1930-4, XVI: 245). This sense of being overshadowed by the glory and grandeur of the Napoleonic career and the age to which he gave his name was felt particularly acutely by many of those writing in the seemingly mundane period after his fall, particularly in France. The Romantic spirit in that country can perhaps be seen as in part an internalization of the aspirations and glory of the Napoleonic age, as is suggested by Alfred de Vigny's comment: "I belong to the generation born with the century, nurtured on the emperor's bulletins, having always before its eyes a naked sword which it was just about to grab when France replaced it in the Bourbon sheath" (Vigny 1953: 6). Within literature itself, this sense of belatedness, of living in an age in which the achievement of glory was no longer possible but in which the Napoleonic model continued to act as a model for inspiration, is felt most strongly in Stendhal's *The Red and the Black*, set in 1830. The novel's hero, Julien Sorel, remains constantly conscious of the Napoleonic example ("For many years, scarcely an hour of Julien's life passed without his telling himself that Bonaparte, an obscure and penniless lieutenant, had made himself master of the world with his sword" [Stendhal 2002: 32]) but is unable to rise through a military career, keeps secret his worship of Napoleon, and chooses the church as the profession through which he hopes to enact the idea of the career open to talent.

The contest between writers and Napoleon was further complicated by the fact that to many Napoleon seemed to bring to the spheres of politics and war the qualities of the artist or poet – genius, creativity, and imagination. Chateaubriand described Napoleon as a "poet in action" and later commented of their first meeting in 1802 that "A prodigious imagination moved this cold politician: he would not have been what he was, if the Muse had not been present: reason realized the ideas of the poet" (quoted in Boorsch 1960: 62, 56). His presentation of Napoleon's power as a product of his ability to combine imagination and reason and to reconcile the spheres of politics and poetics bears comparison with Coleridge's notebook entry of early 1802, "Poet Bonaparte – Layer out of a World-garden" (Coleridge 1957-73, I: 1166), but in Chateaubriand's later accounts his conception moves away from this emphasis on rationality to see Napoleon as a figure of the excessive and continuous creativity that is often now termed romantic irony, as when he describes him as "an extraordinary adventurer, endlessly generating new plans, dreaming up new laws, only feeling fully in charge when he is labouring to disrupt the established order, overturning, destroying in the evening what he created in the morning" (quoted in Martin 2000: 105). For Coleridge, what he came to see as Napoleon's role as a tyrant played an important part in his reformulation of the concept of genius and informed the distinction he ultimately drew between the commanding genius (of which Napoleon was an example), who has an impact on the real world, and the absolute genius, who realizes his creations in the realm of imagination. One of the most striking constructions of Napoleon as the Romantic genius comes from Heinrich Heine, who as a Jew saw Napoleon as a liberating figure on his entry into Düsseldorf in 1811. Heine presents the Emperor as a visionary, able to see into the individual and across time, and a creator who could inspire the writer but whom the writer could never hope to equal:

> He had an eye as clear as the sky, which could read in the hearts of men; it saw all things of this world at once, whereas we others see them only successively and, at that, only by their tinctured shadows. The forehead was not so clear: the spirits of future battles hovered there, and occasionally a movement flashed across his brow: the creative thoughts, the great seven-league thoughts with which the emperor's spirit strode invisibly across the world – and I believe that any one of these thoughts would have given a German writer material enough to last a lifetime! (quoted in Ziolkowski 1960: 98)

Here, Napoleon's domination of Europe becomes not a matter of supplies, armies, and battles, but a triumph of vision, creativity, and imagination.

The impact of Napoleon on the self-conception of major writers of European Romanticism can be seen if we examine the contrasting responses of Madame de Staël, Lord Byron, and Chateaubriand. In the response of de Staël we can trace the attempt to assert the power of the pen over the sword. Initially an admirer of Napoleon, describing him in the late 1790s as "the best republican in France, the most freedom-loving of Frenchmen" and as "that intrepid warrior, the profound thinker, the most extraordinary genius in history" (quoted in Herold 1959: 172, 177), de Staël became increasingly opposed to his regime, particularly for his attempts to curtail the influence of ideologues such as de Staël herself and her lover Benjamin Constant (another increasingly outspoken critic of Bonaparte). Banished by Napoleon first from Paris and then from France, de Staël presented the cultures of other countries, especially those of England and Germany, as alternatives to that of France. While her *De l'Allemagne* (1810) is often seen as the foundation for the first phases of French Romanticism, Napoleon feared that like her other writing it encouraged nationalism, and requested the suppression of "the passages in which she exalts England," commenting that the "unfortunate exaltation has done us enough harm already," before ultimately ordering the destruction of the first edition (quoted ibid., p. 389). As such actions suggest, Napoleon saw de Staël as a real threat to his regime, threatening at one stage that "I shall break her, I shall crush her" and saying of her house at Coppet, a center of liberalism and Romanticism, that it "became a veritable arsenal against me. One went there to win one's spurs" (ibid., pp. 225, 276).

If in de Staël we can see the writer as the opponent of Napoleon, in the writing and career of Lord Byron we have the writer as aspirant to Napoleonic status. Conceiving himself on the grandest scale as a figure of world historical dimensions, and always uncertain about the value of poetry in relation to action, Byron constantly modeled himself on Napoleon, most famously in his commissioning of a copy of the Emperor's carriage for his own exile from Britain in 1816. Yet Byron was always aware of the extent to which he fell short of his imperial model, and as his literary mode and prevailing attitude shifted "from romantic to burlesque" he became increasingly ironic about his Napoleonic ambitions. His most famous moment of textual identification with his hero, when he declares that he has been considered "The grand Napoleon of the realms of rhyme" (*Don Juan* XI, 55), emphasizes that he ruled only in the poetic rather than the political sphere, and his identification is one structured around a likeness of failures rather than achievements, as he goes on to compare the declining popularity of his own works with the defeats that brought Napoleon's reign to an end: "But Juan was my Moscow, and Faliero / My Leipsic, and my Mont Saint Jean seems Cain" (Byron 1980-93, V: 482).

Like Byron, Chateaubriand constantly measured himself against Napoleon, in *Memories from Beyond the Grave* (written during 1811-41 and published 1848-50) making frequent comparisons between his own early life and Bonaparte's extraordinary career: "Napoleon was my age; he had won a hundred battles when I was still languishing in the shadow of these emigrations which were the pedestal of his fortune. Left so far behind him, could I ever catch up with him?" (quoted in Boorsch 1960: 55). Chateaubriand had initially been an admirer of Napoleon, whom he had first met in 1802 and to whom he dedicated the second edition of *Le Génie du Christianisme*, and was nominated by him for an administrative role in Rome, but the execution of the Duc d'Enghien in 1804 prompted Chateaubriand's resignation and the start of his role as an opponent of Bonaparte, attacking him in an article in his paper the *Mercure* in 1807 and then in his pamphlet of 1814 "Of Buonaparte and the Bourbons." Along with de Staël and Constant, he played a major role in the representation of Napoleon as "the Corsican Ogre," and in his *Memories* he sought to combat the increasingly powerful legend. However, as Jean Boorsch has shown, almost a sixth of the *Memories* are focused on Napoleon, and are structured by the repeated "While he...I..." formula (quoted in Boorsch 1960: 57). Yet whereas Byron presented himself as falling short of Napoleonic status, Chateaubriand not only places himself on a par with Napoleon ("in daring to desert Napoleon, I had placed myself at his level") but even sees himself as providing the model for Napoleon himself (as in his account of their journeys to the East, of which he writes "Napoleon takes the path I followed"; quoted in Martin 2000: 102-3). As Andy Martin has written, in an excellent account of the reciprocal relationship between the two men, "Chateaubriand thought of himself as the Napoleon of literature, while Napoleon, conversely, saw himself as the Chateaubriand of political art" (ibid., p. 104).

While writers like Balzac, Byron, Chateaubriand, and Goethe strove to become Napoleons of literature, Napoleon himself longed to become a writer, an element of his personality that has recently been the subject of a fascinating study by Andy Martin. Napoleon, of course, powerfully manipulated his own image through the arts (as in the portraits by David, Gros, and Ingres), but it can be argued that the transformation of Napoleon into both a literary figure and a means of figuring key themes of Romanticism was partly a result of the influence of early Romantic forms on his own self-conception. Napoleon claimed to have read Rousseau's *La Nouvelle Heloïse* at the age of nine and Goethe's *Sorrows of Young Werther* seven times (one critic goes so far as to claim that "it is possible that *Werther* set in motion Napoleon's vital urge towards greatness in action, and helped it to move on a higher level"; Strich 1949: 164), and he had a strong sense of himself as a figure of literary dimensions ("What a novel my life is!" he commented on St Helena; quoted ibid., p. 141). At times Napoleon's own writing can read like Byron *avant la lettre*, as when he writes "Always alone in the midst of men, I come back to dream with myself and to surrender myself to the sharpness of my melancholy" (quoted in Munhall 1960: 4) and "I need solitude and isolation. Splendour wearies me, I am emotionally spent; fame is insipid. At twenty-three I have exhausted every experience" (quoted in O'Flaherty 1969: 257). As Andy Martin has shown, Napoleon's literary conception of himself is strongly felt in his early writings, such as his poem in epic style on a Corsican hero, and this self-conception can be seen to influence the way in which he shaped his own image and career, as in the Egyptian expedition which Martin describes as "from its inception, an overtly literary phenomenon, an exercise in the epic" (Martin 2000: 63). Indeed, in a work published in 1815, Dominique de Pradt presented Napoleon and his career as the enactment of the Romantic spirit of imagination, inspired by, but as lacking in reality as, the Ossian poems of the legendary Gaelic warrior which Napoleon himself carried on his campaigns and incorporated into his own self-mythologizing:

> The Emperor is all system, all illusion, as a man needs must be when he is all imagination. He "ossianizes" in affairs. Whoever followed his career saw him create for himself an imaginary Spain, an imaginary Catholicism, an imaginary England, nay, even an imaginary France... He intoxicates himself with his dreams... Although he deceived much, he was deceived more often than he deceived others. (quoted in Peyre 1960: 26)

Napoleon here becomes the deluded victim of the spirit of Romanticism, rather than its heroic embodiment.

If de Pradt's argument sees Napoleon as, at least in part, a consequence of his own fondness for the proto-Romantic writing of Ossian, it is also important to remember the part that was played in the construction of the Napoleonic legend by the exiled Emperor's own great work, *The Memorial of St Helena*, based on his conversations on St Helena with his secretary Comte Emmanuel de Las Cases and published posthumously in 1823. The *Memorial* became probably the greatest best seller of the nineteenth century (Tulard 1985: 346), and its importance is illustrated in the opening of *The Red and the Black* when Julian Sorel is caught reading it. The *Memorial* is presented as a book for which Julien would die and as part of his personal Koran (Stendhal 2002: 25, 28), and his passionate attachment to it is representative of the influence of the volume in France and of the power of Napoleon's self-presentation. In this fragmentary and anecdotal work, Napoleon presents himself as the champion of the revolution, who sought to defend its benefits in France and to extend them to the oppressed peoples of Europe, and who was forced into war and autocratic rule by the continued aggression of Britain and her allies who wished to restore the prerevolutionary regimes across Europe. The *Memorial* transformed Napoleon's reputation and turned him into a symbol for the people: "So even when I am no more, I will still remain for the peoples the luminary of their rights, my name will be the war cry of their efforts and the emblem of their hopes" (quoted in Herz 1960: 42). Earlier in his career Napoleon had vowed that "In my retirement I shall substitute the pen for the sword" (quoted Martin 2000: 131), and with the *Memorial* he showed just how powerful an instrument the pen could be.

Savior, Satan, Prometheus: Changing Literary Responses to Napoleon

The historian Jean Tulard has argued that the Napoleonic legend was not born on St Helena but "was forged during the first Italian campaign in the newspapers which were destined to raise the morale of the troops, but which taught France about Lodi and Rivoli" (Tulard 1985: 344). Similarly, it is from this Italian campaign of 1796-7 that we can date the start of the literary response to Napoleon's career across Europe, the subject of the remainder of this chapter. For many, Napoleon's defeat of the Austrian forces in Northern Italy represented an act of liberation and an extension of the benefits of the revolution across national borders. The Italian Ugo Foscolo, who fought with Napoleon's army against the Austrians (though who would later lead the radical opposition to Napoleon in Milan), wrote an ode celebrating Bonaparte as a liberator and a force for human brotherhood, as did the German poet Friedrich Hölderlin, while in Britain Walter Savage Landor celebrated Napoleon as "A mortal man above all mortal praise" in his romance poem *Gebir* (1798), transforming him into a messianic figure who was bringing a new world into being through his creation of republican states in Northern Italy (Landor 1937, I: 44). The power of this stage of Napoleon's career is felt most fully in the writing of Stendhal, who would accompany Napoleon during his second Italian campaign of 1800-1, and who described the victories over "old despotism" as "a great and beautiful epoch for Europe" and as the "purest and most brilliant epoch" of Napoleon's life (quoted in O'Flaherty 1969: 258). Stendhal memorably opens *The Charterhouse of Parma* with an exuberant celebration of this campaign and its vitalizing effect on the Italian people:

> On 15 May 1796 General Bonaparte entered Milan at the head of that youthful army which a few days earlier had crossed the bridge at Lodi, and taught the world that, after so many centuries, Caesar and Alexander had a successor. The marvels of courage and genius that Italy witnessed in the course of a few months awakened a slumbering population... (Stendhal 1999: 7)

It is this campaign which has such a strong formative effect on Julien Sorel who listens "with rapture to stories of the battles at the bridge at Lodi, of Arcoli, and of Rivoli, told him by the old Surgeon-major" (Stendhal 2002: 31). But for many writers, Stendhal included, the first Italian campaign represented a high point in Napoleon's career that he would never again equal, especially as he transformed France from a republic into an empire and his regime became increasingly militaristic. Thus, as Pieter Geyl has emphasized, Stendhal's *Life of Napoleon* describes in detail only the Italian campaigns and Stendhal comments that "the truly poetic and perfectly noble part of Bonaparte's life comes to an end with the occupation of Venice" (Geyl 1965: 32-3). Stendhal maintained a careful and discriminating response to Napoleon's career (certainly more complex than the hero worship and identification of his protagonists Sorel and Fabrice del Dongo), but many other writers renounced their support for him at key moments in his career, as we have seen with Chateaubriand and the execution of the Duc d'Enghien. For Landor, who visited Paris during the Peace of Amiens, it was Napoleon's elevation to Consul for Life in 1802 (the celebrations of which he witnessed) that prompted him to remark that "As to the cause of liberty, this cursed nation has ruined it forever" (quoted in Bainbridge 1995: 50), while for William Wordsworth, it was Napoleon's coronation as Emperor in 1804 that finally brought to an end the revolutionary period and marked a return to the pre-1789 forms of church and state. This was a moment when, as he describes in *The Prelude*:

> ...finally to close
> And rivet up the gains of France, a Pope
> Is summoned in to crown an Emperor –
> This last opprobrium, when we see the dog
> Returning to his vomit, when the sun
> That rose in splendour, was alive, and moved
> In exultation among living clouds,
> Hath put his function and his glory off,
> And, turned into a gewgaw, a machine,
> Sets like an opera phantom. (Wordsworth 1979: 408-10)

Wordsworth's disgusted response to the coronation recalls the famous account of Beethoven furiously tearing up the dedication to Napoleon of his "Eroica" symphony upon hearing of Napoleon's elevation of himself to imperial status.

As Napoleon increased his domination of Europe with crushing victories over the other major powers, such as those at Austerlitz in 1805 and Jena in 1806, many writers across Europe sought to inspire opposition to what they saw as his imperial and military regime. In Britain, Walter Scott's enormously popular medieval romances such as *The Lay of the Last Minstrel* (1805) and *Marmion* (1808) were designed to stimulate martial spirit. The Lake poets all contributed to the literary war against the figure they now saw as a tyrant: Wordsworth wrote numerous anti-Napoleonic sonnets dedicated to liberty and national independence, as well as a tract on the Peninsular War; Robert Southey wrote romances such as *The Curse of Kehama* (1810) and *Roderick, The Last of the Goths* (1814) which operated as thinly disguised allegories of the war against France; and Coleridge attacked the French Emperor in both his political journalism and his lectures. The Lake poets transformed the war with Napoleon into an apocalyptic battle between good and evil, with Bonaparte as Satan, a form of representation that would become dominant across Europe and is particularly striking in Russian poetry from 1812, the year of Napoleon's invasion, until his defeat in 1815. In Germany, opposition to Napoleon became linked to the rise of nationalism, and literature played an important role in both movements. August Wilhelm Schlegel (who would enlist in the German army in 1813) appealed for patriotic writing equal to the crisis of the time. His brother Friedrich (who served in the anti-Napoleonic Austrian government) wrote patriotic songs and was on the editorial staff of several patriotic journals, while the patriotic poet Theodore Körner, best known for his collection *Lyre and Sword* (1814), died fighting against Napoleon's forces. Perhaps the most strident of the German anti-Napoleonic writers was Heinrich von Kleist, the author of war songs, who wandered round the battlefield of Aspern reciting poems to inspire the Austrian wounded (Ziolkowski 1960: 95). Kleist used allegory in his *Die Hermannsschlacht* (1809) to present the necessity for a free and united Germany and in his "A German Catechism" he again invoked an apocalyptic register in dictating that Napoleon should be considered as "...a despicable man; the source of all Evil and the end of all Good; a sinner whom the language of mankind does not suffice to indict and in whose accusation, at the Last Judgment, the breath of angels shall expire" (quoted ibid.).

If Napoleon was demonized in writing across Europe during his final decade in power, his image was subject to a remarkable transformation in the 25 years that followed his defeat in 1815, as he was turned from a Satan into a Prometheus, from an oppressive monster into a Christ-like savior, and, broadly speaking, from an incarnation of tyranny into a symbol of liberty. As the greatest and exceptional man of the age, Napoleon became a figure of all that a mortal could hope to achieve, his career prompting examinations of the larger themes of destiny, fate, and the role of the individual in relation to historical, divine, and cosmic forces. Many factors contributed to this transformation, not least the fact of defeat itself which gave the tragic shape of rise and fall to Napoleon's career, while the exile to St Helena made the comparison with Prometheus almost irresistible, bringing with it the idea of punishment for attempting to better the lot of humankind. Napoleon's sufferings on St

Helena enabled poets to present the Romantic themes of melancholy, exile, and alienation on the grandest scale, and many works on the subject suggest a strong degree of authorial self-projection. Numerous poems of the 1820s and 1830s such as Hugo's "The Two Islands" (1825) and Lermontov's "Napoleon" (1829) and "St Helena" (1831) take the island itself as their subject, contrasting the confinement of St Helena with the limitlessness of the surrounding ocean, as in Pushkin's "To the Sea" (1824) in which the boundlessness of the ocean becomes a symbol for Napoleon's character and career (and, more generally, of the Romantic yearning for the infinite):

> His soul was by your spirit haunted,
> In your own image was he framed:
> Like you, immense, profound, undaunted,
> Like you, nocturnal and untamed. (Pushkin 1984: 62)

Indeed, for Heine, the site of Napoleon's exile and death had the symbolic power to fulfill the role of poetry itself, as he wrote in his review of Scott's biography: "The Muses will inspire greater poets [than Scott] to the celebration of their Beloved Napoleon, and if someday men's voices become silent, then the very stones will speak, and the martyr's cliff of St. Helena juts eerily out of the sea, telling his mighty story to the passing centuries" (quoted in Ziolkowski 1960: 99).

The defeat of Napoleon also seemed to many to mark the end of an age greater and more glorious than that which succeeded it. Napoleon seemed to have been defeated by figures of lesser stature (as Heine commented of Wellington, "We see in him only the triumph of stupidity over genius"; quoted in Atkins 1929: 76), and by contrast with the nostalgically viewed stimulations of the Napoleonic age, the period of the Bourbon restoration (and the Orleans monarchy in France after 1830) appeared stagnant and dull, as even Chateaubriand acknowledged: "To descend from Bonaparte and the Empire to what succeeded them is like falling from reality into nothingness, from the top of a mountain into an abyss. Did everything not end with Napoleon?" (quoted in O'Flaherty 1969: 261). In this context, Napoleon started to be seen as a giant among dwarfs, a figure who was too great for the age in which he had lived, an idea found in the poetry of Lermontov and Grillparzer, the latter proposing the epitaph "He was too great because his time was too small" (quoted in Ziolkowski 1960: 100). Moreover, as Chateaubriand also pointed out, it was much easier to indulge in hero worship of Napoleon once the demands of his regime were no longer felt "and the victims' curses, their cries of pain, their howls of anguish, are heard no more" (quoted in Geyl 1965: 26).

Initially it was writers such as Byron and Heine, having held their own personal cults of Napoleon even during the period of his power, who began the literary transformation of him after Waterloo, adopting him as a symbol of the continuing values of the revolution in an age which they now saw as deeply reactionary and oppressive (for Heine, the retraction by the Prussian authorities of the benefits gained by the Jews under the *Code Napoléon* contributed strongly to his support for the Emperor). In "Napoleon's Farewell" of 1815, for example, a supposed translation spoken by the exiled Emperor (that was later translated into Russian by Lermontov), Byron makes Napoleon a symbol of liberty and looks forward to his return:

> Farewell to thee, France! – but when Liberty rallies
> Once more in thy regions, remember me then –
> The violet still grows in the depth of thy valleys;
> Though withered, thy tears will unfold it again –
> Yet, yet, I may baffle the hosts that surround us,
> And yet may thy heart leap awake to my voice –
> There are links which must break in the chain that has bound us,
> *Then* turn thee and call on the Chief of thy choice! (Byron 1980-93, III: 313)

In similar fashion, in his poem "The Grenadiers" of 1819, Heine transforms the sorrow of two soldiers at the defeat of France and the retreat from Moscow with which the poem opens into a joyful conclusion which combines personal resurrection with the return of the Emperor:

> That day will my Emperor ride over my grave,
> Bright swords and lances attending,
> That day will I rise fully armed from my grave,
> The Emperor, the Emperor defending! (Heine 1982: 32)

Heine's poem is one of many which imagines Napoleon's triumph over defeat, exile, and even, after 1821, death; the Emperor's own return from the grave provides the subject for poems such as Joseph Christian von Zedlitz's "The Nocturnal Review" (1829) and Lermontov's "The Ghost Ship" (1840). In one sense, such a return did take place when Napoleon's ashes were brought back to Paris in 1840, at perhaps the highest point of the Napoleonic legend.

It was Napoleon's death in 1821 that stimulated the greatest outpouring of poetry about him, prompting works by Lamartine, Pushkin, Franz Grillparzer, Béranger, Shelley, Victor Hugo, Casimir Delavigne, and Albert von Chamisso. Of the poems on the death of Napoleon, one of the first and certainly the most famous and influential was "Il cinque maggio" (The Fifth of May), written by the Italian Alessandro Manzoni in 1821 (and translated into German by Goethe in 1823). This poem presents many of the themes that would become common in poems on Napoleon of the 1820s and 1830s, including the immense sense of absence left by his death and the unlikelihood that a figure of such importance and greatness will ever be seen again; the global scale of his career; the admiration and hatred he generated; his ability to reconcile "the men of Yesterday/And of To-morrow"; the contrast between his life as Emperor and as a prisoner; and his final exile on "his distant rock, / Mankind's perpetual gazing-stock" (Everett 1910: 232). However, Manzoni's ode is unusual in presenting Napoleon as re-embracing Christian faith at the moment of death.

Consolidating the effect of Napoleon's defeat, exile, and death in the transform-ation of his image was the publication in 1823 of the *Memorial*, and its image of the

Emperor as the hero of the French people was popularized by Jean-Pierre de Béranger in the 1820s in his songs celebrating "the little corporal," written in the voices of the people themselves, in the most famous of which an old woman tells the listening villagers how she had sheltered Napoleon during a campaign and how, on learning of his death, her "sorrow was most bitter! / Was most bitter!" (Hartley 1958: 7). The nationalistic and quasi-religious dimensions of the popular legend of Napoleon as it was conceived in France during this period is well illustrated in Balzac's *Le Médecin de Campagne* of 1832, in which an old soldier gives an account of Napoleon's career and his humbling of kings to a group of peasants, presenting him as a man of destiny who transcended mortal status and had a likeness to Jesus.

The transformation of the image of Napoleon from that of a monster and a devil to a hero of cosmic or divine proportions is seen most strikingly in the shifting response to him of two of the major poets of European Romanticism, Victor Hugo and Alexander Pushkin. In his novel *Les Misérables* (1862), Hugo presents the sudden conversion to Napoleon of Marius, who goes from seeing him as a fabulous monster – the Corsican ogre, the usurper, the tyrant – to seeing him as a hero of quasi-divine status. Hugo had himself undergone a similar conversion, though on a much more protracted timetable. The son of a Royalist mother, Hugo had initially attacked Napoleon in his first pro-Bourbon collection of 1822, but with his mother's death and the development of his relationship with his father, who had been a general in the Grand Army, Hugo increasingly juxtaposed the grandeur and greatness of Napoleon's career with its devastating effect on the world, as in poems like "The Two Islands." The culmination of his transformation of Napoleon into a glorious superhuman hero is fully evident in his ode "To the Column" of 1830, in which Napoleon becomes a figure of Romantic aspiration and seemingly limitless power, akin to the Titan Enceladus who sought to climb Olympus to overthrow Zeus:

> He built this column! – blending, twisting, hammering
> The century into this superhuman thing
>   Stamped with his Roman fist.
> The Alps bowed down beneath his thundering steps,
> The Nile, the Rhine, the Tiber, blazing Austerlitz,
>   Eylau, frozen in mist.
>
> For he, like ancient Enceladus, tried to scale
> The universe's throne, and for twenty years
>   Amassed something awesome,
> Moving earth and heaven with a single word,
> Wagram on Marengo, Champaubert on Arcole,
>   Pelion on Ossa! (Hugo 2001: 35)

Here Hugo makes Napoleon so powerful that he reshapes not only the captured guns of his enemies used in making the column, but the epoch and earth itself, ultimately becoming a figure of cosmic dimensions.

Like Hugo, Alexander Pushkin had initially attacked Napoleon as a destructive and autocratic figure, contributing to the Russian poetic assault on him that followed the invasion of 1812 in his "Reminiscences in Tsarskoe Selo" (1814). But by his 1821 poem "Napoleon," Pushkin was addressing the dead Emperor as "hero" and present- ing him as "a majestic man" who had fulfilled a "wondrous fate" (Pushkin 1984: 42). Though a "vainglorious man" and responsible for the extinction of the French Revolution, Napoleon was redeemed for the "blights and horrors" of his victories by his suffering in exile, and Pushkin concludes his poem by calling on the reader to:

> Hail him! He launched the Russian nation
> Upon its lofty destinies
> And augured ultimate salvation
> For man's long-exiled liberties. (Pushkin 1984: 46)

As this ending emphasizes, Pushkin's conception of Napoleon as embodying the role of Romantic hero, a figure of greatness and genius that could (with some effort) also be made into a powerful symbol of liberty, was also interlinked with his role as a figure against which Russian identity could be defined, a function that Napoleon also fulfilled for Pushkin's fellow Russian poet Michael Lermontov in patriotic poems like "Two Giants" (1832) and "Borodinó" (1837).

The power of the Romantic image of Napoleon in Russian literature in the first half of the nineteenth century, as well as in that of European literature more generally, is testified to by the attempts to undermine it in two of the great novels of the second half of the century, Tolstoy's *War and Peace* (1869) and Dostoyevsky's *Crime and Punishment* (1866). In *War and Peace*, Tolstoy seeks to counter the idea of Napoleon as the great man who makes history, presenting him instead as the vain, pompous, and rather ridiculous puppet of forces over which he has no control. In *Crime and Punishment*, Raskolnikov's justification for his killing of the pawnbroker – "I wanted to become a Napoleon, that's why I killed..." (Dostoyevsky 1991: 483) – serves only to emphasize the distance between Raskolnikov and the status to which he aspires of the man of genius for whom anything is possible, regardless of morality of law. Writing over 30 years before Dostoyevsky, Pushkin had similarly treated with irony the identification with Napo- leon, commenting in *Eugene Onegin* that "Napoleon's our sole inspiration" (1979: 70), and illustrated the dangers of Napoleonic self-conception in his story *The Queen of Spades* (1833) in which the egocentric and unfeeling Hermann (who bears a strong physical resemblance to Napoleon) is destroyed by his own ambition; as for Napoleon, so for Hermann, human will is unable to triumph over fate or destiny. Yet it is also in Pushkin that we find one of the most interesting examinations of the idealizations of Napoleon. His poem "The Hero," written in 1830, presents a dialogue between the Poet and the Friend which begins with the Poet choosing Napoleon as his personal idol:

> It is him, it is him – this warlike stranger,
> He who had all the kings humbled,

> This warrior who was crowned by freedom
> And disappeared like the shadow of the dawn.

Rejecting the standard tropes of Napoleonic hero worship offered by the Friend, the Poet chooses as the moment of Napoleon's greatness his visit to the plague hospital in Jaffa in 1799 during the Egyptian campaign, only to be told by the Friend that this incident is mythical – "A poet's reveries" – and that "The strict historian chases you away." But "The Hero" ends with the poet finding value precisely in what the Friend has constructed as the poetic rather than the historic:

> To the multitude of low truths
> I prefer an illusion that elevates us . . .
> Let the hero keep his heart! What
> Will he be without it? A tyrant . . . [1]

Pushkin's Christ-like conception of his hero in this poem was not one shared by all who contributed to the Romantic vision of Napoleon after Waterloo, but many of them would have understood and agreed with his justification of his own imagining of the Emperor and his transformation of him into a symbolic and legendary figure. While writers such as Hugo, Béranger, Balzac, Heine, Stendhal, Hazlitt, Byron, Manzoni, and Lermontov would have found it difficult to defend their versions of Napoleon against the "strict historian," they would all have avowed that in creating an illusory version, they were elevating not only Napoleon, but themselves and their readers.

NOTE

1 My translation of this poem is taken from Evdokimova (1999: 110-12). Evdokimova provides an excellent discussion of this poem to which I am indebted.

REFERENCES AND FURTHER READING

Primary sources

Byron, George Gordon, Lord (1973-82). *Byron's Letters and Journals*, ed. Leslie Marchand, 12 vols. London: John Murray.

Byron, George Gordon, Lord (1980-93). *The Complete Poetical Works*, ed. Jerome J. McGann and Barry Weller, 7 vols. Oxford: Clarendon Press.

Coleridge, Samuel Taylor (1957-73). *The Notebooks of Samuel Taylor Coleridge*, ed. Kathleen Coburn, 6 vols. New York: Pantheon Books.

Coleridge, Samuel Taylor (1978). *Essays On His Own Times*, ed. David V. Erdman, 3 vols. London: Routledge; Princeton, NJ: Princeton University Press.

Dostoyevsky, Fyodor (1991). *Crime and Punishment*, trans. David McDuff. Harmondsworth, UK: Penguin.

Hartley, Anthony (ed.) (1958). *The Penguin Book of French Verse: 3. The Nineteenth Century*. Harmondsworth, UK: Penguin.

Hazlitt, William (1930-4). *The Complete Works of William Hazlitt*, ed. P. P. Howe, 21 vols. London: J. M. Dent.

Heine, Heinrich (1982). *The Complete Poems: A Modern English Version*, trans. H. Draper. Oxford, Oxford University Press.

Hugo, Victor (2001). *Selected Poetry*, trans. Steven Monte. Manchester: Carcanet.

Landor, Walter Savage (1937). *The Poetical Works of Walter Savage Landor*, ed. Stephen Wheeler, 3 vols. Oxford: Clarendon Press.

Pushkin, Alexander (1979). *Eugene Onegin*, trans. Charles Johnson. Harmondsworth, UK: Penguin.

Pushkin, Alexander (1984). *Collected Narrative and Lyrical Poetry*, trans. Walter Arndt. Ann Arbor, MI: Ardis.

Stendhal (Marie-Henri Beyle) (1999). *The Charterhouse of Parma*, trans. Margaret Mauldon. Oxford: Oxford University Press.

Stendhal (2002). *The Red and the Black*, trans. Roger Gard. Harmondsworth, UK: Penguin.

Vigny, Alfred de (1953). *The Military Necessity*. New York: Grove.

Whately, Richard (1985). *Historic Doubts Relative to Napoleon Bonaparte*, ed. Ralph S. Pomeroy. Berkeley, CA and London: Scolar Press.

Wordsworth, William (1979). *The Prelude: 1799, 1805, 1850*, ed. Jonathan Wordsworth, M. H. Abrams, and Stephen Gill. New York and London: W. W. Norton and Co.

Secondary sources and further reading

Atkins, H. G. (1929). *Heine*. London: Routledge and Sons.

Bainbridge, Simon (1995). *Napoleon and English Romanticism*. Cambridge, UK: Cambridge University Press.

Besser, Gretchen R. (1969). *Balzac's Conception of Genius: The Theme of Superiority in the "Comédie humaine."* Geneva: Librairie Droz.

Boorsch, Jean (1960). "Chateaubriand and Napoleon." *Yale French Studies*, 26: 55-62.

Descotes, Maurice (1967). *La Légende de Napoléon et les écrivains français du XIX siècle*. Paris: Minard.

Evdokimova, Svetlana (1999). *Pushkin's Historical Imagination*. New Haven, CT: Yale University Press.

Everett, William (1910). *The Italian Poets Since Dante*. London: Duckworth and Company.

Geyl, Pieter (1965). *Napoleon: For and Against*, trans. Olive Reiner. Harmondsworth, UK: Penguin.

Guérard, Albert Leon (1924). *Reflections on the Napoleonic Legend*. London: T. Fischer Unwin.

Herold, J. Christopher (1959). *Mistress to an Age: A Life of Madame de Staël*. London: Hamish Hamilton.

Herz, Micheline (1960). "From "The Little Corporal" to "Mongénéral": A Comparison of Two Myths." *Yale French Studies*, 26: 37-44.

Lützeler, Paul Michael (1990). "The Image of Napoleon in European Romanticism." In Gerhart Hoffmeister (ed.), *European Romanticism: Literary Cross-Currents, Modes, and Models*. Detroit: Wayne State University Press, pp. 211-28.

Marceau, Felicien (1976). *Balzac and His World*, trans. Derek Coltman. Westport, CT: Greenwood Press.

Martin, Andy (2000). *Napoleon the Novelist*. Cambridge, UK: Polity.

McCarthy, Mary (1980). *Ideas and the Novel*. London: Weidenfeld and Nicolson.

Munhall, Edgar (1960). "Portraits of Napoleon." *Yale French Studies*, 26: 3-20.

O' Flaherty, Kathleen (1969). "The Genesis of the Napoleonic Legend." *Studies*, 58: 256-66.

Peyre, Henri (1960). "Napoleon: Devil, Poet, Saint." *Yale French Studies*, 26: 21-31.

Plant, Raymond (1983). *Hegel: An Introduction*. Oxford: Blackwell.

Strich, Fritz (1949). *Goethe and World Literature*, trans C. A. M. Sym. London: Routledge and Kegan Paul.

Tulard, Jean (1971). *Le Mythe de Napoléon*. Paris: Librairie Armand Colin.

Tulard, Jean (1985). *Napoleon: The Myth of the Saviour*, trans. Teresa Waugh. London: Methuen.

Wesling, Molly W. (2001). *Napoleon in Russian Cultural Mythology*. New York: Peter Lang.

Yale French Studies (1960). *The Myth of Napoleon*, special issue, 26.

Ziolkowski, Theodore (1960). "Napoleon's Impact on Germany: A Rapid Survey." *Yale French Studies*, 26: 94-105.

27

Orientalism

Diego Saglia

Romantic Approaches to the East

In July 1798 a large expeditionary force led by Napoleon invaded Egypt with the aim of wresting this region from the nominal control of the Ottoman Empire, destabilizing the naval supremacy of the British in the Mediterranean, and disrupting the overland routes to their territories in India. Despite the severe defeat inflicted on the French fleet by Lord Nelson at Aboukir in August, the invasion continued and the occupying power proceeded to an institutional reorganization and a strategic survey of the country. In 1799, during excavations near the Nile Delta, an officer of Engineers discovered a thickly inscribed slab, the Rosetta Stone, that was to become one of the most extraordinary finds of an expedition which combined military and scholarly purposes. Covered in mysterious hieroglyphics (and a Greek translation), this object became a symbol of the enigmatic qualities of the East and of the mission of Western "translators," whose task it was to unfold and explain this complex intersection of cultures. Moreover, as the stone was brought to light during a military operation, it is emblematic of the interconnection between knowledge and power in Romantic-period Orientalism. In fact, the Western fascination for the East was as old as classical antiquity: both the desire for accurate knowledge of the Orient, and hostile visions of it, had powerful cultural precedents in ancient Greek and Roman attitudes. But when, between the eighteenth and nineteenth centuries, the West began to take over increasingly larger portions of Asia, the desire for knowledge became inextricably bound up with practices of control, colonization, and more or less direct exploitation.

Eventually Jean-François Champollion deciphered the inscriptions of the Rosetta Stone in 1821, and published his initial results in *Letter to M. Dacier* (*Lettre à M. Dacier* 1822), generally considered the official beginning of Egyptology. At the same time, this symbolical triumph of Western science over the mysteries of the Orient was linked to a European-wide Egyptian fashion that, from the late eighteenth century onwards, had gradually infiltrated areas of consumer culture such as interior decoration, furniture-making, personal ornaments, and female fashions (Curl 1994). Thus Romantic-period Orientalism kept traces of the "ethnographic" and comparatist attitudes towards the exotic typical of the Enlightenment; yet it also showed a continuing fascination with the decorative and luxurious East typical of eighteenth-century aristocratic exoticism. On the one hand, Romanticism prolonged and modified eighteenth-century images and constructions of the East; on the other, each national tradition developed its own particular version of this Orientalist "addiction." Edward Said's fundamental study *Orientalism* ([1978] 1991) concentrates almost exclusively on Britain and France as the main colonial powers in the nineteenth and early twentieth centuries. Yet, although he feels obliged to overlook "the important contributions to Orientalism of Germany, Italy, Russia, Spain, and Portugal" (Said 1991: 17), he also points out that the Orient is a pervasive and multiform preoccupation. Romantic-period Orientalism in effect laid the foundations of that Europe-wide movement of cultural renovation that Edgar Quinet, in *The Nature of Religions* (*Le Génie des religions* 1841; see Said 1991: 42), called an "Oriental Renaissance," and that later Raymond Schwab defined as a cultural revolution exploding with the arrival of Sanskrit texts in Europe (Schwab 1950).

These epistemological developments were paralleled by transformations in notions of the East as a geographical and strategic whole. For the Romantic period witnessed both the discovery and investigation of new Oriental territories and, conversely, the unavailability of parts of the East to Western scrutiny or control. Whereas distant territories such as China and Japan remained tantalizingly aloof, other countries were gradually added to the geographical and cultural map of the Orient. For instance, Islamic and Ottoman-controlled Albania became prominent after Lord Byron's journey there in 1809. Egypt, its mysterious antiquities and contemporary culture, was an object of interest and fascination, as was the South of Spain and its dazzling architectural remains of Moorish times. Similarly, Africa emerged as an important Orientalist dimension and an adjunct of the East. This was occasioned by the exploration and (re)discovery of the geographical areas between the Islamic North and the unknown interior of the continent, such as the search for the fabled city of Timbuktu, or the explorations of the Niger, the Nile, and Abyssinia, or cultural explorations such as Eugène Delacroix's six-month journey in 1832 as a member of the Comte de Mornay's embassy to the Sultan of Morocco. The geopolitical and geocultural horizons of an East inherited from Enlightenment interests in other civilizations expanded in unprecedented ways between the late eighteenth and early nineteenth centuries. A land of myths and fables that was gradually shedding its fabulous aura, the East evolved into an interlinked cultural and geographic structure to be examined, deciphered, enjoyed, and endlessly represented.

Scholarship, Control, and Consumption

The changes in the cultural map of the Orient owe much to the geopolitics of Northern Africa and Asia in the Romantic period. The East is imagined and represented as a geography to be exploited in economic terms and controlled through military and administrative structures. As this period sees the foundation of the great colonial empires of the later nineteenth and twentieth centuries, actual control of the East is a distinctive feature of a Romantic-period Orientalism which thus suits Said's definition of it as a system for "dominating, restructuring, and having authority" over the East (Said 1991: 3). Nevertheless, several manifestations of Orientalism in this period cannot be merely reduced to one country's actual domination over Eastern territories. In fact, fascination with Oriental cultures was often unrelated to any direct control of colonial territories in the East. As a result, Romantic-period Orientalisms draw on a combination of the scientific and the scholarly, the decorative and the playful, the political, the military, and the economic.

Said usefully points out the variety of, and discrepancies in, Western approaches to the East and highlights the Romantic period as a crucial moment in European relations with the Orient: "The difference between representations of the Orient before the last third of the eighteenth century and those after it (that is, those belonging to what I call modern Orientalism) is that the range of representations expanded enormously in the latter period," because "Europe came to know the Orient more scientifically, [and] to live in it with greater authority and discipline than ever before" (Said 1991: 22). But it must also be observed that Said treats Romantic Orientalism as a prevalently decorative region of the imagination. In his opinion, Pre-Romantic and Romantic figurations of the East "as exotic locale" are steeped in "[s]ensuality, promise, terror, sublimity, idyllic pleasure, intense energy," and thus constitute a "free-floating Orient [that] would be severely curtailed with the advent of academic Orientalism" (pp. 118-19).

In reality, academic Orientalism and the "free-floating Orient" are closely inter-connected phenomena with intersecting developments. For instance, the Romantic period witnessed the foundation of centers of research and academic chairs in Oriental languages. In this way different nations institutionalized new forms of scholarship rooted in eighteenth-century disciplines. As Raymond Schwab observed, it was the translation of the *Zend-Avesta*, the Zoroastrian sacred book, by the French Abraham-Hyacinthe Anquetil-Duperron in 1771 that started the Oriental Renaissance in European Romanticisms. Animated by patriotic and not merely scholarly feelings, in the same year William Jones addressed a public letter to the French Orientalist, accusing him of inaccuracies and defending the achievements of British scholars in this field. Later, in 1784, Jones and other British Orientalists in Calcutta founded the Asiatic Society of Bengal, that in 1788 began publication of its internationally renowned journal *Asiatic Researches*. In France, the Ecole des langues orientales vivantes was founded in Paris in 1795, and Silvestre de Sacy, the first scholar to hold a chair of Arabic, later became its director. Napoleon's 1798 Egyptian expedition led to the creation of the Institut d'Egypte in Cairo which, in turn, was responsible for the publication of the monumental *Description of Egypt* (*Description de l'Egypte*) in 23 volumes between 1809 and 1828. Paris also became an important center of Indian studies when, in 1803, Alexander Hamilton, a member of Jones's Asiatic Society, was obliged to remain in France after the end of the Peace of Amiens. There he continued to work on his edition of the *Hitopadesa* with materials from the Bibliothè-que Nationale. It was in Paris that Hamilton taught Sanskrit to Friedrich Schlegel and thus prepared the ground for the latter's translation of Kalidasa's play *Sakuntala* (fifth century AD) and his fundamental study *On the Language and Wisdom of the Indians* (*Über die Sprache und Weisheit der Indier,* 1808), one of the foundational texts of modern Indology. The Société asiatique de Paris was founded in 1821, while the Royal Asiatic Society of Great Britain and Ireland followed in 1823, under the direction of Henry Thomas Colebrooke. The latter institution was also home to the Oriental Translation Committee, created in 1828 with the aim of encouraging translations from Oriental languages of technical, scientific, legal, and historical works. The first chair of Sanskrit at the Collège de France was created in 1814 and held by Léonard de Chézy; Germany followed in 1818 with a chair for Wilhelm von Humboldt; while the University of Oxford founded one only in 1833.

Said's distinction between Romantic and academic Orientalisms is grounded in restrictive views of Romanticism as a cultural movement awarding pre-eminence to irrational passions and instincts, views that have long been questioned by literary and cultural criticism. This conception, in effect, severely diminishes the relevance of Romantic-period scholarship for fictional production, a combination that is crucial, for instance, in a pivotal text such as Lord Byron's *The Giaour* (1813). This poem narrates a gripping story of love and death complicated by cross-cultural conflict; at the same time, it also reflects on the intricate geopolitical map of age-old tensions between East and West, and is enriched with learned endnotes about the cultural and historical references scattered in the poetry. In addition, Said's definition reduces the multiform manifestations of Romantic-period Orientalism, especially the fact that "The Orient is an integral part of European *material* civilization and culture" (Said 1991: 2). Indeed, the Romantic period also saw the transformation of eighteenth-century aristocratic fashions such as *chinoiserie* and *turquerie* into an increasingly widespread consumption of the Orient through objects imported from the East or recreated in the West – fabrics, foodstuffs, furniture, objects for interior decoration, porcelain and china – as well as the importation and acclimatization of exotic architectural styles (Conner 1979, Sweetman 1987, Sievernich and Budde 1989, MacKenzie 1995). Once again, this (re)production of the East drew on the advances of scholarly Orientalism as, for instance, Wedgwood's Egyptian-style wares were inspired by Dominique Vivant Denon's *Journey to Upper and Lower Egypt* (*Voyage dans la haute et la basse Egypte* 1802) and, later, by the *Description of Egypt.*

European Romantic Orientalisms may thus be described as a plurality of expres-sions of a single, "transdiscursive" phenomenon that elaborated and interfused litera-ture and the arts, history, politics, economics, and military and geopolitical knowledge. Orientalism is a linguistic and extralinguistic fact – located in discourse and material culture – that effected the appropriation and (re)construction of other civilizations, and that proliferated and dispersed across Europe with particular inten-sity from the late eighteenth into the nineteenth century and beyond. Romantic-period Orientalism is part of a multiple system of popular consumption and intense cultural exchanges that developed at a truly international level.

Orientalist Trendsetters

Lord Byron was perhaps the single most important unifying influence on Romantic literary Orientalisms. He was not the earliest practitioner of Orientalist fiction, nor was he the only writer to have direct experience of the East. Nonetheless, his personal legend, his journey to Albania, Greece, and Turkey in 1809-11, and his fascinating Orientalist works – from the first two cantos of *Childe Harold's Pilgrimage* (1812) to the series of "Eastern Tales" (1813-16) – were determining influences on later Romantic treatments in other traditions.

The young Byron traveled to the East as the traditional Grand Tour was no longer practicable since most of Europe had been under Napoleonic control. Unable to obtain the East India Company's permission to visit India, he decided to travel to Greece and Turkey and reach the Levant via Portugal, Spain, and the then unknown land of Albania. This journey opened up new horizons and provided him with materials for later re-elaborations of exotic themes that would greatly add to his fame as a poet. Most importantly this adventurous trip gave him a lifelong passion for the Orient. His travels were rewritten in poetic form in the first two cantos of *Childe Harold's Pilgrimage*, a poetic travelogue that sparked off a vogue for adventures set in exotic lands and a type of brooding, aristocratic hero at odds with society and persecuted by remorse or some unspoken mystery in his past. These ingredients were then re-elaborated in Byron's Eastern tales: *The Giaour* and *The Bride of Abydos* (1813), *The Corsair* and its sequel *Lara* (1814). These works were structurally based on Walter Scott's innovatory revisions of the form of the narrative poem, and proved to be immediate successes, quickly selling thousands of copies. Thematically they combined first-hand observations, an accurate presentation of local color, and a wealth of facts culled from scholarly sources that were generously reproduced in the annotations. Together with introductory remarks and other paratextual materials, such references ensured the presence of the "real" Orient in the poems. And Byron's notes to his works, as well as the catalogues for the sales of his library in 1816 and 1827, confirm the prodigious extent of his knowledge of Orientalist scholarship, including such classics as Barthélemy d'Herbelot's *Bibliothèque orientale* (1697), and Jean Chardin's *Voyages en Perse, et autres lieux de l'Orient* (1686-1711), or recent titles such as Henry William Weber's collection of *Tales of the East* (1812) and Giovan Battista Belzoni's *Observations and Discoveries . . . in Egypt and Nubia* (1820).

Byron famously denied the value of his Orientalist verse in his later narrative poem *Beppo* (1818) and in his letters. He saw these early works as part of a "wrong revolutionary poetical system," his own definition of Romantic poetry from a letter of September 15, 1817 to his publisher John Murray. Nevertheless, Byron's rejection of his own Orientalist production did little to diminish its impact and popularity. His poems enjoyed enormous fame throughout Europe, and unquestionably shaped the exotic imagination of his contemporaries. Delacroix mentioned Byron's works in his journal where, in a note to himself for May 11, 1824, he wrote:

> Poetry is full of riches; always remember certain passages from Byron, they are an unfailing spur to your imagination; they are right for you. The end of the *Bride of Abydos*; *The Death of Selim*, his body tossed about by the waves and that hand – especially that hand – held up by the waves as they break and spend themselves upon the shore. (Delacroix [1893] 1951: 39)

Byron's works provided the sources for some of Delacroix's best-known Orientalist paintings such as "The Combat between the Giaour and the Pasha" (1826) or "The Death of Sardanapalus" (1827). More or less at the same time, the novelist and politician Benjamin Disraeli assessed the European resonance of Byron's tales in his early novel *Vivian Grey* (1826). Here, during a visit to a small German court, the protagonist attends a performance of Byron's *The Corsair* in ballet form, while the actual show is preceded by a discussion of Byron's works that confirms their international success, as well as providing satirical commentary on the Orientalist fashion (book VII, chapters 6-7). Disraeli's is a useful reminder of the diffusion of Byron's tales in the European cultural market well into the nineteenth century and their frequent adaptation through other artistic media.

The crucial importance of Byron's model for those who intended to write Orientalist verse is illustrated by Alexander Pushkin in a letter of January 2, 1822 to P. A. Viazemsky about his own poem *The Fountain of Bakhchisarai*:

> I modelled myself on the Eastern style of speech as far as that is possible for us rational, cold Europeans. Talking of that – do you know why I don't like Moore? Because he is excessively Eastern. He imitates in a childish, ugly fashion the childishness and ugliness of Sadi, Hafiz and Mahomet. A European, even when in raptures over Oriental splendor, should retain the taste and eye of a European – that is why Byron is so delightful in *The Giaour*, *The Bride of Abydos*, etc. (Pushkin 1971: 141)

Pushkin's decision to follow Byron rather than Thomas Moore reveals a basic ideological aspect of Orientalist fiction. For Pushkin the East must be evoked without losing sight of one's Western identity, an assertion which is particularly illuminating in the case of Russian culture and its traditionally intermediate position between Europe and Asia. In addition, Pushkin's words indicate that, in the whole of Europe, Byron's Orientalist poetry had found a competitor in that of his friend Thomas Moore, especially his best-selling poem *Lalla Rookh* (1817). Byron himself, in a letter of 1813, had advised Moore to "Stick to the East; – the oracle, Staël, told me it was the only poetical policy" (Byron 1973-94, III: 101). Moore took his friend's advice and in *Lalla Rookh* produced a complex intersection of prose and verse, complete with learned annotations, that was immediately successful in Britain and everywhere else.

This work is based on a prose frame narrating the princess Lalla Rookh's journey from Delhi to Kashmir, where she is to marry the King of Bokhara. During the long journey the court poet Fadladeen, who is eventually revealed to be the king himself, entertains her with tales that constitute as many inset poetic narratives. The first of these, "The Veiled Prophet of Khorassan," is rich in overtones from the *Arabian Nights* and Gothic atmospheres, and recounts the rise and fall of the mysterious prophet with coded references to Napoleon's career. Another inset narrative is the fairy tale "Paradise and the Peri," the parable-like structure of which, complete with light philosophical moral, re-elaborates some of the features of the traditional genre of the Oriental tale. Another outstanding narrative in Moore's collection is the Byronic tale of thwarted cross-cultural love and revolution in "The Fire-Worshippers." Set against the Muslim conquest of Iran, the poem contains oblique references to the situation of Ireland under British control and to the Irish nationalist rebellion of 1798. Thanks to its multiple voices, Moore's structurally and thematically complex work offers a fascinating combination of different strands of Romantic-period Orientalism: the author's own distinctive admixture of sensuality and sentimentalism, Byron's cross-cultural verse narratives, Gothic aesthetic, and the eighteenth-century moralizing Oriental tale *à la Rasselas*.

Although generally treated as a footnote to Byron's success, Moore's *Lalla Rookh* is, in its own right, an important multilayered version of Romantic Orientalist fiction and a testimony of the dangers of cultural contamination implicit in this kind of exoticism. As Pushkin remarked later in the century, Moore's poem was seen as such a successful adaptation of Eastern themes, structures, and style, as to be judged a quintessentially Oriental text. In an essay for the *Edinburgh Review* of November 1817, the critic Francis Jeffrey praised Moore's work for its literary merits but, at the same time, warned readers against its Oriental excesses. Since its "barbaric ornaments" and "exquisite pictures" were genuinely, yet also dangerously, exotic (Jeffrey 1817: 1, 2), the Eastern fantasies of *Lalla Rookh* came too close to literary and cultural miscegenation. Yet, despite such warnings, the poem was eagerly read, imitated, translated, and, above all, adapted in a variety of other artistic media. Indeed, the contaminating potential of Moore's achievement can be assessed through its popularity and diffusion, as it soon spread all over Europe and appeared in countless translations and adaptations. Amédée Pichot translated it into French in 1820, and Friedrich de la Motte Fouqué produced a German version in 1825. A Polish translation appeared in 1826, and separate tales were published in Dutch (1834), Spanish (1836), and Italian (1838). On January 27, 1821, a German version was performed at court in Berlin by the royal family, with the Grand Duchess of Russia in the part of the heroine; and materials from the poems were used for the librettos of several nineteenth-century operas, including Gaspare Spontini's *Nurmahal* (1822).

Byron's and Moore's works are essential points of reference within the multifaceted array of European Romantic Orientalisms. They provided fashionable models for authors such as Pushkin, as they turned their attention to Eastern themes. In addition,

Byron and Moore stood for two alternative ways of construing the relation between the Western text and the Eastern civilization it aimed to represent. Whereas Moore's *Lalla Rookh* was perceived as an instance of a work invaded and infected by the Orient, and a vehicle of this cultural invasion, Byron's tales described the relationship between East and West as a permanently unresolved, though creatively prolific, tension.

Texts of Knowledge and Texts of Pleasure

The contrast between Byron and Moore reveals the perpetual oscillations of Romantic Orientalism between accuracy, factuality, and scholarly reliability, on the one hand, and the decorative fantasies of a clichéd East of harems, sultans, crescents, and palm-trees, on the other. Both dimensions had eighteenth-century precedents – the Enlightenment's interest in non-European civilizations and the hedonistic East of the *Arabian Nights*. In particular, accuracy in descriptions of the East was reinforced by an increase in scholarly research and the number of travelers' accounts. Professional or occasional travel writers produced a staggering output of narratives about Oriental cultures from a variety of points of view. James Bruce's monumental *Travels to Discover the Source of the Nile* (1790) was controversially received in Great Britain, and many of the author's statements were criticized or disproved by his detractors. Carsten Niebuhr's *Travel through Arabia and other Countries in the East* (in English in 1774-8) was the account of a Danish expedition to the Yemen through Turkey and Egypt by the last surviving member, and was widely read and quoted throughout Europe. Narratives of the British embassy to China, led by Lord Macartney in 1793, were published by Aeneas Anderson in 1795 and George Staunton in 1797. Constantin de Volney's *Travels through Syria and Egypt* (*Voyage en Syrie et en Egypte*) was published in 1787, followed in 1799 by L. F. Cassas's *Picturesque Travels through Syria, Phoenicia, Palestine and Lower Egypt* (*Voyage pittoresque de la Syrie, de la Phoenicie, de la Palestine et de la Basse Egypte*), a monumental enterprise complete with 180 engravings by the artist who accompanied the French Ambassador to the Ottoman Porte on a tour of these provinces. Vivant Denon's *Journey to Upper and Lower Egypt* circulated widely and became an indispensable visual documentary source on these lands. The Swiss traveler Jean Louis Burckhardt's *Travels in Arabia* were published posthumously in English in 1819, and his *Travels in Syria and the Holy Land* appeared in 1822. Giovan Battista Belzoni's archeological and adventurous memoirs, *Narrative of the Operations and Recent Discoveries...in Egypt and Nubia*, were published in 1820.

The accounts of travel writers were accompanied by those of authors and artists, where an investigation of cultural otherness, unfamiliar historical and archeological traditions, or different geographical landscapes doubled as an examination of the divided selfhood of the modern subject, often in imitation of Byron's verse travelogue *Childe Harold's Pilgrimage*. François René de Chateaubriand's pioneering *Journey from Paris to Jerusalem* (*Itinéraire de Paris à Jérusalem*) appeared in 1811, and the large number of French writers who followed him to the East included Gérard de Nerval, Alphonse de Lamartine, and Gustave Flaubert. Delacroix visited Northern Africa between January and June 1832, and David Roberts undertook extensive travels in Egypt, Palestine, and Lebanon between 1838 and 1839. In 1829 Pushkin traveled through Georgia to the Armenian capital Erzurum and published an account of the journey in his travel sketch *Journey to Arzrum* (1836).

As seen above, literary works drew heavily on travel accounts and often included scholarly observations in their notes. Perhaps the foundational instance of this practice is William Beckford's *Vathek*, one of the great intercultural texts of European Romantic Orientalism, originally composed in French, although first published in English in 1786. The rich apparatus of annotations, parallel to the narrative itself, was composed by Beckford's translator, Samuel Henley. When his English version was published without the author's consent, the latter hastened to publish the original and translate the (corrected and expanded) notes into French. For the notes were an intrinsic part of the novel, worthy of being kept and enriched, as they testified to the scholarly research at the basis of Beckford's fiction. Similarly, Robert Southey's long Oriental narrative poems – *Thalaba the Destroyer* (1801) and *The Curse of Kehama* (1810) – contained extensive annotations, often more voluminous than the verse narrative, and designing alternative explorations of the cultural variety of the East which the poetic text merely glimpses at. Notes as assertions of scholarly reliability characterize much Romantic Orientalist verse. The learned annotations in Victor Hugo's *Les Orientales* (1829) were the outcome of a collaboration with the novelist and Oriental specialist Ernest Fouinet who, in 1830, published his own *Selection of Oriental Poems* (*Choix de poésies orientales*). Adam Mickiewicz based his *Crimean Sonnets* (*Sonety Krymskie* 1826) on such philologically reliable collections of Asian verse as Silvestre de Sacy's anthology of Arabic poetry *The Arab Chrestomathy* (*Chrestomathie arabe* 1806, 1826-7), and Joseph von Hammer-Purgstall's *History of Persian Belles Lettres* (*Geschichte der schönen Redekünste Persiens* 1818).

In some cases, the far-fetched lore of Orientalist annotations could even become a major source of literary materials. This is evident in the emergence and diffusion of the figure of the vampire which, from an extensive note in Southey's *Thalaba* on the tales of vampirism common in Eastern Europe and the Ottoman East, was developed by Byron in *The Giaour* and William Polidori in *The Vampyre* (1819). The Oriental demon then traveled to the Continent, where it had already appeared in Goethe's *Bride of Corinth* (*Die Braut von Korinth* 1797), and, especially in France, spawned a series of variations from Cyprien Bérard's *Lord Ruthven, or the Vampires* (*Lord Ruthwen, ou les vampires* 1820), set in Greece, India, and Eastern Europe, to Charles Nodier's *Smarra, or the Demons of the Night* (*Smarra, ou les démons de la nuit* 1821), set in the Greek and thus quasi-Oriental region of Thessaly, with notes on vampirism and travels in Eastern Europe, and Prosper Mérimée's *La Guzla* (1827) where the vampire figure is the Bey of Moina, in Illyria, thus combining folk-tale traits with intimations of political allegory.

If erudite footnotes proved inextricable from Orientalist writing, there were also instances of resistance to this often excessive overloading of fiction with factual references and details. One of the most important dissenting voices was that of Mikhail Lermontov, who refused to burden his Orientalist works with annotations. Thus, although largely founded on fact, his prose tale *Izmail-Bei* (1843) does not present any erudite apparatus, in pointed contrast with the footnoting practices of Russian Orientalist poets of the 1820s and the popular Caucasian tales of Aleksandr Marlinsky such as *Ammalat-Bek* (1832) and *Mulla Nur* (1836) (Layton 1994: 138).

This fictional expansion of the East through annotation indicates that Romantic writers were fully aware that there was no such thing as a single, unified Orient. Moreover it is important to remember that learned references also featured in works seemingly dominated by a "pleasurable" streak – that Orient of adventures, magic, sensuality, and luxury found in Beckford and Byron, and which Said qualifies as a form of decorative and hedonistic Orientalism. In fact, the scientific research under-lying these texts is crucially related to issues of power and control. Most obviously the figure of the harem belongs to a traditionally clichéd East of pleasures and luxury that also doubles as a place of political and ideological tensions (Yeazell 2000). Byron's poems depict the harem as the pivotal place in their intricate structures of East–West conflicts. Similarly, Hugo's *Orientales* presents several explorations of the harem and its sensual and sexual pleasures in a voyeuristic spectacularization of the body of the "other" woman. Several poems in the collection, however, also highlight the political underside of the harem and its links with Oriental despotism, so that sensually charged scenes are often mixed with violent images of the Ottoman repression of Greek revolutionaries. Thus "The Heads of the Seraglio" ("Les Têtes du sérail") is centered on the severed heads of the Greek patriots Canaris, Marco Botzaris, and the Bishop of Missolonghi, on display in the harem by order of the Sultan. As the heads begin to speak, current politics and warfare penetrate the immutable spaces and sounds of the seraglio in a gruesome combination of horror, violence, luxury, and pleasure. Through this paradoxical conjunction Hugo evokes a striking picture of the clash of civilizations represented by the War of Independence in contemporary Greece.

A revolutionary work, Hugo's collection is poised between escapism and sensual abandonment, on the one hand, and an engagement with political and military developments, on the other. This double structure emerges clearly from the Preface, which is an important reflection on Romantic art and one of the manifestos of French Romanticism. It proclaims the freedom to choose one's subject in defiance of neo-classical prescriptions and, as an assertion of literary liberation, it anticipates the Preface to *Cromwell* (1827) and the symbolical "battle" of *Hernani* of 1830. It also defines the Romantics' discovery of the East as a generalized interest with deep roots in current Orientalist scholarship (Hugo [1829, 1831] 1993: 23). Thus, even as Hugo suggests that the Orient is a crucial component of his "useless book of pure poetry" (p. 20, my translation), he simultaneously anchors his project to history, politics, and the War of Greek Independence.

Les Orientales features a sizeable number of poems devoted to sensual pleasure, the harem, and male desire. "The Poet to the Caliph" ("Le Poète au calif") aptly celebrates unbounded male sensuality, will to power, and control through the figure of the

Caliph Noureddin. And yet even more numerous are portraits of women as embodiments of pleasure and sensuality, as in "The Female Captive" ("La Captive"), "Lazzara," and "The Favorite Sultana" ("La Sultane favorite"). The pleasures of the fabulous East of the *Arabian Nights* are evoked in all their sensuousness in "Sarah Bathing" ("Sara la baigneuse") with its hypnotic list of desires:

> Oh! If I were a captain's wife,
> Or a sultana,
> I would take amber-colored baths,
> In a yellow marble basin,
> Near a throne,
> Between two golden griffins! (Hugo 1993: 105, my translation)

Nonetheless, this hedonistic East is invariably placed in a creative tension with the scholarship in the footnotes and an idea of the East as one of the decisive theaters of contemporary international politics and warfare. Pleasure is intertwined with references to the Greek struggle, the French intervention in favor of the Greeks, and the patriotic heroes of this war. In the final part, moreover, the collection returns to the Eastern myth of Napoleon and, as "Bounaberdi" and "He" ("Lui"), the Emperor is depicted as the master of the East and a Messianic figure whose return is invoked by the local populations. In Hugo's *Orientales* the seemingly opposed dimensions of the harem and war are fused in intricate patterns that correct the commonplace view of French Romantic Orientalism as more fictional and reliant on second-hand clichés than British Orientalism (Lowe 1991: 107).

If Hugo's collection interleaves knowledge, pleasure, and geopolitics in fascinating, multifaceted combinations, a comparable intersection is offered by Wolfgang von Goethe's *Western-Eastern Divan* (*West-östlicher Divan*) first published in 1819 and again, in a revised version, in 1827. Goethe's extremely wide-ranging Orientalist work, however, occupies a peculiar place in the context of contemporary European Orientalisms and, specifically, in the varied German Orientalist production that includes such diverse works as Ludwig von Tieck's "idyll" *Almansur* (1790), his play *Alla Moddin* (1790-1), and the Oriental tale *Abdallah* (1792) that shows traces of Beckford's *Vathek*; Friedrich Maximilian Klinger's Oriental tales published between 1795 and 1798; the Danish Adam Gottlob Øhlenslaeger's verse narrative *Aladdin* (1805); the Oriental themes in Novalis's *Heinrich von Ofterdingen* (1799-1802); or the Orientalist gypsy world in Achim von Arnim's *Isabella of Egypt* (*Isabella von Ägypten* 1812). Although broadly related to this tradition, Goethe's collection must be seen as an extremely personal journey of discovery of the East.

Originating from the author's extensive readings, the *Divan* once again highlights the importance of a solid scholarly and philological knowledge of Eastern cultures. The title, modeled on the fourteenth-century Persian poet Hafiz's *Divan* (originally a generic term for "writing"), celebrates the power of literary creation. In addition, Goethe's extensive readings included such landmarks of Orientalism as William

Jones's *Poeseos Asiaticae* (1774), Heinrich Friedrich von Diez's *Annals of Asia* (*Denkwürdigkeiten von Asien* 1811-15), and above all Joseph von Hammer-Purgstall's works: the six-volume *Riches of the Orient* (*Fundgruben des Orients* 1809-18), *History of Persian Belles Lettres* (1818), and the translations from Hafiz in *The Divan of Mohammed Shemseddin Hafiz* (*Der Divan von Mohammed Schemseddin Hafis* 1812-13). Goethe read the latter work in 1814 and, finally able to appreciate the Persian poet's lyrics, received the decisive stimulus for his collection. Furthermore, the pervasive presence of Hafiz in the *Divan* is compounded by echoes of Sadi, Firdusi, Rumi, materials from the *Pand Nameh*, and a large number of other works from Indian, Arabic, Hebrew, Turkish, and Persian literature. Finally the collection is completed by an apparatus of "Notes and Dissertations for a Better Comprehension of the Western-Eastern Divan" ("Noten und Abhandlungen zum besseren Verständnis des west-östlichen Divans") that Goethe intended as a general introduction to Asiatic cultures for the benefit of his readers. The book is ultimately conceived as a complex itinerary of discovery of the East, enriched by a peculiar blend of Western culture, and transfigured through the author's personal experiences.

In effect, the *Divan* masterfully elaborates the common features of Romantic Orientalism with the mature Goethe's views on the theme of the existential journey. The symbolical displacement delineated by the 12 books of the *Divan* is evident from the opening poem, "Hegira" – that is, an emigration or an escape, like the Prophet Muhammad's from Mecca to Medina. The desire to evade, however, is not a refusal of the West or a quest for existential solace in Oriental exoticism. It is rather an escape from conventions, the search for alternative forms of imagination, knowledge, and wisdom. This intention is made plain in the introduction to the "Notes and Dissertations": "The author of the following poems would above all prefer to be considered as a traveler, for whom it is praiseworthy to adapt oneself sympathetically to the customs of a foreign population, try to assimilate its linguistic usage, share its mentality, and understand its manners" (Goethe [1819] 1994, I: 138, my translation). The journey sketched by the collection is both an attempt at reproducing the Orient, its poetry, images, and rhythms, and an exploration of the universal truths of life and experience formulated through the gnomic or emblematic forms of expression that Goethe saw as typical of Eastern literature. This is at its clearest in two of the central poems in the collection: "Ecstatic Longing" ("Selige Sehnsucht") and "Ginkgo Biloba." The former poem draws on Sadi and Hafiz, and climaxes on the famous injunction "Die into becoming!" ("Stirb und werde!"; Goethe 1999: 183) that encapsulates two of the basic themes of the collection: erotic desire and the metaphysical quest for higher meaning. The latter text, instead, takes the exotic tree and its bipartite leaves as symbols of the essential duality and unity of all living beings. The emblematic leaf stands for the multiplicity of the real, that is here expressed with a peculiarly wry sense of wisdom: "I am single, I am double, / And my poems tell you so" (Goethe 1999: 165).

Although Goethe's metaphorical journey through the Orient results in a personal dimension of aesthetic and philosophical reflection, yet once again this project presents features of the Orientalist texts of pleasure (especially the undercurrents of desire in the "Book of Suleika") and the relevance awarded to scholarly and factual details in Orientalist texts of knowledge. Goethe's peculiar elaboration of these two approaches to writing about the Orient ensured the *Divan*'s success and transformed it into a crucial model for younger poets both in Germany and abroad. Its influence was pervasive in August von Platen's collections of *ghazals* (a type of love lyric with a fixed structure, common in Persian, Turkish, and Urdu literature): *Ghazals* (*Ghaselen* 1821), *The Mirror of Hafiz* (*Der Spiegel des Hafis* 1822), *New Ghazals* (*Neue Ghaselen* 1823) and a final volume of *Ghazals* (1834). Von Platen's second 1821 collection of *ghazals* was dedicated to Friedrich Rückert, another practitioner of Orientalist verse, whose *Eastern Roses* (*Östliche Rosen* 1822) is a *divan* that consciously imitates Goethe's collection, as indicated by the opening poem "To Goethe's Western-Eastern Divan" ("Zu Goethes west-östlichem Divan"). An Orientalist scholar, made Professor of Oriental philology at the University of Erlangen in 1826, Rückert was the first German writer to recreate accurately the refined and elaborate poetic form of the *ghazal*, both in his translations from Rumi and Hafiz and in his own original pieces. Finally, Goethe's *Divan* left a deep trace on Théophile Gautier's poetic collection *Enamels and Cameos* (*Emaux et camées* 1852). In the prefatory composition, the French poet, who had already treated Eastern themes in his 1830 collection of *Poems* (*Poésies*), celebrates Goethe's Orientalist verse as an oasis of peace and pure art that may inspire his own visions in this fundamental text of European "art for art's sake."

Internal Orients and the Margins of Europe

In certain Romantic-period cultures the emergence of Orientalism was more specifically a return that brought them to confront their own historical position between East and West. In Russia and Spain, geographically and culturally placed between East and West, authors began to deal with Orientalist themes not as external – literally "exotic" – facts, but rather as constitutive elements in their distinctly multicultural traditions. Thus the contact and "interanimation" between East and West is a particularly relevant component of Russian Romantic Orientalism. In literary terms Russia's historical and cultural division between these two extremes is clearly expressed in Pushkin's choice of Byron over Moore as a poetic model, as we saw in the letter quoted earlier. In many respects, the Orientalism of Russian Romanticism is similar to other contemporary manifestations. It features serious scholarship (the Lazarev institute of Oriental languages was founded in Moscow in 1815, and in the same period Saint Petersburg University started to offer courses in Arabic and Persian), an interest in translations (in the 1840s Vasily Zhukovsky translated episodes from the *Mahabharata* and the *Shah-Nameh* using German intermediate versions), annotated verse narratives based on adventurous love stories, a widespread consumer fashion for the Orient, a gradual imperialist expansion towards the East, and plans for the economic exploitation of these territories. But Russian

Orientalism was in some ways unique, for its East was more properly a South – the regions of Crimea, Georgia, and the Caucasus – that continued to be a socially and politically unstable appendage even after the tsarist conquest and pacification and the building of the Trans-Caucasian military road. These seemingly subjected lands, where in the 1830s fashionable spas were created to cater for the army officers and the leisured classes, were in fact mutinous regions racked by pockets of resistance and guerrilla warfare. An integral part of the empire, as well as an element of destabilization, this Orient was a fascinating and disturbing internal enemy (Layton 1994: 54-70, 71-88).

Choosing Byron's more Western-centered model, Pushkin developed a personal version of the Orientalist verse narrative in his "Southern poems": *The Prisoner of the Caucasus* (*Kavkasky plennik* 1822), *The Fountain of Bakhchisarai* (*Bakhchisaraisky Fontan* 1824), and *The Gypsies* (*Tsygany* 1827). These works are generally structured as cross-cultural romances in which the Russian hero's relationship with an Oriental woman is complicated by a context of revolutions and conflicts. This Byronic formula, however, is given a less predictable treatment in *The Gypsies*. Here the protagonists, the Russian fugitive Aleko and the gypsy Zemfira, represent the familiar gendered distribution of East and West; yet the author avoids awarding cultural or moral superiority to either side in this tragic narrative. In effect Pushkin's Orientalist verse, and *The Gypsies* in particular, is pervasively animated by an "ironic tension between his Oriental subject matter and his 'European eye' " (Greenleaf 1994: 117).

A similar tension emerges powerfully in Mikhail Lermontov's Orientalist works that, although initially based on Pushkin's example, constitute intricate combinations of ethnic and geopolitical discourses, philosophical and existential preoccupations, and a re-elaboration of personal reminiscences. The poet's lifelong passion for the Caucasus was rooted in his childhood experiences in this region and the painful memories of orphanhood. In the lyric "The Caucasus" ("Kavkaz" 1830) Lermontov transfigures his mother into an angel watching over him from the snowy mountain-tops: "You live in my soul, and without you I pine: / You are like one's motherland's music of joy, / Oh Caucasus mine!" (Lermontov 1983: 39). Autobiographical references also appear in his later Orientalist verse, from "The Dagger" ("Kinzhal" 1838), "The Terek's Gifts" ("Dary Tereka" 1839), and "Three Palms (An Oriental Legend)" ("Tri Pal'my, Vostochnoe Skazanie" 1839), to "Mtsyri" (1840). His famous poem "The Demon (An Oriental Tale)" ("Demon, Vostochnaia Povest"), written between 1829 and 1839 and published in 1856, after seven drafts, narrates the tragic love of a fallen angel for the Georgian woman Tamara, who dies after his first fiery embrace. The Caucasus is introduced in draft six (1838) as the appropriately exotic and primitive backdrop to a Byronic tale of impossible love. But the treatment of the Caucasus in this poem also anticipates the landscape and atmospheres of his novel *A Hero of Our Times* (*Geroi nashego vremeni* 1840), although in the latter work the Southern frontier is more carefully presented in the light of the sociocultural and ideological implications of the Russian conquest. The novel's sections are set against the tsarist campaigns to subjugate the Caucasus and combat Chechen resistance, and provide realistic depictions of the "Caucasus line" and the Georgian military road, as well as portraits of the manners and traditions of several mountain tribes, both friendly and hostile. In particular, the tale entitled "Bela" rewrites the usual Byronic cross-cultural love story through a cruel, yet parodic, twist. The protagonist Grigory Pechorin abducts a Circassian princess and takes her to his Russian fort. Nevertheless, unlike the stereotype of the heroic Western liberator, he soon tires of her company and does not prevent her murder by a vengeful tribesman. Thus Lermontov drastically interrupts the imperialist triumphalism and celebration of Western values implied by the cross-cultural romance, and dramatically brings to light the human cost of the tsarist occupation of the South (Layton 2002, Durylin 2002).

The ideological engagement of Lermontov's Orientalist verse is further confirmed by the fact that it contributed to the central intellectual polemic between "Slavophiles" and "Westernizers" in mid-nineteenth-century Russia. In particular, his work was appropriated by the former as a weapon to proclaim and defend the essentially Slavic, and therefore Eastern, quality of Russian culture and literature. In his poem "The Debate" ("Spor" 1841) Lermontov seems to contribute to this attempt at cultural definition by staging the contrast between East and West, or tradition and progress, through a dialogue between the personifications of Elbrus and Kazbek the Great, the two highest mountain peaks in his beloved Caucasus.

Although unrelated to any extensive imperialist and colonizing activity, the Orientalism of Spanish Romantic culture may be considered together with that of Russia because, through the resurgence of the exotic, Spanish culture in the Romantic period also rediscovered its Oriental roots and revalued the presence of an internal Orient in its own history. Moreover, European writers and artists saw the whole of Spain, and not just its Southern regions, as essentially Oriental (not to mention "Romantic") in character. Hugo in the preface to *Les Orientales* famously asserted: "Spain is still the Orient; Spain is half African, Africa is half Asiatic" (Hugo [1829, 1831] 1993: 23, my translation), a notion that the collection develops by including a "Moorish Romance" ("Romance mauresque") on the medieval tale of the half-breed Mudarra and the seven "infantes de Lara," and "Granada," a celebration of the city that was the symbol of Romantic *hispanophilia* (Hoffmeister 1990). Hugo's passion for Oriental Spain was rooted in its popular medieval narrative poetry or *romances*, many of which dealt with the Islamic populations in the South of the peninsula, and which he collectively defined as an "Arabic Iliad" (Hugo 1993: 363).

The fascination of Spain lay in its geocultural ambivalence: it was an East located in the West. It also lay in its combination of the Oriental and the Western, the medieval and the modern, in a syncretic whole that proved an inexhaustible source of inspiration and creativity for European writers. This Eastern past was also attractive for Spanish authors, who had to look no further than their own country to find a treasurehouse of literary materials. Of course, Oriental themes were so ingrained in the national history that neoclassical literature had also often employed Spanish-Moorish themes, as in the tragedies *Don Sancho García* by José de Cadalso (1771) or *Raquel* by Vicente García de la Huerta (1778). As with the later Romantic productions, these works problematized the idea of the cultural and political boundary between Muslims and Christians through the fictionalization of different episodes in the long medieval wars between the Moorish and Christian powers. Orientalist themes continued to be popular in dramatic productions and thus marked the transition towards the modes of Romantic theater. Francisco Martínez de la Rosa's *Morayma* (written in 1818 and published in Paris in 1830) is drawn from Ginés Pérez de Hita's *Civil Wars of Granada* (*Las guerras civiles de Granada* 1595, 1601) and narrates Morayma's persecution by the evil king Boabdil, although it still subscribes to the generic conventions of the eighteenth-century sentimental tragedy and is far from the more explicitly Romantic treatment of Oriental themes in Martínez de la Rosa's later tragedy *Aben Humeya*. First performed in Paris in 1830 as *The Revolt of the Moors* (*La Révolte des Maures*), and in Madrid in 1836, this play elaborates yet another episode in the conflict between Muslims and Christians through the figure of Don Hernando de Valor, Aben Humeya, the leader of the Moors' revolt during the reign of Philip II. Its prologue is one of the central manifestos of Spanish Romanticism and deals especially with notions of local color and historical fidelity.

Yet perhaps the most successful and influential play with Orientalist elements in Romantic-period drama was Juan Eugenio de Hartzenbusch's *The Lovers of Teruel* (*Los amantes de Teruel*). Premiered in 1837, this was one of most successful plays in Spanish Romantic theater, based on a plotline familiar from Boccaccio's *Decameron* and *Siglo de Oro* dramatists such as Tirso de Molina. Hartzenbusch's play chronicles the ill-fated love story between Isabel de Segura and Diego de Marsilla, thwarted by the hatred dividing their families in the thirteenth-century Aragonese town of Teruel near the border with the Moorish kingdom of Valencia. Made prisoner by the Muslims, Diego must return to Teruel in time to claim Isabel as his bride, but Queen Zulima falls in love with him and prevents him from leaving. In the meantime, Isabel is put under pressure by her family to accept another suitor, while Zulima sends a messenger to Teruel to bring news of Diego's death. Isabel marries Rodrigo de Azagra and Marsilla arrives too late to stop her, while Zulima is murdered on the orders of the jealous sultan. Rejected by Isabel, who intends to be faithful to her husband, Marsilla dies of grief, and his beloved dies soon after on seeing his corpse. If Hartenzbusch re-elaborates the traditional plot quite faithfully, his treatment also enhances the Oriental overtones through the figure of the Moorish sultana and the languorous and despotic atmosphere of the court of Valencia.

Moorish themes were also popular in historical novels, from the earliest instance, Rafael Húmara y Salamanca's *Ramiro, Count of Lucena* (*Ramiro, conde de Lucena* 1823), set during the wars of the Reconquest and brimming with Arabic color, to such later examples as Martínez de la Rosa's *Doña Isabel de Solís, Queen of Granada* (*Doña Isabel de Solís, reina de Granada* 1837) and Serafín Estébanez Calderón's sentimental novel *Christians and Moors* (*Cristianos y moriscos* 1838), which tells about a Spanish soldier's love for a converted Moorish woman after the Spanish conquest of Granada. Their love is made impossible by religious and racial conflicts, and their misfortunes and tragic deaths are narrated against the backdrop of detailed evocations of Moorish customs that innovatively combine Romantic historicism and *costumbrismo*, that is, the literary portrayal of manners or customs characteristic of a region or country. In the field of narrative verse, by contrast, the most complex instance is *The Exposed Moor, or Cordoba and Burgos in the Tenth Century* (*El moro expósito, o Córdoba y Burgos en el siglo décimo* 1834) by Angel Saavedra, Duque de Rivas. Written between 1829 and 1833, this epic is composed of 12 *romances históricos* that interweave the tale of Mudarra and the "infantes de Lara" with stories of thwarted cross-cultural love, and evocations of medieval Spain and its multicultural variety. An equally monumental effort of conjuring an entire culture and its geography is José Zorrilla's later, but still essentially Romantic, *Granada, an Oriental Poem* (*Granada, poema oriental* 1852). This incomplete, fragmentary work draws on innumerable Spanish and foreign learned sources, and recounts episodes from the fall of Granada and the rivalries in the Granadan royal family, enriched with secondary narratives and digressions, as well as shorter descriptive pieces about a wealth of Orientalist motifs.

Throughout the early part of the nineteenth century, European literatures were busy "colonizing" Spain with images of an Oriental land of primitive instincts and sensual enjoyments that culminated with Prosper Mérimée's 1843 *Carmen* (Colmeiro 2002). At the same time, however, Spanish literature was equally intent on revitalizing its own geographical, historical, and cultural role within the long European history of dialogues, confrontations, and exchanges between East and West.

Interanimations

As the above *excursus* suggests, in order to piece together the map of European Romantic Orientalisms we need to trace the interlinked development of themes, motifs, and plotlines; the cross-fertilizing influences of scholarly and literary innovations; and the ways in which travel writing contributed to improve knowledge about the East across national and linguistic boundaries. The imaginative space of Romantic Orientalism is composed of innumerable channels of creation, imitation, discovery, and rediscovery. It is the narrative of a fascination with the Orient as a dimension where Western discourse can disperse, as well as an attempt at reconfirming and stressing the dividing line between East and West. In all traditions the temptation of cultural interfusion proved irresistible. William Jones fervently called on Western authors to imitate Oriental literatures in order to renovate their own national heritage. This kind of interanimation visibly emerged in Robert Southey's imitation of the Oriental arabesque in the complex metrical structure of *Thalaba*; the German Romantics' importation of the structure of the *ghazal*; or J. C. L. Simonde de Sismondi's *Historical View of the Literature of the South of Europe* (*De la littérature du midi de l'Europe* 1813) where the origins of Provençal literature, the earliest of modern European literatures, are seen as closely interrelated with the concurrent flourishing of Arabic literature. Resistance to such cross-fertilizations was frequent and linked to fears of racial or cultural miscegenation. Nevertheless, the idea of continuities and interconnections remained very powerful in a period that recognized and valued the productive importance of exchanges and dialogues between civilizations. Friedrich Schlegel's famous *Athenäum* Fragment 116 on "progressive universal poetry" described Romanticism as a culture based on fusion and admixtures. And the East was one of the sources of this cultural convergence as, in the words of Novalis, another member of the Jena group, it was the original fountainhead of civilization. Thus, in an essay of 1789-90 "On Enthusiasm," Novalis remarked: "all I have said here is especially valid for the Orient, the real fatherland of humankind, language, poetry and, therefore, enthusiasm" (Novalis 1960-88, II: 23, my translation).

The Orientalist literature of Romanticism is characterized throughout by international exchanges and intersections between fiction and other art forms. Thus William Jones's English version of *Sakuntala* was translated into German by Johann Georg Adam Forster in 1791, influencing Goethe, Herder, Schiller, and, above all, Friedrich Schlegel, who translated it anew. William Beckford's *Vathek* left traces in Ludwig von Tieck's *Abdallah*, and continued to be read all over Europe well into the nineteenth and twentieth centuries. Thomas Moore's *Lalla Rookh* spawned a series of musical and spectacular versions in several European traditions, including Robert Schumann's choral work "Das Paradies und die Peri" (composed in 1843); Byron's *Corsair* was the source for Schumann's unfinished opera and Hector Berlioz's overture *Le Corsaire* (both composed in 1844), and Giuseppe Verdi's homonymous opera (1848); while *The Giaour* and *Sardanapalus* inspired Delacroix's paintings. The rediscovery of Egypt started by Napoleon's expedition of 1798 began an Egyptian fashion that reached as far as Verdi's *Aida* (1871) and beyond. A distich from Goethe's *Divan* was used by Mickwiecz as an epigraph to his *Crimean Sonnets*. And disciples of the great French Arabist Sylvestre de Sacy contributed to start the teaching of Persian and Arabic at Saint Petersburg University.

In 1800 Friedrich Schlegel observed that "We must seek the highest Romanticism in the Orient" (Schlegel [1800] 1967, II: 320, my translation). If we consider the literary and cultural cross-currents sketched above, this well-known statement may be read as an assessment of the indissoluble links between Romanticisms, Romantic-period cultures, and their multiple versions of the Orient. The variety of interconnected treatments of the East confirms Romanticism as an intercultural dimension that, on the score of Enlightenment cosmopolitanism, brought European traditions together through incessantly proliferating reinventions of the Orient.

References and Further Reading

Butler, M. (1994). "Orientalism." In D. B. Pirie (ed.), *The Penguin History of Literature*, vol. 5: *The Romantic Period*. Harmondsworth, UK: Penguin, pp. 395-447.

Byron, G. G., Lord (1973-94). *Byron's Letters and Journals*, ed. Leslie A. Marchand, 13 vols. London: John Murray.

Colmeiro, J. F. (2002). "Exorcising Exoticism: Carmen and the Construction of Oriental Spain." *Comparative Literature*, 54: 127-44.

Conner, P. (1979). *Oriental Architecture in the West*. London: Thames and Hudson.

Curl, J. S. (1994). *Egyptomania*. Manchester, UK: Manchester University Press.

Delacroix, E. ([1893] 1951). *The Journal of Eugène Delacroix*, ed. Hubert Wellington, trans. Lucy Norton. Oxford: Phaidon.

Durylin, S. (2002). "The Caucasus and Caucasian Peoples in Lermontov's Novel." In Lewis Bagby (ed.), *Lermontov's A Hero of Our Time: A Critical Companion*. Evanston, IL: Northwestern University Press, pp. 124-34.

Goethe, J. W. von ([1819] 1994). *West-Östlicher Divan*, ed. Hendrik Birus, 2 vols. In *Sämtliche Werke*, 40 vols. Frankfurt am Main: Deutscher Klassiker Verlag.

Goethe, J. W. von (1999). *Selected Poetry*, trans. David Luke. London: Libris.

Greenleaf, M. (1994). *Pushkin and Romantic Fashion: Fragment, Elegy, Orient, Irony*. Stanford: Stanford University Press.

Haddad, E. A. (2002). *Orientalist Poetics: The Islamic Middle East in Nineteenth-Century English and French Poetry*. Aldershot, UK: Ashgate.

Hoffmeister, G. (1990). "Exoticism: Granada's Alhambra in European Romanticism." In G. Hoffmeister (ed.), *European Romanticism: Literary Cross-Currents, Modes, and Models*. Detroit: Wayne State University Press, pp. 113-26.

Hugo, V. ([1829, 1831] 1993). *Les Orientales/Les Feuilles d'automne*, ed. Pierre Albouy. Paris: Gallimard.

Jeffrey, F. (1817). "Review of Thomas Moore's *Lalla Rookh*." *The Edinburgh Review*, 29: 1-35.

Layton, S. (1994). *Russian Literature and Empire: Conquest of the Caucasus from Pushkin to Tolstoy*. Cambridge, UK: Cambridge University Press.

Layton, S. (2002). "Ironies of Ethnic Identity." In Lewis Bagby (ed.), *Lermontov's A Hero of Our Time: A Critical Companion*. Evanston, IL: Northwestern University Press, pp. 64-84.

Lermontov, M. (1983). *Major Poetical Works*, ed. and trans. Anatoly Lieberman. London and Canberra: Croom Helm.

Lowe, L. (1991). *Critical Terrains: French and British Orientalisms*. Ithaca, NY and London: Cornell University Press.

MacKenzie, J. (1995). *Orientalism: History, Theory and the Arts*. Manchester, UK: Manchester University Press.

Miller, C. L. (1989). "Orientalism, Colonialism." In Denis Hollier (ed.), *A New History of French Literature*. Cambridge, MA and London: Harvard University Press, pp. 698-705.

Novalis (1960-88). *Schriften*, ed. Paul Kluckhohn and Richard Samuel, 5 vols. Stuttgart: W. Kohlhammer.

Pushkin, A. S. (1971). *Pushkin on Literature*, ed. and trans. Tatiana Wolf. London: Methuen.

Said, E. W. ([1978] 1991). *Orientalism: Western Conceptions of the Orient*. Harmondsworth, UK: Penguin.

Schlegel, F. ([1800] 1967). *Gespräch über die Poesie*. In H. Eichner (ed.), *Kritische-Friedrich-Schlegel-Ausgabe*, vols. 2-3. München, Paderborn, Wien: Verlag Ferdinand Schöning; Zürich: Thomas Verlag.

Schwab, R. (1950). *La Renaissance Orientale*. Paris: Payot.

Sievernich, G. and Budde, H. (eds.) (1989). *Europa und der Orient 800-1900*. Berlin: Bertelsmann Lexikon Verlag.

Sweetman, J. (1987). *The Oriental Obsession: Islamic Inspiration in British and American Art and Architecture 1500-1920*. Cambridge, UK: Cambridge University Press.

Yeazell, R. B. (2000). *Harems of the Mind: Passages of Western Art and Literature*. New Haven, CT and London: Yale University Press.

28

A Continent of Corinnes: The Romantic Poetess and the Diffusion of Liberal Culture in Europe, 1815-50

Patrick Vincent

Recovering the Poetess

During the first half of the nineteenth century, hundreds of women across Europe wrote and published poems we today dismiss as sentimental but that contemporaries considered an integral if albeit minor product of Romanticism. Most of these writers' names and works have long been forgotten; their tears, however, remain emblematic of the romantic poetess. The brunt of criticism aimed at the romantic poetess falls on her abuse of melancholy themes and moods, what Elizabeth Barrett Browning calls in *Aurora Leigh* (1857) her "Elegiac grief, and songs of love, / Like cast-off nosegays picked up on the road, / The worse for being worn" (Barrett Browning 1992: 45). Jerome McGann states that sentimental poetry has always been "something of an embarrassment" in the eyes of high culture (McGann 1996: 1). Yet the motive for the melancholy so frequently expressed in these women poets' elegiac poems on love and death remains unexplained. While critics often think that they know sentimental poetry all too well, dismissing it as excessive, maudlin, or self-indulgent, we have yet to fully understand how such works should be read. In fact, the question returns so insistently in the poems themselves that it must be considered essential to sentimental poetics. As Letitia Landon (1802-38), one of Britain's two most popular poetess figures of that period, writes in an elegy commemorating sister poet Felicia Hemans (1793-1835): "We say the song is sorrowful, but know not / What may have left that sorrow in the song" (Landon 1997: 251).

Thanks to a renewed emphasis on literary-historical research informed by feminist theory, scholars in the last two decades have made significant progress in answering Landon's question. They follow in the footsteps of earlier twentieth-century critics whose pioneering scholarship did much to draw women poets out of the attics, archives, and, most tellingly, out of the literary "remains" so popular in 1830s and 1840s Europe (Larnac 1935, Partridge 1924, Rapgof 1916, Séché 1908a, 1908b, 1910). Scholarship on the poetess today thrives in particular in English departments where many women are now taught in college seminars that until a decade ago acknowledged only six male Romantics (Walker 1982, Mellor 1988, Ross 1989, Leighton 1992, Schor 1994). However, excellent work on Romantic women poets is also being carried out in other national literary fields, suggesting that links may be drawn which transcend national cultures (Heldt 1987, Kirkpatrick 1989, Evers 1991, Kelly 1996a, Finch 2000). As I shall argue, these transnational links which I identify with the poetess were in fact crucial to the way in which women poets imagined themselves. Not only did the poetess serve as a seductive and influential cultural model which gave aspiring women writers in Britain, on the Continent, and in the United States the authority to write and get published, as was the case in Russia for example, where the importation of French women's writing made it acceptable for Russian women to compose verse, but more importantly, the poetess helped foster an international culture that played a significant liberalizing role of *rapprochement* after the demise of the First Empire in 1815, uniting European nations under the banner of tears. I label this liberal ethos the poetess's politics of the feminine and understand it as a sort of ideal third way closer to our own nongovernmental agencies' global humanitarianism than to the nineteenth century's individualism grounded in the family and nation.

Two specifications are necessary regarding my title. The fact that Marceline Desbordes-Valmore (1786-1859), considered one of France's first Romantics, was familiar with the work of Hemans, anthologized as one of Britain's last Romantics, or that the heyday of the romantic poetess in Spain and Russia occurred in the 1840s, reminds us of the inadequacy of the term "Romantic" as a period label (see Michael Ferber's Introduction to this volume). Taking my cue from George Gusdorf, who described "a new sense of European cultural unity" as one of Romanticism's central contributions (Gusdorf 1993, 1: 297), I use this problem-ridden term without capitals to indicate this sense of cultural unity rather than to precisely define a specific period or aesthetic. Even more controversial is the term "poetess" (*poétesse, Dichterin, poetisa, poetessa*). While Samuel Johnson's definition of the poetess as a "female poet," in line with eighteenth-century usage of the term, was arguably neutral, its connotation evolved during the late eighteenth and first half of the nineteenth century into something more self-consciously derogatory, closer to "poetaster" than to "poet." The bourgeois consolidation of the doctrine of separate spheres reinforced the equation of "female" with "feminine," which Alexander Dyce, in his anthology entitled *Specimens of British Poetesses*, usefully summarizes as "her sensibility, her tenderness, her grace" (Dyce 1825: iv). Dyce's title, as opposed to Thomas Campbell's all-male anthology in the same series, *Specimens of English Verse* (1819), highlights the degree to which critics, readers, sometimes even the poets themselves, viewed the poetess as embodied in her work. The poetess's specifically feminine aesthetic, aligned with nineteenth-century domestic ideology and Edmund Burke's category of the Beautiful, was yoked to the materiality of the body – it stemmed from the heart. This heart was expected to be tender, implying, again according to Johnson's dictionary, softness, kindness, susceptibility to impressions, or pathos of expression. What stemmed from the heart could not stem from the mind. In his review of Dyce's *Specimens*, for example, Leigh Hunt writes that the poetess, as the male poets' muse, "condescended, in return, to put on the earthly feminine likeness of some favourite of the other sex" (Hunt 1891: 257). Always derivative, the poetess lacked the originality so central to Romantic aesthetic theory and was barred from the hallowed male poetic tradition. Nowadays, despite efforts to more precisely define the term "poetess" (Blain 1995, Mellor 1997), critics remain wary of employing it, preferring "woman poet" or other more neutral formulations (*femme-poète, Lyrikerin, la poeta, zhenskii poet*). By doing so, however, we endorse the aesthetic and critical movements, Realism and Modernism, most responsible for devaluing those women who found authorization in a culturally sanctioned, feminine poetics. In this chapter, therefore, I find it useful to employ the term "poetess," but always as a figure or pole defined by a specific set of principles: a woman poet can perform, even parody that figure, but she can never *be* a poetess.

"Corinne at Cape Miseno" or the Poetess's Ethos

Whereas women poets in the 1820s and 1830s were commissioned to write ekphrastic poems commenting on gift-book engravings, I want to begin the other way around and use a painting to comment on the visual, indeed theatrical, character of the poetess's performative poetics as well as the ethos which informed her writing. Completed in 1819, the same year that Géricault exhibited his monumental "Raft of the Medusa" at the Paris Salon, François Gérard's "Corinne at Cape Miseno" frames an inspired-looking woman wrapped in a luxurious crimson toga reclined against the fragment of a Roman column and wielding a lyre. A darkened audience clad in various national outfits, including a man in a turban, a British officer, and a mother and child look enraptured in the direction of the painting's well-lighted main subject; in the background a volcano belches menacing black smoke. In the classical harmony of its style and stage props, Gérard's painting is still a long way from Géricault's romantic agony. As in his mentor Jacques-Louis David's public art, Gérard is drawing the portrait of an exemplary republican moral subject. The problem with such an interpretation, however, lies in the painting's historical context – in 1819, France was no longer a republic but a monarchy again, and Napoleon's 1815 defeat largely invalidated the republican symbolism consonant with French neo-Classicism. More-over, republicanism had been even more short-lived for French women, barred from becoming public citizens by the revolutionary government in 1793 and by Napo-leon's 1804 civil code. With no likely reform to look forward to under the Bourbon Restoration, Gérard's glorification in 1819 of a republican heroine must have struck its audience as hopelessly idealistic, or worse, as an anachronism. In fact, after its initial success at the Paris Salon of 1822, the painting was quickly relegated along with its creator to the back provinces of art history, a victim of Gérard's belatedness as a member of David's school.

"Corinne at Cape Miseno," of course, is not an historical painting, but a portrait disguised as literary illustration, deflecting the force of its republicanism. However, inspired by liberal French writer Germaine de Staël's highly popular *Corinne, or Italy* (1807), it depicts the novel's politically charged climactic scene, in which the *improvisatrice* heroine associates the sublime landscape in the vicinity of Naples with the crimes perpetrated against Italy's republican heroes and institutions. An elegiac lament, Corinne's effusion dwells on the way in which women geniuses and poets especially, "whose imagination draws / Its power from loving and from suffering," fall victim to tyranny, and the song clearly foreshadows the heroine's own dramatic finale (de Staël 1850: 228). The story of the painting's commissioning and details of its existence add more layers of significance to Gérard's controversial choice of a republican moral landscape as the painting's subject. Upon Germaine de Staël's death in 1817, Prince Augustus of Prussia suggested to Juliette Récamier that David paint their illustrious friend's portrait (and his own, in the person of Oswald). All agreed except for another writer, Sophie Gay, who felt that the Baron Gérard as a friend of the deceased could more faithfully portray her. This anecdote draws attention to the importance of salon intimacy or what Adela Pinch has called "knowability," the sentimental notion that our ability to sympathize with another lies in the shared familiarity of certain images and affects (Pinch 1996: 165). Instead of directly accepting, David rudely bargained with the prince over the cost of the painting, and a horrified Madame Récamier demanded instead that they commission Gérard, illustrating another important aspect of salon ideology, disinterestedness. In 1821, the Prussian prince gave the painting to Juliette Récamier who exhibited it in her famous drawing room at l'Abbaye-aux-Bois beside a view of moonlit Coppet (Séché 1910: 34). L'Abbaye-aux-Bois through the 1820s and 1830s partly replaced Coppet, Germaine de Staël's castle near Geneva, as an influential salon – the painting therefore served by proxy as a gathering point for politicians, intellectuals, and artists, most notably Chateaubriand, who tested early versions of his *Mémoires d'outre-tombe* on the small circle of Récamier *habitués*. But "Corinne at Cape Miseno" not only drew together France's cosmopolitan elite. The sign of a democratization and commodification of salon culture, the painting was also reproduced as an engraving and printed in 1833 as a frontispiece to the Bentley standard novel edition of the English translation of *Corinne, or Italy*, accompanied by the following passage: "Her friends were impatient to hear her. Even the common people knew her fame, and, as imagination rendered them judges of poetry, they closed silently around" (de Staël 1850: ii).

"Corinne at Cape Miseno" epitomizes values essential to the romantic poetess's ethos, including cosmopolitan sympathy, salon intimacy, and disinterestedness. At the very center of this ethos, of course, presides the poetess, who, like Corinne at the Cape of Miseno, uses her songs to bind together gender, class, and nation under the collective banner of sentiment. Post-1815 Europe was divided by the failure of the

French Revolution, two decades of war, the restoration in many countries of despotic forms of government, and the development of working-class movements. The continent's politically and economically oppressed subjects, whether they were workers marching at Peterloo in 1819, aristocrats demanding constitutional change in Russia's 1825 Decembrist uprising, or Parisians manning the barricades in 1830, all demanded reform. One may argue that the bourgeoisie welcomed sentimental culture because it provided them with a comforting but false sense of social harmony. Among Europe's oppressed subjects, however, were the very same poets who participated in the production of sentiment. These poets sought to re-enact Germaine de Staël's enthusiastic mission, just as Gérard had represented de Staël performing her fictional heroine's role. Originating in Enlightenment moral philosophy, this mission was developed in a number of de Staël's essays, including *On the Influence of Passions on the Happiness of Individuals and Nations* (1796), *On Literature Considered in its Relationship to Social Institutions* (1800), and *On Germany* (1810). But it was her more despairing novel, *Corinne, or Italy,* which most directly inspired the figure of the romantic poetess, the sentimental woman poet who appropriates and subverts limiting social constructions of femininity in order to transform these into a politics of the feminine.

While Gérard's painting shows how women poets imagined their poetry as a well-rehearsed, politically motivated performance, it also reveals contradictions that have undermined the poetess's mission and legacy. First, like the painting's belated neo-Classicism, sentimental poetics went against the grain of developments in aesthetic theory. The poetess did not value originality, but prided herself on speaking with a collective voice, drawing intertextual links with other poets and poems and creating the illusion of expressiveness in order to assert that feelings are common to a knowable community rather than individual and private. Contemporary critics showed little patience with such a performative, public verse, and it remains contrary to our own idea of what lyric poetry is about. Furthermore, in an age of self-interest reflected in utilitarian positivism, in the hegemony of nationalism and in the consolidation of market economics, the poetess's ethos of sympathy appeared increasingly illusory. With the rise of Romantic nationalism in particular, there was a move away from eighteenth-century cosmopolitanism toward a stigmatizing of that same nonnational affiliation as foreignness. The commercialization of literature and poetry's increased circulation and exchange as a commodity, so antithetical to salon ideology's disinterestedness, also forced the poetess to re-evaluate her identity and mission. Commissioned by a prince, decorating the salon of one of the Restoration's most glamorous hostesses, then reprinted in a popular novel series, the trajectory of Gérard's painting approximates the transformation of nineteenth-century women's poetry from polite salon conversation into a popular form of entertainment aimed at middle-class women's magazines and gift-books. These low symbolic productions deepened the rift between high- and middle-brow art as well as women poets' sense that they themselves were industrial workers, a sort of literary proletariat whose tears no longer were the sign of sympathy but rather of commercial value.

Faced with these contradictions and obstacles, it is no surprise that women poets who sought to perform Corinne's politics of the feminine responded most dramatically to the novel's elegiac second half, when the Sapphic plot of fame and love unravels, leading to the heroine's quasi-suicide. Corinne's first improvisation at the Capitol in Rome marks the height of her glory as a woman genius, while her second recitation at the Cape of Miseno foreshadows the novel's melancholy ending. But it is "The Last Song of Corinne," a *recusatio* against patriarchy superficially disguised as Christian renunciation, which especially impressed her readers. Oswald's abandonment of Corinne inscribes the novel in a long literary tradition of self-destructive women, as Lawrence Lipking (1988) has shown, and both male and female contemporaries responded to the death scene because they understood it as a characteristically feminine form of transcendence. Stendhal, for example, described Gérard's portrait of Corinne as an "inspired woman walking to her death along a flowered path." For French critic Charles-Augustin Sainte-Beuve, a prolific commentator on the romantic poetess phenomenon, death was the necessary, sublime resolution to Corinne's passionate morality, crowning her existence, marking her as a saint:

> I like her incapacity to console herself, I like her sentiment which wins over her genius, her frequent invocation to sainthood and to the continuity of ties which alone can stop abrupt separations, and to hear her, at the hour of death, admit in her swan song: "Of all the powers of mind which nature gave, / the power of suffering has been the sole one, / Which I have used to its extent." (Sainte-Beuve 1862: 136)[1]

Sainte-Beuve did not only interpret Corinne's suffering and suicide as a literary convention. Like many women writers, he also understood its historical specificity as well as its socially and politically progressive ramifications. Celebrating Germaine de Staël's conversation skills and tieing these into her republican politics, the critic argues in the same essay that these could only be a product of the still hopeful years of the Directory. For Sainte-Beuve, the writer's republicanism, her dogged belief in perfectibility, and her sympathy for the plight of the unfortunate, all come together in Corinne's dramatic final sacrifice, which expresses the culmination of her creator's life and ideals and her despair of ever seeing these ideals put into practice.

The "last song" is recited not by Corinne herself, but by a young woman who impersonates the dying heroine. Because of the sympathy it inspires, suffering is the most contagious of literary affects, and women poets felt no misgivings about impersonating the dying heroine in their own poetry, creating copies of a copy, simulacra haunted by the ghostly presence of the young woman in white robes. Examples of this sentimental form of literary transmission abound, extending of course beyond poetry to fiction and drama – Germaine de Staël's novel made an impact across Europe (Forsberg 1967, Rossettini 1963). In Germany, Dorothea Schlegel translated *Corinne* almost immediately after its French publication, and although her husband Friedrich received all the credit, her work demonstrates the importance of women translators as cultural mediators in this period. In Italy, where no Romantic woman poet has yet made it into the canon and the most famous last song, "Ultimo Canto di Saffo" (1822) was written by a man, Giacomo Leopardi, *Corinne* nevertheless helped validate the work of real improvisers such as Teresa Bandettini (1763-1837) and Massimina Fantastici (1788-1846). In Russia, where a translation of the novel was published in 1809, Zinaïda Volkonskaya (1792-1862), herself known as the "Corinne of the North" and who died in exile in Rome, addressed an album of verse in French to de Staël where she writes: "Corinne! I follow you in those dark ruins... / It is for you to sing, you whose genius / under a liberal sky has flowed freely" (cited in Rossettini 1963: 60). In Great Britain, Letitia Landon is the woman poet who "followed" Corinne most closely, even adapting Corinne's impro-visations into metrical odes in Isabel Hill's 1833 translation of the novel. France's Delphine Gay (1804-55), named in honor of de Staël's other lovelorn heroine, wrote patriotic odes in the same vein as Corinne's improvisations and was crowned at Rome's Capitol in 1827. Other poets like Felicia Hemans in a "A Parting Song" or French poet Amable Tastu (1798-1885) in "La Gloire" modeled themselves on the poetess figure by quoting from or imitating "The Last Song of Corinne." Even more common was women poets' recourse to themes and motifs associated with *Corinne*: the figures of Corinne, Sappho, or Ariadne; the motif of fame and erotic abandonment; or the theme of Italy and exile.

No matter which strategies they adopted or to what degree they enacted the poetess, all women poets who wanted to perpetuate Germaine de Staël's ethos did so metonymically, expressing their faith in a decentered, collective feminine identity through their embracing of tears and suffering. Felicia Hemans, for example, writes "c'est moi" (that's me) beside a passage on Corinne's pathos-filled finale. France's most famous woman poet, Marceline Desbordes-Valmore, who had often admired Gérard's portrait of Corinne when on her reluctant missions to Madame Récamier for financial help, notes in a letter, "I have howled my sadness for so long, that it has been understood and shared..." (Desbordes-Valmore 1895: 2, 62). One of those women who shared her sadness was Russian poet Evdokia Rostopchina (1812-58), who began her poetic career writing imitations of Desbordes-Valmore's elegies. In Spain, the melancholy poetry of Gertrude Gomez de Avellanada (1814-73) and Carolina Cor-onado (1823-1911) helped shape the poetic identity of sister poets such as Vicenta Garcia Miranda (Kirkpatrick 2002: 511-12). And in a sentimental piece called "Ich denke dein" (I think of you) written in 1792, praised by Goethe, Danish-German poet Friederike Brun (1765-1835) supplicates her listener not to abandon her to oblivion: "Gedenke mein!" (Remember me). Strangely but tellingly, this aristocrat and intimate friend of de Staël and Karl Victor von Bonstetten did find an echo or response to her complaint 30 years later in two popular poems, Hemans's previously cited "A Parting Song" and Landon's "Night at Sea" (1839). When Russian poet Karolina Pavlova (1807-93) asks rhetorically, in a French poem entitled "Les Pleurs des femmes" written in 1840, "Pourquoi donc pleurent-elles tous / Ces pauvres femmes d'ici-bas?" (Why do they all cry, those poor women here below?), she does so with the certitude of knowing that the trope of suffering united her to women poets in Great Britain, across Europe, and all the way to the United States. Addressing a hypothetical male critic, her poem responds to her own question by pointing out that women's tears are a "deuil secret" (a secret loss) men cannot understand, another familiar trope in women's sentimental poetry, but which represents "Ni regret, ni malheur réel" (Neither regret, nor real misfortune) (Pavlova 1964: 503). Pavlova knew that the women poets who filled Europe's periodicals with melancholy verse were not primarily concerned with expressing their own personal condition, but rather wished to voice their collective fear of cultural abandonment and to protest against social and political oppression.

A Continent of Corinnes: The Poetess and Abandonment

Women poets' direct references to the Sappho-Corinne myth were of course the surest sign that they were working in the poetess tradition, enabling them to express their sense of a collective female identity grounded in suffering. German poet Karoline von Günderrode (1780-1806), known as the "female Werther" and often considered the most "authentic" of all romantic poetess figures, killed herself a year before *Corinne* was published, a suicide which unfortunately sealed her reputation as a real-life Corinne. Günderode was well versed in Greek mythology and in one of her poems, "Ariadne auf Naxos," published in *Gedichte und Fantasien* (1804), she assimilates the story of Ariadne to that of Sappho to dramatize the poet's own death wish. As Kari Lokke has argued, however, the poem does not celebrate the pathos of abandonment, but rather conceals it by having the heroine leap voluntarily into the sea, an action which is meant to insure her an immortality not mediated by a male god or poet (Lokke 2002: 97-8). In "Die eine Klage" (The unique complaint) from *Melete* (1806) and her posthumously published "Ist Alles stumm und leer?" (Is everything silent and empty?), the speaker universalizes Ariadne's "Liebe Schmerz" (pain of love), first in the third person, associating it with all those who have felt the "Bittrer Trennung Schmerz" (the pain of bitter separation), then, in the later poem, in the first person, asking: "Kann Lust so schmerzlich sein, / Untreu so herzlich sein?" (Can pleasure be so painful, unfaithfulness so sincere?). To read Günderode's suffering only biographically, as the consequence of her abandonment by Friedrich Creuzer, does an injustice to the universality of the theme which runs through all her work and which links her not only to mythical figures such as Ariadne and Adonis, but also to later women writers who have used Günderode as an emblem for women's oppression. These include poet and prose writer Bettina von Arnim (1785-1859) in her epistolary novel *Die Günderode* (1840), translated by the proto-feminist American writer Margaret Fuller in 1842, and more recently, Christa Wolf's 1979 novella *Kein Ort. Nirgends* (No Place. Nowhere).

Like Ariadne's choice of obscurity in "Ariadne auf Naxos," Günderode's work remained unknown during the poet's lifetime except to a small circle of friends and reviewers, thus respecting the condition of intimacy or knowability so important to salon ideology. Her early death saved her from having to reckon with a contradiction which, as I have argued, is also constitutive of the romantic poetess, namely women poets' increased exposure through commodification to the reading public, this at a time when domestic ideology was wrenching apart the private and public spheres. Beginning in the 1790s in Britain and in the 1810s in France, women were finally able to make a living writing poetry thanks to new literary institutions such as women's magazines and the ubiquitous gift-books. Letitia Landon, one of Britain's first celebrity poets alongside Byron, Moore, and Hemans, actively played up these contradictions as a way to define her poetess identity, drawing parallels between herself and Corinne in poems such as "Corinna" (1821), "The Improvisatrice" (1824), and "Corinne at the Cape of Misena" (1832). In the last, a poem commissioned for an annual entitled *The Amulet*, she gives an ornate description of Gérard's painting followed by a metric translation of Corinne's "Song of Naples." Recycled two years later in Isabel Hill's translation of the novel, the composite nature of this and many other Landon poems suggests that neither organic unity nor originality were a concern. In the poem's second half, she stages a perfectly poised, dramatic poetess surrounded by an adoring crowd, a technique repeated in many other poems including "Sappho" (1822). We are drawn to the crux of Landon's theatrical poetics when she states that "Corinne / Is but another name for her who wrote," then mystifies this statement with the question, "What are the feelings but her own?" Repeatedly flaunting the intertextual, artificial, even commodified quality of sentiment only to reaffirm its expressive truth, the speaker's authority emerges as a shared knowledge of pain, "the truth of sorrow," independent of any precise etiology. Landon marks this community of sufferers as specifically female when she writes of "that keen sense / Of the wide difference between ourselves / And those who are our fellows" (Landon 1997: 143-6).

In France, Adélaïde Dufrénoy was the best-known poetess figure during the Empire and one of the country's first professional *femmes de lettres*. An editor as well as a poet, she mentored the careers of younger women writers including Amable Tastu and Marceline Desbordes-Valmore. Unlike women writers and salon hostesses such as Madame du Deffenand or Madame de Staël, who had participated in Paris's more emancipated aristocratic culture, Dufrénoy had to conform herself to the First Empire's suffocating domestic ideology, in which "modesty" for a woman meant keeping silent. An epistle entitled "Corine à Oswald," written soon after the publication of *Corinne*, on first reading seems to endorse this ideology, opting for the obscurity of love over fame. In the last part of the poem, however, the poet undermines her previous position, not like Günderode, through a self-willed obscurity, but rather by showing off, as Letitia Landon does, Corine's (note the different spelling) performance of an overt and powerful sexuality before Oswald and all male readers:

> The lover whose obscurity
> Reveals her charms in your mind,
> Will she, alas, be more submissive than I?

> Must we hate the arts to remain faithful?
> From a lackluster soul
> Expect only feeble sentiment;
> She'll love you less in her lifetime
> Than I love in a moment. (Dufrénoy 1827: 162)

Sacrificing art and fame also means sacrificing erotic energy, a loss for women, but especially for the men who love those women. Of course, this sexuality falls back into a heterosexual binary, yet for that brief shining moment at least, her Corine is the subject-performer and not simply a passive object of the male gaze. Both Letitia Landon and Adélaïde Dufrénoy, like Germaine de Staël, argue against the necessity of a heroic choice between public and private aspiration. To make their case, they resort to the more liberal sexual norms of the ancien régime, allegorizing literary ambition as erotic desire.

Later French poetess figures, most notably Desbordes-Valmore, Delphine Gay, and Gustave Flaubert's famous lover and correspondent, Louise Colet (1808-76) followed Dufrénoy's lead, writing poems in which abandonment is often a thinly veiled pretext to flaunt their feminized sentiment in public. In her earliest collection, *Elégies, Marie et romances* (1819), a book which helped inaugurate the Romantic movement in France alongside Alphonse de Lamartine's *Méditations* (1820), Desbordes-Valmore enacts the role of the lovelorn poetess in a series of elegies which rehearse over and over her break-up with a mysterious lover named Olivier. There had been a lover, Henri de Latouche, a poet and editor who abandoned the teenage Desbordes-Valmore with a child. But as Yves Bonnefoy argues in his sensitive introduction to the Gallimard edition of Desbordes-Valmore's poetry, it was not so much the relationship itself, or the pain of separation, which marked the poet. Rather, abandonment signified Desbordes-Valmore's own awakening to a previously unthinkable identity as poet (Desbordes-Valmore 1983: 12-13). A real abandonment, in this case an aborted romance in 1827 with Polish poet Adam Mickiewicz, also awakened Russian poet Karolina Pavlova to the same unthinkable identity as poet. Many of Pavlova's best poems, including "10 noyabrya 1840" (November 10, 1840), "Na 10 noyabrya" (On November 10) (1841), and a series of elegies entitled simply "Duma" (Meditation) return to that primary scene of abandonment, but in a more guarded fashion than in Desbordes-Valmore's elegies. In "November 10, 1840," Pavlova calls it an "otherworldy secret; / the seed that does not decay." Like a seed, it grows again and again each year, pointing the speaker back to her past, but also forward, to the moment of divine presence when the two lovers were and will be so perfectly paired that they can communicate silently ("silently calling myself yours"). As in her previously cited poem, "Les Pleurs des femmes," the speaker's "secret loss" here does not reflect either the poet's "regret" or a "real misfortune." Rather, it enables her to express her much vaguer, mystical search for an authentic relationship with the Other: "When the soul, deeply in love, is compelled to state with conviction / to a foreign soul: I believe in you!" (Pavlova 1964: 90).

As nationalism became the dominant ideology, critics began to interpret women poets' cosmopolitan sympathy, their desire for complete reciprocity with the Other, as politically contentious. Many women composed patriotic verse in response: Delphine Gay called herself the "muse of the homeland" (*muse de la patrie*), Amable Tastu published a volume of poems entitled *Chroniques de France* (1829) idealizing French history, and Felicia Hemans wrote schoolboy classics such as "Casabianca" ("The boy stood on the burning deck," 1826) and "The Homes of England" (1828), which established her reputation in Europe and America as *the* poetess of hearth, home, and country. In Britain, in particular, many readers and critics saw Corinne's sexualized discourse as threatening both to the domestic sphere and to the nation. In an often cited comment, Felicia Hemans expresses her frustration at her Irish public's provincial narrow-mindedness: "If I were in higher spirits, I should be strongly tempted to do something *very* strange amongst them, in order to fulfil the ideas I imagine they entertain of that altogether foreign monster, a *Poetess*" (Chorley 1890, 2: 280). Playing on the stock image of the poetess as Corinne, Hemans here positions herself not as a national, but as an international, poet. Recent criticism, most notably by Nanora Sweet (1998), has defended this cosmopolitan version of Hemans, citing the many ambiguities in her work as proof of a real ambivalence in regard to nationalism. In earlier books such as *The Restoration of the Works of Art to Italy* (1816) and *Modern Greece* (1817), the young Hemans contributed to Europe's reformist international current centered around Mediterranean culture and spearheaded on the Continent by liberal intellectuals such as Sismondi and de Staël and William Roscoe in Britain. In "Corinne at the Capitol," published in *Songs of the Affections* (1830), Hemans expresses her ambivalent feelings toward nationalism versus cosmopolitanism. Of of the poem's 48 lines, 44 describe Corinne's coronation scene in glowing language which, as Angela Leighton points out, desexualizes the original, appropriating Corinne's victory for women everywhere (Leighton 1992: 34). "Well may woman's heart beat high / Unto that proud harmony!" the speaker exclaims. But in the last four lines, this victory is severely censured with the sententious statement that "Happier, happier far than thou / With laurel on thy brow, / She that makes the humblest hearth / Lovely but to one on earth!" (Hemans 2002: 355-7).

Evdokia Rostopchina belonged, like Karolina Pavlova, to a transitional era in which Russia's romance with the West was giving way to an increasingly nationalist cultural politics. Contemporaries, aligning themselves either with the Westernizers or the Slavophiles, accused the two women poets of being not Russian enough, or else too Russian. Often described as a haughty German who bored everyone in her salon with her long, dramatic verse recitals, Pavlova tried to defy her critics by flaunting her domesticity, contrasting it with Rostopchina's more scandalous behavior in poems such as "My sovrementsi, grafinya" (We are Contemporaries, Countess, 1847). On the other hand, as a countess, Rostopchina developed aristocratic topoi in her poetry, including salons, balls, and foreign travel, but also relied on sentimental poetry's domesticity to assert a more prescriptive, bourgeois femininity. Drawing on women poets' conventional modesty, Rostopchina signed her early verse like Letitia Landon with a pseudonym or else the abbreviated "Gr-nya E. R. R-na," provoking the critic Vissarion Belinsky to argue that she should let the public know her real self. In a Corinne poem entitled "Moim dvum priatelnitsam" (To my Two Friends), written in 1848, Rostopchina pretends to do just that, but in fact continues to resist such a categorical identity.

> You expected that I would appear
> Before you, inspired like Corinne,
> Armed with a last song, a long song
> To spite your ear.
> [. . .]
> No – you do not have Corinne
> Before you, with her triumphal wreath,
> But a soul, full of tears,
> Familiar with the sufferings of the world! (Rostopchina 1987: 355)

The figure of Corinne is here used to mediate the contradiction between aristocratic and bourgeois, foreign and domestic self. Whereas Hemans's "Corinne at the Capitol" ends up silencing the poetess's more extravagant, public persona, in this poem neither self is sacrificed. By stating that she is "familiar" with the "sufferings of the world," Rostopchina removes a mask, only to reveal another, reaffirming her allegiance not only to Corinne, but also to all women poets, including Pavlova. Her late sentimental poem thus serves as a last stand for Corinne's cosmopolitan ideology of sympathy, for suffering's universal voice, possibly even indicating a gesture of solidarity toward Europe's revolutionaries.

The failure of the 1848 revolutions only amplified the sense of political and social impotence which Europe's women poets felt from the very beginning. Like an actress who performs the play's climactic scene only to discover that her audience is un-moved, the romantic poetess could only regret what she perceived as her own and her sister poets' fruitless efforts at reform. The 1830s and 1840s marked the heyday of farewell and disenchantment poems as well as of elegies written to commemorate dead colleagues. Women's disenchantment poems are moving testaments not just to their sense of failure, but also to the material conditions that dictated these women's identity as poets. The fact that women had less control over these conditions than men, and therefore less hope of being remembered, in part explains why they wrote more disenchantment poems than men and why those poems were so much more despondent. In the footsteps of Corinne, many women wrote last songs which replaced their hope of literary glory with the consolation that their readers, women but also men, might respond to their suffering, thus insuring a collective sense of identity. In "Night at Sea" (1839), for example, Landon reveals her intense fear of not being remembered by her public, as well as her doubts that poetry can in fact insure her own posterity. The dark ocean in the poem separating the speaker from her friends may be interpreted as the new veil cast by industrial literature between writer and reader. As in "The Last Song of Corinne," conversation comes as an anxious response to absence, and the death-like anonymity of the market resembles a salon in which the audience's faces have been darkened. In "La Gloire," which closes Amable Tastu's first volume of poems published in 1826, resignation is expressed even more directly as a testament to the poet's powerlessness in the literary field. The speaker ironically reviews the choices she has made in her career, "opting" for less ambitious, domestic verse, poetry she knows will not outlive her:

> Content with collecting the ephemeral laurel,
> I weaned my pride from thinking of tomorrow:
> I will be satisfied if my songs can cradle
> Wives' and mothers' happiness or sorrow.

In exchange for her renunciation of literary fame, however, the speaker expects another form of consolation, a sense of solidarity among women:

> Let me hope for a triumph so tender,
> Let the songs between us be a secret bond:
> Women of France, let our hearts beat together,
> When we hear the name of our motherland!

This "secret bond" again reminds us of Pavlova's "Les Pleurs des femmes" and of "The Last Song of Corinne," in which the dying poet finds consolation in the knowledge that her subjectivity will be metonymically perpetuated in the form of a young woman. Like the "Last Song" and "Night at Sea," Tastu's poem also closes on a note of regret, "a regret which awakes . . . / . . . the price of the bird's accents." The speaker is uncertain whether such a consolatory formula can save her from cultural oblivion, or whether, like a bird's song, her name will fade away: "The nightingale's song leaves no trace" (Tastu 1858: 158-60).

The "secret bond" which ties women together is actualized most movingly in the many elegies written by women for their sister poets. In Britain, a series of elegies consciously informing one another reveals British women poets' consciousness of a specifically female poetess tradition, as Margaret Linley (1996) has shown. In elegies written for Lucretia Davidson (1833), Elisa Mercoeur (1836), and Delphine Gay (1855), Marceline Desbordes-Valmore also draws sentimental links between herself, other sister poets and artists, and the dead poetess figures she mourns. In the case of Davidson, an American poet who died at 17, these links transcend national borders. What her poems share with the British elegies is their feminized ideology of sympathy, but, even more, their painful realization of this ideology's bankruptcy in the literary marketplace. In "Elisa Mercoeur," the speaker explains how fame leads to death and oblivion far more lucidly than does Hemans in "The Grave of a Poetess" (1828) and with more bitterness:

They then exhausted that living lyre;
Made her read her veiled suffering;
Because the world wants it all when it deigns to listen
And when it says "sing!" one must always sing! (Desbordes-Valmore 1973, 2: 401)

The plight of the romantic poetess is powerfully captured in these four lines. Confusing the woman with her poetry, readers and critics place enormous demands on the "living lyre," requiring that she literally read herself before the public in a verbal undressing which, repeated too many times, leaves nothing to the imagination except the performer's own weariness, her depletion of words. The passage emphasizes the danger of poetry as embodied performance: in the production of symbolic value, the poet is cast as an industrial worker, neither in control of the means of production, nor able to escape the repetitive labor of writing. As I have argued elsewhere, it is precisely against this fate that Karolina Pavlova reacts in "Tri dushi" (Three Souls, 1845), a sort of antielegy which draws parallels between the careers of Delphine Gay, Lucretia Davidson, and Pavlova herself in order to better distinguish the latter from the effusions of a society poet such as Gay, or from Davidson's image as precocious female Chatterton (Vincent 2002). The narrator expresses her desire to be remembered as a serious poet and not simply as a poetess, closing "Three Souls" on a sober, ironic note, admitting the futility of the "heart's useless ardor," yet pursuing her "futile, stubborn dream." Unlike the above elegies, Pavlova here toys with, but ultimately rejects, the Sapphic will-to-dissolution, troped here as a Decembrist wife sacrificing herself for her husband. "Perhaps it would have been better for her / To lose her mind in superficial life / Or to fade out into the steppe..." (Pavlova 1964: 126-7).

Exporting the Poetess: Hemans and Landon in France

Arriving late on the Romantic scene, Pavlova shared affinities with poets such as Elizabeth Barrett, Annette von Droste-Hülshoff, and Louise Ackermann who rejected the romantic poetess persona. All these writers understood that performing Corinne's self-sacrificial heroism was politically ineffectual and had betrayed a generation of women poets. This failure had much to do, ironically, with the romantic poetess's international appeal and great commercial success. Felicia Hemans's and Letitia Landon's reception in France helps us better understand how sentimental culture was transmitted across Europe. Corresponding to two watershed dates in the liberal movement, the 1830 fall of the Bourbons in France and 1832 Reform Bill in Great Britain, the highpoint of sentimental culture was marked by an intense cultural exchange between these two nations. One sign of this development was entrepreneurs launching journals that specialized in reviewing foreign literature, such as Britain's *Foreign Review* and the *Revue britannique*, and opening up retail outlets answering to the new taste for foreign literature: the *Librairie Baudry*, for example, sold French periodicals and books both on the rue du Coq in Paris and from its shop in London's Soho district. In an 1839 essay in the *Revue des deux mondes* (Review of the Two Worlds), Philarète Chasles describes this new current in the cultural relations between Britain and the Continent "as a movement of luxury, of well-being, of cosmopolitanism; a European movement." For Chasles, an important proselytizer of British literature in France, cultural exchange went hand in hand with free trade to mark progress and civilization. However, Chasles also feared, much as John Stuart Mill did in his liberal breviary "On Liberty" (1859), that the forces of modernity helping disseminate culture abroad, including education, free trade, improved communication, and political democracy, were also driving nations to lose their "originality." Hence, if the cosmopolitan current that Chasles describes appears as the realization of Germaine de Staël's dream of a liberal Europe made up of distinct nations, it also reflects a new anxiety today all too familiar: fear of cultural uniformity. According to Chasles, critics but also women poets were to blame for the loss of national originality that went hand in hand with cultural homogenization. After announcing the twilight of a generation of poets, including Scott, Wordsworth, and Southey, the article argues that "all those melodious little voices chirped together in the aviary of English society, which, unable to differentiate them, chose to admire them all at once" (Chasles 1839: 654-6). Both poetesses and critics were seen as lowering poetry's symbolic value by catering to the new market of female middle-class readers. Unlike more avant-garde journals such as the *Muse française*, annuals, called almanacs or *recueils d'étrennes* in France, could bridge the cultural divide, answering to the same rules of decorum on both sides of the Channel. As Marcel Morand writes, the almanacs "certainly contributed to the diffusion of our [French] literature in England, because they presented it in a very acceptable form which offered all the assurances in terms of morality and propriety" (Morand 1933: 204).

Byron, Scott, and Moore were Britain's leading cultural exports, but many prominent British women poets, most noticeably Hemans and Landon, also found their way to France. For example, the *Globe* of March 17, 1827, carried a translation of Felicia Hemans's "Dernières Cérémonies" (Last Rites) whereas Letitia Landon's "Sur un tableau de Hill" (On a Painting by Hill) was used to enliven a review of the 1827 *Forget Me Not* annual. Sainte-Beuve, who liked to draw parallels between women writers from different nations, cites Hemans at least twice. Writing about Marceline Desbordes-Valmore, for example, he mentions the *Memoir of the Life and Writings of Mrs. Hemans* as a model that should be imitated when memorializing "that other tender and passionate poet," Marceline Desbordes-Valmore (Sainte-Beuve 1870: 134-5). Landon's enactment of Corinne, on the other hand, caused less of a ruckus in France than in Britain, and some French critics even defended her exaggerated affect. The very first review of British literature in the *Globe*, for instance, is a front-page, three-column-long article that praises Landon's *The Improvisatrice* (*Globe* 1825). In another *Globe* article on Landon a year later, the reviewer defends the poet against accusations of monotony, basing his argument on the division of spheres: we should allow women to express their feelings, "to seek their inspiration in nature," as long as they do not impinge on the real work of culture (*Globe* 1826).

Because these kinds of reviews condescended toward the work of all women poets, at least one Frenchwoman, Amable Tastu, took Landon more seriously. Perhaps in response to her own popularity in England, Tastu helped disseminate British literature in France, translating Byron and Shakespeare, but also Hemans and Landon. Her second and last collection of poems, *Poésies nouvelles* (New Poems) (1835) contains Hemans's "Les Tombeaux d'une famille" (The Graves of a Household) and "Edith, conte des bois" (Edith, a Tale of the Woods) as well as Landon's "Une chronique d'amour." In the liberal *Revue des deux mondes* of May 15, 1832, Tastu wrote an extended review of Letitia Landon along with a translation of Landon's appropriately titled "The Neglected One." Seven years later, she published a posthumous essay on Felicia Hemans in *Le Temps*. Amable Tastu's articles on Letitia Landon and on Felicia Hemans are a powerful testimony to the links binding women poets across national borders. Besides indicating how well Tastu knew the British poets' work, the articles offers us valuable insight into the ways in which a woman writer could represent herself through the mirror image of a foreign sister poet. This in turn suggests a feminine comparative criticism which claims for sentimental poetry what Germaine de Staël's writing claimed for literature more generally, a means of bringing together gender and nation.

Tastu was well aware of the differences between Landon and Hemans, pointing out in her 1839 review that "Joan of Arc" and "Properzia Rossi," Hemans's poems on fame's unhappiness, "were less well suited to the chaste and severe pen of Madame Hemans than to the poetically passionate talent of her single rival, Miss Landon." Yet in both reviews, she sees the two women performing the same poetical mission. Deriving this mission in the first article from Landon's Preface to *The Venetian Bracelet*, she associates it with Sappho-Corinne, whom Tastu incidentally cites as the "*type réel*" (genuine archetype) of all poetess figures:

> [The mission] that Miss Landon attributes [to the poetess], is the struggle against the heart's egoism and aridity, a result of that refined civilization which hardens all that it polishes. She believes that by awakening our sympathies to the sorrows which only disinterested sentiments can share, we will become less positive, less personal: God grant it that what she said is true! This explains the melancholy which dominates the poetry of Miss Landon, and her inclination toward "grief, disappointment, the fallen leaf, the faded flower, the broken heart and the early grave." (Tastu 1832: 406)

For Landon as interpreted by Amable Tastu, sentimental poetry expresses more than domestic affection or resignation. The poetess struggles against egotism; her suicidal melancholy serves a higher ideal, the spreading of sympathy. Tastu's passage elegantly formulates the poetess's ethos: to make people "less positive, less personal," to achieve what is harder to come by in male Romantic poetry, a decentering or dispersal of subjectivity. In her second review on Hemans, Tastu makes it clear that she also understands this as a decentering of nationalism in exchange for a more cosmopolitan solidarity with people from other classes and countries. Writing of Hemans's "love of country at least as a woman can experience it, that is mixing it with family affections and domestic habits," Tastu universalizes her domestic nationalism, drawing a link between Hemans, herself, and all women. Tastu's favorite work, not surprisingly, is Hemans's *Records of Woman*, a collection that attempts to reconcile romantic nationalism with a more universal subjecthood. The French poet does not see any ambiguity in being patriotic on the one hand, and claiming a more universal identity on the other. According to Tastu, any poetess who receives the same praise lavished on Hemans, that "no man could have written her poetry" and that she "did honor to her sex, her age and her country," has "nobly succeeded in her mission" (Tastu 1839).

The mission evoked in Amable Tastu's reviews of Letitia Landon and Felicia Hemans of course closely echoes Germaine de Staël's own cultural ideal as represented in Gérard's "Corinne at Cape Miseno." The romantic poetess imagined herself, like Corinne in the painting, performing the role of a salon hostess but on a much larger scale, helping through her songs of love and suffering to bring together gender, social class, and nation. The international success of many of these women poets during their lifetime attests to sentimental poetry's contagious power and to the positive effect of that power on European culture. While Tastu's invocation to God in her review of Landon suggests that she herself doubted the effectiveness of such a mission, our rehabilitation of the romantic poetess owes much to our belated realization that by helping to spread sympathy across borders and by protesting against all forms of oppression, these women did contribute in a small way at least to the spread of civil society and democracy. In the expanding community of Europe and in an increasingly globalized but also divided world, the romantic poetess's mission remains as relevant as ever – the poetess embodies hope, the ideal of an authentically liberal and cosmopolitan future.

Note

1 My translation. All translations are mine unless otherwise indicated.

References and Further Reading

Barrett Browning, Elizabeth (1992). *Aurora Leigh*, ed. Margaret Reynolds. Athens: Ohio University Press.

Blain, Virginia (1995). "Letitia Elizabeth Landon, Eliza Mary Hamilton, and the Genealogy of the Victorian Poetess." *Victorian Poetry*, 33 (1): 31-52.

Chasles, Philarète (1839). "De la littérature anglaise actuelle." *La Revue des deux mondes*, 17: 654-86.

Chorley, Henry (1890). *Memorials of Mrs. Hemans*, 2 vols. New York: Thomas Crowell.

Desbordes-Valmore, Marceline (1895). *Correspondance intime*, ed. Benjamin Rivière, 2 vols. Paris: Lemerre.

Desbordes-Valmore, Marceline (1973). *Les Oeuvres poétiques de Marceline Desbordes-Valmore*, ed. M. Bertrand, 2 vols. Grenoble: Presses Universitaires de Grenoble.

Desbordes-Valmore, Marceline (1983). *Poésies*, ed. Yves Bonnefoy. Paris: Gallimard.

Dufrénoy, Adélaide (1827). *Oeuvres de Mme. Dufrénoy*, ed. M. A. Jay. Paris: Librairie Moutardier.

Dyce, Alexander (1825). *Specimens of British Poetesses*. London: T. Rodd, S. Prowett.

Evers, Barbara (1991). *Frauenlyrik um 1800*. Bochum: Universitätsverlag Dr. N. Brockmeyer.

Finch, Alison (2000). *Women's Writing in Nineteenth-Century France*. Cambridge, UK: Cambridge University Press.

Forsberg, Roberta (1967). *Madame de Staël and the English*. New York: Astra Books.

Globe (1825). "*L'Improvisatrice*, de Mlle. Letitia Landon." *Le Globe*, August 9: 737.

Globe (1826). "*Le Troubadour* poème, par Miss Landon." *Le Globe*, 4 (18): 90-1.

Gusdorf, Georges (1993). *Le Romantisme*, 2 vols. Paris: Payot.

Heldt, Barbara (1987). *Terrible Perfection: Women and Russian Literature*. Bloomington: Indiana University Press.

Hemans, Felicia (1827). "Last Rites – Les Dernières Cérémonies." *Le Globe*, 4 (93) March 17.

Hemans, Felicia (2002). *Felicia Hemans: Selected Poems, Letters, Reception Materials*. Princeton, NJ: Princeton University Press.

Hunt, Leigh (1891). "*Specimens of British Poetesses*, by M. Alexander Dyce." In *Men, Women and Books*. London: Smith, Elder.

Kelly, Catriona (1994a). *A History of Russian Women's Writing, 1820-1992*. Oxford: Clarendon Press.

Kelly, Catriona (ed.) (1994b). *An Anthology of Russian Women's Writing, 1777-1992*. Oxford: Oxford University Press.

Kirkpatrick, Susan (1989). *Las Romanticas: Women Writers and Subjectivity in Spain, 1835-1850*. Berkeley: University of California Press.

Kirkpatrick, Susan (ed.) (1992). *Antologica poetica de escritoras del siglo XIX*. Madrid: Castalia.

Kirkpatrick, Susan (2002). "The Uses of Romantic Poetry: Feminine Subjects in Modern Spanish Culture." In Angela Esterhammer (ed.), *Romantic Poetry*. Amsterdam: John Benjamins, pp. 509-24.

Landon, Letitia (1997). *Selected Writings*, ed. Jerome McGann and Daniel Riess. Peterborough, ONT: Broadview Press.

Larnac, Jean (1935). *Histoire de la littérature féminine en France*. Paris: Editions Kra.

Leighton, Angela (1992). *Victorian Women Poets: Writing Against the Heart*. Hemel Hempstead, UK: Harvester/Wheatsheaf.

Linley, Margaret (1996). "Sappho's Conversions in Felicia Hemans, Letitia Landon, and Christina Rossetti." *Prism(s)*, 4: 15-42.

Lipking, Lawrence (1988). *Abandoned Women and Poetic Tradition*. Chicago: University of Chicago Press.

Lokke, Kari (2002). "Poetry as Self-consumption: Women Writers and their Audiences in British and German Romanticism." In Angela Esterhammer (ed.), *Romantic Poetry*. Amsterdam: John Benjamins, pp. 91-111.

Mandell, Laura (ed.) (2003). "The Transatlantic Poetess." Special issue, *Romanticism on the Net*, ed. Michael Eberle-Sinatra. 29-30 (February-May). <http://www.erudit.org/revue/ron/2003/v/n29>.

McGann, Jerome (1996). *The Poetics of Sensibility: A Revolution in Literary Style*. Oxford: Clarendon Press.

Mellor, Anne (1997). "Distinguishing the Poetess From the Woman Poet." In Stephen Behrendt and Harriet Kramer Linkin (eds.), *Approaches to Teaching Romantic Women Poets of the Romantic Period*. New York: Modern Language Association, pp. 63-8.

Mellor, Anne (ed.) (1998) *Romanticism and Feminism*. Bloomington: Indiana University Press.

Morand, Marcel (1933). *Le Romantisme français en Angleterre*. Paris: Honoré Champion.

Partridge, Eric (1924). *The French Romantics' Knowledge of English Literature (1820-1848)*. Paris: Honoré Champion.

Pavlova, Karolina (1964). *Polnoe sobranie stikhotvorenii*, ed. P. P. Gromov and N. M. Gaidenkov. Moscow: Sovietskie Pisatel.

Pinch, Adela (1996). *Strange Fits of Passion: Epistemologies of Emotion, Hume to Austen*. Palo Alto, CA: Stanford University Press.

Rapgof, Boris (1916). *K. Pavlova: Materiali dlia izucheniia*. Petrograd: Tri Rima.

Ross, Marlon (1989). *The Contours of Masculine Desire: Romanticism and the Rise of Women's Poetry*. Oxford: Oxford University Press.

Rossettini, Olga (1963). "Madame de Staël et la Russie." *Rivista di letterature moderne e comparate*, 16 (March): 50-67.

Rostopchina, Evdokia (1987). *Talisman*, ed. and intro. Victor Afanasev. Moscow: Moskovskii Rabochii.

Sainte-Beuve, Charles Augustin (1862). "Mme. de Staël." In *Portraits de Femmes*. Paris: Garnier, pp. 72-145.

Sainte-Beuve, Charles Augustin (1870). *Madame Desbordes-Valmore, sa vie et sa correspondance*. Paris: M. Lévy.

Schor, Esther (1994). *Bearing the Dead: The British Culture of Mourning from the Enlightenment to Victoria*. Princeton, NJ: Princeton University Press.

Séché, Léon (1908a). *Le Cénacle de la Muse Française 1823-1827*. Paris: Mercure de France.

Séché, Léon (1908b). *Les Muses françaises: Anthologie des femmes poètes*. Paris: L. Michaud.

Séché, Léon (1910). *Delphine Gay, Madame de Girardin*. Paris: Mercure de France.

Staël, Germaine de (1850). *Corinne; or Italy*, trans. Isabel Hill with metrical versions of the odes by L. E. Landon. London: Richard Bentley.

Sweet, Nanora (1998). "'Lorenzo's' Liverpool and 'Corinne's' Coppet: The Italianate Salon and Romantic Education." In Thomas Pfau and Robert Gleckner (eds.), *Lessons of Romanticism: A Critical Companion*. Chapel Hill, NC: Duke University Press, pp. 244-60.

Tastu, Amable (1835). "Une jeune poète anglaise: Letitia Landon." *La Revue des deux mondes*, May 15: 406-8.

Tastu, Amable (1839). "Felicia Hemans." *Le Temps*, October 31, no. 3664.

Tastu, Amable (1858). *Poésies complètes*. Paris: Didier.

Uchenova, V. V. (ed.) (1989). *Tsaritsy muz: russkie poetessy XIX-nachala XX vv.* Moscow: Sovremenik.

Vincent, Patrick (2002). "Elegiac Muses: Romantic Women Poets and the Elegy." In Angela Esterhammer (ed.), *Romantic Poetry*. Amsterdam: John Benjamins, pp. 197-221.

Vincent, Patrick (2004). *The Romantic Poetess: European Culture, Politics and Gender, 1820-1840*. Hanover, NH: University Press of New England.

Walker, Cheryl (1982). *The Nightingale's Burden: Women Poets and American Culture before 1900*. Bloomington: Indiana University Press.

29

Lighting Up Night

Lilian R. Furst

Night is a strikingly pervasive theme in European Romanticism. A very large number of lyric poems deal with it, and it is also much favored as the setting for the action in longer narrative and dramatic works, and, of course, in the Gothic novel which flourished on the margins of Romanticism. The theme of night itself as a phase in the 24-hour diurnal cycle brings in its wake a range of other motifs all highly prominent in Romanticism: the moon, evening, twilight, nightingales, dreams, and even mines. Night thus stands at the center of a whole complex of allied topics pivotal to Romanticism.

Night also features frequently in literature's sister arts, music and painting. To cite just a few examples, between 1831 and 1840 Frédéric Chopin (1810-49) composed 21 fantasias which he called *Nocturnes*. Robert Schumann (1810-56) took up the idea from Chopin in his *Variations sur un nocturne de Chopin* (Variations on a Chopin nocturne, 1834) and in 1839 followed this with his *Nachtstücke* (Nightpieces) for the piano. The foremost German Romantic painter, Caspar David Friedrich (1774-1840) repeatedly showed a preference for dark, murky, mysterious, often rather spooky scenes. But the most famous visual portrayals of night are the 14 so-called *Black Paintings*, frightening visions of menacing darkness, painted by the Spaniard Francisco de Goya (1776-1828) executed on the walls of his villa, the Quinto del Sordo, after his recovery from the acute, dangerous illness he suffered in 1819.

The overwhelming profusion of works about night simultaneously creates a problem and prompts a set of questions. The problem stems from the absolute necessity of restricting this unwieldy field through selectivity. Obviously, in the brief span of an essay it is quite impossible to offer a comprehensive survey of the occurrences of night in European Romanticism. Such an endeavor would not even be intellectually rewarding since it would result in a sort of encyclopedic catalogue which could provide scantily annotated information but not foster an understanding of the meaning (or more accurately, meanings) of night for the Romantics. It is more productive to delimit the analysis to some of the main works on night, leaving aside, however reluctantly, such subsidiary strands as evening, the moon, dreams, and so forth. The advantage of this perhaps drastic pruning is to open up space for some crucial questions. Why were the Romantics attracted to night to the point almost of obsessiveness? How did they envisage it? What did it signify for them? What are their primary responses to night? In what ways did they express their feelings? What is the function of night in their writings? The exploration of these questions can lead to a better grasp of the entire thrust and import of the Romantic movement.

In literature night appears in a great variety of guises and genres between the middle of the eighteenth century and the first third of the nineteenth century, roughly the period when Pre-Romanticism and Romanticism predominated. It becomes manifest in discrepant, contradictory images associated at times with melancholy, at others with joy, with turbulence, or with tranquility. So for the Romantic poet night can evoke grief or consolation, depending both on the personal situation and the worldview underlying a specific response. It can function as the physical setting for reflections and/or as the metaphoric correlative to the poet's mood. Night in Romanticism thus spans the spatial, temporal, and psychological dimensions of human existence. Certain perceptions are to the fore at particular phases (for instance, melancholy in mid-eighteenth-century England, and turbulence in the later eighteenth-century German Storm and Stress movement), but it is hard to find a clear, overarching pattern of change. Insofar as a general trend is discernible, it is toward internalization, a drift from night as a primarily physical entity to a greater emphasis on its newer role as a figurative projection of the poet's state. Melancholy, in the forefront early on, wanes only to recur sporadically in later poets; similarly, a sense of tranquility emanates from night at different times. Even if these fluctuations preclude the possibility of a neat, global schema, they testify to the multiple, shifting meanings night held for the Romantics. Their variegated responses also illustrate quite forcefully once more these poets' essential individualism.

Away from Light and Toward Night and Melancholy

In one respect, however, there is a fundamental unity, namely in the pronounced preference for evening, dusk, darkness, and night over the brightness of daylight. This predilection for night must be seen in the larger context of the reversals that the Romantics initiated in the conceptualization of the world; it represents a cardinal facet of their rejection of the belief system that inspired their predecessors, the exponents of the Enlightenment. The very name of this period in literary-philosophical history reveals a core tenet of its faith in what might broadly be termed luminosity, that is, in human beings' capacity to attain mastery of the laws of the universe in which they live. The French and German equivalents to Enlightenment emphasize the same key idea: *Siècle des lumières* means century of lights, while *Aufklärung*, literally illumination, is derived from the adjective *klar*, clear. The Enlightenment upheld the power of the mind to comprehend the world by means of rational inquiry. Dogmatic assumptions inherited from previous ages were subject to a reasoning scrutiny in the quest for clarity. Orderliness, moderation, and above all, intellectual understanding of the processes of the universe were the Enlightenment's guiding principles. Its mentality is epitomized in its apprehension of the world as a mechanism, a sort of clockwork, created and set in motion by a divinity, endlessly repeating itself as programmed, and amenable to decipherment by ratiocination. This aim has its summation in the Enlightenment's grandiose attempt at an encyclopedia that would encompass all knowledge. Edited by Denis Diderot (1713-84) the *Encyclopédie* was begun in 1751 but remained uncompleted.

The Romantics reacted against this cult of rationalism subsumed in the concept of light. Their approach devolved from ideals diametrically opposite to those espoused by the Enlightenment. Reason was ousted by feeling as intuitive insight came to be extolled as the path to a deeper intelligibility beyond the scope of rationalism. Johann Herder (1744-1803), a thinker influential for the young Goethe (1749-1832), coined the term *Einfühlung* (feeling one's way in) to characterize the new method emerging in the later eighteenth century; it sponsored empathy rather than cogitation as the most appropriate means to aspire to a penetration of the mysteries of life. Once the heart came to be valued over the head, the whole purpose and direction of the artistic endeavor was modified. For the Romantics, in contrast to the adherents to the Enlightenment, were most strongly attracted by precisely those areas *not* open to rational comprehension. They sought to fathom the hidden, enigmatic aspects of the world they inhabited, its dark recesses in both the literal and the metaphoric sense. Their fascination with night, with the subconscious strata of the mind as well as with the subterranean realm of the underground mine, are patently expressions of their dominant interests.

A telling comment on the Romantics' way of thinking is contained in an important but little known work with the curious title *Ansichten von den Nachtseiten der Naturwissenschaft* (Views on the Night Sides of the Natural Sciences, 1808) by Gotthilf Heinrich Schubert (1780-1860), a peripheral member of one of the German Romantic circles. In a sequence of 14 lectures Schubert gives an idiosyncratic survey of the history of humankind's relationship to nature. The original state of harmony was broken, he asserts, by the advent of Christianity which silenced the oracles and thereby destroyed "die geheime Gewalt der Natur über den Menschen" (the secret power of nature over human beings; Schubert 1967: 11). He laments the replacement of this former oracular sway by a mechanistic conception: "eine mechanische und handwerksmässige Ansicht einer todten Natur..., in welcher sich wie Würmer, welche ein modernes Gebein benagen nur noch die mechanischen Kräfte bewegen" (a mechanistic and craftsmanlike view of a dead nature..., in which only mechanical forces move like worms gnawing at a modern bone; p. 14). In this strange analogy Schubert equates the modern (Enlightenment) view of the world with a mechanistic, deadened perception of nature. In keeping with his affirmation of the magical and supernatural Schubert endorses magnetism[1] and astrology as the most promising paths to the renewed harmony between the human soul and nature for which the Romantics longed. The impact of such notions as Schubert's was to arouse curiosity about the recondite forces that animate the universe, those dark "night sides" repressed by the Enlightenment.

The earliest manifestations of the role of night are, however, less abstract and more personal. Edward Young's (1683-1765) *The Complaint; or Night Thoughts* (1742), generally referred to by the second part of its title, is unquestionably the work that put night on the map although it predates the period normally considered as Romantic. It is the first of three English works that form the fountainhead of a gentle melancholy, the other two being "Meditations Among the Tombs" (1746) by James Hervey (1714-56) and Thomas Gray's (1716-71) famous "Elegy in a Country Church-yard" (1750). These three were grouped together in a landmark comparative study by the Belgian critic P. Van Tieghem, *La Poésie de la nuit et des tombeaux en Europe au XVIIIè siècle* (The Poetry of Night and Tombs in Europe in the Eighteenth Century, 1921) as the matrix of the stream of poetry that relished melancholy. It is important to realize that at that time melancholy denoted less the depressive mindset with which we associate it today than a mildly pleasurable state induced by contemplation of the transience of life.

Young was already an aging man (59 was much older then than now because the life span was so much shorter) when he composed the *Night Thoughts*; he was also a Doctor of Divinity whose Christian beliefs are much to the fore in the latter six of the work's nine sections. The first three, "On Life, Death, and Immortality," "On Time, Death, and Friendship," and "Narcissa" brought him such fame that their success prompted him to continue the poem, but the later six sections are less well known. They switch from a personal lament to theological argumentation, and are burdened by a prolix oratory. The beginning, however, presents a touching image of a lonely old man who has within a short span lost his wife, his dearest friend, and his daughter, and whose grief excludes him from "Tired Nature's sweet restorer, balmy Sleep" (Young 1975: 1). As the bell strikes 1 a.m., he apostrophizes night:

> Night, sable goddess! from her ebon throne,
> In rayless majesty, now stretches forth
> Her leaden sceptre o'er a slumbering world.
> Silence how dead! and darkness profound!
> Nor eye, nor listening ear, an object finds:
> Creation sleeps. 'Tis as the general pulse
> Of life stood still, and nature made a pause;
> An awful pause! Prophetic of her end. (Young 1975: 2)

Although Young's initial evocation of night is primarily negative, emphasizing the absence of light and movement, it has a certain grandeur in its conceptualization of night as the queen who reigns over a realm of darkness and silence in which the normal course of nature seems as if arrested. Yet that "awful" (i.e., awe-inspiring) pause is also portentous in foreshadowing death. Such an association of night with death draws on the tradition of the *danse macabre*, in which skeletons emerge from their graves at the magic hour of midnight to engage in a bone-rattling dance. This ancient image focuses on the purely physical and horrifying aspects of the link between night and death, whereas for the Romantics night becomes essentially a spiritual experience, and, what is more, one that is welcomed by Young for the visions of his beloved departed that it brings. So here he already anticipates a reversal in the respective evaluation of night and day that will become increasingly important as Romanticism unfolds:

> How populous, how vital, is the grave!
> This is creation's melancholy vault,
> The vale funereal, the sad cypress gloom;
> The land of apparitions, empty shades!
> All, on earth, is shadow, all beyond
> Is substance. (Young 1975: 5)

The temporal reign of night thus forms the setting for the sleepless Young's forlorn reflections on his "hopes and fears" (p. 3) as well as for the appearance of his visions.

Young's intense self-dramatization together with his overblown rhetoric, both of which are likely to strike today's readers as rather excessive, are the very features that drew his contemporaries to his lamentation. Van Tieghem has traced the truly amazing reception of the *Night Thoughts* throughout Europe. Between 1751 and 1844, 23 translations were published in 12 languages: six into German, three into Italian, two each into French, Russian, Danish, and Portuguese, and one each into Dutch, Swedish, Spanish, Polish, Hungarian, and Armenian. The peak of the translations, with seven in the 10 years 1780 to 1790, clearly coincides with the emergence of the Romantic movements in England and in Germany. Imitations were equally numerous in England, Germany, Holland, Russia, Sweden, France, Italy, and Spain. The flood of imitations grew so crass as to elicit ridicule. In the satirical play *Der gestiefelte Kater* (Puss in Boots, 1798) by the German writer Ludwig Tieck (1773-1853) the princess boasts in the first act that she has just composed her *Nachtgedanken* (night thoughts); asked when, she replies: "Gestern Mittag nach dem Essen" (yesterday at midday after lunch; Tieck n.d.: 257). Although such a barb pokes fun at the *Night Thoughts*, it testifies, too, to the work's enormous popularity. Its strong appeal lay in Young's tearful effusion of personal feelings in a fluid, associative manner, in stately verse, and in language rich in imagery. Night enables Young to yield to the free flow of pathos-laden emotions from his tender soul in sharp contrast to the dry, reticent intellectualism of the Enlightenment.

A similar melancholy is also the keynote of the two poems "To Night" (1788) and "The Winter Night" (1796) by Charlotte Smith (1749-1806). However, their literary format is completely different to that of the *Night Thoughts*; in place of Young's expansive diffuseness Smith opts for the highly controlled form of the 14-line sonnet. In both cases the octet serves to set the scene, while the sestet is devoted to the feelings night evokes in the poet. The regular, rigorous rhyme schemes provide a measure of emotional containment lacking in Young. The first and better known of the poems, "To Night," begins with an affirmation of night: "I love thee, mournful, sober-suited Night!" (Smith 1993: 39) in which night, through the unusual adjective, "sober-suited" as well as "mournful," is personified. As in Young's *Night Thoughts*, the physical presence of night is forefronted in the immediate reference to the "pale uncertain light" of the "faint moon, yet lingering in her wane, / And veiled in clouds" (ll. 2-3). The "cold elements" remain "deaf" to the complaint of the poet's "embosom'd grief." Nevertheless, Smith asserts in the sestet, "Tho' no repose in thy dark breast I find, / I still enjoy thee, cheerless as thou art" (ll. 9-10). In a gentle melancholy more accepting of her fate than Young is initially, Smith finds "calm" for her "exhausted breast" in night's "quiet gloom," and "tho' wretched, hopeless" is "resign'd" (ll. 11-12), giving her "sorrows" to "the winds and waves" in hopes of reaching "the ear of Heaven!" (l. 14). Ultimate consolation, this concluding phrase suggests, resides in transcendence, but lament in the quiet darkness of night brings some temporary relief. "To Night" is best read in the context of Smith's extremely trying life; married off at an early age to a spendthrift husband, she wrote a long series of novels to pay off his debts and to support her large family. As a woman in the eighteenth century, she is powerless to do other than accede to her fate and at most to vent her feelings in a discreet manner.

Smith's second night poem, "To Winter Night," also personal in origin, is closer in mood to Young's *Night Thoughts*, though still essentially restrained. The death of her favorite child, Anna Augusta de Foville, in 1795 caused Smith acute grief. The "chill and sullen blast" (Smith 1993: 63, l. 2) of the winter night as she lies sleepless is a figurative re-experiencing in her "sad soul" of "its sorrows past" (ibid., l. 3). Night is now, as for Young, closely coupled with death, and they are seen positively insofar as they allow the poet to exchange her woeful daytime earthly existence "for long and undisturb'd repose" (64, l. 10). Death, prefigured in the darkness of night, is endorsed as a future release from the awareness of loss. The atmosphere of gloom emerges from the sequence of words all of which carry negative connotations: "chill and sullen blast," "sad," "cold and drear," "hollow wind," "exhausted," "the darkest gloom of Middle Winter lours," "suffering," "anguish," "tomb." The outer storminess of this winter night is the metaphoric correlative to the poet's inner pain.

Another melancholy night poem inspired by personal loss is Alphonse de Lamartine's (1790-1896) *Le Lac* (The Lake, 1820) written about his beloved, Julie Charles, who was seriously ill and was shortly to die. As in Smith's two sonnets, night is the time and the scene for Lamartine's grief as he appeals to the waters and the rocks of the lake, where he used to meet his beloved, to recall the memory of the happy hours they had spent there. The poem's 16 four-line stanzas, through the rapid movement of their short lines, bevy of rhetorical questions and repetitions, voice the poet's distress as much in perturbation as in melancholy. Like Young and Smith, Lamartine deplores the transience of life but more with the angry protest of a young man than with the older man's or the woman's acceptance of the inevitable. The incessant motion of the waters and the wind, not stilled at night, mirror the dejected commotion in the poet's mind, which remains unassuaged by night.

Apart from its role as the most influential expression of melancholy, Young's *Night Thoughts* proved exemplary for Romantic writing in another quite different way too, namely in its recourse to a series of nights as a structuring principle. This method of organization recurs in a number of otherwise diverse Romantic works. Like the *Night Thoughts*, William Blake's (1757-1827) *Four Zoas* (written and revised 1795-1804, dated 1797) is divided into nine "Nights." The anonymous *Nachtwachen des Bonaventura*, written in 1804 (*Night Watches of Bonaventura* 1972) is cast into 14 "night watches" held by its first-person narrator, an erstwhile poet who is now earning a steadier living as a nightwatchman. E. T. A. Hoffmann's (1776-1822) *Der goldene Topf* (*The Golden Pot*, 1814) consists of 12 "*Vigilien*" (vigils). A parallel structuration of narratives into "nights" is found in the *Arabian Nights*, which were introduced to the West by the French Orientalist Alphonse Gallard in 1704, but were translated into English only around 1840. On the other hand, two other famous serial narratives, Boccaccio's (1313-75) *Decamerone* (1358) and Chaucer's (1340-1400) *Canterbury Tales* (printed c. 1408, composed 1390-1400) serve to fill days during a plague and a journey respectively. The Romantics' proclivity for night therefore produced an alternative model of narrative continuity.

Night and Turbulence

The potential of night for turbulence that Smith senses in "To Winter Night" and that Lamartine expresses in *Le Lac* is a pronounced theme in Romantic writing as evident in prose and drama as in poetry. Like melancholy, turbulence is at once a physical and a psychological state: physical in the perilous combination of darkness, storminess, thunder, and lightning, and psychological in the responses to these phenomena in agitation, trepidation, and foreboding of an ill fate. The ancient Gaelic warriors in James Macpherson's (1736-96) *Poems of Ossian*, published in 1762, live, love, and fight in constantly dim, cold, misty Northern regions. The Romantics' preference for night and darkness made them gravitate toward this uncharted North as against the familiar warm, sunlit Mediterranean climate that had been the main scenario of Classicism. The Ossianic poems, although they are almost certainly at least partly spurious, that is, fabrications of Macpherson's rather than translations from old Gaelic sources, spawned an entire mythology. Napoleon was entranced by the heroic combats of the Ossianic warriors; the Swiss artist Angelica Kauffman (1741-1807) painted scenes from Ossian, and Felix Mendelssohn (1809-47) composed besides his *Scottish Symphony* (1842) the *Hebrides Overture* (1832), also known as *Fingal's Cave,* in direct reference to a figure in the *Poems of Ossian*. The prevalence of murkiness and tempests is the appropriate milieu for this saga of a tribe doomed to extinction. Much of the action takes place in the dark, and at night the ghosts of ancestors appear, intensifying the eeriness that hangs over the whole collection. The turbulence of combat is infused with melancholy through the incidence of deaths, setbacks, and losses. However, the melancholy is here more active than that of Young or Smith because the poems abound in movement and struggle. So night is here energized from the passive recipient of private griefs into a participatory force instrumental in the unfolding of the plot.

That is also the function of night in Goethe's dramatic ballad *Der Erlkönig* (The Erlking, 1782). Its opening line, "Wer reitet so spät durch Nacht und Wind?" (Who is that riding so late through night and wind?; Goethe 1967 I: 54-5) already arouses anxiety. The turbulence is captured in the galloping rhythm of the horse and the father's desperate efforts to preserve his child from the erlking's allurements. The child's visions of the pursuing erlking, who is alternately caressing and menacing, are explained away in the father's sober interpretations: the erlking's voice is the rustling of the dry leaves, his crown and robe are wisps of cloud, his daughters are the old willows gleaming gray. The erlking's enticements represent both the child's delirium (it is dead in its father's arms on their arrival) and the terrifying aspects of night as the darkness transforms ordinary objects into deceptive, supernatural chimera. The same potential for evil is embodied in the figure of the destructive Queen of the Night in Mozart's *Magic Flute* (1791).

Night is inextricably enmeshed with both evil and turbulence in Goethe's *Faust I* (1775). Its very first word is "Nacht" (night; Goethe 1967 III: 20) as Faust is portrayed in his study recalling the many nights he had spent there in a vain pursuit of knowledge. He is agitated as well as melancholy at the realization of his failure to achieve his aims and by his sense of imprisonment in sterile confines that reek of decay and death, symbolized by the skeletons and bones stashed in the room, presumably the remnants of his endeavor to discover what makes the world go round. Night is for Faust a time of utter despair as he expresses his desire for extinction rather than the dismal state into which he has sunk. In the dark he is beset by thoughts as pessimistic as Young's and Smith's, although (being neither old nor female) his mood is one of rebelliousness.

Night is the setting for several other scenes in *Faust I*. Mephistopheles materializes first as a poodle and then as an itinerant scholar by emerging from a fog ("Nebel"; Goethe 1967 III: 46) that suggests a kind of penumbra. It is under the cover of night that Faust, with the aid of Mephistopheles, kills Valentin, Gretchen's brother who has come to avenge Faust's seduction and abandonment of her. But not only crime takes shelter in the obscurity of night. The uncanny, as in *Der Erkönig*, thrives in the grotesque, obscene "Walpurgisnacht" (III: 121-37), a witches' sabbath in which the darkness is intensified by the nebulousness that shrouds the mountainous area. Faust is troubled by visions of the ghosts of Gretchen and Valentin, but as he flees he lands, in another night scene, in a desolate open field through which a covey of witches is just passing. So throughout *Faust I* night is coupled with at best dubious, more frequently nefarious, and even supernatural doings harmful to human beings. Night acts as the cipher for Faust's confused state of mind; he is as if caught in the enveloping fogginess so that he cannot achieve clarity about his desires until he gives himself over to Mephistopheles, who is himself a manifestation of the power of darkness.

The somberness, turbulence, and mental disorientation of *Faust I* is re-enacted in George Gordon Byron's (1788-1824) verse drama *Manfred* (1817) whose opening scene is specifically designated as taking place at midnight. Manfred is a fusion of the Young of the *Night Thoughts* as his sleepless "vigil" leads him "To look within" (Byron 1970: 390, lines 6-7) and of Faust in his invocation of the "spirits of the unbounded Universe" (line 29). Night is for him, as for Faust, a trigger to despondent reflections and to mysterious visitations. Here again night provokes in the Romantic hero a disturbing blend of melancholy and psychic turmoil as he takes stock of his life and contemplates his profound dissatisfaction with his situation. Even more harrowing than *Manfred* is Byron's poem *Darkness* (1816) in its apocalyptic phantasm: "bright sun extinguish'd and the stars / Did wander darkling in the eternal space, / Rayless, and pathless and the earth / Swung blind and blackening in the moonless air" (Byron 1970: 95, lines 2-5). This horrendous "dream, which was not all a dream" (line 1), dwells on aporias in this voided world: "Seasonless, herbless, treeless, manless, lifeless, / A lump of death – a chaos of hard clay" (l. 71-2). "Darkness" shows the extreme metaphoric negativities that can be the outcome of night's literal blackness.

The most nihilistic among the Romantics' night works is undoubtedly the 1804 work *Die Nachtwachen des Bonaventura* (*The Nightwatches of Bonaventura*), whose authorship has never been definitively established. Like *Faust I* and *Manfred*, *Die Nachtwachen* has as its opening sentence a temporal marker which immediately places it in the realm of night and thereby creates an atmosphere conducive to its strange happenings: "Die Nachtstunde schlug" (The night hour struck; Anon. 1972: 28). Night forms not only the organizational principle of this weird work but also the physical and spiritual context for the random thoughts that flit through the nightwatchman's mind as he makes his rounds. His appearance as a nightwatchman, with pike and horn in hand, is an "abenteuerliche Vermummung" (madcap disguise; ibid.) for his real persona as a poet. He delights in the echo of his footsteps in the deserted town. The eeriness from the hollow resonance of his steps foreshadows the uncanniness of many of his nights in the fitful alternation of moonlight and total darkness. Apart from his own footsteps, a deathly silence reigns: "die Nacht ist still und fast schrecklich, und der kalte Tod steht in ihr wie ein unsichtbarer Geist" (the night is still and almost terrible, and cold death is present in it as an invisible spirit; Anon. 1972: 158). The ideas and images that cross the watchman's mind are just as unstable as the storm clouds. A bizarre medley of assorted notions, tenuously linked by the watchman's associations, they are full of allusions to literary works and philosophical concepts. The fourteenth vigil, for instance, comprises a revision of Hamlet's and Ophelia's relationship in a madhouse, where Ophelia gives birth to a dead child in the depths of a particularly stormy night. Like the storm clouds, the text is in a perpetual state of flux. *Die Nachtwachen des Bonaventura* marks the zenith of the image of night as rife with disruptive turbulence.

Pleasures of Night

But night can also have quite other, far more pleasant meanings for the Romantics as a consoling medium that confers calm and tranquility, especially through communion with nature, at the close of day. Blake's *Songs of Innocence* (1789) offer an example of such a conceptualization in "Night," a lyric in six stanzas of eight lines each with a consistent ABABCCDD rhyme scheme. This predictable regularity itself exerts a soothing effect in contrast to the jaggedness of *Die Nachtwachen des Bonaventura* that repeatedly exposes readers to unexpected jolts. In Blake's idyllic state of innocence all is well at night with nature at rest and at peace. As the evening star shines out, the birds are silent in their nests, and "The moon like a flower / In heaven's high bower / With silent delight / Sits and smiles on the night" (Blake 1966: 118, stanza 1). The poem continues in the same bright vein: angels "pour blessing / And joy without ceasing, / On each bud and blossom / And each sleeping bosom" (p. 119, stanza 2). The angels, "most heedful," act as guardians and comforters to human beings and animals alike, bestowing sleep on those who should be asleep, and taming even the wolves and tigers when they howl for prey. "Tears of gold" flow from "the lion's ruddy eyes" as he lies down beside the bleating lamb (p. 119). The lyric is obviously whimsical and idealized as an evocation of innocence at night, yet precisely in this idyllic quality it is the consummate incarnation of a view of night diametrically opposite to the turbulence represented in several other Romantic works. In Blake's *Songs of Experience* (1789-94), in which many of the poems are, as it were, darkened responses to those in the *Songs of Innocence* – for example the pairs "Infant Joy" and "Infant Sorrow" (pp. 118 and 217), "The Blossom" and "The Sick Rose" (pp. 115-16 and 213), and the two "Holy Thursday" poems (pp. 122 and 211-12) – the closest counterpart to "Night" is "The Tyger" (p. 210), who burns bright "In the forests of the night," inspiring fear through his fiery ferocity embodied in the sequence of the poem's unresolvable rhetorical questions. For Blake, night has thus two entirely different faces, corresponding respectively to the states of innocence and experience.

Victor Hugo (1802-85) too sees night under two starkly contrasting aspects. The 1837 work *Nuits de juin* (June nights; 2001: 108) is a brief lyric as uncomplicated in its content as in its form, consisting of two four-line stanzas with an ABABCDCD rhyme scheme. Eyes shut, in a dozing state, the poet is conscious of the heightened pleasantness of nature in the dark: the intoxicating scent of the flowers, the purity of the stars under the heavenly dome, and the soft, pale half-light of dawn awaiting the time of its return. Night is here perceived subjectively through the poet's impressions; although it is a physical presence, it is made vague and shadowy through the slumber filtering it. Nine years later Hugo's *Nuit* (2001: 540-2) seems a negative rejoinder. In the same verse form but twice as long as *Nuit de juin*, it is dominated by the image of nature suspended in fear during the "noire énigme" (black enigma; IV: 1) that is night. All the words are oppressive: "épouvante" (fright), "morne" (dismal), "frémissant" (trembling), "effroi" (dread). The poem dwells on the terror attributed to night, when nature in the darkness is "livrée aux mystères sans nombre" (given over to countless mysteries; II:1). The primordially and perhaps irrationally menacing quality of night is cogently summoned up here.

Much more commonly, however, the Romantics envisage night as solacing, a phase of release from the demands of day when nature and the poet may shelter in a comforting respite. For Goethe in *Wanderers Nachtlied I* (Wanderer's Night Song, 1776; 1967 I: 42) night is a deliverance from the "Schmerz und Lust" (pain and striving; line 6) of his daytime existence. The eight-line poem was written during a tortured phase in Goethe's life when he felt constrained by the pressures imposed on him in his native Frankfurt; the long walks he took at night as a means of escape and release earned him the nickname of "the wanderer." The poem is addressed to night, which is apostrophized as heaven's gift to humanity, the source of sweet peace, a balm to sufferers who are weary of daytime's struggles. The poet begs night to bring its consoling calm to him too. There is no attempt at any physical description of night; the apprehension is wholly subjective as Goethe, with utmost economy, sketches his inner landscape. This progressive turning inward onto the poet's vision is one of the most important changes wrought by the Romantics. *Wanderers Nachtlied II*[2] (1967 I: 42), one of the best-known poems in German, is even more compressed and intense, consisting of eight very short lines. Again night is extolled as the fountainhead of a quiescence that is about to spread from the motionless treetops and the hushed birds into the poet's heart. The slow, stately movement suggested by the preponderance of long, dark vowels is the incarnation of that quietness. The concord between nature and poet is the key to the serenity of this remarkable paean to night.

Goethe's contemporary, Friedrich Hölderlin (1770-1843) projects a similar perception of night, though in a quite different form, in his ode *Brot und Wein* (Bread and Wine, 1807; 1970: 290) whose first section was originally published as *Nacht*. Rather unusually for the Romantics, this poem takes place in an urban setting, as its first words indicate: "Ringsum ruhet die Stadt" (The town is at rest all around): its inhabitants are on their way home after the day's work, the busy market is cleared of its produce and flowers, and torches light up the streets. The day's normal activities are thus implicitly contrasted with what Young called the "pause" ushered in by nightfall. In the darkness Hölderlin registers sounds, not sights: a string instrument from a distant garden, a fountain freshly welling up by scented flowerbeds, the pealing of bells, and the watchman's proclamation of the hours. The appearance of the moon throws an aura of mystery, secrecy, and sadness, but also beauty over the scene. The majestic rhythm of Hölderlin's blank verse evokes the peace that night brings; the "pause" is not, as for Young, "awful," but restful and inviting.

The emotions in William Wordsworth's (1770-1850) "A Night-Piece" (1969: 146-7) are more powerful. Composed in 1798 and published in 1815, it portrays, like Goethe's *Wanderers Nachtlied I*, a lone "pensive traveller" (line 9) at night. The 26-line poem falls into three parts of unequal length. The first seven lines form a kind of overture to the main section of 15 lines that lead into a four-line coda which evaluates the central experience. Opening in mid-line with "– The sky is overcast," the preamble describes a night obscured "With a continuous cloud of texture close, / Heavy and wan" (lines 2-3). The moon is "A dull, contracted circle" (line 4) that yields light only "feebly" (line 5). These initial lines vividly convey the dreariness of an oppressive enclosure in darkness. Then the sudden, almost startling transformation occurs in the "pleasant, instantaneous gleam" (line 8) as the moon, now "clear...and the glory of heaven" (line 13), accompanied by a multitude of stars, illuminates the "blue-black vault" (line 14). So in this central section the emergence of the moon and stars as the clouds disperse effects a radical change in the outer scene which has its counterpart in the poet's mood. The oppressive stasis that permeates the opening section gives way to a sense of liberation in the recurrent images of movement: the moon, which previously could be seen only "indistinctly" through a "veil of clouds" (line 3) now "sails along" (line 14); the stars, "sharp" and "bright," "wheel away" "fast" (lines 15-16) and "roll along" (line 19). Even as "the Vision closes" (line 23), the traveler's mind is suffused with a "delight" (line 24) "Which slowly settles into peaceful calm" (line 25). The congruence of man and nature, a cardinal Romantic theme, is here demonstrated by the sympathy between the outer and the inner constellation. The peace at night, for which Goethe's wanderer longs, is heightened in Wordsworth's poem into a feeling of "delight." Night is no longer equated with death; instead it adumbrates the possibility of loveliness.

Wordsworth's "delight" is intensified in Percy Bysshe Shelley's (1792-1822) 1820 ode "To Night" (1928: 84) into a state of exuberant exaltation. In the five stanzas, each of seven lines, the poet begs "beloved Night" (V: 5) to "Come soon, soon!" (V: 7). Twice he exclaims: "I sighed for thee" (III: 2 and 7). For Shelley night is far preferable to "weary Day" (III: 5) which lies "heavy on flower and tree" (III: 4), "Lingering like an unloved guest" (III: 6). The capitalization of "Night" and "Day" points to the personification manifest also in the attribution to night of "a mantle gray / Star-wrought!" (II: 1-2), of "hair" that blinds "the eyes of Day" (II: 3), and of an "opiate wand" (II: 6) that weaves dreams. Shelley's exhilaration at the swiftness of night's flight is captured in the ethereal lightness and speed of his verse.

From Dejection to Buoyancy

In recording the transition from a dejected to a more buoyant perception of night, Wordsworth's and Shelley's poems exemplify a trend in Romantic writing about night. The earlier works emphasize melancholy and turbulence as the major feelings inspired by night. By contrast, many (though by no means all) the later works focus on its more positive, attractive facets. For instance, *Um Mitternacht* (At Midnight, 1827; 1969: 19-20) by Eduard Mörike (1804-75) has the quality of a folk song through the refrain on which both its eight-line stanzas close: the waters of the spring sing even in their nightly sleep "Vom Tage / Vom heute gewesenen Tage" (of the day / Of the day just gone; lines 7-8, 15-16). But although night turns its back on day, there is no need for a refuge, no sense of bitterness at the trials and tribulations of daytime. The friendly calm with which night descends on the land is immediately highlighted in the lyric's initial word: "Gelassen" (calmly) as night leans dreamily ("träumend"; line 2) on the mountain walls. The image of the golden scales of time, poised at midnight in perfect equilibrium conjures up the repose of that absolutely even balance. The hours themselves are personified as they are said to sing an ancient lullaby sweetly under the darkened heavens. The soothing sound of this lullaby melds with the unbroken flow of the waters from the spring to evoke the utmost tranquility without abrupt movements or hectic feelings. At midnight the universe is becalmed as if night were casting a trance of an almost magical stillness. The very simple rhyme scheme of ABABCDCD together with the concluding repetition and the long, dark vowels (as in Goethe's *Wanderers Nachtlied II*) have an enchanting effect on the reader like that of night over the earth. Night is here anthropomorphized as a benign force in human life.

Closely related to Mörike in both mood and manner are the numerous night lyrics of Joseph von Eichendorff (1788-1857) whose poems clearly stand in the tradition of the folk song. Folk songs, along with folktales, were of particular interest to the second generation of German Romantics (the *Hochromantik*, that is, High Romantics), who saw in them valuable relics of the Germanic cultural heritage which they wanted to recuperate as part of a growing national (and subsequently nationalistic) consciousness. Ludwig Achim von Arnim (1781-1831) and Clemens Brentano (1778-1842) compiled a landmark collection under the title *Des Knaben Wunderhorn* (Youth's Wondrous Horn, 1805). Many of Eichendorff's night lyrics resemble folk songs in their directness, use of simple language, regular ABABCDCD rhyme schemes, and frequently short lines. The impression of artlessness and facility is accentuated by the avoidance of any complexity in either form or feeling. These are essentially *Stimmungsgedichte* (poems of mood) whose generic plurals elicit emotion-laden atmospheres rather than specific visual scenes. The iconography concentrates on the moon, birds, and flowers, which in various combinations form the material for Eichendorff's celebration of night. Occasionally an element of sentimentality creeps in, for instance in his overuse of diminutives which prettify excessively, or, in his later poems, a strain of melancholy as night leads to intimations of the grave. Generally, however, Eichendorff revels in the beauties of night, proclaiming, for instance, in *Nachtfeier* (Celebration of Night, 1810; 1966: 116) "mir ist so wohl zur Stunde" (I feel so well at this hour; line 5). Far from filling him with "Grausen" (horror; line 19), as it does some, night has the impact of restoring and refreshing him ("laben und erfrischen"; line 20). In *Mondnacht* (Moonlit Night, 1827; 1966: 218), the heavens are personified as kissing the earth at night, spreading enchantment over the shimmering blossom, the softly swaying ears of corn, and the quietly rustling woods. The single sustained metaphor of heaven's caress of the earth supports the entire poem as if its eight lines were uttered in one musical melody. The perception of night as comforting, auspicious, and full of bewitching pleasures reaches its apogee in Eichendorff.

A positive apprehension of night is implicit too in Ann Radcliffe's (1764-1823) "Night," from her 1791 novel *The Romance of the Forest* (1931: 348-50). In some ways this poem harks back to Young's *Night Thoughts* in its vestiges of preciosity in a phrase such as "bright with ensanguine hue" (V: 3) or in its reference to "Fancy's touch" (VII: 3). Like Young, Radcliffe also savors "the melancholy charm [that] steals o'er the mind" (IX: 1) together with the "pleasing dread" which fills the soul as "the glooms in forms terrific sweep / And rouse the thrilling horrors of the dead!" (II: 2-4). But Radcliffe goes beyond Young in her enthusiastic welcome of the "shades" (III: 3) of night and especially its "visionary powers" (I: 4). Whereas for Young visions of his departed companions are merely compensations for the darkness of night, for Radcliffe night's "sweet romantic visions" (VIII: 4) are its primary attraction. The same adjective, "sweet," is applied to night's "accents" (IX: 4) that provoke "the rising rapture" (IX: 2) with which the poet greets night. The melancholy, so pervasive and central to Young, is here replaced by a sense of elation at the gifts night offers.

Radcliffe's poem foreshadows in its stance if not in its form the *Hymnen an die Nacht* (Hymns to Night, 1798) by Novalis (Friedrich von Hardenberg, 1771-1801). Radcliffe's format is clearly conservative in its succession of 10 four-line stanzas each with an ABAB rhyme scheme. Novalis, on the other hand, is highly innovative, indeed experimental. The very word that he chose to designate his work, "hymns," points to the quasi-religious fervor that pulsates through this sequence of six long dithyrambs which were cast predominantly in verse in the original manuscript but printed in the Romantics' journal, *Das Athenäum* as prose poems. The actual typographical format in which the *Hymnen* were presented is of little consequence since there are only minimal verbal differences between the two versions. Fundamental to both is the pronounced incantatory tone characteristic of religious professions of faith and conducive to the work's haunting musical cadences. Novalis himself came from a family of Pietists, a sect that invested belief in an ardent personal relationship with God. When his bride died of consumption at an early age, he vented his grief in the *Hymnen* in which he elaborated a radical reversal of the meanings of day and night.

The *Hymnen* open on an eloquent tribute to the wonders displayed by daylight: which living person cannot but love above all else the manifold beauties nature affords to the senses? Formulated as a rhetorical question that anticipates an affirmative answer, this praise of light represents a contrasting frame to the main argument of the *Hymnen* heralded by Novalis's statement: "Abwärts wende ich mich zu der heiligen, unausprechlichen, geheimnisvollen Nacht" (I turn away to holy, inexpressible, secret-laden night; 1953 I: 339). From the perspective of this immersion in night, the daylight world now strikes Novalis as dim, distant, poor, and childish ("arm und kindisch"; p. 400) compared to the raptures of night. In a powerful panegyric to night, Novalis acclaims the infinite eyes that night opens up in us ("die unendlichen Augen die Nacht in uns geöffnet"; ibid.) for granting him visions of his lost beloved, who is to him the lovely sun of night ("liebliche Sonne der Nacht"; p. 401).

This vision that lights up night for Novalis is the basis for his revaluation of the roles of day and night. He becomes dedicated to night ("der Nacht Geweihte"; p. 401), eagerly awaiting the return of its timeless, spaceless domain. This idea of a complete reversal of the conventional evaluation of day and night, which had been mooted over half a century earlier by Young, becomes for Novalis an ecstatic creed. He repeatedly resorts to the image of a rebirth to describe his sensations: "mit einem Male riss das Band der Geburt – des Lichtes Fessel" (suddenly the umbilical cord tore – the shackles of light; p. 402), releasing his newborn spirit to feel "den ewigen, unwandelbaren Glauben an den Himmel der Nacht und sein Licht, die Geliebte" (the eternal, immutable belief in the heaven of night and its sun, the beloved; p. 302). Later, in the fifth and sixth of the *Hymnen*, Novalis expands this personal epiphany to all humanity's salvation through the coming of Christ, a revelation as potent as that which he experienced in his vision at his bride's grave. In the closing lines of the cycle the poet is received, as night descends, into the arms of the holy trinity of his beloved, Jesus, and the Divine Father.

Novalis also accomplishes another equally crucial transformation in the *Hymnen*: the total disappearance of night as a physical environment. Only in the opening tribute to light is there fleeting mention in very generalized terms of the phenomena of the outer world: the plants, the animals, the glittering stones, clouds, breezes, and human beings, the kings of the universe. There is no corresponding panorama of the scenery of night, in fact it has no scenery, no substantive existence, as it were. The night of the *Hymnen* is devoid of the features familiar in the great majority of night poetry, the moon, the stars, the clouds which so frequently form the setting for the poet's reflections. In the *Hymnen* night is as if disembodied; it envelops the poet as an exclusively spiritual medium in which he experiences his visions. The passage into night is not part of the public, expected diurnal rhythm; much rather it is a mysterious process, a private occult gift bestowed on the poet. These are the words in which Novalis addresses night about that esoteric transition: "Hast auch du ein Gefallen an uns, dunkle Nacht? Was hälst du unter deinem Mantel, das mir unsicht-bar kräftig an die Seele geht? Köstlicher Balsam träuft aus deiner Hand, aus dem Bündel Mohn. Die schweren Flügel des Gemüts hebst du empor. Dunkel und unaussprechlich fühlen wir uns bewegt" (Do you too, dark night, take pleasure in us? What do you hold beneath your cloak that affects my soul with invisible power? Precious balsam drips from your hand, from the bundle of poppies. You raise the heavy wings of the spirit. We feel ourselves moved in a dark, inexpressible manner; 1953: 400).

The coming of night is for Novalis a psychological crossing into another world peopled by his beloved as well as Jesus and God. By stripping night of its tangible presence, Novalis internalizes it so that it becomes an imaginative projection of the poet's mind, a means of transcendence, the gateway to that higher poetic realm to which the Early German Romantics (*Frühromantiker*) aspired.

Like Novalis's *Hymnen,* another extensive cycle of night poems, Alfred de Musset's (1810-57) sequence of four *Nuits* (1835-7), published toward the close of the Ro-mantic period, are, except for their titles, wholly devoid of references to night as a physical entity. It has been erased to function exclusively as the context for the poet's visions. Visions and melancholy are two major elements which Musset's poems share, almost a century after Young's *Night Thoughts*, like Radcliffe's "Night," with this predecessor. In other respects, however, Musset's *Nuits* differ basically from previous night poetry. They are linked externally by the seasons: *Nuit de mai* (May 1835), *Nuit de décembre* (December 1835), *Nuit d'août* (August 1836), and *Nuit d'octobre* (October 1837) as well as internally by a narrative that maps the poet's progress from a dejected silence to a capacity to accept suffering and to go on living and writing.

All four poems pivot on the poet's visions; three of them (May, August, and October) record confrontations with the Muse, while the fourth (December) conjures up a changing figure "Qui me ressemblait comme un frère" (who resembled me like a brother; Musset 1975: 54-6), as the closing line of several stanzas proclaims, an other who finally identifies himself as "La Solitude." With this persona, as with the Muse, the poet engages in extended dialogues. The originality of the *Nuits* lies in the use of this dialogic format in the exchanges between the poet and his visions in a dramatic lyricism unlike that of any of the other night poems. The Muse generally speaks in the traditional French verse form of the alexandrine, repeatedly urging the poet to take up his lyre again, whereas the poet responds in shorter lines, insisting that his sorrows silence him. By the last of the series, the poet comes to concede the role of suffering as necessary to the genesis of poetry, an insight that is embodied in the at least partial reversal of the verse pattern as he, like the Muse, reassumes the prescribed alexandrine.

Musset's *Nuits* clearly reiterate a number of motifs familiar in Romantic night poetry, notably melancholy, the incursion of visions, and a certain amount of agitation. But night exists here solely as a temporal phase conducive to the elaboration of the poet's state of mind. Even more than in Novalis's *Hymnen an die Nacht*, the inner landscape prevails to the exclusion of the outer. Instead of describing or personifying night, as much Romantic writing does, Novalis's *Hymnen* and Musset's *Nuits* turn it into the occasion for the exploration of the poet's subconscious. "Nach innen geht der geheimnisvolle Weg" (Inwards leads the mysterious path), Novalis asserted in the 18th of his *Blütenstaub* (Pollen Dust, 1798) pieces, a collection of fragments that summarized his ideology. He went on to profess: "In uns, oder nirgends ist die Ewigkeit mit ihren Welten, die Vergangenheit und die Zukunft. Die Aussenwelt ist die Schattenwelt" (Within us or nowhere lies eternity and its worlds, the past and the future. The outer world is a world of shadows; 1953 I: 310-11).

In this belief, extreme though it may seem, Novalis delineates one of the major, perhaps *the* major trend of Romantic writing, whether it be about one of the seasons or about night. The Romantics were strongly drawn inward into their own subjectivity. The foremost attraction of night for them was the opportunity it affords, under the cover of darkness, for this journey into the self. Night reduces the claims made on the individual by the outer world by effacing its sights and colors in favor of a realm of shadows in which the poet is set free to plumb his or her own psyche. The feelings unveiled in this situation range from melancholy to joy, from turbulence to tranquility, but varied as they are, all are unleashed by the withdrawal into night.[3]

NOTES

1 Magnetism was a theory propagated by Franz Anton Mesmer (1734-1815) who held that an imponderable fluid permeated the entire universe, infusing both matter and spirit with its vital force. Good health depended on the proper distribution of this fluid to achieve equilibrium.

2 Titled *"Ein Gleiches"* (The Same) in the standard Hamburg edition of Goethe's works.

3 I would like to record my gratitude to Michael Ferber and Inger S. Brodey for helping me to locate several of the texts, and to Jocelyn M. Dawson and Janice H. Koelb for library work.

REFERENCES

Primary sources

Anon ([1804] 1972). *Night Watches of Bonaventura,* trans. and ed. Gerald Gillespie. Edinburgh: Edinburgh University Press.

Blake, William (1966). *Complete Writings,* ed. Geoffrey Keynes. London and New York: Oxford University Press.

Byron, George Gordon (1970). *Poetical Works,* ed. Frederick Page, rev. John Jump. London and New York: Oxford University Press.

Eichendorff, Joseph von (1966). *Werke.* Munich: Hanser.

Goethe, Johann Wolfgang von (1967). *Werke,* 14 vols. Hamburg: Christian Wegner.

Hölderlin, Friedrich. *Sämtliche Gedichte,* ed. Detlev Luders. Hamburg: Athenäum Verlag.

Hoffmann, Ernst Theodor Amadeus (1967). *Werke.* Hamburg: Hofmann & Campe.

Hugo, Victor (2001). *Selected Poems,* trans. and ed. E. H. and M. Blackmore. Chicago and London: University of Chicago Press.

Lamartine, Alphonse de (1981). *Méditations poétiques,* ed. Marius-François Guyard. Paris: Gallimard.

Macpherson, James (1846). *Poems of Ossian.* Edinburgh: Geddes.

Mörike, Eduard (1969). *Werke.* Berlin and Weimar: Aufbau.

Musset, Alfred de (1975). *Oeuvres complètes,* ed. Edmond Bire. Paris: Garnier; reprint Nendeln/Liechtenstein: Kraus.

Novalis (Hardenberg, Friedrich von) (1953). *Dichtungen.* Heidelberg: Lambert Schneider.

Radcliffe, Ann (1931). *The Romance of the Forest, Three Eighteenth-Century Romances.* New York: Scribner's Sons.

Schubert, Gotthilf Heinrich (1967). *Ansichten von den Nachtseiten der Naturwissenschaft.* Darmstadt: Wissenschaftliche Buchgesellschaft.

Shelley, Percy Bysshe (1928). *Works,* ed. Roger Ingpen and Walter E. Peck. New York: Scribner's Sons.

Smith, Charlotte (1993). *Poems,* ed. Stuart Curran. New York and Oxford: Oxford University Press.

Tieck, Ludwig (n.d.). *Werke,* ed. Gotthold Ludwig Klee. Leipzig: Bibliographisches Institut.

Wordsworth, William (1969). *Poetical Works,* ed. Ernest de Selincourt, rev. Thomas Hutchinson. London and New York: Oxford University Press.

Young, Edward (1975). *Night Thoughts or The Complaint and The Consolation,* ed. Robert Essick and Jenijoy LaBelle. Mineola, NY: Dover.

Secondary sources

Van Tieghem, P. (1921). *La Poésie de la nuit et des tombeaux en Europe au XVIIIe siècle.* Paris: Rieder.

30

Romantic Opera

Benjamin Walton

Every nation wants to see represented on stage only its own average and superficial aspects; unless you provide it with heroes, music, or fools. (Friedrich Schlegel, *Philosophical Fragments* [1797] 1994)

Halfway through "Der Dichter und der Komponist," E. T. A. Hoffmann's dialogue on the aesthetics of Romantic opera, the composer figure Ludwig elaborates his conception of the ideal Romantic plot by retelling Carlo Gozzi's dramatic fairy tale *Il Corvo* (The Raven). To summarize Hoffmann's summary, the story begins with the shooting of the eponymous bird, an act which unleashes a monster from a grotto who places a curse on the bird's assassin, Millo, King of Frattambrosa. This curse dictates that in retribution for the killing, Millo must find a wife with hair as red as the raven's blood, eyebrows as black as the raven's feathers, and skin as white as the marble tomb on which the raven landed, or else go insane. Millo's brother Jennaro sets out in search of such a woman, finds her, abducts her, survives a storm, chances upon a pair of magnificent falcons and a stallion, and is then informed by two doves that the animals and the kidnapped princess Armilla are also cursed in a particularly cunning way: if Millo receives them he will die, and if he does not then Jennaro will be turned to stone. The remainder of the plot is given over to getting round the difficulties that this curse presents, but all Jennaro's efforts to try to save his brother from death while retaining his own animate existence appear instead to Millo like evidence of extreme jealousy. Jennaro is sentenced to death as a result, and to prove his innocence has to confide in his brother. This too is forbidden by the curse, and he is duly made into a statue. Only the appearance of Norand, Armilla's sorcerer father, can bring things to a happy end, and then only after Armilla has killed herself in order to return Jennaro to fleshly life (on Norand's instructions), leading Millo in turn to prepare himself for suicide from despair. Norand's final appearance causes the vault in which the action is taking place to be suffused with light: "the great, mysterious prophecy has been fulfilled; all sorrow is at an end; Armilla, touched by Norand, comes back to life and everything ends happily" (Charlton 1989: 188-209, quote p. 199).

Hoffmann's own protagonists are quick to praise the way in which the unfolding of the plot carries the force of poetic truth, allowing the incredible to become credible: "Millo's action in killing the raven knocks, as it were, at the bronze portal of the shadowy spirit-realm, so that it swings open with a clang and the spirits emerge into the world and enmesh men in the mysterious fate that governs their own movements" (Charlton 1989: 199). For Hoffmann this was the same spirit-realm in which music resided, and which could raise language into the heightened sphere of musical expression, allowing poet and composer to unite in the revelation of the "ultimate sublimity" to which successful Romantic art gave access. In this way Romantic opera, "with its fairies, spirits, miracles, and transformations" becomes "the only true sort" of opera, "for only in the realm of romanticism is music at home" (Charlton 1989: 196).

The force and clarity of Hoffmann's aesthetic formulations, however, cannot entirely bridge the (Romantically picturesque) chasm between his celebration of this paradigmatic narrative and the modern reader's likely bewilderment faced with a plot that multiplies its magical resources in a way that seems less mysterious than unhinged. Such a gulf, made still deeper by the disappearance of almost all self-described Romantic repertory from later canons of operatic performance, points towards a general problem with the idea of operatic Romanticism that goes beyond simple changes in the audience's capacity to suspend disbelief. Through the writings of Hoffmann and many of the other German Romantics, instrumental music would become the perfect Romantic artform in the early years of the nineteenth century, and would remain synonymous with ideals of heightened expression and emotional communion long after they had become outdated and unpopular in the other arts. In operatic history, however, Romanticism has tended instead to appear as an awkward transitional stage, typically narrated through its shortcomings and premonitions of future better developments. In good Romantic fashion, Romantic opera is always becoming, always moving towards a distant, fleetingly glimpsed perfect form.

In this sense, and despite Hoffmann's own career as an operatic composer (as well as conductor, critic, novelist, playwright, theater manager, and designer), the place of *Il Corvo* as a nonexistent opera, awaiting the perfect music, is symbolically significant in an age that thrived on the aesthetic frisson of imaginary sounds.[1] Textless instrumental music could be easily conceived untethered from the sources of its production, celebrated as the ideal Romantic art in its separation from the specificity of language and the mundanity of daily life. Opera, on the other hand, however supernatural, was harder to render equally unearthly, since its libretto and its physical realization – the scenery, props, costumes, and singers – all served to distract from the ideal. Indeed, as with Romantic drama, it could be argued that some of the most successful Romantic operas were those freed from the complicated, messy business of actual staging, and which could exist instead in other forms, whether as operatic tales like Hoffmann's Romanticized fantasy on *Don Giovanni* (1813) or Balzac's decidedly Hoffmannesque *Massimilla Doni* (1839), or else in musical works at one remove from opera such as

Liszt's operatic paraphrases or Berlioz's hybrid unstageable operas of the mind, *Roméo et Juliette* (1839) and *La Damnation de Faust* (1846).[2] While Romanticism propelled music to the top of the aesthetic hierarchy, opera could only partake wholeheartedly in the same discourse through being transformed into literary fantasy or honorary instrumental music.

Several matters arise from this disparity between the real and the imaginary that will be explored in this chapter. First, it indicates that the history of Romantic opera occupies a significant place in the history of desire for operatic reform, a narrative that runs in parallel with the genre itself, from seventeenth-century censorship and the *querelle des bouffons* through Gluck, Wagner, Brecht, and Boulez. In the case of Romantic opera, this reformative aspect leads to some unexpected aesthetic anomalies, with demands for dramatic unity contrasting with absurdly magical plots, or stripped-down simplicity of musical style trumping the potential (but uncontrollable) emotional force of vocal virtuosity. Furthermore, Romantic works such as those listed above by Balzac or Berlioz (or Romantically themed operas by Verdi or Wagner) point towards the problematic chronology of operatic Romanticism, with music's much-remarked belatedness in catching up with intellectual trends leading to a broadly conceived Romantic aesthetic that only begins around 1810 and then spreads easily into the 1830s, 1840s, and beyond. It is after all the ninth volume of the comprehensive *New Oxford History of Music*, on the period from 1830-90, that is named "The Age of Romanticism." The eighth, meanwhile, largely covering the period of literary Romanticism, is named after a single figure, whose instrumental music comprehensively dwarfs his single problematic opera: Ludwig van Beethoven (Abraham 1982, 1990).

The dominance of Beethoven, then and now, has generated an entire critical tradition debating whether the composer is "Classic" or "Romantic," as well as emphasizing the newfound aesthetic prestige of the symphony over the continuing social prestige of opera.[3] Yet to address only such stylistic and generic matters is to ignore the larger issue of national identity, both concealed and implied by titling a history of early nineteenth-century music "The Age of Beethoven." The celebration of certain types of instrumental music carried national implications, and Hoffmann's prescription for operatic Romanticism in "Der Dichter" came in large part from a desire for the creation of a German national opera that could rival the French and Italian equivalents whose works dominated German stages throughout the late eighteenth and early nineteenth centuries. In this way compositional choices combined with national aspirations and prejudices to produce different versions of "Romantic opera" embodying a variety of positive and negative suppositions about the vexed term "Romanticism." Examination of the three major national traditions – of Germany, France, and Italy – can shed light on some of these differences and crosscurrents. And by remaining largely within the earlier (age of Beethoven) chronology of mainstream Romantic history, it becomes possible to map out a few relatively delimited moments when opera and the history of Romanticism intersect in revealing ways.

Germany

Romantic opera was born in Germany, insofar as the first operas to name themselves "Romantic" appeared there. Three early works by the three key early Romantic composers were performed or were begun in 1808: Ludwig Spohr's *Alruna, die Eulenkönigin* (Alruna, Queen of the Owls), Carl Maria von Weber's *Silvana* (completed 1810), and Hoffmann's own *Der Trank der Unsterblichkeit* (The Immortality Potion).[4] All are *Singspiele*, alternating closed musical numbers with spoken dialogue, and have appropriately Romantic supernatural plots. Yet as Edward Dent pointed out in *The Rise of Romantic Opera*, such plots were by no means an invention of the early nineteenth century, and can be traced with ease back through Handel and beyond (Dent 1976: 24-5). More pressing, for Dent, is to discover when plots of a certain kind become linked to what could be described as "Romantic music." Here, immediately, familiar dilemmas about definitions begin to surface. Dent himself defines Romantic style as the incursion of comic elements into the tragic, but sees the question ultimately related to performance style: "Opera became Romantic...because audiences wanted to hear trivial music sung by first-rate singers" (Dent 1976: 15). Others have been less damning, but histories of Romantic music are filled with stylistic pronouncements such as Dent's about what (or who) is Romantic and what (or who) is not, relying on a fixed (if not always well-founded) notion of Romantic style only partially connected to cultural context. In these terms, it becomes possible to draw up a kind of taxonomy of operatic Romanticism that includes not only magical plots, but also an increased use of the orchestra, particularly to evoke natural or supernatural events; the presence of reminiscence motives (musical signs that return in various contexts); the symbolic use of different tonalities; a tendency to blur formal boundaries in favor of continuous music; and the adoption of straightforward folk-like material. Musically speaking, one of the most important predecessors here is Mozart's *Die Zauberflöte* (1791), whose multilayered plot and deceptively simple music generated a rash of sequels and related pieces in the years following its premiere, and which together with *Don Giovanni* serve as "parent works of romantic opera."[5] Equally important, however, are the French works from the 1790s and 1800s of Etienne-Jean Méhul, Luigi Cherubini, and Jean-François Le Sueur, many of which both Weber and Hoffmann conducted, and which frequently include recurring thematic material and strikingly novel use of the orchestra (Méhul's *Uthal* [1806] with its violinless scoring being only the most famous example).

However revealing in terms of the history of genre it might be to uncover the non-German and inescapably hybrid roots of German attempts to establish a national opera, it is only once in the German context that the idea of a *Romantic* opera becomes an explicit aim. When Spohr, Hoffmann, and Weber call their works Romantic in 1808 it still signifies a type of plot above all. Already in 1802, however, an article by Franz Horn had appeared in the newly founded *Allgemeine musikalische Zeitung* which announced in proto-Hoffmannian terms that by its nature "true opera is essentially romantic. It allows the most exuberant harmonic vitality and extravagant flights of fancy to glide smoothly past us, and, uplifted by the sweet sounds of music, we perceive the sublimest impulses of that vitality with greater clarity than can ever happen in a mere drama" (quoted in Charlton 1989: 185). In line with this more far-reaching and inclusive version of Romantic operatic potential, Hoffmann's next work, *Aurora* (1811-12), was conceived in explicitly more ambitious terms as a "grosse romantische Oper," thereby uniting the Romantic *Singspiel* tradition with the national project for a grand opera involving large forces and classical or historical subject matter to rival French examples. The plot was indeed classical in inspiration and indebted to Gluck, whose *Iphigénie en Aulide* (1774) Hoffmann had declared in an 1810 review in *Allgemeine musikalische Zeitung* (reprinted in Charlton 1989: 255-62) as "true musical drama" and a better model for composition than the "high Romantic" style of Mozart (pp. 259, 261).

Hoffmann's opera was never performed during his lifetime, but its aims of dramatic and musical unity, in line with Romantic theories of the fusion of the arts (from writers such as Wackenroder and Schelling), would recur as a rallying cry for German opera throughout the period, receiving perhaps their most famous pre-Wagnerian articulation in Weber's review of Hoffmann's subsequent and most accomplished opera *Undine* (1816).[6] After praising Hoffmann's use of the orchestra and his attempts to create continuous musical development, Weber announced that: "Of course when I speak of opera I am speaking of the German ideal, namely a self-sufficient work of art in which every feature and every contribution by the related arts are moulded together in a certain way and dissolve, to form a new world" (Warrack 1981: 201). Such a description resonates as a celebration of the German Romantic operatic dream, music's expressive potency mixed with the other arts in a revelatory synthesis. And the connections here with later Wagnerian thought are impossible to ignore, not least because it was largely Wagner's transformation of such Romantic ideals that has granted these earlier works their eternally transitional status in operatic history. Yet however ideologically driven such narratives about Wagner's successful completion of the Romantic project might be, with inadequate opera successfully converted into superior music drama, it is hard to refute the Wagnerian suspicion that in the time of Weber and Hoffmann practice often failed to fulfill what theory prescribed, in a way that fits neatly with contemporary national stereotyping. As Madame de Staël put it in 1813 in her phenomenally influential work *De l'Allemagne* (On Germany), written to educate the French about their neighbors, "In general the Germans conceive art better than they practise it" (de Staël 1871, 2: 162). This is clear enough with Hoffmann's *Undine* which, despite a considerably less convoluted plot than *Il Corvo*, is hard to credit with the organic wholeness that Weber describes. Indeed, Weber's review criticizes the libretto (by Friedrich de la Motte Fouqué, author of the original popular *Undine* tale of 1811) for a lack of clarity brought about by the librettist's overfamiliarity with his own story, but he sees it compensated for by music "so powerful from beginning to end that one can grasp the whole work after a single hearing and individual details simply disappear" (Warrack 1981: 203).

When Weber wrote his *Undine* review he was midway through a decade-long operatic hiatus between the single act *Abu Hassan* (1811) and *Der Freischütz*, begun in 1817 but not premiered until 1821. Weber's writings of that period, whether reviews or introductions to works which he conducted in Prague and Dresden, thereby become a forum for working out the theoretical bases for future success. True to this task, the eventual arrival of *Freischütz* left earlier Romantic repertory to fade from view next to the dazzling triumph of a work that remains the symbol of all Romantic opera, and even "the true originator of German musical romanticism" (Whittall 1987: 31). Here the branches of the Romantic taxonomy come together in a form that generated enormous enthusiasm at its premiere in Berlin and then throughout the German states and northern Europe. The boundary between the human and supernatural realms explored in *Undine* and also in Spohr's *Faust* (premiered in Prague, 1816) is integral to the plot, which concerns the huntsman Max's attempts to win his beloved Agathe in a shooting contest through the use of magic bullets obtained from the devil in the terrifying Wolf's Glen at midnight. As in *Undine*, it is the orchestra that holds the task of depicting the magical. In contrast to Hoffmann's work, however, where the world of the water sprites has a moral clarity lacking in human affairs, Weber's supernatural realm is entirely malignant. Consequently, his musical representation of the glen is structured tonally on the notes of the diminished seventh chord that acts throughout the work as a recurrent sign of evil, and timbrally through a use of tremolo strings, timpani rolls, and spooky woodwind interjections that would map out the musical domain of terror for many years to come. Yet the use of the orchestra also signifies beyond the devil's realm. Again, Madame de Staël paraphrases received opinion adroitly: "the Germans excel in instrumental music; the knowledge that it requires and the patience necessary to perform it well come completely naturally to them" (de Staël 1871, 2: 164). As with Hoffmann, pronounced use of the orchestra thereby becomes a national statement, pitting German instrumental expertise against the innate vocal facility (or, for their detractors, fatuity) which marked the character of the Italians. As John Warrack writes, resurrecting the dichotomy for the late twentieth century, Weber's emphasis on the orchestra in *Der Freischütz* came "from deep in his German heritage" (Warrack 2001: 305).

The orchestra was by no means the only Romantic signifier in the work bound up with German identity. The emphasis on natural life, on hunting, and the social dynamics between the strata of village society, all pointed towards an idealized rustic imagery that was reinforced by the folk-like quality of much of the music. The inspiration for this, as in other Romantic works, actually came primarily from French opéra-comique models.[7] Yet its transplantation to the forests of Bohemia, together with the serendipitous timing of its premiere in Berlin only weeks after the opening of Spontini's French imperial *Olympie*, secured the work's rapid progression from engaging *Singspiel* to totem of Romantic nationhood, as a work which "succeeded where attempts by Tieck, Brentano, Schlegel, Arnim and Werner had failed – in bringing Romanticism into the theatre" (Warrack 1976: 227).[8]

Whatever the achievements of *Der Freischütz*, it was nevertheless still not the grand Romantic through-composed generically synthesized opera of Weber's imagination. When this arrived in the autumn of 1823 in the form of *Euryanthe*, it was received poorly and has remained "one of the most problematic works in the annals of opera" (Tusa 1991: 1). Much has traditionally been blamed on the libretto, by Helmina von Chézy, which takes a plot about a pair of lovers threatened by the jealousy and scheming of another pair, and weighs it down with twists and absurdities. Weber played his part in contributing to the textual problems, suggesting the insertion of the supernatural in the form of the ghost of a dead lover, and the appearance in Act 3 of a giant serpent reminiscent of the monster in *Il Corvo*. Moreover, he incited von Chézy to challenge him with her verses, to "heap difficulty upon difficulty" because "*Euryanthe* must be something new! Must stand alone on its peak!" (Warrack 1976: 284).

The fault was not with the libretto alone, however, since Weber's musical realization also received repeated criticism for the lack of the very qualities that he had celebrated in *Undine*. In short, the work was not sufficiently unified, and presented too close a reading of isolated dramatic moments at the expense of the expression of the whole. John Daverio has offered an intriguing defense of Weber in this respect, mapping the tension (outlined by Weber's critics) between the competing Romantic aesthetics of self-sufficient melodic expression and dramatic truth onto Friedrich Schlegel's reading of allegory and symbol (Daverio 1993). Where general Romantic philosophy celebrated the mystical unity of part and whole in symbol at the expense of the unpromising metonymic doubling of allegory, Schlegel saw allegory's potential as a way towards the infinite, hinting at the inexpressible in the gaps and fractures which it generated. Similarly, then, for Daverio, in its very failure to unite dramatic and musical requirements, *Euryanthe* confronts the false unity of the symbol with the generative potential of Schlegelian allegory. Weber's opera is both designed to work as music alone (the symbolic unity) and as dramatic accompaniment (allegorizing the plot), and the ultimate incompatibility of the two functions as self-critique, thus placing the opera within the critical tradition of the early Jena Romantics. As a result, *Euryanthe* becomes the embodiment of Romantic opera through its shortcomings, which gesture towards a forever unattainable ideal.

France

It is perhaps hard now, in the age of boxed sets and critical editions, to recover quite how unself-evident the idea of aesthetic unity would have seemed to the early nineteenth-century operagoer, at a time when works were routinely changed from city to city and from singer to singer with little sense of an original, inalterable text. In this light, it is not especially surprising that the first time that part of *Euryanthe* was heard in Paris, it was a retexted version of the Act 2 love duet "Hin nimm die Seele mein" interpolated into an arrangement of *Freischütz* named *Robin des Bois*. Yet the burgeoning status of *Freischütz* as the quintessence of German Romantic art has granted this particular restaging the reputation of an indefensibly barbaric act, with its own negative reception history to mirror the positive one of the original work.[9] This is largely thanks to the vitriolic account given by Hector Berlioz in his *Memoirs*, in which the French arranger, the critic François-Henri-Joseph Blaze (better known as Castil-Blaze) is labeled a "veterinary surgeon of music" who "hacked and mutilated" Weber's work in adapting it to French tastes (Berlioz 1969: 102, 99). But alongside such contempt for the treatment of the piece, Berlioz's account also points to another justification for the lasting significance of the Parisian *Freischütz* over all the other various adaptations and parodies performed throughout Europe.[10] Berlioz admits that he found himself intoxicated by the music, even in its sadly altered state, seduced by its power away from his previous classical love, the operas of Gluck, to the irresistible enchantments of Weber's new style. In other words, the performance of *Robin* introduced Berlioz, and by extension French musical culture, to the unbridled joys of Romantic music.

Such a narrative contains an element of truth. *Robin* was not the first German opera to be put on in Paris; there had been arrangements of both *Die Zauberflöte* (as *Les Mystères d'Isis*, first performed in 1801) and Winter's *Das unterbrochene Opferfest* (*Le Sacrifice interrompu*). But Mozart's work, which included parts from *Don Giovanni* and *La Clemenza di Tito*, was not perceived as "German," and Winter's tale of ancient Peru, also from the 1790s, which opened at the Odéon two months before *Robin*, was rapidly overshadowed by Weber's supernatural diversions.[11] Weber's music, on the other hand, even in its rearranged form, was experienced through the filter of presuppositions about its Teutonic difficulty and obscurity. Dramatically, too, despite a shift in location from Bohemia to Yorkshire (a move that tied in with contemporary enthusiasm for Walter Scott), the Wolf's Glen (or rather St Dunstan's Abbey) at midnight remained markedly un-Parisian. As Heine described in *The Romantic School*, his account of the history of German Romanticism for a French audience (updating Madame de Staël):

> Between twelve and one, the hour that has been allotted to ghosts from time imme-morial, the full stream of life is still roaring through the streets of Paris, in the opera the thundering finale is just sounding, out of the Variétés and the Théâtre-Gymnase come streaming the merriest groups, and the boulevards are thronging with rollicking, laughing, bantering crowds, and everybody goes to the soirées. How unhappy a poor ghost would feel spooking amidst this animated multitude! (Heine 1985: 96-7)

The appearance of *Robin* can be placed near the start of an influx of German "Romantic" material in the late 1820s that included a clutch of theatrical adaptations of Goethe's *Faust* around 1827, the appearance of Hoffmann's tales in translation from 1829, and a number of supernatural operas, from François-Adrien Boieldieu's hugely popular Scott-inspired opéra-comique *La Dame Blanche* (1825) to Giacomo Meyer-beer's *Robert le Diable* (begun 1827, premiered 1831), complete with its ballet of ghostly nuns.[12] Given French tendencies to amalgamate varieties of north European exoticism (as seen in *Robin*'s change of location), the famous English Shakespeare productions from 1827 can also be added to this list. Furthermore, the following year saw the start of the phenomenally successful Beethoven symphony concerts at the Conservatoire. In Berlioz's words: "I had just had the successive revelations of Shakespeare and Weber. Now at another point on the horizon I saw the giant form of Beethoven rear up. Beethoven opened before me a new world of music, as Shakespeare had revealed a new universe of poetry" (Berlioz 1969: 120). In this way, Weber's opera also shows the way towards a (largely unoperatic) French musical Romanticism in the undeniably Romantic figure of Berlioz, whose *Symphonie fantastique* premiere in December 1830 becomes a musical equivalent of the famous first performance of Hugo's *Hernani* that February or indeed of the revolution that overthrew the Restoration regime over three days in late July.

There is, however, an alternative story of operatic Romanticism in France, which turns against the idea that Romantic music must conform to the German model. *Der Freischütz*, after all, appeared at a low point for the German Romantics, who, "once so influential on the other national movements" by the 1820s had found "middle age, seclusion, and sagging esteem" (Paulin 1985: 216). In France, meanwhile, the mid-1820s saw Romantic debates in full spate, based to a large extent on questions of theatrical reform foreign to the German context, but deeply enmeshed with developments in the popular theaters, including those like the Odéon (venue for *Robin*) which performed both classical spoken theater and "Romantic" opera. Moreover, the appearance of the French *Freischütz* in 1824-5 coincided with a shift from the medievalist royalist Romanticism of the early 1820s to the modern liberal Romanticism of the second half of the decade.[13] In its setting, Weber's Romantic opera appealed to the former, but without any deeper national meaning. As Heine put it, "in France the Gothic fad was simply a fad, and it served only to heighten the pleasure of the present" (Heine 1985: 124). Musically, meanwhile, the work came closer to the latter, its balance of tuneful melodies and progressive harmonies becoming in itself a sign of French Romanticism as defined by Stendhal, most musical of the liberal Romantics: "the art of presenting people with ... works which, in the present state of their needs and beliefs, will give them the greatest possible pleasure" (Stendhal [1823] 1970: 39, my translation).

If *Robin* marks a notable transformation of German Romanticism into a French equivalent, reactions to the more unfamiliar types of "Germanic" musical expression within the piece nevertheless varied. Stendhal himself, for instance, in a poorly disguised "anonymous" letter to the Romantic journal *Le Globe*, announced that while the huntsmen's chorus, the waltz, the drinking song, and selected other moments in *Robin* were good, the rest was "overworked and unintelligible."[14] For Stendhal, this meant above all that it did not sound enough like the inescapable soundtrack of post-Napoleonic Europe, the music of his beloved Gioachino Rossini.

In some ways Rossini, like Wagner, has haunted this chapter throughout. When Weber rewrote his description of true operatic unity from the *Undine* review in his unfinished novel *Tonkünstlers Leben*, he altered the first sentence to read "Of course when I speak of opera I am speaking of the German *and French* ideal" (my italics). French opera could thus for the most part be securely acknowledged as a potential model. Italian opera, however, remained the poorly repressed Other, ridiculed but none the less threatening in its tuneful fecundity and perceived lack of concern for dramatic truth. And from 1815 or so that Italian threat was embodied by Rossini, the most popular composer in Europe, whose works spread through Austro-Germany first to Vienna and then from 1818 to Hoffmann's Berlin. "At the present moment the danger lies . . . with the sirocco of Rossini blowing from the south," wrote Weber in *Tonkünstlers Leben* (Warrack 1981: 338), while Hoffmann railed against "the grotesque leaps and roulades of Rossini and his ilk, of the clumsy violin figures, and of the odious trills that often take the place of melody and then incite female singers to a surfeit of gurgling" (Charlton 1989: 441). Of course, Rossini's influence could not easily be ignored completely in the quest for popular success, but it is notable that in *Euryanthe* the music closest to Rossinian forms and levels of vocal virtuosity is granted to the evil characters Lysiart and Eglantine, whereas the good, wholesome Agathe and Adolar receive less adventurous music.[15] More generally the Rossinian aesthetic – cast as overornamented and formally straitjacketed – became anti-Romantic by default, and doubly cursed for its incessant popularity.

In France, Rossini's similar rise to ubiquity from 1819 caused an equivalent outburst of nationalist condemnation, but within the contours of French Romanticism (and largely thanks to Stendhal, exiled back to Paris from Italy in 1821) it was resistance to the Italian style that was for the most part derided as un-Romantic, indicating support for the moribund French repertoire at the Opéra instead of the scintillating Rossinian modernity relished by the young dilettanti at the Théâtre-Italien next door.[16] And their youthfulness was important; much of French Romanticism from the mid-1820s involved playing out a generational struggle around which the binaries of Romantic debate collected: present versus past, liberal versus royalist, cosmopolitan versus nationalist, Romantic versus classic. The transition from political to artistic categories was easily made, and in these terms the implied and oft-repeated comparison that opened Stendhal's premature and exhilaratingly prolix 1824 biography of Rossini was not an idle one: "Napoleon is dead; but a new conqueror has already shown himself to the world" (Stendhal 1985: 3).

Within the dominance of the German Romantic paradigm, the attention given to Rossini in Paris during the Restoration becomes for later historians a sign of poor musical taste. In the words of Jean Mongrédien: "Today we may be somewhat surprised that some of the better authors of the 1820s and 1830s considered Rossini to be one of them" (Mongrédien 1996: 136-7). Yet the surprise only exists within a strict conception of Romanticism borrowed from other contexts, and thereby risks missing Rossini's multiple significance for Romanticism in Paris. In the first place, the very sound of his music – its frenetic pace, its deafening, percussion-saturated volume – offered an addictively appealing accompaniment for modern (and therefore Romantic) French existence, as memorably described by art critic Etienne-Jean

Delécluze: "Lord Byron, Rossini and Cayenne pepper, these are the three stimulants that people must now have to avoid falling into a numbness that resembles death" (Delécluze 1948: 76, my translation). Furthermore, as hinted at above, the foreignness of his (and Weber's) music offered a welcome release from deadening French traditions, while pointing towards a Stendhalian (and Staëlian) cosmopolitanism in which German harmony (represented by Weber) and Italian melody (Rossini) could merge in Paris, "more than ever the capital of Europe" (Stendhal 1985: 126, translation modified).

In the *Undine* review, Weber blames the tumultuous circumstances of life under Napoleon for the poor quality and "pointless stage spectacle" of contemporary theater (Warrack 1981: 202). Similarly, the poet and the composer in Hoffmann's dialogue are brought together in the midst of war and they both regard aesthetic speculation as a welcome escape from its horrors, art clearly held apart from political life. In the Restoration, however, for the "generation of 1820" brought up on tales of Napoleonic glory only to come of age under the restored *ancien régime*, art and politics were inescapably intertwined.[17] And this generated Rossini's ultimate Romantic importance, when, after his move to Paris in 1824, he was given the task of transforming French grand opera. The results of this – two revisions of earlier pieces and a single new work – were statistically fewer than his government sponsors had hoped, but dramatically and musically they lie at the heart of political Romanticism. All depict narratives of popular revolt through painstakingly accurate scenic effects and massed choruses. The first, *Le Siège de Corinthe* (1826, adapted from *Maometto II*) drew on the enormous contemporary interest in the Greek War of Independence and included both a memorable blessing of the Greek flags and a devastating tragic finale. Meanwhile, his last opera, *Guillaume Tell* (1829), in many ways offered a single-handed response to Stendhal's call for the French union of Italian and German opera, providing a work with hunters' choruses, rural peasant dances, orchestral scene-painting, and patriotic oath-swearing, all combined with reconceived Italian vocal writing. The piece also included an uprising on stage that later generations would connect effortlessly to the following year's revolution in the Parisian streets. In its own time, this link was not so appealingly straightforward, and Rossini's work, like the Neapolitan uprising in Gustave Auber's equally famed *La Muette de Portici* from the previous year (a performance of which supposedly triggered the Belgian revolution of 1830), could be interpreted in various ways according to temperament and political inclination.[18] Whatever Rossini's personal aesthetics (and his later pronouncements are far from Romantically inclined), his French works managed to bring together many of the multiple strands of French Romantic concern, and thereby to offer something for everyone. Even Berlioz, having initially rejected Rossini's inclusive approach as evidence of his "usual mixture of art, habit, experience and audience manipulation," in 1834 declared *Tell* a 'splendid work,' and (more tellingly) "a sign of those greater and nobler capacities whose development the requirements of the sensual people for whom he has written for until now [i.e., the Italians and French] have necessarily made impossible."[19] Even Rossini, in other words, could become an honorary German.

Italy

Three years after introducing Germany to France with *De l'Allemagne*, the indefatigable Madame de Staël published an article ("On the Manner and Usefulness of Translations," 1816) that single-handedly launched Romantic debate in Italy.[20] In outline, and in advance of similar French squabbles, de Staël's proposal – that Italians should borrow more from other European countries as a means to rejuvenate native literature – led to an outpouring of pamphlets classically defending Italian traditions or Romantically supporting the need for innovation. (See Piero Garofalo's chapter in this volume.) Almost nowhere in all the responses was there mention of opera, and indeed de Staël's only reference in her original polemic dismissed it as obviously absurd. Rossini's use of Shakespeare in *Otello* (1816) or Scott in *La donna del lago* (1819) nevertheless indicate some awareness of the literary stakes at the time, while many of his post-1816 works, mostly written for the Teatro San Carlo in Naples, romantically explore the blurring of formal and generic conventions. Any concerted Italian Romantic movement dwindled during the 1820s in the face of Austrian censorship, however, and as a result many historians have claimed that Italian Romanticism never really occurred at all. Yet by the late 1820s the influence of French liberal Romanticism did make its way back to Italy, combined with Hugo's ideas on theatrical reform, and this time opera played a much more striking role. This manifested itself primarily through matters of libretto choice, notably towards plots taken from recent history or set in distant lands and reliant on extremes of violence or emotion. But musically, too, there were signs of change, and here once again Rossini becomes a central yet ambiguous figure. In the words of Giuseppe Mazzini, the voice of politicized Romanticism in the 1830s and 1840s, Rossini ("the Napoleon of a musical era") had "achieved in music what Romanticism had achieved in literature" (Mazzini [1836] 2001: 53). Yet for Mazzini Rossini had failed to form a new style, and it was vital for the subsequent generation of composers to escape the temptation of imitation. By 1835-6, when Mazzini described his hopes for opera, this was not news. As in Germany, but for very different reasons, the instant challenge in the years following Rossini's move to Paris had been to find new means of expression that broke away from the Rossinian mold. Again as with German developments, one way to do this was to turn away from the virtuosic ornamentation that was such a feature of Rossini's style. Nor is the national comparison far-fetched, since the opera by Vincenzo Bellini that most strongly took such a course, *La Straniera* (premiered in Milan, 1829), was pronounced "philosophical" by contemporary critics, transparent code for "German," and Bellini was granted a privileged place within the canons of German Romanticism (Smart 2001: 198). In this work and his earlier *Il Pirata* (premiered in Milan, 1827), notably bloodthirsty plots joined a vocal style that mixed recitative and aria to form a "canto declamato" which relied on largely syllabic setting in place of Rossini's melismatic style.

  The image of the young, blond Bellini, famously described by Heine as "a sigh in dancing pumps" (quoted in Rosselli 1996: 54-5) added to his Romantic credentials, which were further bolstered by later stories of his wholeheartedly Romantic identification with his characters during composition and by his premature death. Yet after *La Straniera*, Bellini's operas such as *Norma* (premiered in Milan, 1831) and *Beatrice di Tenda* (Venice, 1833) become less obviously Romantic both in terms of plot and formal experimentation, leading to Mazzini's assessment that Bellini, like Rossini, could not represent the future of Italian opera. Various reasons could be proposed for the course of Bellini's development that move away from Mazzini's narrative, but in part the issue undoubtedly involved the hardening of Romanticism into one of a range of different stylistic options. Similarly, Bellini's older rival, Gaetano Donizetti, reserved his most experimental music for plots of dramatic intensity such as *Lucrezia Borgia* (based on the play by Hugo, premiered in Milan in 1833) and *Lucia di Lammermoor* (Naples, 1835), but it was counted as only one musical style among many. In a sense, then, Romantic opera had returned to its beginnings in Germany as a plot-based generic choice, and one in which increasingly audiences through the 1830s throughout Europe were less interested. But there is also another striking continuity here. In the midst of describing the disunity of modern opera, Mazzini produces a flood of prose in which operatic shortcomings get recast as an infernal dance, a *ronde du sabbat*:

> An opera is a thing that has no name: it is the witches' prophecy in *Macbeth*, the intermezzo in *Faust*...a mosaic, a gallery, a mishmash, a typically contradictory succession of varied and independent thoughts, without link, which spin like ghosts within the narrow limits of an enchanted circle...like the fantastic race through field and dale described in a ballad by Bürger...(Mazzini [1836] 2001, 46, my translation)

In other words, bad opera is as Romantic as Romantic German poetry, and although this coincides well enough with Mazzini's generally guarded opinion of Romanticism as something destructive of old rules rather than constructive of new ones, his imagery also indicates negatively what Hoffmann had claimed 20 years earlier: that Romantic opera is the only true sort of opera. In this sense, its absence from the Italian debates of 1816 or from French writings on dramatic reform in the 1820s bears witness not only to its relatively low aesthetic status in these countries, but to the fact that it, like the repertoire of the popular theaters, already paid little attention to the traditional unities that Romantic theorists wished to overthrow. Moreover, its dramatic realization often conflicted with musical expression and actively supplanted it. The Wolf's Glen, for example, received continual developments during the run of *Robin* in Paris to retain its effect, and Weber's own carefully conceived staging, including a wooden owl with glowing eyes, caused him aesthetic doubts and proved susceptible to parody both at the time and for many decades afterwards.[21] One response to such material demands was to turn away from the disillusioning reality of props and scenery back to the suggestive intangibility of notes; in Beethoven's words (as reported by Weber's son), "one must *hear* that kind of thing, only hear" (quoted in Warrack 1976: 235). Another is to side with Arthur Schopenhauer, who praised Rossini's distance from plot developments as a successful separation of words and music that thereby makes opera aesthetically equivalent to Romantic instrumental music (Rossini as unexpected Romantic once more). A better solution, perhaps, is to embrace opera's frequently absurd contingency, to recognize that it is the unreformed opera, the opera of vocal excess as much as of incredible plots (which is to say, all opera) that comes closest to Romantic ideals; each performance, like Daverio's reading of *Euryanthe*, inherently revealing the impossibility of perfection.

NOTES

1 There were operas written on *Il Corvo*, at least one of which (by Johann Peter Pixis, 1822) was apparently inspired directly by Hoffmann's account. None, however, seems to have had any great success. Charlton (1989: 186-7) provides a list of operatic Gozzi settings written between 1777 and 1838. See also Rusack (1930).

2 On the Berlioz works see Albright (2001).

3 Leon Plantinga, in a recent review of Maynard Solomon's (2003) *Late Beethoven: Music, Thought, Imagination*, writes that when "Solomon declines to tell us whether Beethoven belongs essentially to a 'Classical' or a 'Romantic' period or school, he is surely right. The reason is not so much that this composer presents a unique and perplexing case, but rather that the question itself rests on shaky foundations" (Plantinga 2004: 4).

4 Weber's very first opera, *Das Waldmädchen* (1800), parts of which were reused in *Silvana*, was in fact entitled a "romantisch-komische Oper."

5 See Warrack (2001: 239). The *Zauberflöte* sequels and imitators (including a number of operas based on *The Tempest*) are described on pp. 178-87.

6 On early Romantic theories of the union of the arts see Kwon (2003).

7 On the opéra-comique roots of *Freischütz* see Warrack (1976: 224-6) and Dahlhaus (1989: 68-9).

8 Curiously enough the performance of *Olympie* took place with a libretto adapted by none other than Hoffmann. See Charlton (1989: 421, 431). On the importance of *Freischütz* for narratives of German Romantic opera, see Finscher (1983-4).

9 For a balanced and detailed recent consideration of the arrangement and its reception see Everist (2002: 252-71).

10 On the parodies of *Freischütz* see Servières (1906).

11 The premiere of Winter's work took place in Vienna in 1796. On its French arrangement see Everist (2002: 251).

12 On French theatrical versions of Faust and the progression of German Romanticism within Restoration France see Hibberd (2001); on the French reception of Hoffmann in France see Teichmann (1961). On *Robert le Diable* see Brzoska (2003).

13 For a detailed overview of this process see Bray (1932).

14 In *Le Globe*, 5 April 1825, 1 (90): 452. On the attribution to Stendhal see Walton (2001: 80 n. 29).

15 Michael Tusa, in his monograph of *Euryanthe*, emphasizes the formal alterations from the Italian models, but the similarities (and vocal styles) are more striking (Tusa 1991: 37).

16 The first performance of a work by Rossini in Paris (*L'italiana in Algeri*) actually came in 1817, but was a failure. See Walton (2004).

17 On the generational politics of the Restoration see Spitzer (1987).

18 On *La Muette* see Hibberd (2004). On the political role of the opera see Slatin (1979).

19 Berlioz's initial response came in a letter of August 21, 1829 (two weeks after the premiere); see Berlioz (1995: 58). The more considered opinion comes from the extensive review published in the *Gazette musicale*, 1

(1834), and is reprinted in Solie (1998: 84-99, quote p. 84).

20 On this debate and later Romantic operatic developments in Italy see Tomlinson (1986).

21 On the popular phantasmagoric background to the scene, as well as Weber's concerns about the lower-class roots of the staging in the light of his ambitions for German opera see Newcomb (1995).

REFERENCES AND FURTHER READING

Abraham, Gerald (ed.) (1982, 1990). *The Age of Beethoven, 1790-1830,* and *Romanticism, 1830-1890,* vols. 8 and 9 of *The New Oxford History of Music.* Oxford: Oxford University Press.

Albright, Daniel (2001). *Berlioz's Semi-operas: Roméo et Juliette and La Damnation de Faust.* Rochester, NY: University of Rochester Press.

Berlioz, Hector (1969). *The Memoirs of Hector Berlioz, Member of the French Institute, Including His Travels in Italy, Germany, Russia and England: 1803-1865,* ed. and trans. David Cairns. London: Gollancz.

Berlioz, Hector (1995). *Selected Letters of Berlioz,* ed. Hugh Macdonald, trans. Roger Nichols. London: Faber and Faber.

Bray, René (1932). *Chronologie du romantisme, 1804-1830.* Paris: Boivin.

Brzoska, Matthias (2003). "Robert le Diable and Les Huguenots." In David Charlton (ed.), *The Cambridge Companion to Grand Opera.* Cambridge, UK: Cambridge University Press, pp. 189-207.

Charlton, David (ed.) (1989). *E. T. A. Hoffmann's Musical Writings: Kreisleriana, The Poet and the Composer, Music Criticism,* trans. Martyn Clarke. Cambridge, UK: Cambridge University Press.

Dahlhaus, Carl (1989). *Nineteenth-Century Music,* trans. J. Bradford Robinson. Berkeley and Los Angeles: University of California Press.

Daverio, John (1993). "*Euryanthe* and the Artwork as Critique." In *Nineteenth-Century Music and the German Romantic Ideology.* New York: Schirmer Books, pp. 89-126.

Delécluze, Etienne-Jean (1948). *Journal de Delécluze, 1824-1828,* ed. Robert Baschet. Paris: Bernard Grasset.

Dent, Edward (1976). *The Rise of Romantic Opera,* ed. Winton Dean. Cambridge, UK: Cambridge University Press.

Everist, Mark (2002). *Music Drama at the Paris Odéon, 1824-1828.* Berkeley and Los Angeles: University of California Press.

Finscher, Ludwig (1983-4). "Weber's *Freischütz:* Conceptions and Misconceptions." *Journal of the Royal Musical Association,* 110: 79-90.

Heine, Heinrich (1985). "The Romantic School," trans. Helen Mustard. In *The Romantic School and Other Essays,* ed. Jost Hermand and Robert C. Holub. New York: Continuum, pp. 1-127.

Hibberd, Sarah (2001). "'Cette diablerie philosophique': *Faust* criticism in Paris c.1830." In Roger Parker and Mary Ann Smart (eds.), *Reading Critics Reading: Opera and Ballet Criticism in France from the Revolution to 1848.* Oxford: Oxford University Press, pp. 111-36.

Hibberd, Sarah (2004). "La Muette and Her Context." In David Charlton (ed.), *The Cambridge Companion to Grand Opera.* Cambridge, UK: Cambridge University Press, pp. 149-67.

Kwon, Chung-Sun (2003). *Studie zur Idee des Gesamtkunstwerks in der Frühromantik.* Frankfurt: Peter Lang.

Mazzini, Giuseppe ([1836] 2001). *Filosofia della musica,* ed. Luigi Salvatorelli. Naples: Pagano.

Mongrédien, Jean (1996). *French Music from the Enlightenment to Romanticism: 1789-1830,* trans. Sylvain Frémaux. Portland, OR: Amadeus Press.

Newcomb, Anthony (1995). "New Light(s) on Weber's Wolf's Glen Scene." In Thomas Bauman and Marita McClymonds (eds.), *Opera and the Enlightenment.* Cambridge, UK: Cambridge University Press, pp. 61-88.

Paulin, Roger (1985). *Ludwig Tieck: A Literary Biography.* Oxford: Clarendon Press.

Plantinga, Leon (2004). "Beethoven the Classical-Romantic." *Times Literary Supplement,* May 28: 3-4.

Rosselli, John (1996). *The Life of Bellini.* Cambridge, UK: Cambridge University Press.

Rusack, Hedwig (1930). *Gozzi in Germany. A Survey of the Rise and Decline of the Gozzi Vogue in Germany*. New York: Columbia University Press.

Schlegel, Friedrich (1994). *Philosophical Fragments*, trans. Peter Firchow. Minneapolis, University of Minnesota Press.

Servières, Georges (1906). "Les Contrefaçons et parodies du 'Freischütz'." *Le Guide musical* 52: 267-70, 288-90, 307-12, 327-33.

Slatin, Sonia (1979). "Opera and Revolution: *La Muette de Portici* and the Belgian Revolution of 1830 Revisited." *Journal of Musicological Research*, 3: 45-62.

Smart, Mary Ann (2001). "Bellini." In Stanley Sadie (ed.), *The New Grove Dictionary of Music and Musicians*, 2nd edn. London: Macmillan, vol. 3, pp. 194-212.

Solie, Ruth (ed.) (1998). *Source Readings in Music History, Volume 6, The Nineteenth Century*, trans. Oliver Strunk. New York: W. W. Norton.

Spitzer, Alan B. (1987). *The French Generation of 1820*. Princeton, NJ: Princeton University Press.

Staël, Germaine de ([1813] 1871). *De l'Allemagne*. In *Oeuvres complètes*. Paris: Firmin Didot.

Stendhal (Marie-Henri Beyle) ([1823] 1970). "Ce que c'est que le romanticisme." In *Racine et Shakspeare*, ed. Pierre Martino. Paris: Garnier-Flammarion, pp. 39-48.

Stendhal (1985). *The Life of Rossini*, trans. Richard N. Coe, 2nd edn. London: John Calder.

Teichmann, Elizabeth (1961). *La Fortune d'Hoffmann en France*. Geneva: E. Droz.

Tomlinson, Gary (1986). "Italian Romanticism and Italian Opera: An Essay in Their Affinities." *19th-Century Music*, 10: 43-60.

Tusa, Michael C. (1991). *Euryanthe and Carl Maria von Weber's Dramaturgy of German Opera*. Oxford: Oxford University Press.

Walton, Benjamin (2001). "The Professional Dilettante: Ludovic Vitet and *Le Globe*." In Roger Parker and Mary Ann Smart (eds.), *Reading Critics Reading: Opera and Ballet Criticism in France from the Revolution to 1848*. Oxford: Oxford University Press, pp. 69-85.

Walton, Benjamin (2004). "Rossini and France." In Emanuele Senici (ed.), *The Cambridge Companion to Rossini*. Cambridge, UK: Cambridge University Press, pp. 25-36.

Warrack, John (ed.) (1981). *Carl Maria von Weber: Writings on Music*, trans. Martin Cooper. Cambridge, UK: Cambridge University Press.

Warrack, John (1976). *Carl Maria von Weber*, 2nd edn. Cambridge, UK: Cambridge University Press.

Warrack, John (2001). *German Opera: From the Beginnings to Wagner*. Cambridge, UK: Cambridge University Press.

Whittall, Arnold (1987). *Romantic Music: A Concise History from Schubert to Sibelius*. London: Thames and Hudson.

31
At Home with German Romantic Song

James Parsons

Origins

Given that Romanticism was and is a great convergence of contradictions, it is hardly surprising that one of the era's most pre-eminent musical genres – the *Lied*, or German song – is itself a crossroads of competing interests. Simply to speak of musical Romanticism presupposes that what one is talking about reflects a kind of declaration of independence wherein music's too great reliance on words once and for all was severed. Whereas Johann Christoph Gottsched could declare in 1754 that music without words "lacks a soul and is incomprehensible" (Gottsched 1754: 207), E. T. A. Hoffmann, listening to Beethoven's purely instrumental Fifth Symphony in 1810, exulted in a "spirit world of the infinite" (Hoffmann 1963: 37). Harking to such, Hoffmann and his contemporaries found in music a beacon for all of the arts, given their belief that music fashions meaning from its own constituent elements, a condition anticipated in 1798 when Friedrich Schlegel asked, "Does not pure instrumental music appear to create its own text?" (Schlegel 1967: 254).[1] Ironically, it is only against this backdrop that the *Lied*, predicated as it is on the union of words and music, came into full flower. But the paradoxes do not end here, for the resulting merger of dissimilar elements is at once the most private yet potentially the most universalizing of musical mediums.

Although *Lied* devotees likely would downplay the genre's incongruities – insisting that this or that song by Schubert, Schumann (both Robert and Clara), Brahms, or Wolf is a perfect synthesis of constituent elements – the reality behind such a statement is at once more interesting and, in an historical sense, messy. What follows is thus a celebration of all that is untidy, contradictory, and, in a word, Romantic, in a body of music that frequently is anything but orderly or problem-free.

Even the *Lied*'s origins, until recently a matter of certainty, are no longer as easy to pinpoint as once they were. As the story typically has been told – itself an outgrowth of Romantic mythmaking – Franz Schubert (1797-1828), the greatest German song composer, single-handedly invented the genre in Vienna when, as a precocious youth of 17 on October 19, 1814, he conceived *Gretchen am Spinnrade* (Gretchen at the Spinning Wheel). Propitiously, the poem Schubert set was by none other than Johann Wolfgang Goethe (1749-1832), sage of Weimar, author of the 1774 best-selling novel *Die Leiden des jungen Werther* (The Sorrows of Young Werther), and, as time went on, the poet whose works were most often set by *Lied* composers. While there is no question that this *Lied* is one of the most exquisite in all music, one must recall that nothing is created in a vacuum. This is not to dispute Schubert's achievement, but merely to affirm that he stood on the shoulders of earlier composers. As Schlegel put it, "the historian is a prophet facing backwards" (Schlegel 1967: 176); in many ways Schubert is similarly positioned, for what he prophesied was possible because of his awareness of German song before him: standing higher, he saw further.

To understand this, it is necessary to come to terms with the way in which Schubert engaged with the past while moving beyond it. Simply stated, in an age when virtuoso singing was encountered exclusively in the opera house, the *Lied*, beginning in the 1740s, was directed toward a growing middle class in possession of leisure time. Seizing on the financial promise of a new market yet aware that its success depended on a song's accessibility, composers responded with *Lieder* marked by diatonic, foursquare melodies circumscribed by moderate ranges, simple keyboard accompaniments that could be performed by the singers themselves, and strophic form. (One of the oldest musical forms, strophic design obtains when each strophe of a poem is set to the same music; another common form is modified strophic, one where consecutive stanzas are set to varied versions of the same music. When substantially different music is used for different poetical strophes, the resulting musical form is known as through-composed.) Schubert himself memorably reveals strophic song's worth in one of his most approachable *Lieder*, his 1815 setting of Goethe's "Heidenröslein" (Wild Rose). A work that has attained folk song status in German-speaking lands, its allure in part derives from it conflictedness. In Goethe's poem and Schubert's setting, darker concerns lie beneath the unruffled façade. In the former this is revealed in the thinly veiled intimation of sexual violence. In the latter the self-consciously naïve approach to song is at odds with the voice's recurring high Gs. Casting a pall over the lower range of the rest of the song, the note's repetitions insinuate, like a schoolyard taunt, that the boy may not possess the wherewithal, as he says, to "break" (*brechen*) the rose. As so often with Schubert, he makes his point with admirable economy. Although I have no ready statistics, common sense dictates that many of the composer's more than 600 *Lieder* are strophic; predictably enough, history has favored the exceptions to this rule, as the river of prose devoted to *Erlkönig* and *Gretchen am Spinnrade* attest. Remarkable though these songs are, I should not wish to do without the strophic *Frühlingslaube* (Faith in Spring, 1820, Ludwig Uhland [1787-1862]), a work of quiet grandeur all the more moving for its formal straightforwardness.

Case Study: Schubert's *Der Wegweiser*

Der Wegweiser (The Signpost), the 20th of 24 songs from Schubert's *Winterreise* (Winter Journey, 1827), in turn a setting of Wilhelm Müller's (1794-1827) poetic cycle *Die Winterreise* (1822-4), goes far in illustrating its composer's reliance on conventional Lied approaches while concurrently embarking on new ones. To be sure, more than a little of the poignancy radiating from Schubert's setting derives from the way in which Müller inverts a literary stock in trade. The wanderer, a familiar *Aufklärung* (Enlightenment) figure, is recast for a new age. Unlike the hero of Goethe's 1794 *Wilhelm Meisters Lehrjahre* (Wilhelm Meister's Apprenticeship), who joyously proclaims his most enduring ambition to be "the harmonic development of my personality," that is, self-synthesis or enlightenment, Müller's wayfarer is different (Goethe 1995: 175). The first words of the cycle's opening poem *Gute Nacht* (Good Night) make this clear: "Fremd bin ich eingezogen, Fremd zieh' ich wieder aus" (A stranger I arrived, a stranger I depart). Scorned by love, the wanderer embarks on a journey of self-discovery, ending not in sunny sanguinity but unremitting gloom. No circle of friends around a cozy fire awaits him. Instead, as the concluding song *Der Leiermann* (The Hurdy-gurdy Man) discloses, he is joined by snarling dogs and a mute hurdy-gurdy player who, barefoot on the ice, plays on and on, a stark indication that the journey into madness is inexhaustible.

In *Der Wegweiser* the listener encounters the lamentable pilgrim traveling "a road from which no one has returned." The song's title ironically summarizes his plight: he longs for companionship yet all he finds are signposts revealing the *possibility* of such. For large stretches Schubert relies on diatonicism (that is, only notes within the key), syllabic text setting, and accompanimental textures reminiscent of eighteenth-century song. What intrigues is the way he does and does not partake of the *Lied* aesthetic from the previous century. Müller's poem, arranged in four four-line stanzas, would have been set by earlier composers strophically; not Schubert, though he alludes to strophic form. The second strophe begins with a close reference to the first, the change being that the music is in the parallel major instead of minor (an effect not unlike seeing a scene first in darkness, then in light). The third strophe returns to G Minor yet its second half interjects notable changes. In the concluding fourth Schubert recalls the opening strophe by rhythmic means alone; while the vocal lines in the first and fourth strophes are subtly different, their rhythms are identical. The similar–dissimilar relationship between the first and last strophes underscores a major point. Strophic song brings with it the possibility that song might continue forever and that, issuing from a "broken record technique," one's hope might be granted. In *Der Wegweiser* Schubert moves in the opposite direction. Far from suggesting song's ceaselessness, the intimation of strophic design reveals that song possesses limits (even though Schubert's cycle is not yet complete), a deft musical equivalent of the old parlor trick where one opens progressively smaller and smaller boxes – only now the last contains not a pleasant surprise but a mocking empty container.

Schubert buttresses this impression by additional means. Whereas the vocal line in the first strophe passes over many different notes, in the concluding fourth it becomes caught on a single note, like an insect on fly-paper. Mirroring the way Müller closes in on his protagonist, Schubert starts the final strophe with 15 repetitions of the same note – the voice's G – a claustrophobic analogue to the poem's progression. While the wayfarer starts the song with the possibility, however slight, of pursuing other paths, by the end those options one by one have disintegrated. Schubert's depiction of this mounting desolation provides the *Lied* with one of its masterstrokes, one showing him extending the intentionally limited harmonic vocabulary of his tuneful predecessors. As the voice begins tolling away on the reiterated Gs in measure 57, the piano sounds the notes $c^{\#}$-e-g-$b^{\flat}$, a fully diminished chord that should rise by half step in the next measure to a major dominant (d-$f^{\#}$-a), but rather progresses to a tonic G Minor chord in second inversion. In measure 59 the piano's harmonies of $e^{\flat}$-g-$b^{\flat}$ set the scene for $a^{\flat}$-c-$e^{\flat}$; instead, the right hand sustains the harmonies from measure 59 while the left hand moves by half step up to E-natural. Schubert continues this tactic of chords pointing in one direction yet unexpectedly resolved for the next four measures. The effect is like doors slamming. The remainder of the strophe further narrows the net. In measure 67 the piano's incessant Gs drop an octave, plummeting into a hole that further restricts the wanderer's field of vision in the last 17 measures before broadening to quarter and half note repetitions of the same note in the last six bars. The piano's outer voices draw in as well (mm. 69-74). The upper line chromatically descends from F to C while the lowest line chromatically rises from B-natural to E-natural, as if in anticipation of the walls closing in on the protagonist of Edgar Allan Poe's *The Pit and the Pendulum* (1842).

For many, Schubert's relationship to the past is antagonistic. For Eric Sams, Schubert's song facility was "practically without ancestry" (Sams 1980: 774). Charles Rosen is even more emphatic. After Schubert's "first tentative experiments the principles on which most of his songs are written are almost entirely new; they are related to the *Lieder* of the past only by negation: they annihilate all that precedes" (Rosen 1972: 454). While one sympathizes with such viewpoints, according to my précis of *Der Wegweiser*, founded as it is on showing how Schubert refers to the past while looking to the future, the judgments of a Rosen or Sams cast Schubert in overly oedipal terms. A master of human psychology, Schubert hems in his wanderer by simultaneously suggesting strophic design while withholding it. Not only is the eighteenth-century *Lied* marked by shared characteristics, it is supremely emblematic of domesticity, given that the home was this music's chief habitat. Paradoxically invoking German song's domestic association, Schubert adds another layer of meaning. Singing of signposts pointing toward towns and people, his wanderer – from within song – learns that the *Lied*'s most reassuring of outcomes no longer holds true, for here song does not bring people together in consanguinity.

In contrast, Schubert's unjustly neglected *Am Fenster* (At the Window, 1826, Johann Gabriel Seidl [1804-75]) finds the composer harnessing words and music in support of the *Lied*'s more customary role: a safe haven for intimacy, a sheltering sonic space for individual subjectivity. While the protagonist sings "dear, familiar walls, you enclose me within your coolness," it is equally true that what comforts is the protective realm of verse and tone. Two other poems set to music by Schubert, both in 1817 and by Franz von Schober (1796-1882), reaffirm the point: *Trost im Liede* (Consolation in Song) and *An die Musik* (To Music). The former speaks of "comfort on the wings of harmony," while the latter lauds music's ability to transport one to "a better world." *Der Wegweiser* is doubly disturbing because not only does it not lead to "a better world," it goes against another grain, one wherein German song, together with a great many other modes of creative expression, came to be thought of as an essential in the late eighteenth- and nineteenth-century German formulation of self-cultivation known to Germans as *Bildung*. As Goethe reveals in perhaps the most celebrated *Bildungsroman*, or educational novel, his previously mentioned *Wilhelm Meisters Lehrjahre*, such a forging of self depends on the equilibrium of opposing elements, be they head and heart, nature and reason, the earthly here and now and the boundless beyond. Writers and poets idealized this spiritual harmony in many ways. Justinus Kerner (1786-1862) makes this the subject of his 1826 "Sehnsucht nach der Waldgegend" (Longing for the Woodlands), set two years later by Robert Schumann (1810-56) as one of 12 songs comprising his Opus 35, when he reveals what can happen when such harmony is lacking. Deprived of the "wondrous forest," that is nature, where "in the twilight places bird song and silver stream" inspired "many a song fresh and bright," Kerner's protagonist is "desolate and mute." The songs of yore "seldom stir," a condition not unlike "the mere half-song of the bird parted from tree and leaf." Schumann, who at 18 professed the credo that "song unites the highest, word and tone" (Eismann 1956, 1: 18), adroitly captures the alienation that ensues when a person lacks the unity of *Bildung*. At the start the voice's longer note values halt the instrument's momentum. In the second strophe the harmony drifts from the G Minor tonic to F Major in a single measure at the mention of the forest's "twilight places." Removed from this environment, its memory disquiets. Responding to this, voice and piano, although often doubled in this section, just as frequently shadow each other at the distance of an eighth note. In view of the long Lied tradition in which the keyboard's right hand doubles the vocal melody, the effect troubles, for it announces that a thing that should act as one does not.

Lied Sensibility

It is intriguing to observe how enduring this "*Lied* sensibility" has been. A late addition to a long tradition, the 1929 *Reisebuch aus den österreichischen Alpen* (Travel Diary From the Austrian Alps) by Ernst Krenek (1900-91), a cycle of 20 songs set to the composer's own texts, confirms German song's dual potential as a habitat for subjectivity and *Bildung*. Krenek begins: "I now set out,...looking for self and homeland." In a great many *Lieder* one senses that all one has to do to make something better is sing. *Der Wegweiser* possesses the intensity it does because

Schubert thwarts this expectation. More typically, Beethoven (1770-1827), in his stirring Opus 46 *Adelaide* (1794-5) exults in song's orphic vitality. Friedrich Matthisson (1761-1831), whose poem of the same name Beethoven sets, molds four four-line strophes each of which reflects the young man's love for the absent Adelaide. In the first stanza, alone in a spring garden, the gently flowing *Zauberlicht* (magic light) and *Blütenzweige* (swaying blossoms), a symbolic kiss between heaven and earth, remind him of Adelaide and prompt him to say her name. In the next stanza a lifetime is compressed into 20 words, the references to sparkling stream, Alpine snow, and the star-strewn skies affirming the infinity of this love and bringing with it the second articulation of the beloved's name. Still separated from the object of his affections in the third strophe the youth no longer simply senses her in nature's semblance. He "hears" her in the evening breeze, in the bells of the lily of the valley rustling in the grass, in the rushing water and, most tellingly, from the nightingales who sing the name "Adelaide!" Nature merges with song to provide a more perfect existence. In the last strophe, even though the young man has died, love perseveres: "A blossom will spring from the ashes of my heart, and clearly on every crimson petal will shine, Adelaide!" Matthisson constructs his poem so that each of the four strophes ends with "Adelaide." Beethoven responds with a formal scheme matching the poem's progression from the mundane world in the first strophe, unbounded nature in the second, sounding nature in the third calling out "Adelaide," to love outstripping death's silence in the fourth. Like Matthisson's poem, Beethoven creates the allusion that his song will endure forever. While the poem can only suggest this with its imagery of the heart's ashes sprouting a blossom on which the beloved's name will be written, Beethoven, in a move calculated to prove the power of song, has the vocalist sing the name "Adelaide" not four times but 14. The persona may be parted from Adelaide, but in repeatedly singing her name he wills her into existence.

Beethoven's devotion to song and his inclination to turn to it to plot a path toward self-cultivation have gone unobserved for too long. In one of his most ground-breaking works, the Ninth Symphony (1824) with its finale that adds voices for the first time to the previously instrumentally sacrosanct symphony, song lies at the heart of the movement's fusion of the contained here and now and the endless sublime. Noteworthy, too, is the fact that Schiller's 1786 poem "An die Freude" (Ode to Joy, revised 1803) was set to music some 50 times before Beethoven, in a style in keeping with eighteenth-century German song; this too has received little comment (Parsons 2002). Given the "Ode to Joy" tune's studied simplicity there is little doubt that Beethoven knew at least some of these previous settings. In the event, Beethoven lifts the melody from the body of eighteenth-century *Lieder*, namely his own, for the choral finale's principal tune is a reworking of his *Gegenliebe* (Mutual Love, 1794 or 1795, Gottfried August Bürger [1747-94]). German song thus animates one of Romanticism's most ambitious projects, elevated from its humble domestic origins to the realm of full orchestra, vocal quartet, and chorus and where it leads, as Schiller proclaims, to "der Unbekannte" (the unknown one) whose throne is among the stars. Other Romantics followed Beethoven's example, using the *Lied* as a transmuted vocal presence in instrumental works that, while quoting the tune of an earlier song, do so without words. Just as Keats in his "Ode on a Grecian Urn" (1819) reveres the vessel because it silently emits the past's "melodies . . . unheard" given its ability to "express / A flowery tale more sweetly than our rhyme," (ll. 11 and 3/4), Schubert, in a number of songs, absorbs the *Lied* into nonvocal works. Those who know the words to his *Der Tod und das Mädchen* (Death and the Maiden, 1817, Matthias Claudius [1740-1815]), in which the character of death in part reveals "I am not cruel, you shall sleep softly in my arms," will find deeper meaning when, listening to the second movement of Schubert's 1824 D-Minor String Quartet (nicknamed "Death and the Maiden"), they discover that he quotes the earlier song. One can only ponder the autobiographical allusions informing the later work, which Schubert wrote shortly after being diagnosed in 1822 with an illness (in all likelihood syphilis) that he believed forever changed his life (McKay 1996: 164-207, Gibbs 2000: 91-114). Mendelssohn, Brahms, Mahler, and Richard Strauss, among others, added to and extended the practice of referencing *Lieder* in instrumental compositions.

Beethoven again explores the *Lied's* potential for orphic dynamism in his Opus 98 song cycle *An die ferne Geliebte* (To the Distant Beloved, 1816). (The song cycle, an important Lied subgenre, is defined most pithily as three or more poems in which coherence obtains through poetry, music, or the interaction between the two.) Another work concerned with lovers unwillingly parted, as in *Adelaide* all nature unites to right this wrong. At the end of the cycle's first song, the text, by Alois Isidor Jeitteles (1794-1858) says: "At the sound of songs all time and space recede." The final sixth song returns to the same melody heard in the first, thereby making clear that while the lover is still without his beloved that song, as previously averred, can annul this separation. In support of this, the last song begins slowly and with straight quarter notes before quickening in tempo and note values, exuberantly ending with the words:

> Dann vor diesen Liedern weichet,
> Was geschieden uns so weit,
> Und ein lieben Herz erreichet
> Was ein Liebend Herz geweiht!
>
> (Then these songs will overcome,
> what so far parts us,
> and a loving heart will attain
> what a loving heart has offered!)

While I have yet to encounter a sanctioned term for the concept I have dubbed the "German *Lied* sensibility," by whatever name, it provided the German-speaking lands with an enduring lyric preoccupation. So complete was its sway that on occasion it was singled out for ironic critique. Joseph von Eichendorff (1788-1857), one of German Romanticism's major figures, does this and more in his poem "Der wandernde Musikant" (The Wandering Minstrel), first issued as an insertion in his novella

Aus dem Leben eines Taugenichts (Memoirs of a Good-For-Nothing, 1826). Just as Müller reverses the Enlightenment wanderer in his *Die Winterreise*, Eichendorff, writing two years after Müller, transposes him. Whereas Müller's sojourner craves companionship, Eichendorff's is a confirmed loner. In the second strophe Eichendorff inventively calls on Müller's wayfarer. Glossing the final song of *Winterreise*, in which the piteous hurdy-gurdy player stands barefoot on the ice cranking his rasping instrument, Eichendorff's minstrel declares that he too knows "some lovely old songs" which he performs "in der Kälte, ohne Schuh'" (in the cold, without shoes), not knowing where he will spend the night. Set to music by Hugo Wolf (1860-1903) in sardonic folk vein in 1888 (as *Der Musikant*), at the mention of "in der Kälte" Wolf obliges with a surprisingly remote key change to underscore the minstrel's fretful resolve. Throughout Wolf's *Lied* his drone harmonies subtly evoke those from Schubert's *Der Leiermann*. But unlike Müller's hapless musician and, even more to the point his wayfarer, Eichendorff's catches the eye of many a pretty girl. Whereas Müller's protagonist yearns for this, Eichendorff's is made uncomfortable by the prospect of affection, for such would snuff out his life-giving proclivity for song. If only he were not a rascal, he sings; but he is and so he moves on, bidding his would-be conquest better luck elsewhere. May you find husband, house, and yard elsewhere he intones, for "Wenn wir zwei zusammen wären, möcht mein Singen mir vergeh'n" (If we two were together, I would forget how to sing).

Eichendorff's (and Wolf's) sentiments prove to be the exception, for more times than not song's sanctuary was deemed a boon to love and creativity, not a hindrance. While Eichendorff's roving musician dislikes the role of husband and the prospect of house and yard – containment metaphors all – Schumann suggests the opposite in the eight *Lieder* comprising his song cycle, Opus 42. A setting of Adelbert von Chamisso's (1781-1838) *Frauenliebe und -leben* (Woman's Love and Life, 1831), Schumann's songs are but a fraction of the bounteous lyric floodtide by which he broke through personal and artistic crises in 1840 with almost 125 *Lieder*. Compositional motivations and the undeniable musical appeal of his songs notwithstanding, whether because of their female subordination, the incongruity of a man professing (presuming?) to understand a woman's point of view, or the Biedermeier ethos, Chamisso's poems have vexed recent critics (Solie 1992). Although all three topics are beyond this study, one point that does invite scrutiny is the fact that Schumann ends with Chamisso's eighth poem. Omitting the final ninth, Schumann's setting colors our impression of his woman in ways that seem never to have been adequately addressed. Concluding after the woman learns of her husband's death, it is hard to imagine her not a perpetual victim. Yet Chamisso's closing poem clarifies that she perseveres and at length makes peace with her life before blessing her granddaughter on the occasion of her wedding.

A subject open to interpretation, Schumann's decision to alter Chamisso's cycle surely was not arbitrary. At least in this song cycle his approach anticipates an aspect of cinema where a literary source is adapted as a film script. Throughout his *Frauenliebe und -leben* Schumann enlivens Chamisso's poems in ways individual to music. In the first song, in which the woman proclaims her all-embracing infatuation with her beloved, even though Schumann begins in a major key (B^b), the deliberate tempo (Larghetto) and shared yet frequently unaligned rhythmic motives between voice and piano tinge his portrayal with apprehension, a mood he skillfully expands upon in calling on the rhythm of the sarabande. A dance associated with the past, the sarabande, to most Germans and surely Schumann, would have conjured up the old Baroque dance suite, above all those by Johann Sebastian Bach (and especially his French and English Suites). As in many a Bach sarabande, Schumann emphasizes beat two yet with a twist; whereas Bach frequently uses the pattern quarter note, dotted quarter, eighth note (or some variant thereof), Schumann responds with quarter, quarter, *eighth rest*, eighth. At exactly the point in the rhythmic formula most emblematic of the sarabande, Schumann, in the piano part, responds not with rhythmic expansion, but its opposite, silence. Janus-faced, his music recalls the past while stressing something absent. At the same time, the piano's first seven notes sonically recycle themselves, the phrase's last chord being rhythmically and harmonically identical to the first. Inexorably looping (a strategy not unlike the incessant 16th-note figuration Schubert gives the piano in *Gretchen am Spinnrade* and which portrays the young girl's restless state of mind and her duty at the spinning wheel), Schumann's music restrains not just his protagonist but also us, his listeners. In so doing, he delineates a charged space that undermines one's ability to know if the woman is remembering past events or presently living them. Schumann again calls upon music's ability to capture a mood, situation, or sound from the real world in the fifth song. While Chamisso never explicitly mentions the marriage, poeticizing the subject in the reference to "blossoming myrtle" (the traditional German wedding flower), Schumann makes the ritual the song's centerpiece. Before the woman sings a note the piano portrays her joyous yet restive outlook in a riot of stylized church bells; just as significantly, after the voice falls silent at song's end the piano breaks into a solemn wedding march.

For all its irrefutably beautiful music that captures the essence of the composer's trademark *Innigkeit* – that untranslatable term meaning inwardness and intimacy – the most frequently commented upon aspect of Schumann's cycle is its ending. Eschewing Chamisso's ninth poem, Schumann deploys an extended piano postlude that recapitulates the music of the first song. Many have remarked on the similarity of this gesture and the conclusion of Beethoven's *An die ferne Geliebte*, which, as has been seen, brings back the music for the first song at the end of the cycle's final sixth. Schumann in fact prepares the way for the Beethoven association in his sixth song. There, following a strophe by Chamisso that he cuts (where the woman announces her pregnancy to her husband), Schumann tailors his music so as to be reminiscent of the music Beethoven fashions for the first line of the third strophe of his cycle's sixth song. The musical recollection surely is meant to underscore a shared poetical outlook. Beethoven's melody sets the words "Und du singst was ich gesungen" (And you sing that which I sing); Schumann's, at the moment he looks back to Beethoven, reveals "Bleib' an meinem Herzen, / Fühle dessen Schlag" (Stay by my heart, feel it beating).

With this connection in place, when Schumann recalls the music of his cycle's first song at the end of *Frauenliebe und -leben* it is not merely an homage to Beethoven or an epilogue. The recollected song (now minus words) certainly invites both responses, yet it eloquently invites poetical persona and listener to remember the sentiments of the opening song. Moreover, in invoking Beethoven as Schumann does it is difficult not to consider how Beethoven's *An die ferne Geliebte* ends, with the wish that "these songs will overcome, what so far parts us, and a loving heart will attain what a loving heart has offered!" Schumann was no clairvoyant, looking into the future to see that he would die before his beloved future wife Clara Wieck (1819-96). Nevertheless, when Schumann composed *Frauenliebe und -leben* on July 11 and 12, 1840 – and all the *Lieder* from his celebrated 1840 *Liederjahr* – song obviously offered him the means to conquer the distance then separating him from Clara and the challenges her father Friedrich Wieck then was perpetrating in an effort to keep them apart. Mindful of this, it may be that Schumann's reading of Chamisso's cycle does not seek to keep the woman forever a victim or to constrain her according to gender roles no longer acceptable. Rather the *Lied*, and all that Schumann draws on in his cycle, triumphantly announce that each time the first song's intriguing opening motive is initiated – one also to be heard at the cycle's end – it is empowered to dissolve the distance of time and place. The boxes mentioned in relation to *Der Wegweiser* no longer are empty: the woman's thoughts fill the otherwise unspecified room within a comforting home in which she is enclosed, just as her memories engender a kind of inner life bounded by poem and music and the knowledge of what the two together might achieve. Fanciful although this interpretation may at first seem, it nevertheless is supported in a generalized sense by contemporaneous assessments of the *Lied*. The philosopher Friedrich Theodor Vischer (1807-87) asserted in his *Ästhetik oder Wissenschaft des Schönen* (1846–57): "Song is something that grows from nature; it can generate itself from life" (Wiora 1971: 15). If this is so, why is it not equally true, as Beethoven and Schumann seem to say, that "song can generate life"?

Whereas Beethoven, Schubert, and Schumann turned to *Lieder* to distill the existing world, the songs of Louis Spohr (1784-1859), and to a lesser extent of Robert Franz (1815-92), now seem not just pretty but merely so. While such an aesthetic found room at the full table that was Romanticism, in the modern world, as John Galsworthy (1867-1933) phrases it in the opening chapter of his book *To Let* (1921), from *The Forsyte Saga*, "People are tired – the bottom's tumbled out of sentiment" (Galsworthy 1978: 666). This is not to suggest that the poets and composers who contributed to the *Lied*, not to mention the singers, pianists, and audiences who brought it to life, lacked discrimination. As the nineteenth century progressed home music making's long-standing authority joined with other concerns – especially the ambitions of a burgeoning middle class who displayed their acquisition of culture with pianos in their parlors – to make the *Lied* big business. What is remembered nowadays is not the type of song that captivated well-fed burghers, and which usually reached them through a half-open door from the music room (and a cloud of cigar smoke), but rather what satisfies our current ideas of what is worth admitting to the pantheon of artistic permanence. For the Romantics themselves one can be certain that Spohr's Opus 154 *Sechs deutsche Lieder* (Six German Songs, 1857) were held by many to be the equal of the two songs by Johannes Brahms (1833-97) making up his glorious Opus 91 (1864-84). That both collections enlarge the *Lied*'s time-honored forces – violin for Spohr, viola for Brahms – would have been greeted as so much the better. Whereas Brahms could turn more into a virtue, with Spohr the outcome appears contrived, given that the added agent overwhelms. Even in the set's third song, *Töne* (Tones, R. Otto), the text of which admonishes "Hear, then, these strings' soft entreaty," the violin part sounds more like a fugitive from a Paganini violin capriccio than anything inspired by Otto's poem.

Yet if Spohr represents a vanished world, then what is it about the many nineteenth-century German *Lieder* that have not disappeared that allow them to continue speaking to us across an almost incalculable cultural divide? Throughout this chapter I have stressed German song's role as sanctuary, one reflected in the genre's privileged themes and the way it gave voice (literally) to subjectivity and a view of nature where fragrant flowers, babbling brooks, and murmuring forests habitually interact with humanity. Friedrich Schlegel yearned for a time when "all art should become science and all science art; poetry and philosophy should be made one" (Schlegel 1967: 160). In music, "the most romantic of all the arts" according to Hoffmann (Hoffmann 1963: 34), Romanticism attained this oneness. Musing on this topic over the course of a lifetime, Jean Paul Richter (1763-1825) concluded that since "the Romantic is beauty without limit," it follows that music "is romantic poetry for the ear" given that sound knows no limits. Music, in fact, is "poetry for the ear," because "a sound never sounds alone, but always threefold, blending, as it were, the romantic quality of the future and the past into the present" (Hoeckner 1997: 60-1). Of all the ironies that could have been uncovered in this chapter, the most ironic is this: in German Romanticism song is unlimited beauty made manifest by the simultaneously limited yet unlimited borders of verse and song.

Uniquely endowed by nature, it follows that when Romantic *Lieder* summon nature it is not to witness indifferently the dejected wanderer or yearning lover but as an ally or source of consolation. At its best, nature joyously links with love to produce more songs, a message overflowing from Goethe's famous 1771 poem "Maifest" (May Celebration), set to music by Beethoven some time before 1796 as *Maigesang* (May Song), Opus 52, No. 4. Although many things are at work in Goethe's poem, one of the most obvious is its verbal energy, a feature made plain in the nine clipped four-line strophes alternating five- and four-syllable lines. Beethoven responds to the poem's rhythmic momentum by binding Goethe's stanzas three at a time. So tightly wound is this construction there is hardly a moment for the singer to breathe as nature's attributes are listed; especially felicitous is the description that from every twig buds are bursting "und tausend Stimmen aus dem Gesträuch" (and a thousand voices from the bushes). In recompense for the demands placed on the singer, Beethoven ends each three-strophe unit with a piano interlude that interjects a cascade of thirds in the right hand and thirds and sixths in the left. Thirds and sixths, of course, are the bread and butter of musical harmony and thus a reference to the concord Goethe insists upon in linking nature, love, and song.

From Home to Concert Hall

Just as Romanticism changed from within and without as the nineteenth century progressed, so, too, did the *Lied*. This especially is to be seen in the genre's abode; whereas for more than a century the preserve of German song had been the home, concert halls – symbols of civic pride that increasingly were seen as temples of art – began luring previously domestic and chamber music genres. The adjustments required to adapt a *Lied* to large halls became a concern for many, the fear being that a genre founded on intimate expression might not survive larger quarters. At first the modifications were nominal: piano Lieder simply moved to symphony halls. In the period 1870-80, however, the incongruity of having an orchestra on hand yet not playing during the performance of songs saw the introduction of orchestral *Lieder*. Above all in the symphonic songs of Gustav Mahler (1860-1911) and Richard Strauss (1864-1949) there appears to have been something in the challenge of retaining the *Lied*'s close associations and combining them with the comparatively more public utterance of the symphony that meshed with these composers' innate talents. In Mahler's resplendent *Das Lied von der Erde* (The Song of the Earth, 1908), past and future converge while drawing on the strengths of the symphony and the *Lied*, a fusion Mahler had been moving towards all his life. The texts, German translations by Hans Bethge (1876-1946) of Chinese poetry, expose another synthesis. The first five songs pertain to earthly life while the last looks upward to the sun setting behind the mountain, the rising moon, the distant horizon's gleaming blue. Poetical imagery and musical means highlight the work's deliberate imbalance. Not only do the first five songs form a subsection, they begin and end respectively in A Minor and A Major. Transcending the earth's cares in the sixth song, Mahler responds with a lengthening of musical time – one that aspires to eternity – whereby it lasts almost as long as the first five. A further parallel is the concluding *Lied*'s movement from C Minor to C Major. Harking back to the first five songs' trajectory from A Minor to A Major, C Minor and C Major are conjoined in the charged sonority with which the last song dissolves – appropriately enough on the words "ewig, ewig" (forever, forever). In view of the theme I have pursued here, what Mahler extols at the end of *Das Lied von der Erde* does not surprise, for beyond the here and now there is another home. "Ich wandle nach der Heimat, meiner Stätte, Ich werde niemals in der Ferne schweifen" (I travel to my homeland, my abode, I will never again roam to distant lands).

The leave-taking at the heart of the final movement of Mahler's cycle is not unlike that at the end of Strauss's *Im Abendrot* (At Twilight), the song that traditionally concludes his *Vier letzte Lieder* (Four Last Songs, 1948). Despite the stylistic dissimilarities between the two songs and their separation in time by 40 years, they are related spiritually given that both are moving summaries of their composers' emotional and musical worlds. Thus it is enticing to view them as requiems for German song. Especially in the latter, written the same year as the invention of the Frisbee and the first issue of *TV Guide*, the temptation to regard the *Lied* in retrospective terms is strong. Eichendorff's poem portrays a couple walking side by side after life's long journey; the last line asks: "Is this perhaps death?" Once the poetical question is sounded the 84-year-old composer quotes from a work of his written a half century earlier, the symphonic poem *Tod und Verklärung* (Death and Transfiguration, 1889). Words and music dovetail in a particularized lament, one that has inspired many critics to surmise that the gesture is a farewell to the Lied. According to one writer it is not just the one song that signals this but all four comprising the set: "Strauss could reasonably have thought his *Vier letzte Lieder...* bore their epithet for the genre" (Griffiths 2000: 680). Or, as another would have it, "Strauss's return late in life to the Lied – when it was of minor importance in the modern world – is further evidence of his conservative nostalgia for things past," a yearning that "reminds one also of the past significance of the Lied" (Kravitt 1996: 245). Strauss may have intended this yet it is by no means certain that everyone after him agrees the genre has lost its vitality. As long as people sing, new songs will be written just as old ones, even if they sometimes are German and from the century before last, will be listened to with pleasure and for profit. A wise man (Steiner 1997: 75) recently wrote, "Song leads us home to where we have not yet been."

NOTE

1 My translation. All translations are mine unless otherwise indicated.

REFERENCES AND FURTHER READING

Agawu, V. K. (1992). "Theory and Practice in the Analysis of the Nineteenth-Century Lied." *Music Analysis*, 11: 3-36.

Dürr, W. (2002). *Das deutsche Sololied im 19. Jahrhundert: Untersuchungen zur Sprache und Musik*, 2nd edn. Wilhelmshaven: Florian Noetzel.

Eismann, G. (1956). *Robert Schumann: Ein Quellenwerk über sein Leben und Schaffen*, 2 vols. Leipzig: Breitkopf & Härtel.

Galsworthy, J. (1978). *The Forsyte Saga*. Harmondsworth, UK: Penguin.

Garlington, A. S., Jr. (1989). "Richard Strauss's *Vier letzte Lieder*: The Ultimate *opus ultimatum*." *The Musical Quarterly*, 73: 79-93.

Gibbs, C. H. (2000). *The Life of Schubert*. Cambridge, UK: Cambridge University Press.

Goethe, J. W. (1995). *Wilhelm Meister's Apprenticeship*, trans. E. A. Blackall. Princeton, NJ: Princeton University Press.

Gottsched, J. C. (1754). *Auszug aus des Herrn Batteux schönen Künsten*. Leipzig: B. C. Breitkopf.

Griffiths, P. (2000). "Lieder. The Twentieth Century." In S. Sadie (ed.), *The New Grove Dictionary of Music and Musicians*, rev. edn. London and New York: Macmillan, vol. 14, pp. 678-80.

Hoeckner, B. (1997). "Schumann and Romantic Distance." *Journal of the American Musicological Society*, 50: 55-132.

Hefling, S. E. (2000). *Mahler: Das Lied von der Erde*. Cambridge, UK: Cambridge University Press.

Hoffmann, E. T. A. (1963). *Schriften zur Musik: Aufsätze und Rezensionen*. Munich: Winkler.

Kravitt, E. F. (1996). *The Lied: Mirror of Late Romanticism*. New Haven, CT: Yale University Press.

McKay, E. N. (1996). *Franz Schubert: A Biography*. Oxford: Clarendon Press.

Muxfeldt, K. (2001). "*Frauenliebe und Leben* Now and Then." *19th-Century Music*, 25: 27-48.

Parsons, J. (2002). "Deine Zauber binden wieder: Beethoven, Schiller, and the Joyous Reconciliation of Opposites." *Beethoven Forum*, 9: 1-53.

Parsons, J. (2004). "The Eighteenth-Century Lied." In J. Parsons (ed.), *The Cambridge Companion to the Lied*. Cambridge, UK: Cambridge University Press, pp. 35-62.

Reed, J. (1985). *The Schubert Song Companion*. Manchester: Manchester University Press.

Rosen, C. (1972). *The Classical Style*. New York: W. W. Norton.

Sams, E. (1980). "Schubert." In S. Sadie (ed.), *The New Grove Dictionary of Music and Musicians*. London: Macmillan, vol. 16, pp. 752-811.

Schlegel, F. (1967). *Kritische Friedrich-Schlegel-Ausgabe*. Munich: Ferdinand Schöningh, vol. 2.

Seelig, H. (1996). "The Literary Context: Goethe as Source and Catalyst." In R. Hallmark (ed.), *German Lieder in the Nineteenth Century*. New York: Schirmer Books, pp. 1-30.

Solie, R. A. (1992). "Whose Life? The Gendered Self in Schumann's *Frauenliebe* Songs." In S. P. Scher (ed.), *Music and Text: Critical Inquiries*. Cambridge, UK: Cambridge University Press, pp. 219-40.

Steiner, G. (1997). *Errata: An Examined Life*. New Haven, CT: Yale University Press.

Youens, S. (1992). *Hugo Wolf: The Vocal Music*. Princeton, NJ: Princeton University Press.

Youens, S. (1991). *Retracing a Winter's Journey: Franz Schubert's Winterreise*. Ithaca, NY: Cornell University Press.

Youens, S. (2001). "Words and Music in France and Germany." In J. Samson (ed.), *The Cambridge History of Nineteenth-Century Music*. Cambridge, UK: Cambridge University Press, pp. 460-99.

Wiora, W. (1971). *Das deutsche Lied: Zur Geschichte und Ästhetik einer musikalischen Gattung*. Wolfenbüttel and Zurich: Möseler.

32

The Romantic System of the Arts

Michael Ferber

If "the modern system of the arts," to borrow the phrase Kristeller uses in his well-known essay, was in place by the middle of the eighteenth century and if it was structured according to the neoclassical hierarchy of the arts and genres, can we rightly say "the Romantic system of the arts" succeeded and replaced it? Even the neoclassical "system," no doubt, was various and uneven, appearing the less systematic the closer one examines it, containing or failing to contain contrary or anomalous trends which indeed sometimes anticipate Romanticism itself. Nonetheless, a coherent pattern of artistic and literary theory and practice, an ideal system of norms, prevailed in Europe as part of the general cultural hegemony of France. It was contested, but it prevailed: it was backed by the patronage, academies, and tastes of the *ancien régime*, not only of the nobility but of the high bourgeoisie. Many of the Romantics' experiments or innovations in all the arts and in every country met with fierce attacks from this establishment, and not a few were compared to or blamed on the political upheavals that began in 1789. With due allowance for complications and counter-trends, then, I will assume the active presence of the modern neoclassical system as I try to describe, briefly enough to convey a sense of the whole of it, the "Romantic system" that was in large part a reaction against the one in place.[1]

But was the new system really anything so coherent as a system? Blake felt he had to create a system or be enslaved by another man's (*Jerusalem*, 10.20), while Friedrich Schlegel wrote, "It is equally fatal to have a system and not to have a system. One must try to combine them" (*Athenaeum Fragments* #53, Schlegel [1798] 1991: 24). We should remember Blake's bitter struggle to make headway against a rigid system of styles, techniques, taste, patronage, and commercial practices, but in the spirit of Schlegel's paradoxical advice we may grant that the movements we try to trace toward a new system may sometimes be better described simply as movements away from an old system, and that since there were so many of these movements, what emerged in the end may have been less a new system than a new systemlessness. By that point, however, we seem to have gone past Romanticism, or past its heroic phase, which was as constructive as it was destructive. From its formative and "high" phases, then, I think we can abstract an ideal type of Romantic theory and practice in literature, music, and painting.

The Lyric

Insofar as we are dealing with a system of interconnections it is somewhat arbitrary where we begin. Let it be the "renaissance of the Renaissance" in literature: the explosion of lyric poetry – Pindaric odes, hymns, songs, elegies, sonnets, *canzoni liberi*, blank-verse epistles or "conversation" poems, and so on – in great quantities and of a quality still thought to set the standard in most European countries two centuries later. The sonnet revival alone is almost definitive of Romanticism, although, like every other single distinctive feature, it leaves out a few prominent figures. In England the sonnet had been in eclipse since Milton (Gray wrote one, Collins and Goldsmith none), when Thomas Edwards published 13 of them in 1748; Thomas Warton followed soon afterward, and then Charlotte Smith, William Lisle Bowles, Cowper, Wordsworth, Coleridge, and Lamb made the sonnet the central form it has remained until recently. Wordsworth's public debut was a Shakespearean sonnet, and by the end of his life he had written over five hundred sonnets, mainly Miltonic; a few of them, with a few by Shelley and Keats, rank among the glories of the form. Byron despised the "whining" Petrarchan mode and vowed never to write one, but he broke his vow once or twice. Felicia Hemans began with sonnets, published translations of sonnets from Portuguese, Spanish, and Italian, and composed several sequences near the end of her life; there was another cycle by Mary Robinson. Among the English writers now considered canonical only Blake, despite his early Spenserian imitations, never wrote any.[2]

In Germany the revival began with Bürger, better known for launching the great vogue of the *Kunstballade* or "literary ballad," another hallmark of Romanticism; he wrote a set of Petrarchan sonnets to the memory of his beloved (1789). The revival continued with A. W. Schlegel, Eichendorff, Tieck, and virtually all the Romantics; Goethe got into it with a score of sonnets; he and Schlegel each wrote one called "Das Sonett," while Tieck wrote a set called "Die Kunst der Sonette," not unlike the sonnets on the sonnet by Wordsworth, Burns, and Keats. In France the revival, like Romanticism generally, got a late start: Lamartine, Hugo, Vigny, and Musset wrote only a handful, and it was not until the second generation, that of Nerval, Gautier, and Baudelaire, that the sonnet rose to prominence, and greatness. Sainte-Beuve, however, wrote several dozen, including eight "imitations" of sonnets by Wordsworth and several of sonnets by Bowles and Lamb. In Italy the 12 sonnets of Foscolo (1803), and in Poland the "Crimean Sonnets" of Mickiewicz (1826), are ranked among their most accomplished works. Pushkin and some of his contemporaries wrote a few sonnets, but most of them seem to have neglected the form, ultimately perhaps because Russia had never had a Renaissance. It is notable, however, that the famous stanza of *Eugene Onegin* (1823-31) has 14 lines, and is sometimes called "the Pushkin sonnet."[3]

The Pindaric ode, public, prophetic, solemn, even sublime, had not been as dormant as the sonnet, but it was dramatically revived by Joseph Warton and William Collins in 1746; in his "Advertisement" to his odes Warton described them as "an attempt to bring back Poetry into its right channel." It came to seem the most characteristic Romantic form.[4] The first six poems of Blake's first printed book, *Poetical Sketches*, are brief odes to the seasons, the evening star, and morning. Coleridge wrote odes even earlier than he wrote sonnets; they culminated in "Dejection: An Ode" and "To William Wordsworth." Wordsworth hesitated to name "Lines Written a Few Miles above Tintern Abbey" an ode, but an ode it is, if not a Pindaric one like the "Intimations" ode. Shelley wrote quite a few, notably the "Ode to the West Wind," though its stanzas are *terza rima* sonnets. Byron produced odes to Napoleon and to Venice. The late odes of Keats, of course, are the warrant of his place among the English poets. Some of Goethe's earliest poems are odes that are meant to seem spontaneous and inspired; his "Wanderers Sturmlied" even names Pindar twice. Hölderlin's odes are less weighty than his poems labeled hymns and elegies, but these latter are not far from odes themselves, and they are his greatest works; they derive from a careful study of Pindar in Greek. Novalis's *Hymns to the Night* (1800) were not called odes, perhaps because of their religious mode, but in form they are odelike. The young Hugo published 72 odes from 1816 to 1828, moving from historical subjects to more personal ones, including the celebration of "the poet" himself. Lamartine and others continued writing odes while Hugo moved on to other forms, though he returned to them later in new and expanded modes. The young Nerval tried a few odes, and then produced about 20 "little odes" (*odelettes*) in the 1830s. Looking back in 1871 Banville could write that the ode in France "has absorbed all the poetic genres. . . . It has become all of modern poetry" (quoted in Porter 1978: 75).

The elegy was nearly as central. To the stimulus of Gray's "Elegy Written in a Country Churchyard" (1750) and of the other English "Graveyard" poems, as well as of the mournful Ossian (1760 and after), Germans from Klopstock onward responded with elegies, of which the most influential was Schiller's "The Gods of Greece" (1788) and the most accomplished and complex those of Hölderlin, such as "Menon's Lament for Diotima" and "Bread and Wine" (both 1800-1). Using various forms Wordsworth became the great English Romantic elegist, from "Michael" and the "Lucy" poems to "Elegiac Stanzas" and "Extempore Effusion on the Death of James Hogg." In France the term *élégie* had long been associated with love, but with its revival by André Chénier (rediscovered in 1819) it gained a melancholy in part inspired by Gray. With Desbordes-Valmore and Lamartine the elegy takes a prominent part at the opening of Romanticism.

Poems on the death of other poets, though they had a tradition going back to Moschus's lament for Bion (translated by Shelley), grew in numbers and in psychological depth throughout Europe. Chatterton's apparent suicide provoked poems by Coleridge, Keats, and D. G. Rossetti, not to mention a play by Vigny (1835); Keats's death led to Shelley's "Adonais"; Byron's "Lament of Tasso" started a Europe-wide vogue; Byron's own death prompted even more elegies, from Elizabeth Barrett to Dionysius Solomos, from Müller to Vigny, and including Pushkin's farewell poem "To the Sea"; Pushkin's death in turn led to many more, most notably Lermontov's scathing "The Death of a Poet" (1837); and it was his verses at the funeral of Larra (1837) that launched the young Zorrilla's career.[5]

As a development out of both the ode and the elegy, finally, we find what M. H. Abrams has called "the greater Romantic lyric": the meditation by a solitary poet outdoors, moving from description of nature to inner resolution or insight and back again. Besides the examples he gives – such as Coleridge's "Frost at Midnight," Wordsworth's "Intimations" ode, and Schiller's "Der Spaziergang" ("The Walk," 1795) – we might add Lamartine's *Méditations poétiques* (1820), Leopardi's "The Broom" (written 1836), perhaps Pushkin's "To Ovid" (1821), though we could also call these elegies in the broad sense. Lamartine's use of "meditation" to name this longer lyric form was not unique: the first poem of Gautier's *Poésies* (1830) is "Méditation," and Lermontov wrote a celebrated one in 1839 (Abrams 1965).[6]

Lyric poetry, then, flourished and grew in prestige. It is tempting to assert that the shorter forms overthrew the longer forms, epic and drama, and usurped their rank in the hierarchy of genres, but the epic and drama retained much of their prestige, and many of the Romantic poets wrote, or aspired to write, both of them. Yet it is striking that the poets very often "lyricized" them both, and other forms as well. *The Prelude* and *The Excursion*, for all their Miltonic spirit, lack the "epic breadth" and objectivity even of Milton, let alone Homer and Virgil; they are philosophical and/or autobiographical and often turn on moments of epiphany presented with lyric intensity. The nearly 4,700 lines of Byron's *Childe Harold's Pilgrimage* are in Spenserian stanzas, which lend themselves to self-contained meditative moments, while his "Turkish Tales" are gathered into various units which allow both rapid narrated action and lyrical digressions or reflections. Pushkin's "southern" tales, inspired by Byron, are more lyrical yet: plot is less central, and a dreamlike mystery suffuses the half-told events. Vigny's characteristic *poème*, which in his day meant "narrative poem," was a much shorter form than the epic, free of machinery and national themes. Hugo called it the "little epic"(*petite épopée*); it might justly be called a lyrical epic. The whole of Blake's *Milton*, which clanks with cosmic machinery, nonetheless is said to take place in a moment, in "the pulsation of an artery," like a lyric. The ballad attracted the Romantics as a sort of lyrical epic; they went on, under the inspiration of Bürger's "Lenore" especially, to relyricize the ballad itself – in the *Lyrical Ballads* (1798), Mary Robinson's *Lyrical Tales* (1800), the *Ballades* of Hugo (1823-8), and some of the more direct responses to Bürger, such as Zhukovsky's "Svetlana" (1813), Mickiewicz's "Romanticality" (1822), Pushkin's "The Bridegroom" (1825), and Deschamps' "La Noce de Léonore" (1825).[7]

As for drama, Jerome McGann has well said, "The separation of the drama from the theatre is an index of Romanticism itself" (McGann 1989: 39 n. 2): this withdrawal into closet drama, into a theater of the mind, could be described as a lyricization, in stance if not in form. To his unactable *Prometheus Unbound* Shelley gave the subtitle

"Lyrical Drama," a term sometimes used to refer to opera, and indeed what is opera, which grew in importance during this period, but lyrical drama? And what better term for Goethe's *Faust*, as its numerous musical versions by Romantic composers attest? Tieck's *Genoveva* (1800), with its allegorical characters, stress on mood or atmosphere, and vague plot, won high praise from other Romantics, but was criticized by Schiller and others for its lack of "plastic" or dramatic form (see Paulin 1985: 122-3). Mickiewicz's *Forefathers' Eve* (1823, 1832) is a closet drama, or scenes from a drama, with the subtitle "A Poem." It is true that many poets tried to write stageable pieces that might attract audiences and make money; moreover many of the battles over Romanticism in France, like those in Germany earlier over *Sturm und Drang*, were staged on the stage, as it were, notably in the nightly brouhahas at performances of Hugo's *Hernani* (1830). Still, most Romantic plays seem to need the "poetic" sympathy of a reader in his or her study; on stage they are vulnerable to ridicule if the slightest misstep breaks the spell.

In all this we may see the culmination of the century-long process, especially in England, of what Anne Williams (1984) calls "lyric appropriations" of other genres (epistle, satire, elegy, pastoral, even – with Wordsworth – tragedy). It was attended with theories that made the lyric, or moments of lyric, the quintessence of poetry. Coleridge's thought that "a poem of any length neither can be, nor ought to be, all poetry" (1983, 2: 15) seems to identify "poetry" with brief lyrical moments; Poe would later push this thought to an extreme. Leopardi thought lyric the only true poetry; the epic was really a set of hymns. And several Romantics agreed with the historical argument that all genres, including epic and drama, arose from lyrical forms, particularly the ode. As long as "Ossian" was taken as authentic, it seemed to vouch for the lyrical origins of epic; though billed as fragments of a lost epic cycle, none of them narrated much action and most of them were elegies. Bürger argued that the "lyric" and "epic-lyric" (ballad, romance) were one and the same; Foscolo thought the earliest poetry was lyrical; Hugo chose the ode as the form to deploy at first "because it was in this form that the inspiration of the earliest poets formerly appeared to the earliest peoples" (from the preface to the 1823 edition of the *Odes*, my translation).

The Rise of Music

The elevation of the lyric, the form most closely tied to music, and its infusion into the other genres, corresponds to a shift in the reigning system of the "sister arts" whereby music replaced painting as poetry's favorite sister. This shift was most prominent in Germany, where most Romantic writers ranked music first among the arts. Indeed Hölderlin, Jean Paul, Hoffmann, Clemens Brentano, Lenau, and Grillparzer were all musicians. Hoffmann thought music the highest art and perhaps the only Romantic one (Neubauer 1986: 205). "No color is as Romantic as a tone," Jean Paul wrote (quoted in Meyer 1989: 6). Kleist regarded the art of music "as the algebraic formula of all the others" (Neubauer 1986: 192). Schelling grandly defined music as the form in which "the real unity purely as such becomes potence and symbol" and is thus somehow more fundamental than painting, which takes "the ideal unity in its discernibleness as its symbol"; in a virtually Pythagorean manner he posits the ultimate significance of rhythm, harmony, and melody to be "the first and purest forms of movement in the universe" (Schelling 1989: 109, 126, 117). We are not far here from Schopenhauer's privileging of music as the direct copy of "the Will" and Nietzsche's attributing to music a Dionysian wisdom. Though Wackenroder's and Tieck's *Outpourings of an Art-Loving Friar* (1797) deals mainly with painters and painting, the final chapter is devoted to "the Tone-Poet Joseph Berglinger"; in sections published posthumously Wackenroder claims music is the most wonderful of the arts because "it depicted human feeling in a superhuman manner." Novalis praises music as the art that shows most clearly how the spirit "poeticizes" objects (Behler 1993: 246, 202). Heine declares music to be "art's final word" (quoted in Junod 2000: 28). Music pervades Brentano's work, literally and metaphorically, and many of his leading characters are musicians; in a review of an opera he asks, "Is a poet conceivable who is no musician?" (Fetzer 1974: 26). His poem "Phantasie" (a title used by many composers) has stanzas "orchestrated" for various instruments (ibid., p. 94); Tieck does something similar.

René Wellek has argued that "the hierarchy of arts differs in Germany and England, as does the hierarchy of genres in literature" (Wellek 1965: 27) but he may have exaggerated the difference. Even in unmusical England something of the new esteem for music shows itself among the poets. Wordsworth's "Peele Castle" may be one of the great examples of *ekphrasis* or description of painting, but he also wrote "The Power of Music" and, more important, claimed "The mind of man is fashioned and built up / Even as a strain of music" (1799 *Prelude* ll. 67-8). Though he was interested in paintings and made efforts to see them, Coleridge believed that a man of mere talent could incorporate imagery into poetry, "But the sense of musical delight, with the power of producing it, is a gift of imagination" (Coleridge 1983, 2: 20); "Music seems to have an *immediate* communion with my Life" (Coburn 1951: 214; see also Woodring 1978). Keats was fascinated by a Grecian urn, but was surely even more rapt by the song of a nightingale, and even within the silent, entirely visual world of the urn Keats responds to "unheard" melodies that reach the "spirit." As for nightingales, it is not beside the point that many Romantic poems of every nation are devoted to songbirds, and that the songbirds often stand for poets. Aeolian harps, too, vibrate in Romantic verse from Ireland to Russia. Musical metaphors pervade Shelley's poetry; indeed he invents a musical metaphysic where, for instance, Prometheus's beloved, Asia, follows music to find him, as if floating in a boat on a stream of air; their "wordless converse" when they meet is a kind of melody; at his liberation a great long sound transforms the human race; and the final act is a joyous choral dance celebrating the musicalization of the cosmos. Byron wrote "Hebrew Melodies" and many other songs while he dismissed painting as "the most artificial and unnatural" of the arts (Marchand 1975-82, 5: 213); he described the silent experience of the sublime as "a tone, / The soul and source of music, which makes known / Eternal harmony" (*Childe Harold*, 3. 90). Even Blake the engraver and painter composed tunes for his *Songs* and sang them well, according to contemporaries, and it is a bard's song that precipitates the plot of his epic *Milton*.

To Madame de Staël music is the foremost of the arts, and the highest praise of her heroine Corinne's poetry is that it is an "intellectual melody" (*Corinne*, ch. 2). George Sand shared her view, and several of her novels are devoted to music or musicians. The rise of Romantic poetry in France, it is true, has been linked to a revival of pictorialism, and painters and poets inspired one another in their clubs or *cénacles*; Sainte-Beuve in "Le Cénacle" notes the presence of a painter "with ardent palette" at the gathering of poets and cries, "Fraternité des arts!" It is also true that poetry everywhere had long taken for granted the union of music with verse and had no need to assert it – within poetry poems are "songs" and poets "singers" holding "lyres" – but music gradually appears more and more often as the explicit ideal. Lamartine names a volume of poems *Harmonies* (1830); an old air transports Nerval in "Fantaisie" to another time and place. Imagery similar to Shelley's can be found in Baudelaire's "La Musique." Even a poem often cited as the quintessence of pictorialism has a musical title and, one might argue, a musical method, Gautier's "Symphonie en Blanc Majeur." Music in French poetry reaches its peak, though late, in Verlaine's "Art Poétique": "Music before everything."[8]

Not everyone, even in Germany, placed music higher than poetry – Kant did not, for instance, and for Hegel poetry was the most inward and spiritual of the arts – but it became common to rank that poetry highest that is most like music. At the same time the words "poetry" and "poetic" took on both a broader sense and a normative one: "poetic" became the highest term of praise for a work of any art. The Schlegels and others in their circle routinely called the prose they most admired "poetry," notably Goethe's *Wilhelm Meister*: here everything is "poetry, high pure poetry" and "This marvellous prose is prose, and yet it is poetry" (from F. Schlegel's review of *Wilhelm Meister*). Coleridge agreed: "poetry of the highest kind may exist without metre" (Coleridge 1983, 2: 15). As if in a pre-emptive reversal of Matthew Arnold's famous description of Pope and Dryden as "classics of our prose," Mme de Staël wrote, "In France our greatest lyric poets are perhaps our great prose writers, Bossuet, Pascal, Fénelon, Buffon, Jean-Jacques, etc." (in *De l'Allemagne*, 2.9). Vigny wrote, "*Ivanhoe* is a historical novel. But one could just as well say: *Ivanhoe* is a poem without the marvelous and without verse" (in *Journal d'un poète* [1829]).

Diderot had used "poetic" in art criticism and many others followed him in nineteenth-century France. Of that painter attending the gathering of poets, Sainte-Beuve wrote, "He is a poet, too." To cite a late instance, Charles Tillot, writing of Delacroix's ceiling paintings in 1851, said: "There he has shown himself to be what he truly is: both painter and poet at once" (quoted in Jobert 1998: 217). In England Constable wrote in a letter, "It is the business of a painter not to contend with nature & put this scene . . . on a canvas of a few inches, but to make something out of nothing, in attempting which he must almost of necessity become poetical" (cited in Rosen 1995: 173).

Novalis thought music "poeticized" objects, as we saw, and at the same time Tieck introduced the concept of the "poetic" into music criticism; in an almost paradoxical formula, he said a good symphony is "purely poetic" if it is "absolute," that is, without words (Dalhaus 1989: 68-9). But then music is itself a language, deeper and truer than the one we speak, just as poetry is a language within or beyond everyday language. Friedrich Schlegel thought it possible that purely instrumental music tends toward philosophy (Schlegel 1991: 444). "Music speaks the most universal language which arouses the soul in freedom," Schumann believed, "without specific constraints, yet the soul feels itself at home in it" (quoted in Meyer 1989: 66). Carl August Griesinger, the biographer of Haydn, after hearing a performance of Beethoven's *Eroica* in 1804, wrote, "Here is more than Haydn and Mozart, here the symphony-poem [*Simphonie-Dichtung*] is brought to a higher plateau" (quoted in Sipe 1998: 54, see also p. 77). Beethoven called himself a *Tondichter*, "tone poet." Mendelssohn and others wrote "songs without words"; Chopin, whom Heine called "the great genius tone-poet" (quoted in Bernstein 1998: 61), composed *ballades* and *nocturnes*, both literary forms, for piano alone; and another literary form adopted by composers was the *romance* (German *Romanze*), the word coming from Spanish, where it means "ballad." Schumann planned at one point to give his piano *Fantasie* opus 17 the name *Dichtungen* ("Poems"): "I think it a very noble and significant term for musical compositions" (see Marston 1992: 6). He named his opus 21 piano pieces *Novelletten*. One of his *Kinderszenen* is "The Poet Speaks"; it is in the voice of a piano recitative that he speaks. Liszt composed 12 "symphonic poems," and many composers followed him; he wrote that instrumental music is "a poetic language" (quoted in Junod 2000: 29).[9]

At work in many of these claims for it is a concept of poetry more abstract and basic than its ordinary use; it hearkens to its Greek etymology (*poiein* means "to make"). *Poesie* is Schelling's term for the creative power, whether in humans or in the Absolute; lying within nature, for instance, is "a poem that lies enclosed in a secret marvelous cipher" that only poets can read and interpret (quoted in Wellek 1981: 76). This idea became common among Romantics. Jean Paul called music "romantic poetry through the ear," while for Solger, "*die Poesie* is the universal art" (quoted in Lindenberger 2000: 371, 372).[10] In "A Defence of Poetry" Shelley makes *to poiein* one of the two modes of mental action, and defines poetry "in a general sense" as "the expression of the Imagination." Thoreau writes in *Walden*, "The morning wind forever blows, the poem of creation is uninterrupted; but few are the ears that hear it" (Thoreau 1992: 57).[11]

Painting

With the lyricizing of literature, the exalting of music, and the poeticizing of all the arts, we would expect the musicalizing of painting. And indeed as some painters got more "painterly" and coloristic, departing from the fine brushwork and more "sculpturesque" manner of the neoclassical standard, their work was perceived as musical. A character of Brentano's praises certain paintings for having "much harmony and music" in them (Fetzer 1974: 82). The painter Runge, like Goethe, speculated on "the analogy of color and tone," and at times posited a kind of abstract "inner music" as fundamental to all the arts: "there must be music through words in a beautiful poem, just as there must be music in a beautiful picture and in a beautiful building" (Bisanz 1970: 74).

The arrival of Beethoven's music in France in 1828 excited the "Young France" circle and evoked a fresh look at all the arts; the term "poetic" arose, notably in Berlioz's Beethoven essays (Schrade 1942). In the minds of French artists and critics music and painting each served as the paradigm for the other. Corot the landscapist loved Mozart, Beethoven, and Weber, and analyzed symphonies as pictures (Champa 1991). If *ut pictura musica* took its place beside the older *ut pictura poesis*, that is, if painting became the norm for music as it had been for poetry, the Horatian formula was increasingly often reversed to *ut musica pictura*, so that painting no less than poetry reoriented itself toward music. Music is "the most powerful of all the arts," Delacroix wrote (quoted in Kagan 1986). He also said, "Harmony in music exists not only in the makeup of the chords, but also in their relationships, in what I would call, if need be, their auditory reflections. Well, painting works the same way!" (quoted in Jobert 1998: 34). Baudelaire often praised Delacroix's musical character: "These wonderful *chords* of color often give one ideas of melody and harmony, and the impression that one takes away from his pictures is often, as it were, a musical one" (quoted in Honour 1979: 120). The English culmination of this thinking arrives in Pater's *The Renaissance* (1873), where after describing how each art draws from the other arts to overcome its limitations he concludes that "All art constantly aspires toward the condition of music . . . music being the typical, or ideally consummate art" ("The School of Giorgione"). As the most abstract or nonrepresentational of the arts, of course, music would become the closer sister to painting to the extent that painting itself became abstract. Thus it seems inevitable that the notorious near-abstract painting by Whistler's should have the musical title *Nocturne in Black and Gold* (1875), though it was only one of at least six "Nocturne" paintings; he also painted several "Symphonies" and "Harmonies," titles aimed at directing the viewer to the paintings' purely formal properties.[12]

Friedrich Schlegel warned painters against becoming too sculpturesque (Honour 1979: 127-8), and his was a common view; de Staël summed up German opinion this way: "In various German works ancient poetry has been compared to sculpture and romantic [Christian, modern] poetry to painting" (*De l'Allemagne* 2.11). Gautier thought sculpture was the least Romantic of the arts (Honour 1979: 127-8). As for the practice of sculpture itself, perhaps because the achievement of the Greeks and the high Renaissance still seemed unsurpassable, it is generally agreed that it responded least to the Romantic aesthetic, and it is hard to recall a notable Romantic sculptor until, perhaps, Rodin.[13]

The "Selving" of the Arts

The theory and practice of painterliness corresponded to the demand, heard mainly in Germany, that music become purely or "absolutely" music, music without words and without "program." Related to this demand, I think, is the often noted feature of Romantic music that it does not transcribe well from one instrument or ensemble to another – notwithstanding Liszt's genius at making piano reductions of symphonies. Bach's music often sounds equally right on many different instruments, but increasingly in this era transcriptions sound less and less appropriate or "natural." (Beethoven's piano version of his violin concerto is a case in point.) The sheer sound or sonority, the timbre or "color" of the instrument or orchestration, now seems of the essence; each "form" has one unique sonic embodiment. This Romantic characteristic seconds the idea that music has an inner nature that composers seek to express.[14]

As painting becomes most itself, drawing from its most characteristic means, it comes to resemble music. As music and painting each become most themselves, they grow "poetic." We might then ask if there is a trend within poetry and its theory that corresponds to this self-intensification or "selving," as Hopkins might say of it. Does poetry become more poetic? It is not hard to find distinctions drawn between poetry and verse, the one internal and essential, the other superficial and technical, and the extension of "poem," as we saw, to certain great works of prose – to the point where Rimbaud (in a letter to Paul Demeny, 1871) calls *Les Misérables* "a true poem" (though presumably not a lyric!), and Emerson calls Swedenborg's system a "poem" even though he concedes there was an "entire want of poetry" in its author (Emerson 1983: 682, 688). Nor is it unusual to find certain poems, or passages of poems, praised as expressions of the true poetic genius, of "poetry" in the deep Schellingian sense. This usage has much to do with the expressivist turn in Romantic aesthetic theory, the shift from mirror to lamp and fountain as the root metaphors for art's origin or purpose, but we might consider here another possible poeticizing of poetry, though it is difficult to name and describe. It is an intensity of poetic means, such as the compression of imagery or metaphor into a simultaneously elevated, even religious, rhetorical tone, of the sort we find in Wordsworth's "Simplon Pass" section of *The Prelude* or in Shelley's "Ode to the West Wind." Or, in more understated poems such as Keats's "To Autumn," Hugo's "Demain, dès l'aube" (Tomorrow, at Dawn), or Pushkin's "I loved you once," an implied richness of feeling economically yet completely offered in seemingly perfect forms. What such poems or passages share, perhaps, is indeed sheer feeling, as well as unusually salient musical effects (self-consciously so in the Shelley and Keats poems); no doubt the liberation from rhymed couplets and neoclassical conventions of decorum, as well as the growing prestige of lyric as the essential poetic genre, gave room for the heart and the ear together.

Composite or Hybrid Forms

To go further in specifying this sort of intensification might take us into the mists of Romantic theorizing at its vaguest. If we grant, however, that something like this is evident, and explicitly attempted, in many characteristic poems, paintings, and musical pieces, we must also grant the ambition, if not always the fulfillment, of what seems to be the opposite goal: the composite work of art or *Gesamtkunstwerk*. Perhaps it was only modesty or insufficient skill that kept most masters of one art from trying to combine it with others, but there were prominent exceptions: Berlioz and Wagner, among other composers, wrote their own libretti or songs, Blake was poet and painter, and Hugo made some remarkably effective and innovative water colors and ink drawings. The ideal of the total work of art was widely attractive. Blake also sang his "illuminated" texts, and Runge hoped to exhibit his *Times of Day* series in a specially designed Gothic building along with poetry and music – "an abstract painterly fantastic-musical poem with choirs" (quoted in Bisanz 1970: 1975). Opera, especially with its conventional interlude of ballet, was already a proto-*Gesamtkunstwerk* well before Wagner. Shelley may have intended his *Prometheus Unbound* as something of the sort; he had recently heard about a ballet based on Beethoven's *Creatures of Prometheus*. Though its full extent was not known until 1832, Goethe's *Faust* loomed as an extraordinary epic drama that contained the whole history of literary and musical, if not visual, forms, including folk songs, church liturgy, the masque or "triumph," Greek drama, and indeed opera. To reconcile this distinctively Romantic trend with the purification or intensification we have just discussed is not beyond Romantic theory itself, which might claim that it is just through their return to their individual essences that the arts discover or recover their true commonality one with another – to which Pater and others would add that their source and ultimate end is music. It would be interesting, too, to see how far Runge's obviously churchlike setting for his project could be generalized: to the extent that Romanticism is "spilt religion," in T. E. Hulme's dismissive phrase (Hulme 1924: 118), an infusion of religious emotion and symbolism into the arts as well as nature, the "total work of art" could be seen as an attempt at a new version of the traditional church, in which music, poetry, painting, sculpture, stained-glass windows, and even incense and wine had long been combined to appeal to all the senses.

As for music, we must acknowledge another important tendency that is even less well recuperated by theories of "absolute" art, and that is, of course, the great growth of opera and the rise of the *Lied*, to name only two instances of the continuing marriage of word and music. The final movement of Beethoven's final symphony, having on one interpretation surveyed and dismissed the three purely instrumental earlier movements, declares that only a combination of chorus and quartet is adequate to the themes of joy and faith. That great example remained something of an exception, but opera also, shall we say, intensified – grew more dramatic and emotional, intertwined action more closely with arias (Wagner's "endless melody" being one extreme), and enhanced its orchestral power, lighting, scenery, and sheer length. We may also find in some works of Liszt and Berlioz a kind of "closet opera" comparable to the mental theater of Romantic writers. (See Benjamin Walton's chapter in this volume.) As for the art-song or *Lied*, it is one of the glories of German Romanticism – not only the six hundred by Schubert but also those by Beethoven, Schumann, Wolf, and Brahms. The practice of "through-composing" instead of repeating strophes or stanzas brought poetic text and music closer; changes in melody, rhythm, key, mode, and harmony allowed music to serve the text in a newly intimate and "expressive" way, thus confirming the thesis that "poetry" is the quintessential art. But these resources also made music an interpreter of the text and, sometimes, when the setting seemed perfect, its master – to the point where audiences familiar with the song cannot imagine the text without it. As Charles Rosen has put it, one of the greatest achievements of the Romantics is "the elevation of the song from a minor genre to the vehicle of the sublime" (Rosen 1995: 124). Nor is this only a German practice; the French equivalent is the *mélodie*, pioneered by Berlioz, who set many texts by French Romantic poets. (See James Parsons' chapter in this volume.)

This may be the place to consider that most hybrid of literary forms, the novel. The Schlegels believed that the novel was not a prose epic, or even primarily a narrative genre, but a distinctively modern, composite form with its own origin and character. As "modern" in their parlance is at times nearly synonymous with "Romantic," the novel seems to become the central Romantic "genre." Indeed *romantisch* in German could mean "novel-like," the adjectival derivative of *Roman*, "novel"; Friedrich Schlegel, Tieck, and other Romantics sometimes used the term in that sense.[15] They admired Goethe's *Wilhelm Meister*, in which narrative often yields to philosophical dialogues, letters, or songs, and the plot has so many coincidences and mysterious events that it can only be taken as allegorical or symbolic. Novalis's *Heinrich von Ofterdingen*, F. Schlegel's *Lucinde* (1799), Hölderlin's *Hyperion* (1796), Hoffmann's *Life and Opinions of the Tomcat Murr*, Brentano's *Godwi* (subtitled "A Novel Run Wild") (1801), not to mention the unclassifiable short fictions of Jean Paul, are as much fantasias on their themes as long tales. Vigny's *Stello* (1832) is really three accounts of suffering poets, told by the same intrusive and digressive narrator; each chapter of Karolina Pavlova's *A Double Life* (1848) is divided between prose, which tells the outward events of the heroine's dull life, and poetry, which reports her dreams. The novels of Scott, Dumas, Hugo, and Balzac are more or less realist narratives, sometimes epic in scope and length, but we can discern a trend within many Romantic novels, especially in Germany, toward reducing narrative, suspending action, meditating and dreaming on the theme, and flowering into songs. May we not call this development a lyricizing of the novel? Jean Paul called the novel a "poetic encyclopedia" (quoted in Wellek 1981: 104). Novalis, who eventually dismissed *Wilhelm Meister* for being too prosaic, insisted "A novel must be poetic through and through" (quoted in Blackall 1983: 16). Hugo was later to say that Scott was "picturesque but prosaic," whereas the novel ought to be "picturesque but poetic" (ibid.) Lyric infiltrates from within, one might say, in many Romantic novels, but it also imposes itself from without in Byron's *Don Juan* and Pushkin's *Eugene Onegin*, both, to borrow the latter's subtitle, "novels in verse" – not the blank verse, hexameters, or heroic couplets usually deployed in epics but tightly rhymed lyrical stanzas.

The Rise of Shorter Forms

At this point we have returned to where we started, with the rise of the lyric, but from here we can pursue another pattern. What is there in the other arts to correspond to the new stature of the shorter forms in literature? In music, there is no doubt about the symphony's continuing pre-eminence; in fact, after Beethoven hugely expanded its form with the *Eroica*, and German theorists advocated pure music, it grew in prestige. Opera, too, as we have said, grew in popularity and range. But the Romantics did indeed give new weight to short forms, and not only to songs. Beethoven's *Bagatelles* and Schubert's *Moments musicaux* pointed the way, but Chopin is the supreme example – his impromptus, scherzi, preludes, nocturnes, polonaises, mazurkas, waltzes, and études for piano are all brief, some less than a minute long – just as he is the most "absolute" of composers in almost never writing any music for words. To these we may add the intermezzi, caprices, album leaves, and rhapsodies of several other composers. Schumann's sets of piano pieces, the *Davidsbündlertänze*, *Carnaval*, *Kinderszenen*, *Waldszenen*, and so on, resemble collections of lyric poems, say *Songs of Innocence* or *Lyrical Ballads*, with some unity of theme or spirit; Liszt's *Années de pèlerinage* is similar. So with the song cycle, often based on poem sets themselves – Schubert's *Winterreise*, Schumann's *Dichterliebe*, or Berlioz' *Nuits d'été* – which rivaled the opera or symphony in status.

With these belongs another characteristic contribution of Romantic music, the overture. Weber, Schumann, Mendelssohn, and Berlioz all wrote fine examples, Mendelssohn's "Hebrides" Overture (opus 26) being perhaps the most celebrated, and while they may be performed as the first piece of an evening's concert, they are really overtures to nothing, despite their titles. They are miniature symphonies, sometimes with a vague "program" but often merely gesturing to a subject through their titles, freer than symphonic movements in form, shorter than "symphonic poems." We may set these next to the preludes of Chopin, preludes to nothing but other preludes. It is tempting to compare them to the greatest work of Wordsworth, *The Prelude*, but that is hardly a short form and its title is posthumous; closer in spirit is Lamartine's "Les Préludes" (1822), a poem comprising several short sections in different meters and rhyme schemes. (One of Liszt's symphonic poems is named after it, though not originally inspired by it.)

In painting, it began to be possible to exhibit sketches and studies, or at least exhibit works which unsympathetic critics dismissed as merely sketches and studies, but which more sympathetic viewers, in the Romantic spirit, appreciated for their freshness, their nearness to their originating inspiration. The shift in the hierarchy of genres that corresponds to the rise of lyrics and overtures is the rise of the landscape, which had ranked at most third in the traditional system behind history painting and portraiture. In 1787 the *Sturm und Drang* novelist Wilhelm Heinse predicted that "Landscape painting will, in the end, supercede all other genres" (quoted in Vaughan 1994: 41). Runge, though often in an allegorical manner, Friedrich and Carus in Germany, Constable and Turner in England, took steps to bring that about. They made the landscape genre distinctively Romantic and tutored generations of eyes to see landscape itself as "Romantic," as it used to be "picturesque." We must note in fairness, however, that Delacroix never questioned the traditional hierarchy, almost never painted landscapes (though his skill in it is visible in his backgrounds), and sought and received great commissions for historical, allegorical, and even religious paintings in public buildings (though he was also, by that time, no longer sympathetic to Romanticism as he understood it). The turn toward nature in eighteenth-century literature had much to do with this trend, of course, and it was seconded by the early Romantics: Runge was a pupil of the poet Kosegarten, whose nature poems were in the spirit of Thomson, Gray, and Ossian, but also a friend of Tieck, whose novel *Franz Sternbalds Wanderungen* is filled with enthusiastic descriptions of landscape. Kosegarten was also an influence on Friedrich. Constable knew Wordsworth personally and admired his poetry; Thomson was a favorite of Turner, who also appreciated Wordsworth and, much later, Shelley. To round out this account we should add Charles Rosen's observation that, if "The creation of the song cycle is a parallel to the replacement of epic poetry by landscape poetry and the elevation of landscape painting to the commanding position previously held by historical and religious painting," it is partly due to the sources of the songs themselves, for "It was the lyric poetry of landscape that was the chief inspiration in the development of the *Lied*" (Rosen 1995: 125).

One way in which shorter, lyrical forms in literature partly dislodged the central position of epic was through a new appreciation of the fragment. Here probably the paradigm is Macpherson's *Fragments of Ancient Poetry* (1760), given out as surviving pieces of an ancient epic cycle by the Scottish bard Ossian. To his few readers today Ossian is tediously static – we would like a little more epic action – but the supposed fragments tend to be lyrical, elegiac, and not very long by epic standards. Soon there was a new trend, the publishing of new work deliberately left unfinished. Goethe's *Faust, ein Fragment* (1790) is the great German example, but there were many others. By 1798 Friedrich Schlegel was theorizing about the fragment, in which he saw the typical modern form: "Many of the works of the ancients have become fragments. Many modern works are fragments as soon as they are written" (Schlegel 1991: 24). He published his theories, fittingly, as *Critical Fragments* (1798) and *Athenaeum Fragments* (1800). Though they are writing about Jena Romanticism only, Lacoue-Labarthe and Nancy have recently claimed that "the fragment is the romantic genre *par excellence*" (Lacoue-Labarthe and Nancy 1988: 40). To mention another instance, Karoline von Günderode published *Poetic Fragments* under a pseudonym in 1805.

The best-known English example is Coleridge's "Kubla Khan: Or, A Vision in a Dream. A Fragment" (1797, first published in 1816), but he also published other apparently incomplete poems, a volume of poems called *Sibylline Leaves*, and an almost comically fragmentary *Biographia Literaria*. Wordsworth included "A Fragment" in the *Lyrical Ballads* of 1800, later called "The Danish Boy." Even better known in its day than "Kubla Khan" was Byron's *The Giaour: A Fragment of a Turkish Tale* (1813). Keats's *Hyperion: A Fragment* (1820) was said to be published "contrary to the wish of the author," but there was certainly little risk of opprobium by this time: fragments were everywhere: Isabella Lickbarrow's "On Sensibility: A Fragment," Leigh Hunt's "Paganini. A Fragment," and so on. In his *Nouvelles Méditations* (1823) Lamartine included an "epic fragment" and a "dramatic fragment." Alfred de Musset's *Le Saule, fragment* (1830-1, published in 1850) is really a set of fragments; it is appropriate that it contains a verse translation of Ossian's hymn to the evening star. Mickiewicz published "Part II" and "Part IV" of his dramatic "poem" *Forefathers' Eve* in 1823; they seemed to have little to do with each other. In 1832 he published a "Part III" that seemed to have little to do with either of the earlier parts. Many of Pushkin's early poems are called "fragment" (*otryvok*), and he was often criticized (or praised) for his fragmentariness; even *Eugene Onegin* seems to have been abandoned rather than completed.[16] The Hungarian Romantic Vörösmarty has been described recently as "the first major Hungarian poet to publish works that were meant to remain fragments" (Szegedy-Maszák 2002: 56-7). And we might add Emerson's notoriously choppy apothegmatic style; "I am a fragment," he wrote, "and this is a fragment of me" ("Experience," see Buell 2002: 109-14).

It is worth noting that probably the earliest use of "fragment" to refer to a kind of work of art is found in Petrarch's Latin title, *Rerum vulgarium fragmenta*, to his *Rime sparse* ("Scattered Rhymes") or *Canzoniere*. Friedrich Schlegel called them "classical fragments of a novel." But they also, of course, launched the sonnet, and the sonnet sequence, into the European repertory of forms. It may be more than a coincidence, then, that the Romantic sonnet revival took place alongside the vogue for the fragment. Schlegel claimed that the sonnet is "the most perfect form for a romantic fragment" (quoted in Fechner 1969: 337). (See Elizabeth Wanning Harries's chapter in this volume.) It would seem to be part of this tendency to smaller, and even fragmentary, forms that the Romantics usually wrote individual sonnets and seldom sonnet cycles, which had been the Renaissance norm, and that some of their sonnets reached toward the sublime, which had been the domain of epic, drama, and the Pindaric ode.[17]

Unfinished painting was not often exhibited, but sketches and studies gained acceptance, as we noted, though they correspond more to first drafts than fragments. Blake's first book, with a title befitting the work of a visual artist, *Poetical Sketches* (1783), does contain a few parts of a work, but most poems are complete and not at all sketchy. Yet Delacroix could write in his 1853 journal, of a friend who loved music, "We spoke of Chopin. He told me that his improvisations were much bolder than his finished compositions. It is the same, no doubt, with a study for a painting compared with the finished picture. No, one doesn't spoil a painting by finishing it! Perhaps there is less room for the imagination than in a sketchy work" (quoted in Jobert 1998:

34). J. L. Koerner has argued that Friedrich's finished paintings of a thicket of firs or grove of oaks are like fragments in their separation from foreground and background, their invitation to the observer to complete their context in his or her mind (Koerner 1990: 26). In music, aside from improvisations and "impromptus" (written down and published!), something like a deliberate fragment appears among the Romantics: Rosen notes that several pieces by Chopin and Schumann, for instance, are fragmentary in a musical sense, ending on a dominant seventh, or beginning in such ambiguous tonality as to sound like a transition (Rosen 1995: 78-86). Schumann's fragmentary *Kreisleriana* was inspired by Hoffmann's fragmentary stories of the same name, about the musical genius Johannes Kreisler, and perhaps by the equally fragmentary *Tomcat Murr*.

To end this survey of the Romantic system with the fragment certainly puts into question the notion of system itself. How systematic was all this shifting and transforming of genres? Was it not more a constellation than a system – an illusion of the distant observer? One can find examples or pronouncements to illustrate every move, but one can find counterexamples and counterpronouncements as well. While many Romantics thought epic grew from lyric, Schelling thought elegy, at least, descended from epic. Delacroix conserved the traditional hierarchy in painting, Berlioz was untouched by German theories of absolute music (most of his instrumental music has a "program"), and so on. Nonetheless I think I have shown that the elements of Romantic theory and practice do not merely accommodate our projections of lines and shapes, like a group of stars, but share a gravitational field like a family of planets and moons. Rosen and Zerner have suggested that "The Romantic movement might with some justice be defined as a progressive abolition of the hierarchy of genres and of the distinction between central and marginal forms" (Rosen and Zerner 1984: 35). The planets, on this view, including such asteroids and comets as fragments and preludes, grew equal to one another and no longer revolved around a common sun. This may be true, but the Romantic movement lasted many decades, and the abolition of the hierarchy was indeed "progressive"; the waning of the gravitational field took time. What I have traced is a set of interconnected rotations or transpositions within the traditional neoclassical system; after turn succeeded turn, no doubt, turbulence or centrifugal forces broke enough bonds that nothing resembling a system remained. Since the late nineteenth century the arts have been continually reinventing themselves and little has been taken for granted. From 1770 to about 1850, however, their cosmos was not altogether chaotic. The Romantics of that period brought about, in the strict sense of the word, a revolution in the arts, and it was the final one.

NOTES

1   Kristeller describes the system of "the five major arts of painting, sculpture, architecture, music and poetry," whereas I shall deal almost exclusively with painting, music, and poetry. He does not discuss the hierarchies within the arts. We might note here that the Romantic

rejection of neo-Classicism often accompanied a renewed attention to and admiration for the classics, especially Greek. For a recent discussion of some of the complexities of these relations, see Fry (2000).

2   Harold Bloom writes, "That English Romanticism, as opposed to Continental, was a renaissance of the Renaissance, is happily now a critical commonplace" (Bloom 1971: 4). But at least some countries on the Continent also knew this second Renaissance. On the sonnet and other forms in England, see Curran (1986). Blake's "To the Evening Star" (1783) is sometimes considered a sonnet, as it has 14 lines, but it is rhymeless and does not observe the usual stanza breaks. See also Feldman and Robinson (1999).

3   See Gendre (1996, part 3 ch. 1). The "late start" of Romanticism in France has been much debated; it might be better to think of it as a second start, with Chateaubriand and Madame de Staël representing the first, which failed to take hold. In the homeland of Petrarch the sonnet had never died out, but Alfieri, a "pre-Romantic," was unusually devoted to it.

4   On the early ode in English see Cohen (2001).

5   "Elegy" has two meanings, often confused, each ancient: (1) a poem in the "elegiac distich" (hexameter plus pentameter), used for almost any subject, and (2) a poem or song of mourning. Schiller's "Der Spaziergang" (1795), a poem of great importance for Romanticism, was titled "Elegie" in its first version; it is an elegy mainly in the technical sense, but it approaches the broad sense that Schiller offers in *On Naïve and Sentimental Poetry*: a poem where nature is represented as lost or the ideal as unattainable. See Ziolkowski (1980). In Russia, Küchelbecker complained in 1824 that the melancholic, private elegy had replaced the inspired, public ode as the prevalent poetic form. See Leighton (1987: 55-68).

6   Abrams adds "Der Spaziergang" to his category of "greater romantic lyric" (Abrams

1971: 453-7). Lamartine's originality, Paul Bénichou writes, is, "even while working in the existing poetic genres, to have finally erased the boundaries between them and mixed their tones in the flexible and multiform genre of the *méditation*" (Bénichou 1999: 113).

7   On Vigny and the *poème*, Hugo and the ode, and Lamartine and the elegy, see the chapters on these writers in Bénichou (1999) and in Porter (1978). André Chénier, whom the French Romantics recognized as a forerunner, may have invented the short *poème*; see Porter (1978: 47-8).

8   On painting and poetry see Gilman (1958, ch. 6).

9   F. Schlegel also wrote, "Many musical compositions are merely translations of poems into the language of music" (Schlegel 1991: 392). A sort of dialectical reversal of the song without words appears in the title Verlaine gives to his 1874 collection of poems, *Romances sans paroles*!

10 Lindenberger gives several more examples of the broad use of "poetry."

11 On *Poesie* in the Schlegels see Beiser (2003: 15-18).

12 Whistler's musically titled paintings had subtitles in a referential or imitative mode as well, such as "Old Battersea Bridge."

13 Brown (2001) devotes only five pages to sculpture (and five to architecture), against 400 to painting, drawing, etching, etc.

14 On the high value of sonority or timbre for Romantic music, see Einstein (1947: 7-8) and Rosen (1995: 38-40). It is thus fitting that Berlioz, in many other ways the quintessential Romantic composer, is highly regarded for his genius at orchestration.

15 On the word *romantisch* see Eichner (1972: 102-3).

16 On Pushkin see Greenleaf (1994: 1-3, 206ff); she considers *Onegin* to be "a deliberately fabricated Romantic fragment poem."

17 See Harries (1994: 11). See also Balfour (2002) on the "sublime sonnet."

REFERENCES AND FURTHER READING

Abrams, M. H. (1971). *Natural Supernaturalism.* New York: Norton.

Abrams, M. H. (1965). "Structure and Style in the Greater Romantic Lyric." In Frederick W. Hilles and Harold Bloom (eds.), *From Sensibility to Romanticism.* London: Oxford University Press, pp. 527-60.

Balfour, Ian (2002). "The Sublime Sonnet in European Romanticism." In Angela Esterhammer (ed.), *Romantic Poetry.* Amsterdam: Benjamins, pp. 181-95.

Behler, Ernst (1993). *German Romantic Literary Theory.* Cambridge, UK: Cambridge University Press, 1993.

Beiser, Frederick C. (2003). *The Romantic Imperative: The Concept of Early German Romanticism.* Cambridge, MA: Harvard University Press.

Bénichou, Paul (1999). *The Consecration of the Writer, 1750-1830*, trans. Mark K. Jensen. Lincoln: University of Nebraska Press.

Bernstein, Susan (1998). *Virtuosity of the Nineteenth Century.* Stanford, CA: Stanford University Press.

Bisanz, Rudolf M. (1970). *German Romanticism and Philipp Otto Runge.* DeKalb: Northern Illinois University Press.

Blackall, Eric A. (1983). *The Novels of the German Romantics.* Ithaca, NY: Cornell University Press.

Bloom, Harold (1971). "First and Last Romantics." In *The Ringers in the Tower.* Chicago: University of Chicago Press, pp. 3-11.

Brown, David Blayney (2001). *Romanticism.* London: Phaidon.

Buell, Lawrence (2002). *Emerson.* Cambridge, MA: Harvard University Press.

Champa, Kermit (1991). *The Rise of Landscape Painting in France: Corot to Monet.* Manchester, NH: Currier Gallery.

Coburn, Kathleen (ed.) (1951). *Inquiring Spirit: A New Presentation of Coleridge from his Published and Unpublished Writings.* New York: Pantheon.

Cohen, Ralph (2001). "The Return to the Ode." In John Sitter (ed.), *The Cambridge Companion to Eighteenth Century Poetry.* Cambridge, UK: Cambridge University Press, pp. 225-48.

Coleridge, Samuel Taylor (1983). *Biographia Literaria*, ed. James Engell and W. Jackson Bate. Princeton, NJ: Princeton University Press.

Curran, Stuart (1986). *Poetic Form and British Romanticism.* New York: Oxford University Press.

Dahlhaus, Carl (1989). *The Idea of Absolute Music*, trans. Roger Lustig. Chicago: University of Chicago Press.

Eichner, Hans (1972). "Germany/Romantisch – Romantik – Romantiker." In Hans Eichner (ed.), *'Romantic' and Its Cognates / The European History of a Word.* Toronto: University of Toronto Press, pp. 98-156.

Einstein, Alfred (1947). *Music in the Romantic Era.* New York: Norton.

Emerson, Ralph Waldo ([1850] 1983). "Swedenborg; or, The Mystic." In Joel Porte (ed.), *Ralph Waldo Emerson: Essays and Lectures.* New York: Library of America, pp. 661-89.

Fechner, Jürg-Ulrich (1969). *Das deutsche Sonnett.* Munich: Wilhelm Fink.

Feldman, Paula R. and Robinson, Daniel (eds.) (1999). *A Century of Sonnets: The Romantic Era Revival.* New York: Oxford University Press.

Fetzer, John F. (1974). *Romantic Orpheus: Profiles of Clemens Brentano.* Berkeley: University of California Press.

Fry, Paul H. (2000). "Classical Standards in the Period." In Marshall Brown (ed.), *The Cambridge History of Literary Criticism, Vol. 5: Romanticism.* Cambridge: Cambridge University Press, pp. 7-28.

Gendre, André (1996). *Evolution du sonnet français.* Paris: Presses Universitaires de France.

Gilman, Margaret (1958). *The Idea of Poetry in France.* Cambridge, MA: Harvard University Press.

Greenleaf, Monika (1994). *Pushkin and Romantic Fashion: Fragment, Elegy, Orient, Irony.* Stanford, CA: Stanford University Press.

Harries, Elizabeth Wanning (1994). *The Unfinished Manner: Essays on the Fragment in the Later Eighteenth Century.* Charlottesville: University Press of Virginia.

Honour, Hugh (1979). *Romanticism*. New York: Harper.

Hulme, T. E. (1924). *Speculations: Essays on Humanism and the Philosophy of Art*. New York: Harcourt Brace.

Jobert, Barthélémy (1998). *Delacroix*. Princeton, NJ: Princeton University Press.

Junod, Philippe (2000). "The New *Paragone*: Paradoxes and Contradictions of Pictorial Musicalism." In Marsha L. Morton and Peter L. Schmunk (eds.), *The Arts Entwined: Music and Painting in the Nineteenth Century*. New York: Garland, pp. 23-46.

Kagan, Andrew (1986). "Ut Pictura Musica, I: to 1860." *Arts Magazine*, 60: 86-91.

Koerner, Joseph Leo (1990). *Caspar David Friedrich and the Subject of Landscape*. New Haven, CT: Yale University Press.

Kristeller, Paul Oskar (1965). "The Modern System of the Arts." In *Renaissance Thought II. Papers on Humanism and the Arts*. New York: Harper, pp. 163-227.

Lacoue-Labarthe, Philippe and Nancy, Jean-Luc (1988). *The Literary Absolute: The Theory of Literature in German Romanticism*, trans. Philip Barnard and Cheryl Lester. Albany: State University of New York Press.

Leighton, Lauren Gray (ed.) (1987). *Russian Romantic Criticism*. Westport, CT: Greenwood Press.

Lindenberger, Herbert (2000). "Literature and the Other Arts." In Marshall Brown (ed.), *The Cambridge History of Literary Criticism, Vol. 5: Romanticism*. Cambridge, UK: Cambridge University Press, pp. 362-86.

Marchand, Leslie (ed.) (1975-82). *Byron's Letters and Journals*, 12 vols. Cambridge, MA: Harvard University Press.

Marston, Nicholas (1992). *Schumann: Fantasie, Op. 17*. Cambridge, UK: Cambridge University Press.

McGann, Jerome J. (1989). *Towards a Literature of Knowledge*. Chicago: University of Chicago Press.

Meyer, Leonard (1989). *Style and Music*. Philadelphia: University of Pennsylvania Press.

Neubauer, John (1986). *The Emancipation of Music from Language*. New Haven, CT: Yale University Press.

Paulin, Roger (1985). *Ludwig Tieck: A Literary Biography*. Oxford: Clarendon Press.

Porter, Laurence M. (1978). *Renaissance of the Lyric in French Romanticism: Elegy "Poème" and Ode*. Lexington, KY: French Forum.

Rosen, Charles (1995). *The Romantic Generation*. Cambridge, MA: Harvard University Press.

Rosen, Charles and Zerner, Henri (1984). *Romanticism and Realism*. New York: Viking.

Schelling, Friedrich W. J. (1989). *The Philosophy of Art*, trans. Douglas W. Stott. Minneapolis: University of Minnesota Press.

Schlegel, Friedrich ([1798] 1991). *Athenaeum Fragments*. In *Philosophical Fragments*, trans. Peter Firchow. Minneapolis: University of Minnesota Press.

Schrade, Leo (1942). *Beethoven in France*. New Haven, CT: Yale University Press.

Sipe, Thomas (1998). *Beethoven: Eroica Symphony*. Cambridge, UK: Cambridge University Press.

Szegedy-Maszák, Mihály (2002). "Vörösmarty and the Poetic Fragment in Hungarian Romanticism." In Angela Esterhammer (ed.), *Romantic Poetry*. Amsterdam: Benjamins, pp. 55-61.

Thoreau, Henry (1992). *Walden and Resistance to Civil Government*, ed. William Rossi, 2nd edn. New York: Norton.

Vaughan, William (1994). *German Romantic Painting*, 2nd edn. New Haven, CT: Yale University Press.

Wellek, René (1965). "German and English Romanticism: A Confrontation." In *Confrontations*. Princeton, NJ: Princeton University Press, pp. 3-33.

Wellek, René (1981). *A History of Modern Criticism 1750-1950*, vol. 2, *The Romantic Age*. Cambridge, UK: Cambridge University Press, 1981.

Williams, Anne (1984). *Prophetic Strain: The Greater Lyric in the Eighteenth Century*. Chicago: University of Chicago Press.

Woodring, Carl (1978). "What Coleridge Thought of Pictures." In Karl Kroeber and William Walling (eds.), *Images of Romanticism*. New Haven, CT: Yale University Press, pp. 91-106.

Ziolkowski, Theodore (1980). *The Classical German Elegy, 1795-1950*. Princeton, NJ: Princeton University Press.

Index

CPSIA information can be obtained at www.ICGtesting.com
Printed in the USA
BVOW09*1711310316

442399BV00016B/133/P